Eight Plays
by
Henrik Isben

A Doll's House
Ghosts
An Enemy of the People
The Wild Duck
Rosmersholm
The Lady from the Sea
Hedda Gabler
The Master Builder

Modern Library
College Editions

Eight Plays
by
Henrik Ibsen

A Doll's House
Ghosts
An Enemy of the People
The Wild Duck
Rosmersholm
The Lady from the Sea
Hedda Gabler
The Master Builder

Translated, with an Introduction, by
Eva Le Gallienne

THE MODERN LIBRARY
New York
Distributed by McGraw-Hill, Inc.

First Edition

Library of Congress in Publication Data

Ibsen, Henrik, 1828–1906.
Eight plays by Henrik Ibsen.
    Contents: A doll's house—Ghosts—An
enemy of the people—[etc.]
    1. Le Galliene, Eva, 1899-
II. Title.
PT8854.L4   1981   839.8'226   81-8671
ISBN 0-07-554342-7   AACR2

Manufactured in the United States of America

Contents

Introduction

In a letter to Fredrik Gjertsen, written in 1872, Ibsen has this to say about translating: "To translate well is a difficult matter. It is not simply a question of rendering the meaning, but also, to a certain extent, of remodelling the expression and the metaphors, of accommodating the outward form to the structure and requirements of the language into which one is translating. . . . The foreign effect which it [the foreign meter] produces on the language acts like a disturbing melody coming between the reader and the sense of what he is reading."

In the first English translations of Ibsen's plays, largely the work of William Archer, this "foreign effect" continuously gets in the way. Archer's devotion to Ibsen as an artist made him over-conscientious; he clung assiduously to the letter, translating many of the Norwegian idioms so literally that they frequently fail to convey Ibsen's thought. They present a series of stumbling blocks to the reader's mind and tongue twisters to the actor. Instead of translating the meaning, they confuse it and occasionally falsify it. This "disturbing melody" undoubtedly contributed to the notion that Ibsen's plays are "difficult" and "obscure."

Archer's style gives little hint of the clarity, the powerful economy—what Huneker calls the "dramatic stenography"—of the original. His dialogue reflects the conventional stage clichés of his time. He was, after all, a Victorian littérateur, whereas Ibsen was an innovator and a genius. Ibsen's writing has the austerity, the clean, uncompromising beauty of a Viking ship; and his ideas were so startling, so provocative, that even the tempering gentility of Archer's prose could not prevent them from revolutionizing not only plays and players, but the pattern of thought of men and women everywhere.

It would be wrong, however, to minimize the immense service Archer performed in introducing Ibsen to the English-speaking world. Nor should one underestimate the difficulties of the task.

I feel that it is impossible to translate adequately Ibsen's poetic dramas, particularly *Brand* and *Peer Gynt*. The rhythm, the very *sound* of the language, is inextricably bound up with the thought, the passion, the satire, the mysticism. It is like blood pulsing through the body; there is no life without it. The prose plays, on the other hand—the so-called "social plays," which started with *The Pillars of Society* in 1877 and ended eleven plays later with *When We Dead Awaken* in 1899—should on the face of it seem easier. Yet one despairs of ever being able to convey that deceptively simple, lucid style, that spare, frugal prose that is yet so alive with poetry. And so one begins to feel that to translate Ibsen's prose adequately is impossible, too!

I first began to translate some of Ibsen's plays because I wanted to act in them. Fortunately, I was able, through my Scandinavian background, to read them in the original, and I realized the shortcomings of the Archer versions—the only ones then available.

I believe the fact of my being an actress helped me to convey Ibsen's thoughts in phrases that rang true on the stage, that sounded like the speech of human beings speaking in their own tongue rather than in a translation from a foreign language. When I read these versions myself, I felt that they "played well," to use an actor's term.

I was also keenly aware that Ibsen was above all a poet, and I tried my best to keep a sense of rhythm in the dialogue—for this sense of rhythm is very marked in the original.

There was a period—in the 1920s, 1930s, and 1940s—when Ibsen's plays were considered "box office poison." This was a fallacy, largely fostered by the type of newspaper critic who automatically used such terms as "museum pieces" or "dusty relics" when referring to the plays. But those of us who produced and acted in them found them popular with audiences all over the country. In recent years there has been a tremendous revival of interest in the plays. It is now universally acknowledged that Ibsen's ideas were almost incredibly ahead of his time.

Ibsen once wrote, "The minority is always right," and went on to say, "I mean that minority which leads the van, and pushes on to points which the majority has not yet reached." He most certainly led "the van" and in many ways continues to do so.

Ibsen's earlier plays were said to be reminiscent of Oehlenschläger, Schiller, and Wergeland, and, although Ibsen was always unwilling to acknowledge the influence of others, it is probable that he—in common with most young poets—reflected in his writing much that he had read and admired. His development was slow, and it took him many years to arrive at a style and a way of thinking that were peculiarly and passionately his own.

He was forty by the time he wrote *Peer Gynt*; and he was in his fiftieth year when he wrote *The Pillars of Society*, the first of the "social plays" which were to make him world famous and which, to the English-speaking world, constitute his most important and familiar work. It is on these plays that the great bulk of English criticism and commentary has been focused. Ibsen was hailed as the chief exponent of the "well-built" play, a term flattering at first but, in recent years, tinged with a patronizing disdain. Much has been written of Ibsen's great debt to Scribe, and the influence of Hebbel, and even of Dumas fils, has been interminably discussed.

Ibsen has given no definite clue, not even the smallest hint, to help us pin down any of these conjectures. A young woman said of him during his Grimstad days when he was in his teens, "He went about Grimstad like an enigma secured with seven seals"; and the stage manager of the Royal Theatre in Copenhagen described him in 1852 as "a small, close-mouthed Norwegian with wide-awake eyes." "A small, shy woodchuck" was another description of him during his Bergen years. Later on, in the 1890s, when he had become "the Great Silent One," he was usually referred to as "the Sphinx of the North." But from first to last in his long life the sense of reserve—of almost pathological secrecy—seems to have been a trait in his nature universally recognized.

There is one influence, however, that—particularly to a worker in the theatre—demands no proof, no corroboration from Ibsen or from anyone else, for it is self-evident. For five years, from 1851 until 1856, he was stage manager and official dramatic poet of the theatre in Bergen; and from 1857 to 1862, for another five years, he was director of the Norwegian Theatre in Christiania (Oslo): ten consecutive years of practical theatre work. What better way for a young playwright to learn his craft! With the exception of Shakespeare and Molière, no other playwright of modern times has had a comparable opportunity.

His duties at Bergen—apart from being the theatre poet and being obliged to write at least one play a year—seem to have been those of stage manager and assistant director. He was given no real authority and was often contemptuous of the plays presented there. He attended all the rehearsals, marking down positions and stage business; he followed the script—we are told of his insistence on the actors' keeping strictly to the written text, a fact that no doubt added little to his popularity.

I have examined some of his prompt copies, preserved at the old Bergen theatre, now a museum, and have often held them up as an example to stage managers of my own, who felt it beneath their dignity to keep their scripts in proper order; but it was not beneath the dignity of a genius to do so.

As official poet, Ibsen had the opportunity to see five of his early plays produced in Bergen; of these five only *The Feast at Solhaug* was successful. It was Ibsen's first theatrical triumph, and in answer to the applause he made a speech in which he said: "Your appreciation shall strengthen me in my work toward the aim for which I am striving, and which *I shall attain.*" And we are told he laid peculiar stress upon the final words.

In Christiania, Ibsen was given full authority as director, but only two of his plays were presented there—*Lady Inger of Östraat* and *The Vikings at Helgeland*. These five years were full of struggle and discouragement. He tried in vain to raise the level of the plays as well as of the acting and productions; but his attempts ended in failure, and in 1862 the theatre was forced to close. Yet in spite of the defeat of Ibsen's program, which filled him with a bitter sense of humiliation, an invaluable groundwork had been laid in these ten years for the work that lay ahead. One can be sure that nothing escaped those "wide-awake" eyes of his.

The art of the theatre must be practiced. No amount of theory or speculation can take the place of actually being a part of the work itself. The constant daily closeness to the actors, the opportunity to watch night after night the reaction of the audiences, the incessant planning of stage business and scenic effects—no wonder Ibsen's craftsmanship became superlative. Even if other influences existed, they could only be incidental compared to this.

The word *realism* is closely connected with Henrik Ibsen. But he was realistic in the sense that a great painter might be called realistic: he did not agree with what he called "photographic art." He resented being classed with realists such as Zola, for instance, of whom he said: "Zola goes down into the sewer to take a bath: I, in order to cleanse it." Halvdan Koht in his excellent *Life of Ibsen* rightly says: "He resembled Flaubert more than he did Zola. He was a romanticist who had become realist—a man who thought romantically, but wrote realistically. He did not wish—did not even wish to seem—merely to study society in all the forms and consequences of vice and lust. The thing which filled his mind was the individual man, and he measured the worth of a community according as it helped or hindered a man in being himself. He had an ideal standard which he placed upon the community, and it was from this measuring that his social criticism proceeded."

The most important difference between Ibsen's plays and the theatre pieces that preceded them was the light Ibsen's plays cast on the inner, secret lives of the characters presented in them. The effects he created were not dependent—or depended very little—on ordinary dramatic action. They were dramas of the mind, of the spirit. Most of the action had already taken place before the rise of the curtain, and the drama lay in the effect of this action, the results of it, the response to it. Ibsen's plays remind one of an iceberg: the greater part of it lies hidden beneath the surface. This is the quality above all others that presents such a challenge to the actor. External virtuosity is not enough; his plays demand a subtler, a far more delicate technique. One might almost say that the most important part of the actor's performance lies in what is *not* said. It can never be a question of mere words and gestures; the inner content is what counts. From start to finish of the play the actor must sustain a consistent, unbroken line of thought. Ibsen demands of his interpreters the most absolute concentration, and he demands it of his audiences, too. He must have agreed with the words embossed in gold letters above the proscenium arch of the Royal Theatre in Copenhagen: "Ej blot til Lyst"—"Not only for amusement." To him the theatre was a place of truth, of ruthless analysis, a place where the minds and souls of human beings were revealed with an honesty that sometimes seems unbearably harsh and with a perception that is uncannily clairvoyant. If people find his plays "difficult" and "obscure," the fault lies with the people, not with Ibsen. His meaning, even in his later plays with their slant toward mysticism, is never blurred or devious. Only one must listen and observe. Then the reward is very great. But one must not expect compromise from Ibsen, and he makes no concessions. As Huneker says: "It is his aloofness that his audiences resent most of all." Ibsen did not write to please.

It is not surprising that most of the Ibsen pioneers have been women; in nearly every country they were the first to introduce his plays. In England it was Janet Achurch and Elizabeth Robins; in America, Modjeska and Mrs. Fiske; in France, Réjane; in Italy, Duse. A great actress once thanked Ibsen for creating such wonderful roles for women, to which he angrily replied: "I have never created roles. I have written of human beings and human destinies." But the fact remains, whether he liked it or not, that to a great actress the Ibsen repertoire is as stimulating and rewarding as the Shakespearean repertoire is to a great actor. The range and variety of Ibsen's portraits of women are incomparable. His grasp of the intricacies of female psychology is miraculous. Especially in his later plays, when he dealt more and more with the hidden subconscious forces of human beings, he became increasingly absorbed in his studies of the feminine mind. It was perhaps the poet in him that gave him such a sensitive understanding of the mysterious invisible life of these women he portrayed—so mercilessly and yet so delicately. Björnstjerne Björnson once used the expression "We women and poets," and Ibsen might well have used it, too. It was indeed as if he had the power to transmute himself and in his imagination actually to become these women of whom he wrote, so intimate and so accurate in every small detail is his knowledge of them.

The women of the sagas, with their wild, deep natures, had always held a great fascination for him; and something of their sharply individual, fearless spirit—warm and strong at the same time—undoubtedly crept into many of the women in Ibsen's plays; they are a combination of ice and flame. And the woman he married, Suzannah Thoresen, was, according to Koht, "the embodiment of Saga womanhood."

It is probably this quality of fearless individualism that makes the Ibsen women seem so strange, even distasteful, to many people. Such a monument of hypocrisy, such comfortable fallacies, have been built up about women, particularly in plays and novels. In most fiction—especially when Ibsen's plays first made their appearance—women were either blondly good or darkly bad. But to treat a woman as a rounded human being capable at once of courage and cowardice, tenderness and cruelty, honesty and deceit, self-sacrifice and merciless rapacity—in short, as a creature whose being was torn by the torments of spiritual as well as of emotional conflict—was startling in the extreme. No wonder these plays have such appeal to women on both sides of the footlights. Here is a man who sees women as they really are; he never spares them, yet he understands them. And by focusing on them the light of uncompromising honesty, he accepts them as man's equal.

Not that Ibsen's plays are exclusively—or even preponderantly—concerned with women. His gallery of men is equally impressive. But with Ibsen, woman was for the first time in the modern theatre allowed to dominate the stage as a full-fledged individual, interesting and complete in herself, quite apart from the men with whom she shared the action; and to the Victorian mind, this must have seemed shocking and unseemly. One critic described Ibsen's women as "without affection, an unlovable, unlovely and detestable crew"; and another dismissed them pompously as a lot of "crazed, hysterical geese."

Ibsen's plays have suffered from labels arbitrarily attached to them both by ardent admirers and horrified detractors: *A Doll's House* is

a play about the emancipation of women; *Ghosts* is a play about venereal disease; *Hedda Gabler* is a play about a neurotic monster;
The Master Builder is a play about an insane elderly man who falls
in love with a young girl and crashes to his death from the top of a
tower. Such labels are, of course, oversimplifications of mere externals, and they are grossly misleading.

Ibsen himself clearly states that he was not a feminist. He did believe, however, that women had an equal right with men to develop as individuals and become—if they had it in them to do
so—complete human beings. In *A Doll's House* he was concerned
with the problem of woman's position in society.

In his notes for this "modern tragedy," as he called it, Ibsen
writes: "A woman cannot be herself in the society of the present
day, which is an exclusively masculine society, with laws framed by
men and with a judicial system that judges feminine conduct from a
masculine point of view."

The theme in the play that interested Ibsen most was not that of
woman's freedom—her so-called emancipation—but that of the
different ethical codes by which men and women live. To Nora it
was right and natural to commit forgery to save her husband's life.
Any other behavior would have been unthinkable. She would have
done anything to save or shield anyone she loved. When in the last
act Torvald exclaims "One doesn't sacrifice one's honor for love's
sake," she replies with perfect truth, "Millions of women have
done so."

In the eight years of their life together Nora and Torvald "have
never once sat down seriously and tried to get to the bottom of anything," and when, at Nora's insistence, they finally do so in the famous last scene of the play, Nora suddenly realizes that she "has
been living with a stranger." There has never been any understanding between them and never can be until she is given the
chance to stand alone and sort out for herself the true and false in
life. She has accepted without question the masculine point of view
on everything: on religion, on the law, on every phase of human
behavior. Her attitude to all such things has been dictated to her,
and she now discovers that this world she has been living in was a
fictitious world and that instead of spiritual truths, she has been

offered sugarplums and playthings. She has been denied her dignity as a woman—as a human being—and it is mainly this that causes her rebellion.

Ibsen was accused of being an enemy to the "sacred ties of marriage." People could not understand that to him marriage was so sacred that he believed it must be based on a spiritual communion—mere "living together" was not enough. He felt that a man and a woman should, ideally, go through life together as perfect equals, in perfect honesty, free to develop—each in his own way—into a complete human entity. As Nietzsche said: "What is freedom? To have the will to be responsible for one's self."

In 1879 no one had dared to face this issue boldly and present it with such uncompromising impartiality; for Ibsen nowhere takes sides—he simply shows us the situation and leaves us to judge it as we choose.

What is dated about this issue? It still exists today.

In performance *A Doll's House* often seems to "date" because the Noras and the Torvalds are not young enough. They should be very young and very much in love. Torvald's pomposity, his priggishness, his delight in his own masculine superiority become intolerable—not to say incredible—in an older man; but they are not so surprising in a young one. Then they become funny and human and almost touching. And Nora's flightiness, her sense of mischief, her naïveté, her delight in Torvald and her fear of him, her romping with the children, her little vanities, her pathetic faith in "the wonderful thing," her pride in her own cleverness—all these traits, both good and bad, are only lovable and engaging if the part is played by a young woman. And this, too, makes her sudden growing up seem logical.

Usually the age of the entire cast is much too old. The Krogstad–Mrs. Linde situation makes no sense unless it gives promise of a fruitful, happy life. And Dr. Rank's is the tragedy of a man still in the prime of life.

There is a tendency, too, to anticipate the ending. The play should be attacked lightly and at a brisk tempo. And one should not minimize the comedy, for there is much comedy in most of Ibsen's plays—a fact too often forgotten and another reason why the plays are usually condemned as heavy and depressing. Huneker—God bless him!—has this to say on the subject: "His warmest admirers deny him the gift of humor, but we believe that he is the greatest humorist, as well as dramatist, of the nineteenth century. . . . Why, Aristophanes, Jonathan Swift, Dumas fils, and Calvin (who was fond of roasting his religious foes) rolled into one is about the happiest formula we can express for the tense-lipped old humorist from Norway!"

Koht tells us that from his early Grimstad days Ibsen had been a lover of Holberg's comedies, "finding in them much of the love of irony, the sense of the ludicrous, which he himself possessed."

This element of humor, this sense of satire are difficult to translate, and there is scarcely a trace of that sort of thing in the Archer versions. Then, too, Ibsen has suffered from his legend. The terrible old man of the North fills actors and audiences alike with such awe that they are apt to consider it a sacrilege if one points out that there was laughter behind those formidable whiskers!

Even Dr. Rank has wit and humor. It may be the dry humor of disillusionment, but it is telling all the same, and it is a mistake to play him in a macabre, ghoulish manner. The beginning of the scene between Rank and Nora in the second act is pure high comedy; it acts as a kind of counterpoint to the hidden seriousness beneath and thereby heightens it. It is a good example of the dramatic realism of Ibsen's method.

In performance Ibsen's plays have often been accused of monotony. If this is true, the fault lies in the acting and direction. There is no monotony in the material; it is as many-faceted, as mercurial, as life itself.

A *Doll's House* caused a violent commotion when it first appeared. As Huneker said: "That slammed door reverberated across the roof of the world." Nervous managers thought that with a different ending the success of the play might be assured. H. L. Mencken astonishingly asserts that Ibsen "even agreed to write a new ending to the play." This is categorically refuted in several of Ibsen's letters. In an open letter to a Norwegian newspaper, *National Tidende*, dated February 17, 1880, Ibsen writes: "Sir, in your esteemed paper I have read a letter from Flensburg, in which it is stated that *A Doll's House* (in German, *Nora*) has been acted there, and that the conclusion of the play has been changed—the alteration having been made, it is asserted, by my orders. This last statement is untrue. Immediately after the publication of *Nora*, I received from my translator . . . the information that he had reason to fear that an 'adaptation' of the play, giving it a different ending, was about to be published and that this would probably be chosen in preference to the original by several of the North German theatres. In order to prevent such a possibility, I sent to him, for use in case of absolute necessity, a draft of an altered last scene. . . . This change I myself, in a letter to my translator, stigmatize as 'barbaric violence' done to the play. Those who make use of the altered scene do so entirely against my wish. As long as no literary convention exists between Germany and the Scandinavian countries, we Scandinavian authors enjoy no protection from the law. . . . Our dramatic works are exposed to acts of violence at the hands of translators, theatrical directors, stage managers, and actors at the smaller theatres. When my works are threatened I prefer, taught by experience, to commit the act of violence myself, instead of leaving them to be treated and 'adapted' by less careful and less skillful hands."

When an Italian manager made a similar request, Ibsen replied: "The fact is I cannot possibly directly authorize any change whatever in the ending of the drama. I may almost say it was for the sake of the last scene that the whole play was written. . . . I cannot formally authorize, or approve, such a proceeding."

In those days, however, when no international copyright law existed, Ibsen was powerless to forbid such "acts of violence." This puts an entirely different complexion on the whole affair. I only mention it at such length because Mencken's statement is such a fantastic distortion of Ibsen's character; it was not in his nature to compromise where his artistic ideals were involved.

If *A Doll's House* caused a commotion, *Ghosts* caused what Archer termed "a frenzy of execration."

Clement Scott, an eminent London critic of the period, compared *Ghosts* to "an open drain, a loathsome sore unbandaged, a dirty act done publicly, a lazar house with all its doors and windows open." Again, it was Ibsen's honesty that offended the prudish hypocrisy of the Victorian mind: if the things that the play dealt with in fact existed, they must be kept carefully hidden. Ibsen, however, believed that it was his mission, and that of the theatre generally, to bring all human problems into the open, that only by facing them boldly could one hope to eradicate the ills of society.

Once more we have the label firmly attached: "a play about venereal disease." But is it only that? Is it even primarily that?

In studying the play closely it seems to me it was in Mrs. Alving that Ibsen was most interested: the rebellion and evolution of Mrs. Alving. It is she who is put on trial, and the real tragedy lies in her struggle to escape from the spiritual, as well as the physical, heritage of the past. "I must work my way through to freedom!" she exclaims to Pastor Manders in the second act.

In one of his notes for *Ghosts*, Ibsen wrote: "Marriage for external reasons, even when these are religious or moral, brings a Nemesis upon the offspring," and from this, Koht concludes, I think rightly: "Oswald was branded with disease, not because the father was a beast, but because the mother had obeyed the *immoral ethics* of society. It was, from the first, this sin of the mother's which avenged itself. . . . The starting point for Ibsen was not at all the *medical* fact, but a purely *ethical* principle—as was always the case with him."

How much more interesting this makes the play! And, again, we find that we cannot hope to grasp the core of Ibsen's meaning by skimming the surface and taking his plays at mere face value.

Ghosts, in spite of its stark austerity that puts one in mind of a Greek tragedy, has flashes of sardonic humor that save it from remoteness. Ibsen revenged himself with evident glee on the members of the official Norwegian Church, who had so often attacked him from the pulpit. His Pastor Manders is a merciless portrait, in the richest vein of satire—and must be played as such. Manders's scene with Engstrand in the second act is broadly comic, and Engstrand himself is a rogue worthy of Shakespeare. But the overall impact of the play is terrifying—it freezes the blood. And how does it end? Archer tells us that he once asked Ibsen this question.

Ibsen thought a moment. Then he smiled and said: "I don't know. Each one must find that out for himself. I should never dream of deciding so delicate a question. But what is your opinion?"

In a letter to his publisher Frederik Hegel, dated 1882, Ibsen wrote: "As regards *Ghosts*, I feel certain that the minds of the good people at home will soon be opened to its real meaning. All the infirm, decrepit creatures who have fallen upon the work, thinking to crush it, will themselves be crushed by the verdict of the history of literature."

Ibsen wrote *An Enemy of the People* as a direct answer to the mass of hypocritical nonsense and abuse that had been showered upon *Ghosts*. He poured out all his contempt in this "merry comedy." In a letter to his publisher he wrote: "I have enjoyed writing this play. . . . Dr. Stockmann and I got on so very well together; we agree on so many subjects. But the doctor is a more muddle-headed person than I am; and because of this and other peculiarities of his, people will stand hearing a good many things from him, which they perhaps would not have taken in good part if they had been said by me."

An Enemy of the People has always been one of Ibsen's most popular plays, perhaps because it is essentially conventional in form and treatment. The fact that Dr. Stockmann is portrayed as a comedy character part, "muddle-headed" as Ibsen says, takes the curse off his violent attacks on the "mob and the masses." People are willing to accept such things from a man at whose personal foibles and eccentricities they are invited to laugh. And certainly in this play the humor is broad and inescapable enough. The action is straightforward, and the characters are drawn with bold and simple strokes— there is nothing oblique or devious about them. Ibsen had been disgusted and disappointed by the attacks the so-called liberal press had hurled against *Ghosts*. He had expected abuse from the conservatives, but he had confidently looked to the liberals for support. Now, in *An Enemy of the People,* he retaliates and heaps contempt and ridicule upon the liberal newspapers of the time through his hilarious caricatures of the editor, reporter, and printer of *The People's Monitor*. It was never wise to invoke Ibsen's

anger. These portraits are as vivid and as full of sardonic rage as
Daumier's drawings of the law courts. The dart of Ibsen's vitriolic
pen must have drawn blood from many a contemporary journalist.

It was a good many years before anyone dared to present *Ghosts*
on the stage, but *An Enemy of the People* was immediately produced not only in Scandinavia and Germany, but in England,
where it was among Beerbohm Tree's most notable successes. In
this country it still ranks among the most popular of Ibsen's works.

An Enemy of the People is almost completely dominated by Doctor
Stockmann, and for once Ibsen lets the women fade into the background. His next play, *The Wild Duck*, is also primarily a man's
play.

In June 1884 Ibsen wrote to his friend Theodor Caspari: "All this
winter I've been revolving some new crazy fancies ['Galskaber' in
the original, an almost untranslatable expression] in my brain; I
went on doing it until they assumed dramatic form; and now I have
just completed a play in five acts—that is to say, the rough draft of
it; now comes the elaboration, the more energetic individualiza-
tion of the persons and their mode of expression."

By the end of the year the play was finished. Ibsen called it *The
Wild Duck*. Many critics have considered it Ibsen's finest work. It
is true that the exposition is handled clumsily, and one could
wish—especially if one happens to be the producer—that the entire action could have taken place in Hjalmar Ekdal's studio, for the
first-act dinner-party scene at old Werle's house, introducing many
minor characters who never appear again, presents a painful problem in performance. Then, too, the subject of Hedvig's hereditary
weakness of the eyes seems unnecessarily overstressed, and Mrs.
Sörby's remark about Werle's imminent blindness strikes one as a
trifle pat—a most convenient coincidence. But these are minor
faults in a wonderful play. It is a marvelous comedy! Yes, *comedy*—in spite of little Hedvig's pathetic death. Such a mixture of
moods was an extremely daring innovation in the 1880s, when
plays were firmly labeled "tragic" or "comic" and it was not considered proper to blend the two.

Hermann J. Weigand, author of *The Modern Ibsen*, perceptively writes: "*The Wild Duck* does not begin as a comedy and end as a tragedy. It is a comedy from start to finish. Ibsen injects tragedy into comedy, to make comedy but the more poignant. With Ibsen we must look down from the heights upon the human menagerie assembled in the studio, and we must keep a close tether on our emotions."

And how vivid and human are the members of that "human menagerie"! For once even Ibsen himself had to admit that he had written a play full of rare acting opportunities, for in a letter to his publisher Hegel he refers to the manuscript of *The Wild Duck* in these words: "For the last four months I have worked at it every day; and it is not without a certain feeling of regret that I part from it. Long, daily association with the persons in this play has endeared them to me, in spite of their manifold failings; and I am not without hope that they may find good and kind friends among the great reading public; and more particularly among the actor tribe—to whom they offer roles which will well repay the trouble spent on them." This is a most unusual concession on Ibsen's part. He did not usually think in terms of the "actor tribe."

But the "actor tribe" certainly responded with enthusiasm, and *The Wild Duck* has always been a favorite among theatre people. It is not surprising, for even the minor characters are drawn with uncanny perception. As for Hjalmar Ekdal, he is surely one of the greatest comedy parts ever written. But how difficult to play! It takes a great actor to avoid the pitfall of being consciously funny in the role, for Hjalmar, of course, takes himself most seriously. It is this that makes him so deliciously human. He is totally unaware of the comic aspect of punctuating his most grandiloquent statements by large mouthfuls of bread and butter. Ibsen's stage directions are specific on this score. In the second act, for instance, Hjalmar is holding forth on the subject of Old Ekdal: "You don't seem to understand how humiliating it is for a man like me to see his old father treated like a servant. But someday the pendulum will swing the other way; it won't be long now—I feel it! (*Takes another sandwich*) I have a sacred duty in life, and I intend to perform it to the full!" And, in the last act, when Hjalmar sees himself at his most desperate and tragic, the pattern is repeated: "Poor lonely old man. (*He takes some bread and butter and smoked tongue, and finishes his cup of coffee*) . . . Those two scoundrels! Vicious, infamous brutes! I'll have to pick up a hat somewhere on the way. (*Takes some more bread and tongue*) Something will have to be done about it. I've no desire to risk my life. (*Looks for something on the tray*)." Gina asks, "What are you looking for?" and he answers, "Butter." In the hands of a bad actor such things can easily become mere buffoonery.

Hjalmar's return from the dinner party (and here we see one of the chief values of that awkward first act) is hilariously funny. From that point on we can never take him seriously again, no matter how seriously he takes himself, no matter how often he carries on about his "integrity as a human being" or refers complacently to his "ardent, sensitive temperament." When, in the last act, Gregers urges him to uphold the standard of the ideal against which his comfort-loving, shallow nature rebels so furiously, one can't help feeling sorry for Hjalmar as he exclaims: "I wasn't made to bear unhappiness, Gregers. I need security; I must be surrounded by peace and comfort." And when Gregers reminds him of his mythical invention, his childlike answer—"That's a doubtful proposition, I'm afraid. . . . What on earth do you expect me to invent? Other people have invented practically everything already"—is touchingly human. This is comedy based on timeless human foibles. This is why "in spite of manifold failings," as Ibsen said, there is something so endearing about the man. This is the quality that inspires the kind of devotion Gina and Hedvig feel for him, and Gregers Werle, too—that Gregers Werle who is the counterpart of Lona Hessel in *Pillars of Society*, the dark obverse of the same medal. For in this play Ibsen chooses to present the seeker after truth as a meddlesome neurotic. Lona is an eminently sane and healthy person, whereas Gregers Werle is warped and sickly—a pathological case. As Relling says: "Can't you see the fellow's mad? He's a crackpot—a lunatic!" It's true that in this play "the lie" does not affect society as a whole, but only the immediate family life of Hjalmar, Gina, and little Hedvig. Here it is a personal matter, involving only the domestic happiness of the Ekdal household. And it is the personal happiness of individuals that Relling, with his mixture of kindness and cynicism, wishes to preserve: "Rob the average man of his basic lie and you rob him of his happiness as well." An unadmirable point of view, perhaps, and one with which, as a rule, Ibsen would have disagreed. But in this play the playwright chooses to build up a strong defense in favor of it. He uses the character of Gina as witness to the fact that evasion of the truth does not always prevent a human being from being basically good and honest. Gina is the salt of the earth, a peasant woman born to serve, touching in her devotion but by no means blind to Hjalmar's faults—far from it. She understands him thoroughly—sees through him—yet accepts and loves him. This is a woman's job according to her lights. There is nothing of the rebellious "Ibsen woman" in Gina Ekdal. She knows precisely how to handle Hjalmar. Her shrewd common sense never fails her, even when she is most exasperated and unhappy.

Hedvig is in many ways like her mother. She has a precocious understanding of her father's weaknesses, yet she adores him. Her one desire is to please him, and, like her mother, she studies his every mood. His absurd flamboyance appeals to her; life is never dull to Hedvig when Hjalmar is around. His cruel behavior to her in the last act of the play is almost unbearable to watch. Yet one feels that had it not been for Gregers Werle's meddling, the child would have managed to weather the storm; her natural sanity would have enabled her to survive. But Werle's unhealthy suggestions, against which she instinctively rebels ("but I didn't think so much of it—after I'd slept on it"), come at a moment in her life when, as the pragmatic Relling says, "young girls are apt to behave strangely." She kills herself out of bewildered misery and despair, thinking her beloved father hates her. She perhaps found it impossible to sacrifice her precious wild duck on the altar of her love for him—as Gregers had suggested—and decides to sacrifice herself instead.

The Wild Duck is so filled with fascinating people that one is tempted to touch on all of them: the eccentric, tragicomic figure of Old Ekdal; even poor "daemonic" Molvik, who spouts his drunken nonsense at the very moment of Hedvig's poignant death. It is best to meet them in the play itself, for Ibsen has brought them to life so completely that to attempt to comment on them is an unnecessary impertinence.

Much has been written about the "symbolism" of *The Wild Duck*, that symbolism so often associated with Ibsen's work and which he always indignantly denied. Critics have asked: "What is the hidden meaning of the wild duck, the attic-forest, and Old Ekdal's ancient gun that can no longer shoot?" I may be naïve but, for the life of me, I can't see why they shouldn't be just what they seem to be. Old Ekdal, broken by disgrace and ruin, uses the attic-forest as an escape from the reality he cannot bear to face. It is the "basic lie" that permits him to go on living. As Relling says, "He discovered the cure for himself, you see."

To Hjalmar the attic-forest is a means of avoiding the routine work of earning the family living. He leaves such boring things to the faithful Gina and spends blissful hours puttering away, perfecting his "improvements." Most men have a touch of Peter Pan about them and resent the tiresome business of "growing up." When Gregers asks him about the old gun, Hjalmar answers, "It won't fire any more. It's fun to have it, though; we take it apart, grease it, give it a good cleaning—and then put it together again." And he adds rather sheepishly, "That is—*Father* does; he likes puttering about with things like that." But it is obvious that Hjalmar delights in these things, too. When Old Ekdal comes out of the attic carrying the dead rabbit, Hjalmar's remark to him "And you skinned it without waiting for me!" is surely proof enough.

To the child Hedvig it is only natural that the attic, with its old desk complete with pigeonholes, its "great big clock," its paint box, and the books filled with marvelous pictures, as well as the doves, hens, rabbits, and her pet wild duck—her pride and joy—should be a magical world. She is an only child and spends much time alone. And there, in the "boundless deep" of the old attic, she can enter the secret realm of her own imagination. Yet she is perfectly sane and realistic about it all: "After all, it's only an old attic," she says to Gregers. And when he replies "How can you be so certain?" she "is silent and looks at him open-mouthed." It is only Gregers, "the crackpot," who tends to attach a symbolic meaning to the "wild duck's world."

It's easy to see that to Gina the attic-forest is only another cross to bear. One can imagine her efforts to combat the dirt and smells. Hjalmar solemnly tells Gregers: "These contraptions are all my own invention. . . . Gina doesn't like the hens and rabbits to get into the studio, so it's important to keep all this in running order." Poor Gina!

We have proof that Ibsen took pleasure in deliberately mystifying his readers and his critics—particularly the latter. He was well aware of his growing reputation as a "juggler of symbols." In the letter to his publisher that accompanied the manuscript of *The Wild Duck,* he wrote: "My critics will, at any rate, find several things to squabble about and several things to interpret." We can almost see the malicious grin that lurked behind those formidable whiskers.

In *Rosmersholm*, the play that followed *The Wild Duck*, Ibsen created one of the most complicated and provocative female characters in dramatic literature—Rebekka West.

Rosmersholm is extraordinary, maddening, and fascinating, and so packed with hidden forces, half statements, shadowy innuendoes, that it seems constantly to shift before our eyes like quicksand or a mirage. We have to be alert to catch its meaning. But perhaps we should not attempt to analyze it with our brains, for our brains rebel at it. Rather we should abandon ourselves to its curious magic as to some strange anodyne. There is poison in the play—a sickly spirit of defeat.

Technically it is a masterpiece. The gradual unfolding of the themes—Rosmer's spiritual aspiration coupled with his inability to act (a vacillation of the will reminiscent of Hamlet's), the extraordinarily timeless political discussions, the psychological murder, the implication of incest, the counterdevelopment of Rosmer's and Rebekka's love, the spirit of the dead wife hovering over the whole, revenging herself on the living, driving them inexorably on to the final tragedy—takes shape little by little as each piece of the puzzle is fitted into place. It is an enthralling process. Whether we like the play or not, we cannot be indifferent to it.

At first Ibsen's thought seems to have centered upon Rosmer.

But as the work took shape, the focus shifted and it is the two women who dominate the play, the one dead and the other so appallingly alive. Huneker has described Rebekka in these words: "As cunning as Becky Sharp, as amorous as Emma Bovary, as ambitious as Lady Macbeth, Rebekka West is the most complete portrait of a designing woman that we know of; she is more trouble-breeding than Hedda Gabler."

The play is somber and brooding. Yet far from being dull in texture, it is curiously iridescent. It is perhaps the most Nordic of all Ibsen's plays; one feels it could never take place in a southern land—any more than Macbeth could. In a peculiar way it reminds one of Macbeth, although it is entirely different. One gets a picture of pale, lurid skies, and the air seems full of the rustle of wings as though unseen evil forces hovered over the play, heralding inevitable retribution. And, like Macbeth, it is an extraordinarily penetrating study of two sick minds.

Against this atmosphere—with its quality of surrealism—Ibsen places the firmly realistic figure of Professor Kroll, another of his savagely satiric portraits; and in Mortensgaard he indulges in another gibe at the liberal press. That fantastic tragicomic ruin of a man, Ulrik Brendel, appears—though unconsciously—as a kind of instrument of fate; and Mrs. Helseth, with her crude, peasant awareness of occult forces, provides a sort of link between this world and the surrealistic one.

Although at first glance this play might appear to be one of Ibsen's most "difficult" works, in the hands of two actresses of genius—Duse and Mrs. Fiske—it took its place among Ibsen's most notable stage successes. Given a great interpreter to match the greatness of the play, *Rosmersholm* casts an almost hypnotic spell over an audience.

Ibsen's next play, *The Lady from the Sea*, is also typically Nordic in atmosphere and feeling, and it, too, deals with mysterious psychic powers. But the play that followed, probably his most famous play and the most popular in the Ibsen repertoire—*Hedda Gabler*—bears the stamp of no particular country and no particular time. Ibsen wrote of it himself: "It was not really my desire to deal in this play with so-called problems. What I principally wanted to do was to depict human beings, human emotions and human destinies."

The subject matter of *Hedda Gabler* is essentially undramatic—Henry James described it as "the picture not of an action but of a condition." Yet there are few plays that have such power to grip and hold an audience. *Hedda Gabler* is the psychological study of a woman, a fascinating, tragic, hateful woman, a woman of the world—well bred, of subtle intellect, cultivated, exquisite. But this calm, polished, cold (Ibsen called her "ice-cold") exterior hides a demon, and it is vitally important to the performance of the play that the demon *be* hidden. There have been actresses—some of them great—who have played Hedda as an exotic *femme fatale*. But this is to make nonsense of the play. Ibsen has taken the trouble—which he does not always do—of describing Hedda specifically: "She is a woman of twenty-nine. Her face and figure show breeding and distinction. Her complexion is pale and opaque. Her eyes are steel-gray and express a cold, unruffled repose. Her hair is an agreeable medium-brown, but not especially abundant." The point is that she must not be in any way spectacular.

Ibsen's description provides a definite clue to his intention. Unless Hedda is able to convince people, to charm them, to inspire confidence in them—before proceeding to destroy them—there is no play. And is it conceivable that a good, solid bourgeois professor like George Tesman—blissfully under the thumbs of his two beloved aunts—would ever have become involved to the point of marriage with a neurotic, scheming monster? It is precisely in the gradual revelation of Hedda's true nature that the excitement of the play lies.

The two principal motivating factors in the pattern of Hedda's behavior are her environment—the stuffy middle-class atmosphere in which she finds herself trapped—and her pregnant condition—which her fastidious, twisted nature finds unbearably offensive. In a note on the play Ibsen says: "Her physiological condition is the cause of her psychosis."

In different circumstances, surrounded by beauty and wealth, the center of a circle of brilliant, stimulating people, Hedda might have been a different person. It is her own spiritual poverty, her malign egoism, that generates the boredom that causes her to destroy herself and others. She is a creature without aim or purpose in life, a parasite on society, and all her potential virtues have become warped and atrophied. There is a "fallen angel" quality about her, and that, in spite of our dislike for her, fills us with pity—we are appalled at such tragic waste.

Perhaps in no other play has Ibsen's craftsmanship been so unerring. From a slow beginning the play gradually builds in tempo and the tension mounts until it becomes almost unbearable. One feels as if one were climbing up a spiral—faster and higher, faster and higher—until the final pistol shot, with its sense of release. The play is so closely knit, the dialogue so pointed, the characters drawn with such fullness yet such economy of means, that not one word—nor one silence— is superfluous; it is dangerous to attempt to cut any of Ibsen's plays, but to cut *Hedda Gabler* is impossible.

Archer sums up the play in these perceptive words: "Of all Ibsen's works, *Hedda Gabler* is the most detached, the most objective—a character study pure and simple. It is impossible—or so it seems to me—to extract any sort of general idea from it. . . . The poet does not even pass judgment on his heroine; he simply paints her full-length portrait with scientific impassivity. But what a portrait! How searching in insight, how brilliant in coloring, how rich in detail!"

Surely no one (unless it might be one of those curious people who seem to think it a mark of superiority never to use their brains) can pretend not to understand the play *Hedda Gabler*. As for Hedda the woman, only in the sense that one can never fully understand another human being could one fail to understand her; Ibsen has made her live so completely.

But *The Master Builder* is another matter. Here is a play that asks a hundred questions and leaves us to supply the answers. No two critics have ever agreed on Ibsen's precise meaning.

Professor Weigand writes: "The whole dramatic situation, the progress of the action and the catastrophe are seen to hinge upon

the fact that the two characters who exclusively occupy the foreground of the stage are to some degree deranged."

To H. L. Mencken, the play means merely: "that a man of fifty-
five or sixty is an ass to fall in love with a flapper of seventeen."

Georg Brandes, on the other hand, has this to say: "It gives one
at one and the same time a sense of enthrallment and a sense of de-
liverance. This is a play that echoes and re-echoes in our minds
long after we have read it. . . . Great is its art, profound and rich in
its symbolic language. . . . Ibsen's intention has been to give us by
means of real characters, but in half-allegorical form, the tragedy of
a great artist who has passed the prime of life."

In my opinion *The Master Builder* is a great poem (in order to
fully appreciate this it may be necessary to read it in the original),
and one does not expect a poem to provide logical explanations of
its meaning. It opens up doors in the mind leading to vistas along
which our thoughts wander, fascinated, occasionally bewildered,
but constantly stimulated. Perhaps the fact that the play is written
in what seems to be a realistic manner—"by means of real characters"—may mislead us; and certainly in performance the play must
be treated realistically. To approach the play with heavy, slow,
symbolic solemnity is to defeat it entirely. On the contrary, the attack must be light and swift; the tempos should vary constantly to
match the play's mercurial quality of thought. And one cannot too
greatly stress the importance of the comedy. The first scene between Solness and Hilda is full of mischief, of sheer fun. It is
Hilda's impertinent cocksureness, her exuberance, her delight in
herself and in the fact of living that is so attractive to the master
builder—he "who cannot live without joy in life."

Of all Ibsen's plays, this is the one that seems most timeless. It
could just as well have been written yesterday or fifty years from
now. Perhaps this explains its continuing appeal to youth. For in a
way it is a hymn to youth, and not always a flattering one, for Ibsen
was well aware of the terrible ruthlessness of youth. When he
wrote the play, he had just rescued himself from his infatuation
with a young Austrian girl in whose company he had spent much
time a year or so earlier. Koht says: "She had appeared to him as
coming out of fairyland, and he had called her 'the Princess'. But

sometimes chills had run through him, for he seemed to see a beast of prey or a troll behind the fair exterior." Hilda Wangel is frequently referred to as "a bird of prey," and she herself makes no attempt to hide the troll in her—she rather glories in it. There is a great deal of Ibsen himself in the character of Solness. The playwright even admitted publicly on one occasion that "he [Solness] is a man who is somewhat related to me." There is much that is autobiographical about this play.

Like all great poetry—all great music, too, for that matter—*The Master Builder* may reveal itself to one in a flash at a first reading or a first hearing, or it may grow on one slowly over the years, as one grows up to it. It would be disappointing if great things were too easy.

"Punctually on the stroke of one, there, entering the doorway, was the dour and bristling presence known to all the world in caricature . . . the great ruff of white whisker, ferociously standing out all round his sallow, bilious face, as if dangerously charged with electricity . . . the immaculate silk hat, the white tie, the frock-coated martinet's figure dressed from top to toe in old-fashioned black broadcloth, at once funereal and professional, the trousers concertinaed, apparently with dandiacal design, at the ankles, over his highly polished boots, the carefully folded umbrella—all was there apparitionally before me; a forbidding, disgruntled, tight-lipped presence, starchily dignified, straight as a ramrod; there he was, as I hinted, with a touch of grim dandyism about him, but with no touch of human kindness about his parchment skin or fierce badger eyes. He might have been a Scotch elder entering the kirk."

My father, Richard Le Gallienne, described Henrik Ibsen in the above words when he went to interview the great man in Oslo in the late 1890s, and this is the picture that comes to mind when the name of Henrik Ibsen is mentioned today. One immediately wonders: How could such a man have been a poet, an artist? How was it possible for this starched, stuffy, respectable "Scotch elder" to penetrate, as few other writers have ever done, the most complex, secret motives of the human mind and spirit?

We must not forget the "enigma sealed with seven seals" of his Grimstad days. This forbidding exterior was the armor Ibsen chose to wear both as a very young man to hide his basic insecurity and shyness and as an old man to hide the vulnerability of his sensitive, poetic nature.

Like all great artists, Ibsen was a creature of a thousand facets. To say one "knows" such a man is always incorrect. One may know a certain aspect of him—that is all. It is doubtful if anyone knew *all* of Henrik Ibsen except, possibly, his wife. The chief clue to his complete personality lies in the characters he portrayed in his works, for there was a part of himself in all of them.

In a speech to Oslo students in 1874 Ibsen made a very important and revealing statement: "All I have written . . . I have mentally lived through. . . . Partly I have written on that which only by glimpses, and at my best moments, I have felt stirring vividly within me as something great and beautiful. I have written on that which, so to speak, has stood higher than my daily self. . . . But I have also written on the opposite, on that which to introspective contemplation appears as the dregs and sediments of one's own nature. . . . Yes, gentlemen, nobody can poetically present that to which he has not to a certain degree and at least at times the model within himself."

In reading some of the biographies that have been written about Ibsen (of which I think Koht's is probably the best), one finds passages on his high ideals, his aspiration, his moral indignation, his indomitable will, his relentless search after truth in his own soul, and one thinks: "Ah, yes! Brand, of course!" Then one comes across descriptions of violent, savage behavior, of cowardice in the face of danger, of colossal boastings, and of a black-bearded man lying drunk in the gutter, and who could this be but Peer Gynt?

Ibsen's delight in titles and decorations is worthy of Mayor Stockmann or George Tesman. Yet he can write to Björnson, referring to a request for sorely needed financial aid made to the Norwegian parliament: "You say that the Storthing *must* grant my petition. Do you really believe it will? I have an impression that my new work will not dispose the members more charitably towards me; but hang me if I can or will, on that account, suppress a single line, no matter what these 'pocket-edition' souls think of it. Let me rather be a beggar all my life!" This sounds more like Dr. Stockmann than his brother Peter!

In another letter we catch a glimpse of Master Builder Solness: "There is, of course, a certain satisfaction in becoming so well known in these different countries. But it gives me no sense of happiness. And what is it really worth—the whole thing?"

There are traces of Ibsen in Lovborg as well as in Tesman, in Rosmer as well as in Kroll. And Koht even goes so far as to say of Hedda Gabler: "The mysterious one, who carries the contrasts and the strife within her. In this feminine soul Ibsen has laid down much of that which strove within himself."

It is easy to see why a man of this complex, paradoxical nature should have chosen the dramatic form as his medium. Since in his own being he experienced and understood so many widely divergent impulses, was throughout his life constantly torn by violent conflicts of mind and spirit, he could honestly and positively agree with the many different points of view, the opposite patterns of behavior, of the characters he created in his plays. This is what makes Ibsen's men and women so alive and so convincing and is also perhaps the reason why his work, in reality so personal, nevertheless seems so objective. He shows us the situations, reveals the human beings, but never imposes judgment. He was himself too well aware of the infinite convolutions of the human soul. He knew there were always at least two sides to any problem, and the last words he was heard to speak were "On the contrary."

Alfred Kerr, a well-known German critic who was present at the imposing funeral with which the Norwegian state honored its great poet, wrote: "The ruling men in Norway had a daemon among them, and they buried a grandee." But it was both Peer Gynt and Mayor Stockmann that lay in that coffin.

Ibsen once wrote to a Norwegian student association: "Support from the young is dearer to me than support from anyone else. Moreover I hope confidently that the years shall never bring me to the point where I should feel a stranger among the intellectual younger generation."

It is now three quarters of a century since Henrik Ibsen's death, yet I know that at this time it is still the "intellectual younger generation" that appreciates Ibsen most. Even here and now he would not feel a stranger among the young, for he, perhaps more than any other writer of the nineteenth century, "allied himself most closely with the future."

Eva Le Gallienne
Weston, Connecticut
September 1981

Chronology

1828   Born in Skien, Norway—March 20.

1836   His father's business failed.

1843   Becomes apprentice to apothecary in Grimstad.

1849   Completed his first play, *Catiline,* under the pen name of Brynjolf Bjarme. His first poem appeared in *Christiania-Posten.*

1850   Ole Schulerud published *Catiline*. Ibsen moves to Christiania to enter the University. *The Warrior's Barrow* staged at the Christiania Theatre.

1851   With Botten-Hansen and Vinje edits a literary and political free-lance paper, *Andhrimner.* Abandons pen name and from now on writes under his own name.
November 6. Signs contract with the Bergen Theatre as dramatic author and stage manager.

1852   First trip abroad to Copenhagen and Dresden.

1853   *St. John's Night* produced at the Bergen Theatre.

1855   *Lady Inger of Östraat.*

1856   *The Feast at Solhaug.* First success. Meets Susannah Thoresen. *Olaf Liljekrans.*

1857   Becomes artistic director of The Christiania Norwegian Theatre.

1858   Marriage to Susannah Thoresen. *The Vikings at Helgeland* produced in Christiania.

1859   Birth of his son Sigurd.

1862   Failure of the Christiania Theatre. *Love's Comedy*.

1863   *The Pretenders*.

1864   Leaves Norway for Italy. Settles in Rome.

1865   *Brand*.

1867   *Peer Gynt*.

1868   Moves to Dresden.

1869   *The League of Youth*. Visit to Stockholm. Sent as Norwegian delegate to Egypt for the opening of the Suez Canal.

1873   *Emperor and Galilean*.

1874   Visit to Norway.

1875   Settles in Munich.

1876   *Emperor and Galilean*, first of his plays to be translated into English by Miss Catherine Ray.

1877   *Pillars of Society*.

1878   Visit to Rome.

1879   *A Doll's House*.

1881   *Ghosts*.

1882   *An Enemy of the People*.

1884   *The Wild Duck*.

1885   Visit to Norway. Settles once again in Munich.

1886   *Rosmersholm*.

1887   Visit to Denmark and Sweden. Returns to Munich.

1888   *The Lady from the Sea*.

1890   *Hedda Gabler*.

1891   Moves to Norway. Settles in Christiania.

1892   *The Master Builder*.

1894   *Little Eyolf*.

1896   *John Gabriel Borkman*.

1898   Celebration of his seventieth birthday. Visits Stockholm.

1899   *When We Dead Awaken*. Opening of the new National Theatre in Christiania.

1900   Suffers first paralytic stroke.

1906   May 23. Ibsen's death.

A Doll's House

A PLAY IN THREE ACTS

1879

CHARACTERS

TORVALD HELMER, *a lawyer*

NORA, *his wife*

DOCTOR RANK

MRS. KRISTINE LINDE

NILS KROGSTAD, *an attorney*

HELMER'S THREE SMALL CHILDREN

ANNE-MARIE,* *nurse at the Helmers*

HELENE, *maid at the Helmers*

A PORTER

The action takes place in the Helmer residence.

*For stage purposes, often ANNA-MARIA.

ACT ONE

SCENE: *A comfortable room furnished with taste, but not expensively. In the back wall a door on the right leads to the hall, another door on the left leads to* HELMER'S *study. Between the two doors a piano. In the left wall, center, a door; farther downstage a window. Near the window a round table with an armchair and a small sofa. In the right wall upstage a door, and further downstage a porcelain stove round which are grouped a couple of armchairs and a rocking chair. Between the stove and the door stands a small table. Engravings on the walls. A whatnot with china objects and various bric-a-brac. A small bookcase with books in fancy bindings. The floor is carpeted; a fire burns in the stove. A winter day.*

NORA: Be sure and hide the Christmas tree carefully, Helene, the children mustn't see it till this evening, when it's all decorated.
(To the PORTER, *taking out her purse)* How much?
PORTER: Fifty, Ma'am.
NORA: Here you are. No—keep the change.
(The PORTER *thanks her and goes.* NORA *closes the door. She laughs gaily to herself as she takes off her outdoor things. Takes a bag of macaroons out of her pocket and eats a couple, then she goes cautiously to the door of her husband's study and listens)* Yes—he's home. *(She goes over to the table right, humming to herself again.)*
HELMER *(From his study)*: Is that my little lark twittering out there?
NORA *(Busily undoing the packages)*: Yes, it is.
HELMER: Is that my little squirrel bustling about?
NORA: Yes.

3

HELMER: When did my squirrel get home?

NORA: Just this minute. (*She puts the bag of macaroons back in her pocket and wipes her mouth*) Oh, Torvald, do come in here! You must see what I have bought.

HELMER: Now, don't disturb me! (*A moment afterwards he opens the door and looks in—pen in hand*) Did you say "bought"? That—all *that*? Has my little spendthrift been flinging money about again?

NORA: But, Torvald, surely this year we ought to let ourselves go a bit! After all, it's the first Christmas we haven't had to be careful.

HELMER: Yes, but that doesn't mean we can afford to *squander* money.

NORA: Oh, Torvald, we can squander a bit, can't we? Just a little tiny bit? You're going to get a big salary and you'll be making lots and lots of money.

HELMER: After the first of the year, yes. But remember there'll be three whole months before my salary falls due.

NORA: We can always borrow in the meantime.

HELMER: Nora! (*Goes to her and pulls her ear playfully*) There goes my little featherbrain! Let's suppose I borrowed a thousand crowns today, you'd probably squander it all during Christmas week; and then let's suppose that on New Year's Eve a tile blew off the roof and knocked my brains out—

NORA (*Puts her hand over his mouth*): Don't say such frightful things!

HELMER: But let's suppose it happened—then what?

NORA: If anything as terrible as *that* happened, I shouldn't care whether I owed money or not.

HELMER: But what about the people I'd borrowed from?

NORA: Who cares about them? After all they're just strangers.

HELMER: Oh, Nora, Nora! What a little woman you are! But seriously, Nora, you know my feelings about such things. I'll have no borrowing—I'll have no debts! There can be no freedom—no, nor beauty either—in a home based upon loans and credit. We've held out bravely up to now, and we shall continue to do so for the short time that remains.

NORA (*Goes toward the stove*): Just as you like, Torvald.

HELMER (*Following her*): Come, come; the little lark mustn't droop her wings. Don't tell me my little squirrel is sulking! (*He opens his purse*) Nora! Guess what I have here!

NORA (*Turns quickly*): Money!

HELMER: There you are! (*He hands her some notes*) Don't you suppose I know that money is needed at Christmas time.

NORA (*Counts the notes*): Ten, twenty, thirty, forty. Oh thank you, thank you, Torvald—this'll last me a long time!

HELMER: Better see that it does!

NORA: Oh, it will—I know. But do come here. I want to show you everything I've bought, and all so cheap too! Here are some new clothes for Ivar, and a little sword—and this horse and trumpet are for Bob, and here's a doll for Emmy—and a doll's bed. They're not worth much, but she's sure to tear them to pieces in a minute anyway. This is some dress material and handerchiefs for the maids. Old Anne-Marie really should have had something better.

HELMER: And what's in that other parcel?

NORA (*With a shriek*): No, Torvald! You can't see that until this evening!

HELMER: I can't, eh? But what about you—you little squanderer? Have you thought of anything for yourself?

NORA: Oh, there's nothing I want, Torvald.

HELMER: Of course there is!—now tell me something sensible you'd really like to have.

NORA: But there's nothing—really! Except of course—

HELMER: Well?

NORA (*She fingers the buttons on his coat; without looking at him*): Well—If you really want to give me something—you might —you might—

HELMER: Well, well, out with it!

NORA (*Rapidly*): You might give me some money, Torvald—just anything you feel you could spare; and then one of these days I'll buy myself something with it.

HELMER: But Nora—

NORA: Oh, please do, dear Torvald—I beg you to! I'll wrap it up in beautiful gold paper and hang it on the Christmas tree. Wouldn't that be fun?

HELMER: What's the name of the bird that eats up money?

NORA: The Spendthrift bird—I know! But do let's do as I say, Torvald!—it will give me a chance to choose something I really need. Don't you think that's a sensible idea? Don't you?

HELMER (*Smiling*): Sensible enough—providing you really *do* buy something for yourself with it. But I expect you'll fritter it away on a lot of unnecessary household expenses, and before I know it you'll be coming to me for more.

NORA: But, Torvald—

HELMER: You can't deny it, Nora dear. (*Puts his arm round her waist*) The Spendthrift is a sweet little bird—but it costs a man an awful lot of money to support one!

NORA: How can you say such nasty things—I save all I can!

HELMER: Yes, I dare say—but that doesn't amount to much!

NORA (*Hums softly and smiles happily*): You don't know, Torvald, what expenses we larks and squirrels have!

HELMER: You're a strange little creature; exactly like your father. You'll go to any lengths to get a sum of money—but as soon as you have it, it just slips through your fingers. You don't know yourself what's become of it. Well, I suppose one must just take you as you are. It's in your blood. Oh, yes! such things are hereditary, Nora.

NORA: I only wish I had inherited a lot of Father's qualities.

HELMER: And I wouldn't wish you any different than you are, my own sweet little lark. But Nora, it's just occurred to me—isn't there something a little—what shall I call it—a little guilty about you this morning?

NORA: About me?

HELMER: Yes. Look me straight in the eye.

NORA (*Looking at him*): Well?

HELMER (*Wags a threatening finger at her*): Has my little sweet-tooth been breaking rules today?

NORA: No! What makes you think that?

HELMER: Are you sure the sweet-tooth didn't drop in at the confectioner's?

NORA: No, I assure you, Torvald—

HELMER: She didn't nibble a little candy?

NORA: No, really not.

HELMER: Not even a macaroon or two?

NORA: No, Torvald, I assure you—really—

HELMER: There, there! Of course I'm only joking.

NORA (*Going to the table right*): It would never occur to me to go against your wishes.

HELMER: Of course I know that—and anyhow—you've given me your word—(*Goes to her*) Well, my darling, I won't pry into your little Christmas secrets. They'll be unveiled tonight under the Christmas tree.

NORA: Did you remember to ask Dr. Rank?

HELMER: No, it really isn't necessary. He'll take it for granted he's to dine with us. However, I'll ask him, when he stops by this morning. I've ordered some specially good wine. I am so looking forward to this evening, Nora, dear!

NORA: So am I— And the children will have such fun!

HELMER: Ah! How nice it is to feel secure; to look forward to a good position with an ample income. It's a wonderful prospect—isn't it, Nora?

NORA: It's simply marvelous!

HELMER: Do you remember last Christmas? For three whole weeks—you locked yourself up every evening until past midnight—making paper flowers for the Christmas tree—and a lot of other wonderful things you wanted to surprise us with. I was never so bored in my life!

NORA: I wasn't a bit bored.

HELMER (*Smiling*): But it all came to rather a sad end, didn't it, Nora?

NORA: Oh, do you have to tease me about that again! How could I help the cat coming in and tearing it all to pieces.

HELMER: Of course you couldn't help it, you poor darling! You meant to give us a good time—that's the main thing. But it's nice to know those lean times are over.

NORA: It's wonderful!

HELMER: Now I don't have to sit here alone, boring myself to death; and you don't have to strain your dear little eyes, and prick your sweet little fingers—

NORA (*Claps her hands*): No, I don't—do I, Torvald! Oh! How lovely it all is. (*Takes his arm*) I want to tell you how I thought we'd arrange things after Christmas. (*The doorbell rings*) Oh there's the bell. (*Tidies up the room a bit*) It must be a visitor—how tiresome!

HELMER: I don't care to see any visitors, Nora—remember that.

HELENE (*In the doorway*): There's a lady to see you, Ma'am.

NORA: Well, show her in.

HELENE (*To* HELMER): And the Doctor's here too, Sir.

HELMER: Did he go straight to my study?

HELENE: Yes, he did, Sir.

(HELMER *goes into his study.* HELENE *ushers in* MRS. LINDE *who is dressed in traveling clothes, and closes the door behind her.*)

MRS. LINDE (*In subdued and hesitant tone*): How do you do, Nora?

NORA (*Doubtfully*): How do you do?

MRS. LINDE: You don't recognize me, do you?

NORA: No, I don't think—and yet—I seem to—(*With a sudden outburst*) Kristine! Is it really you?

MRS. LINDE: Yes; it's really I!

NORA: Kristine! And to think of my not knowing you! But how could I when—(*More softly*) You've changed so, Kristine!

MRS. LINDE: Yes I suppose I have. After all—it's nine or ten years—

NORA: Is it *that* long since we met? Yes, so it is. Oh, these last eight years have been such happy ones! Fancy your being in town! And imagine taking that long trip in midwinter! How brave you are!

MRS. LINDE: I arrived by the morning boat.

NORA: You've come for the Christmas holidays, I suppose—what fun! Oh, what a good time we'll have! Do take off your things.

You're not cold, are you? (*Helping her*) There; now we'll sit here by the stove. No, you take the arm-chair; I'll sit here in the rocker. (*Seizes her hands*) Now you look more like yourself again. It was just at first—you're a bit paler, Kristine—and perhaps a little thinner.

MRS. LINDE: And much, much older, Nora.

NORA: Well, perhaps a *little* older—a tiny, tiny bit—not much, though. (*She suddenly checks herself; seriously*) Oh, but, Kristine! What a thoughtless wretch I am, chattering away like that—Dear, darling Kristine, do forgive me!

MRS. LINDE: What for, Nora, dear?

NORA (*Softly*): You lost your husband didn't you, Kristine! You're a widow.

MRS. LINDE: Yes; my husband died three years ago.

NORA: Yes, I remember; I saw it in the paper. Oh, I *did* mean to write to you, Kristine! But I kept on putting it off, and all sorts of things kept coming in the way.

MRS. LINDE: I understand, dear Nora.

NORA: No, it was beastly of me, Kristine! Oh, you poor darling! What you must have gone through!— And he died without leaving you anything, didn't he?

MRS. LINDE: Yes.

NORA: And you have no children?

MRS. LINDE: No.

NORA: Nothing then?

MRS. LINDE: Nothing— Not even grief, not even regret.

NORA (*Looking at her incredulously*): But how is that possible, Kristine?

MRS. LINDE (*Smiling sadly and stroking her hair*): It sometimes happens, Nora.

NORA: Imagine being so utterly alone! It must be dreadful for you, Kristine! I have three of the loveliest children! I can't show them to you just now, they're out with their nurse. But I want you to tell me all about yourself—

MRS. LINDE: No, no; I'd rather hear about you, Nora—

NORA: No, I want you to begin. I'm not going to be selfish today.

I'm going to think only of you. Oh! but one thing I *must* tell you. You haven't heard about the wonderful thing that's just happened to us, have you?

MRS. LINDE: No. What is it?

NORA: My husband's been elected president of the Joint Stock Bank!

MRS. LINDE: Oh, Nora— How splendid!

NORA: Yes; isn't it? You see, a lawyer's position is so uncertain, especially if he refuses to handle any cases that are in the least bit—shady; Torvald is very particular about such things—and I agree with him, of course! You can imagine how glad we are. He's to start at the Bank right after the New Year; he'll make a big salary and all sorts of percentages. We'll be able to live quite differently from then on—we'll have everything we want. Oh, Kristine! I'm so happy and excited! Won't it be wonderful to have lots and lots of money, and nothing to worry about!

MRS. LINDE: It certainly would be wonderful to have enough for one's needs.

NORA: Oh, not just for one's *needs*, Kristine! But heaps and heaps of money!

MRS. LINDE (*With a smile*): Nora, Nora, I see you haven't grown up yet! I remember at school you were a frightful spendthrift.

NORA (*Quietly; smiling*): Yes; that's what Torvald always says. (*Holding up her forefinger*) But I haven't had much chance to be a spendthrift. We have had to work hard—both of us.

MRS. LINDE: You too?

NORA: Oh yes! I did all sorts of little jobs: needlework, embroidery, crochet—that sort of thing. (*Casually*) And other things as well. I suppose you know that Torvald left the Government service right after we were married. There wasn't much chance of promotion in his department, and of course he had to earn more money when he had me to support. But that first year he overworked himself terribly. He had to undertake all sorts of odd jobs, worked from morning till night. He couldn't stand it; his health gave way and he became deathly ill. The doctors said he absolutely *must* spend some time in the South.

MRS. LINDE: Yes, I heard you spent a whole year in Italy.

NORA: Yes, we did. It wasn't easy to arrange, I can tell you. It was just after Ivar's birth. But of course we had to go. It was a wonderful trip, and it saved Torvald's life. But it cost a fearful lot of money, Kristine.

MRS. LINDE: Yes, it must have.

NORA: Twelve hundred dollars! Four thousand eight hundred crowns! That's an awful lot of money, you know.

MRS. LINDE: You were lucky to have it.

NORA: Well, you see, we got it from Father.

MRS. LINDE: Oh, I see. Wasn't it just about that time that your father died?

NORA: Yes, it was, Kristine. Just think! I wasn't able to go to him—I couldn't be there to nurse him! I was expecting Ivar at the time and then I had my poor sick Torvald to look after. Dear, darling Papa! I never saw him again, Kristine. It's the hardest thing I have had to go through since my marriage.

MRS. LINDE: I know you were awfully fond of him. And after that you went to Italy?

NORA: Yes; then we had the money, you see; and the doctors said we must lose no time; so we started a month later.

MRS. LINDE: And your husband came back completely cured?

NORA: Strong as an ox!

MRS. LINDE: But—what about the doctor then?

NORA: How do you mean?

MRS. LINDE: Didn't the maid say something about a doctor, just as I arrived?

NORA: Oh, yes; Dr. Rank. He's our best friend—it's not a professional call; he stops in to see us every day. No, Torvald hasn't had a moment's illness since; and the children are strong and well, and so am I. (*Jumps up and claps her hands*) Oh Kristine, Kristine! How lovely it is to be alive and happy! But how disgraceful of me! Here I am talking about nothing but myself! (*Seats herself upon a footstool close to* KRISTINE *and lays her arms on her lap*) Please don't be cross with me— Is it really true, Kristine, that you didn't love your husband? Why did you marry him, then?

MRS. LINDE: Well, you see—Mother was still alive; she was bed-

ridden; completely helpless; and I had my two younger brothers
to take care of. I didn't think it would be right to refuse him.

NORA: No, I suppose not. I suppose he had money then?

MRS. LINDE: Yes, I believe he was quite well off. But his business
was precarious, Nora. When he died it all went to pieces, and
there was nothing left.

NORA: And then—?

MRS. LINDE: Then I had to struggle along as best I could. I had a
small shop for a while, and then I started a little school. These
last three years have been one long battle—but it is over now,
Nora. My dear mother is at rest— She doesn't need me any
more. And my brothers are old enough to work, and can look
after themselves.

NORA: You must have such a free feeling!

MRS. LINDE: No—only one of complete emptiness. I haven't a
soul to live for! (*Stands up restlessly*) I suppose that's why I felt I
had to get away. I should think here it would be easier to find
something to do—something to occupy one's thoughts. I might
be lucky enough to get a steady job here—some office work, perhaps—

NORA: But that's so terribly tiring, Kristine; and you look so tired
already. What you need is a rest. Couldn't you go to some nice
watering-place?

MRS. LINDE (*Going to the window*): I have no father to give me the
money, Nora.

NORA (*Rising*): Oh, please don't be cross with me!

MRS. LINDE (*Goes to her*): My dear Nora, you mustn't be cross
with me! In my sort of position it's hard not to become bitter.
One has no one to work for, and yet one can't give up the struggle. One must go on living, and it makes one selfish. I'm
ashamed to admit it—but, just now, when you told me the good
news about your husband's new position—I was glad—not so
much for your sake as for mine.

NORA: How do you mean? Oh of course—I see! You think Torvald
might perhaps help you.

MRS. LINDE: That's what I thought, yes.

NORA: And so he shall, Kristine. Just you leave it to me. I'll get him in a really good mood—and then bring it up quite casually. Oh, it would be such fun to help you!

MRS. LINDE: How good of you, Nora dear, to bother on my account! It's especially good of you—after all, you've never had to go through any hardship.

NORA: I? Not go through any—?

MRS. LINDE (*Smiling*): Well— Good Heavens—a little needlework, and so forth— You're just a child, Nora.

NORA (*Tosses her head and paces the room*): You needn't be so patronizing!

MRS. LINDE: No?

NORA: You're just like all the rest. You all think I'm incapable of being serious—

MRS. LINDE: Oh, come now—

NORA: You seem to think I've had no troubles—that I've been through nothing in my life!

MRS. LINDE: But you've just told me all your troubles, Nora dear.

NORA: I've only told you trifles! (*Softly*) I haven't mentioned the important thing.

MRS. LINDE: Important thing? What do you mean?

NORA: I know you look down on me, Kristine; but you really shouldn't. You take pride in having worked so hard and so long for your mother.

MRS. LINDE: I don't look down on anyone, Nora; I can't help feeling proud and happy too, to have been able to make Mother's last days a little easier—

NORA: And you're proud of what you did for your brothers, too.

MRS. LINDE: I think I have a right to be.

NORA: Yes, so do I. But I want you to know, Kristine—that I, too, have something to be proud of.

MRS. LINDE: I don't doubt that. But what are you referring to?

NORA: Hush! We must talk quietly. It would be dreadful if Torvald overheard us! He must never know about it! No one must know about it, except you.

MRS. LINDE: And what is it, Nora?

NORA: Come over here. (*Draws her down beside her on sofa*) Yes, I have something to be proud and happy about too. I saved Torvald's life, you see.

MRS. LINDE: Saved his life? But how?

NORA: I told you about our trip to Italy. Torvald would never have recovered if it hadn't been for that.

MRS. LINDE: Yes, I know—and your father gave you the necessary money.

NORA (*Smiling*): That's what everyone thinks—Torvald too; but—

MRS. LINDE: Well—?

NORA: Papa never gave us a penny. I raised the money myself.

MRS. LINDE: All that money! You?

NORA: Twelve hundred dollars. Four thousand eight hundred crowns. What do you think of that?

MRS. LINDE: But, Nora, how on earth did you do it? Did you win it in the lottery?

NORA (*Contemptuously*): The lottery! Of course not! Any fool could have done that!

MRS. LINDE: Where did you get it then?

NORA (*Hums and smiles mysteriously*): H'm; tra-la-la-la.

MRS. LINDE: You certainly couldn't have borrowed it.

NORA: Why not?

MRS. LINDE: A wife can't borrow without her husband's consent.

NORA (*Tossing her head*): Oh I don't know! If a wife has a good head on her shoulders—and has a little sense of business—

MRS. LINDE: I don't in the least understand, Nora—

NORA: Well, you needn't. I never said I borrowed the money. I may have got it in some other way. (*Throws herself back on the sofa*) Perhaps I got it from some admirer. After all when one is as attractive as I am—!

MRS. LINDE: What a mad little creature you are!

NORA: I'm sure you're dying of curiosity, Kristine—

MRS. LINDE: Nora, are you sure you haven't been a little rash?

NORA (*Sitting upright again*): Is it rash to save one's husband's life?

MRS. LINDE: But mightn't it be rash to do such a thing behind his back?

NORA: But I couldn't tell him—don't you understand that! He

wasn't even supposed to know how ill he was. The doctors didn't tell him—they came to me privately, told me his life was in danger and that he could only be saved by living in the South for a while. At first I tried persuasion; I cried, I begged, I cajoled—I said how much I longed to take a trip abroad like other young wives; I reminded him of my condition and told him he ought to humor me—and finally, I came right out and suggested that we borrow the money. But then, Kristine, he was almost angry; he said I was being frivolous and that it was his duty as my husband not to indulge my whims and fancies—I think that's what he called them. Then I made up my mind he must be saved in spite of himself—and I thought of a way.

MRS. LINDE: But didn't he ever find out from your father that the money was not from him?

NORA: No; never. You see, Papa died just about that time. I was going to tell him all about it and beg him not to give me away. But he was so very ill—and then, it was no longer necessary—unfortunately.

MRS. LINDE: And you have never confided all this to your husband?

NORA: Good heavens, no! That's out of the question! He's much too strict in matters of that sort. And besides—Torvald could never bear to think of owing anything to me! It would hurt his self-respect—wound his pride. It would ruin everything between us. Our whole marriage would be wrecked by it!

MRS. LINDE: Don't you think you'll ever tell him?

NORA (*Thoughtfully; half-smiling*): Perhaps some day—a long time from now when I'm no longer so pretty and attractive. No! Don't laugh! Some day when Torvald is no longer as much in love with me as he is now; when it no longer amuses him to see me dance and dress-up and act for him—then it might be useful to have something in reserve. (*Breaking off*) Oh, what nonsense! That time will never come! Well—what do you think of my great secret, Kristine? Haven't I something to be proud of too? It's caused me endless worry, though. It hasn't been easy to fulfill my obligations. You know, in business there are things called installments, and quarterly interest—and they're dreadfully hard

to meet on time. I've had to save a little here and there, wherever I could. I couldn't save much out of the housekeeping, for of
course Torvald had to live well. And I couldn't let the children go
about badly dressed; any money I got for them, I spent on them,
the darlings!

MRS. LINDE: Poor Nora! I suppose it had to come out of your own
allowance.

NORA: Yes, of course. But after all, the whole thing was my doing.
Whenever Torvald gave me money to buy some new clothes, or
other things I needed, I never spent more than half of it; I always
picked out the simplest cheapest dresses. It's a blessing that almost anything looks well on me—so Torvald never knew the difference. But it's been hard sometimes, Kristine. It's so nice to
have pretty clothes—isn't it?

MRS. LINDE: I suppose it is.

NORA: And I made money in other ways too. Last winter I was
lucky enough to get a lot of copying to do. I shut myself up in my
room every evening and wrote far into the night. Sometimes I
was absolutely exhausted—but it was fun all the same—working
like that and earning money. It made me feel almost like a man!

MRS. LINDE: How much have you managed to pay off?

NORA: Well, I really don't know exactly. It's hard to keep track of
things like that. All I know is—I've paid every penny I could
scrape together. There were times when I didn't know which
way to turn! (Smiles) Then I used to sit here and pretend that
some rich old gentleman had fallen madly in love with me—

MRS. LINDE: What are you talking about? What old gentleman?

NORA: I'm just joking! And then he was to die and when they
opened his will, there in large letters were to be the words: "I
leave all my fortune to that charming Nora Helmer to be handed
over to her immediately."

MRS. LINDE: But who is this old gentleman?

NORA: Good heavens, can't you understand? There never was any
such old gentleman; I just used to make him up, when I was at
the end of my rope and didn't know where to turn for money.
But it doesn't matter now—the tiresome old fellow can stay
where he is as far as I am concerned. I no longer need him nor his

money; for now my troubles are over. (*Springing up*) Oh, isn't it wonderful to think of, Kristine. No more troubles! No more worry! I'll be able to play and romp about with the children; I'll be able to make a charming lovely home for Torvald—have everything just as he likes it. And soon spring will be here, with its great blue sky. Perhaps we might take a little trip—I might see the ocean again. Oh, it's so marvelous to be alive and to be happy!

(*The hall doorbell rings.*)

MRS. LINDE (*Rising*): There's the bell. Perhaps I had better go.

NORA: No, no; do stay! It's probably just someone for Torvald.

HELENE (*In the doorway*): Excuse me, Ma'am; there's a gentleman asking for Mr. Helmer—but the doctor's in there—and I didn't know if I should disturb him—

NORA: Who is it?

KROGSTAD (*In the doorway*): It is I, Mrs. Helmer.

(MRS. LINDE *starts and turns away to the window.*)

NORA (*Goes a step toward him, anxiously; in a low voice*): You? What is it? Why do you want to see my husband?

KROGSTAD: It's to do with Bank business—more or less. I have a small position in the Joint Stock Bank, and I hear your husband is to be the new president.

NORA: Then it's just—?

KROGSTAD: Just routine business, Mrs. Helmer; nothing else.

NORA: Then, please be good enough to go into his study.

(KROGSTAD *goes. She bows indifferently while she closes the door into the hall. Then she goes to the stove and tends the fire.*)

MRS. LINDE: Who was that man, Nora?

NORA: A Mr. Krogstad—he's a lawyer.

MRS. LINDE: I was right then.

NORA: Do you know him?

MRS. LINDE: I used to know him—many years ago. He worked in a law office in our town.

NORA: Yes, so he did.

MRS. LINDE: How he has changed!

NORA: He was unhappily married, they say.

MRS. LINDE: Is he a widower now?

NORA: Yes—with lots of children. There! That's better! (*She closes the door of the stove and moves the rocking chair a little to one side.*)

MRS. LINDE: I'm told he's mixed up in a lot of rather questionable business.

NORA: He may be; I really don't know. But don't let's talk about business—it's so tiresome.

(DR. RANK *comes out of* HELMER'S *room.*)

RANK (*Still in the doorway*): No, no, I won't disturb you. I'll go in and see your wife for a moment. (*Sees* MRS. LINDE) Oh, I beg your pardon. I seem to be in the way here, too.

NORA: Of course not! (*Introduces them*) Dr. Rank—Mrs. Linde.

RANK: Well, well, I've often heard that name mentioned in this house; didn't I pass you on the stairs when I came in?

MRS. LINDE: Yes; I'm afraid I climb them very slowly. They wear me out!

RANK: A little on the delicate side—eh?

MRS. LINDE: No; just a bit overtired.

RANK: I see. So I suppose you've come to town for a good rest—on a round of dissipation!

MRS. LINDE: I have come to look for work.

RANK: Is that the best remedy for tiredness?

MRS. LINDE: One has to live, Doctor.

RANK: Yes, I'm told that's necessary.

NORA: Oh, come now, Dr. Rank! You're not above wanting to live yourself!

RANK: That's true enough. No matter how wretched I may be, I still want to hang on as long as possible. All my patients have that feeling too. Even the *morally* sick seem to share it. There's a wreck of a man in there with Helmer now—

MRS. LINDE (*Softly*): Ah!

NORA: Whom do you mean?

RANK: A fellow named Krogstad, he's a lawyer—you wouldn't know anything about him. He's thoroughly depraved—rotten to the core— Yet even he declared, as though it were a matter of paramount importance, that he must live.

NORA: Really? What did he want with Torvald?

RANK: I've no idea; I gathered it was some Bank business.

NORA: I didn't know that Krog—that this man Krogstad had anything to do with the Bank?

RANK: He seems to have some sort of position there. (*To* MRS. LINDE) I don't know if this is true in your part of the country—but there are men who make it a practice of prying about in other people's business, searching for individuals of doubtful character—and having discovered their secret, place them in positions of trust, where they can keep an eye on them, and make use of them at will. Honest men—men of strong moral fiber—they leave out in the cold.

MRS. LINDE: Perhaps the weaklings need more help.

RANK (*Shrugs his shoulders*): That point-of-view is fast turning society into a clinic.

(NORA, *deep in her own thoughts, breaks into half-stifled laughter and claps her hands*.)

RANK: Why should that make you laugh? I wonder if you've any idea what "society" is?

NORA: Why should I care about your tiresome old "society"? I was laughing at something quite different—something frightfully amusing. Tell me, Dr. Rank—will all the employees at the Bank be dependent on Torvald now?

RANK: Is *that* what strikes you as so amusing?

NORA (*Smiles and hums*): Never you mind! Never you mind! (*Walks about the room*) What fun to think that we—that Torvald—has such power over so many people. (*Takes the bag from her pocket*) Dr. Rank, how about a macaroon?

RANK: Well, well!— Macaroons, eh? I thought they were forbidden here.

NORA: These are some Kristine brought—

MRS. LINDE: What! I—

NORA: Now, you needn't be so frightened. How could you possibly know that Torvald had forbidden them? He's afraid they'll spoil my teeth. Oh, well—just for once! Don't you agree, Dr. Rank? There you are! (*Puts a macaroon into his mouth*) You must have one too, Kristine. And I'll have just one—just a tiny one, or at most two. (*Walks about again*) Oh dear, I am so happy! There's just one thing in all the world that would give me the greatest pleasure.

RANK: What's that?

NORA: It's something I long to say in front of Torvald.

RANK: What's to prevent you?

NORA: Oh, I don't dare; it isn't nice.

MRS. LINDE: Not nice?

RANK: It might be unwise, then; but you can certainly say it to us. What is it you so long to say in front of Torvald?

NORA: I'd so love to say "Damn!—damn!—damn it all!"

RANK: Have you gone crazy?

MRS. LINDE: Good gracious, Nora—

RANK: Go ahead and say it—here he comes!

NORA (*Hides the macaroons*): Hush—sh—sh.

(HELMER *comes out of his room; he carries his hat and over-coat.*)

NORA (*Going to him*): Well, Torvald, dear, did you get rid of him?

HELMER: He has just gone.

NORA: Let me introduce you—this is Kristine, who has just arrived in town—

HELMER: Kristine? I'm sorry—but I really don't—

NORA: Mrs. Linde, Torvald, dear—Kristine Linde.

HELMER: Oh yes! I suppose you're one of my wife's school friends?

MRS. LINDE: Yes; we knew each other as children.

NORA: Imagine, Torvald! She came all that long way just to talk to you.

HELMER: How do you mean?

MRS. LINDE: Well, it wasn't exactly—

NORA: Kristine is tremendously good at office-work, and her great dream is to get a position with a really clever man—so she can improve still more, you see—

HELMER: Very sensible, Mrs. Linde.

NORA: And when she heard that you had become president of the Bank—it was in the paper, you know—she started off at once; you *will* try and do something for Kristine, won't you. Torvald? For my sake?

HELMER: It's by no means impossible. You're a widow, I presume?

MRS. LINDE: Yes.

HELMER: And you've already had business experience?

MRS. LINDE: A good deal.

HELMER: Then, I think it's quite likely I may be able to find a place for you.

NORA (*Clapping her hands*): There, you see! You see!

HELMER: You have come at a good moment, Mrs. Linde.

MRS. LINDE: How can I ever thank you—?

HELMER (*Smiling*): Don't mention it. (*Puts on his overcoat*) But just now, I'm afraid you must excuse me—

RANK: I'll go with you. (*Fetches his fur coat from the hall and warms it at the stove.*)

NORA: Don't be long, Torvald, dear.

HELMER: I shan't be more than an hour.

NORA: Are you going too, Kristine?

MRS. LINDE (*Putting on her outdoor things*): Yes; I must go and find a place to live.

HELMER: We can all go out together.

NORA (*Helping her*): How tiresome that we're so cramped for room, Kristine; otherwise—

MRS. LINDE: Oh, you mustn't think of that! Good bye, dear Nora, and thanks for everything.

NORA: Good bye for the present. Of course you'll come back this evening. And you too, Dr. Rank—eh? If you're well enough? But of course you'll be well enough! Wrap up warmly now! (*They go out talking, into the hall; children's voices are heard on the stairs*) Here they come! Here they come! (*She runs to the outer door and opens it. The nurse,* ANNE-MARIE, *enters the hall with the children*) Come in, come in—you darlings! Just look at them, Kristine. Aren't they sweet?

RANK: No chattering in this awful draught!

HELMER: Come along, Mrs. Linde; you have to be a mother to put up with this!

(DR. RANK, HELMER, *and* MRS. LINDE *go down the stairs;* ANNE-MARIE *enters the room with the children;* NORA *comes in too, shutting the door behind her.*)

NORA: How fresh and bright you look! And what red cheeks! Like apples and roses. (*The children chatter to her during what follows*) Did you have a good time? Splendid! You gave Emmy and Bob a ride on your sled? Both at once? You *are* a clever boy, Ivar! Let me hold her for a bit, Anne-Marie. My darling little doll-baby. (*Takes the smallest from the nurse and dances with her*) All right, Bobbie! Mama will dance with you too. You threw snow-balls, did you? I should have been in on that! Never mind, Anne; I'll undress them myself—oh, do let me—it's such fun. Go on into the nursery, you look half-frozen. There's some hot coffee in there on the stove. (*The nurse goes into the room on the left. NORA takes off the children's things and throws them down anywhere, while the children all talk together*) Not really! You were chased by a big dog? But he didn't bite you? No; dogs don't bite tiny little doll-babies! Don't touch the packages, Ivar. What's in them? Wouldn't you like to know! No. No! Careful! It might bite! Come on, let's play. What will we play? Hide-and-seek? Let's play hide-and-seek. Bob, you hide first! Do you want me to? All right! I'll hide first then.

(*She and the children play, laughing and shouting, all over the room and in the adjacent room to the left. Finally NORA hides under the table; the children come rushing in, look for her, but cannot find her, hear her half-suppressed laughter, rush to the table, lift up the cover and see her. Loud shouts of delight. She creeps out, as though to frighten them. More shouts. Meanwhile there has been a knock at the door leading into the hall. No one has heard it. Now the door is half-opened and KROGSTAD appears. He waits a little—the game continues.*)

KROGSTAD: I beg your pardon, Mrs. Helmer—

NORA (*With a stifled scream, turns round and half jumps up*): Oh! What do you want?

KROGSTAD: Excuse me; the outer door was ajar—someone must have forgotten to close it—

NORA (*Standing up*): My husband is not at home, Mr. Krogstad.

KROGSTAD: I know that.

NORA: Then, what do you want here?

KROGSTAD: I want a few words with you.

NORA: With—? (*To the children, softly*) Go in to Anne-Marie.

What? No—the strange man won't do Mama any harm; when he's gone we'll go on playing. (*She leads the children into the right hand room, and shuts the door behind them; uneasy, in suspense*) You want to speak to me?

KROGSTAD: Yes, I do.

NORA: Today? But it's not the first of the month yet—

KROGSTAD: No, it is Christmas Eve. It's up to you whether your Christmas is a merry one.

NORA: What is it you want? Today I can't possibly—

KROGSTAD: That doesn't concern me for the moment. This is about something else. You have a few minutes, haven't you?

NORA: I suppose so; although—

KROGSTAD: Good. I was sitting in the restaurant opposite, and I saw your husband go down the street—

NORA: Well?

KROGSTAD: —with a lady.

NORA: What of it?

KROGSTAD: May I ask if that lady was a Mrs. Linde?

NORA: Yes.

KROGSTAD: She's just come to town, hasn't she?

NORA: Yes. Today.

KROGSTAD: Is she a good friend of yours?

NORA: Yes, she is. But I can't imagine—

KROGSTAD: I used to know her too.

NORA: Yes, I know you did.

KROGSTAD: Then you know all about it. I thought as much. Now, tell me: is Mrs. Linde to have a place in the Bank?

NORA: How dare you question me like this, Mr. Krogstad—you, one of my husband's employees! But since you ask—you might as well know. Yes, Mrs. Linde is to have a position at the Bank, and it is I who recommended her. Does that satisfy you, Mr. Krogstad?

KROGSTAD: I was right, then.

NORA (*Walks up and down*): After all, one has a little influence, now and then. Even if one is only a woman it doesn't always follow that—people in subordinate positions, Mr. Krogstad, ought really to be careful how they offend anyone who—h'm—

KROGSTAD: —has influence?

NORA: Precisely.

KROGSTAD (*Taking another tone*): Then perhaps you'll be so kind, Mrs. Helmer, as to use your influence on *my* behalf?

NORA: What? How do you mean?

KROGSTAD: Perhaps you'll be good enough to see that I *retain* my subordinate position?

NORA: But, I don't understand. Who wants to take it from you?

KROGSTAD: Oh, don't try and play the innocent! I can well understand that it would be unpleasant for your friend to associate with me; and I understand too, whom I have to thank for my dismissal.

NORA: But I assure you—

KROGSTAD: Never mind all that—there is still time. But I advise you to use your influence to prevent this.

NORA: But, Mr. Krogstad, I *have* no influence—absolutely none!

KROGSTAD: Indeed! I thought you just told me yourself—

NORA: You misunderstood me—*really* you did! You must know my husband would never be influenced by me!

KROGSTAD: Your husband and I were at the University together—I know him well. I don't suppose he's any more inflexible than other married men.

NORA: Don't you dare talk disrespectfully about my husband, or I'll show you the door!

KROGSTAD: The little lady's plucky.

NORA: I'm no longer afraid of you. I'll soon be free of all this—after the first of the year.

KROGSTAD (*In a more controlled manner*): Listen to me, Mrs. Helmer. This is a matter of life and death to me. I warn you I shall fight with all my might to keep my position in the Bank.

NORA: So it seems.

KROGSTAD: It's not just the salary; that is the least important part of it— It's something else— Well, I might as well be frank with you. I suppose you know, like everyone else, that once—a long time ago—I got into quite a bit of trouble.

NORA: I have heard something about it, I believe.

KROGSTAD: The matter never came to court; but from that time on, all doors were closed to me. I then went into the business with which you are familiar. I had to do something; and I don't think I've been among the worst. But now I must get away from all that. My sons are growing up, you see; for their sake I'm determined to recapture my good name. This position in the Bank was to be the first step; and now your husband wants to kick me back into the mud again.

NORA: But I tell you, Mr. Krogstad, it's not in my power to help you.

KROGSTAD: Only because you don't really want to; but I can compel you to do it, if I choose.

NORA: You wouldn't tell my husband that I owe you money?

KROGSTAD: And suppose I were to?

NORA: But that would be an outrageous thing to do! (*With tears in her voice*) My secret—that I've guarded with such pride—such joy! I couldn't bear to have him find it out in such an ugly, hateful way—to have him find it out from you! I couldn't bear it! It would be too horribly unpleasant!

KROGSTAD: Only unpleasant, Mrs. Helmer?

NORA (*Vehemently*): But just you do it! You'll be the one to suffer; for then my husband will *really* know the kind of man you are—there'll be no chance of keeping your job then!

KROGSTAD: Didn't you hear my question? I asked if it were only unpleasantness you feared?

NORA: If my husband got to know about it, he'd naturally pay you off at once, and then we'd have nothing more to do with you.

KROGSTAD (*Takes a step towards her*): Listen, Mrs. Helmer: Either you have a very bad memory, or you know nothing about business. I think I'd better make the position clear to you.

NORA: What do you mean?

KROGSTAD: When your husband fell ill, you came to me to borrow twelve hundred dollars.

NORA: I didn't know what else to do.

KROGSTAD: I promised to find you the money—

NORA: And you did find it.

KROGSTAD: I promised to find you the money, on certain conditions. At that time you were so taken up with your husband's illness and so anxious to procure the money for your journey, that you probably did not give much thought to details. Perhaps I'd better remind you of them. I promised to find you the amount in exchange for a note, which I drew up.

NORA: Yes, and I signed it.

KROGSTAD: Very good. But then I added a clause, stating that your father would stand sponsor for the debt. This clause your father was to have signed.

NORA: Was to—? He did sign it.

KROGSTAD: I left the date blank, so that your father himself should date his signature. You recall that?

NORA: Yes, I believe—

KROGSTAD: Then I gave you the paper, and you were to mail it to your father. Isn't that so?

NORA: Yes.

KROGSTAD: And you must have mailed it at once; for five or six days later you brought me back the document with your father's signature; and then I handed you the money.

NORA: Well? Haven't I made my payments punctually?

KROGSTAD: Fairly—yes. But to return to the point: That was a sad time for you, wasn't it, Mrs. Helmer?

NORA: It was indeed!

KROGSTAD: Your father was very ill, I believe?

NORA: Yes—he was dying.

KROGSTAD: And he did die soon after, didn't he?

NORA: Yes.

KROGSTAD: Now tell me, Mrs. Helmer: Do you happen to recollect the date of your father's death: the day of the month, I mean?

NORA: Father died on the 29th of September.

KROGSTAD: Quite correct. I have made inquiries. Now here is a strange thing, Mrs. Helmer—(*Produces a paper*) something rather hard to explain.

NORA: What do you mean? What strange thing?

KROGSTAD: The strange thing about it is, that your father seems to have signed this paper three days after his death!

NORA: I don't understand—

KROGSTAD: Your father died on the 29th of September. But look at this: his signature is dated October 2nd! Isn't that rather strange, Mrs. Helmer? (NORA *is silent*) Can you explain that to me? (NORA *continues silent*) It is curious, too, that the words 'October 2nd' and the year are not in your father's handwriting, but in a handwriting I seem to know. This could easily be explained, however; your father might have forgotten to date his signature, and someone might have added the date at random, before the fact of your father's death was known. There is nothing wrong in that. It all depends on the signature itself. It is of course genuine, Mrs. Helmer? It was your father himself who wrote his name here?

NORA (*After a short silence, throws her head back and looks defiantly at him*): No, it wasn't. *I* wrote father's name.

KROGSTAD: I suppose you realize, Mrs. Helmer, what a dangerous confession that is?

NORA: Why should it be dangerous? You will get your money soon enough!

KROGSTAD: I'd like to ask you a question: Why didn't you send the paper to your father?

NORA: It was impossible. Father was too ill. If I had asked him for his signature, he'd have wanted to know what the money was for. In his condition I simply could not tell him that my husband's life was in danger. That's why it was impossible.

KROGSTAD: Then wouldn't it have been wiser to give up the journey?

NORA: How could I? That journey was to save my husband's life. I simply couldn't give it up.

KROGSTAD: And it never occurred to you that you weren't being honest with me?

NORA: I really couldn't concern myself with that. You meant nothing to me— In fact I couldn't help disliking you for making it all so difficult—with your cold, business-like clauses and conditions—when you knew my husband's life was at stake.

KROGSTAD: You evidently haven't the faintest idea, Mrs. Helmer, what you have been guilty of. Yet let me tell you that it was nothing more and nothing worse that made me an outcast from society.

NORA: You don't expect me to believe that you ever did a brave thing to save your wife's life?

KROGSTAD: The law takes no account of motives.

NORA: It must be a very bad law, then!

KROGSTAD: Bad or not, if I produce this document in court, you will be condemned according to the law.

NORA: I don't believe that for a minute. Do you mean to tell me that a daughter has no right to spare her dying father worry and anxiety? Or that a wife has no right to save her husband's life? I may not know much about it—but I'm sure there must be something or other in the law that permits such things. You as a lawyer should be aware of that. You don't seem to know very much about the law, Mr. Krogstad.

KROGSTAD: Possibly not. But business—the kind of business we are concerned with—I *do* know something about. Don't you agree? Very well, then; do as you please. But I warn you: if I am made to suffer a second time, you shall keep me company. (*Bows and goes out through the hall*.)

NORA (*Stands a while thinking, then tosses her head*): What nonsense! He's just trying to frighten me. I'm not such a fool as all that! (*Begins folding the children's clothes. Pauses*) And yet—? No, it's impossible! After all—I only did it for love's sake.

CHILDREN (*At the door, left*): Mamma, the strange man has gone now.

NORA: Yes, yes, I know. But don't tell anyone about the strange man. Do you hear? Not even Papa!

CHILDREN: No, Mamma; now will you play with us again?

NORA: No, not just now.

CHILDREN: But Mamma! You promised!

NORA: But I can't just now. Run back to the nursery; I have so much to do. Run along now! Run along, my darlings! (*She pushes them gently into the inner room, and closes the door behind them. Sits on the sofa, embroiders a few stitches, but soon pauses*) No! (*Throws down the work, rises, goes to the hall door and calls out*) Helene, bring the tree in to me, will you? (*Goes to table, right, and opens the drawer; again pauses*) No, it's utterly impossible!

HELENE (*Carries in the Christmas tree*): Where shall I put it, Ma'am?

NORA: Right there; in the middle of the room.

HELENE: Is there anything else you need?

NORA: No, thanks; I have everything.

(HELENE, *having put down the tree, goes out.*)

NORA (*Busy dressing the tree*): We'll put a candle here—and some flowers here—that dreadful man! But it's just nonsense! There's nothing to worry about. The tree will be lovely. I'll do everything to please you, Torvald; I'll sing for you, I'll dance for you—

(*Enter* HELMER *by the hall door, with a bundle of documents.*)

NORA: Oh! You're back already?

HELMER: Yes. Has somebody been here?

NORA: No. Nobody.

HELMER: That's odd. I just saw Krogstad leave the house.

NORA: Really? Well—as a matter of fact—Krogstad was here for a moment.

HELMER: Nora—I can tell by your manner—he came here to ask you to put in a good word for him, didn't he?

NORA: Yes, Torvald.

HELMER: And you weren't supposed to tell me he'd been here— You were to do it as if of your own accord—isn't that it?

NORA: Yes, Torvald; but—

HELMER: Nora, Nora! How could you consent to such a thing! To have dealings with a man like that—make him promises! And then to lie about it too!

NORA: Lie!

HELMER: Didn't you tell me that nobody had been here? (*Threatens with his finger*) My little bird must never do that again! A song-bird must sing clear and true! No false notes! (*Puts arm around her*) Isn't that the way it should be? Of course it is! (*Lets her go*) And now we'll say no more about it. (*Sits down before the fire*) It's so cozy and peaceful here! (*Glances through the documents*.)

NORA (*Busy with the tree, after a short silence*): Torvald!

HELMER: Yes.

NORA: I'm so looking forward to the Stenborgs' fancy dress party, day after tomorrow.

HELMER: And I can't wait to see what surprise you have in store for me.

NORA: Oh, it's so awful, Torvald!

HELMER: *What* is?

NORA: I can't think of anything amusing. Everything seems so silly, so pointless.

HELMER: Has my little Nora come to *that* conclusion?

NORA (*Behind his chair, with her arms on the back*): Are you very busy, Torvald?

HELMER: Well—

NORA: What are all those papers?

HELMER: Just Bank business.

NORA: Already!

HELMER: The board of directors has given me full authority to do some reorganizing—to make a few necessary changes in the staff. I'll have to work on it during Christmas week. I want it all settled by the New Year.

NORA: I see. So that was why that poor Krogstad—

HELMER: H'm.

NORA (*Still leaning over the chair-back and slowly stroking his hair*): If you weren't so very busy, I'd ask you to do me a great, great favor, Torvald.

HELMER: Well, let's hear it! Out with it!

NORA: You have such perfect taste, Torvald; and I do so want to look well at the fancy dress ball. Couldn't you take me in hand, and decide what I'm to be, and arrange my costume for me?

HELMER: Well, well! So we're not so self-sufficient after all! We need a helping hand, do we?

NORA: Oh, please, Torvald! I know I shall *never* manage without your help!

HELMER: I'll think about it; we'll hit on something.

NORA: Oh, how sweet of you! (*Goes to the tree again; pause*) Those red flowers show up beautifully! Tell me, Torvald; did that Krogstad do something very wrong?

HELMER: He committed forgery. Have you any idea of what that means?

NORA: Perhaps he did it out of necessity?

HELMER: Or perhaps he was just fool-hardy, like so many others. I am not so harsh as to condemn a man irrevocably for one mistake.

NORA: No, of course not!

HELMER: A man has a chance to rehabilitate himself, if he honestly admits his guilt and takes his punishment.

NORA: Punishment—

HELMER: But that wasn't Krogstad's way. He resorted to tricks and evasions; became thoroughly demoralized.

NORA: You really think it would—?

HELMER: When a man has that sort of thing on his conscience his life becomes a tissue of lies and deception. He's forced to wear a mask—even with those nearest to him—his own wife and children even. And the children—that's the worst part of it, Nora.

NORA: Why?

HELMER: Because the whole atmosphere of the home would be contaminated. The very air the children breathed would be filled with evil.

NORA (*Closer behind him*): Are you sure of that?

HELMER: As a lawyer, I know it from experience. Almost all cases of early delinquency can be traced to dishonest mothers.

NORA: Why—only mothers?

HELMER: It usually stems from the mother's side; but of course it can come from the father too. We lawyers know a lot about such things. And this Krogstad has been deliberately poisoning his own children for years, by surrounding them with lies and hypocrisy—that is why I call him demoralized. (*Holds out both hands to her*) So my sweet little Nora must promise not to plead his cause. Shake hands on it. Well? What's the matter? Give me your hand. There! That's all settled. I assure you it would have been impossible for me to work with him. It literally gives me a feeling of physical discomfort to come in contact with such people. (NORA *draws her hand away, and moves to the other side of the Christmas tree.*)

NORA: It's so warm here. And I have such a lot to do.

HELMER (*Rises and gathers up his papers*): I must try and look through some of these papers before dinner. I'll give some thought to your costume too. Perhaps I may even find something to hang in gilt paper on the Christmas tree! (*Lays his hand on her head*) My own precious little song-bird! (*He goes into his study and closes the door after him.*)

NORA (*Softly, after a pause*): It can't be—! It's impossible. Of course it's impossible!

ANNE-MARIE (*At the door, left*): The babies keep begging to come in and see Mamma.

NORA: No, no! Don't let them come to me! Keep them with you, Anne-Marie.

ANNE-MARIE: Very well, Ma'am. (*Shuts the door.*)

NORA (*Pale with terror*): Harm my children!—Corrupt my home! (*Short pause. She throws back her head*) It's not true! I know it's not! It could never, never be true!

                                                   CURTAIN

ACT
TWO

SCENE: *The same room. In the corner, beside the piano, stands the Christmas tree, stripped and with the candles burnt out.* NORA'S *outdoor things lie on the sofa.* NORA, *alone, is walking about restlessly. At last she stops by the sofa, and picks up her cloak.*

NORA (*Puts the cloak down again*): Did someone come in? (*Goes to the hall and listens*) No; no one; of course no one will come today, Christmas Day; nor tomorrow either. But perhaps— (*Opens the door and looks out*) No, there's nothing in the mailbox; it's quite empty. (*Comes forward*) Oh nonsense! He only meant to frighten me. There won't be any trouble. It's all impossible! Why, I— I have three little children!

(ANNE-MARIE *enters from the left, with a large cardboard box.*)

ANNE-MARIE: Well—I found the box with the fancy dress clothes at last, Miss Nora.

NORA: Thanks; put it on the table.

ANNE-MARIE (*Does so*): I'm afraid they're rather shabby.

NORA: If I had my way I'd tear them into a thousand pieces!

ANNE-MARIE: Good gracious! They can be repaired—just have a little patience.

NORA: I'll go and get Mrs. Linde to help me.

ANNE-MARIE: I wouldn't go out again in this awful weather! You might catch cold, Miss Nora, and get sick.

NORA: Worse things might happen— How are the children?

ANNE-MARIE: The poor little things are playing with their Christmas presents; but—

NORA: Have they asked for me?

ANNE-MARIE: They're so used to having Mamma with them.

NORA: I know, but, you see, Anne-Marie, I won't be able to be with them as much as I used to.

ANNE-MARIE: Well, little children soon get used to anything.

NORA: You really think so? Would they forget me if I went away for good?

ANNE-MARIE: Good gracious!—for good!

NORA: Tell me something, Anne-Marie—I've so often wondered about it—how could you bear to part with your child—give it up to strangers?

ANNE-MARIE: Well, you see, I had to—when I came to nurse my little Nora.

NORA: Yes—but how could you *bear* to do it?

ANNE-MARIE: I couldn't afford to say "no" to such a good position. A poor girl who's been in trouble must take what comes. Of course *he* never offered to help me—the wicked sinner!

NORA: Then I suppose your daughter has forgotten all about you.

ANNE-MARIE: No—indeed she hasn't! She even wrote to me—once when she was confirmed and again when she was married.

NORA (*Embracing her*): Dear old Anne-Marie—you were a good mother to me when I was little.

ANNE-MARIE: But then my poor little Nora *had* no mother of her own!

NORA: And if ever my little ones were left without—you'd look after them, wouldn't you?—Oh, that's just nonsense! (*Opens the box*) Go back to them. Now I must— Just you wait and see how lovely I'll look tomorrow!

ANNE-MARIE: My Miss Nora will be the prettiest person there! (*She goes into the room on the left*.)

NORA (*Takes the costume out of the box, but soon throws it down again*): I wish I dared go out—I'm afraid someone might come. I'm afraid something might happen while I'm gone. That's just silly! No one will come. I must try not to think— This muff needs cleaning. What pretty gloves—they're lovely! I must put it out of my head! One, two, three, four, five, six— (*With a scream*) Ah! They're here! (*Goes toward the door, then stands irresolute*. MRS. LINDE *enters from the hall, where she has taken off her things*.)

NORA: Oh, it's you, Kristine! There's no one else out there, is there? I'm so glad you have come!

MRS. LINDE: I got a message you'd been asking for me.

NORA: Yes, I just happened to be passing by. There's something I want you to help me with. Sit down here on the sofa. Now, listen: There's to be a fancy dress ball at the Stenborgs' tomorrow evening—they live just overhead—and Torvald wants me to go as a Neapolitan peasant girl, and dance the tarantella; I learned it while we were in Capri.

MRS. LINDE: So you're going to give a real performance, are you?

NORA: Torvald wants me to. Look, here's the costume; Torvald had it made for me down there. But it's all torn, Kristine, and I don't know whether—

MRS. LINDE: Oh, we'll soon fix that. It's only the trimming that has come loose here and there. Have you a needle and thread? Oh, yes. Here's everything I need.

NORA: It's awfully good of you!

MRS. LINDE (*Sewing*): So you're going to be all dressed up, Nora—what fun! You know—I think I'll run in for a moment—just to see you in your costume— I haven't really thanked you for last night. I had such a happy time!

NORA (*Rises and walks across the room*): Somehow it didn't seem as nice to me as usual. I wish you'd come to town a little earlier, Kristine. Yes—Torvald has a way of making things so gay and cozy.

MRS. LINDE: Well—so have you. That's your father coming out in you! But tell me—is Doctor Rank always so depressed?

NORA: No; last night it was worse than usual. He's terribly ill, you see—tuberculosis of the spine, or something. His father was a frightful man, who kept mistresses and all that sort of thing—that's why his son has been an invalid from birth—

MRS. LINDE (*Lets her sewing fall into her lap*): Why, Nora! what do you know about such things?

NORA (*Moving about the room*): After all—I've had three children; and those women who look after one at childbirth know almost as much as doctors; and they love to gossip.

MRS. LINDE (*Goes on sewing; a short pause*): Does Doctor Rank come here every day?

NORA: Every single day. He's Torvald's best friend, you know—
always has been; and he's *my* friend too. He's almost like one of
the family.

MRS. LINDE: Do you think he's quite sincere, Nora? I mean—isn't
he inclined to flatter people?

NORA: Quite the contrary. What gave you that impression?

MRS. LINDE: When you introduced us yesterday he said he had
often heard my name mentioned here; but I noticed afterwards
that your husband hadn't the faintest notion who I was. How
could Doctor Rank—?

NORA: He was quite right, Kristine. You see Torvald loves me so
tremendously that he won't share me with anyone; he wants me
all to himself, as he says. At first he used to get terribly jealous if I
even mentioned any of my old friends back home; so naturally I
gave up doing it. But I often talk to Doctor Rank about such
things—he likes to hear about them.

MRS. LINDE: Listen to me, Nora! In many ways you are still a
child. I'm somewhat older than you, and besides, I've had much
more experience. I think you ought to put a stop to all this with
Dr. Rank.

NORA: Put a stop to what?

MRS. LINDE: To the whole business. You said something yesterday about a rich admirer who was to give you money—

NORA: One who never existed, unfortunately. Go on.

MRS. LINDE: Has Doctor Rank money?

NORA: Why yes, he has.

MRS. LINDE: And he has no one dependent on him?

NORA: No, no one. But—

MRS. LINDE: And he comes here every single day?

NORA: Yes—I've just told you so.

MRS. LINDE: It's surprising that a sensitive man like that should be
so importunate.

NORA: I don't understand you—

MRS. LINDE: Don't try to deceive me, Nora. Don't you suppose I
can guess who lent you the twelve hundred dollars?

NORA: You must be out of your mind! How could you ever think such a thing? Why, he's a friend of ours; he comes to see us every day! The situation would have been impossible!

MRS. LINDE: So it wasn't he, then?

NORA: No, I assure you. Such a thing never even occurred to me. Anyway, he didn't have any money at that time; he came into it later.

MRS. LINDE: Perhaps that was just as well, Nora, dear.

NORA: No—it would never have entered my head to ask Dr. Rank— Still—I'm sure that if I did ask him—

MRS. LINDE: But you won't, of course.

NORA: No, of course not. Anyway—I don't see why it should be necessary. But I'm sure that if I talked to Doctor Rank—

MRS. LINDE: Behind your husband's back?

NORA: I want to get that thing cleared up; after all, that's behind his back too. I must get clear of it.

MRS. LINDE: That's just what I said yesterday; but—

NORA (*Walking up and down*): It's so much easier for a man to manage things like that—

MRS. LINDE: One's own husband, yes.

NORA: Nonsense. (*Stands still*) Surely if you pay back everything you owe—the paper is returned to you?

MRS. LINDE: Naturally.

NORA: Then you can tear it into a thousand pieces, and burn it up—the nasty, filthy thing!

MRS. LINDE (*Looks at her fixedly, lays down her work, and rises slowly*): Nora, you are hiding something from me.

NORA: You can see it in my face, can't you?

MRS. LINDE: Something's happened to you since yesterday morning, Nora, what is it?

NORA (*Going towards her*): Kristine—! (*Listens*) Hush! Here comes Torvald! Go into the nursery for a little while. Torvald hates anything to do with sewing. Get Anne-Marie to help you.

MRS. LINDE (*Gathers the things together*): Very well; but I shan't leave until you have told me all about it. (*She goes out to the left, as* HELMER *enters from the hall.*)

NORA (*Runs to meet him*): Oh, I've missed you so, Torvald, dear!

HELMER: Was that the dressmaker—?

NORA: No, it was Kristine. She's helping me fix my costume. It's going to look so nice.

HELMER: Wasn't that a good idea of mine?

NORA: Splendid! But don't you think it was good of me to let you have your way?

HELMER: Good of you! To let your own husband have his way! There, there, you crazy little thing; I'm only teasing. Now I won't disturb you. You'll have to try the dress on, I suppose.

NORA: Yes—and I expect you've work to do.

HELMER: I have. (*Shows her a bundle of papers*) Look. I've just come from the Bank— (*Goes towards his room.*)

NORA: Torvald.

HELMER (*Stopping*): Yes?

NORA: If your little squirrel were to beg you—with all her heart—

HELMER: Well?

NORA: Would you do something for her?

HELMER: That depends on what it is.

NORA: Be a darling and say 'Yes', Torvald! Your squirrel would skip about and play all sorts of pretty tricks—

HELMER: Well—out with it!

NORA: Your little lark would twitter all day long—

HELMER: She does that anyway!

NORA: I'll pretend to be an elf and dance for you in the moonlight, Torvald.

HELMER: Nora—you're surely not getting back to what we talked about this morning?

NORA (*Coming nearer*): Oh, Torvald, dear, I do most humbly beg you—!

HELMER: You have the temerity to bring that up again?

NORA: You must give in to me about this, Torvald! You *must* let Krogstad keep his place!

HELMER: I'm giving his place to Mrs. Linde.

NORA: That's awfully sweet of you. But instead of Krogstad— couldn't you dismiss some other clerk?

HELMER: This is the most incredible obstinacy! Because you were thoughtless enough to promise to put in a good word for him, am I supposed to—?

NORA: That's not the reason, Torvald. It's for your own sake. Didn't you tell me yourself he writes for the most horrible newspapers? He can do you no end of harm. Oh! I'm so afraid of him—

HELMER: I think I understand; you have some unpleasant memories—that's why you're frightened.

NORA: What do you mean?

HELMER: Aren't you thinking of your father?

NORA: Oh, yes—of course! You remember how those awful people slandered poor father in the newspapers? If you hadn't been sent to investigate the matter, and been so kind and helpful—he might have been dismissed.

HELMER: My dear Nora, there is a distinct difference between your father and me. Your father's conduct was not entirely unimpeachable. But mine is; and I trust it will remain so.

NORA: You never know what evil-minded people can think up. We could be so happy now, Torvald, in our lovely, peaceful home—you and I and the children! Oh! I implore you, Torvald—!

HELMER: The more you plead his cause the less likely I am to keep him on. It's already known at the Bank that I intend to dismiss Krogstad. If I were to change my mind, people might say I'd done it at the insistence of my wife—

NORA: Well—what of that?

HELMER: Oh, nothing, of course! As long as the obstinate little woman gets her way! I'd simply be the laughing-stock of the whole staff; they'd think I was weak and easily influenced—I should soon be made to feel the consequences. Besides—there is one factor that makes it quite impossible for Krogstad to work at the Bank as long as I'm head there.

NORA: What could that be?

HELMER: His past record I might be able to overlook—

NORA: Yes, you might, mightn't you, Torvald—?

HELMER: And I'm told he's an excellent worker. But unfortunately we were friendly during our college days. It was one of those impetuous friendships that subsequently often prove embarrassing. He's tactless enough to call me by my first name—regardless of the circumstances—and feels quite justified in taking a familiar tone with me. At any moment he comes out with "Torvald" this, and "Torvald" that! It's acutely irritating. It would make my position at the Bank intolerable.

NORA: You're surely not serious about this, Torvald?

HELMER: Why not?

NORA: But—it's all so petty.

HELMER: Petty! So you think I'm petty!

NORA: Of course not, Torvald—just the opposite; that's why—

HELMER: Never mind; you call my motives petty; so I must be petty too! Petty! Very well!—We'll put an end to this now—once and for all. (HELMER *goes to the door into the hall and calls* HELENE.)

NORA: What do you want?

HELMER (*Searching among his papers*): I want this thing settled. (HELENE *enters*) Take this letter, will you? Get a messenger and have him deliver it at once! It's urgent. Here's some money.

HELENE: Very good, Sir. (*Goes with the letter*.)

HELMER (*Putting his papers together*): There, little Miss Obstinacy.

NORA (*Breathless*): Torvald—what was in that letter?

HELMER: Krogstad's dismissal.

NORA: Call her back, Torvald! There's still time. Call her back! For my sake, for your own sake, for the sake of the children, don't send that letter! Torvald, do you hear? You don't realize what may come of this!

HELMER: It's too late.

NORA: Too late, yes.

HELMER: Nora, dear; I forgive your fears—though it's not exactly flattering to me to think I could ever be afraid of any spiteful nonsense Krogstad might choose to write about me! But I forgive you all the same—it shows how much you love me. (*Takes her in his arms*) And that's the way it should be, Nora darling. No matter what happens, you'll see—I have strength and courage for us both. My shoulders are broad—I'll bear the burden.

NORA (*Terror-struck*): How do you mean?

HELMER: The whole burden, my darling. Don't you worry any more.

NORA (*With decision*): No! You mustn't—I won't let you!

HELMER: Then we'll share it, Nora, as man and wife. That is as it should be. (*Petting her*) Are you happy now? There! Don't look at me like a frightened little dove! You're just imagining things, you know— Now don't you think you ought to play the tarantella through—and practice your tambourine? I'll go into my study and close both doors, then you won't disturb me. You can make all the noise you like! (*Turns round in doorway*) And when Rank comes, just tell him where I am. (*He nods to her, and goes with his papers to his room, closing the door.*)

NORA (*Bewildered with terror, stands as though rooted to the ground, and whispers*): He'd do it too! He'd do it—in spite of anything! But he mustn't—never, never! Anything but that! There must be some way out! What shall I do? (*The hall bell rings*) Dr. Rank—! Anything but that—anything, *anything* but that!

(NORA *draws her hands over her face, pulls herself together, goes to the door and opens it.* RANK *stands outside hanging up his fur coat. During the following scene, darkness begins to fall.*)

NORA: How are you, Doctor Rank? I recognized your ring. You'd better not go in to Torvald just now; I think he's busy.

RANK: How about you? (*Enters and closes the door.*)

NORA: You know I always have an hour to spare for you.

RANK: Many thanks. I'll make use of that privilege as long as possible.

NORA: What do you mean—as long as possible?

RANK: Does that frighten you?

NORA: No—but it's such a queer expression. Has anything happened?

RANK: I've been expecting it for a long time; but I never thought it would come quite so soon.

NORA: What is it you have found out? Doctor Rank, please tell me!

RANK (*Sitting down by the stove*): I haven't much time left. There's nothing to do about it.

NORA (*With a sigh of relief*): Oh! Then—it's about you—?

RANK: Of course. What did you think? It's no use lying to one's self. I am the most miserable of all my patients, Mrs. Helmer. These past few days I've been taking stock of my position—and I find myself completely bankrupt. Within a month, I shall be rotting in the church-yard.

NORA: What a ghastly way to talk!

RANK: The whole business is pretty ghastly, you see. And the worst of it is, there are so many ghastly things to be gone through before it's over. I've just one last examination to make, then I shall know approximately when the final dissolution will begin. There's something I want to say to you: Helmer's sensitive nature is repelled by anything ugly. I couldn't bear to have him near me when—

NORA: But Doctor Rank—

RANK: No, I couldn't bear it! I won't have him there—I shall bar my door against him— As soon as I am absolutely certain of the worst, I'll send you my visiting-card marked with a black cross; that will mean the final horror has begun.

NORA: Doctor Rank—you're absolutely impossible today! And I did so want you to be in a good humor.

RANK: With death staring me in the face? And why should I have to expiate another's sins! What justice is there in that? Well—I suppose in almost every family there are some such debts that have to be paid.

NORA (*Stopping her ears*): Don't talk such nonsense! Come along! Cheer up!

RANK: One might as well laugh. It's really very funny when you come to think of it—that my poor innocent spine should be made to suffer for my father's exploits!

NORA (*At table, left*): He was much addicted to asparagus-tips and paté de foie gras, wasn't he?

RANK: Yes; and truffles.

NORA: Oh, of course—truffles, yes. And I suppose oysters too?

RANK: Oh, yes! Masses of oysters, certainly!

NORA: And all the wine and champagne that went with them! It does seem a shame that all these pleasant things should be so damaging to the spine, doesn't it?

RANK: Especially when it's a poor miserable spine that never had any of the fun!

NORA: Yes, that's the biggest shame of all!

RANK (*Gives her a searching look*): H'm—

NORA (*A moment later*): Why did you smile?

RANK: No; you were the one that laughed.

NORA: No; you were the one that smiled, Doctor Rank!

RANK (*Gets up*): You're more of a rogue than I thought you were.

NORA: I'm full of mischief today.

RANK: So it seems.

NORA (*With her hands on his shoulders*): Dear, dear Doctor Rank, don't go and die and leave Torvald and me.

RANK: Oh, you won't miss me long! Those who go away—are soon forgotten.

NORA (*Looks at him anxiously*): You really believe that?

RANK: People develop new interests, and soon—

NORA: What do you mean—new interests?

RANK: That'll happen to you and Helmer when I am gone. You seem to have made a good start already. What was that Mrs. Linde doing here last evening?

NORA: You're surely not jealous of poor old Kristine!

RANK: Yes, I am. She will be my successor in this house. When I'm gone she'll probably—

NORA: Sh—hh! She's in there.

RANK: She's here again today? You see!

NORA: She's just helping me with my costume. Good heavens, you *are* in a unreasonable mood! (*Sits on sofa*) Now do try to be good, Doctor Rank. Tomorrow you'll see how beautifully I'll dance; and then you can pretend I'm doing it all to please you—and Torvald too, of course—that's understood.

RANK: (*After a short silence*): You know—sitting here talking to you so informally—I simply can't imagine what would have become of me, if I had never had this house to come to.

NORA (*Smiling*): You really *do* feel at home with us, don't you?

RANK (*In a low voice—looking straight before him*): And to be obliged to leave it all—

NORA: Nonsense! You're not going to leave anything.

RANK (*In the same tone*): And not to be able to leave behind one even the smallest proof of gratitude; at most a fleeting regret—an empty place to be filled by the first person who comes along.

NORA: And supposing I were to ask you for—? No—

RANK: For what?

NORA: For a great proof of your friendship.

RANK: Yes?—Yes?

NORA: No, I mean—if I were to ask you to do me a really tremendous favor—

RANK: You'd really, for once, give me that great happiness?

NORA: Oh, but you don't know what it is.

RANK: Then tell me.

NORA: I don't think I can, Doctor Rank. It's much too much to ask—it's not just a favor—I need your help and advice as well—

RANK: So much the better. I've no conception of what you mean. But tell me about it. You trust me, don't you?

NORA: More than anyone. I know you are my best and truest friend—that's why I can tell you. Well then, Doctor Rank, there is something you must help me prevent. You know how deeply, how intensely Torvald loves me; he wouldn't hesitate for a moment to give up his life for my sake.

RANK (*Bending towards her*): Nora—do you think he is the only one who—?

NORA (*With a slight start*): Who—what?

RANK: Who would gladly give his life for you?

NORA (*Sadly*): I see.

RANK: I was determined that you should know this before I—went away. There'll never be a better chance to tell you. Well, Nora, now you know, and you must know too that you can trust me as you can no one else.

NORA (*Standing up; simply and calmly*): Let me get by—

RANK (*Makes way for her, but remains sitting*): Nora—

NORA (*In the doorway*): Bring in the lamp, Helene. (*Crosses to the stove*) Oh, dear Doctor Rank, that was really horrid of you.

RANK (*Rising*): To love you just as deeply as—as someone else does; is that horrid?

NORA: No—but the fact of your telling me. There was no need to do that.

RANK: What do you mean? Did you know—?

(HELENE *enters with the lamp; sets it on the table and goes out again.*)

RANK: Nora—Mrs. Helmer—tell me, did you know?

NORA: Oh, how do I know what I knew or didn't know. I really can't say— How could you be so clumsy, Doctor Rank? It was all so nice.

RANK: Well, at any rate, you know now that I stand ready to serve you body and soul. So—tell me.

NORA (*Looking at him*): After this?

RANK: I beg you to tell me what it is.

NORA: I can't tell you anything now.

RANK: But you must! Don't punish me like that! Let me be of use to you; I'll do anything for you—anything within human power.

NORA: You can do nothing for me now. Anyway—I don't really need help. I was just imagining things, you see. Really! That's all it was! (*Sits in the rocking chair, looks at him and smiles*) Well—you're a nice one, Doctor Rank! Aren't you a bit ashamed, now that the lamp's been lit?

RANK: No; really not. But I suppose I'd better go now—for good?

NORA: You'll do no such thing! You must come here just as you always have. Torvald could never get on without you!

RANK: But how about *you*?

NORA: You know I always love to have you here.

RANK: Yes—I suppose that's what misled me. I can't quite make you out. I've often felt you liked being with me almost as much as being with Helmer.

NORA: Well—you see— There are the people one loves best—and yet there are others one would almost rather *be* with.

RANK: Yes—there's something in that.

NORA: When I was still at home, it was of course Papa whom I loved best. And yet whenever I could, I used to slip down to the servants' quarters. I loved being with them. To begin with, they never lectured me a bit, and it was such fun to hear them talk.

RANK: I see; and now you have me instead!

NORA (*Jumps up and hurries toward him*): Oh, dear, darling Doctor Rank. I didn't mean it like that! It's just that now, Torvald comes first—the way Papa did. *You* understand—!
(HELENE *enters from the hall.*)

HELENE: I beg your pardon, Ma'am— (*Whispers to* NORA, *and gives her a card.*)

NORA (*Glancing at card*): Ah! (*Puts it in her pocket.*)

RANK: Anything wrong?

NORA: No, nothing! It's just—it's my new costume—

RANK: Isn't that your costume—there?

NORA: Oh, that one, yes. But this is a different one. It's one I've ordered—Torvald mustn't know—

RANK: So *that's* the great secret!

NORA: Yes, of course it is! Go in and see him, will you? He's in his study. Be sure and keep him there as long as—

RANK: Don't worry; he shan't escape me. (*Goes into* HELMER'S *room.*)

NORA (*To* HELENE): He's waiting in the kitchen?

HELENE: Yes, he came up the back stairs—

NORA: Why didn't you tell him I was busy?

HELENE: I did, but he insisted.

NORA: He won't go away?

HELENE: Not until he has spoken to you, Ma'am.

NORA: Very well, then; show him in; but quietly, Helene—and don't say a word to anyone; it's about a surprise for my husband.

HELENE: I understand, Ma'am. (*She goes out.*)

NORA: It's coming! It's going to happen after all! No, no! It can't happen. It *can't!*
(*She goes to* HELMER'S *door and locks it.* HELENE *opens the hall door for* KROGSTAD, *and shuts it after him. He wears a traveling-coat, boots, and a fur cap.*)

NORA (*Goes towards him*): Talk quietly; my husband is at home.

KROGSTAD: What's that to me?

NORA: What is it you want?

KROGSTAD: I want to make sure of something.

NORA: Well—what is it? Quickly!

KROGSTAD: I suppose you know I've been dismissed.

NORA: I couldn't prevent it, Mr. Krogstad. I did everything in my power, but it was useless.

KROGSTAD: So that's all your husband cares about you! He must realize what I can put you through, and yet, in spite of that, he dares to—

NORA: You don't imagine my husband knows about it?

KROGSTAD: No—I didn't really suppose he did. I can't imagine my friend Torvald Helmer showing that much courage.

NORA: I insist that you show respect when speaking of my husband, Mr. Krogstad!

KROGSTAD: With all due respect, I assure you! But am I right in thinking—since you are so anxious to keep the matter secret—that you have a clearer idea today than you had yesterday, of what you really did?

NORA: Clearer than *you* could ever give me!

KROGSTAD: Of course! I who know so little about the law—!

NORA: What do you want of me?

KROGSTAD: I just wanted to see how you were getting on, Mrs. Helmer. I've been thinking about you all day. You see—even a mere money-lender, a cheap journalist—in short, someone like me—is not entirely without feeling.

NORA: Then prove it; think of my little children.

KROGSTAD: Did you or your husband think of mine? But that's not the point. I only wanted to tell you not to take this matter too seriously. I shan't take any action—for the present, at least.

NORA: You won't, will you? I was sure you wouldn't!

KROGSTAD: It can all be settled quite amicably. It needn't be made public. It needn't go beyond us three.

NORA: But, my husband must never know.

KROGSTAD: How can you prevent it? Can you pay off the balance?

NORA: No, not immediately.

KROGSTAD: Have you any way of raising the money within the next few days?

NORA: None—that I will make use of.

KROGSTAD: And if you had, it would have made no difference. Even if you were to offer me the entire sum in cash—I still wouldn't give you back your note.

NORA: What are you going to do with it?

KROGSTAD: I shall simply keep it—I shall guard it carefully. No one, outside the three of us, shall know a thing about it. So, if you have any thought of doing something desperate—

NORA: I shall.

KROGSTAD: —of running away from home, for instance—

NORA: I shall!

KROGSTAD: —or perhaps even something worse—

NORA: How could you guess that?

KROGSTAD: —then put all such thoughts out of your head.

NORA: How did you know that I had thought of *that*?

KROGSTAD: Most of us think of *that*, at first. I thought of it, too; but I didn't have the courage—

NORA (*Tonelessly*): I haven't either.

KROGSTAD (*Relieved*): No; you haven't the courage for it either, have you?

NORA: No! I haven't, I haven't!

KROGSTAD: Besides, it would be a very foolish thing to do. You'll just have to get through one domestic storm—and then it'll all be over. I have a letter for your husband, here in my pocket—

NORA: Telling him all about it?

KROGSTAD: Sparing you as much as possible.

NORA (*Quickly*): He must never read that letter. Tear it up, Mr. Krogstad! I will manage to get the money somehow—

KROGSTAD: Excuse me, Mrs. Helmer, but I thought I just told you—

NORA: Oh, I'm not talking about the money I owe you. Just tell me how much money you want from my husband—I will get it somehow!

KROGSTAD: I want no money from your husband.

NORA: What *do* you want then?

KROGSTAD: Just this: I want a new start; I want to make something of myself; and your husband shall help me do it. For the past eighteen months my conduct has been irreproachable. It's been a hard struggle—I've lived in abject poverty; still, I was content to work my way up gradually, step by step. But now I've been kicked out, and now I shall not be satisfied to be merely reinstated—taken back on sufferance. I'm determined to make something of myself, I tell you. I intend to continue working in the Bank—but I expect to be promoted. Your husband shall create a new position for me—

NORA: He'll never do it!

KROGSTAD: Oh, yes he will; I know him—he'll do it without a murmur; he wouldn't dare do otherwise. And then—you'll see! Within a year I'll be his right hand man. It'll be Nils Krogstad, not Torvald Helmer, who'll run the Joint Stock Bank.

NORA: That will never happen.

KROGSTAD: No? Would you, perhaps—?

NORA: Yes! I have the courage for it now.

KROGSTAD: You don't frighten me! A dainty, pampered little lady such as you—

NORA: You'll see, you'll see!

KROGSTAD: Yes, I dare say! How would you like to lie there under the ice—in that freezing, pitch-black water? And in the spring your body would be found floating on the surface—hideous, hairless, unrecognizable—

NORA: You can't frighten me!

KROGSTAD: You can't frighten me either. People don't do that sort of thing, Mrs. Helmer. And, anyway, what would be the use? I'd still have your husband in my power.

NORA: You mean—afterwards? Even if I were no longer—?

KROGSTAD: Remember—I'd still have your reputation in my hands! (NORA *stands speechless and looks at him*) Well, I've given you fair warning. I wouldn't do anything foolish, if I were you. As soon as Helmer receives my letter, I shall expect to hear from him. And just remember this: I've been forced back into my former way of life—and your husband is responsible. I shall never forgive him for it. Good-bye, Mrs. Helmer.

(*Goes out through the hall.* NORA *hurries to the door, opens it a little, and listens.*)

NORA: He's gone. He didn't leave the letter. Of course he didn't—
that would be impossible! (*Opens the door further and further*)
What's he doing? He's stopped outside the door. He's not going
down the stairs. Has he changed his mind? Is he—? (*A letter falls
into the box.* KROGSTAD'S *footsteps are heard gradually
receding down the stairs.* NORA *utters a suppressed shriek, and
rushes forward towards the sofa table; pause*) It's in the letter-
box! (*Slips shrinkingly up to the hall door*) It's there!— Torvald,
Torvald—now we are lost!

(MRS. LINDE *enters from the left with the costume.*)

MRS. LINDE: There, I think it's all right now. If you'll just try it
on—?

NORA (*Hoarsely and softly*): Come here, Kristine.

MRS. LINDE (*Throws down the dress on the sofa*): What's the matter with you? You look upset.

NORA: Come here. Do you see that letter? Do you see it—in the
letter-box?

MRS. LINDE: Yes, yes, I see it.

NORA: It's from Krogstad—

MRS. LINDE: Nora—you don't mean Krogstad lent you the money!

NORA: Yes; and now Torvald will know everything.

MRS. LINDE: It'll be much the best thing for you both, Nora.

NORA: But you don't know everything. I committed forgery—

MRS. LINDE: Good heavens!

NORA: Now, listen to me, Kristine; I want you to be my witness—

MRS. LINDE: How do you mean "witness"? What am I to—?

NORA: If I should go out of my mind—that might easily happen—

MRS. LINDE: Nora!

NORA: Or if something should happen to me—something that
would prevent my being here—!

MRS. LINDE: Nora, Nora, you're quite beside yourself!

NORA: In case anyone else should insist on taking all the blame
upon himself—the whole blame—you understand—

MRS. LINDE: Yes, but what makes you think—?

NORA: Then you must bear witness to the fact that that isn't true.
I'm in my right mind now; I know exactly what I'm saying; and I

tell you nobody else knew anything about it; I did the whole thing on my own. Just remember that.

MRS. LINDE: Very well—I will. But I don't understand at all.

NORA: No—of course—you couldn't. It's the wonderful thing—It's about to happen, don't you see?

MRS. LINDE: What "wonderful thing"?

NORA: The wonderful—wonderful thing! But it must never be allowed to happen—never. It would be too terrible.

MRS. LINDE: I'll go and talk to Krogstad at once.

NORA: No, don't go to him! He might do you some harm.

MRS. LINDE: There was a time—he would have done anything in the world for me.

NORA: He?

MRS. LINDE: Where does he live?

NORA: How do I know—? Yes— (*Feels in her pocket*) Here's his card. But the letter, the letter—!

HELMER (*From his study; knocking on the door*): Nora!

NORA (*Shrieks in terror*): Oh! What is it? What do you want?

HELMER: Don't be frightened! We're not coming in; anyway, you've locked the door. Are you trying on?

NORA: Yes, yes, I'm trying on. I'm going to look so pretty, Torvald.

MRS. LINDE (*Who has read the card*): He lives just round the corner.

NORA: But it won't do any good. It's too late now. The letter is in the box.

MRS. LINDE: I suppose your husband has the key?

NORA: Of course.

MRS. LINDE: Krogstad must ask for his letter back, unread. He must make up some excuse—

NORA: But this is the time that Torvald usually—

MRS. LINDE: Prevent him. Keep him occupied. I'll come back as quickly as I can. (*She goes out hastily by the hall door.*)

NORA (*Opens* HELMER'S *door and peeps in*): Torvald!

HELMER (*In the study*): Well? May one venture to come back into one's own living-room? Come along, Rank—now we shall see— (*In the doorway*) Why—what's this?

NORA: What, Torvald dear?

HELMER: Rank led me to expect some wonderful disguise.

RANK (*In the doorway*): That's what I understood. I must have been mistaken.

NORA: Not till tomorrow evening! Then I shall appear in all my splendor!

HELMER: But you look quite tired, Nora, dear. I'm afraid you've been practicing too hard.

NORA: Oh, I haven't practiced at all yet.

HELMER: You ought to, though—

NORA: Yes—I really should, Torvald! But I can't seem to manage without your help. I'm afraid I've forgotten all about it.

HELMER: Well—we'll see what we can do. It'll soon come back to you.

NORA: You will help me, won't you, Torvald? Promise! I feel so nervous—all those people! You must concentrate on me this evening—forget all about business. *Please*, Torvald, dear— promise me you will!

HELMER: I promise. This evening I'll be your slave—you sweet, helpless little thing—! Just one moment, though—I want to see— (*Going to hall door.*)

NORA: What do you want out there?

HELMER: I just want to see if there are any letters.

NORA: Oh, don't, Torvald! Don't bother about that now!

HELMER: Why not?

NORA: *Please* don't, Torvald! There aren't any.

HELMER: Just let me take a look— (*Starts to go.*)
(NORA, *at the piano, plays the first bars of the tarantella.*)

HELMER (*Stops in the doorway*): Aha!

NORA: I shan't be able to dance tomorrow if I don't rehearse with you!

HELMER (*Going to her*): Are you really so nervous, Nora, dear?

NORA: Yes, I'm terrified! Let's rehearse right away. We've plenty of time before dinner. Sit down and play for me, Torvald, dear; direct me—guide me; you know how you do!

HELMER: With pleasure, my darling, if you wish me to. (*Sits at piano.*)

(NORA *snatches the tambourine out of the box, and hurriedly drapes herself in a long parti-colored shawl; then, with a bound, stands in the middle of the floor and cries out.*)

NORA: Now play for me! Now I'll dance!

(HELMER *plays and* NORA *dances.* RANK *stands at the piano behind* HELMER *and looks on.*)

HELMER (*Playing*): Too fast! Too fast!

NORA: I can't help it!

HELMER: Don't be so violent, Nora!

NORA: That's the way it *should* be!

HELMER (*Stops*): No, no; this won't do at all!

NORA (*Laughs and swings her tambourine*): You see? What did I tell you?

RANK: I'll play for her.

HELMER (*Rising*): Yes, do—then I'll be able to direct her.

(RANK *sits down at the piano and plays;* NORA *dances more and more wildly.* HELMER *stands by the stove and addresses frequent corrections to her; she seems not to hear. Her hair breaks loose, and falls over her shoulders. She does not notice it, but goes on dancing.* MRS. LINDE *enters and stands spellbound in the doorway.*)

MRS. LINDE: Ah—!

NORA (*Dancing*): We're having such fun, Kristine!

HELMER: Why, Nora, dear, you're dancing as if your life were at stake!

NORA: It is! It is!

HELMER: Rank, stop! This is absolute madness. Stop, I say!

(RANK *stops playing, and* NORA *comes to a sudden standstill.*)

HELMER (*Going toward her*): I never would have believed it. You've forgotten everything I ever taught you.

NORA (*Throws the tambourine away*): I told you I had!

HELMER: This needs an immense amount of work.

NORA: That's what I said; you see how important it is! You must work with me up to the very last minute. Will you promise me, Torvald?

HELMER: I most certainly will!

NORA: This evening and all day tomorrow you must think of nothing but me. You mustn't open a single letter—mustn't even *look* at the mail-box.

HELMER: Nora! I believe you're still worried about that wretched man—

NORA: Yes—yes, I am!

HELMER: Nora— Look at me—there's a letter from him in the box, isn't there?

NORA: Maybe—I don't know; I believe there is. But you're not to read anything of that sort now; nothing must come between us until the party's over.

RANK (*Softly, to* HELMER): Don't go against her.

HELMER (*Putting his arm around her*): Very well! The child shall have her way. But tomorrow night, when your dance is over—

NORA: Then you'll be free.

(HELENE *appears in the doorway, right.*)

HELENE: Dinner is served, Ma'am.

NORA: We'll have champagne, Helene.

HELENE: Very good, Ma'am. (*Goes out.*)

HELMER: Quite a feast, I see!

NORA: Yes—a real feast! We'll stay up till dawn drinking champagne! (*Calling out*) Oh, and we'll have macaroons, Helene—lots of them! Why not—for once?

HELMER (*Seizing her hand*): Come, come! Not so violent! Be my own little lark again.

NORA: I will, Torvald. But now—both of you go in—while Kristine helps me with my hair.

RANK (*Softly, as they go*): Is anything special the matter? I mean—anything—?

HELMER: No, no; nothing at all. It's just this childish fear I was telling you about. (*They go out to the right.*)

NORA: Well?

MRS. LINDE: He's gone out of town.

NORA: I saw it in your face.

MRS. LINDE: He'll be back tomorrow evening. I left a note for him.

NORA: You shouldn't have bothered. You couldn't prevent it anyway. After all, there's a kind of joy in waiting for the wonderful thing to happen.

MRS. LINDE: I don't understand. What *is* this thing you're waiting for?

NORA: I can't explain. Go in and join them. I'll be there in a moment.

(MRS. LINDE *goes into the dining room.* NORA *stands for a moment as though pulling herself together; then looks at her watch.*)

NORA: Five o'clock. Seven hours till midnight. Twenty-four hours till the next midnight and then the tarantella will be over. Twenty-four and seven? I've thirty-one hours left to live.

(HELMER *appears at the door, right.*)

HELMER: Well! What has become of the little lark?

NORA (*Runs to him with open arms*): Here she is!

CURTAIN

ACT
THREE

SCENE: *The same room. The table, with the chairs around it, has been moved to stage-center. A lighted lamp on the table. The hall door is open. Dance music is heard from the floor above.* MRS. LINDE *sits by the table absent-mindedly turning the pages of a book. She tries to read, but seems unable to keep her mind on it. Now and then she listens intently and glances towards the hall door.*

MRS. LINDE (*Looks at her watch*): Where can he be? The time is nearly up. I hope he hasn't— (*Listens again*) Here he is now. (*She goes into the hall and cautiously opens the outer door; cautious footsteps are heard on the stairs; she whispers*) Come in; there is no one here.

KROGSTAD (*In the doorway*): I found a note from you at home. What does it mean?

MRS. LINDE: I simply *must* speak to you.

KROGSTAD: Indeed? But why here? Why in this house?

MRS. LINDE: I couldn't see you at my place. My room has no separate entrance. Come in; we're quite alone. The servants are asleep, and the Helmers are upstairs at a party.

KROGSTAD (*Coming into the room*): Well, well! So the Helmers are dancing tonight, are they?

MRS. LINDE: Why shouldn't they?

KROGSTAD: Well—why not!

MRS. LINDE: Let's have a talk, Krogstad.

KROGSTAD: Have we two anything to talk about?

MRS. LINDE: Yes. A great deal.

KROGSTAD: I shouldn't have thought so.

MRS. LINDE: But then, you see—you have never really understood me.

KROGSTAD: There wasn't much to understand, was there? A woman is heartless enough to break off with a man, when a better match is offered; it's quite an ordinary occurrence.

MRS. LINDE: You really think me heartless? Did you think it was so easy for me?

KROGSTAD: Wasn't it?

MRS. LINDE: You really believed that, Krogstad?

KROGSTAD: If not, why should you have written to me as you did?

MRS. LINDE: What else could I do? Since I was forced to break with you, I felt it was only right to try and kill your love for me.

KROGSTAD (*Clenching his hands together*): So that was it! And you did this for money!

MRS. LINDE: Don't forget I had my mother and two little brothers to think of. We couldn't wait for you, Krogstad; things were so unsettled for you then.

KROGSTAD: That may be; but, even so, you had no right to throw me over—not even for their sake.

MRS. LINDE: Who knows? I've often wondered whether I did right or not.

KROGSTAD (*More softly*): When I had lost you, I felt the ground crumble beneath my feet. Look at me. I'm like a shipwrecked man clinging to a raft.

MRS. LINDE: Help may be nearer than you think.

KROGSTAD: Help was here! Then you came and stood in the way.

MRS. LINDE: I knew nothing about it, Krogstad. I didn't know until today that I was to replace *you* at the Bank.

KROGSTAD: Very well—I believe you. But now that you do know, will you withdraw?

MRS. LINDE: No; I'd do you no good by doing that.

KROGSTAD: "Good" or not—I'd withdraw all the same.

MRS. LINDE: I have learnt to be prudent, Krogstad—I've had to. The bitter necessities of life have taught me that.

KROGSTAD: And life has taught me not to believe in phrases.

MRS. LINDE: Then life has taught you a very wise lesson. But what about deeds? Surely you must still believe in them?

KROGSTAD: How do you mean?

MRS. LINDE: You just said you were like a shipwrecked man, clinging to a raft.

KROGSTAD: I have good reason to say so.

MRS. LINDE: Well—I'm like a shipwrecked *woman* clinging to a raft. I have no one to mourn for, no one to care for.

KROGSTAD: You made your choice.

MRS. LINDE: I *had* no choice, I tell you!

KROGSTAD: What then?

MRS. LINDE: Since we're both of us shipwrecked, couldn't we join forces, Krogstad?

KROGSTAD: You don't mean—?

MRS. LINDE: Two people on a raft have a better chance than one.

KROGSTAD: Kristine!

MRS. LINDE: Why do you suppose I came here to the city?

KROGSTAD: You mean—you thought of me?

MRS. LINDE: I can't live without work; all my life I've worked, as far back as I can remember; it's always been my one great joy. Now I'm quite alone in the world; my life is empty—aimless. There's not much joy in working for one's self. You could help me, Nils; you could give me something and someone to work for.

KROGSTAD: I can't believe all this. It's an hysterical impulse—a woman's exaggerated craving for self-sacrifice.

MRS. LINDE: When have you ever found me hysterical?

KROGSTAD: You'd really be willing to do this? Tell me honestly—do you quite realize what my past has been?

MRS. LINDE: Yes.

KROGSTAD: And you know what people think of me?

MRS. LINDE: Didn't you just say you'd have been a different person if you'd been with me?

KROGSTAD: I'm sure of it.

MRS. LINDE: Mightn't that still be true?

KROGSTAD: You really mean this, Kristine, don't you? I can see it in your face. Are you sure you have the courage—?

MRS. LINDE: I need someone to care for, and your children need a mother. We two need each other, Nils. I have faith in your fundamental goodness. I'm not afraid.

KROGSTAD (*Seizing her hands*): Thank you—thank you, Kristine. I'll make others believe in me too—I won't fail you! But—I'd almost forgotten—

MRS. LINDE (*Listening*): Hush! The tarantella! You must go!

KROGSTAD: Why? What is it?

MRS. LINDE: Listen! She's begun her dance; as soon as she's finished dancing, they'll be down.

KROGSTAD: Yes—I'd better go. There'd have been no need for all that—but, of course, you don't know what I've done about the Helmers.

MRS. LINDE: Yes, I do, Nils.

KROGSTAD: And yet you have the courage to—?

MRS. LINDE: I know you were desperate—I understand.

KROGSTAD: I'd give anything to undo it!

MRS. LINDE: You can. Your letter's still in the mail-box.

KROGSTAD: Are you sure?

MRS. LINDE: Quite, but—

KROGSTAD (*Giving her a searching look*): Could that be it? You're doing all this to save your friend? You might as well be honest with me! Is that it?

MRS. LINDE: I sold myself once for the sake of others, Nils; I'm not likely to do it again.

KROGSTAD: I'll ask for my letter back unopened.

MRS. LINDE: No, no.

KROGSTAD: Yes, of course. I'll wait till Helmer comes; I'll tell him to give me back the letter—I'll say it refers to my dismissal—and ask him not to read it—

MRS. LINDE: No, Nils; don't ask for it back.

KROGSTAD: But wasn't that actually your reason for getting me to come here?

MRS. LINDE: Yes, in my first moment of fear. But that was twenty-four hours ago, and since then I've seen incredible things happening here. Helmer must know the truth; this wretched business must no longer be kept secret; it's time those two came to a thorough understanding; there's been enough deceit and subterfuge.

KROGSTAD: Very well, if you like to risk it. But there's one thing I can do, and at once—

MRS. LINDE (*Listening*): You must go now. Make haste! The dance is over; we're not safe here another moment.

KROGSTAD: I'll wait for you downstairs.

MRS. LINDE: Yes, do; then you can see me home.

KROGSTAD: Kristine! I've never been so happy! (KROGSTAD *goes out by the outer door. The door between the room and the hall remains open.*)

MRS. LINDE (*Arranging the room and getting her outdoor things together*): How different things will be! Someone to work for, to live for; a home to make happy! How wonderful it will be to try!—I wish they'd come— (*Listens*) Here they are! I'll get my coat— (*Takes bonnet and cloak.* HELMER'S *and* NORA'S *voices are heard outside, a key is turned in the lock, and* HELMER *drags* NORA *almost by force into the hall. She wears the Italian costume with a large black shawl over it. He is in evening dress and wears a black domino, open.*)

NORA (*Stuggling with him in the doorway*): No, no! I don't want to come home; I want to go upstairs again; I don't want to leave so early!

HELMER: Come—Nora dearest!

NORA: I beg you, Torvald! Please, *please*—just one hour more!

HELMER: Not one single minute more, Nora darling; don't you remember our agreement? Come along in, now; you'll catch cold. (*He leads her gently into the room in spite of her resistance*.)

MRS. LINDE: Good evening.

NORA: Kristine!

HELMER: Why, Mrs. Linde! What are you doing here so late?

MRS. LINDE: Do forgive me. I did so want to see Nora in her costume.

NORA: Have you been waiting for me all this time?

MRS. LINDE: Yes; I came too late to catch you before you went upstairs, and I didn't want to go away without seeing you.

HELMER (*Taking* NORA'S *shawl off*): And you *shall* see her, Mrs. Linde! She's worth looking at I can tell you! Isn't she lovely?

MRS. LINDE: Oh, Nora! How perfectly—!

HELMER: Absolutely exquisite, isn't she? That's what everybody said. But she's obstinate as a mule, is my sweet little thing! I don't know what to do with her. Will you believe it, Mrs. Linde, I had to drag her away by force?

NORA: You'll see—you'll be sorry, Torvald, you didn't let me stay, if only for another half-hour.

HELMER: Do you hear that, Mrs. Linde? Now, listen to this: She danced her tarantella to wild applause, and she deserved it, too, I must say—though, perhaps, from an artistic point of view, her interpretation was a bit too realistic. But never mind—the point is, she made a great success, a phenomenal success. Now—should I have allowed her to stay on and spoil the whole effect? Certainly not! I took my sweet little Capri girl—my capricious little Capri girl, I might say—in my arms; a rapid whirl round the room, a low curtsey to all sides, and—as they say in novels—the lovely apparition vanished! An exit should always be effective, Mrs. Linde; but I can't get Nora to see that. Phew! It's warm here. (*Throws his domino on a chair and opens the door to his*

room) Why—there's no light on in here! Oh no, of course—
Excuse me— (*Goes in and lights candles.*)

NORA (*Whispers breathlessly*): Well?

MRS. LINDE (*Softly*): I've spoken to him.

NORA: And—?

MRS. LINDE: Nora—you must tell your husband everything—

NORA (*Tonelessly*): I knew it!

MRS. LINDE: You have nothing to fear from Krogstad; but you
must speak out.

NORA: I shan't.

MRS. LINDE: Then the letter will.

NORA: Thank you, Kristine. Now I know what I must do. Hush—!

HELMER (*Coming back*): Well, have you finished admiring her,
Mrs. Linde?

MRS. LINDE: Yes, and now I must say good-night.

HELMER: Oh—must you be going already? Does this knitting belong to you?

MRS. LINDE (*Takes it*): Oh, thank you; I almost forgot it.

HELMER: So you knit, do you?

MRS. LINDE: Yes.

HELMER: Why don't you do embroidery instead?

MRS. LINDE: Why?

HELMER: Because it's so much prettier. Now watch! You hold the
embroidery in the left hand—so—and then, in the right hand,
you hold the needle, and guide it—so—in a long graceful
curve—isn't that right?

MRS. LINDE: Yes, I suppose so—

HELMER: Whereas, knitting can never be anything but ugly.
Now, watch! Arms close to your sides, needles going up and
down—there's something Chinese about it!— That really was
splendid champagne they gave us.

MRS. LINDE: Well, good-night, Nora; don't be obstinate any
more.

HELMER: Well said, Mrs. Linde!

MRS. LINDE: Good-night, Mr. Helmer.

HELMER (*Accompanying her to the door*): Good-night, good-
night; I hope you get home safely. I'd be only too glad to—but

you've such a short way to go. Good-night, good-night. (*She goes;* HELMER *shuts the door after her and comes forward again*) Well—thank God we've got rid of her; she's a dreadful bore, that woman.

NORA: You must be tired, Torvald.

HELMER: I? Not in the least.

NORA: But, aren't you sleepy?

HELMER: Not a bit. On the contrary, I feel exceedingly lively. But what about you? You seem to be very tired and sleepy.

NORA: Yes, I am very tired. But I'll soon sleep now.

HELMER: You see! I was right not to let you stay there any longer.

NORA: Everything you do is always right, Torvald.

HELMER (*Kissing her forehead*): There's my sweet, sensible little lark! By the way, did you notice how gay Rank was this evening?

NORA: Was he? I didn't get a chance to speak to him

HELMER: I didn't either, really; but it's a long time since I've seen him in such a jolly mood. (*Gazes at* NORA *for a while, then comes nearer her*) It's so lovely to be home again—to be here alone with you. You glorious, fascinating creature!

NORA: Don't look at me like that, Torvald.

HELMER: Why shouldn't I look at my own dearest treasure?—at all this loveliness that is mine, wholly and utterly mine—mine alone!

NORA (*Goes to the other side of the table*): You mustn't talk to me like that tonight.

HELMER (*Following*): You're still under the spell of the tarantella—and it makes you even more desirable. Listen! The other guests are leaving now. (*More softly*) Soon the whole house will be still, Nora.

NORA: I hope so.

HELMER: Yes, you do, don't you, my beloved. Do you know something—when I'm out with you among a lot of people—do you know why it is I hardly speak to you, why I keep away from you, and only occasionally steal a quick glance at you; do you know why that is? It's because I pretend that we love each other in secret, that we're secretly engaged, and that no one suspects there is anything between us.

NORA: Yes, yes; I know your thoughts are always round me.

HELMER: Then, when it's time to leave, and I put your shawl round your smooth, soft, young shoulders—round that beautiful neck of yours—I pretend that you are my young bride, that we've just come from the wedding, and that I'm taking you home for the first time—that for the first time I shall be alone with you—quite alone with you, in all your tremulous beauty. All evening I have been filled with longing for you. As I watched you swaying and whirling in the tarantella—my pulses began to throb until I thought I should go mad; that's why I carried you off—made you leave so early—

NORA: Please go, Torvald! Please leave me. I don't want you like this.

HELMER: What do you mean? You're teasing me, aren't you, little Nora? Not want me—! Aren't I your husband—?

(*A knock at the outer door.*)

NORA (*Starts*): Listen—!

HELMER (*Going toward the hall*): Who is it?

RANK (*Outside*): It is I; may I come in a moment?

HELMER (*In a low tone, annoyed*): Why does he have to bother us now! (*Aloud*) Just a second! (*Opens door*) Well! How nice of you to look in.

RANK: I heard your voice, and I thought I'd like to stop in a minute. (*Looks round*) These dear old rooms! You must be so cozy and happy here, you two!

HELMER: I was just saying how gay and happy you seemed to be upstairs.

RANK: Why not? Why shouldn't I be? One should get all one can out of life; all one can, for as long as one can. That wine was excellent—

HELMER: Especially the champagne.

RANK: You noticed that, did you? It's incredible how much I managed to get down.

NORA: Torvald drank plenty of it too.

RANK: Oh?

NORA: It always puts him in such a jolly mood.

RANK: Well, why shouldn't one have a jolly evening after a well-spent day?

HELMER: Well-spent! I'm afraid mine wasn't much to boast of!

RANK (*Slapping him on the shoulder*): But mine was, you see?

NORA: Did you by any chance make a scientific investigation, Doctor Rank?

RANK: Precisely.

HELMER: Listen to little Nora, talking about scientific investigations!

NORA: Am I to congratulate you on the result?

RANK: By all means.

NORA: It was good then?

RANK: The best possible, both for the doctor and the patient—certainty.

NORA (*Quickly and searchingly*): Certainty?

RANK: Absolute certainty. Wasn't I right to spend a jolly evening after that?

NORA: You were quite right, Doctor Rank.

HELMER: I quite agree! Provided you don't have to pay for it, to-morrow.

RANK: You don't get anything for nothing in this life.

NORA: You like masquerade parties, don't you, Dr. Rank?

RANK: Very much—when there are plenty of amusing disguises—

NORA: What shall we two be at our next masquerade?

HELMER: Listen to her! Thinking of the next party already!

RANK: We two? I'll tell you. You must go as a precious talisman.

HELMER: How on earth would you dress that!

RANK: That's easy. She'd only have to be herself.

HELMER: Charmingly put. But what about you? Have you decided what you'd be?

RANK: Oh, definitely.

HELMER: Well?

RANK: At the next masquerade party I shall be invisible.

HELMER: That's a funny notion!

RANK: There's a large black cloak—you've heard of the invisible cloak, haven't you? You've only to put it around you and no one can see you any more.

HELMER (*With a suppressed smile*): Quite true!

RANK: But I almost forgot what I came for. Give me a cigar, will you, Helmer? One of the dark Havanas.

HELMER: Of course—with pleasure. (*Hands cigar case.*)

RANK (*Takes one and cuts the end off*): Thanks.

NORA (*Striking a wax match*): Let me give you a light.

RANK: I thank you. (*She holds the match. He lights his cigar at it*) And now, I'll say good-bye!

HELMER: Good-bye, good-bye, my dear fellow.

NORA: Sleep well, Doctor Rank.

RANK: Thanks for the wish.

NORA: Wish me the same.

RANK: You? Very well, since you ask me— Sleep well. And thanks for the light. (*He nods to them both and goes out.*)

HELMER (*In an undertone*): He's had a lot to drink.

NORA (*Absently*): I dare say. (HELMER *takes his bunch of keys from his pocket and goes into the hall*) Torvald! What do you want out there?

HELMER: I'd better empty the mail-box; it's so full there won't be room for the papers in the morning.

NORA: Are you going to work tonight?

HELMER: No—you know I'm not.—Why, what's this? Someone has been at the lock.

NORA: The lock—?

HELMER: Yes—that's funny! I shouldn't have thought that the maids would— Here's a broken hair-pin. Why—it's one of yours, Nora.

NORA (*Quickly*): It must have been the children—

HELMER: You'll have to stop them doing that— There! I got it open at last. (*Takes contents out and calls out towards the kitchen*) Helene?—Oh, Helene; put out the lamp in the hall, will you? (*He returns with letters in his hand, and shuts the door to the hall*) Just look how they've stacked up. (*Looks through them*) Why, what's this?

NORA (*At the window*): The letter! Oh, Torvald! No!

HELMER: Two visiting cards—from Rank.

NORA: From Doctor Rank?

HELMER (*Looking at them*): Doctor Rank, physician. They were right on top. He must have stuck them in just now, as he left.

NORA: Is there anything on them?

HELMER: There's a black cross over his name. Look! What a grue-some thought. Just as if he were announcing his own death.

NORA: And so he is.

HELMER: What do you mean? What do you know about it? Did he tell you anything?

NORA: Yes. These cards mean that he has said good-bye to us for good. Now he'll lock himself up to die.

HELMER: Oh, my poor friend! I always knew he hadn't long to live, but I never dreamed it would be quite so soon—! And to hide away like a wounded animal—

NORA: When the time comes, it's best to go in silence. Don't you think so, Torvald?

HELMER (*Walking up and down*): He'd become such a part of us. I can't imagine his having gone for good. With his suffering and loneliness he was like a dark, cloudy background to our lives—it made the sunshine of our happiness seem even brighter— Well, I suppose it's for the best—for him at any rate. (*Stands still*) And perhaps for us too, Nora. Now we are more than ever dependent on each other. (*Takes her in his arms*) Oh, my beloved wife! I can't seem to hold you close enough. Do you know something, Nora. I often wish you were in some great danger—so I could risk body and soul—my whole life—everything, everything, for your sake.

NORA (*Tears herself from him and says firmly*): Now you must read your letters, Torvald.

HELMER: No, no; not tonight. I want to be with you, my beloved wife.

NORA: With the thought of your dying friend—?

HELMER: Of course— You are right. It's been a shock to both of us. A hideous shadow has come between us—thoughts of death and decay. We must try and throw them off. Until then—we'll stay apart.

NORA (*Her arms round his neck*): Torvald! Good-night! Good-night!

HELMER (*Kissing her forehead*): Good-night, my little song-bird; Sleep well! Now I'll go and read my letters. (*He goes with the letters in his hand into his room and shuts the door.*)

NORA (*With wild eyes, gropes about her, seizes* HELMER'S *domino, throws it round her, and whispers quickly, hoarsely, and brokenly*): I'll never see him again. Never, never, never. (*Throws her shawl over her head*) I'll never see the children again. I'll never see them either—Oh the thought of that black, icy water! That fathomless—! If it were only over! He has it now; he's reading it. Oh, not yet—please! Not yet! Torvald, good-bye—! Good-bye to you and the children!

(*She is rushing out by the hall; at the same moment* HELMER *flings his door open, and stands there with an open letter in his hand*.)

HELMER: Nora!

NORA (*Shrieks*): Ah—!

HELMER: What does this mean? Do you know what is in this letter?

NORA: Yes, yes, I know. Let me go! Let me out!

HELMER (*Holds her back*): Where are you going?

NORA (*Tries to break away from him*): Don't try to save me, Torvald!

HELMER (*Falling back*): So it's true! It's true what he writes? It's too horrible! It's impossible—it can't be true.

NORA: It *is* true. I've loved you more than all the world.

HELMER: Oh, come now! Let's have no silly nonsense!

NORA (*A step nearer him*): Torvald—!

HELMER: Do you realize what you've done?

NORA: Let me go—I won't have you suffer for it! I won't have you take the blame!

HELMER: Will you stop this play-acting! (*Locks the outer door*) You'll stay here and give an account of yourself. Do you understand what you have done? Answer me! Do you understand it?

NORA (*Looks at him fixedly, and says with a stiffening expression*): I think I'm beginning to understand for the first time.

HELMER (*Walking up and down*): God! What an awakening! After eight years to discover that you who have been my pride and joy—are no better than a hypocrite, a liar—worse than that—a criminal! It's too horrible to think of! (NORA *says nothing, and continues to look fixedly at him*) I might have known what to expect. I should have foreseen it. You've inherited all your father's lack of principle—be silent!—all of your father's lack of principle, I say!—no religion, no moral code, no sense of duty. This is my punishment for shielding him! I did it for your sake; and this is my reward!

NORA: I see.

HELMER: You've destroyed my happiness. You've ruined my whole future. It's ghastly to think of! I'm completely in the power of this scoundrel; he can force me to do whatever he likes, demand whatever he chooses; order me about at will; and I shan't dare open my mouth! My entire career is to be wrecked and all because of a lawless, unprincipled woman!

NORA: If I were no longer alive, then you'd be free.

HELMER: Oh yes! You're full of histrionics! Your father was just the same. Even if you "weren't alive," as you put it, what good would that do me? None whatever! He could publish the story all the same; I might even be suspected of collusion. People might say I was behind it all—that I had prompted you to do it. And to think I have you to thank for all this—you whom I've done nothing but pamper and spoil since the day of our marriage. Now do you realize what you've done to me?

NORA (*With cold calmness*): Yes.

HELMER: It's all so incredible, I can't grasp it. But we must try and come to some agreement. Take off that shawl. Take it off, I say! Of course, we must find some way to appease him—the matter must be hushed up at any cost. As far as we two are concerned, there must be no change in our way of life—in the eyes of the world, I mean. You'll naturally continue to live here. But you won't be allowed to bring up the children—I'd never dare trust them to you—God! to have to say this to the woman I've loved so tenderly— There can be no further thought of happiness between us. We must save what we can from the ruins—we can save appearances, at least— (*A ring;* HELMER *starts*) What can that be? At this hour! You don't suppose he—! Could he—? Hide yourself, Nora; say you are ill.

(NORA *stands motionless.* HELMER *goes to the door and opens it.*)

HELENE (*Half dressed, in the hall*): It's a letter for Mrs. Helmer.

HELMER: Give it to me. (*Seizes the letter and shuts the door*) It's from him. I shan't give it to you. I'll read it myself.

NORA: Very well.

HELMER: (*By the lamp*); I don't dare open it; this may be the end—for both of us. Still—I must know. (*Hastily tears the letter open; reads a few lines, looks at an enclosure; with a cry of joy*) Nora! (NORA *looks inquiringly at him*) Nora!—I can't believe it—I must read it again. But it's true—it's really true! Nora, I am saved! I'm saved!

NORA: What about me?

HELMER: You too, of course; we are both of us saved, both of us. Look!—he's sent you back your note—he says he's sorry for what he did and apologizes for it—that due to a happy turn of events he— Oh, what does it matter what he says! We are saved, Nora! No one can harm you now. Oh, Nora, Nora—; but let's get rid of this hateful thing. I'll just see— (*Glances at the I.O.U.*) No, no—I won't even look at it; I'll pretend it was all a horrible dream. (*Tears the I.O.U. and both letters in pieces. Throws them into the fire and watches them burn*) There! Now it's all over— He said in his letter you've known about this since Christmas Eve— you must have had three dreadful days, Nora!

NORA: Yes. It's been very hard.

HELMER: How you must have suffered! And you saw no way out but—No! We'll forget the whole ghastly business. We'll just thank God and repeat again and again: It's over; all over! Don't you understand, Nora? You don't seem to grasp it: It's over. What's the matter with you? Why do you look so grim? My poor darling little Nora, I understand; but you mustn't worry— because I've forgiven you, Nora; I swear I have; I've forgiven everything. You did what you did because you loved me—I see that now.

NORA: Yes—that's true.

HELMER: You loved me as a wife should love her husband. You didn't realize what you were doing—you weren't able to judge how wrong it was. Don't think this makes you any less dear to me. Just you lean on me; let me guide you and advise you; I'm not a man for nothing! There's something very endearing about a woman's helplessness. And try and forget those harsh things I said just now. I was frantic; my whole world seemed to be tumbling about my ears. Believe me, I've forgiven you, Nora—I swear it—I've forgiven everything.

NORA: Thank you for your forgiveness, Torvald. (*Goes out, to the right*.)

HELMER: No! Don't go. (*Looking through the doorway*) Why do you have to go in there?

NORA (*Inside*): I want to get out of these fancy-dress clothes.

HELMER (*In the doorway*): Yes, do, my darling. Try to calm down now, and get back to normal, my poor frightened little songbird. Don't you worry—you'll be safe under my wings—they'll protect you. (*Walking up and down near the door*) How lovely our home is, Nora! You'll be sheltered here; I'll cherish you as if you were a little dove I'd rescued from the claws of some dreadful hawk. You'll see—your poor fluttering little heart will soon grow calm again. Tomorrow all this will appear in quite a different light—things will be just as they were. I won't have to keep on saying I've forgiven you—you'll be able to sense it. You don't really think I could ever drive you away, do you? That I could even so much as reproach you for anything? You'd understand if you could see into my heart. When a man forgives his wife whole-heartedly—as I have you—it fills him with such tenderness, such peace. She seems to belong to him in a double sense; it's as though he'd brought her to life again; she's become more than his wife—she's become his child as well. That's how it will be with us, Nora—my own bewildered, helpless little darling. From now on you mustn't worry about anything; just open your heart to me; just let me be both will and conscience to you. (NORA *enters in everyday dress*) What's all this? I thought you were going to bed. You've changed your dress?

NORA: Yes, Torvald; I've changed my dress.

HELMER: But what for? At this hour?

NORA: I shan't sleep tonight.

HELMER: But, Nora dear—

NORA (*Looking at her watch*): It's not so very late— Sit down,

Torvald; we have a lot to talk about. (*She sits at one side of the table*.)

HELMER: Nora—what does this mean? Why that stern expression?

NORA: Sit down. It'll take some time. I have a lot to say to you. (HELMER *sits at the other side of the table*.)

HELMER: You frighten me, Nora. I don't understand you.

NORA: No, that's just it. You don't understand me; and I have never understood you either—until tonight. No, don't interrupt me. Just listen to what I have to say. This is to be a final settlement, Torvald.

HELMER: How do you mean?

NORA (*After a short silence*): Doesn't anything special strike you as we sit here like this?

HELMER: I don't think so—why?

NORA: It doesn't occur to you, does it, that though we've been married for eight years, this is the first time that we two—man and wife—have sat down for a serious talk?

HELMER: What do you mean by serious?

NORA: During eight whole years, no—more than that—ever since the first day we met—we have never exchanged so much as one serious word about serious things.

HELMER: Why should I perpetually burden you with all my cares and problems? How could you possibly help me to solve them?

NORA: I'm not talking about cares and problems. I'm simply saying we've never once sat down seriously and tried to get to the bottom of anything.

HELMER: But, Nora, darling—why should you be concerned with serious thoughts?

NORA: That's the whole point! You've never understood me—A great injustice has been done me, Torvald; first by Father, and then by you.

HELMER: What a thing to say! No two people on earth could ever have loved you more than we have!

NORA (*Shaking her head*): You never loved me. You just thought it was fun to be in love with me.

HELMER: This is fantastic!

NORA: Perhaps. But it's true all the same. While I was still at home I used to hear Father airing his opinions and they became my opinions; or if I didn't happen to agree, I kept it to myself—he would have been displeased otherwise. He used to call me his doll-baby, and played with me as I played with my dolls. Then I came to live in your house—

HELMER: What an expression to use about our marriage!

NORA (*Undisturbed*): I mean—from Father's hands I passed into yours. You arranged everything according to your tastes, and I acquired the same tastes, or I pretended to—I'm not sure which—a little of both, perhaps. Looking back on it all, it seems to me I've lived here like a beggar, from hand to mouth. I've lived by performing tricks for you, Torvald. But that's the way you wanted it. You and Father have done me a great wrong. You've prevented me from becoming a real person.

HELMER: Nora, how can you be so ungrateful and unreasonable! Haven't you been happy here?

NORA: No, never. I thought I was; but I wasn't really.

HELMER: Not—not happy!

NORA: No; only merry. You've always been so kind to me. But our home has never been anything but a play-room. I've been your doll-wife, just as at home I was Papa's doll-child. And the children in turn, have been my dolls. I thought it fun when you played games with me, just as they thought it fun when I played games with them. And that's been our marriage, Torvald.

HELMER: There may be a grain of truth in what you say, even though it is distorted and exaggerated. From now on things will be different. Play-time is over now; tomorrow lessons begin!

NORA: Whose lessons? Mine, or the children's?

HELMER: Both, if you wish it, Nora, dear.

NORA: Torvald, I'm afraid you're not the man to teach me to be a real wife to you.

HELMER: How can you say that?

NORA: And I'm certainly not fit to teach the children.

HELMER: Nora!

NORA: Didn't you just say, a moment ago, you didn't dare trust them to me?

HELMER: That was in the excitement of the moment! You mustn't take it so seriously!

NORA: But you were quite right, Torvald. That job is beyond me; there's another job I must do first: I must try and educate myself. You could never help me to do that; I must do it quite alone. So, you see—that's why I'm going to leave you.

HELMER (*Jumping up*): What did you say—?

NORA: I shall never get to know myself—I shall never learn to face reality—unless I stand alone. So I can't stay with you any longer.

HELMER: Nora! Nora!

NORA: I am going at once. I'm sure Kristine will let me stay with her tonight—

HELMER: But, Nora—this is madness! I shan't allow you to do this. I shall forbid it!

NORA: You no longer have the power to forbid me anything. I'll only take a few things with me—those that belong to me. I shall never again accept anything from you.

HELMER: Have you lost your senses?

NORA: Tomorrow I'll go home—to what *was* my home, I mean. It might be easier for me there, to find something to do.

HELMER: You talk like an ignorant child, Nora—!

NORA: Yes. That's just why I must educate myself.

HELMER: To leave your home—to leave your husband, and your children! What do you suppose people would say to that?

NORA: It makes no difference. This is something I *must* do.

HELMER: It's inconceivable! Don't you realize you'd be betraying your most sacred duty?

NORA: What do you consider that to be?

HELMER: Your duty towards your husband and your children— I surely don't have to tell you that!

NORA: I've another duty just as sacred.

HELMER: Nonsense! What duty do you mean?

NORA: My duty towards myself.

HELMER: Remember—before all else you are a wife and mother.

NORA: I don't believe that anymore. I believe that before all else I am a human being, just as you are—or at least that I should try and become one. I know that most people would agree with you,

Torvald—and that's what they say in books. But I can no longer be satisfied with what most people say—or what they write in books. I must think things out for myself—get clear about them.

HELMER: Surely your position in your home is clear enough? Have you no sense of religion? Isn't that an infallible guide to you?

NORA: But don't you see, Torvald—I don't really know what religion is.

HELMER: Nora! How *can* you!

NORA: All I know about it is what Pastor Hansen told me when I was confirmed. He taught me what he thought religion was— said it was *this* and *that.* As soon as I get away by myself, I shall have to look into that matter too, try and decide whether what he taught me was right—or whether it's right for *me*, at least.

HELMER: A nice way for a young woman to talk! It's unheard of! If religion means nothing to you, I'll appeal to your conscience; you must have some sense of ethics, I suppose? Answer me! Or have you none?

NORA: It's hard for me to answer you, Torvald. I don't think I know—all these things bewilder me. But I *do* know that I think quite differently from you about them. I've discovered that the law, for instance, is quite different from what I had imagined; but I find it hard to believe it can be right. It seems it's criminal for a woman to try and spare her old, sick, father, or save her husband's life! I can't agree with that.

HELMER: You talk like a child. You have no understanding of the society we live in.

NORA: No, I haven't. But I'm going to try and learn. I want to find out which of us is right—society or I.

HELMER: You are ill, Nora; you have a touch of fever; you're quite beside yourself.

NORA: I've never felt so sure—so clear-headed—as I do tonight.

HELMER: "Sure and clear-headed" enough to leave your husband and your children?

NORA: Yes.

HELMER: Then there is only one explanation possible.

NORA: What?

HELMER: You don't love me any more.

NORA: No; that is just it.

HELMER: Nora!— What are you saying!

NORA: It makes me so unhappy, Torvald; for you've always been so kind to me. But I can't help it. I don't love you any more.

HELMER (*Mastering himself with difficulty*): You feel "sure and clear-headed" about this too?

NORA: Yes, utterly sure. That's why I can't stay here any longer.

HELMER: And can you tell me how I lost your love?

NORA: Yes, I can tell you. It was tonight—when the wonderful thing didn't happen; I knew then you weren't the man I always thought you were.

HELMER: I don't understand.

NORA: For eight years I've been waiting patiently; I knew, of course, that such things don't happen every day. Then, when this trouble came to me—I thought to myself: Now! Now the wonderful thing will happen! All the time Krogstad's letter was out there in the box, it never occurred to me for a single moment that you'd think of submitting to his conditions. I was absolutely convinced that you'd defy him—that you'd tell him to publish the thing to all the world; and that then—

HELMER: You mean you thought I'd let my wife be publicly dishonored and disgraced?

NORA: No. What I thought you'd do, was to take the blame upon yourself.

HELMER: Nora—!

NORA: I know! You think I never would have accepted such a sacrifice. Of course I wouldn't! But my word would have meant nothing against yours. That was the wonderful thing I hoped for, Torvald, hoped for with such terror. And it was to prevent that, that I chose to kill myself.

HELMER: I'd gladly work for you day and night, Nora—go through suffering and want, if need be—but one doesn't sacrifice one's honor for love's sake.

NORA: Millions of women have done so.

HELMER: You think and talk like a silly child.

NORA: Perhaps. But you neither think nor talk like the man I want to share my life with. When you'd recovered from your fright —and you never thought of me, only of yourself—when you had nothing more to fear—you behaved as though none of this had happened. I was your little lark again, your little doll—whom you would have to guard more carefully than ever, because she was so weak and frail. (*Stands up*) At that moment it suddenly dawned on me that I had been living here for eight years with a stranger and that I'd borne him three children. I can't bear to think about it! I could tear myself to pieces!

HELMER (*Sadly*): I see, Nora—I understand; there's suddenly a great void between us— Is there no way to bridge it?

NORA: Feeling as I do now, Torvald—I could never be a wife to you.

HELMER: But, if I were to change? Don't you think I'm capable of that?

NORA: Perhaps—when you no longer have your doll to play with.

HELMER: It's inconceivable! I *can't* part with you, Nora. I can't endure the thought.

NORA (*Going into room on the right*): All the more reason it should happen. (*She comes back with outdoor things and a small traveling-bag, which she places on a chair.*)

HELMER: But not at once, Nora—not now! At least wait till tomorrow.

NORA (*Putting on cloak*): I can't spend the night in a strange man's house.

HELMER: Couldn't we go on living here together? As brother and sister, if you like—as friends.

NORA (*Fastening her hat*): You know very well that wouldn't last, Torvald. (*Puts on the shawl*) Good-bye. I won't go in and see the children. I know they're in better hands than mine. Being what I am—how can I be of any use to them?

HELMER: But surely, some day, Nora—?

NORA: How can I tell? How do I know what sort of person I'll become?

HELMER: You are my wife, Nora, now and always!

NORA: Listen to me, Torvald—I've always heard that when a wife deliberately leaves her husband as I am leaving you, he is legally freed from all responsibility towards her. At any rate, I release you now from all responsibility. You mustn't feel yourself bound, any more than I shall. There must be complete freedom on both sides. Here is your ring. Now give me mine.

HELMER: That too?

NORA: That too.

HELMER: Here it is.

NORA: So—it's all over now. Here are the keys. The servants know how to run the house—better than I do. I'll ask Kristine to come by tomorrow, after I've left town; there are a few things I brought with me from home; she'll pack them up and send them on to me.

HELMER: You really mean it's over, Nora? *Really* over? You'll never think of me again?

NORA: I expect I shall often think of you; of you—and the children, and this house.

HELMER: May I write to you?

NORA: No—never. You mustn't! Please!

HELMER: At least, let me send you—

NORA: Nothing!

HELMER: But, you'll let me help you, Nora—

NORA: No, I say! I can't accept anything from strangers.

HELMER: Must I always be a stranger to you, Nora?

NORA (*Taking her traveling-bag*): Yes. Unless it were to happen—the most wonderful thing of all—

HELMER: What?

NORA: Unless we both could change so that— Oh, Torvald! I no longer *believe* in miracles, you see!

HELMER: Tell me! Let *me* believe! Unless we both could change so that—?

NORA: —So that our life together might truly be a marriage. Goodbye. (*She goes out by the hall door.*)

HELMER (*Sinks into a chair by the door with his face in his hands*): Nora! Nora! (*He looks around the room and rises*) She is gone! How empty it all seems! (*A hope springs up in him*) The most wonderful thing of all—?

(*From below is heard the reverberation of a heavy door closing.*)

Ghosts

**A DOMESTIC TRAGEDY
IN THREE ACTS**

1881

CHARACTERS

MRS. HELENE ALVING, *the widow of Captain (Chamberlain) Alving*

OSVALD ALVING, *her son; a painter*

PASTOR MANDERS

JAKOB ENGSTRAND, *a carpenter*

REGINE ENGSTRAND,* *a member of the Alving household*

> *The action takes place on Mrs. Alving's country estate on one of the large fjords in the west of Norway.*

*For stage purposes, often REGINA.

ACT
ONE

SCENE: *A spacious garden-room; in the left wall a door, and in the right wall two doors. In the center of the room a round table, with chairs about it. On the table lie books, periodicals and newspapers. In the foreground to the left a window, and by it a small sofa, with a work-table in front of it. In the background, the room is continued into a somewhat narrower conservatory, the walls of which are formed by large panes of glass. In the right-hand wall of the conservatory is a door leading down into the garden. Through the glass wall a gloomy fjord landscape is faintly visible, veiled by steady rain.*

ENGSTRAND, *the carpenter, stands by the garden door. His left leg is somewhat bent; he has a clump of wood under the sole of his boot.* REGINE, *with an empty garden syringe in her hand, hinders him from advancing.*

REGINE (*In a low voice*): Well—what is it you want? No!—stay where you are—you're dripping wet!

ENGSTRAND: It's only God's rain, my child.

REGINE: It's the devil's rain, that's what it is!

ENGSTRAND: Lord, how you talk, Regine! (*Limping a few steps into the room*) But, here's what I want to tell you—

REGINE: Don't go clumping about with that foot of yours! The young master's upstairs asleep.

ENGSTRAND: Asleep at this hour—in broad daylight?

REGINE: It's none of your business.

ENGSTRAND: Now—look at *me*—I was on a bit of a spree last night—

REGINE: That's nothing new!

81

ENGSTRAND: Well—we're all frail creatures, my child—

REGINE: We are that!

ENGSTRAND: And temptations are manifold in this world, you see—but that didn't prevent me from going to work at half past five as usual!

REGINE: That's as it may be—and now, get out! I can't stand here having a rendezvous with you.

ENGSTRAND: What's that?

REGINE: I don't want anyone to see you here—so get out!

ENGSTRAND (*Comes a few steps nearer*): Damned if I go till I've had a talk with you. Listen—I'll be through with my work at the school-house this afternoon—then I'm going right back to town by the night boat—

REGINE (*Mutters*): A pleasant journey to you!

ENGSTRAND: Thank you, my child! Tomorrow's the opening of the Orphanage, they'll all be celebrating—sure to be a lot of drinking too—I'll prove to them that Jakob Engstrand can keep out of the way of temptation—

REGINE: Ha! . . .

ENGSTRAND: Lots of grand people'll be here—Pastor Manders is expected from town—

REGINE: He gets here today.

ENGSTRAND: There—you see! Damned if I give *him* a chance to say anything against me!

REGINE: So that's it, is it?

ENGSTRAND: That's what?

REGINE (*Gives him a searching look*): What are you going to try and put over on him this time?

ENGSTRAND: Are you crazy? As if I'd try and put anything over on *him!* No—Pastor Manders has been too good a friend to me—and that's just what I want to talk to you about. As I was saying, I'm going back home tonight—

REGINE: You can't go soon enough to please me!

ENGSTRAND: But I want you to come with me, Regine.

REGINE (*Open-mouthed*): I, go with *you?*

ENGSTRAND: Yes—I want you to come home with me.

REGINE (*Scornfully*): You'll never get me to do that!

ENGSTRAND: Well—we'll see.

REGINE: Yes! You'll see all right! After being brought up here by Mrs. Alving—treated almost like one of the family—do you suppose I'd go home with you—back to that kind of a house? You're crazy!

ENGSTRAND: What kind of talk's that! You'd defy your own father, would you?

REGINE (*Mutters, without looking at him*): You've said often enough I'm no concern of yours—

ENGSTRAND: Never mind about that—

REGINE: Many's the time you've cursed at me and called me a—Fi donc!

ENGSTRAND: When did I ever use a foul word like that?

REGINE: I know well enough whàt word you used!

ENGSTRAND: Well—maybe—when I wasn't feeling quite myself—hm. Temptations are manifold in this world, Regine!

REGINE: Pah! . . .

ENGSTRAND: And then your mother used to drive me crazy—I had to find some way to get back at her. She put on so many airs: (*Mimicking her*) "Let me go, Engstrand! Leave me alone! Don't forget I spent three years in Chamberlain Alving's house at Rosenvold!" (*Laughs*) God Almighty! She never got over the Captain being made Chamberlain while she was working here!

REGINE: Poor mother! You certainly hounded her into her grave!

ENGSTRAND (*Shrugging his shoulders*): Oh, of course! I'm to blame for everything!

REGINE (*Under her breath as she turns away*): Ugh! And then that leg of yours!

ENGSTRAND: What did you say, my child?

REGINE: Pied de mouton!

ENGSTRAND: What's that? English?*

REGINE: Yes.

ENGSTRAND: Yes—well; you've certainly got educated here—and that may come in handy too.

---

*In performance this should be changed to "German," since the characters are speaking in English.

REGINE (*After a short silence*): Why do you want me to go back with you?

ENGSTRAND: Why wouldn't a father want his only child with him? Aren't I a lonely, deserted widower?

REGINE: Oh, don't talk rubbish to me! Why do you want me with you?

ENGSTRAND: Well—I'll tell you—I'm thinking of setting up in a new line of business—

REGINE (*Whistles*): What, again! What is it this time?

ENGSTRAND: You'll see—this time it'll be different. Christ Almighty—!

REGINE: Stop your swearing! (*She stamps her foot.*)

ENGSTRAND: Sh! You're right, my child. Well—what I wanted to say was—I've managed to save quite a bit of money—from this work on the Orphanage—

REGINE: You have, have you? So much the better for you.

ENGSTRAND: There's nothing to spend your money on in this God-forsaken hole—

REGINE: Well?

ENGSTRAND: So I thought I'd invest it in a paying concern. I thought of starting a sort of tavern—for seamen—

REGINE: Ugh!

ENGSTRAND: A really high-class tavern, you know—none of your cheap dives. No—by God! I'd cater to Captains and First-mates—really high-class people.

REGINE: And I suppose I'd be expected to—

ENGSTRAND: Oh, you could be a great help, Regine. You wouldn't have to do anything—it wouldn't be hard on you, my child— you'd have everything your own way!

REGINE: Oh yes, of course!

ENGSTRAND: After all there must be some women in the house— that goes without saying. We'd have to have a bit of fun in the evenings, singing and dancing—and that sort of thing. You've got to remember—these poor fellows are sailors— wanderers on the seas of the world. (*Comes nearer to her*) Don't be a fool and stand in your own way. What future is there for you out here? What good's all this education the Mrs. has paid for? You're to look after the kids in the new Orphanage I hear—is that a job for you? Do you want to wear yourself to the bone looking after a lot of dirty brats?

REGINE: If things turn out as I hope—well—it could be—it could be—

ENGSTRAND: What "could be"?

REGINE: You keep your nose out of that! How much money did you save?

ENGSTRAND: I'd say—in all—close to two hundred dollars.

REGINE: Not so bad!

ENGSTRAND: Enough to get me started, my child.

REGINE: Do I get any of it?

ENGSTRAND: You do not!

REGINE: Not even enough to buy myself a new dress?

ENGSTRAND: You come with me—you'll get plenty of new dresses then!

REGINE: I can get them myself, if I set my mind to it.

ENGSTRAND: But a father's guiding hand is a good thing, Regine. There's a nice little house right on Harbor Street—not much money down either—it'd be like a kind of Seamen's Home, you know.

REGINE: But I don't want to live with you! I don't want to have anything to do with you! So now—get out!

ENGSTRAND: You wouldn't be with me for long, my child—I know that well enough. All you've got to do is use your wits—you've turned into a handsome wench—do you know that?

REGINE: Well—what of it?

ENGSTRAND: Before you know it, some First-mate'll come along—maybe even a Captain.

REGINE: I don't intend to marry any such trash. Sailors have no "savoir vivre."

ENGSTRAND: Well—I couldn't say about that—

REGINE: I tell you I know all about sailors. I wouldn't think of marrying one of them!

ENGSTRAND: Who says you'd have to marry? You can make it pay just the same. (*More confidentially*) That Englishman—the one with the yacht—he gave three hundred dollars, he did—and she wasn't any better looking than you are.

REGINE (*Goes towards him*): Get out of here!

ENGSTRAND (*Retreating*): Now, now! You wouldn't hit me, would you?

REGINE: You just say anything against Mother, and you'll see whether I'd hit you or not! Get out, I say! (*She pushes him towards the garden door*) And don't bang the door; young Mister Alving—

ENGSTRAND: Is asleep—I know! Why should you be so worried about him? (*In a lower tone*) God—Almighty! You don't mean to tell me that he—?

REGINE: You must be out of your head—you fool! Go on now—get out this minute. No—not that way—here comes Pastor Manders; the back stairs for you!

ENGSTRAND (*Goes toward door right*): All right—I'll go. But listen—you have a talk with him—he'll tell you what you owe your father—for I am your father after all, you know; I can prove that by the Church Register.

(*He goes out through the other door that* REGINE *has opened for him and closes after him. She glances at herself quickly in the mirror, fans herself with her handkerchief and straightens her collar; then she sets about tending the flowers.* PASTOR MANDERS *enters the conservatory by the garden door. He wears an overcoat, carries an umbrella and has a small traveling-bag slung over his shoulder.*)

MANDERS: Good-day, Miss Engstrand.

REGINE (*Turning in glad surprise*): Well! Good-day, Pastor Manders! Fancy! So the steamer's in, is it?

MANDERS (*He comes into the room*): Yes—just docked. Dreadful weather we've had these last few days.

REGINE (*Following him*): It's a blessing for the farmers, Pastor Manders.

MANDERS: Quite right, Miss Engstrand! We city-folk never think of that. (*He begins taking off his overcoat.*)

REGINE: Do let me help you! My goodness! It's soaking wet! I'll just hang it in the hall—and, let me take your umbrella—I'll open it up—so it'll dry quicker.

(*She goes out with the things by the second door on the right.* MANDERS *puts his traveling-bag on a chair with his hat. Meanwhile,* REGINE *comes in again.*)

MANDERS: It's very pleasant to be indoors. And how are things going here? All well, I trust?

REGINE: Yes—many thanks.

MANDERS: I expect you've been very busy with tomorrow's preparations.

REGINE: Yes—there's been so much to do!

MANDERS: And Mrs. Alving is at home, I hope?

REGINE: Oh yes, indeed. She just went upstairs to give the young master his hot chocolate.

MANDERS: Tell me—I heard down at the pier that Osvald had come home—

REGINE: He arrived the day before yesterday—we didn't expect him until today.

MANDERS: In good health and spirits, I trust?

REGINE: Yes, thank you, he seems to be—but dreadfully tired after his journey. He came straight through from Paris—without a stop; I mean, he came the whole way without a break. I think he's taking a little nap—so we must talk very quietly.

MANDERS: Sh! We'll be still as mice!

REGINE (*She moves an armchair up to the table*): Do sit down, Pastor Manders, and make yourself comfortable. (*He sits; she places a footstool under his feet*) There! How does that feel?

MANDERS: Most comfortable, thank you! (*He looks at her*) Do you know, Miss Engstrand, I really believe you've grown since I saw you last.

REGINE: Do you think so, Pastor Manders? Mrs. Alving says I've filled out too.

MANDERS: Filled out, eh? Yes, yes—perhaps a little—just suitably.

(*Short pause.*)

REGINE: Shall I tell Mrs. Alving you're here?

MANDERS: Thank you—there's no hurry, my dear child—Well—tell me, my dear Regine, how is your father getting on out here?

REGINE: Pretty well, thank you, Mr. Manders.

MANDERS: He came in to see me last time he was in town.

REGINE: Did he really? He's always so grateful for a talk with you, Mr. Manders.

MANDERS: I suppose you see him regularly, every day?

REGINE: I?— Oh, yes—of course.— Whenever I have time—that
is—

MANDERS: I'm afraid your father is not a very strong character,
Miss Engstrand. He badly needs a guiding hand.

REGINE: Yes, I dare say he does, Mr. Manders.

MANDERS: He needs someone near him—someone he can lean
on—whose judgment he respects. He admitted as much, quite
candidly, last time he came to see me.

REGINE: Yes—he said something of the sort to me. But I don't
know if Mrs. Alving would want to let me go—especially now
that we'll have the Orphanage to manage. And I really couldn't
bear to leave Mrs. Alving—she's always been so good to me.

MANDERS: But a daughter's duty, my dear child—of course, we
would first have to gain Mrs. Alving's consent.

REGINE: But would it be quite the thing, at my age, to keep house
for a single man?

MANDERS: What do you mean? My dear Miss Engstrand, it's a
question of your own father!

REGINE: Yes, I know—but all the same—of course if it were a
proper kind of house—belonging to a real gentleman—

MANDERS: Why—my dear Regine—!

REGINE: Oh, I mean a man I could look up to—respect—become
attached to—as though I were really his daughter—

MANDERS: But, my dear child—

REGINE: Then I'd gladly live in town again—for I'm often very
lonely here—and you know yourself, Mr. Manders, what it is to
be alone in the world. And I'm capable and willing—though I say
it myself as shouldn't. Mr. Manders—I suppose you couldn't
find me a position of that sort?

MANDERS: I? No—I'm really afraid I can't.

REGINE: But, you will think of me, dear, dear Mr. Manders—
you'll keep me in mind in case—

MANDERS: (*Gets up*): Yes, yes—of course, Miss Engstrand—

REGINE: Because, you see—if I could only—

MANDERS: Would you be so kind as to tell Mrs. Alving I am here?

REGINE: I'll go and call her at once, Mr. Manders.

(*She goes out left*. MANDERS *paces up and down the room a cou-*

*ple of times, then stands for a moment upstage with his hands be-
hind his back looking out into the garden. Then he comes back to
the table, picks up a book and glances at the title page. He gives a
start and examines some of the others.)*

MANDERS: Hm!— Well—well! Really!

(MRS. ALVING *comes in by the door left followed by* REGINE
who immediately goes out by the first door on the right.)

MRS. ALVING *(With outstretched hand)*: Welcome, dear Mr. Manders!

MANDERS: Good-day, Mrs. Alving. Well—here I am—as I promised.

MRS. ALVING: And punctual as usual!

MANDERS: I had great trouble getting away. As you know—I m
chairman of so many organizations—and what with my committee meetings—

MRS. ALVING: I'm all the more grateful to you for coming so
promptly. Now we shall be able to get all our business settled before dinner. But, where is your luggage?

MANDERS *(Hastily)*: I left my things down at the Inn—I'll put up
there for the night.

MRS. ALVING *(Repressing a smile)*: Can't I really persuade you to
spend the night here this time?

MANDERS: No, no, Mrs. Alving—thank you all the same—but I
prefer to stay there as usual. It's so convenient—right by the
pier, you know.

MRS. ALVING: Well—just as you wish! I should have thought, that
perhaps, at our age—!

MANDERS: Ah—yes, of course—you will have your little joke!
Well—I suppose you're radiantly happy today—what with tomorrow's ceremony—and having Osvald home again—

MRS. ALVING: Yes—isn't it wonderful! He hasn't been home for
over two years, you know. And he's promised to spend the whole
winter with me!

MANDERS: Has he really? That's a nice filial gesture—for I'm sure
his life in Rome and Paris must offer many attractions.

MRS. ALVING: Yes, no doubt—but after all, he has his mother
here. God bless him—he still has a place in his heart for me.

MANDERS: It would be regrettable indeed if separation and his interest in such a thing as Art, were to interfere with his natural affections.

MRS. ALVING: That's true. But fortunately, there's no danger of that with him. I'll be curious to see if you recognize him after all these years—he'll be down presently—he's just having a little rest upstairs. But—do sit down, dear Mr. Manders.

MANDERS: Thank you. You're sure I'm not disturbing you?

MRS. ALVING (*Sits by table*): Of course not!

MANDERS: Splendid—then suppose we get down to business. (*He goes to the chair and takes a bundle of papers out of his traveling-bag. Then sits down at the table opposite* MRS. ALVING. *He tries to arrange a space on which to lay out the papers*) Now first of all there's the question of— (*Breaks off*) Tell me, Mrs. Alving—what are those books doing here?

MRS. ALVING: These? I happen to be reading them.

MANDERS: You really read this sort of thing?

MRS. ALVING: Of course I do.

MANDERS: Do you feel that this type of reading makes you any better—any happier?

MRS. ALVING: It gives me a certain confidence.

MANDERS: Extraordinary! How do you mean?

MRS. ALVING: It seems to clarify and confirm many things I've thought about myself. The strange thing is, Mr. Manders, there's really nothing new in any of these books; they deal with subjects that most of us think about and believe in; though I dare say most people don't take the trouble to look into them very deeply—or face them very honestly.

MANDERS: But, good Heavens—you don't seriously believe that most people—?

MRS. ALVING: I most emphatically do.

MANDERS: But surely not here—surely not *our* kind of people—

MRS. ALVING: Yes! "Our kind of people" too.

MANDERS: Well—I really must say—!

MRS. ALVING: But, what precisely do you object to in these books?

MANDERS: Object to? You don't imagine I waste my time delving into such subjects!

MRS. ALVING: Then you're condemning them without knowing them?

MANDERS: I've read quite enough about these books to disapprove of them.

MRS. ALVING: But, how can you form an opinion if you haven't—?

MANDERS: My dear Mrs. Alving—in some things it is wiser to depend on the opinion of others. That is the way our world functions—and it is best that it should be so. Otherwise, what would become of Society?

MRS. ALVING: Well—you may be right.

MANDERS: I don't deny that such books may have a certain fascination. And I don't blame you for wishing to familiarize yourself with certain intellectual trends which, I understand, are current in the sophisticated world where your son has been allowed to roam so freely. But—

MRS. ALVING: But—?

MANDERS (*Lowering his voice*): But one doesn't discuss such things openly, Mrs. Alving. There is no reason to give an account to all and sundry of what one reads, or thinks, in the privacy of one's own room.

MRS. ALVING: Certainly not—I agree with you—

MANDERS: Think of your new responsibilities towards the Orphanage. When you decided to found it, your feelings on certain subjects were decidedly at variance with those you now entertain—unless I am greatly mistaken.

MRS. ALVING: I grant you that. But, let's get back to the Orphanage, Mr. Manders.

MANDERS: By all means—only, remember: caution, my dear Mrs. Alving! And now—to work! (*Opens an envelope and takes out some papers*) You see these papers—?

MRS. ALVING: The deeds?

MANDERS: Yes—all in order at last! I had great trouble in getting them in time. I had to bring strong pressure to bear on the authorities; they are painfully conscientious when it comes to property settlements of any kind, but here they are at last. (*Turns over the papers*) This is the deed of conveyance for that part of the Rosenvold estate known as the Solvik property, together with all the newly erected buildings, the school, the teacher's house and the chapel. And here is the Charter of the Institution: "Charter of the Orphanage in memory of Captain Alving."

MRS. ALVING (*After examining the papers at some length*): That all seems clear—

MANDERS: I used the title "Captain" instead of "Court Chamberlain"—it seemed less ostentatious.

MRS. ALVING: Whatever you think best.

MANDERS: Here is the bank-book controlling the invested capital—the interest on which will be used to defray the running expenses of the institution.

MRS. ALVING: Thank you—you'll take charge of that, won't you?

MANDERS: Certainly, if you wish. For the time being, I think it would be wise to leave the entire sum in the bank—the interest is not very attractive it's true—but we could then take our time and later on find a good mortgage—it would of course have to be a first mortgage and on unexceptionable security—we can afford to take no risks—but we can discuss that matter at a later date.

MRS. ALVING: Yes, dear Mr. Manders—I leave all that to you.

MANDERS: I'll keep a sharp look-out. Now, there's something else—I've meant to take it up with you several times.

MRS. ALVING: And what is that?

MANDERS: The question of insurance. Do you wish me to take out insurance on the Orphanage or not?

MRS. ALVING: Well of course it must be insured!

MANDERS: Just a moment, Mrs. Alving—let us examine the matter more carefully.

MRS. ALVING: But, everything I own is insured—my house and its contents—the livestock—everything.

MANDERS: Your personal property, of course. All my things are insured too. But this is quite a different matter. The Orphanage is dedicated to a high spiritual purpose—

MRS. ALVING: Yes, but—

MANDERS: As far as I am personally concerned, I can't see the slightest objection to safe-guarding ourselves against all possible risks—

MRS. ALVING: I quite agree—

MANDERS: But what about public opinion?

MRS. ALVING: Public opinion—?

MANDERS: Are there any groups of people here—people who matter, I mean—who might take exception to it?

MRS. ALVING: What do you mean by "people who matter"?

MANDERS: I mean men of wealth and influence whose opinion it might be unwise to overlook.

MRS. ALVING: I see what you mean—yes, there may be a few people here who might object—

MANDERS: There, you see! In town I think there might be a strong feeling against it—among my colleagues for instance, and some of the more influential members of their congregations; it could be implied that we hadn't sufficient faith in Divine Providence.

MRS. ALVING: But, surely, Mr. Manders, you have no such feeling—

MANDERS: Oh, as far as I am personally concerned, I have no qualms in the matter; but we might not be able to prevent our action from being interpreted in an erroneous and unfortunate light—and this in turn might reflect on the work of the Orphanage.

MRS. ALVING: Of course, if that were to be the case—

MANDERS: And I admit, I can't quite overlook the embarrassing—I might even say difficult position—I should find myself in. In town this Orphanage has been much discussed by the leading citizens. They are well aware of the benefits that would accrue to the town from such an institution—its existence would undoubtedly reduce to an important degree the yearly sums they are expected to donate to charitable works. And, since I have been your adviser in this matter—your business representative from the beginning—most of the blame and criticism would inevitably fall on me—

MRS. ALVING: I wouldn't want you to be exposed to that.

MANDERS: Not to speak of the attacks that would unquestionably be made against me by certain newspapers—

MRS. ALVING: That settles it, Mr. Manders—we'll say no more about it!

MANDERS: Then, we decide against insurance?

MRS. ALVING: Yes—we'll let that go.

MANDERS (*Leaning back in his chair*): But, on the other hand, Mrs. Alving, suppose there *should* be an accident—one never knows—would you be prepared to make good the damage?

MRS. ALVING: No, I must tell you quite frankly, that would be out of the question.

MANDERS: In that case we are assuming a very grave responsibility.

MRS. ALVING: Well—do you see anything else to do?

MANDERS: I'm afraid not—I don't really see that there's anything else we *can* do; we don't want to be placed in a false position—and we have no right to arouse the antagonism of the Community.

MRS. ALVING: Especially you—as a clergyman.

MANDERS: We must simply have faith that our institution will be under the special protection of Providence.

MRS. ALVING: Let us hope so, Mr. Manders.

MANDERS: Then—we'll let it go?

MRS. ALVING: By all means.

MANDERS: As you wish. (*Makes a note*) No insurance.

MRS. ALVING: It's strange you should happen to bring this up today—

MANDERS: I've often meant to discuss it with you—

MRS. ALVING: Because only yesterday we nearly had a fire down there.

MANDERS: What!

MRS. ALVING: Nothing came of it, fortunately—some wood-shavings caught fire—in the carpenter's shop—

MANDERS: Where Engstrand works?

MRS. ALVING: Yes. They say he's often very careless with matches—

MANDERS: Poor man—he has so much on his mind—so many worries. I'm happy to say he's decided to turn over a new leaf.

MRS. ALVING: Indeed? Who told you that?

MANDERS: He assured me so himself. I'm very glad—he's such an excellent worker.

MRS. ALVING: Yes—when he's sober.

MANDERS: That unfortunate weakness! He tells me it relieves the pain in that poor leg of his. Last time he came to see me in town, he was really very touching. He was so grateful to me for getting him this work here—where he could be near Regine.

MRS. ALVING: I don't think he sees much of her

MANDERS: Oh yes, he sees her every day—he told me so himself.

MRS. ALVING: Well—it's possible.

MANDERS: He realizes the need of someone near him, to help him when temptation gets too strong for him. That's what is so endearing about Jakob Engstrand—he admits how weak he is—and is so anxious to reform. Mrs. Alving—suppose it should become a real necessity for him to have Regine home with him again—?

MRS. ALVING (*Rises quickly*): Regine—?

MANDERS: I urge you not to oppose it.

MRS. ALVING: I most certainly would oppose it! And besides— Regine is to work at the Orphanage.

MANDERS: But—he *is* her father after all—

MRS. ALVING: I know only too well the kind of father he is! No! She shall never go back to him while I have anything to say in the matter!

MANDERS (*Gets up*): But, my dear Mrs. Alving, why be so violent about it! It's a great pity that you misjudge Engstrand so. One would think you were actually afraid—

MRS. ALVING (*More calmly*): That's not the point. I am looking after Regine now and she will stay here with me. (*Listens*) Sh! Dear Mr. Manders, let's not discuss this any further. (*Her face lights up with joy*) Here comes Osvald. We'll think about *him* now.

(OSVALD ALVING *enters left. He has on a light overcoat and is carrying his hat. He is smoking a large Meerschaum pipe.*)

OSVALD (*Standing in the doorway*): Oh, I'm sorry—I thought you were in the library—I didn't mean to disturb you. (*Comes in*) How do you do, Mr. Manders!

MANDERS (*Stares at him*): Well, what an amazing—!

MRS. ALVING: What do you think of him, Mr. Manders?

MANDERS: Can it really be—?

OSVALD: Yes—it's the Prodigal Son, Mr. Manders!

MANDERS: My dear boy—!

OSVALD: Or the wandering son returned to the fold—if you prefer.

MRS. ALVING: He's only joking, Mr. Manders— He's referring to your disapproval of an artist's career.

MANDERS: We are not infallible in our judgments; certain steps may seem to us dangerous that turn out in the end to be— (*Shakes hands with him*) So, welcome! Welcome home, my dear Osvald!—I may still call you Osvald, I trust?

OSVALD: What else should you call me, Mr. Manders?

MANDERS: Splendid!—I was just going to say—you must not imagine, my dear Osvald, that I unconditionally condemn the artist's life. I dare say there are many who succeed, in spite of everything, in preserving their integrity of character.

OSVALD: Let us hope so!

MRS. ALVING (*Beaming with pleasure*): Well—this one's managed to do so, Mr. Manders—you've only to look at him to see that!

OSVALD (*Pacing the room*): There, there—Mother, dear—never mind—!

MANDERS: Yes, fortunately, that's undeniable! And you've begun to make quite a name for yourself. I've often seen you mentioned in the papers, and always most favorably. Though recently I haven't seen so much about your work.

OSVALD (*Going up to the conservatory*): No—I haven't done much painting lately.

MRS. ALVING: Even an artist needs to rest now and then.

MANDERS: Most understandable— At such times you gather new strength, for even finer work.

OSVALD: Quite so— Will dinner be ready soon, Mother?

MRS. ALVING: In half an hour, dear. There's nothing wrong with his appetite, thank God!

MANDERS: And I see he's partial to tobacco too.

OSVALD: I found this old pipe of Father's up in his study—

MANDERS: Oh—so that accounts for it!

MRS. ALVING: How do you mean?

MANDERS: When Osvald came in just now—with that pipe in his mouth—I thought for a moment it was his father come to life again.

OSVALD: Really?

MRS. ALVING: How can you say that! Osvald takes after me.

MANDERS: Yes—perhaps; but, still, there's something about his mouth—something in the expression—that reminds me very strongly of Alving—especially when he smokes.

MRS. ALVING: I don't see it at all—Osvald's mouth is much more sensitive. There's something almost ascetic about it.

MANDERS: It's true—some of my colleagues have a similar expression.

MRS. ALVING: But put down your pipe now, Osvald, dear. I don't allow smoking in this room.

OSVALD (*Puts down the pipe*): Very well, Mother. I only wanted to try it; I smoked it once before you see—when I was a child.

MRS. ALVING: *You* did?

OSVALD: Yes—I was very little at the time—I remember I went up to Father's study one evening; he was in a very gay, jolly mood.

MRS. ALVING: How could you possibly remember? It's so long ago!

OSVALD: Oh, but I do! I remember it very distinctly; he sat me on his knee and told me to smoke his pipe: Smoke, Son, he said—go on, Son—have a good smoke; so I smoked away with all my might, until I felt deathly ill and great beads of perspiration stood out on my forehead. He thought it was very funny. I remember he roared with laughter at me.

MANDERS: What a very odd thing to do!

MRS. ALVING: It's a lot of nonsense. Osvald must have dreamed it.

OSVALD: No, Mother, I assure you I didn't! Don't you remember, you came in and rushed me off to the nursery. And then I was sick—and I noticed you'd been crying—I suppose it *was* rather odd—did Father often play tricks like that?

MANDERS: He was a great joker in his young days.

OSVALD: Yet think of all the good he did. The fine and useful things he was able to accomplish—though he died comparatively young.

MANDERS: Yes—you have a fine heritage, Osvald Alving. It should be a great incentive to you!

OSVALD: Yes, you're right! Indeed it should.

MANDERS: And it was good of you to come home for the ceremony tomorrow.

OSVALD: That's the least I could do for Father's memory.

MRS. ALVING: And he plans to stay here for a while—that's the nicest thing of all!

MANDERS: Yes, I understand you intend to spend the winter here.

OSVALD: I plan to stay here indefinitely, Mr. Manders. It's so good to be home again!

MRS. ALVING (*Beaming*): Yes, it is, isn't it, dear?

MANDERS (*Looks at him sympathetically*): You were very young when you left home, my dear Osvald.

OSVALD: A little too young, perhaps.

MRS. ALVING: What nonsense! It's good for a strong healthy boy—especially an only child—to get away from home. Much better than being petted and spoiled by doting parents!

MANDERS: I think that is open to debate, Mrs. Alving. A home and parents are still a child's best refuge.

OSVALD: I'm inclined to agree with Mr. Manders there.

MANDERS: Take your own son here as an example—there's no harm in discussing it before him—what has been the result in his case? Here he is, twenty-three or twenty-four years old, and he has never yet known what a normal, well-regulated home can be.

OSVALD: I beg your pardon, Mr. Manders—you're quite wrong in that.

MANDERS: Really? But, I thought you'd been living exclusively in artistic circles.

OSVALD: So I have.

MANDERS: And mostly among the younger artists, I believe.

OSVALD: Quite right.

MANDERS: But surely the majority of such people are in no position to found a home and family.

OSVALD: Most of them are in no position to get married—that's true enough—

MANDERS: That's just what I say—

OSVALD: But that doesn't necessarily mean that they can't have homes of their *own*—and many of them have—very comfortable and well-run homes too.

(MRS. ALVING, *who has been listening attentively, nods in agreement but says nothing.*)

MANDERS: I'm not thinking of bachelor-establishments; when I use the word "home" I mean a family—a home where a man lives with his wife and children.

OSVALD: Or with his children—and their mother.

MANDERS (*With a start, clasping his hands*): Good Heavens!

OSVALD: Well?

MANDERS: —lives with—with—his children's mother!

OSVALD: Would you rather he abandoned her?

MANDERS: Then you're speaking of illegal unions—dissolute relationships—!

OSVALD: I've never noticed anything especially dissolute in the lives these people lead.

MANDERS: How can any decent young man or woman possibly degrade themselves by living openly in such shameful circumstances!

OSVALD: Well—what do you expect them to do? A poor young artist—a poor young girl—marriage is an expensive business—what do you expect them to do?

MANDERS: I would expect them to resist temptation, Mr. Alving—to part before it is too late.

OSVALD: That's a lot to expect of young people in love, Mr. Manders.

MRS. ALVING: Indeed it is!

MANDERS (*Persistently*): And to think that the authorities put up with such behavior—that it should be openly tolerated. (To MRS. ALVING) You see how right I was to be concerned about your son. Living in circles where such rampant immorality prevails, where it's taken for granted, one might say—

OSVALD: Let me tell you something, Mr. Manders—I've spent many a Sunday at some of these "illegal homes"—as you call them—

MANDERS: On a Sunday too—!

OSVALD: Sunday happens to be a holiday—I've never once heard a single vulgar or indecent word—nor have I ever witnessed any behavior that could possibly be called immoral. But do you know when and where I *have* met with such behavior?

MANDERS: No! God forbid!

OSVALD: Then permit me to tell you: When some of your highly-respected citizens—your model fathers and husbands from back home here—when they take a trip abroad to "see a bit of life"—when *they* condescend to honor us poor artists with their presence—then you would see "rampant immorality" if you like! These respectable gentlemen could tell us about things that we had never even dreamed of!

MANDERS: You dare imply that honorable men here from home—?

OSVALD: You must have heard these same "honorable men" when they get safely home again, hold forth on the outrageous immorality that prevails abroad?

MANDERS: Of course I have.

MRS. ALVING: I've heard them too—

OSVALD: Well you may take their word for it! They speak with true authority! (*Clutches his head in his hands*) It's an outrage that that free and beautiful life should be distorted by their filth!

MRS. ALVING: Don't get so excited, Osvald. It's bad for you.

OSVALD: You're right, Mother. It's bad for me I know—it's just that I'm so tired. I think I'll take a little walk before dinner. Forgive me, Mr. Manders—I shouldn't have let go like that. I know you can't possibly understand my feelings. (*He goes out by the up-stage door right.*)

MRS. ALVING: Poor boy!

MANDERS: You may well say so!— That he should have sunk to this! (MRS. ALVING *looks at him in silence.* MANDERS *paces up and down*) He called himself the Prodigal Son—Tragic!—Tragic! (MRS. ALVING *continues to look at him silently*) And what do you say to all this?

MRS. ALVING: I say Osvald was right in every word he said.

MANDERS (*Stops pacing*): Right?— You mean you agree to such principles?

MRS. ALVING: Living here alone all these years, I've come to the same conclusions—but I've never put my thoughts into words— Well—now my boy can speak for me.

MANDERS: You are greatly to be pitied, Mrs. Alving!—I have always had your best interests at heart; for many years I have advised you in business matters; for many years I have been your friend and your late husband's friend; as your spiritual adviser I once saved you from a reckless and fool-hardy action; and it is as your spiritual adviser that I now feel it my duty to talk to you with the utmost solemnity.

MRS. ALVING: And what have you to say to me, as my "spiritual adviser," Mr. Manders?

MANDERS: Look back over the years—it's appropriate that you should do so today, for tomorrow is the tenth anniversary of your husband's death and his Memorial will be unveiled; tomorrow I shall speak to the crowd assembled in his honor—but today I must speak to you alone.

MRS. ALVING: I'm listening.

MANDERS: You had been married scarcely a year when you took the step that might have wrecked your life: You left house and home and ran away from your husband—yes, Mrs. Alving, ran away—and refused to go back to him in spite of all his entreaties.

MRS. ALVING: I was miserably unhappy that first year—don't forget that.

MANDERS: What right have we to expect happiness in this life? It is the sign of a rebellious spirit— No! Mrs. Alving, we are here to do our duty, and it was your duty to stay with the man you had chosen and to whom you were bound in Holy Matrimony.

MRS. ALVING: You know the kind of life Alving led in those days; his dissipation—his excesses—

MANDERS: It's true, I heard many rumors about him—and had those rumors been true, I should have been the first to condemn his conduct at that time; but it is not a wife's place to judge her husband; your duty was to resign yourself and bear your cross with true humility. But you rebelled against it and instead of giving your husband the help and support he needed, you deserted him, and by so doing jeopardized your own good name and reputation—and that of others too.

MRS. ALVING: Of "others"? Of *one*, you mean.

MANDERS: It was highly imprudent to come to me, of all people, for help.

MRS. ALVING: But why? Weren't you our "spiritual adviser" as well as our friend?

MANDERS: All the more reason. You should go down on your knees and thank God that I found the necessary strength of mind to dissuade you from your reckless purpose, to guide you back to the path of duty, and home to your husband.

MRS. ALVING: Yes, Mr. Manders—that was certainly your doing.

MANDERS: I was merely an instrument in God's hand. And, as I had foreseen—once you had returned to your duties, and humbled your spirit in obedience—you were repaid an hundredfold. Alving reformed entirely, and remained a good and loving husband to the end of his days. He became a real benefactor to this whole community, and he allowed you to share, as his fellow-worker, in all his enterprises—and a very able fellow-worker too—I am aware of that, Mrs. Alving—I must pay you that tribute; but now I come to the second great error of your life.

MRS. ALVING: What do you mean by that?

MANDERS: You first betrayed your duty as a wife—you later betrayed your duty as a mother.

MRS. ALVING: Ah—!

MANDERS: All your life you have been possessed by a willful, rebellious spirit. Your natural inclinations always led you toward the undisciplined and lawless. You could never tolerate the slightest restraint; you have always disregarded any responsibility—carelessly and unscrupulously—as though it were a burden you had a right to cast aside. It no longer suited you to be a wife—so you left your husband. The cares of motherhood were too much for you—so you sent your child away to be brought up by strangers.

MRS. ALVING: That's true—I did do that.

MANDERS: And for that reason you are now a stranger to him.

MRS. ALVING: No! No! I'm not!

MANDERS: Of course you are! How could you be otherwise? And now you see the result of your conduct. You have much to atone for; you were guilty as a wife, Mrs. Alving, you failed your husband miserably—you are seeking to atone for that by raising this Memorial in his honor; how are you going to atone for your failure towards your son? It may not be too late to save him: by redeeming yourself—you may still help him to redemption! I warn you! (*With raised forefinger*) You are guilty as a mother, Mrs. Alving. I felt it my duty to tell you this.

(*Pause.*)

MRS. ALVING (*Slowly, with great control*): I have listened to you talk, Mr. Manders. Tomorrow you will be making speeches in my husband's honor; I shall not make any speeches tomorrow; but now I intend to talk to you—just as frankly—just as brutally—as you have talked to me!

MANDERS: Of course—it's natural that you should try and justify your conduct.

MRS. ALVING: No—I only want to make a few things clear to you.

MANDERS: Well?

MRS. ALVING: You've just talked a great deal about my married life after you—as you put it—"led me back to the path of duty." What do you really know about it? From that day on you never set foot inside our house—you who had been our closest friend—

MANDERS: But, you and your husband left town, immediately afterwards—

MRS. ALVING: And you never once came out here to see us during my husband's lifetime. It wasn't until this Orphanage business, that you felt compelled to visit me.

MANDERS (*In a low uncertain tone*): If that is meant as a reproach, my dear Helene, I beg you to consider—

MRS. ALVING: —that in your position you had to protect your reputation! After all—I was a wife who had tried to leave her husband! One can't be too careful with such disreputable women!

MANDERS: My dear!—Mrs. Alving—what a gross exaggeration!

MRS. ALVING: Well—never mind about that—the point is this: your opinions of my married life are based on nothing but hearsay.

MANDERS: That may be so—what then?

MRS. ALVING: Just this: that now, Manders, I am going to tell you the truth! I swore to myself that one day I would tell it to you—to you alone!

MANDERS: Well? And what is the truth?

MRS. ALVING: The truth is this: My husband continued to be a depraved profligate to the day of his death.

MANDERS (*Feeling for a chair*): What did you say?

MRS. ALVING: After nineteen years of marriage—just as depraved, just as dissolute—as he was the day you married us.

MANDERS: How can you use such words—!

MRS. ALVING: They are the words our doctor used.

MANDERS: I don't understand you.

MRS. ALVING: It's not necessary that you should.

MANDERS: I can't take it in. You mean—that this seemingly happy marriage—those long years of comradeship—all that was only a pretense—to cover up this hideous abyss?

MRS. ALVING: That is just exactly what it was—nothing else.

MANDERS: But—it's inconceivable—I can't grasp it! How was it possible to—? How could the truth remain concealed?

MRS. ALVING: My life became one long fight to that end: After Osvald was born, Alving seemed to me a little better—but it didn't last long! And then I had to fight for my son as well: I was determined that no living soul should ever know the kind of father my boy had— As a matter of fact, you know how charming Alving could be—it was hard for people to think ill of him. He was one of those fortunate men whose private lives never seem to damage their public reputation. But then, Manders—I want you to know the whole story—then the most horrible thing of all happened.

MANDERS: How could anything be worse than—?

MRS. ALVING: I knew well enough all that was going on—and I put up with it as long as I didn't have to see it—but, when I was faced with it here—in my own home—!

MANDERS: Here?

MRS. ALVING: Yes—in this very house. The first time I became aware of it, I was in there— (*Points to the down-stage door right*) in the dining room—I was busy with something, and the door was ajar—then I heard the maid come up from the garden with water for the plants—

MANDERS: Yes?

MRS. ALVING: In a few moments, I heard Alving come in after her—he said something to her in a low voice—and then I heard— (*With a short laugh*) it still rings in my ears—it was so horrible, and yet somehow so ludicrous—I heard my own servant-girl whisper: "Let me go, Mr. Alving!— Leave me alone!"

MANDERS: But he couldn't have meant anything by it, Mrs. Alving—believe me—I'm sure he didn't—!

MRS. ALVING: I soon found out what to believe: My husband had his way with the girl, and there were—consequences, Mr. Manders.

MANDERS (*As though turned to stone*): To think—that in this house—!

MRS. ALVING: I had been through a lot in this house! Night after night—in order to keep him home—I sat up in his study with him—pretending to join him in his private drinking-bouts. I sat there alone with him for hours on end listening to his obscene, senseless talk—I had to struggle with him—fight with sheer brute force—in order to drag him to his bed.

MANDERS (*Shaken*): How were you able to endure all this?

MRS. ALVING: I had to endure it—I had my little boy to think of. But when I discovered this final outrage—with a servant—in our own house—! That was the end. From that day on I became master here. I took full control—over him and over everything. Alving didn't dare say a word—he knew he was in my power. It was then I decided to send Osvald away. He was nearly seven and was beginning to notice things and ask questions, as children do. This I could not endure, Manders. I felt the child would be poisoned in this sordid, degraded home. That's why I sent him away. Now perhaps you understand why I never let him set foot in this house as long as his father was alive. What you could never understand—is what agony it was to have to do it!

MANDERS: To think of all you have been through—!

MRS. ALVING: I could never have stood it if I hadn't had my work. For I can honestly say I have worked! Alving received all the praise—all the credit—but don't imagine he had anything to do with it! The increase in the value of our property—the improvements—all those fine enterprises you spoke of—all that was *my* work. All he did was to sprawl on the sofa in his study reading old newspapers. In his few lucid moments I did try to spur him to some effort—but it was no use. He sank back again into his old habits and then spent days in a maudlin state of penitence and self-pity.

MANDERS: And you're building a Memorial to such a man—?

MRS. ALVING: That's what comes of having a bad conscience.

MANDERS: A bad—? What do you mean?

MRS. ALVING: It seemed to me inevitable that the truth must come out, and that people would believe it; so I decided to dedicate this Orphanage to Alving—in order to dispel once and for all any possible rumors—any possible doubts.

MANDERS: You've fully succeeded in that.

MRS. ALVING: But I had another reason: I didn't want my son to inherit anything whatsoever from his father.

MANDERS: I see—so you used Alving's money to—?

MRS. ALVING: Precisely. The money that has gone into the Orphanage amounts to the exact sum—I've calculated it very carefully—to the exact sum of the fortune, that once made people consider Lt. Alving a good match.

MANDERS: I understand you.

MRS. ALVING: I sold myself for that sum. I don't want Osvald to touch a penny of it. Everything he has will come from me—everything!

(OSVALD *enters from the door up-stage right. He has left his hat and coat outside.*)

MRS. ALVING (*Goes toward him*): Back already, dear?

OSVALD: Yes—what can one do—out in this everlasting rain! But I hear dinner's nearly ready—splendid!

(REGINE *enters from the dining room carrying a small parcel.*)

REGINE: This parcel just came for you, Mrs. Alving. (*Hands her the parcel.*)

MRS. ALVING (*With a glance at* MANDERS): Ah! The songs for tomorrow's ceremony, I expect.

MANDERS: Hm—

REGINE: And dinner is served, Mrs. Alving.

MRS. ALVING: Good; we'll be there in a moment. I just want to see—

REGINE (*To* OSVALD): Would you like red or white wine, Mr. Alving?

OSVALD: Both, by all means, Miss Engstrand.

REGINE: Bien— Very good, Mr. Alving. (*Exits into dining room.*)

OSVALD: Let me help you uncork it— (*Follows her into the dining room, half closing the door.*)

MRS. ALVING (*Who has opened the parcel*): Yes—just as I thought—the songs for tomorrow, Mr. Manders.

MANDERS (*Clasping his hands*): How I shall ever have the courage to make my speech tomorrow—!

MRS. ALVING: You'll manage—somehow.

MANDERS (*Softly, so as not to be heard in the dining room*): It would never do to arouse suspicion—

MRS. ALVING (*Quietly but firmly*): No— And from tomorrow on, I shall be free at last—the long, hideous farce will be over—I shall forget that such a person as Alving ever lived in this house—there'll be no one here but my son and me.

(*The noise of a chair being overturned is heard from the dining room—at the same time* REGINE'S *voice.*)

REGINE'S *voice* (*In a sharp whisper*): Osvald!—Are you mad?— Let me go!

MRS. ALVING (*Stiffens with horror*): Ah—!

(*She gazes distractedly at the half-open door.* OSVALD *is heard coughing and humming a tune—then the sound of a bottle being uncorked.*)

MANDERS (*In agitation*): But what *is* all this? What's the *matter*, Mrs. Alving?

MRS. ALVING (*Hoarsely*): Ghosts—Those two in the conservatory—Ghosts—They've come to life again!

MANDERS: What do you mean? Regine—? Is *she*—?

MRS. ALVING: Yes—Come— Not a word!

(*She takes* MANDERS' *arm and goes falteringly towards the dining room.*)

CURTAIN

ACT
TWO

SCENE: *The same room. The landscape is still shrouded in rain
and mist.* MANDERS *and* MRS. ALVING *enter from the dining
room.*

MRS. ALVING (*In the doorway, calls back into the dining room*):
Aren't you coming too, Osvald?

OSVALD (*Off stage*): No, thanks; I think I'll go out for a bit.

MRS. ALVING: Yes, do, dear; I think it's cleared up a little.
(*She closes the dining room door, crosses to the hall door and
calls*) Regine!

REGINE (*Off stage*): Yes, Mrs. Alving?

MRS. ALVING: Go down to the laundry and help them with the
wreaths.

REGINE: Very well, Mrs. Alving.
(MRS. ALVING *makes sure that* REGINE *has gone and then
closes the door.*)

MANDERS: You're sure he can't hear us in here?

MRS. ALVING: Not with the door shut—besides, he's going out.

MANDERS: I'm still so overcome. I don't know how I managed to
eat a morsel of that delicious food.

MRS. ALVING (*In suppressed anguish, pacing up and down*): No—
Well—what's to be done?

MANDERS: What's to be done indeed? I wish I knew what to suggest— I don't feel competent to deal with a crisis of this sort.

MRS. ALVING: One thing I'm convinced of—that, so far, nothing
serious has happened.

MANDERS: God forbid!— But it's a shameful business all the same.

MRS. ALVING: It's just a foolish whim on Osvald's part; I'm sure of that.

MANDERS: As I said before—I have no experience in such things—but I can't help thinking—

MRS. ALVING: One thing's clear: she must leave this house at once—before it's too late.

MANDERS: That goes without saying.

MRS. ALVING: But where can she go? We certainly wouldn't be justified in—

MANDERS: She must go home to her father, of course.

MRS. ALVING: To whom—did you say?

MANDERS: To her— But of course. Engstrand isn't her— Good Heavens, Mrs. Alving—all this is impossible—there must be some mistake!

MRS. ALVING: I'm afraid there is no mistake, Manders. The girl confessed to me herself. And Alving didn't deny it; so the only thing we could do was to try and hush the matter up.

MANDERS: Yes—I suppose so.

MRS. ALVING: The girl left my service at once and was given a handsome sum to keep her mouth shut. She then took matters into her own hands—went back to town and renewed an old friendship with the carpenter, Engstrand. She hinted that she had money—told him some cock-and-bull story about a foreigner with a yacht—the outcome of all this was, that they were married in great haste. You married them yourself, I believe.

MANDERS: But—I can't understand it! I remember distinctly Engstrand coming to arrange about the wedding: He was overcome with confusion—and kept reproaching himself bitterly for his and his fiancée's shameless behavior.

MRS. ALVING: Well—I suppose he had to take the blame on himself.

MANDERS: I certainly never would have believed Jakob Engstrand capable of such duplicity—and to me of all people! I shall have to teach him a good lesson, I can see that—The immorality of such a marriage—and for money too! How much did the girl receive?

MRS. ALVING: Three hundred dollars.

MANDERS: It's almost unbelievable—for a paltry three hundred dollars—consenting to marry a loose woman.

MRS. ALVING: What about me? Didn't I marry a "loose" man?

MANDERS: What on earth are you talking about!

MRS. ALVING: Was Alving any better when he married me, than the girl Johanna was when she married Engstrand?

MANDERS: But—good Heavens—the two cases are utterly different—

MRS. ALVING: Perhaps not so very different, after all. There was a colossal difference in the price—that's true enough! A paltry three hundred dollars as against a large fortune.

MANDERS: But there *can* be no comparison in this instance! Your decision was based on the advice of relatives and friends—as well as the promptings of your heart.

MRS. ALVING (*Without looking at him*): My heart, as you call it, was involved elsewhere at the time—as I thought you knew.

MANDERS (*In a reserved tone*): Had I known any such thing, I should not have been a constant visitor in your husband's house.

MRS. ALVING: One thing is certain; I never really consulted my own feelings in the matter.

MANDERS: Perhaps not—but you consulted your mother—your two aunts—all those nearest to you—as was only right.

MRS. ALVING: Yes—those three! They were the ones that settled the whole business for me. As I look back on it, it seems incredible. They pointed out, in the most forceful terms, that it would be nothing short of folly to refuse an offer of such magnificence! Poor Mother. If she only knew what that "magnificence" has led to.

MANDERS: No one can be held responsible for the outcome— The fact remains, that your marriage in every way conformed to the strictest rules of law and order.

MRS. ALVING (*At the window*): All this talk about law and order!—I often think all the suffering in the world is due to that.

MANDERS: That is a very wicked thing to say, Mrs. Alving.

MRS. ALVING: That may be; but I will not be bound by these responsibilities, these hypocritical conventions any longer—I simply cannot! I must work my way through to freedom.

MANDERS: What do you mean by that?

MRS. ALVING (*Drumming on the windowpane*): I should never have lied about Alving—but I didn't dare do anything else at the time—and it wasn't only for Osvald's sake—it was for my own sake too. What a coward I've been!

MANDERS: A coward?

MRS. ALVING: A coward, yes— I could just hear what people would say if they found out the truth: Poor man! One can hardly blame him with a wife like that! She tried to leave him, you know!

MANDERS: They would have been justified to some extent.

MRS. ALVING (*Looking at him steadily*): If I'd had the strength I should have taken Osvald into my confidence; I should have said: Listen, my son, your father was a corrupt, contaminated man—

MANDERS: Good God—!

MRS. ALVING: And then I should have told him the whole story—word for word—just as I told it to you.

MANDERS: You horrify me, Mrs. Alving!

MRS. ALVING: I know—God, yes!—I know!—I'm horrified myself at the thought of it!— That's how much of a coward I am.

MANDERS: How can you call yourself a coward for doing what was merely your duty? Have you forgotten that a child should love and honor his father and mother?

MRS. ALVING: Don't let us talk in generalities! Let us ask: Should Osvald love and honor Captain Alving?

MANDERS: You're his mother—how could you find it in your heart to shatter his ideals?

MRS. ALVING: Oh—ideals, ideals! What about the Truth?— If only I weren't such a coward!

MANDERS: You shouldn't scoff at ideals, Mrs. Alving—they have a way of avenging themselves. God knows—Osvald doesn't seem to have many—unfortunately. But his father seems to be somewhat of an ideal to him.

MRS. ALVING: Yes, that's quite true.

MANDERS: Your letters must be responsible for that feeling in him—you must have fostered it.

MRS. ALVING: Yes. I was treading the path of duty and obedience, Mr. Manders—I therefore lied to my son, religiously, year after year. What a coward—what a coward I was!

MANDERS: You have fostered a happy illusion in your son's mind, Mrs. Alving—you shouldn't underestimate its value.

MRS. ALVING: Its value may turn out to be dubious, who knows? But I won't tolerate any nonsense with Regine—he mustn't be allowed to get her into trouble.

MANDERS: Good Heavens, no—that would be unthinkable!

MRS. ALVING: If I thought she would really make him happy—if he were really serious about it—

MANDERS: What do you mean?

MRS. ALVING: Oh, but he couldn't be—Regine could never be enough for him—

MANDERS: What are you talking about?

MRS. ALVING: If I weren't such a miserable coward I'd say to him: marry her—come to any arrangement you like with her—only be honest about it!

MANDERS: A marriage between them—? How could you condone anything so abominable—so unheard of!

MRS. ALVING: Unheard of, you say? Why not face the truth, Manders? You know there are dozens of married couples out here in the country who are related in the same way.

MANDERS: I refuse to understand you.

MRS. ALVING: But you *do* understand me all the same!

MANDERS: There may be a few instances—family life is not always as blameless as it should be, unfortunately. But in nine cases out of ten the relationship is unsuspected—or at worst, unconfirmed. Here—on the other hand— That you a mother, should be willing to allow your son—!

MRS. ALVING: But I'm *not* willing to allow it—that's just what I'm saying— I wouldn't allow it for anything in the world.

MANDERS: Only because you're a coward—as you express it. But if you weren't a coward—! Such a revolting marriage—God forgive you!

MRS. ALVING: We're all of us descended from that kind of marriage—so they say. And who was responsible for that arrangement, Mr. Manders?

MANDERS: I refuse to discuss these matters with you, Mrs. Alving—you are in no fit state to touch on such things— How you can have the effrontery to call yourself a coward for not—!

MRS. ALVING: I'll tell you what I mean by that; I live in constant fear and terror, because I can't rid myself of all these ghosts that haunt me.

MANDERS: Ghosts, you say?

MRS. ALVING: Yes— Just now, when I heard Regine and Osvald in there—I felt hemmed in by ghosts— You know, Manders, the longer I live the more convinced I am that we're all haunted in this world—not only by the things we inherit from our parents—but by the ghosts of innumerable old prejudices and beliefs—half-forgotten cruelties and betrayals—we may not even be aware of them—but they're there just the same—and we can't get rid of them. The whole world is haunted by these ghosts of the dead past; you have only to pick up a newspaper to see them weaving in and out between the lines— Ah! if we only had the courage to sweep them all out and let in the light!

MANDERS: So this is the result of all this reading of yours—this detestable, pernicious, free-thinking literature!

MRS. ALVING: You're mistaken, my dear Manders. It was you who first goaded me into thinking—I shall always be grateful to you for that.

MANDERS: I?

MRS. ALVING: Yes. When you forced me to obey what you called my conscience and my duty; when you hailed as right and noble what my whole soul rebelled against as false and ugly—that's when I started to analyze your teachings; that's when I first started to *think*. And one day I saw quite clearly that all that you stand for—all that you preach—is artificial and dead—there's no life or truth in it.

MANDERS (*Softly, with emotion*): So that's all I achieved by the hardest struggle of my life.

MRS. ALVING: I'd call it your most ignominious defeat.

MANDERS: It was a victory over myself, Helene; my greatest victory.

MRS. ALVING: It was a crime against us both.

MANDERS: The fact that by my entreaties I persuaded you to return to your lawful husband, when you came to me distracted and overwrought crying: "Here I am. Take me!" You consider that a crime?

MRS. ALVING: Yes; I think it was.

MANDERS: There is no possible understanding between us.

MRS. ALVING: Not any more, at any rate.

MANDERS: You have always been to me—even in my most secret thoughts—another man's wife.

MRS. ALVING: You really believe that, Manders?

MANDERS: Helene—!

MRS. ALVING: It's so easy to forget one's feelings!

MANDERS: I don't forget. I am exactly the same as I always was.

MRS. ALVING (*With a change of tone*): Oh, don't let's talk any more about the old days! Now you're up to your eyes in committee meetings and advisory boards—and I sit out here and battle with ghosts—the ghosts within myself and those all around me.

MANDERS: Those around you, I can at least help you to conquer. After the dreadful things you've said to me today, I couldn't dream of leaving a young, unprotected girl alone in your house.

MRS. ALVING: I think the best thing would be to arrange a good match for her—don't you agree?

MANDERS: Unquestionably. It would be best for her in every respect. Regine has reached the age when—of course, I know very little about these things—

MRS. ALVING: Yes—she developed early.

MANDERS: So it seemed to me. I remember thinking when I prepared her for Confirmation, that she was remarkably well-developed for a child of her age. For the present she had better go home, under her father's care—but, of course, Engstrand isn't— How could he—*he* of all people—conceal the truth from me!

(*There is a knock at the hall door.*)

MRS. ALVING: Who can *that* be? Come in!

(ENGSTRAND *appears in the doorway; he is in his Sunday clothes*)

ENGSTRAND: I most humbly beg pardon—but—

MRS. ALVING: Oh, it's you, Engstrand.

ENGSTRAND: None of the maids seemed to be about—so I took the liberty of knocking, Ma'am—

MRS. ALVING: Oh, very well—come in. Do you wish to speak to me?

ENGSTRAND (*Coming in*): No—thank you all the same, Mrs. Alving. But—if I might have a word with the Reverend—

MANDERS (*Pacing up and down*): With me—eh? So you want to talk to me, do you?

ENGSTRAND: I'd be most grateful—

MANDERS (*Stopping in front of him*): Well—what is it?

ENGSTRAND: It's just this, Sir; we're being paid off down there— and many thanks to you, Ma'am—our work's all finished; and, I thought how nice and helpful it would be to all of us who've worked together so hard and faithfully—if we could have a few prayers this evening.

MANDERS: Prayers?— Down at the Orphanage?

ENGSTRAND: Yes, Sir; of course if it isn't convenient to you, Sir—

MANDERS: Oh, it's convenient enough—but—hm—

ENGSTRAND: I've taken to saying a few prayers myself down there of an evening—

MRS. ALVING: *You* have?

ENGSTRAND: Yes—now and then; we can all do with a little edification, I thought; but I'm just a simple, humble fellow—I'm not much good at it, God help me! But as long as the Reverend happened to be here—I thought—

MANDERS: Look here, Engstrand; I must first ask you a question: Are you in a proper state of mind for prayer? Have you a clear untroubled conscience?

ENGSTRAND: God help me! Perhaps we'd better not talk about my conscience, Mr. Manders.

MANDERS: That is exactly what we must talk about. Well—answer me!

ENGSTRAND: Well, Sir—of course, now and then, it does trouble me a bit—

MANDERS: I'm glad you admit that at least. Now—will you be so kind as to tell me honestly—what is the truth about Regine?

MRS. ALVING (*Rapidly*): Mr. Manders!

MANDERS (*Calming her*): I'll handle this—

ENGSTRAND: Regine! —Lord, how you frightened me! (*Gives* MRS. ALVING *a look*) There's nothing wrong with Regine, is there?

MANDERS: It is to be hoped not. But what I mean is this: What is your true relationship to Regine? You pretend to be her father, do you not?

ENGSTRAND (*Uncertain*): Yes—hm—well, Sir—you know all about me and poor Johanna—

MANDERS: No more prevarication, please! Your late wife confessed the whole truth to Mrs. Alving before she left her service.

ENGSTRAND: Do you mean to say she—? Oh, she did, did she?

MANDERS: Yes; so it's no use lying any longer, Engstrand.

ENGSTRAND: Well! And after her swearing up and down—

MANDERS: Swearing, you say—?

ENGSTRAND: I mean, she gave me her solemn word, Sir.

MANDERS: And all these years you've kept the truth from me— from *me*, who have always had the utmost faith in you!

ENGSTRAND: Yes, Sir—I'm afraid I have.

MANDERS: Have I deserved that, Engstrand? Haven't I always done everything in my power to help you? Answer me—haven't I?

ENGSTRAND: Yes, Sir. Things would often have looked pretty black for me, if it hadn't been for Mr. Manders.

MANDERS: And this is how you repay me! You cause me to enter erroneous statements in the Church Register, and withhold from me for years the truth which it was your duty to impart to me. Your conduct has been inexcusable, Engstrand; from now on, I shall have nothing more to do with you.

ENGSTRAND (*With a sigh*): Yes, Sir; I suppose that's how it has to be!

MANDERS: I don't see how you can possibly justify your conduct.

ENGSTRAND: We felt it better not to add to her shame by talking about it. Supposing you'd been in poor Johanna's place, Mr. Manders—

MANDERS: I!

ENGSTRAND: Lord bless me! I don't mean that the way it sounds! What I mean is: suppose you had done something you were ashamed of in the eyes of the world, as they say; we men oughtn't to judge a poor woman too hard, Mr. Manders.

MANDERS: But I don't judge her—it's *you* I'm accusing.

ENGSTRAND: Mr. Manders, would you allow me to ask you just one little question?

MANDERS: Very well—what is it?

ENGSTRAND: Shouldn't a decent honorable man help those who've gone astray?

MANDERS: Well—naturally—

ENGSTRAND: And isn't a man bound to keep his word of honor?

MANDERS: Yes, of course, but—

ENGSTRAND: Well—you see, after Johanna got into trouble with that Englishman—or maybe he was American—or one of those Russians even—anyway, she came back to town. Poor thing—she'd already refused me twice; she only had eyes for the handsome fellows—and, of course, I had this deformed leg of mine. You remember, Sir, I was once rash enough to enter one of those dance-halls—one of those dives where sailors spend their time drinking and carousing, as they say—I was just trying to persuade them to try another kind of life—

MRS. ALVING (*By the window*): Hm—

MANDERS: Yes, I know, Engstrand; those dreadful men threw you downstairs; I remember your telling me of that tragic experience; you bear your deformity with honor.

ENGSTRAND: I don't mean to brag about it, Sir. Well—anyway,

she came to me, and confided her whole trouble to me, with
tears and lamentations—it broke my heart to listen to her—

MANDERS: Did it, indeed, Engstrand! Well—and then—?

ENGSTRAND: Well, then I said to her, I said: that American is
wandering on the seas of the world; and you, Johanna, are a
sinful fallen creature, I said. But, Jakob Engstrand, I said, stands
here on two solid legs, I said; of course I only meant that in a
manner of speaking, you know, Sir—

MANDERS: Yes, yes—I understand—go on—

ENGSTRAND: Well then, Sir, I married her—I made her an honest
woman—so no one would know of her reckless behavior with
that foreigner—

MANDERS: All of that was very right and good of you, Engstrand;
but I cannot condone your consenting to accept money—

ENGSTRAND: Money? Me? Not a penny—

MANDERS (*In a questioning tone, to* MRS. ALVING): But—?

ENGSTRAND: Oh yes—wait a bit—now I remember. Johanna did
say something about some money she had—but I refused to hear
anything about it! Get Thee behind me, Satan, I said; it's Mam-
mon's gold (or bank-notes or whatever it was), we'll throw it back
in the American's face, I said; but, of course, he had disappeared, Sir—disappeared over the vast ocean, you see—

MANDERS: Yes—I see—my dear Engstrand—

ENGSTRAND: Yes, Sir; and then Johanna and I agreed that every
penny of that money should go to the child's upbringing; and
that's where it went, Sir; and I can account for every cent of it.

MANDERS: But this puts things in an entirely different light—

ENGSTRAND: That's the way it was, Mr. Manders. And, though I
say it myself, I've tried to be a good father to Regine—to the best
of my ability, that is—you know what a weak man I am,
Sir—unfortunately—

MANDERS: Yes, yes—I know, dear Engstrand—

ENGSTRAND: I can truly say I gave the child a decent upbringing
and made poor Johanna a good and loving husband; but it never
would have occurred to me to go to you, Mr. Manders, and brag
about it and pat myself on the back for doing a good action; I'm
not made like that. And most of the time, unfortunately, I've

little enough to brag about. When I go and talk to you, Sir, it's
mostly to confess my sins and weaknesses. For, as I said just
now, my conscience troubles me quite a bit, Mr. Manders—

MANDERS: Give me your hand, Jakob Engstrand.

ENGSTRAND: Oh—Lord, Sir!—

MANDERS: Come now—no nonsense! (*Grasps his hand*) There!

ENGSTRAND: I most humbly ask you to forgive me, Sir—

MANDERS: On the contrary—it's I who must ask your forgiveness—

ENGSTRAND: Oh, no, Sir!

MANDERS: Most certainly—and I do so with all my heart. Forgive
me, dear Engstrand, for so misjudging you. I wish I might give
you some proof of my sincere regret and of the esteem in which I
hold you—

ENGSTRAND: You'd really like to do that, Sir?

MANDERS: It would give me the greatest of pleasure.

ENGSTRAND: Well—it just happens—there is something you
could do for me, Sir; I've managed to put by a bit of money from
my earnings here, and I'm thinking of opening a kind of Seamen's Home when I get back to town, Sir—

MRS. ALVING: You—*what*?

ENGSTRAND: It'd be like a kind of refuge for them, you see,
Ma'am. These poor sailors have so many temptations when they
get to port—I thought in my house, they'd find a father's care—

MANDERS: What do you say to that, Mrs. Alving?

ENGSTRAND: Of course, I haven't much capital to go on—and I
thought if I could just find a helping hand—

MANDERS: I shall give it some thought. I find your scheme most
interesting. But now, go and get everything ready—light the
lights—and prepare for our little celebration. Now I feel sure
you are in a fit state for prayer, my dear Engstrand—

ENGSTRAND: Yes—I really believe I am. Well, goodbye, Mrs.
Alving, and thank you for everything; be sure and take good care
of Regine for me. (*Wipes away a tear*) Poor Johanna's child—it's
strange how she's managed to creep into my heart—but, she
has—there's no denying it! (*He bows and goes out by the hall
door.*)

MANDERS: Well—what do you think of him now, Mrs. Alving? It certainly puts things in an entirely different light.

MRS. ALVING: It does indeed!

MANDERS: It just shows you how careful one must be in judging one's fellow-men. And what a satisfaction to find oneself mistaken! What do you say now?

MRS. ALVING: I say you're a great big baby, Manders, and always will be!

MANDERS: *I!*

MRS. ALVING (*Puts her hands on his shoulders*): Yes; and I say I should like very much to give you a big hug!

MANDERS (*Hastily drawing back*): Good Heavens— What ideas you have!

MRS. ALVING (*With a smile*): Oh, you needn't be afraid of me!

MANDERS (*By the table*): You have such an extravagant way of expressing yourself! I'll just gather up all these documents and put them in my bag. (*He does so*) There! Keep an eye on Osvald when he returns; I'll leave you for the present—but I'll come back and see you later. (*He takes his hat and goes out through the hall door.*)

MRS. ALVING (*Gives a sigh, glances out of the window, straightens up one or two things in the room and is about to go into the dining room but stops in the doorway and gives a low exclamation*): Osvald—are you still there?

OSVALD (*From the dining room*): I'm just finishing my cigar.

MRS. ALVING: I thought you'd gone out for a walk.

OSVALD: In this kind of weather?

(*Noise of a glass clinking.* MRS. ALVING *leaves the door open, and sits down on the sofa with some knitting.*)

OSVALD (*Off stage*): Was that Mr. Manders who went out just now?

MRS. ALVING: Yes, he went down to the Orphanage.

OSVALD: Hm—

(*The clinking of a bottle on a glass is heard again.*)

MRS. ALVING (*With an uneasy glance*): Osvald dear—be careful with that liqueur—it's quite strong, you know.

OSVALD: It'll do me good, Mother! I feel so chilly.

MRS. ALVING: Wouldn't you rather come in here with me?

OSVALD: You don't allow smoking in there, you said.

MRS. ALVING: I don't mind a cigar, dear.

OSVALD: Very well, then I'll come in—I'll just have another little drop—there! (*He comes in smoking a cigar. Closes the door after him. A short silence*) Where did Mr. Manders go?

MRS. ALVING: I just told you; he went down to the Orphanage.

OSVALD: Oh, yes—so you did.

MRS. ALVING: It's not good for you to sit so long at table, Osvald, dear.

OSVALD (*Holding his cigar behind his back*): But it's so cozy, Mother. (*He pats her face and caresses her*) You don't know what it means: To be home! To sit at my mother's table—in my mother's own room—to eat my mother's delicious food—!

MRS. ALVING: My dear, dear boy!

OSVALD (*Walks up and down impatiently*): And what on earth is there to do here? I can't seem to settle to anything—

MRS. ALVING: Can't you?

OSVALD: In this gloomy weather—never a ray of sunshine. (*Paces up and down*) God! Not to be able to work—!

MRS. ALVING: Perhaps you shouldn't have come home, Osvald.

OSVALD: I had to come, Mother.

MRS. ALVING: But, if you're unhappy, Osvald. You know I'd ten times rather give up the joy of having you here, than—

OSVALD (*Stopping by the table*): Tell me honestly, Mother— is it really such a joy to you to have me home again?

MRS. ALVING: How can you ask such a thing!

OSVALD (*Crumpling up a newspaper*): I should have thought you didn't much care one way or the other.

MRS. ALVING: How have you the heart to say that to me, Osvald?

OSVALD: After all—you managed to live without me all these years.

MRS. ALVING: That's true—I've managed to live without you— (*A pause. Twilight is falling gradually.* OSVALD *paces up and down. He has put out his cigar. He suddenly stops in front of* MRS. ALVING.)

OSVALD: May I sit beside you on the sofa, Mother?

MRS. ALVING (*Making room for him*): Of course, dear.

OSVALD (*Sits beside her*): There's something I must tell you.

MRS. ALVING (*Anxiously*): Well?

OSVALD (*Staring in front of him*): I don't think I can bear it any longer.

MRS. ALVING: Bear what? What is it?

OSVALD (*As before*): I somehow couldn't bring myself to write to you about it—and, since I've been home—

MRS. ALVING (*Grips his arm*): Osvald—what is it?

OSVALD: All day yesterday and again today, I've tried to get rid of the thought—free myself of it—but I can't—

MRS. ALVING (*Rising*): You must be honest with me, Osvald—

OSVALD (*Pulls her down on the sofa again*): No, don't get up! Sit still! I'll try and tell you. I've complained a lot about being tired after my journey—

MRS. ALVING: Yes—well, what of that—?

OSVALD: But that isn't really what's the matter with me; this is no ordinary fatigue—

MRS. ALVING (*Tries to get up*): You're not ill, are you, Osvald?

OSVALD (*Pulling her down again*): No, don't get up, Mother. Try and be calm. I'm not really ill either—not in the usual sort of way— (*Clasping his head in his hands*) It's a kind of mental breakdown, Mother—I'm destroyed—I'll never be able to work again. (*He hides his face in his hands, and lets his head fall into her lap—shaking with sobs.*)

MRS. ALVING (*Pale and trembling*): Osvald! It's not true! Look at me!

OSVALD (*Looking up in despair*): I'll never be able to work again! Never—never! I'll be like a living corpse! Mother—can you imagine anything more frightful—?

MRS. ALVING: But, my darling! How could such a dreadful thing happen to you?

OSVALD (*Sitting up again*): That's just it—I don't know! I can't possibly imagine! I've never lived a dissipated life—not in any kind of way—you must believe that, Mother—I haven't!

MRS. ALVING: I believe that, Osvald.

OSVALD: And yet, in spite of that—this ghastly thing has taken hold of me!

MRS. ALVING: It'll come out all right, my darling. It's just over-work—believe me!

OSVALD (*Dully*): Yes—I thought that too at first—but it's not so.

MRS. ALVING: Tell me all about it.

OSVALD: Yes, I will.

MRS. ALVING: When did you first notice anything?

OSVALD: It was just after I went back to Paris—after my last visit here. I started to get terrible headaches—all up the back of my head—it was as if an iron band was screwed round my head—from the neck up—

MRS. ALVING: And then—?

OSVALD: At first I thought it was just the usual kind of headache I'd always had—since I was a child—

MRS. ALVING: Yes—?

OSVALD: But it wasn't that—I soon found that out. I was no longer able to work. I'd start on a new picture and all my strength would suddenly fail me—it was as though I were paralyzed; I couldn't concentrate—and I felt sick and dizzy; it was the most ghastly sensation; at last I went to see a doctor—and then I found out the truth.

MRS. ALVING: What do you mean?

OSVALD: He was one of the best doctors there. I described to him just how I felt—and then he started asking me all sorts of questions—questions about things that seemed to have no bearing on the case—I couldn't make out what he was driving at—

MRS. ALVING: Well—?

OSVALD: At last he said: your constitution has been undermined from birth; he used the word "vermoulu."

MRS. ALVING (*Anxiously*): What did he mean by that?

OSVALD: I didn't know what he meant either; I asked him to explain. And do you know what he said—that cynical old man—? (*Clenching his fist*) Oh!—

MRS. ALVING: No—what?

OSVALD: He said: the sins of the fathers are visited upon the children.

MRS. ALVING (*Rises slowly*): The sins of the fathers—!

OSVALD: I almost hit him in the face.

MRS. ALVING (*Pacing the floor*): The sins of the fathers—

OSVALD (*With a sad smile*): Can you believe it? Of course I assured him that such a thing was out of the question—but he paid no attention—he repeated what he'd said. I had some of your letters with me—and I had to translate to him the parts that referred to Father—

MRS. ALVING: Yes—?

OSVALD: Then he had to admit he must be on the wrong tack. And then I learned the truth—the incredible truth! The sort of life I'd been leading—gay and carefree, but innocent enough I thought—had been too much for my strength; I should have been more careful. So, you see, I've brought it on myself—

MRS. ALVING: No! You mustn't believe that, Osvald!

OSVALD: He said that was the only possible explanation. My whole life ruined—thrown away—through my own carelessness. All that I dreamt of achieving, of accomplishing—I dare not think of it—I mustn't think of it! If I could only live my life over again—if I could wipe it all out and start afresh! (*He flings himself face downward on the sofa. After a pause looks up, leaning on his elbows*) It wouldn't be so bad if it was something I'd inherited—if it were something I couldn't help. But, deliberately—out of carelessness—out of shameful stupidity to throw away happiness, health—everything that's worthwhile in this world—my future—my whole life—!

MRS. ALVING: No—no! It's impossible, Osvald—my darling—my boy! (*Bending over him*) It's not true—it's not as desperate as that—!

OSVALD (*Jumping up*): Oh, Mother, you don't know! And to think I should bring you such unhappiness! I've often hoped and prayed that you didn't care much about me, after all—

MRS. ALVING: Not care about you, Osvald? You're all I have in the world—you're the only thing on earth that matters to me—

OSVALD (*Takes both her hands and kisses them*): Yes, Mother, I know; when I'm home I realize that—and it makes it doubly hard for me. Well—now you know all about it; don't let's discuss it any more today; I can't bear to dwell on it too long. (*Paces about the room*) Give me something to drink, Mother.

MRS. ALVING: To drink? What do you want, Osvald?

OSVALD: Oh, it doesn't matter—anything! You must have something in the house—

MRS. ALVING: Yes, but Osvald—don't you think—?

OSVALD: Don't refuse me, Mother—be a dear! I must have something to help me drown these agonizing thoughts! (*He goes up to the conservatory and looks out*) Oh, it's so dark—so terribly dark! (MRS. ALVING *goes to the bell-pull and rings*) This incessant rain! It may go on for weeks—for months! Never a ray of sunshine! I never remember seeing any sunshine here!

MRS. ALVING: You're not thinking of leaving me, Osvald?

OSVALD (*With a deep sigh*): I'm not thinking of anything, Mother; I'm not capable of thinking— (*In a low voice*) I've had to give that up!

(REGINE *comes in from the dining room*.)

REGINE: Did you ring, Mrs. Alving?

MRS. ALVING: Yes; bring in the lamp.

REGINE: At once, Mrs. Alving—I have it ready. (*She goes out*.)

MRS. ALVING (*Goes to* OSVALD): Don't keep anything from me, Osvald.

OSVALD: I won't, Mother. (*Goes to the table*) It seems to me I've been very frank with you.

(REGINE *brings in the lamp and puts it on the table*.)

MRS. ALVING: Oh, and Regine—you might bring us a half bottle of champagne.

REGINE: Very good, Mrs. Alving. (*She goes out*.)

OSVALD (*Takes her face in his hands*): That's right, Mother! I knew you wouldn't let me go thirsty!

MRS. ALVING: My own poor boy! As if I could refuse you anything!

OSVALD (*Eagerly*): You really mean that, Mother?

MRS. ALVING: What?

OSVALD: That you couldn't refuse me anything?

MRS. ALVING: But, my dear Osvald—

OSVALD: Sh!

(REGINE *enters with a small tray on which are a bottle of champagne and two glasses; she sets it down on the table*.)

REGINE: Shall I open it, Mrs. Alving?

OSVALD: No thanks—I'll do it myself.

(REGINE *goes out*.)

MRS. ALVING (*Sits down at the table*): Osvald—be honest with me—what is it you don't want me to refuse you—?

OSVALD (*Busy opening the bottle*): First, let's have a glass of wine— (*He opens the bottle and pours out one glass and is about to pour another*.)

MRS. ALVING (*Puts her hand over the glass*): Thanks—not for me.

OSVALD: For me, then! (*He empties his glass, refills it and empties it again; he sits down at the table*.)

MRS. ALVING (*Expectantly*): Well—

OSVALD: Mother, tell me—what was the matter with you and Mr. Manders at dinner, just now? Why were you so quiet and solemn?

MRS. ALVING: Oh—did you notice that?

OSVALD: Yes. Hm— (*A pause*) Mother, what do you think of Regine?

MRS. ALVING: What do I think of her?

OSVALD: Don't you think she's wonderful?

MRS. ALVING: You don't know her as well as I do, Osvald—

OSVALD: Well—what of that?

MRS. ALVING: I should have taken charge of her sooner—I'm afraid she spent too many years at home—

OSVALD: But she's so wonderful to look at, Mother! (*Fills up his glass*.)

MRS. ALVING: She has many grave faults, Osvald—

OSVALD: As if that mattered—! (*He drinks*.)

MRS. ALVING: But I'm fond of her all the same; I feel responsible for her. I wouldn't have anything happen to her for all the world.

OSVALD (*Jumps up*): Mother! The one thing that could save me, is Regine!

MRS. ALVING (*Rising*): What do you mean?

OSVALD: I mean I can't endure this agony alone!

MRS. ALVING: But I'm here to help you, Osvald—

OSVALD: Yes, I know; I thought that would be enough—that's why I came home to you; but it's no use; I see that now. My life here would be intolerable.

MRS. ALVING: Osvald—!

OSVALD: I must live a different sort of life; that's why I must go away again. I don't want you to see it happening to me—

MRS. ALVING: But you can't go away when you're so ill, Osvald.

OSVALD: If it were just an ordinary illness, of course I'd stay home, Mother; I know you're the best friend I have in the world—

MRS. ALVING: You do know that—don't you?

OSVALD (*Moves about the room restlessly*): But it's the anguish, the remorse, the deadly fear—oh—that terrible fear!

MRS. ALVING (*Follows after him*): Fear? Fear of what?

OSVALD: Don't ask me any more about it! I don't know—I can't de-scribe it to you— (MRS. ALVING *goes to the bell-pull and rings*) What do you want?

MRS. ALVING: I want my boy to be happy, that's what I want—I won't let you suffer here! (*To* REGINE) More champagne, Regine! A whole bottle!

(REGINE *goes.*)

OSVALD: Mother!

MRS. ALVING: We country-people know how to live too—you'll see.

OSVALD: Isn't she wonderful to look at? So beautifully built! So ra-diant with health.

MRS. ALVING (*Sitting down at the table*): Sit down, Osvald; let's talk quietly for a moment—

OSVALD (*Sits down*): You don't know about it, Mother—but I haven't been quite fair to Regine—

MRS. ALVING: Not fair—?

OSVALD: No—it was just thoughtlessness on my part—nothing se-rious; but last time I was home—

MRS. ALVING: Yes—?

OSVALD: She kept on asking questions about Paris—I told her a bit about my life there—and one day I said to her, quite casually: "Perhaps you'd like to go there and see it all for yourself, Regine—"

MRS. ALVING: Well—?

OSVALD: Then she blushed and got quite excited and said she'd give anything to go; then I said, perhaps some day it might be arranged—or something of that sort—

MRS. ALVING: I see.

OSVALD: Of course I'd forgotten all about it; but the other day, when I arrived, I asked her if she was glad I intended to spend such a long time here—

MRS. ALVING: Yes—?

OSVALD: And then she looked at me so strangely and said: "Then what about my trip to Paris?"

MRS. ALVING: Her trip—?

OSVALD: Yes—it seems she'd taken me quite seriously; she'd been thinking about it all this time—thinking about *me*. She'd even tried to teach herself some French—

MRS. ALVING: So that was why—

OSVALD: I'd never noticed her much before, Mother—but suddenly I saw her there—so beautiful—so vital—she stood there as though waiting to come into my arms—

MRS. ALVING: Osvald—!

OSVALD: I suddenly realized that she could save me; she was so full of the joy of life!

MRS. ALVING (*Startled*): Joy of life—? Is there salvation in that? (REGINE *comes in with the champagne.*)

REGINE: Excuse me for being so long, Mrs. Alving. I had to go down to the cellar— (*Puts the bottle on the table.*)

OSVALD: Fetch another glass.

REGINE (*Looks at him surprised*): Mrs. Alving has a glass, Sir.

OSVALD: Yes—but fetch one for yourself, Regine. (REGINE *starts and gives a quick frightened glance at* MRS. ALVING) Well?

REGINE (*Softly, with hesitation*): Do you wish me to, Mrs. Alving?

MRS. ALVING: Fetch the glass, Regine.

(REGINE *goes into the dining room.*)

OSVALD (*Looking after her*): Have you noticed her walk, Mother—so strong—so sure.

MRS. ALVING: This can't be allowed to happen, Osvald.

OSVALD: But it's all settled—you must see that—there's no use forbidding it. (REGINE *comes in with an empty glass and keeps it in her hand*) Sit down, Regine. (REGINE *looks questioningly at* MRS. ALVING.)

MRS. ALVING: Sit down. (REGINE *sits on a chair by the dining*

room door, with the empty glass in her hand) Osvald—What
were you saying about the joy of life?

OSVALD: Yes—the joy of life, Mother—you don't know much
about that here at home. I could never find it here.

MRS. ALVING: Not here with me?

OSVALD: No. Never at home. But you don't understand that.

MRS. ALVING: Yes—I believe I'm beginning to understand it
—now.

OSVALD: That—and the joy of work. They're really the same thing
you know. But of course, you don't know anything about that
here either.

MRS. ALVING: No; you may be right. Tell me more about it.

OSVALD: Well—I simply mean that here people look on work as a
curse—as a kind of punishment. They look on *life* as a wretched,
miserable business—to be got through as soon as possible—

MRS. ALVING: I know—a "vale of tears"—we do our best to make
it so—

OSVALD: But, you see, abroad, people don't look at it like that.
They don't believe in that old-fashioned preaching any longer.
The mere fact of being alive in this world seems to them joyous
and marvelous. You must have noticed, Mother, everything I
paint is filled with this joy of life; always and forever the joy of
life! My paintings are full of light, of sunshine, of glowing happy
faces. That's why I'm afraid to stay here, Mother.

MRS. ALVING: Afraid? What are you afraid of—here with me?

OSVALD: I'm afraid that all the strongest traits in my nature would
become warped here—would degenerate into ugliness.

MRS. ALVING (*Looks at him intently*): You really believe that is
what would happen?

OSVALD: Yes—I'm convinced of it! Even if I lived the same life
here as I live abroad—it still wouldn't *be* the same life.

MRS. ALVING (*Who has listened intently, rises; a thoughtful look
in her eyes*): Now I see it! It's all becoming clear to me—

OSVALD: What do you see?

MRS. ALVING: The whole pattern—for the first time, I see it—and
now I can speak.

OSVALD (*Rising*): I don't understand you, Mother.

REGINE (*Who has risen too*): Perhaps I'd better go—

MRS. ALVING: No, no—stay where you are. Now I can speak. Now you must know everything, Osvald—and then you can choose. Osvald! Regine!

OSVALD: Sh! Here comes Manders.

MANDERS (*Enters from hall door*): Well—I must say—we've had a most edifying time—

OSVALD: So have we.

MANDERS: There can be no doubt about it— We must make it possible for Engstrand to start that seamen's home of his. Regine must go back with him; she can be most helpful—

REGINE: No thank you, Mr. Manders!

MANDERS (*Notices her for the first time*): What—? You in here? And with a glass in your hand?

REGINE (*Hastily puts down her glass*): Pardon!

OSVALD: Regine is going with me, Mr. Manders.

MANDERS: Going with you—?

OSVALD: Yes; as my wife—if she insists on that.

MANDERS: But—good Heavens—!

REGINE: It's no fault of mine, Mr. Manders—

OSVALD: Or if I decide to stay here—she'll stay too.

REGINE (*Involuntarily*): Stay here—!

MANDERS: I am amazed at you, Mrs. Alving.

MRS. ALVING: None of this will happen—for now I can tell the truth at last.

MANDERS: But you won't—you can't!

MRS. ALVING: I can and I will—and nobody's ideals will be the worse for it.

OSVALD: Mother, what is all this—what are you hiding from me?

REGINE (*Listening*): Mrs. Alving—Listen!—I hear people shouting out there. (*She goes up to the conservatory.*)

OSVALD (*Going to the window stage left*): What's happening? What's that glare in the sky?

REGINE (*Calls out*): It's the Orphanage—the Orphanage is on fire!

MRS. ALVING (*Going to the window*): On fire—?

MANDERS: On fire—? Impossible! I've just come from there.

OSVALD: Give me my hat!—Oh never mind— Father's Orphanage! (*He runs out into the garden.*)

MRS. ALVING: My shawl, Regine! The whole place is in flames!

MANDERS: How horrible! It's a judgment, Mrs. Alving— a judgment on this house.

MRS. ALVING: Yes—undoubtedly, Manders. Come, Regine.
(MRS. ALVING *and* REGINE *hurry out through the hall door.*)

MANDERS (*Clasping his hands*): And to think it's not insured!
(*He follows them as the curtain falls.*)

ACT
THREE

SCENE: *The room as before. All the doors stand open. The lamp
is still burning on the table. It is dark out of doors; there is only a
faint glow from the fire in the background to the left.*

AT RISE: MRS. ALVING, *with a shawl over her head, stands in the
conservatory looking out.* REGINE, *also with a shawl on, stands a
little behind her.*

MRS. ALVING: Nothing left—burned to the ground!

REGINE: The cellar is still in flames.

MRS. ALVING: Why doesn't Osvald come?—there's no hope of saving anything.

REGINE: Shall I take his hat down to him?

MRS. ALVING: Is he out there without it?

REGINE (*Pointing to the hall*): Yes—it's hanging in the hall—

MRS. ALVING: No—leave it—he'll be back in a moment— I think
I'll go and look for him. (*Exits to the garden.*)

MANDERS (*Enters from hall*): Isn't Mrs. Alving here?

REGINE: She just went down to the garden.

MANDERS: What a night—I've never gone through anything as dreadful!

REGINE: It's a terrible thing, Mr. Manders!

MANDERS: Don't speak of it!— I can't bear the thought of it.

REGINE: But how could it possibly have happened?

MANDERS: Oh, don't ask me, Miss Engstrand—how should I know! You're not implying—? Isn't it enough that your father should—?

REGINE: What's he been up to—?

MANDERS: He's driven me half mad—

ENGSTRAND (*Enters through hall*): Oh there you are, Mr. Manders—

MANDERS (*Turning around with a start*): Must you follow me in here too!

ENGSTRAND: Oh, Mr. Manders!— Such a terrible thing, Sir—!

MANDERS (*Pacing up and down*): Yes, yes! We know! We know!—

REGINE: What's the meaning of this?

ENGSTRAND: It was all due to the prayer meeting, you see! (*Aside to* REGINE) We've hooked the old fool now, my girl! (*Aloud*) That poor Mr. Manders should be the cause of such a calamity—and through my fault too!

MANDERS: But I tell you, Engstrand—

ENGSTRAND: No one touched the lights but you, Sir!

MANDERS (*Standing still*): That's what *you* claim—but I could swear I never went *near* the lights!

ENGSTRAND: But I saw you with my own eyes, Sir!— I saw you snuff one of the candles and throw the bit of wick right into a pile of shavings!

MANDERS: You say you *saw* this?

ENGSTRAND: So help me God, Sir!

MANDERS: Incredible!— I'm not in the habit of snuffing candles with my fingers.

ENGSTRAND: No Sir—I thought at the time it didn't look quite like you. It'll be quite a serious thing, won't it, Sir?

MANDERS (*Walks restlessly back and forth*): Don't ask me about it!

ENGSTRAND (*Follows him about*): You hadn't insured the place, had you, Sir?

MANDERS (*Still pacing*): I told you I hadn't!

ENGSTRAND (*Following him*): Hadn't insured it!— And then to go and set the whole place on fire like that! Lord! What a bit of bad luck, Sir!

MANDERS (*Wipes the perspiration from his brow*): You may well say so, Engstrand.

ENGSTRAND: A charitable institution too! A place dedicated, you might say, to the good of the Community!— It's likely the papers won't treat you any too kindly, Mr. Manders.

MANDERS: That's just it! That's what I'm thinking about—all the spiteful attacks and accusations! That's the worst part of the whole business—I can't bear the thought of it!

MRS. ALVING (*Enters from the garden*): He won't come—he can't seem to tear himself away.

MANDERS: Oh, it's you, Mrs. Alving.

MRS. ALVING: Well, Manders! You got out of making your speech after all!

MANDERS: I'd be only too glad to make it!

MRS. ALVING (*In a subdued tone*): It's all for the best; that poor Orphanage could never have brought good to anyone!

MANDERS: You really feel that?

MRS. ALVING: Well—don't you?

MANDERS: All the same—it's a great tragedy.

MRS. ALVING: Nonsense! Now—let's discuss it from a business point of view— Are you waiting for Mr. Manders, Engstrand?

ENGSTRAND (*By the hall door*): Yes, Ma'am, I am.

MRS. ALVING: Well then—sit down.

ENGSTRAND: I'd rather stand, thank you, Ma'am.

MRS. ALVING (*To* MANDERS): I suppose you'll be leaving by the next boat?

MANDERS: Yes—there's one in an hour.

MRS. ALVING: Please take all the documents with you—I don't want to hear another word about it! I've other things to think about now.

MANDERS: Mrs. Alving—

MRS. ALVING: I'll arrange to send you Power of Attorney and you can wind things up as you think best.

MANDERS: I'll be glad to look after it for you. Of course now, the original terms of the bequest will have to be radically altered.

MRS. ALVING: Naturally—

MANDERS: I would suggest making the actual land over to the Parish under the circumstances; it's not without value, and could be used for many purposes. As to the interest on the capital—I feel sure I can find some worthy project in need of support—something that would prove beneficial to the life of the community.

MRS. ALVING: Do anything you like with it—it makes no difference to me.

ENGSTRAND: You might give a thought to my Seamen's Home, Mr. Manders.

MANDERS: To be sure. A good suggestion. Well worth looking into.

ENGSTRAND (*Aside*): Looking into! That's a good one!

MANDERS (*With a sigh*): Of course I may not be long in charge of these affairs; public opinion may compel me to withdraw; there will naturally be an investigation to determine the cause of the fire; it all depends on the outcome of that.

MRS. ALVING: What *are* you talking about, Manders?

MANDERS: It's impossible to tell what that outcome will be.

ENGSTRAND (*Coming closer*): Oh no it's not, Mr. Manders! Don't forget *me*—don't forget Jakob Engstrand!

MANDERS: But—I don't see—

ENGSTRAND (*In a low voice*): And Jakob Engstrand is not one to desert a benefactor in his hour of need—as they say!

MANDERS: But, my dear man—how could you possibly—?

ENGSTRAND: Jakob Engstrand won't desert you, Sir! He'll be like a guardian angel to you, Sir!

MANDERS: But I could never consent—!

ENGSTRAND: You'll have nothing to do with it, Sir. It wouldn't be the first time I'd taken the blame for others.

MANDERS: Jakob! (*Wringing his hands*) You're one in a million! I'll see that you get funds for your Seamen's Home—You can count on that. (ENGSTRAND *tries to thank him but is overcome with emotion*; MANDERS *slings his traveling-bag over his shoulder*) And now—let's be off. We'll travel together, of course.

ENGSTRAND (*At the hall door, aside to* REGINE): You'd better come with me, hussy! You'll live like a Queen!

REGINE (*Tosses her head*): Merci! (*She fetches* MANDERS' *things from the hall.*)

MANDERS: Goodbye, Mrs. Alving. May the Spirit of Truth and Righteousness soon enter into this house.

MRS. ALVING: Goodbye, Manders. (*She goes to meet* OSVALD *who enters from the garden.*)

ENGSTRAND (*As he and* REGINE *help* MANDERS *with his coat*): Goodbye, my dear child. And if anything should happen to you, remember Jakob Engstrand's always there—you know where to find him. Harbor Street—you know! (*To* MRS. ALVING *and* OSVALD) My home for poor Seamen shall be called "Captain Alving's Haven" and if it turns out the way I want it, Ma'am—I humbly hope it may prove worthy of Captain Alving's memory!

MANDERS (*In the doorway*): Hm—yes. Come along my dear Engstrand. Goodbye again—goodbye! (*They exit through the hall.*)

OSVALD (*Goes toward the table*): What does he mean? What "home" is he talking about?

MRS. ALVING: It's some sort of a hostel he and Manders are thinking of starting.

OSVALD: It'll only burn down—just like this one.

MRS. ALVING: Why do you say that?

OSVALD: Everything will be burnt. Father's memory will be wiped out. I shall soon be burnt up too.

(REGINE *looks at him in amazement.*)

MRS. ALVING: Osvald!— You poor boy! You shouldn't have stayed down there so long.

OSVALD (*Sits down at the table*): I expect you're right about that.

MRS. ALVING: Your face is wet, Osvald; let me dry it for you. (*Wipes his face with her handkerchief.*)

OSVALD (*Indifferently*): Thanks, Mother.

MRS. ALVING: You must be tired, Osvald. You'd better get some sleep.

OSVALD (*Apprehensively*): No! No! I don't want to sleep! I never sleep—I only pretend to— (*Dully*) I'll sleep soon enough!

MRS. ALVING (*Looking at him anxiously*): I'm afraid you're really ill, my darling!

REGINE (*Intently*): Is Mr. Alving ill?

OSVALD (*Impatiently*): And close the doors!—I want all the doors closed!—this terrible fear—

MRS. ALVING: Close the doors, Regine.

(REGINE *closes the doors and remains standing by the one to the hall.* MRS. ALVING *takes off her shawl, and* REGINE *does likewise.*)

MRS. ALVING (*Draws up a chair and sits next to* OSVALD): There!—I'll sit here beside you.

OSVALD: Yes—do, Mother. And Regine must stay here too—she must never leave me. You'll be there to help me, won't you, Regine?

REGINE: I don't understand—

MRS. ALVING: —there to help you?

OSVALD: Yes—when the time comes.

MRS. ALVING: Can't you trust your mother to do that?

OSVALD: You? (*Smiles*) You'd never do it. (*With a melancholy laugh*) You! (*Looks at her gravely*) And yet you're the only one who has the right to do it. Why are you always so formal with me, Regine? Why don't you call me Osvald?

REGINE (*In a low voice*): Mrs. Alving might not like it.

MRS. ALVING: You may soon have a right to—so sit down with us, Regine. (REGINE *hesitates, then sits down quietly at the far side of the table*) And now, my darling, I'm going to free you from this torment; you won't have to bear this dreadful burden any longer.

OSVALD: You're going to free me, Mother?

MRS. ALVING: Yes—from this remorse, this sense of guilt, this self-reproach—

OSVALD: —Do you think you can do that?

MRS. ALVING: Yes, I believe I can now. Earlier this evening you were talking about the joy of life—and suddenly everything became clear to me; I saw my whole life in a new light.

OSVALD (*Shaking his head*): I don't understand this.

MRS. ALVING: You should have known your father when he was a young lieutenant. He was filled with that joy of life, I can tell you!

OSVALD: Yes—so I've heard.

MRS. ALVING: He seemed to radiate light and warmth—he was filled with a turbulent, joyous vitality.

OSVALD: Well—?

MRS. ALVING: And this boy, so full of the joy of life—he was like a boy then—was cooped up in this drab little provincial town—which could offer him no real joy—only dissipation. He had no real aim in life—no work that could stimulate his mind or feed his spirit—nothing but a dull, petty, routine job. He found no one here who understood that pure joy of life that was in him; what friends he had were bent on idling their time away or drinking themselves into a stupor—

OSVALD: Mother—!

MRS. ALVING: And so, the inevitable happened.

OSVALD: The inevitable?

MRS. ALVING: You told me a little while ago, what would happen to you if you stayed here.

OSVALD: Do you mean by that—that Father—?

MRS. ALVING: Your poor father could find no outlet for that overpowering joy of life that was in him—and I'm afraid I brought him no happiness either.

OSVALD: Why, Mother?

MRS. ALVING: All my life I'd been taught a great deal about duty—that seemed the all-important thing. Everything was reduced to a question of duty—*my* duty—*his* duty—your poor father—I'm afraid I must have made home intolerable for him, Osvald.

OSVALD: Why did you never write me about all this?

MRS. ALVING: You were his son—I felt it would be wrong to talk to you about it; you see, I didn't see things clearly then.

OSVALD: How did you see them?

MRS. ALVING (*Slowly*): I was aware of one thing only; that your father was a broken, dissolute man, long before you were born.

OSVALD (*A smothered cry*): Ah! (*He rises and goes to the window.*)

MRS. ALVING: And day in and day out I was tormented by the thought that Regine actually had the same rights in this house that you have.

OSVALD (*Turns quickly*): Regine!

REGINE (*Jumps up and says in a choking voice*): I—!

MRS. ALVING: Yes. Now you know everything—both of you.

OSVALD: Regine!

REGINE (*To herself*): So mother was—*that* sort of woman.

MRS. ALVING: Your mother had many fine qualities, Regine.

REGINE: She was that sort all the same. There've been times when I guessed she might be—but—Mrs. Alving! Please allow me to leave at once.

MRS. ALVING: You really want to go, Regine?

REGINE: I certainly do, Mrs. Alving.

MRS. ALVING: Of course you must do as you wish, but—

OSVALD (*Goes to* REGINE): Leave now? But you belong here.

REGINE: Merci, Mr. Alving—I suppose I can call you Osvald now—though this wasn't the way I wanted it to happen.

MRS. ALVING: Regine—I haven't been honest with you—

REGINE: No! You certainly haven't, Mrs. Alving! If I'd known that Osvald was a sick man—And now that there can never be anything serious between us—No! I can't waste my time out here in the country looking after invalids.

OSVALD: Not when it's your own brother, Regine?

REGINE: I should say not! I'm poor—all I have is my youth—I can't afford to waste it. I don't want to be left stranded. I have some of that "joy of life" in me too, Mrs. Alving!

MRS. ALVING: No doubt. But don't throw yourself away, Regine.

REGINE: If I do—I *do*—that's all! If Osvald takes after his father, I take after my mother, I suppose. —May I ask, Mrs. Alving, if Mr. Manders knows about all this?

MRS. ALVING: Mr. Manders knows everything.

REGINE (*Rapidly putting on her shawl*): Then I'd better try and catch that boat. Mr. Manders is such a kind man, he's sure to help me. It seems to me I have a right to some of that money too—a better right than that filthy old carpenter.

MRS. ALVING: You're welcome to it, Regine.

REGINE (*With a hard look*): And I must say, Mrs. Alving—it seems to me I also had a right to a decent up-bringing—one suited to a gentleman's daughter. (*Tosses her head*) Well—what do I care! (*Casts a bitter glance at the unopened bottle*) Some day I may be drinking champagne with the best of them—who knows?

MRS. ALVING: If you should ever need a home, Regine—come to me.

REGINE: No thank you, Mrs. Alving! Mr. Manders'll look after me I'm sure. And if the worst comes to the worst, I know of a place where I'd be quite at home.

MRS. ALVING: Where do you mean?

REGINE: In Captain Alving's Hostel, of course!

MRS. ALVING: Be careful, Regine! Don't destroy yourself!

REGINE: What do I care!—Well—goodbye! (*She bows to them and goes out through the hall*.)

OSVALD (*Stands at the window gazing out*): Has she gone?

MRS. ALVING: Yes.

OSVALD (*Mutters to himself*): How stupid it all is!

MRS. ALVING (*Stands behind him and puts her hands on his shoulders*): Osvald—my dear; has it been a very great shock to you?

OSVALD (*Turns his face towards her*): All that about Father, you mean?

MRS. ALVING: Yes, your poor father!—I'm afraid it's been too much for you.

OSVALD: Why do you say that? It was a great surprise to me, I admit; but after all, it doesn't really matter.

MRS. ALVING (*Withdraws her hands*): Not matter? That your father was so unspeakably unhappy?

OSVALD: I feel sorry for him of course—as I would for anyone who suffered.

MRS. ALVING: No more than that?—But he was your *father* Osvald.

OSVALD (*Impatiently*): Father! Father! I never *knew* my father. The only thing I remember about him is that he once made me sick!

MRS. ALVING: What a dreadful thought! But surely a child must have some love for his father, in spite of everything.

OSVALD: Even if he owes his father nothing? Even if he never knew him? Come now, Mother! You're too broadminded to believe in that superstitious nonsense!

MRS. ALVING: Superstitious nonsense—you think that's all it is?

OSVALD: Of course, Mother—you must see that. It's one of those old-fashioned illusions people go on clinging to—

MRS. ALVING (*Shaken*): Ghosts—

OSVALD (*Paces up and down*): Yes—call them ghosts if you like.

MRS. ALVING (*In a burst of emotion*): Osvald— Then you don't love me either!

OSVALD: Well, at least I know *you*—

MRS. ALVING: You know me—yes; but is that all?

OSVALD: I know how much you care for me; I should be grateful to you for that. And now that I'm ill, you can be of great help to me.

MRS. ALVING: I can—can't I, Osvald? I'm almost glad you're ill—since it's brought you home to me. I understand—you don't belong to me yet—I'll have to win you.

OSVALD (*Impatiently*): Oh, don't let's have a lot of phrases, Mother! You must remember I'm ill. I can't be bothered with other people; I've got to think about myself.

MRS. ALVING (*Gently*): I'll be very quiet and patient, Osvald.

OSVALD: And, for God's sake, *happy*, Mother!

MRS. ALVING: Yes, my darling—you're right. (*Goes to him*) And you've no more doubts, no more remorse? I've freed you of all that?

OSVALD: Yes, Mother, you have. But who's to free me of the terror—?

MRS. ALVING: Terror!

OSVALD (*Pacing up and down*): Regine would have done it, if I'd asked her.

MRS. ALVING: I don't understand. What is this terror—and what has Regine to do with it?

OSVALD: Mother—is it very late?

MRS. ALVING: It's early morning. (*She goes to the conservatory and looks out*) The dawn is just breaking. It's going to be a lovely day, Osvald! In a little while you'll see the sun!

OSVALD: I'll be glad of that. Perhaps after all there are lots of things I could be glad about, Mother—lots of things I'd like to live for—

MRS. ALVING: Of course there are!

OSVALD: And even if I'm not able to work—

MRS. ALVING: You'll soon be able to work again, you'll see. Now that you're rid of all those depressing, gloomy thoughts.

OSVALD: Yes—it's good that you were able to wipe out that obsession. Now, if I can just get over this other— (*Sits down on the sofa*) Come here, Mother. I want to talk to you—

MRS. ALVING: Yes, Osvald. (*She pushes an armchair over near the sofa and sits close to him.*)

OSVALD: Meanwhile the sun is rising. And now that you know—I don't feel—so afraid any more.

MRS. ALVING: Now that I know—what?

OSVALD (*Without listening to her*): Mother—didn't you say a little while ago that there was nothing in this world you wouldn't do for me, if I asked you?

MRS. ALVING: Yes—of course I did.

OSVALD: And you stand by that, Mother?

MRS. ALVING: You can depend on me, my darling. You're the only thing on earth I have to live for.

OSVALD: Well then—listen, Mother; you have a strong, gallant spirit—I know that; I want you to sit quite still while I tell you something.

MRS. ALVING: What dreadful thing are you going to—?

OSVALD: Don't scream or get excited, do you hear? Promise me! We'll sit here and talk it over quietly. Promise!

MRS. ALVING: Yes, yes—I promise! Tell me what it is!

OSVALD: Well then—listen: this fatigue of mine—my inability to work—all of that is not the *essence* of my illness—

MRS. ALVING: How do you mean?

OSVALD: You see—my illness *is* hereditary—it— (*Touches his forehead and speaks very quietly*) It is centered—*here*.

MRS. ALVING (*Almost speechless*): Osvald! No—no!

OSVALD: Don't scream, Mother—I can't stand it! It's lurking here—lying in wait—ready to spring at any moment.

MRS. ALVING: How horrible—!

OSVALD: Quiet, Mother!—Now you understand the state I'm in.

MRS. ALVING (*Springing up*): It's not true, Osvald—it's impossible!

OSVALD: I had one attack while I was abroad—it didn't last long. But when I realized the condition I'd been in, I was filled with unspeakable terror—and I could think of nothing but getting home to you.

MRS. ALVING: So that's what you mean by "the terror"!

OSVALD: Yes—unspeakable, sickening terror! If it had only been an ordinary illness—even a fatal one—I wouldn't have minded so much—I'm not afraid of death—though I should like to live as long as possible—

MRS. ALVING: You will, Osvald—you must!

OSVALD: But there's something so utterly revolting about this! To become a child again—a helpless child—to have to be fed—to have to be—oh! It's too ghastly to think of!

MRS. ALVING: I'll be here to look after you, Osvald.

OSVALD (*Jumping up*): No, never; I won't stand it! I can't endure the thought of lingering on like that—of growing old like that—old and gray-haired like that! And you might die and I should be left alone. (*Sits down in* MRS. ALVING'S *chair*) For the doctor said I might live for years, you see. He called it "Softening of the brain" or something of the sort. (*With a sad smile*) Charming expression! It makes one think of cherry-colored velvet curtains—soft and delicate to stroke—

MRS. ALVING (*Screams*): Osvald!

OSVALD (*Springs up and paces up and down*): And now you've taken Regine away from me—if only I had her. She'd have been willing to help me, I know.

MRS. ALVING (*Goes to him*): What do you mean by that, my darling?—You know I'd give my life to help you—

OSVALD: I recovered from that attack abroad—but the doctor said that the next time—and there's bound to be a "next time"—it would be hopeless.

MRS. ALVING: How could he be so brutal—!

OSVALD: I insisted on the truth—I made him tell me. I explained that I had certain arrangements to make (*With a cunning smile*) and so I had. (*Takes a small box from his breast pocket*) Do you see this, Mother?

MRS. ALVING: What is it?

OSVALD: Morphine tablets—

MRS. ALVING (*Looks at him in terror*): Osvald—

OSVALD: I managed to save up twelve of them—

MRS. ALVING (*Snatching at it*): Give me the box, Osvald!

OSVALD: Not yet, Mother. (*Puts the box back in his pocket.*)

MRS. ALVING: I can't endure this!

OSVALD: You must endure it, Mother. If only Regine were here— I'd have explained to her how matters stood; I'd have asked her to help me put an end to it; she'd have done it, I know.

MRS. ALVING: Never!

OSVALD: Oh yes she would! If she'd seen that ghastly thing take hold of me—if she'd seen me lying there like an imbecile child—beyond help—hopelessly, irrevocably lost—

MRS. ALVING: Regine would never have done it!

OSVALD: Oh yes! She'd have done it! Regine has such a magnificently light and buoyant nature. She wouldn't have put up long with an invalid like me!

MRS. ALVING: Then I can only thank God Regine is not here!

OSVALD: Yes, but then you'll have to help me, Mother.

MRS. ALVING (*With a loud scream*): I!

OSVALD: Who has a better right?

MRS. ALVING: I—your mother.

OSVALD: For that very reason.

MRS. ALVING: I, who gave you life!

OSVALD: I didn't ask you for life—and what kind of a life did you give me! I don't want it—take it back again!

MRS. ALVING: Help—help! (*She runs out into the hall.*)

OSVALD (*Following her*): Don't leave me! Where are you going?

MRS. ALVING (*In the hall*): I must fetch a doctor, Osvald—let me out!

OSVALD (*In the hall*): You shall not go out—and no one shall come in.

(*Sound of a key turning in the lock.*)

MRS. ALVING (*Re-entering the room*): Osvald—Osvald! My little
one!

OSVALD (*Follows her in*): Mother—if you love me—how can you
bear to see me suffer this agony of fear!

MRS. ALVING (*After a moment's silence, in a firm voice*): I give you
my word, Osvald.

OSVALD: Then, you will—?

MRS. ALVING: Yes—If it becomes necessary—but it won't become
necessary! That's impossible!

OSVALD: Let us hope so—Meanwhile we'll live together as long as
we can. Thank you, Mother (*He sits in the armchair that* MRS.
ALVING *had moved to the sofa.*)

(*Day breaks; the lamp is still burning on the table.*)

MRS. ALVING (*Approaching him cautiously*): Do you feel calmer
now?

OSVALD: Yes.

MRS. ALVING (*Bends over him*): This has all been a nightmare,
Osvald—just something you've imagined. It's been a dreadful
strain, but now you're home with me and you'll be able to get
some rest. I'll spoil you as I did when you were a tiny little
boy—you shall have everything you want. There! The attack's
over now—You see how easily it passed. It's not so serious—I
was sure it couldn't be! And it's going to be such a lovely day,
Osvald. Bright sunshine! Now you'll really be able to see your
home.
(*She goes to the table and puts out the lamp. The sun rises. The
glaciers and peaks in the background are bathed in the bright
morning light.*)

OSVALD (*Immovable in his armchair with his back to the view outside, suddenly speaks*): Mother—give me the sun.

MRS. ALVING (*By the table, looks at him in amazement*): What did
you say?

OSVALD (*Repeats in a dull toneless voice*): The sun— The sun.

MRS. ALVING (*Goes to him*): Osvald—what's the matter with you?
(OSVALD *seems to crumple up in the chair; all his muscles relax;
his face is expressionless—his eyes vacant and staring.*)

MRS. ALVING (*Trembling with terror*): What is it? (*Screams*) Osvald! What's the matter with you? (*Throws herself on her knees beside him and shakes him*) Osvald! Osvald! Look at me! Don't you know me?

OSVALD (*Tonelessly as before*): The sun— The sun.

MRS. ALVING (*Springs up in despair, tears at her hair with both hands and screams*): I can't bear it! (*Whispers, paralyzed with fear*) I can't bear it! Never! (*Suddenly*) Where did he put them? (*Passes her hand rapidly over his breast*) Here! (*Draws back a couple of steps and cries*) No; no; no!—Yes! No; no! (*She stands a few steps away from him, her hands clutching her hair, and stares at him in speechless terror.*)

OSVALD (*Immovable as before*): The sun— The sun.

CURTAIN

An Enemy
of the People

A PLAY IN FIVE ACTS

1882

CHARACTERS

DR. TOMAS STOCKMANN, *physician at the Baths*

MRS. KATRINE STOCKMANN, *his wife*

PETRA, *their daughter, a schoolteacher*

EJLIF

MORTEN } *their sons, aged thirteen and ten*

PETER STOCKMANN, *the doctor's elder brother; Mayor and Chief of Police; Chairman of the Board at the Baths*

MORTEN KIIL, *owner of a tannery; Mrs. Stockmann's foster-father*

HOVSTAD, *editor of* The People's Monitor

BILLING, *his colleague on the paper*

CAPTAIN HORSTER

ASLAKSEN, *a printer*

Citizens of various types and standing; some women and a number of schoolboys

The action takes place in a town on the South Coast of Norway.

ACT ONE

SCENE: *Evening.* DOCTOR STOCKMANN'S *living room. It is decorated and furnished simply but neatly. In the side wall right are two doors, the upstage door leading to the hall and the one downstage to the doctor's study. In the opposite wall, facing the hall door, a door leading to the other rooms of the house. Against this wall, in the center of it, stands the stove: further downstage a sofa above which hangs a mirror, and in front of it an oval table: on this table is a lighted lamp with a shade. In the back wall, an open door leads to the dining room. The table is laid for supper and a lighted lamp stands on it.*

BILLING *is seated at the supper table; he has a napkin tucked under his chin.* MRS. STOCKMANN *stands by the table and places a dish of cold roast beef before him. The other seats round the table are empty; the table is in disorder, as though a meal had recently been finished.*

MRS. STOCKMANN: I'm afraid you'll have to put up with a cold meal, Mr. Billing; you were an hour late, you know.

BILLING (*Eating*): Never mind. It's delicious—absolutely delicious.

MRS. STOCKMANN: Stockmann is very strict about having his meals on time.

BILLING: It doesn't matter a bit. In fact I think food tastes even better when one's alone and undisturbed.

MRS. STOCKMANN: Well—as long as you enjoy it—(*Turns toward the hall door, listening*) That may be Mr. Hovstad—perhaps he's come to join you.

BILLING: Very likely.

149

(THE MAYOR, PETER STOCKMANN, *enters. He wears an overcoat and the gold-braided cap of his office. He carries a cane.*)

THE MAYOR: Good evening, Sister-in-law.

MRS. STOCKMANN: Well! Good evening. (*She comes forward into the living room*) So, it's you! How nice of you to look in.

THE MAYOR: I happened to be passing by, and so— (*With a glance toward the dining room*) Oh—you have company, I see.

MRS. STOCKMANN (*Slightly embarrassed*): No, no—not really. Mr. Billing just happened to drop in. Won't you join him for a bite to eat?

THE MAYOR: No, thank you—nothing for me! I never eat hot food at night—not with my digestion.

MRS. STOCKMANN: Oh, just for once! It surely couldn't hurt you.

THE MAYOR: I'm much obliged—but, no! I stick to my tea and bread and butter; it's much better for you—and it's more economical too.

MRS. STOCKMANN (*Smiling*): I hope you don't think Tomas and I are extravagant!

THE MAYOR: I know *you're* not, my dear; far be it from me to think that of *you*. (*Points to the doctor's study*) Is he home?

MRS. STOCKMANN: No. He went for a little walk after supper—with the boys.

THE MAYOR: Is that good for one's health, I wonder? (*Listens*) Here he comes now.

MRS. STOCKMANN: No, I don't think it can be he. (*A knock at the door*) Come in! (HOVSTAD *comes in from the hall*) Oh, it's Mr. Hovstad.

HOVSTAD: You must excuse me; I was held up at the printer's. Good evening, Mr. Mayor.

THE MAYOR (*Bowing rather stiffly*): Good evening. You're here on business, I presume?

HOVSTAD: Yes, partly. It's about an article for the paper.

THE MAYOR: I thought as much. I hear my brother has become quite a prolific contributor to *The People's Monitor*.

HOVSTAD: He's kind enough to write a piece for us now and then; whenever he has anything particular on his mind.

MRS. STOCKMANN (*To* HOVSTAD): But don't you want to—? (*She points toward the dining room.*)

THE MAYOR: It's natural, I suppose, that he should want to reach the kind of people who understand his point-of-view. Not that I have any personal objection to your paper, Mr. Hovstad—you may rest assured of that.

HOVSTAD: No—of course not.

THE MAYOR: We have a fine spirit of mutual tolerance here in our town, I'm glad to say; a truly co-operative spirit; it comes, of course, from the great common interest we all share—an interest that naturally concerns all right-thinking citizens.

HOVSTAD: The Baths, of course.

THE MAYOR: Precisely. Those splendid Mineral Baths of ours! You mark my words, Mr. Hovstad; the whole life of our community will center more and more around the Baths—there can be no doubt of that!

MRS. STOCKMANN: That's just what Tomas says.

THE MAYOR: The way the town has grown in these past two years is quite extraordinary. People are prosperous; housing-developments are springing up; the value of property is soaring; there's life and activity everywhere!

HOVSTAD: And far less unemployment too.

THE MAYOR: That's true, of course; and that's a great load off the upper classes; taxes for home-relief have already been reduced—and they will be reduced still further if we have a really prosperous summer; a good rush of visitors—plenty of invalids to give the Baths a reputation—

HOVSTAD: I hear there's a good chance of that.

THE MAYOR: Every day inquiries about living quarters —apartments and so forth—keep pouring in. Things look highly promising.

HOVSTAD: Then the doctor's article will be most timely.

THE MAYOR: So he's been writing again, has he?

HOVSTAD: This is something he wrote during the winter. It's an article about the Baths—strongly recommending them, and laying particular stress on the excellence of sanitary conditions here.

But I didn't use it at the time—I held it over.

THE MAYOR: Why? Was he indiscreet, as usual?

HOVSTAD: No, nothing like that; I only thought it would be better to hold it over till the spring, when people start thinking about summer plans.

THE MAYOR: Very sensible; highly sensible, Mr. Hovstad.

MRS. STOCKMANN: Tomas never spares himself where the Baths are concerned.

THE MAYOR: As one of the staff that's no more than his duty.

HOVSTAD: And, after all, it was his idea in the first place.

THE MAYOR: His idea? Was it indeed? I know some people are of that opinion. But it seems to me I too had at least a modest share in the enterprise.

MRS. STOCKMANN: That's what Tomas always says.

HOVSTAD: Of course, Mr. Mayor, that's undeniable; you put it all on a practical basis—you made the whole thing possible; we all know that. I simply meant that the initial idea was Dr. Stockmann's.

THE MAYOR: My brother has had plenty of ideas in his time—unfortunately; but it takes a very different type of man to work them out. I should have thought the members of this household would be among the first to—

MRS. STOCKMANN: My dear Peter—

HOVSTAD: You surely don't—?

MRS. STOCKMANN: Do go in and have some supper, Mr. Hovstad; my husband is sure to be home directly.

HOVSTAD: Thank you; I think I will have just a bite. (*He goes into the dining room.*)

THE MAYOR (*Lowering his voice*): It's amazing! These people who come from peasant stock never seem to lose their want of tact.

MRS. STOCKMANN: Now, why should you be upset? You and Tomas are brothers—isn't it natural that you should share the honor?

THE MAYOR: One would think so, yes; but a share is not enough for some people, it seems.

MRS. STOCKMANN: What nonsense! You and Tomas get on so well together. (*Listening*) I think I hear him now. (*She goes and opens the hall door.*)

DR. STOCKMANN (*Is heard laughing; he shouts in a loud voice, from the hall*): Here's another visitor for you, Katrine. Isn't this splendid, eh? Hang your coat up there on the peg, Captain Horster. But, I forgot—you don't wear an overcoat, do you? What do you think of this, Katrine? I met him on the street—I had a hard time persuading him; at first he wouldn't hear of coming up! (CAPTAIN HORSTER *enters and bows to* MRS. STOCKMANN) In with you, boys! They're starving again, Katrine! Come along, Captain Horster; you must try a piece of our roast-beef— (*He forces* CAPTAIN HORSTER *into the dining room;* EJLIF *and* MORTEN *follow them.*)

MRS. STOCKMANN: But, Tomas, don't you see—!

DR. STOCKMANN (*Turns in the doorway*): Oh, it's you, Peter! (*Goes to him and holds out his hand*) Well, now this is really splendid!

THE MAYOR: I can only stay a minute—

DR. STOCKMANN: Nonsense! We'll have some hot toddy in a moment. You haven't forgotten the toddy, have you, Katrine?

MRS. STOCKMANN: Of course not! I've got the water boiling. (*She goes into the dining room.*)

THE MAYOR: Toddy, too—!

DR. STOCKMANN: Yes; let's sit down and be comfortable.

THE MAYOR: Thank you; I don't care for drinking parties.

DR. STOCKMANN: But this isn't a party!

THE MAYOR: It seems to me— (*He glances toward the dining room*) It's incredible the amount of food they can get through!

DR. STOCKMANN (*Rubs his hands*): Yes—it does one good to see young people eat! They're always hungry! That's the way it should be—they must keep up their strength. They've got things to stir up—they have to build the future!

THE MAYOR: May I ask what there is that requires "stirring up" —as you call it?

DR. STOCKMANN: You'll have to ask the young people about that—when the time comes. Of course we shan't live to see it. A couple of old fogies like you and me—

THE MAYOR: A fine way to talk, I must say!

DR. STOCKMANN: You mustn't mind my nonsense, Peter. I'm in such high spirits today. It makes me so happy to be a part of all this fertile, teeming life. What a wonderful age we live in! A whole new world is springing up around us!

THE MAYOR: Do you really think so?

DR. STOCKMANN: Of course you can't appreciate it as well as I do . You've spent your whole life surrounded by all this—you take it all for granted. But after being stuck away for years in that dreadful little hole up North—never seeing a soul—never exchanging a stimulating word with anyone—I feel as though I'd suddenly been transported into the heart of some great metropolis!

THE MAYOR: I should hardly call it a metropolis—

DR. STOCKMANN: Oh, I know it may seem small compared to lots of other places; but there's life here—there's a future—there are innumerable things to work and strive for; that's what's important, after all. (*Calls out*) Katrine! Did the postman bring anything for me?

MRS. STOCKMANN (*From the dining room*): No—he didn't come today.

DR. STOCKMANN: And to be getting a good salary, Peter! That's something you appreciate when you've lived on starvation-wages as long as we have—

THE MAYOR: Oh, come now—

DR. STOCKMANN: Things were often very hard for us up there, let me tell you; but now we can live like princes! Today, for instance, we had roast beef for dinner; and then we had it for supper too. Don't you want to taste it? At least let me show it to you—do come and see it!

THE MAYOR: Certainly not!

DR. STOCKMANN: Well—come over here then. Look! Isn't our new table-cover handsome?

THE MAYOR: Yes—I noticed it.

DR. STOCKMANN: And we have a lamp-shade too; Katrine has been saving up for them. It makes the room look much more cozy. Don't you think so? Stand over here—no, no; not over there—here! That's right! You see how it concentrates the light? I think it's quite magnificent! What do you think?

THE MAYOR: Of course, if one can afford such luxuries—

DR. STOCKMANN: Oh, we can afford them now. Katrine says I earn almost as much as we spend.

THE MAYOR: Almost—!

DR. STOCKMANN: Besides, a man of science should live in a certain amount of style. I'll bet you a mere county commissioner spends more money a year than I do.

THE MAYOR: Well—I should hope so! A high-ranking government official—!

DR. STOCKMANN: Take an ordinary business man, then. I'll bet you a man like that spends ever so much more—

THE MAYOR: Such things are purely relative—

DR. STOCKMANN: As a matter of fact I don't squander money, Peter. But I do so enjoy inviting people to my home—I can't resist it; I was an exile for so long, you see. I feel the need of company—buoyant, active people—liberal-minded people—like those young fellows enjoying their food in there. To me, that makes life worth while. I wish you'd make a point of getting to know Hovstad—

THE MAYOR: That reminds me—Hovstad was telling me just now he plans to publish another article of yours.

DR. STOCKMANN: Of mine?

THE MAYOR: Yes—about the Baths. An article you wrote last winter.

DR. STOCKMANN: Oh, that one! I'd rather that didn't appear just now.

THE MAYOR: Why not? This seems to me to be the ideal time for it.

DR. STOCKMANN: Yes—under ordinary circumstances— (*Paces across the room.*)

THE MAYOR (*Follows him with his eyes*): What is there so unusual about circumstances now?

DR. STOCKMANN (*Stands still*): I'm afraid I can't tell you about it just now, Peter—not this evening, at any rate. The circumstances may turn out to be in the highest degree unusual, you see. On the other hand it may all amount to nothing—just an illusion on my part.

THE MAYOR: You sound very mysterious. Are you keeping somehing from me? Is anything the matter? As chairman of the Bath Committee I demand the right to—!

DR. STOCKMANN: And I demand the right to—! Oh, don't let's fly off the handle, Peter.

THE MAYOR: I am not in the habit of "flying off the handle," as you express it. But I must emphatically insist that all matters concerning the Baths be handled in a business-like manner, and through the proper channels. I shall not tolerate devious or underhanded methods.

DR. STOCKMANN: When have I ever used devious or underhanded methods?

THE MAYOR: You have an incorrigible tendency to take things into your own hands; in a well-ordered community that is equally reprehensible. The individual must subordinate himself to Society as a whole; or, more precisely, to those authorities responsible for the well-being of that Society.

DR. STOCKMANN: That may be so; but I can't see how the devil it concerns me!

THE MAYOR: That is where you are wrong, my dear Tomas; I can't seem to get that into your head! But be careful; sooner or later you'll have to pay for it. Now I've warned you. Goodbye.

DR. STOCKMANN: You're out of your mind, I tell you! You're on the wrong track entirely—!

THE MAYOR: I am seldom on the wrong track. Moreover—I take strong exception to—! (*Bows in the direction of the dining room*) Goodbye, Katrine. Good-day, Gentlemen. (*He goes.*)

MRS. STOCKMANN (*Coming into the sitting room*): Has he gone?

DR. STOCKMANN: Yes—and in a towering rage too!

MRS. STOCKMANN: Tomas, dear! What did you do to him this time?

DR. STOCKMANN: Nothing at all! He can't very well expect me to give him an account of things—before they happen.

MRS. STOCKMANN: An account of what things?

DR. STOCKMANN: Never mind about that now, Katrine— It's very odd that the postman didn't come.

(HOVSTAD, BILLING and HORSTER *have risen from table and come into the sitting room;* EJLIF *and* MORTEN *follow presently.*)

BILLING (*Stretching himself*): What a meal! Strike me dead if I don't feel like a new man!

HOVSTAD: His Honor didn't seem in a very sunny mood this evening.

DR. STOCKMANN: It's his stomach; his digestion's bad, you know.

HOVSTAD: I think he found it hard to digest us! He has no great love for *The People's Monitor*, I gather.

MRS. STOCKMANN: I thought you seemed to get on very well.

HOVSTAD: Only a temporary truce, I fear me!

BILLING: A truce, yes. That's the word for it.

DR. STOCKMANN: We mustn't forget poor Peter is a lonely bachelor. He has no home to be happy in. Business—nothing but business! And then that damned tea he's always filling himself up with. Now then, boys! Draw your chairs up to the table! Katrine—what about that toddy!

MRS. STOCKMANN (*Going towards the dining room*): I'm just getting it.

DR. STOCKMANN: You sit here on the sofa with me, Captain Horster. We don't often have the chance of seeing you!— Go on, boys! Sit down!
(*They sit down at the table.* MRS. STOCKMANN *brings in a tray with kettle, glasses, decanters, etc.*)

MRS. STOCKMANN: There you are! Now help yourselves. There's Arrak, rum, and this is cognac.

DR. STOCKMANN (*Taking a glass*): We're ready for it! (*While the toddy is being mixed*) Now—the cigars. Ejlif, you know where the box is. And Morten can get my pipe. (*The boys go into the room right*) I have a suspicion Ejlif sneaks a cigar now and then—but I pretend not to notice. (*Calls*) And my smoking-cap, Morten! Do you know where I left it, Katrine? Oh, he's found it. (*The boys bring in the various things*) Now, my friends, help yourselves! I stick to my pipe, you know; many's the long cold trip, up there in the North, that *this* has kept me company. (*They clink glasses*) Your health! It's a damn sight pleasanter to be sitting here in this warm comfortable room!

MRS. STOCKMANN (*Sits and starts to knit*): Are you sailing soon, Captain Horster?

HORSTER: I hope to be ready next week.

MRS. STOCKMANN: And you're going to America?

HORSTER: That's the intention.

BILLING: Then you won't be able to vote in the town election.

HORSTER: Oh, there's to be an election, is there?

BILLING: Didn't you know?

HORSTER: No—I don't bother about such things.

BILLING: You mean you have no interest in public affairs?

HORSTER: I don't know anything about them.

BILLING: Still—one ought at least to vote.

HORSTER: Even if you understand nothing about it?

BILLING: Not understand? How do you mean? Society is like a ship; it's up to every man to put his hand to the helm.

HORSTER: That may be all right on shore; but it would never do at sea.

HOVSTAD: Sailors rarely take an interest in public matters.

BILLING: Yes—it's amazing!

DR. STOCKMANN: Sailors are like birds of passage; North or South—every place is home to them! All the more reason for us to redouble our activities. Will there be anything of public interest in tomorrow's paper, Mr. Hovstad?

HOVSTAD: Nothing of local interest—no. But the day after tomorrow I thought I'd use your article.

DR. STOCKMANN: Oh, blast it, the article—of course! I'm afraid you'll have to hold it for a while.

HOVSTAD: Really? But we happen to have lots of space—and it seemed to me so timely.

DR. STOCKMANN: I dare say you're right—but you'll have to hold it all the same. I'll explain about it later—

(PETRA, *wearing a hat and cloak, enters from the hall; she carries a number of exercise books under her arm.*)

PETRA: Good evening.

DR. STOCKMANN: Oh, it's you, Petra. Good evening.

(*General greetings.* PETRA *takes off her hat and cloak and puts them, with the exercise books, on a chair by the door.*)

PETRA: So while I slave away at school—you sit here enjoying yourselves!

DR. STOCKMANN: Now you must come and enjoy yourself too.

BILLING: May I mix you a little drink?

PETRA (*Goes to the table*): Thanks, I'll do it myself; you always make it too strong. Oh—by the way, Father, I have a letter for you. (*Goes to the chair where she left her things.*)

DR. STOCKMANN: A letter! From whom?

PETRA (*Looking in the pocket of her cloak*): I met the postman on my way out—

DR. STOCKMANN (*Rises and goes towards her*): You might have given it to me before!

PETRA: I really didn't have time to run upstairs again. Here it is.

DR. STOCKMANN (*Seizing the letter*): Let me see—let me see, child. (*He reads the address*) Yes! This is it!

MRS. STOCKMANN: Is it the one you've been expecting, Tomas?

DR. STOCKMANN: Yes. I must go in and read it at once. What about a light, Katrine? I suppose there's no lamp in my study again!

MRS. STOCKMANN: Oh, yes there is! It's already lighted on the desk.

DR. STOCKMANN: Good. Excuse me a moment— (*He goes into his study, right.*)

PETRA: What's all that about, Mother?

MRS. STOCKMANN: I don't know; these last few days he's done nothing but ask for the postman.

BILLING: Perhaps it's from one of his patients out of town—

PETRA: Poor father! He's getting to be frightfully busy. (*Mixes her toddy*) Ah! This will be most welcome!

HOVSTAD: Have you been teaching at night school again this evening?

PETRA (*Sipping her drink*): Two hours, yes.

BILLING: And four hours this morning at the girls' school—?

PETRA (*Sitting down at the table*): Five.

MRS. STOCKMANN: And you have some exercises to correct this evening as well, I see.

PETRA: Quite a lot.

HORSTER: You seem to keep busy too!

PETRA: Yes—but I like it. It's good to feel thoroughly exhausted!

BILLING: Do you enjoy that?

PETRA: It makes one sleep so well.

MORTEN: You must be a great sinner, Petra.

PETRA: A sinner?

MORTEN: Yes—or you wouldn't have to work so hard. Work is a punishment for our sins—that's what Mr. Rörlund always says

EJLIF: How can you be such a fool! Believing all that nonsense!

MRS. STOCKMANN: Now, now—Ejlif!

BILLING (*Laughing*): That's a good one!

HOVSTAD: Shouldn't you like to work hard, Morten?

MORTEN: No, I shouldn't.

HOVSTAD: What do you want to do when you grow up?

MORTEN: I want to be a Viking.

EJLIF: You'd have to be a heathen, then.

MORTEN: Well—so I'd *be* a heathen!

BILLING: Good for you, Morten! That's the spirit!

MRS. STOCKMANN (*Makes a sign to him*): I'm sure you don't really mean that, Mr. Billing!

BILLING: Strike me dead if I don't! I'm a heathen and I'm proud of it. You'll see—we'll all be heathens before long.

MORTEN: Then we could do anything we liked, couldn't we?

BILLING: Well—I don't know about that, Morten—

MRS. STOCKMANN: You'd better run along, boys; you must have home-work to do.

EJLIF: Couldn't I stay a little bit longer—?

MRS. STOCKMANN: No—you couldn't. Now, run along—both of you.

(*The boys say goodnight and go into the room, left.*)

HOVSTAD: Do you think it's bad for them to hear that sort of talk?

MRS. STOCKMANN: I don't know; but I know I don't like it.

PETRA: Don't be so stuffy, Mother!

MRS. STOCKMANN: That's all very well—but I don't. Not in one's own home at any rate.

PETRA: All this hypocrisy! At home we're taught to hold our tongues; and at school we have to teach the children lies!

HORSTER: Teach them lies?

PETRA: Yes, of course—We have to teach all kinds of things we don't believe a word of!

BILLING: That's true enough.

PETRA: If I had enough money, I'd start a school myself—then I'd run things quite differently.

BILLING: Well—as far as the money goes—

HORSTER: If you're really serious about that, Miss Stockmann, I'd be glad to provide the necessary space; my father's old house is practically empty, and there's a huge dining-room on the ground floor that would—

PETRA: Oh, I don't suppose anything will come of it—but, thanks, all the same!

HOVSTAD: I've a feeling Miss Petra is more likely to take up journalism. And, that reminds me—have you had a chance to read that English story you promised to translate for us?

PETRA: No, not yet. But I'll get it done for you in time—don't worry.

(DR. STOCKMANN *comes in from his study with the letter open in his hand.*)

DR. STOCKMANN (*Flourishing the letter*): Well! Here's some news that will make the town sit up and take notice!

BILLING: News?

MRS. STOCKMANN: What sort of news, Tomas?

DR. STOCKMANN: A great discovery, Katrine!

HOVSTAD: Really?

MRS. STOCKMANN: A discovery of yours, you mean?

DR. STOCKMANN: Of mine—yes! (*Paces up and down*) And I defy them this time to call me a crack-pot, and laugh it off as nonsense. They won't dare! They simply won't dare!

PETRA: What is it, Father? Tell us!

DR. STOCKMANN: Just give me time, and I'll tell you all about it. I do wish Peter were here! It only goes to show how blind we are—just like a lot of moles!

HOVSTAD: What do you mean Doctor?

DR. STOCKMANN: It's the general opinion that this town of ours is an exceedingly healthy place—isn't that true?

HOVSTAD: Of course.

DR. STOCKMANN: A quite exceptionally healthy place, as a matter of fact; a place to be highly recommended, not only to ordinary inhabitants, but to invalids as well—

MRS. STOCKMANN: My dear Tomas—

DR. STOCKMANN: And, as such, we have duly praised and recommended it; I myself have sung its praises innumerable times—not only in *The People's Monitor*, but in many pamphlets too—

HOVSTAD: Well—what then?

DR. STOCKMANN: And these Mineral Baths that have been called "the pulse of the town"—its "nerve center"—and the devil only knows what else besides—

BILLING: "The throbbing heart of our city" I remember I once called them—in a somewhat convivial mood—

DR. STOCKMANN: Yes—that too. Well—do you know what these Baths are? These precious, magnificent Baths that have been established at such great expense—can you guess what they really are?

HOVSTAD: No—what?

MRS. STOCKMANN: Tell us, Tomas!

DR. STOCKMANN: They're nothing but a pest hole!

PETRA: The Baths, Father?

MRS. STOCKMANN (*At the same time*): Our Baths!

HOVSTAD (*Simultaneously*): But, Doctor—!

BILLING: This is incredible!

DR. STOCKMANN: I tell you the whole institution is a whited-sepulcher, spreading poison; it's a menace to the Public Health! All that filth from the tanneries up at Milldale—and you know what a stench there is around there!—seeps into the feed-pipes of the pump-room; and, not only that, but this same poisonous offal seeps out into the beach as well.

HOVSTAD: In the salt-water baths, you mean?

DR. STOCKMANN: Precisely.

HOVSTAD: How can you be sure of all this, Doctor?

DR. STOCKMANN: I've made the most painstaking investigations. I'd suspected something of the sort for quite some time, you see. I was struck by the curious amount of illness among the visitors at the Baths last year—there were several cases of typhoid and gastric fever—

MRS. STOCKMANN: Yes, I remember.

DR. STOCKMANN: At first we took it for granted that the visitors brought the infection with them; but later—this past winter—I began to think differently. I set to work to analyze the water, as best I could—

MRS. STOCKMANN: So that's what you've been working at!

DR. STOCKMANN: Yes—I've worked very hard at it, Katrine, but I didn't have the necessary equipment here; so I finally sent samples of the drinking-water and the sea-water by the beach to the laboratories at the university, and asked them to give me a full analysis.

HOVSTAD: And is that what you just received?

DR. STOCKMANN (*Showing the letter*): Yes—here it is! It proves beyond the shadow of a doubt the presence of decayed animal-matter in the water—millions of infusoria. The use of this water, both internally and externally, is in the highest degree danger-ous to health.

MRS. STOCKMANN: What a blessing you found it out in time!

DR. STOCKMANN: It is indeed, Katrine!

HOVSTAD: What do you propose to do about it, Doctor?

DR. STOCKMANN: Set things straight, of course.

HOVSTAD: You think that can be done?

DR. STOCKMANN: It *must* be done. Otherwise the Baths are en-tirely useless—ruined! But there's no need for that to happen; I'm quite clear as to how we should proceed.

MRS. STOCKMANN: To think of your keeping all this secret, Tomas, dear!

DR. STOCKMANN: You wouldn't have had me rushing all over town gabbing about it before I was absolutely certain, would you? I'm not as mad as all that, you know!

PETRA: But, surely, to us—

DR. STOCKMANN: I couldn't say a word to a living soul! But tomor-row you can run and tell that badger of yours all about it—

MRS. STOCKMANN: Oh, Tomas!

DR. STOCKMANN: Well—your grandfather, then. That'll give the old man something to gape at! He thinks I'm cracked in the head—and a lot of other people think so too, I've noticed. But I'll show them! Yes—this time I'll show them! (*Walks up and down rubbing his hands*) What a commotion there'll be in the town, Katrine! Think of it; they'll have to re-lay all the waterpipes.

HOVSTAD (*Rising*): All the waterpipes—?

DR. STOCKMANN: Well—naturally. The intake must be moved
much higher up; I always said it was down too low.

PETRA: You were right after all, Father.

DR. STOCKMANN: Yes—you remember, Petra? I sent in a protest
before they even started on the work; but, of course, at that
time, no one listened to me. Well—I'll let them have it now! I've
prepared a report for the Board of Directors; it's been ready for a
week—I was only waiting for this. (*Points to the letter*) I'll send it
off at once. (*Goes into his study and returns with a manuscript*)
Look! Four closely written pages! And I'll enclose this letter too.
A paper, Katrine! Something to wrap this up in. Good. And now
give this to—to—what the devil is that girl's name! To the
maid—*you* know! Tell her to deliver it to the Mayor immediately!

(MRS. STOCKMANN *takes the package and goes out through the
dining room.*)

PETRA: What do you think Uncle Peter will say, Father?

DR. STOCKMANN: What *can* he say? He can't fail to be pleased
that such an important fact has come to light.

HOVSTAD: May we announce this in *The People's Monitor*?

DR. STOCKMANN: I'd be most grateful if you would.

HOVSTAD: It's important that the public should know of this without delay.

DR. STOCKMANN: It is indeed!

MRS. STOCKMANN (*Returning*): She's gone with it.

BILLING: Strike me dead if you're not hailed as the leading citizen
of our community, Dr. Stockmann!

DR. STOCKMANN (*Walks up and down in high glee*): Oh, nonsense! I only did my duty. I simply was lucky enough to spot
it—that's all. But still—

BILLING: Hovstad, don't you think the town should get up some
sort of a demonstration in Dr. Stockmann's honor?

HOVSTAD: I shall certainly propose it.

BILLING: I'll talk it over with Aslaksen.

DR. STOCKMANN: No, no—my dear friends! You mustn't bother
with such nonsense; I won't hear of it! And, I warn you,

Katrine—if the Board of Directors should think of offering me a raise in salary—I shall refuse it. I simply won't accept!

MRS. STOCKMANN: You're quite right, Tomas, dear.

PETRA (*Raising her glass*): Your health, Father!

HOVSTAD *and* BILLING: Your good health, Doctor!

HORSTER (*Clinks glasses with him*): I hope this brings you joy.

DR. STOCKMANN: Thank you, thank you—my dear, dear friends! I can't tell you how happy I am—! It's a wonderful thing to feel you've deserved well of your own hometown, and of your fellow-citizens. Hurrah, Katrine!

(*He puts his arms round her and whirls her round the room. MRS. STOCKMANN screams and struggles to free herself. Laughter, applause and cheers for the doctor. The two boys poke their heads in the door to see what is going on.*)

CURTAIN

ACT
TWO

SCENE: *The doctor's living room. The door to the dining room is closed. Morning.* MRS. STOCKMANN, *carrying a sealed letter in her hand, comes in from the dining room, goes to the door of the doctor's study and peeps in.*

MRS. STOCKMANN: Are you in there, Tomas?

DR. STOCKMANN (*From the study*): Yes, I just got back. (*Enters*) Do you want me?

MRS. STOCKMANN: Here's a letter from your brother. (*Hands it to him.*)

DR. STOCKMANN: Now—let's see. (*Opens the envelope and reads*) "The manuscript forwarded to me is returned herewith—" (*He reads on, mumbling to himself*) Hm.

MRS. STOCKMANN: Well? What does he say?

DR. STOCKMANN: Just that he'll be up to see me around noon.

MRS. STOCKMANN: You must be sure and be home, then.

DR. STOCKMANN: I can easily manage that; I've made all my morning calls.

MRS. STOCKMANN: I can't help wondering how he'll take it.

DR. STOCKMANN: He's sure to be annoyed that it was I, and not he, who discovered the whole business.

MRS. STOCKMANN: That's what I'm afraid of.

DR. STOCKMANN: He'll be glad at heart, of course. But still—; Peter's always so damnably resentful when anyone else does anything for the good of the town.

MRS. STOCKMANN: I know. I think it would be nice if you made a point of letting him share the honor; you might even imply that it was he who put you on the track—

DR. STOCKMANN: That's all right as far as I'm concerned. All I care about is getting the thing cleared up.

(*Old* MORTEN KIIL *sticks his head in at the hall door.*)

MORTEN KIIL (*Slyly*): Is—is all this true?

MRS. STOCKMANN (*Goes toward him*): Well! Here's Father.

DR. STOCKMANN: So it is! Good morning, Father-in-law!

MRS. STOCKMANN: Do come in.

MORTEN KIIL: If it's true, I will; otherwise I'll be off again.

DR. STOCKMANN: If what's true?

MORTEN KIIL: All this nonsense about the water-works. Well? Is it?

DR. STOCKMANN: Of course it's true. But how did *you* find out about it?

MORTEN KIIL: From Petra. She ran in to see me on her way to school—

DR. STOCKMANN: Oh, did she?

MORTEN KIIL: Yes, indeed; and she told me—at first I thought she must be joking! But that's not like Petra, come to think of it.

DR. STOCKMANN: Of course not! She'd never joke about a thing like that.

MORTEN KIIL: You never know; and I don't like to be made a fool of. So it really is true, is it?

DR. STOCKMANN: Unquestionably. Do sit down, Father. (*Forces him down on the sofa*) Well—what do you think? It's a lucky thing for the town, isn't it?

MORTEN KIIL (*With suppressed laughter*): A lucky thing for the town?

DR. STOCKMANN: Yes, that I made this discovery in time—

MORTEN KIIL (*As before*): Oh, of course! Of course!—I must say I never thought you'd try your monkey-tricks on your own brother!

DR. STOCKMANN: Monkey-tricks—!

MRS. STOCKMANN: Father, dear—!

MORTEN KIIL (*Rests his hands and chin on the top of his cane and blinks slyly at the doctor*): Let me see—what was it now? Oh! yes—the waterpipes are full of little animals—isn't that it?

DR. STOCKMANN: Infusoria, yes.

MORTEN KIIL: And Petra said there were a lot of them—whole swarms of them.

DR. STOCKMANN: Certainly; hundreds of thousands of them.

MORTEN KIIL: And yet no one can see them—isn't that the story?

DR. STOCKMANN: Of course no one can see them.

MORTEN KIIL (*With quiet chuckling laughter*): I'll be damned if this isn't the best thing you've hit on yet!

DR. STOCKMANN: What do you mean?

MORTEN KIIL: You'll never get the Mayor to believe this nonsense!

DR. STOCKMANN: We shall see.

MORTEN KIIL: You think he's as crazy as all that?

DR. STOCKMANN: I'm confident that the whole town will be as crazy as all that.

MORTEN KIIL: The whole town! Yes—I wouldn't put it past them. And it'll serve them right, too—teach them a lesson. We old-timers aren't good enough for them—oh, no! They think them-

selves so clever! They hounded me out of the Town
Council—hounded me out like a dog, that's what they did! But
they'll get paid back now! Just you go on playing your monkey-
tricks with them, Stockmann—

DR. STOCKMANN: But, Father—listen—!

MORTEN KIIL (*Rising*): Give 'em all the monkey-tricks you can
think of, say I! If you can put this over on the Mayor and his
cronies—so help me, I'll give a hundred crowns to charity!

DR. STOCKMANN: Very handsome of you.

MORTEN KIIL: Mind you, I've little enough to spare! But just you
put this over, and next Christmas I'll give fifty crowns to charity!
(HOVSTAD *enters from the hall*.)

HOVSTAD: Good morning! (*Pausing*) Oh, excuse me—

DR. STOCKMANN: No—come in; come in.

MORTEN KIIL (*Chuckling again*): Is *he* in on this?

HOVSTAD: What do you mean?

DR. STOCKMANN: Yes, of course he is.

MORTEN KIIL: I might have known it! He's to put it in his paper.
Ah! You're a good one, Stockmann! Well—I'm off. I'll leave you
two together.

DR. STOCKMANN: No, Father; don't go yet.

MORTEN KIIL: Yes—I'll be off. Just you think up all the monkey-
tricks you can. You can be damn sure you won't lose by it!
(*He goes;* MRS. STOCKMAN *goes with him*.)

DR. STOCKMANN (*Laughing*): What do you think—? The old man
doesn't believe a word about the water-works!

HOVSTAD: Oh, was that what you were talking about?

DR. STOCKMANN: Yes. I suppose you've come about that, too?

HOVSTAD: Yes, I have. Have you a few moments, Doctor?

DR. STOCKMANN: As many as you like.

HOVSTAD: Have you heard anything from the Mayor yet?

DR. STOCKMANN: No, not yet. But he's to be here presently.

HOVSTAD: Since I left here last night I've thought a great deal
about this matter.

DR. STOCKMANN: You have?

HOVSTAD: Yes. As a doctor and a man of science you naturally
think of this business of the water-works as a thing apart. I mean

by that—you probably haven't stopped to realize how many other things it may involve.

DR. STOCKMANN: In what way—? Let's sit down, my dear fellow. No—here on the sofa. (HOVSTAD *sits down on the sofa and* STOCKMANN *in an armchair on the other side of the table*) So—you think—?

HOVSTAD: You said last night that the water was polluted by decayed matter in the soil.

DR. STOCKMANN: The trouble comes from that poisonous swamp by the tanneries at Milldale. I'm convinced of that.

HOVSTAD: Forgive me, Doctor—but I think the trouble comes from poison of quite another sort.

DR. STOCKMANN: What poison do you mean?

HOVSTAD: I mean the poison that is polluting and contaminating our whole community.

DR. STOCKMANN: What the devil do you mean by that?

HOVSTAD: Little by little the whole town has come under the control of a pack of bureaucrats.

DR. STOCKMANN: Oh, come now—they're not all bureaucrats.

HOVSTAD: Perhaps not—but those of them who are not bureaucrats are the friends and hangers-on of those who are. We are under the thumb of a small clique of powerful men; it's the old established families, the men of wealth and position, who rule the town.

DR. STOCKMANN: But, remember—they are also men of ability and insight.

HOVSTAD: I suppose it was their ability and insight that controlled the installation of the water-system?

DR. STOCKMANN: That was a colossal piece of stupidity, I grant you. But it will be corrected now.

HOVSTAD: Do you think that will be such a simple matter?

DR. STOCKMANN: Simple or not, it must be done.

HOVSTAD: Yes; especially if the press exerts its influence.

DR. STOCKMAN: That won't be necessary, I assure you; I'm certain that my brother—

HOVSTAD: Excuse me, Doctor, but I want you to know that I intend to publicize the matter.

DR. STOCKMANN: In the newspaper?

HOVSTAD: Yes. When I took over *The People's Monitor*, it was with the thought of breaking up this ring of obstinate old reactionaries who now have full control.

DR. STOCKMANN: With the result that you nearly wrecked the paper—you told me that yourself.

HOVSTAD: We were obliged to draw in our horns for a while—that's true enough; if these particular men had been put out of office at that time, the Bath scheme might have fallen through entirely. But now that danger's over; the Baths are an accomplished fact—and we can afford to do without these high and mighty gentlemen.

DR. STOCKMANN: Do without them, yes; but still, we have a lot to thank them for.

HOVSTAD: Oh, we shall make a point of acknowledging the debt! But a journalist of my liberal turn of mind cannot be expected to let an opportunity like this go by. This myth of official infallibility must be exploded. That kind of superstition must be rooted out.

DR. STOCKMANN: There I agree with you entirely, Mr. Hovstad; if it's a superstition, we must get rid of it!

HOVSTAD: I hesitate to attack the Mayor—since he's your brother; on the other hand, I'm sure you feel as I do, that truth comes first.

DR. STOCKMANN: Undoubtedly—of course. (*Vehemently*) But, all the same!

HOVSTAD: I don't want you to think ill of me. I'm no more egotistical—no more ambitious—than the majority of men.

DR. STOCKMANN: My dear fellow—! No one says you are.

HOVSTAD: I come of a very humble family, Dr. Stockmann; and my knowledge of the common people has been gained through personal experience. I know their needs—I understand their aims. It's because they wish to develop their own ability, knowledge and self-respect, that they claim the right to share in the responsibilities of government—

DR. STOCKMANN: That's very understandable—

HOVSTAD: Yes. And it seems to me a journalist would incur a heavy responsibility by failing to seize the slightest chance of furthering the emancipation of the down-trodden masses. Oh! I know the powers-that-be will call this anarchy. But, let them! I shall at least have done my duty.

DR. STOCKMANN: Quite so—quite so, dear Mr. Hovstad. Still —damn it all—you must remember—! (*A knock at the door*) Come in!

(ASLAKSEN, *the printer, appears at the hall door. He is shabbily but respectably dressed in a black suit with a slightly crumpled white necktie. He carries a silk hat and gloves.*)

ASLAKSEN (*Bowing*): Excuse me, Doctor, if I intrude—

DR. STOCKMANN (*Rising*): Well—well! It's Mr. Aslaksen!

ASLAKSEN: Yes, it's me, Doctor—

HOVSTAD (*Gets up*): Do you want me, Aslaksen?

ASLAKSEN: No; I didn't even know you were here. It's the doctor I—

DR. STOCKMANN: What can I do for you?

ASLAKSEN: Is it true, what Mr. Billing tells me, that you're planning to improve our water-system?

DR. STOCKMANN: For the Baths, yes.

ASLAKSEN: Just as I thought; then I'd like you to know, Doctor, that I shall support this plan with all my might.

HOVSTAD (*To the doctor*): You see!

DR. STOCKMANN: I'm most grateful to you, I'm sure; but—

ASLAKSEN: You never know—we small middle-class men might be very useful to you. We form what you might call a solid majority in the town; if we really make up our minds to it, that is. And it's always a good thing to have the support of the majority, Dr. Stockmann.

DR. STOCKMANN: That's unquestionably true; but I can't conceive that any special measures will be necessary in this case. The matter is so simple—so straightforward—

ASLAKSEN: It might be helpful all the same. I know the local authorities very well. Suggestions from people outside their immediate circle are not looked upon too favorably by the powers-that-be. So I thought it might be a good idea if we arranged a demonstration of some sort.

HOVSTAD: I quite agree.

DR. STOCKMANN: A demonstration? But what form would this demonstration take?

ASLAKSEN: Oh, it would be conducted with the utmost moderation, Doctor; I strive for moderation in all things; moderation is a citizen's prime virtue—at least in my opinion.

DR. STOCKMANN: Your moderation is well-known, dear Mr Aslaksen.

ASLAKSEN: I think I may safely say it is. And to us small middle-class men, this business of the water-works is of very great importance. Our Baths bid fair to become a small gold mine, as it were. Many of us count on them to provide us with a means of livelihood—the home-owners especially; so we naturally wish to support the Baths in every possible way. Now, since I happen to be chairman of the Home-owners Association—

DR. STOCKMANN: Yes—?

ASLAKSEN: —and also an active worker in the Temperance Society—you know of course, Doctor, that I'm a temperance man—?

DR. STOCKMANN: That goes without saying—

ASLAKSEN: Then I need hardly tell you that I am in constant touch with a great number of my fellow-citizens. And since my reputation is that of a prudent, law-abiding man—as you yourself remarked—I have a certain influence in the town; a kind of modest authority—though I do say so myself.

DR. STOCKMANN: I'm well aware of that.

ASLAKSEN: So—should it be advisable—it would be a comparatively simple matter for me to get up some sort of a petition.

DR. STOCKMANN: A petition?

ASLAKSEN: Yes—a petition of thanks; of thanks to you, on behalf of the townspeople, for having taken up this all-important matter. It goes without saying that it must be worded with suitable moderation; it would never do to offend the authorities, or any of the men in power. But, if we keep this in mind, I see no reason for any possible objection.

HOVSTAD: Well—even if they did object—!

ASLAKSEN: No, no! There must be nothing in it to offend the powers-that-be, Mr. Hovstad. We can't afford to antagonize the

men who control our destinies. I've seen plenty of that in my
time—no good ever comes of it. But no one could object to a citizen expressing his opinion freely—provided it is couched in
temperate terms.

DR. STOCKMANN: I am delighted, my dear Mr. Aslaksen, to know
I can count on the support of my fellow-townsmen; I can't tell
you how happy this makes me! And now—how about a glass of
sherry?

ASLAKSEN: No—many thanks; I never indulge in spirits.

DR. STOCKMANN: Well—you surely won't refuse a glass of beer?

ASLAKSEN: Thank you—but I never touch anything so early in the
day. Now I'll be on my way; I must talk to some of the home-
owners, and set about preparing public opinion.

DR. STOCKMANN: It's extremely kind of you, Mr. Aslaksen; but I
can't conceive that all this preparation should be necessary. The
issue is clear—I can't see any room for disagreement.

ASLAKSEN: The authorities have a way of functioning very slowly,
Dr. Stockmann. Oh, far be it from me to blame them—!

HOVSTAD: We'll give them a good stirring up in the paper tomorrow—

ASLAKSEN: But I beg you, Mr. Hovstad—no violence! If you wish
to get results, you must use moderation. Take my advice; I speak
from experience. Well—now I'll say goodbye. Remember, Doctor, we—of the middle-class—stand behind you to a man. The
solid majority is on your side.

DR. STOCKMANN: I'm most grateful to you, Mr. Aslaksen. (*Holds
out his hand*) Goodbye, goodbye!

ASLAKSEN: Are you coming to the office, Mr. Hovstad?

HOVSTAD: I'll be there presently. There are still a couple of things
I'd like to discuss.

ASLAKSEN: Very well. (*He bows and goes out;* DR. STOCKMANN
shows him into the hall.)

HOVSTAD (*As the doctor re-enters*): Well—now what do you say,
Doctor? Don't you agree it's high time we put a stop to all this
half-hearted, cowardly, shilly-shallying?

DR. STOCKMANN: Are you referring to Aslaksen?

HOVSTAD: Yes, I am. He's been infected by the poison too, you

see—though he's not a bad sort, in his way. He's typical of most
people around here; always wavering, always on the fence. They
never dare take a definite stand—they're too full of doubts, and
scruples, and caution.

DR. STOCKMANN: He seems like a thoroughly well-intentioned
man.

HOVSTAD: Intentions may be all very well—but give me a man
with some self-confidence, some self-assurance.

DR. STOCKMANN: Yes—I agree with you there.

HOVSTAD: I'm going to use this opportunity to inject a little back-
bone into their good intentions. This servile worship of the
"Powers-that-be" must be wiped out. The inexcusable bungling
about the water-works must be fully exposed. Every single voter
must be made aware of it.

DR. STOCKMANN: Very well; as long as you think it's for the good
of the Community. But I must speak to my brother first.

HOVSTAD: Meanwhile—I'll be writing my editorial. And if the
Mayor refuses to take action—

DR. STOCKMANN: That's inconceivable.

HOVSTAD: Perhaps not so inconceivable as you might think. But
suppose he does—

DR. STOCKMANN: Then, my dear Mr. Hovstad—if that should
happen—you may print my full report, word for word—just as it
is.

HOVSTAD: Is that a promise?

DR. STOCKMANN (*Hands him the manuscript*): Look—here it is;
take it with you. There's no harm in your reading it; you can return it to me later on.

HOVSTAD: Very good; I shall do so. Goodbye for now, dear Doctor.

DR. STOCKMANN: Goodbye. But, you'll see, this whole thing will
be cleared up quite simply, Mr. Hovstad; I'm confident of that.

HOVSTAD: Well—we shall see. (*He bows and goes out through the
hall.*)

DR. STOCKMANN (*Goes to the dining room and looks in*):
Katrine—! Oh! Are you back, Petra?

PETRA (*Enters the sitting room*): Yes; I just got back from school.

MRS. STOCKMANN (*Enters*): Hasn't he been here yet?

DR. STOCKMANN: Peter? No. But I had a long talk with Hovstad. He's quite excited about my discovery. He feels its implications are even more important than I thought. He's placed his newspaper at my disposal—in case I should require it.

MRS. STOCKMANN: But do you think you will?

DR. STOCKMANN: No! I'm sure I shan't. Still—it's very flattering to have the support of an enlightened, independent paper, such as his. I had a visit from the chairman of the Home-owners Association, too.

MRS. STOCKMANN: Really? What did he want?

DR. STOCKMANN: He, too, wanted to assure me of his support. They're all ready to stand by me, in case of need. Do you know what I have on my side, Katrine?

MRS. STOCKMANN: On your side? No—what?

DR. STOCKMANN: The solid majority.

MRS. STOCKMANN: And is that a good thing for you, Tomas, dear?

DR. STOCKMANN: A good thing! Well—I should hope so! (*He rubs his hands and paces up and down*) What a wonderful thing it is to feel in such close harmony with one's fellowmen!

PETRA: And to know one's doing good and valuable work!

DR. STOCKMANN: Especially when it's for your own home town, Petra.

MRS. STOCKMAN: There's the bell.

DR. STOCKMANN: That must be he. (*A knock at the door*) Come in!

THE MAYOR (*Enters from the hall*): Good morning.

DR. STOCKMANN: I'm glad to see you, Peter.

MRS. STOCKMANN: Good morning, Brother-in-law. And how are you today?

THE MAYOR: Thank you—only so-so. (*To the doctor*) Last night, after office-hours, I received a long dissertation from you on the subject of the Baths.

DR. STOCKMANN: Have you read it?

THE MAYOR: Yes—I have.

DR. STOCKMANN: Well—what do you think of it?

THE MAYOR (*With a side glance*): Hm—

MRS. STOCKMANN: Come along, Petra. (*She and* PETRA *go into the room left.*)

THE MAYOR: Why did you find it necessary to carry on these investigations behind my back?

DR. STOCKMANN: As long as I wasn't absolutely sure, I—

THE MAYOR: Then you think you're absolutely sure now?

DR. STOCKMANN: Didn't my report convince you of that?

THE MAYOR: Is it your intention to submit this report to the Board of Directors as an official document?

DR. STOCKMANN: Of course. Something must be done about it; and at once.

THE MAYOR: In your customary manner, you make use of some very strong expressions. You say among other things, that what we offer our visitors is nothing short of poison.

DR. STOCKMANN: But, Peter—what else can you call it? I tell you—whether you drink it or bathe in it—the water is poison! We can't do this to poor sick people who come here in good faith expecting to be cured!

THE MAYOR: You conclude your report by stating that a sewer must be built to carry off the alleged impurities at Milldale, and that the entire water-system must be redesigned and re-installed.

DR. STOCKMANN: Can you think of any other solution?

THE MAYOR: I found a pretext for calling on the town engineer this morning, and brought the matter up—in a joking way, of course—as something we should perhaps consider some time in the future.

DR. STOCKMANN: In the future!

THE MAYOR: He laughed at the extravagance of the suggestion—I naturally let him think it was my own idea. Have you taken the trouble to find out the cost of these proposed alterations? I gathered from the engineer it would amount to several hundred thousand crowns.

DR. STOCKMANN: As much as that?

THE MAYOR: Yes. But that's not the worst of it. The work would take at least two years.

DR. STOCKMANN: Two years? Two whole years?

THE MAYOR: At least. And what's to happen to the Baths in the meantime? Are we to close them? We'd have no alternative. You don't imagine people would go on coming here if it were rumored that the waters were injurious to the health?

DR. STOCKMANN: But, Peter—that's just what they are.

THE MAYOR: And that this should happen now—just when the Baths are beginning to gain a reputation. Other towns in this vicinity might qualify equally well as health resorts. They'd bend every effort to divert this stream of visitors from us, to them; why shouldn't they? And we should be left stranded. All the money that has been invested in this costly undertaking would be wasted; most likely the whole scheme would have to be abandoned. The town would be completely ruined—thanks to you!

DR. STOCKMANN: Ruined—!

THE MAYOR: The only future the town has is through the Baths—the only future worth mentioning, that is! You know that as well as I do.

DR. STOCKMANN: Well? What do you think should be done?

THE MAYOR: I find myself unconvinced by your report. I cannot fully persuade myself that conditions are as critical as your statement represents.

DR. STOCKMANN: If anything they're worse! At least they will be, during the summer, when the hot weather sets in.

THE MAYOR: I repeat that in my opinion you greatly exaggerate the situation. I am certain that a competent physician would find adequate steps to take—would be able to counteract any harmful agents, should their presence be definitely established.

DR. STOCKMANN: I see. And then—?

THE MAYOR: The present water-system is an established fact and must, of course, be treated as such. At some future time the Directors might see their way clear—provided the cost was not too exorbitant—to inaugurate certain improvements.

DR. STOCKMANN: You don't imagine I could ever be party to such a swindle?

THE MAYOR: Swindle?

DR. STOCKMANN: Swindle, yes! It would be the worst kind of trickery—an out and out crime against Society!

THE MAYOR: I've already told you, I've not been able to persuade myself of the existence of any imminent danger.

DR. STOCKMANN: Yes, you have! You couldn't possibly have done otherwise. My report is so obviously clear and convincing. You understand the situation perfectly, Peter, but you simply refuse to face it. You were responsible for the placement of the Baths and the water-works—it was you who insisted on putting them where they are. It was a damnable mistake and now you refuse to admit it. Do you think I don't see through you?

THE MAYOR: And what if it were so? If I am concerned with protecting my reputation, it's only for the good of the town. I cannot possibly direct affairs in a manner conducive to the general welfare as I see it, unless my integrity and authority are unassailable. For this reason—among others—I consider it imperative that your report should not be brought to the notice of the Board of Directors. It must be withheld for the sake of the community. Later on I will bring the matter up for discussion and we will go to work quietly and see what can be done. Meanwhile not a word—not a breath—about this unfortunate business must be allowed to leak out.

DR. STOCKMANN: I'm afraid that can hardly be prevented, my dear Peter.

THE MAYOR: It must and shall be prevented.

DR. STOCKMANN: It's no use, I tell you; too many people know of it already.

THE MAYOR: Know of it! Who? Surely not those fellows from *The People's Monitor*—?

DR. STOCKMANN: Yes—they know about it too. The free press will certainly see to it that you're made to do your duty.

THE MAYOR: You're an incredibly rash man, Tomas. Hasn't it occurred to you that all this might have serious consequences for you?

DR. STOCKMANN: Consequences—for me?

THE MAYOR: For you—and those dear to you, yes.

DR. STOCKMANN: What the devil do you mean by that?

THE MAYOR: As your brother, I've always been ready and willing to help you—I think I may say that?

DR. STOCKMANN: You have indeed—and I thank you for it.

THE MAYOR: I don't ask for thanks. In a way I was forced into it—for my own sake. By helping you to greater financial security I had hoped to keep you in check, to some extent.

DR. STOCKMANN: Do you mean to tell me you only did it for your own sake?

THE MAYOR: In a way, I said. It's extremely awkward for an official, when his closest relative is continuously compromising himself.

DR. STOCKMANN: You think I do that, do you?

THE MAYOR: Yes, you do—unfortunately; I daresay you're not even aware of it. You have a restless, violent, rebellious nature, and you can't resist going into print indiscriminately on any and all subjects. No sooner does a thought strike you than you dash off an article to the newspaper—or you write a whole pamphlet on the subject.

DR. STOCKMANN: Surely if one has new ideas, it's one's duty to share them with the public!

THE MAYOR: Believe me, the public has no need of new ideas; it's better off without them. The best way to serve the public is to give it what it's used to.

DR. STOCKMANN: That's a very bald statement!

THE MAYOR: For once I must be frank with you. I've tried to avoid it hitherto, because I know how irritable you are; but it's time I told you the truth, Tomas. You don't realize how you antagonize people by this intolerant attitude of yours. You criticize the authorities—you even criticize the Government; you do nothing but find fault. And then you complain of being slighted—of being persecuted. With your difficult nature, what can you expect?

DR. STOCKMANN: Oh—so I'm difficult too, am I?

THE MAYOR: Yes, Tomas; you are an extremely difficult man to get along with. I speak from experience. You seem to forget that you have me to thank for your present position as medical adviser to the Baths—

DR. STOCKMANN: I was entitled to that position—it belonged to me by right! It was I who first saw the possibility of creating a

health resort here, and I was the only one at that time who believed in it. I fought for the idea single-handed for many years. I
wrote about it—publicized it—

THE MAYOR: That is undeniable. But at that time the scheme was
premature. Living as you did then, in that out-of-the-way corner
of the world, you naturally couldn't be a judge of that. But later,
when circumstances seemed more favorable, I—and the
others—took the matter in hand—

DR. STOCKMANN: Yes. And a fine mess you made of it! You took
my splendid plan and ruined it. And now the results of your cleverness and shrewdness are all too obvious.

THE MAYOR: Only one thing is obvious, in my opinion: you feel
the need to be belligerent—to strike out at your superiors; that's
an old habit of yours. You refuse to submit to the slightest authority; you regard anyone above you as a personal enemy, and
are prepared to use every conceivable weapon against him. I
have now pointed out to you what is at stake for the town as a
whole—and consequently for me personally. I warn you, Tomas,
I shall be completely ruthless unless you accept certain conditions.

DR. STOCKMANN: What conditions?

THE MAYOR: Since you have seen fit to go round gossiping about a
subject, which should, of course, have been treated with the
utmost discretion as an official secret, it is too late to hush the
matter up. There are bound to be all sorts of rumors, and
malicious-minded people will of course elaborate them. It will
therefore be necessary for you publicly to refute them.

DR. STOCKMANN: I? But how? I don't understand.

THE MAYOR: We shall expect you, on further investigation, to
come to the conclusion that the situation is not nearly as pressing
or as dangerous as you had at first imagined.

DR. STOCKMANN: Oh! You expect that of me, do you?

THE MAYOR: Furthermore we will expect you to make a public
statement expressing your faith in the management's integrity
and in their intention to take thorough and conscientious steps to
remedy any possible defects.

DR. STOCKMANN: But that's out of the question, Peter. No

amount of patching or tinkering can put this matter right; I tell
you I *know!* It is my firm and unalterable conviction—

THE MAYOR: As a member of the staff you have no right to personal
convictions.

DR. STOCKMANN (*With a start*): No right to—?

THE MAYOR: Not as a member of the staff—no! As a private
individual—that's of course another matter. But as a subordinate
in the employ of the Baths you have no right openly to express
convictions opposed to those of your superiors.

DR. STOCKMANN: This is too much! Do you mean to tell me that as
a doctor—a scientific man—I have no right to—!

THE MAYOR: But this is not purely a scientific matter; there are
other questions involved—technical and economic questions.

DR. STOCKMANN: To hell with all that! I insist that I am free to
speak my mind on any and all questions!

THE MAYOR: You are free to do anything you please—as long as it
doesn't concern the Baths. But we forbid you to touch on that
subject.

DR. STOCKMANN (*Shouts*): Forbid it—you! A bunch of—!

THE MAYOR: *I* forbid it. I personally—your superior in chief. And
when I give an order I expect to be obeyed.

DR. STOCKMANN (*Controlling himself*): By God! If you weren't
my brother, Peter—!

PETRA (*Flings open the door*): Don't put up with this, Father!

MRS. STOCKMANN (*Following her*): Petra! Petra!

THE MAYOR: So! We've been listening at doors, have we?

MRS. STOCKMANN: You talked so loud—we couldn't very well
help hearing—

PETRA: That's not true. I was listening on purpose.

THE MAYOR: Well—I can't say I'm sorry—

DR. STOCKMANN (*A step toward him*): You talked to me in terms
of forbidding—of forcing me to obedience—

THE MAYOR: I had to; you gave me no choice.

DR. STOCKMANN: So you expect me to recant in public.

THE MAYOR: We consider it imperative that you issue a statement
along the lines indicated.

DR. STOCKMANN: And what if I refuse?

THE MAYOR: Then—in order to reassure the public—we shall have to issue a statement ourselves.

DR. STOCKMANN: Very well. I shall attack you in the newspapers; I shall use every means to prove that I am right and that you are wrong. What do you say to that?

THE MAYOR: In that case I shall not be able to prevent your dismissal.

DR. STOCKMANN: What—!

PETRA: Dismissal! Father!

MRS. STOCKMANN: Dismissal!

THE MAYOR: I shall be obliged to advise the Board to give you your notice and to see that you have no further connection with the Baths.

DR. STOCKMANN: You would dare do that!

THE MAYOR: It is you who force me to it.

PETRA: Uncle! This is a disgraceful way to treat a man like Father!

MRS. STOCKMANN: Do be quiet, Petra!

THE MAYOR (*Looking at* PETRA): So! We already presume to have opinions, do we? I suppose it's only natural. (*To* MRS. STOCKMANN) Sister-in-law, you seem to be the only sensible member of this household. I advise you to use what influence you have on your husband; try and make him realize what this will mean both for his family—

DR. STOCKMANN: My family is my own concern!

THE MAYOR: I repeat—both for his family, and for the town he lives in.

DR. STOCKMANN: I'm the one who has the good of the town at heart—you know that perfectly well! This is my home town and I love it. That's why I want to expose this dangerous situation that, sooner or later, must come to light.

THE MAYOR: And in order to prove your love for it you insist on destroying the town's one hope of prosperity?

DR. STOCKMANN: But it's a *false* hope, man! Are you mad? Do you want the town to grow rich by selling filth and poison? Must its prosperity be founded on a lie?

THE MAYOR: That's worse than nonsense—it's downright libelous!

Only an enemy of Society could insinuate such things against his native town.

DR. STOCKMANN (*Steps towards him*): You dare to—!

MRS. STOCKMANN (*Throws herself between them*): Tomas!

PETRA (*Seizes her father's arm*): Steady, Father!

THE MAYOR: I refuse to expose myself to violence. You've been warned. I advise you to remember what you owe to yourself and to your family. Goodbye. (*He goes.*)

DR. STOCKMANN: They expect me to put up with that kind of treatment, do they? And in my own house too! What do you say to that, Katrine?

MRS. STOCKMANN: It's disgraceful, Tomas, I know—it's shameful—

PETRA: I wish I could have a talk with Uncle—!

DR. STOCKMANN: I suppose it's my own fault; I should have stood up to them long ago—held my own—defied them! An enemy of Society, am I? I'm damned if I'll put up with that!

MRS. STOCKMANN: Remember, Tomas—your brother has the power on his side—

DR. STOCKMANN: But I have the right on mine!

MRS. STOCKMANN: The right—yes, I daresay; but what good is right against might?

PETRA: Mother! How can you talk like that!

DR. STOCKMANN: Might, might! Don't talk nonsense, Katrine. In a free society to be *right* is what counts! I have the free press behind me, and the solid majority on my side—you heard what Aslaksen said. Isn't that might enough for you?

MRS. STOCKMANN: But, Tomas—you're surely not thinking of—?

DR. STOCKMANN: Of what?

MRS. STOCKMANN: Of going against your brother's wishes?

DR. STOCKMANN: What the devil do you expect me to do? What else *can* I do if I'm to stick up for what's honest and right?

PETRA: That's what I'd like to know!

MRS. STOCKMANN: But you know it won't be of any use! If they won't do it—they won't!

DR. STOCKMANN: Just give me time, Katrine. I'll succeed in the end—you'll see.

MRS. STOCKMANN: You'll succeed in getting dismissed—that's what it'll end with.

DR. STOCKMANN: In any case I shall have done my duty to Society—even though I am supposed to be its enemy!

MRS. STOCKMANN: But what about your family, Tomas? What about those dependent on you? Would you be doing your duty to us?

PETRA: Oh, do stop putting us first, Mother!

MRS. STOCKMANN: It's all very well for you to talk—you can manage alone, if need be. But what about the boys, Tomas? And yourself? And me?

DR. STOCKMANN: You must be stark, raving mad, Katrine! If I were such a coward as to kow-tow to Peter and his blasted crew—do you think I'd ever again have a moment's happiness?

MRS. STOCKMANN: I don't know about that; but God preserve us from the sort of happiness we'll have if you persist in defying them! We'll have nothing to live on; you'll be jobless, penniless—just as you were in the old days. We can't go through that again! Be sensible, Tomas; think of the consequences!

DR. STOCKMANN (*Struggling with himself and clenching his hands*): It's disgraceful that these damned bureaucrats should be able to do this to a free, honorable man! Don't you agree, Katrine?

MRS. STOCKMANN: They've treated you abominably—there's no doubt about that. But there's so much injustice in the world—one must just put up with it. Think of the boys, Tomas! Look at them! What's to become of them? You surely wouldn't have the heart to—

(EJLIF *and* MORTEN *have entered while she speaks; they carry their schoolbooks.*)

DR. STOCKMANN: The boys—! (*Firmly and decisively*) I don't care if the whole world crumbles, I refuse to be a slave to any man! (*He goes towards his study.*)

MRS. STOCKMANN (*Follows him*): Tomas! What are you going to do?

DR. STOCKMANN (*At the door*): When my boys grow up to be free men, I want to be able to look them in the face! (*He goes into his study.*)

MRS. STOCKMANN (*Bursting into tears*): God help us all!

PETRA: Father's wonderful, Mother! He'll never give in!

CURTAIN

ACT THREE

SCENE: *The editorial office of* The People's Monitor. *The entrance door is in the background to the left; in the same wall to the right another door with glass panes, through which can be seen the composing-room. A door in the wall right. A large table stands in the middle of the room covered with papers, newspapers and books. Down left a window and by it a desk with a high stool. A couple of armchairs by the table; other chairs along the walls. The room is dingy and cheerless, the furniture old and the armchairs dirty and torn. In the composing-room some printers can be seen at work; further back a hand-press is in operation.*

HOVSTAD *is seated at the desk writing. In a few moments* BILLING *enters from the door right, with the doctor's manuscript in his hand.*

BILLING: Well, I must say—!

HOVSTAD (*Still writing*): Have you read it?

BILLING (*Laying the ms. on the desk*) I have indeed!

HOVSTAD: The doctor has courage, hasn't he? It's a strong statement!

BILLING: Strong! Strike me dead—it's positively crushing! Every word has the impact of a sledge-hammer.

HOVSTAD: It'll take more than one blow to knock those fellows out.

BILLING: That's true enough; but we'll keep on pounding at them and one of these days they'll come crashing down. As I sat there reading that article I could almost hear the revolution thundering in the distance.

HOVSTAD (*Turning round*): Careful! Don't let Aslaksen hear that.

BILLING: Aslaksen is a chicken-hearted milksop—he hasn't an ounce of manly feeling in him! But you'll insist on having your own way this time, won't you? You'll definitely use the doctor's statement?

HOVSTAD: If the Mayor doesn't give in—yes.

BILLING: It'd be a damn nuisance if he did!

HOVSTAD: Well—fortunately we're bound to gain by the situation in any case. If the Mayor doesn't agree to the doctor's proposition he'll have all the little people on his neck—the Home-owners Association, and all the rest of them. And if he does agree to it, all the rich people will be up in arms; all the people who've hitherto been his chief supporters—including of course those who have the biggest investment in the Baths—

BILLING: Yes; I suppose it would cost them a pretty penny to make the alterations—

HOVSTAD: There's no doubt of that! And once the reactionary party is split up, we can continue to expose the Mayor's total in-efficiency, and convince the public that the Liberals must be brought to power, for the general good of the community.

BILLING: Strike me dead if that isn't the truth! I feel it—I feel it—the revolution is approaching!

(*A knock at the door.*)

HOVSTAD: Hush! (*Calls out*) Come in!

(DR. STOCKMANN *enters from the door upper left.*)

HOVSTAD (*Going to meet him*): Ah, here's the doctor now. Well?

DR. STOCKMANN: You may go ahead and print it, Mr. Hovstad.

HOVSTAD: So it's really come to that, has it?

BILLING: Hurrah!

DR. STOCKMANN: Yes—it's come to that; so print away, I say! They've asked for war, now let them have it.

BILLING: War to the death, I hope; war to the death!

DR. STOCKMANN: This first article is only the beginning; I have four or five others in mind—my head's bursting with ideas. Where's Aslaksen?

BILLING (*Calling into the printing room*): Oh, Aslaksen! Come here a minute, will you!

HOVSTAD: Four or five others, you say? On the same subject?

DR. STOCKMANN: Oh, by no means; they'll deal with quite different matters. They all stem from the water-works and the sewerage-system, of course—one thing leads to another. It's exactly like trying to patch up an old building.

BILLING: Strike me dead—that's the truth! You do a bit here and a bit there, but the whole thing's so rotten, you end by tearing it down!

ASLAKSEN (*Enters from the printing room*): Tearing down! Surely, Doctor, you're not thinking of tearing down the Baths!

HOVSTAD: No, of course not. You needn't be alarmed.

DR. STOCKMANN: We were talking about something quite different. Well—what do you think of my article, Mr. Hovstad?

HOVSTAD: I think it's an absolute masterpiece—

DR. STOCKMANN: Yes, isn't it—? I'm so glad you agree!

HOVSTAD: It's clear and to the point—anyone could follow it; there's no need to be a specialist. You'll have every intelligent man on your side.

ASLAKSEN: And the prudent ones as well, I hope.

BILLING: Prudent—and imprudent too! Pretty nearly the whole town in fact—

ASLAKSEN: In that case, I think we might safely venture to print it.

DR. STOCKMANN: Well—I should hope so!

HOVSTAD: It'll be in tomorrow morning.

DR.STOCKMANN: Splendid! There's no time to lose, you know. By the way, Mr. Aslaksen, there's one thing I'd like to ask you; you'll supervise the printing of the article yourself, won't you?

ASLAKSEN: Indeed I will.

DR. STOCKMANN: It's very precious, remember. We don't want any errors; every word is important. I'll drop in again presently—you might let me see a proof. I can't wait to have the thing in print—to get it launched.

BILLING: It'll be a bombshell!

DR. STOCKMANN: I want every enlightened citizen to read it and judge for himself. You've no idea what I've been through today. I've been exposed to every kind of pressure; my rights as an individual have been threatened—

BILLING: Your rights—!

DR. STOCKMANN: Yes! I was expected to crawl and humble myself. My deepest—my most sacred convictions were to be sacrificed for purely personal ends—

BILLING: Strike me dead! This is an outrage!

DR. STOCKMANN: But this time they've gone too far—and they shall be told so in no uncertain terms! I shall set up my headquarters here at *The People's Monitor*, and continue to attack them daily—

ASLAKSEN: But, just a minute—

BILLING: Hurrah! It's war—war!

DR. STOCKMANN: I'll run them into the ground; smash them to pieces—wipe them out! I'll show the public what they really are—that's what I'll do!

ASLAKSEN: But you will use moderation, my dear Doctor; attack—but prudently.

BILLING: No! Don't spare the dynamite!

DR. STOCKMANN: It's no longer merely a question of sewers and water-works, you see; it's a question of cleaning up the whole community—

BILLING: That's the way to talk!

DR. STOCKMANN: All those old fogies must be kicked out of office, no matter what position they may hold. I have such a clear perspective on everything today; I don't see all the details yet, but I'll soon work them out. What we need, my friends, is young and vital leaders—new captains at the outposts.

BILLING: Hear, hear!

DR. STOCKMANN: If we stand together, we're bound to win. This whole revolution will be launched quite smoothly—like a new ship gliding down the ways. Don't you believe that?

HOVSTAD: I believe we have every hope of putting the right people into power at last.

ASLAKSEN: And if we proceed with caution, I see no reason why we should run into any danger.

DR. STOCKMANN: Who the hell cares about danger! This is a matter of truth and conscience!

HOVSTAD: You deserve every support, Doctor.

ASLAKSEN: Dr. Stockmann is a true friend of the town; a friend of Society—that's what he is.

BILLING: Strike me dead! He's a friend of the People, Aslaksen!

ASLAKSEN: I'm sure the Home-owners Association will use that as a slogan.

DR. STOCKMANN: My dear friends—I can't thank you enough for all your loyalty; it does me good to hear you. My sainted brother called me something very different; but he'll be repaid—with interest! I'll be off now—I have to see a poor devil of a patient—but I'll be back. Take good care of my article, won't you, Mr. Aslaksen? And don't cut out any exclamation-marks! You can even add a few if you like! Well—goodbye for now; I'll be back shortly. Goodbye.

(*General goodbyes as they accompany him to the door; he goes.*)

HOVSTAD: He can be exceedingly useful to us.

ASLAKSEN: Yes, providing he sticks to this matter of the Baths; if he goes beyond that, it might be unwise to follow him.

HOVSTAD: Hm; it all depends on—

BILLING: You're always so damned frightened, Aslaksen.

ASLAKSEN: Frightened? Yes, when it comes to attacking the local authorities I am frightened, Mr. Billing. I've learned in a hard school, you see. National politics however are another matter; in such things you wouldn't find me frightened, I assure you—even if you were to pit me against the Government itself.

BILLING: I dare say not; that's where you're so inconsistent.

ASLAKSEN: Where the good of the town is concerned, I am very conscientious. There's no harm in attacking the Government—what does the Government care? Those men at the top are unassailable. But the local authorities are different—they can be dismissed; and should their power fall into the hands of inexperienced men, not only the Home-owners but the entire community would suffer.

HOVSTAD: If the People are never allowed self-government how can they ever gain experience? Haven't you thought of that?

ASLAKSEN: When one has vested interests, Mr. Hovstad, one must protect them. A man can't think of everything.

HOVSTAD: Vested interests! Then I hope I never have any!

BILLING: Hear, hear!

ASLAKSEN (*With a smile*): Hm. (*Points to the desk*) There was a time when Commissioner Stensgaard sat in that editor's chair, if you remember.

BILLING (*Spitting*): Pooh! That turncoat!

HOVSTAD: Well—I'm no weathercock, and never will be!

ASLAKSEN: A politician should never say "never" about anything, Mr. Hovstad. And as for you, Mr. Billing—I understand you've applied for the post of secretary to the Town Council; hadn't you better use a little caution?

BILLING: I—!

HOVSTAD: Billing—is this true?

BILLING: As a matter of fact, it is. I'm only doing it to spite the Big-wigs, mind you!

ASLAKSEN: Well—it's no business of mine. I may be accused of cowardice and inconsistency, but my political record is an open book. I've never changed in any way—except, possibly, to become more moderate. My heart is, and always has been, with the People; I must admit, however, that my common-sense inclines me towards the side of the authorities, to some extent; the local authorities, I mean.

(*He goes into the printing office.*)

BILLING: Shouldn't we try and get rid of him, Hovstad?

HOVSTAD: Do you know of anybody else who'd be willing to pay our expenses?

BILLING: It's damnable to have no capital!

HOVSTAD (*Sits down at the desk*): Yes; we'd be all right if we had that!

BILLING: Why don't you talk to Dr. Stockmann?

HOVSTAD (*Looking through some papers*): What good would that do? He hasn't a penny.

BILLING: No—but he has connections; old Morten Kiil—"the badger" as they call him.

HOVSTAD (*Writing*): You really think he has money?

BILLING: Strike me dead—of course he has! And Stockmann's family is bound to get part of it. The old man's sure to provide for—for the children, at any rate.

HOVSTAD (*Half turning*): Are you counting on that?

BILLING: What do you mean—"counting?" You know I never count on anything.

HOVSTAD: You're wise. And you'd better not count on that job as secretary either; I assure you, you won't get it.

BILLING: Do you suppose I don't know that? That's the very reason I've applied for it. A slight of that sort fires the spirit of rebellion in one—gives one a fresh supply of vitriol, as it were; and that's a very necessary thing in a God-forsaken hole like this where nothing really stimulating ever seems to happen.

HOVSTAD (*Still writing*): Yes, yes; I know, I know.

BILLING: But—one of these days they'll hear from me, I promise you!—Well—I'd better go in and write that appeal to the Homeowners Association. (*He goes into the room on the right.*)

HOVSTAD (*At the desk: he bites the end of his penholder and says slowly*): Hm.— I see.— So that's it.(*A knock at the door*) Come in!

(PETRA *enters from the back, left.*)

HOVSTAD (*Rising*): Well! It's you, is it? What are you doing here?

PETRA: You must excuse me for—

HOVSTAD (*Pushes an armchair forward*): Do sit down.

PETRA: No thanks; I can only stay a minute.

HOVSTAD: Is it a message from your father—?

PETRA: No, I've come on my own account. (*Takes a book out of her coat pocket*) I've brought back that English story.

HOVSTAD: Brought it back—why?

PETRA: Because I don't want to translate it after all.

HOVSTAD: But you gave me a definite promise—

PETRA: I know; but I hadn't read it then. You haven't read it, have you?

HOVSTAD: No—I don't read English; but—

PETRA: That's what I thought; so I felt I should advise you to look around for something else. (*Putting the book on the table*) This would never do for *The People's Monitor*.

HOVSTAD: Why not?

PETRA: Because it's against everything you stand for.

HOVSTAD: Well, as far as that goes—

PETRA: No—you don't see my point; this story claims that there's a supernatural power looking after all the so-called good people in the world, so that everything turns out well for them in the end—whereas all the so-called bad people get punished.

HOVSTAD: Splendid! Just what the public wants.

PETRA: Yes; but you surely wouldn't want to be the one to give them such nonsense. You don't believe a word of it yourself; you know perfectly well that's not the way things really happen.

HOVSTAD: You're right, of course; but, you see, a publisher can't always do as he pleases—he often has to cater to the public in minor matters. Politics, after all, are the main thing—to a newspaper at any rate; if I want to steer people towards a more liberal way of thinking, I can't afford to scare them off. If they come across a nice moral tale like that tucked away somewhere in the back pages of the paper they feel safer, and they're more willing to accept what we give them on the front page.

PETRA: But that's disgusting! I'm sure you'd never play a trick like that. You're not a hypocrite!

HOVSTAD (*Smiling*): I'm glad you think so well of me. As a matter of fact it's Billing's idea, not mine.

PETRA: Billing's!

HOVSTAD: Yes; at least he was talking along those lines only the other day. It was Billing who wanted to print the story; I don't know anything about it.

PETRA: Mr. Billing! But that seems impossible; he has such a modern point of view!

HOVSTAD: Well, you see—Billing is a man of many parts. He's now decided he wants to become secretary to the Town Council—or so I hear.

PETRA: I don't believe that for a moment, Mr. Hovstad. He could never lower himself to that!

HOVSTAD: You'd better ask him about it.

PETRA: I never would have thought such a thing of Mr. Billing.

HOVSTAD (*Looks at her intently*): No? Is it really such a surprise to you?

PETRA: Yes, indeed it is. And yet—perhaps it isn't really. I don't know what to think—

HOVSTAD: We newspaper men are worthless fellows, Miss Petra.

PETRA: Do you really mean that?

HOVSTAD: Yes; at least, I sometimes think so.

PETRA: That may be true as far as ordinary petty everyday matters are concerned. But now that you're involved in a great cause—

HOVSTAD: You mean this business about your father?

PETRA: Yes, of course. It must give you a proud feeling; a sense of being worth more than just ordinary people.

HOVSTAD: You're right; I do feel a bit like that today.

PETRA: I'm sure you must. What a wonderful career you've chosen! To be a pioneer; to promote the truth; to fight for bold ideas—new ways of thinking! The mere fact of coming to the defense of someone who's been wronged—

HOVSTAD: Especially when that someone is—I don't quite know how to put it—

PETRA: When he's so true and honorable, you mean?

HOVSTAD (*In a low voice*): Yes; and especially when he happens to be your father.

PETRA (*Suddenly taken aback*): You mean—? Oh, no!

HOVSTAD: Yes, Petra—Miss Petra.

PETRA: Is that your reason—? Is that what matters most to you? Then, it isn't the thing itself; the truth means nothing to you—and my father's generosity of soul means nothing either!

HOVSTAD: Yes, of course it does, but—

PETRA: Thank you, Mr. Hovstad. You've said more than enough. I shall never trust you again in anything.

HOVSTAD: Come now—you mustn't be too hard on me! Even if it is mainly for your sake—

PETRA: What makes me angry is that you haven't been honest with my father. You let him think you were concerned with the truth, with the good of the community, when all the time—! You've made fools of us both, Mr. Hovstad. You're not at all the sort of man you pretended to be. I shall never forgive you for it—never!

HOVSTAD: I wouldn't be too caustic, Miss Petra; this is not the time for that.

PETRA: Not the time? Why not?

HOVSTAD: Because your father can't very well get on without my help.

PETRA: I see. So you're that sort of a person too.

HOVSTAD: No, no—really I'm not! I didn't think what I was saying; you must believe me!

PETRA: I know what to believe, I assure you. Goodbye.

ASLAKSEN (*Enters hurriedly and mysteriously from the printing office*): Hell and damnation, Mr. Hovstad—! (*Sees* PETRA) Oh, I beg your pardon—

PETRA: There's the book. Get someone else to do it for you. (*Goes towards the main entrance.*)

HOVSTAD (*Following her*): But, Miss Petra—

PETRA: Goodbye. (*She goes*)

ASLAKSEN: Mr. Hovstad, listen!

HOVSTAD: Well—what is it? What's the matter?

ASLAKSEN: It's the Mayor! He's out in the printing office.

HOVSTAD: The Mayor?

ASLAKSEN: Yes; he says he wants to talk to you. He came in the back way—didn't want to be seen, I suppose.

HOVSTAD: What does this mean, I wonder? Wait a minute—I'll go myself— (*He goes toward the printing office, opens the door, bows and invites* THE MAYOR *to come in.*)

HOVSTAD: Be on the look-out, Aslaksen, and see that no one—

ASLAKSEN: I understand— (*He goes into the printing office.*)

THE MAYOR: I don't suppose you expected to see me here, Mr. Hovstad.

HOVSTAD: No, I can't say I did.

THE MAYOR (*Looking round*): A nice place you have here; most comfortable.

HOVSTAD: Well—

THE MAYOR: You must forgive me for dropping in like this, and taking up your time.

HOVSTAD: I'm only too delighted, Mr. Mayor; always at your service. Let me take your things— (*Takes* THE MAYOR'S *hat and cane and puts them on a chair*) And now—won't you sit down?

THE MAYOR (*Sits by the table*): Thanks. (HOVSTAD *sits down at the table also*) I've been faced with—with a very troubling matter today, Mr. Hovstad.

HOVSTAD: Really? But, of course, you must have so many duties—

THE MAYOR: It concerns my brother, Mr. Hovstad.

HOVSTAD: Dr. Stockmann?

THE MAYOR: Yes. He's written a sort of memorandum to the directors of the Baths, alleging that there are certain defects in the establishment.

HOVSTAD: Really? Has he?

THE MAYOR: Hasn't he told you? I thought he said—

HOVSTAD: Now I come to think of it, I believe he did mention—

ASLAKSEN (*Enters from the printing office*): I'd better have that manuscript—

HOVSTAD (*With annoyance*): It's over on the desk.

ASLAKSEN: Ah, yes—here it is.

THE MAYOR: But surely— Isn't that—?

ASLAKSEN: It's Dr. Stockmann's article.

HOVSTAD: Oh—was that what you were referring to?

THE MAYOR: Precisely— What do you think of it?

HOVSTAD: I've only just glanced at it—and, of course, I'm not an expert—

THE MAYOR: And yet you intend to print it?

HOVSTAD: I can't very well refuse anything signed by—

ASLAKSEN: I've nothing to do with editing the paper, Mr. Mayor.

THE MAYOR: No, of course not.

ASLAKSEN: I just do the printing.

THE MAYOR: I understand.

ASLAKSEN: So—if you'll excuse me— (*Goes towards the press-room.*)

THE MAYOR: Just one moment, Mr. Aslaksen. With your permission, Mr. Hovstad—?

HOVSTAD: Of course.

THE MAYOR: Mr. Aslaksen—you seem to me to be a discreet and sensible man.

ASLAKSEN: It's very kind of you to say so—

THE MAYOR: And a man of widespread influence too.

ASLAKSEN: Only among the little people, Your Honor.

THE MAYOR: It's the small taxpayers who form the majority—here, as everywhere.

ASLAKSEN: That's true enough.

THE MAYOR: And I've no doubt you are familiar with the general trend of sentiment among them. Are you not?

ASLAKSEN: I think I may say I am, Your Honor.

THE MAYOR: Well—since there appears to be such a fine feeling of self-sacrifice among the poorer classes—

ASLAKSEN: How do you mean?

HOVSTAD: Self-sacrifice?

THE MAYOR: It indicates an admirable sense of public-spirit. I find it a little surprising, I admit; but then I don't know the public sentiment as well as you do.

ASLAKSEN: But, Your Honor—

THE MAYOR: And it will entail no small sacrifice to the town, I can assure you.

HOVSTAD: To the town?

ASLAKSEN: I don't understand; surely, this concerns the Baths—

THE MAYOR: At a rough preliminary estimate, the alterations Dr. Stockmann has in mind will cost in the neighborhood of two hundred thousand crowns.

ASLAKSEN: That's a lot of money; but—

THE MAYOR: A municipal loan will naturally be necessary.

HOVSTAD (Rising): You surely can't mean that the town—?

ASLAKSEN: You mean the townspeople would have to pay for it out of their own pockets?

THE MAYOR: My dear Mr. Aslaksen, where else should the money come from?

ASLAKSEN: I should think the owners of the Baths would be responsible.

THE MAYOR: The owners are not prepared to increase their investment at this time.

ASLAKSEN: Are you quite sure of that?

THE MAYOR: I have positive information to that effect. So if these alterations are to be made, the town itself will have to pay for them.

ASLAKSEN: But then, damn it all, Mr. Hovstad—excuse me, Your Honor—this puts the matter in quite a different light!

HOVSTAD: It does indeed.

THE MAYOR: The worst part of it is we shall be obliged to close down the Baths for a couple of years.

HOVSTAD: Close them? Completely close them?

ASLAKSEN: For two years!

THE MAYOR: Yes; it will take at least two years to do the work.

ASLAKSEN: But, damn it! We could never survive that, Your Honor; we home-owners depend on these visitors—what are we to live on in the meantime?

THE MAYOR: That is a difficult question to answer, Mr. Aslaksen. But what's to be done? Once people get this notion into their heads that the waters are tainted, that the whole place is a pest-hole—we can hardly expect them to come here.

ASLAKSEN: Then you think it's no more than a notion?

THE MAYOR: Try as I will, I can't persuade myself to think other-wise.

ASLAKSEN: Then it's downright inexcusable of Dr. Stockmann—I beg pardon, Your Honor, but—

THE MAYOR: Unfortunately you're quite right, Mr. Aslaksen; my brother has always been an exceedingly rash man.

ASLAKSEN: And yet you are prepared to back him up in this, Mr. Hovstad!

HOVSTAD: But, who would ever have thought that—!

THE MAYOR: I've drawn up a short statement on the matter, inter-preting the facts from a more rational point of view; I've also indi-cated ways in which any small defects that might conceivably exist can be taken care of within the scope of the present financial budget.

HOVSTAD: Have you it with you?

THE MAYOR (*Feeling in his pocket*): Yes; I thought I'd better bring it in case you—

ASLAKSEN (*Quickly*): Damn it—there he is!

THE MAYOR: Who? My brother?

HOVSTAD: Where?

ASLAKSEN: Coming through the press-room.

THE MAYOR: This is unfortunate! I don't want to run into him here—yet there are several things I'd still like to talk to you about.

HOVSTAD (*Pointing to the door on the right*): Wait in there for a moment.

THE MAYOR: But—?

HOVSTAD: There's no one in there but Billing.

ASLAKSEN: Quick, Your Honor! Here he comes!

THE MAYOR: Very well; get rid of him as soon as you can, though. (*He goes out by the door right which* ASLAKSEN *opens, and closes after him.*)

HOVSTAD: Pretend to be busy, Aslaksen. (*He sits down and starts to write.* ASLAKSEN *goes through a pile of newspapers on a chair, right.*)

DR. STOCKMANN (*Enters from the composing-room*): Well—Here I am, back again. (*Puts down his hat and stick.*)

HOVSTAD (*Writing*): Already, Doctor? Get on with what we were just talking about, Aslaksen. We've no time to waste today.

DR. STOCKMANN (*To* ASLAKSEN): No proofs yet, I hear.

ASLAKSEN (*Without turning round*): You could hardly expect them yet, Doctor.

DR. STOCKMANN: No, of course not. It's just that I'm impatient—you can understand that; I can't wait to see the thing in print.

HOVSTAD: It'll be another hour at least; wouldn't you say so, Aslaksen?

ASLAKSEN: I'm afraid so, yes.

DR. STOCKMANN: Never mind; I'll come back. I don't mind coming back twice if need be. What's a little inconvenience compared to the welfare of the town—! (*Starts to go but stops and comes back*) By the way, there's something I must discuss with you.

HOVSTAD: I'm afraid, just now, you must excuse me, Doctor—

DR. STOCKMANN: It'll only take a moment. I was just thinking; when people read this article of mine tomorrow morning, and realize I devoted my whole winter to working for the good of the town—

HOVSTAD: But, after all, Doctor—

DR. STOCKMANN: Oh, I know what you're going to say—it was no more than my duty as a citizen—I know that as well as you do. But my fellow-townsmen—well, bless their hearts, they're so fond of me, you see—

ASLAKSEN: Yes—they've thought very highly of you up to now—

DR. STOCKMANN: I know; that's why I'm so afraid they might —what I mean is this: the people, especially the poorer classes, are bound to take this article of mine as a rousing call to action—as a summons to run things for themselves from now on—

HOVSTAD (*Rising*): As a matter of fact, Doctor, I think I ought to tell you—

DR. STOCKMANN: I knew it! I was sure they'd be up to something. But I won't hear of it, I tell you! So if they're planning anything like that—

HOVSTAD: Like what?

DR. STOCKMANN: Oh, I don't know—a parade, or a banquet, or a testimonial dinner of some sort—I count on you to put a stop to it. You, too, Mr. Aslaksen—remember now!

HOVSTAD: Excuse me, Doctor; I think you'd better know the truth once and for all—

(MRS. STOCKMANN *enters from the rear door, left*.)

MRS. STOCKMANN (*Seeing the doctor*): Just as I thought!

HOVSTAD (*Goes towards her*): You here too, Mrs. Stockmann?

DR. STOCKMANN: What the devil do you want here, Katrine?

MRS. STOCKMANN: You know very well what I want.

HOVSTAD: Won't you sit down? Or perhaps you'd rather—

MRS. STOCKMANN: Thanks—but please don't bother about me; and forgive my coming here to fetch my husband. I'm the mother of three children, let me tell you.

DR. STOCKMANN: Don't talk nonsense! As if we didn't all know that!

MRS. STOCKMANN: You don't seem to be giving much thought to it—otherwise you wouldn't be so anxious to ruin us all!

DR. STOCKMANN: You must be stark raving mad, Katrine! Just because he has a wife and children, can't a man stand up for the truth? Be a useful citizen? Serve the town he lives in?

MRS. STOCKMANN: If you'd only use a little moderation, Tomas!

ASLAKSEN: That's what I always say: everything in moderation!

MRS. STOCKMANN: It's very wrong of you, Mr. Hovstad, to lure my husband away from house and home; persuading him to get mixed up in all this—making a fool of him!

HOVSTAD: I don't make a fool of anyone—

DR. STOCKMANN: A fool! You think I let people make a fool of me!

MRS. STOCKMANN: Yes, Tomas—you do! Oh, I know you're the cleverest man in town, but you're easily fooled all the same. (*To* HOVSTAD) Don't you realize he'll lose his position if you print that article of his—

ASLAKSEN: What!

HOVSTAD: As a matter of fact, Dr. Stockmann—

DR. STOCKMANN (*Laughing*): They can't do a thing to me—they'd never dare! Don't forget, my dear, the solid majority is with me.

MRS. STOCKMANN: More's the pity. You'd be better off without it!

DR. STOCKMANN: Don't talk nonsense, Katrine; go home and tend to your house-work and leave Society to me. What is there to be afraid of! Can't you see how happy and confident I am? (*Rubs his hands and walks up and down*) The truth will conquer—I'm convinced of it. The people will band together in the cause of truth and freedom, and nothing can stop them—! (*Stops suddenly by a chair*) Why—what the devil's this doing here?

ASLAKSEN (*Realizing*): Oh, Lord.

HOVSTAD (*The same*): Hm—

DR. STOCKMANN (*He picks up* THE MAYOR'S *cap and holds it gingerly aloft*): The crown of authority, is it not?

MRS. STOCKMANN: It's the Mayor's cap!

DR. STOCKMANN: And the staff of office, too! But what the devil are they doing here?

HOVSTAD: You might as well know—

DR. STOCKMANN: Ah, I see! He came to try and win you over. Well—he chose the wrong customer for once! I suppose he caught sight of me in the office and— (*Bursts out laughing*) Did he turn tail, Mr. Aslaksen?

ASLAKSEN (*Hurriedly*): Yes, Doctor, he—he turned tail.

DR. STOCKMANN: Ran off and left his stick and— But, wait a minute—that's not a bit like Peter. What have you done with him? Oh, of course—he's hiding in there. Now you're going to see something, Katrine!

MRS. STOCKMANN: Please, Tomas—!

ASLAKSEN: Be careful, Doctor!

(DR. STOCKMANN *has put on* THE MAYOR'S *cap and seized his stick; he goes to the door, flings it open and makes a military salute.* THE MAYOR *enters, flushed with anger, followed by* BILL-ING.)

THE MAYOR: What is the meaning of these antics?

DR. STOCKMANN: Show some respect, Peter, if you please, (*Struts up and down*) I'm in authority now!

MRS. STOCKMANN (*Almost in tears*): Tomas—for heaven's sake!

THE MAYOR (*Following him*): Give me my cap and stick!

DR. STOCKMANN (*As before*): You may be chief of police, but I'm the Mayor—I'm king of the whole town!

THE MAYOR: Take off that cap, I tell you. Don't you realize it's a badge of office!

DR. STOCKMANN: Listen to him! We've roused the spirit of democracy—do you think a bit of gold braid can frighten me? To-morrow the revolution starts, I'd have you know. You threatened to dismiss me, did you? Well now it's my turn to dismiss you—I'm going to kick you out of office! And if you don't think I can do it, you'll soon find out! The power is on my side—the power of an aroused public! Hovstad and Billing here will thunder away at you in the *Monitor*, and Aslaksen will lead the entire Home-owners Association into battle—!

ASLAKSEN: No, Doctor; I'll do nothing of the sort.

DR. STOCKMANN: Nonsense! Of course you will—

THE MAYOR: I see; so perhaps Mr. Hovstad will decide to join the rebels after all?

HOVSTAD: No, Your Honor.

ASLAKSEN: Mr. Hovstad's no fool; he's not likely to ruin both himself and the paper for the sake of a delusion.

DR. STOCKMANN (*Looks from one to the other*): What does this mean?

HOVSTAD: You've presented this whole matter in a false light, Doctor; that is why I cannot possibly give you my support.

BILLING: After what the Mayor so kindly explained to me just now—

DR. STOCKMANN: A false light, eh? Leave that part of it to me—you just print my article; I'll prove the truth of every word of it.

HOVSTAD: I shall not print it. I neither can, nor will, nor dare.

DR. STOCKMANN: Not *dare?* But that's absurd. You're the editor, aren't you? Don't you control your own paper?

ASLAKSEN: No—the subscribers do.

THE MAYOR: Fortunately—yes.

ASLAKSEN: Public opinion, majority interests, the Home-owners Association and other similar groups—they control the paper.

DR. STOCKMANN (*Calmly*): And they would all be against me, you think?

ASLAKSEN: Unquestionably. If your article were printed it would mean the ruin of the town.

DR. STOCKMANN: I see.

THE MAYOR: And now, my cap and stick!

(DR. STOCKMANN *takes off the cap and lays it on the table; he places the stick beside it*.)

THE MAYOR (*Picking them up*): Your term of office came to rather an abrupt end, didn't it?

DR. STOCKMANN: This is not the end, Peter—believe me. (*To* HOVSTAD) So you find it impossible to print my article in the *Monitor?*

HOVSTAD: Quite impossible; apart from anything else, consideration for your family would—

DR. STOCKMANN: Kindly leave my family to me, Mr. Hovstad.

THE MAYOR (*Takes a manuscript from his breast pocket*): This will put the necessary facts before the public. It is an official statement; I trust you to deal with it accordingly.

HOVSTAD (*Taking the manuscript*): Very good. We shall take care of it; it will appear without delay.

DR. STOCKMANN: But mine will be suppressed. Do you think you can suppress the truth? You'll find it's not so easy! Mr. Aslaksen, please take my manuscript and print it as a pamphlet—at my own expense—I'll publish it myself. I want four hundred copies; no, five—better make it six.

ASLAKSEN: I can't possibly use my printing-press for such a purpose, Doctor—not if you were to pay me its weight in gold. I dare not offend public opinion. No one in town will print it, I assure you.

DR. STOCKMANN: Then give it back to me.

HOVSTAD (*Hands it to him*): Gladly.

DR. STOCKMANN (*Takes up his hat and stick*): But you won't be able to suppress it all the same! I'll call a public meeting—I'll read it to the people myself; my fellow-townsmen are going to hear the truth!

THE MAYOR: It won't be any good; not a single hall will be available to you.

ASLAKSEN: Not one—I'll vouch for that.

BILLING: That's true—strike me dead if it isn't!

MRS. STOCKMANN: But this is disgraceful, Tomas! Why are they suddenly all against you?

DR. STOCKMANN: I'll tell you why. It's because all the men in this town are a lot of old women—just like you! They think of nothing but themselves; they don't care a damn about the general good!

MRS. STOCKMANN: Then I'll show them here's at least one old woman who knows how to be a man. I'll stand by you, Tomas!

DR. STOCKMANN: Well said, Katrine! Nothing can stop me; if I can't rent a hall, I'll hire a drum and march through the town with it. I'll read my statement at the corner of every street, of every square—the people are going to know the truth!

THE MAYOR: You can't do that! Are you a raving lunatic?

DR. STOCKMANN: Yes, I am!

ASLAKSEN: No one will go with you, Doctor Stockmann.

BILLING: Strike me dead—I'm sure of that!

MRS. STOCKMANN: Don't give in now, Tomas. I'll ask the boys—they'll go with you.

DR. STOCKMANN: That's a splendid thought!

MRS. STOCKMANN: Morten would be delighted—and I'm certain Ejlif would go too.

DR. STOCKMANN: Yes—and then there's Petra! And you, Katrine!

MRS. STOCKMANN: Oh, no; it wouldn't do for me to go. But I tell you what I'll do—I'll watch you from the window.

DR. STOCKMANN (*Throws his arms round her*): Thanks! Well —the fight is on, gentlemen! We'll see if you and your chicanery can prevent an honest citizen from cleaning up the town he lives in! Come, Katrine!

(*He and* MRS. STOCKMANN *go out by the door upper left*.)

TH E MAYOR (*Shakes his head thoughtfully*): He's managed to turn her head at last! Now she's as mad as he is.

CURTAIN

ACT
FOUR

SCENE: *A large old-fashioned room in* CAPTAIN HORSTER'S *house. Open double doors in the back wall lead to an anteroom. In the wall left are three windows; in the center of the opposite wall is a platform on which stands a small table with two candles, a carafe of water, a glass and a bell placed on it. Sconces between the windows provide the general lighting. Down left a small table with a candle, and a chair beside it. Down right a door and near it a couple of chairs.*

There is a large gathering of townspeople of various types. Among the crowd are seen a few women and schoolboys. People continue to stream in from the anteroom until the main room is quite full.

FIRST MAN (*As he bumps into another one*): You're here too, are you, Lamstad?

SECOND MAN: I never miss a public meeting.

ANOTHER MAN: I see you've brought your whistle.

SECOND MAN: Of course; haven't you?

THIRD MAN: I should hope so! Skipper Evensen said he was going to bring his big horn!

SECOND MAN: That Evensen's a good one, he is!
(*Laughter in the group.*)

FOURTH MAN (*Joining them*): Tell me—what's going on here this evening?

SECOND MAN: Doctor Stockmann and the Mayor are holding a debate.

FOURTH MAN: But the Mayor's his brother, isn't he?

FIRST MAN: That makes no difference; Doctor Stockmann's not afraid of anyone.

THIRD MAN: But he's all wrong; it says so in the *Monitor*.

SECOND MAN: He must be wrong this time; no one would let him have a hall—not the Home-owners Association, nor the Citizens' Club either.

FIRST MAN: Even the Baths refused him.

SECOND MAN: That's not surprising.

A MAN (*In another group*): Whom do we support in this business?

ANOTHER MAN (*In the same group*): Just keep an eye on Aslaksen and do as he does.

BILLING (*With a portfolio under his arm pushes his way through the crowd*): Excuse me, gentlemen. May I get by please? I'm reporting for *The People's Monitor*. Thanks—thank you! (*He sits at the table left.*)

A WORKMAN: Who's he?

ANOTHER WORKMAN: Don't you know him? That's Billing—he writes for Aslaksen's paper.
(CAPTAIN HORSTER *ushers in* MRS. STOCKMANN *and* PETRA *through the door down right.* EJLIF *and* MORTEN *follow them.*)

CAPTAIN HORSTER: I thought this would be a good place for you to sit; it'll be easy for you to slip away if anything should happen.

MRS. STOCKMANN: Will there be any disturbance, do you think?

HORSTER: It's hard to say—with all these people. But don't be anxious—just sit here quietly.

MRS. STOCKMANN (*Sitting down*): It was so kind of you to let Stockmann have the room.

HORSTER: Since nobody else would, I thought I—

PETRA (*Who has also seated herself*): And it was brave of you too, Captain Horster.

HORSTER: I don't see anything specially brave about it.

(HOVSTAD *and* ASLAKSEN *enter at the same time, but separately, and make their way through the crowd.*)

ASLAKSEN (*Going up to* HORSTER): Isn't Doctor Stockmann here yet?

HORSTER: He's waiting in there.

(*A movement in the crowd by the door at the back of the room.*)

HOVSTAD (*To* BILLING): Here comes the Mayor! Look!

BILLING: Yes—strike me dead! So he's put in an appearance after all!

(MAYOR STOCKMANN *advances graciously through the crowd, bowing to right and left. He takes his stand near the wall on the left. A moment later* DR. STOCKMANN *enters from the door down right. He wears a black frock coat and a white tie. There is scattered applause countered by subdued hissing. Then, silence.*)

DR. STOCKMANN (*In a low tone*): How do you feel, Katrine?

MRS. STOCKMANN: I'm all right, thank you, dear. (*Whispers to him*) Don't lose your temper, Tomas!

DR. STOCKMANN: Don't worry—I'll keep myself in hand. (*Looks at his watch, mounts the platform and bows*) It's a quarter past; I'm going to begin— (*Takes out his manuscript.*)

ASLAKSEN: Wait! We must elect a chairman first.

DR. STOCKMANN: That won't be necessary.

SEVERAL GENTLEMEN (*Shouting*): Yes! Yes!

THE MAYOR: By all means; of course we must have a chairman.

DR. STOCKMANN: But I've called this meeting to read a paper, Peter.

THE MAYOR: All the same—your paper is likely to cause discussion.

SEVERAL VOICES IN THE CROWD: A chairman! We want a chairman!

HOVSTAD: The general voice seems to be in favor of a chairman.

DR. STOCKMANN (*Controlling himself*): Oh, very well— Let the "general voice" have its way.

ASLAKSEN: Perhaps the Mayor will honor us?

THREE GENTLEMEN (*Clapping*): Bravo! Bravo!

THE MAYOR: Many thanks. But for various obvious reasons, I must decline. However, we are fortunate in having in our midst a man who, I am certain, will be acceptable to all. I refer, of course, to the chairman of the Home-owners Association—Mr. Aslaksen.

MANY VOICES: Yes! Yes! Long live Aslaksen! Hurrah for Aslaksen!

(DR. STOCKMANN *takes his manuscript and leaves the platform.*)

ASLAKSEN: Since my fellow-citizens are pleased to show me this signal mark of confidence—who am I to refuse?

(*Applause and cheers.* ASLAKSEN *ascends the platform.*)

BILLING (*Making notes*): Mr. Aslaksen elected by acclamation—

ASLAKSEN: And now—since I stand here as your chairman—allow me to say a few brief words to you. I am a quiet peace-loving man, gentlemen; a man in favor of discreet moderation, and of—and of—moderate discretion. All those who know me are aware of that.

SEVERAL VOICES: Yes, yes! To be sure, Aslaksen!

ASLAKSEN: I have learned in the great common school of life and of experience, that moderation is the citizen's prime virtue—a virtue from which he reaps the highest benefits—

THE MAYOR: Hear! Hear!

ASLAKSEN: —and that discretion and moderation are also the best servants of Society. Allow me therefore to suggest to our respected fellow-citizen who has seen fit to call this meeting, that he take note; let us hope he will bend every effort to keep within the bounds of moderation.

A MAN (*By the door*): I propose a toast to the Temperance Society! Hurrah!

A VOICE: Shame! Shame!

VOICES: Sh! Quiet!

ASLAKSEN: No interruptions if you please, gentlemen!—Does anyone wish to offer any observations?

THE MAYOR: Mr. Chairman!

ASLAKSEN: The Mayor has the floor!

THE MAYOR: Because of my close relationship to the present medical adviser to the Baths—a relationship of which most of you are undoubtedly aware—I should have preferred not to speak here this evening. But my position as Chairman of the Board, as well as my deep concern for the welfare of the town, force me to make this motion. I think I may venture to assume that not a single soul here present would condone the spreading of exaggerated and irresponsible statements concerning the sanitary conditions of our Baths and of our town.

MANY VOICES: No, no! Never! Certainly not! We protest!

THE MAYOR: I therefore move that this meeting pass the following resolution: Dr. Stockmann cannot be allowed to read his paper or to address this assembly on this particular subject.

DR. STOCKMANN (*Flaring up*): Cannot be allowed—! What do you mean?

MRS. STOCKMANN (*Coughing*): Hm, hm!

DR. STOCKMANN (*Controlling himself*): So, I'm not to be allowed; I see.

THE MAYOR: I have acquainted the Public with the relevant facts through my statement in *The People's Monitor*, so that all right-thinking citizens may have no difficulty in forming their own judgment. It will be clearly seen that the doctor's report on the situation—apart from being a direct vote of censure against the leading men in the community—simply means saddling the tax-payers with a totally unnecessary outlay of at least one hundred thousand crowns.

(*Cries of protest and scattered whistles.*)

ASLAKSEN (*Rings the bell*): Order, order, gentlemen! I beg to second the Mayor's motion. I share the opinion that there are other motives behind the doctor's agitation; he may talk about the Baths, but his real aim is nothing short of revolution—the complete overthrow of the parties now in power. No one doubts the doctor's integrity of purpose—there can be no two opinions about that. I too am in favor of self-government by the People, provided it doesn't result in too great a burden on the tax-payer;

in this case that is precisely what would occur. For this reason—well, damn it—excuse me, gentlemen!—on this occasion I cannot possibly side with Dr. Stockmann. You can pay too high a price—even for gold. At all events, that's my opinion. (*Loud applause from all sides.*)

HOVSTAD: I too should like to make my position clear in this matter. At first Dr. Stockmann's agitation met with considerable favor in many quarters and I did my best to give it my impartial support. It soon appeared however that we had been misled; that the facts had been presented in a false light—

DR. STOCKMANN: False—!

HOVSTAD: —an ambiguous light, if you prefer. The Mayor's report leaves no doubt on that score. I trust no one here questions my liberal principles; on the great political issues of the day, the views of *The People's Monitor* are well-known to you all. But I have learned from men of judgment and experience that when it comes to purely local matters, a newspaper should proceed with a certain amount of caution.

ASLAKSEN: I whole-heartedly endorse the speaker's views.

HOVSTAD: In the matter now under discussion public opinion is quite obviously against Dr. Stockmann. Now—what is a publisher's first and foremost duty, gentlemen? Is it not to work in harmony with his readers? Is he not obligated—by a tacit mandate, as it were—to serve indefatigably and tenaciously the interests of the majority? Or am I mistaken?

MANY VOICES: No, no! Hovstad is right!

HOVSTAD: It has not been easy, I assure you, to break with a man in whose home I have been a frequent guest of late. A man who up to this very day has enjoyed the unqualified goodwill of his fellow-citizens. A man whose only, or perhaps one should say whose chief fault, consists in following his heart rather than his head.

A FEW SCATTERED VOICES: That's true! Hurrah for Dr. Stockmann!

HOVSTAD: But my duty to Society has forced me, much against my will, to make this break. And there's another consideration that impels me to oppose him, and try, if I can, to stop him on the rash course on which he is embarked: consideration for his family, gentlemen—

DR. STOCKMANN: Stick to the sewers and water-works!

HOVSTAD: —consideration for his wife, and for his helpless children.

MORTEN: Does he mean us, Mother?

MRS. STOCKMANN: Hush!

ASLAKSEN: I shall now put the Mayor's resolution to a vote.

DR. STOCKMANN: That won't be necessary! I don't intend to speak about the filth and corruption of the Baths this evening. No! You're going to hear about something very different.

THE MAYOR (*Half to himself*): Now what's he up to?

A DRUNKEN MAN (*Near the main entrance*): I'm entitled to pay taxes—so I suppose I'm entitled to an opinion too. And it is my irrefutable and incomprehensible opinion that—

SEVERAL VOICES: Silence over there!

OTHERS: He's drunk! Throw him out!

(*The drunken man is put out.*)

DR. STOCKMANN: May I speak?

ASLAKSEN (*Ringing the bell*): Dr. Stockmann has the floor.

DR. STOCKMANN: I'd like to have seen anyone try—even a few days ago—to gag me as I've been gagged this evening. I should have fought like a lion for what I know to be my sacred rights. But that doesn't matter to me now. Now I have more important things to say.

(*The people crowd closer round him.* MORTEN KIIL *appears among the crowd.*)

DR. STOCKMANN (*Continuing*): I've done a lot of thinking these past days—turning things over in my mind, till my brain seemed all muddled and confused—

THE MAYOR (*Coughing*): Hm—!

DR. STOCKMANN: But gradually things straightened out, and I saw them in their true perspective. That's why I'm here this evening. I'm going to expose many things to you, my friends! The fact that our water-works are poisoned and that our health-resort is nothing but a pest-hole is comparatively unimportant compared to the discovery I'm about to reveal now.

MANY VOICES: No mention of the Baths! We won't listen! Leave them out of it!

DR. STOCKMANN: I've just told you—I'm going to speak about a great discovery I've made in these past days—and this is it: The very sources of our spiritual life are poisoned, and our whole community is founded on a pestilential lie!

A MURMUR OF AMAZED VOICES: What's he saying?

THE MAYOR: How dare he—!

ASLAKSEN (*His hand on the bell*): I call upon the speaker to moderate his language!

DR. STOCKMANN: No man could love his native town more than I've loved mine! I was very young when I left here, and distance, memory and homesickness combined to cast a kind of aura round the place and round its people. (*Scattered applause and expressions of approval*) I spent many years in the far North, in a God-forsaken hole of a place. I used to visit the few starving wretches scattered about in that rocky wilderness, and I often thought a horse-doctor would have served their purpose better than a man of science like myself.

(*Murmurs throughout the room.*)

BILLING (*Laying down his pen*): Strike me dead! I've never heard such—

HOVSTAD: An insult to honest country-folk!

DR. STOCKMANN: Just wait a minute! —All that time I don't think anyone could have accused me of forgetting my home town. I sat there brooding over an idea—like an eider-duck on her eggs—and what I finally hatched out was the plan for our Baths. (*Applause and protests*) And when at last fate was kind enough to make my return home possible—I felt as though my every wish had been fulfilled. I still had one wish, though; an ardent, unwavering, passionate desire to serve my home town and my fellow-citizens.

THE MAYOR (*Gazing into space*): A strange way to show it—!

DR. STOCKMANN: I was supremely happy—basking in joyous illusions. Then, yesterday morning—no, the preceding evening to be exact—I received a mental jolt; my eyes were suddenly wide open and the first thing I saw was the colossal stupidity of our reigning authorities—

(*Noise, cries and laughter.* MRS. STOCKMANN *coughs repeatedly.*)

THE MAYOR: Mr. Chairman!

ASLAKSEN (*Ringing his bell*): By virtue of my office—!

DR. STOCKMANN: Let the expression pass, Mr. Aslaksen—there's no need to be petty! I simply mean that the whole disgraceful situation at the Baths was suddenly revealed to me—a mess for which the so-called leading men of the town must take the blame. These leading men—I'm sick of them and all their works! They're like a lot of goats let loose in a young orchard —destroying everything; they stand in the way of free men and hamper them at every turn. For my part I'd like to see them exterminated together with all other predatory creatures—

(*Uproar in the room.*)

THE MAYOR: Mr. Chairman—can such things be allowed?

ASLAKSEN (*His hand on the bell*): Dr. Stockmann—!

DR. STOCKMANN: I can't conceive why it should have taken me so long to see through these gentlemen; every single day I've had a prime example before my very eyes—my brother Peter—empty of ideas and filled with prejudice—

(*Laughter, noise and catcalls.* MRS. STOCKMANN *coughs.* ASLAKSEN *violently rings his bell.*)

THE DRUNKEN MAN (*Who has returned*): Are you referring to me? My name's Pettersen all right—but I'll be damned if—

ANGRY VOICES: Throw him out! Throw that drunk out!

(*They throw him out again.*)

THE MAYOR: Who was that person?

A BYSTANDER: I don't know him, Your Honor.

ANOTHER MAN: He's not from around here.

A THIRD MAN: He must be that lumber-dealer from— (*The rest is inaudible.*)

ASLAKSEN: The man was unquestionably intoxicated. Proceed, Dr. Stockmann; but with moderation, if you please!

DR. STOCKMANN: Well, fellow-citizens, I shall say no more about our leading men. And if anyone imagines, after what I have just said, that I'm here to attack these gentlemen this evening, he is quite wrong I assure you. You see, I cherish the comfortable conviction that these reactionaries, these relics of another age, are busily engaged in cutting their own throats—they don't need a doctor to help them. And besides, they are not the worst menace to Society; it is not primarily due to them that our spiritual well-being is endangered, and that the very ground we stand on reeks with corruption. They are not the most dangerous enemies to truth and freedom!

CRIES FROM ALL SIDES: Who then? Who do you mean? Name them! Name them!

DR. STOCKMANN: Oh, I shall name them—never fear! You see, that is my great discovery; I made it yesterday. (*Raising his voice*) In our Society, the worst enemy to truth and freedom is the majority. Yes! The damnable, solid, liberal majority—that's the great menace! There's your answer!

(*Great commotion in the room. Most of the audience are shouting, stamping and whistling. A few old gentlemen exchange covert glances and seem to be enjoying the situation.* MRS. STOCKMANN *gets up anxiously;* EJLIF *and* MORTEN *advance threateningly towards the schoolboys who are making catcalls.* ASLAKSEN *rings his bell and calls for order.* HOVSTAD *and* BILLING *both try to speak but are drowned out. At last quiet is restored.*)

ASLAKSEN: The speaker is requested to withdraw this outrageous statement.

DR. STOCKMANN: Never, Mr. Aslaksen—never! This same great majority robs me of my freedom, and wishes to prevent me from stating the truth!

HOVSTAD: The majority is always right.

BILLING: Yes—but, strike me dead—truth is right too!

DR. STOCKMANN: The majority is never right—never, I tell you!

That's one of those social lies against which every free, intelligent man ought to rebel. What does the majority consist of—of wise men or of fools? I think we must all of us agree that from one end of the world to the other the proportion is overwhelmingly in favor of the fools. And are wise men to be ruled by fools? What could be more senseless! (*Uproar and yells*) You can shout me down if you like, but you can't deny it! The majority has the power, unfortunately—but right is on the side of people like me—of the few—of the individual. It's the minority that's always right! (*Renewed commotion*.)

HOVSTAD: Ha, ha! Dr. Stockmann has turned aristocrat!

DR. STOCKMANN: I've said I won't waste any words on that little rear-guard of puny, narrow-chested, self-important men—the stream of life has already left them far behind. I'm thinking of the few—those rare spirits among us who have had the vision to recognize the truth in new ideas, new ways of thought—and have made those ways their own. These men are in the vanguard—so far ahead that the solid majority can't begin to reach them; and there they fight for new-born truths—too new and too daring to be accepted by that sacred majority of yours.

HOVSTAD: Now he's a revolutionist!

DR. STOCKMANN: Yes, by Heaven, I am, Mr. Hovstad! I intend to revolt against the lie that truth belongs exclusively to the majority. And what are these truths the majority worships? They're truths so old and worn—they're practically decrepit. And when a truth reaches that age you can hardly tell it from a lie! (*Laughter and jeers*) You can believe me or not as you like; but truths are not such tough old Methuselahs as most people imagine. A normal, ordinary truth is good for, say, seventeen or eighteen—at most twenty years; seldom more. And truths as venerable as that are nothing but skin and bones; yet it isn't until then that the great majority adopts them and prescribes them to Society as wholesome spiritual food. But there's not much nourishment in that kind of a diet, I assure you; as a doctor you can take my word for that. These tired old truths are as rancid and moldy as last year's bacon; they're the cause of all that moral scurvy that plagues Society.

ASLAKSEN: Our honored speaker appears to have strayed somewhat from his subject.

THE MAYOR: I heartily endorse the chairman's observation.

DR. STOCKMANN: You must be mad, Peter! I'm doing my best to stick to my subject; I'm saying that it's the masses—that damnable solid majority—that poison the sources of our spiritual life and corrupt the very ground we walk on.

HOVSTAD: I see; in other words you condemn the great majority of liberal-minded men for having sense enough to rely on truths that are fundamental and conclusive.

DR. STOCKMANN: My dear Mr. Hovstad, don't speak about fundamental truths! The truths endorsed by the great majority of men today were considered fundamental by the vanguard in our grandfather's time; they are no longer endorsed by the vanguard of today. There's only one fundamental truth, in my opinion—and that is that Society cannot live a healthy life based on truths that have become old and spineless.

HOVSTAD: Can't you be more explicit? Instead of this vague talk, give us some examples of these so-called spineless truths you say we base our lives on.

(*Approval from several parts of the room.*)

DR. STOCKMANN: I could give you innumerable examples—but one will serve: the fundamental truth which, though basically a lie, you and your *People's Monitor* and its adherents swear by all the same—

HOVSTAD: —which is?

DR. STOCKMANN: A doctrine inherited from your grandparents, and that you thoughtlessly go on proclaiming far and wide; the doctrine that the common herd, the crowd, the masses, are the very flower of the people—in fact *are* the people—and that the uncouth man, the vulgar man, the ignorant and unevolved, have the same right to condemn and sanction, to govern and counsel, as the intellectually and spiritually distinguished few.

BILLING: Well—strike me dead! I've never—!

HOVSTAD (*Shouting at the same time*): Take note of this, citizens!

ANGRY VOICES: Aren't we the people? Are we to have no say?

A WORKMAN: A man who talks like that deserves to be kicked out!

OTHERS: Throw him out!

A MAN (*Shouting*): Now's the time to blow your horn, Evensen! (*The deep notes of a horn are heard; whistles, catcalls and uproar.*)

DR. STOCKMANN (*As the noise subsides*): Be reasonable! Can't you endure the truth? I don't expect you all to agree with me—but I certainly thought Mr. Hovstad would calm down and back me up. Mr. Hovstad lays claim to being a free-thinker—

SEVERAL VOICES (*Subdued and astonished*): A free-thinker, did he say? What? Hovstad a free-thinker?

HOVSTAD: I dare you to prove it, Dr. Stockmann! Have I ever said so in black and white?

DR. STOCKMANN: No, damn it—you've never had the courage! Well, I don't want to get you into trouble; I'm the one who's the free-thinker, Mr. Hovstad. And now—let me prove to you all, scientifically, that *The People's Monitor* makes fools of you and leads you by the nose when it tells you that you , the masses, the crowd, are the flower of the people. That's just a journalistic lie! The masses are only the raw material from which a People can be made. (*Murmurs, laughter and general disturbance*) It's the same thing in all other forms of life. Fine animals are created by breeding and selection. Take an ordinary common hen, for instance—she's not much good for eating, and her eggs are not much better than a crow's eggs—or a raven's; she can't be compared with a really fine strain of poultry. But now take a Japanese or Spanish hen—a pheasant or a turkey—and you'll soon see the difference! Or in the case of dogs—so closely related to mankind; think first of a common ordinary cur—one of those filthy, ragged, plebian mongrels that haunt the gutters and dirty up the side-walks; and compare that mongrel with a pedigreed poodle, bred for generations from the finest stock, used to good food and accustomed to well-modulated voices and the sound of music. Don't you suppose the poodle's brain shows a marked superior-

ity? Of course it does! A trainer can take a poodle pup like that
and teach it the most fantastic tricks—things a common mongrel
could never dream of learning!

(Noise and laughter.)

A MAN *(Shouting)*: Are you comparing us with dogs?

ANOTHER: We're not animals, Doctor!

DR. STOCKMANN: Of course you are! We're all animals, my friend!
What are we else? But there aren't many well-bred animals
among us. There's a tremendous difference between poodle-
men and mongrel-men. And it's so ridiculous—Mr. Hovstad
agrees with me entirely as long as it's four-legged animals we're
talking of—

HOVSTAD: An animal's an animal—and there's an end of it!

DR. STOCKMANN: Perhaps; but as soon as I apply the rule to two-
legged animals, Mr. Hovstad rebels; he no longer has the courage of his convictions—he refuses to think things through to the
end; so he turns the rule upside down and proclaims in the *Monitor* that the ordinary hen and the common cur are the prize specimens in the menagerie. And that's the way it'll always be, while
we allow the cur in us to triumph, instead of working our way up
to some sort of spiritual distinction.

HOVSTAD: I make no pretense of being distinguished in any way; I
come from simple peasant stock and I'm proud of it. I'm proud to
belong to those common people you're insulting!

SOME WORKMEN: Hurrah for Hovstad! Hurrah! Hurrah!

DR. STOCKMANN: The kind of common people I mean don't necessarily come from the lower classes; they're crawling and
swarming all around us—you often find them in the very top
ranks of Society. You've only to look at that smug, respectable
Mayor of yours! He's about as low as any man that ever walked
on two feet—

THE MAYOR: I must protest against these personal remarks!

DR. STOCKMANN: —and that has nothing to do with the fact that
one of our ancestors was a disgusting old pirate from somewhere
in Pomerania—

THE MAYOR: Pure invention! Utterly groundless!

DR. STOCKMANN: —no! It's because he thinks the thoughts of his superiors in office, and kow-tows to their opinions. And people who do that are common in spirit; that's why, in spite of his magnificence, my brother Peter is so fundamentally lacking in distinction, and is consequently so anti-liberal.

THE MAYOR: Mr. Chairman—!

HOVSTAD: So it seems you have to be a liberal to be distinguished! That's a new point of view if you like!

(Laughter)

DR. STOCKMANN: Yes, that's part of my new discovery too. And there's something else: I've discovered that morality and liberalism are almost precisely the same thing. That's why I consider it downright inexcusable of The People's Monitor to go on proclaiming day in and day out that morality and liberalism are the sole monopoly of the mob and the masses; and that culture automatically generates vice and spiritual depravity—just as the filth from the Milldale Tanneries generates the poison that pollutes our water-works. (Noise and interruptions) And yet this same People's Monitor prates about raising the masses to a higher level! Why, damn it—if the Monitor's premise were really sound, raising them to a higher level would be equivalent to hurling them straight to perdition! Fortunately the theory that culture demoralizes is just another of those lies handed down from the past. No! Stupidity, poverty and ugliness are the true evils—they're demoralizing if you like! And to live in a house that is never aired, and where the floors are never swept—my wife, incidentally, claims that floors should be scrubbed every day, but that's a debatable point—that's demoralizing too! Lack of oxygen weakens the moral fiber. And there must be precious little oxygen in the houses around here, if the moral fiber of our citizens is so feeble that the great majority of them are anxious and willing to build the future of our town on a foundation of hypocrisy and lies!

ASLAKSEN: This is an insult to the entire community—we shall not tolerate it!

A GENTLEMAN: I move that the speaker be called to order!

EAGER VOICES: Yes, yes! He's right! Sit down! Sit down!

DR. STOCKMANN (Flaring up): Then I shall shout it from the

house-tops! I'll write to all the newspapers! I'll let the whole country know of the situation here!

HOVSTAD: Dr. Stockmann is evidently bent on ruining the town.

DR. STOCKMANN: I love my native town so much that I'd rather see it ruined than prosper on a lie!

ASLAKSEN: There's a statement for you!

(Noise and catcalls. MRS. STOCKMANN *coughs in vain; the doctor no longer hears her.)*

HOVSTAD *(Shouting above the tumult)*: You're an enemy to this whole community, or you couldn't talk so lightly of the ruin of the town!

DR. STOCKMANN *(With growing excitement)*: A community based on lies and corruption deserves to be destroyed! Men who live on lies should be wiped out like a lot of vermin. This poison will spread throughout the country, and eventually the whole country will deserve to be destroyed; and, should it ever come to that, I'd say from the bottom of my heart: let it be destroyed, and let all its people perish!

A MAN *(In the crowd)*: He's the People's enemy—that's what he is!

BILLING: Strike me dead! Did you hear that? The Voice of the People!

THE WHOLE CROWD *(Shouting)*: Yes, yes, yes! He's an enemy of the People! He's a traitor to his country! He's against the People!

ASLAKSEN: As a citizen of this town, and as a human being, I am deeply shocked by what I have heard here tonight. I must regretfully concur with the sentiments expressed by so many of my fellow-citizens, and I move that those sentiments be formulated in the following resolution: "This meeting hereby declares the former medical adviser to the Baths, Dr. Tomas Stockmann, to be an enemy of the People."

(Thunders of applause and cheers. A number of people crowd around DR. STOCKMANN, *jeering and booing.* MRS. STOCKMANN *and* PETRA *have risen.* MORTEN *and* EJLIF *exchange blows with some of the schoolboys who have joined in the jeering. Some grownups separate them.)*

DR. STOCKMANN *(To the jeering crowd)*: Fools! You fools! I tell you that—

ASLAKSEN (*Ringing his bell*): Doctor Stockmann is out of order! A formal vote must now be taken. However, out of consideration for personal feelings, it will be by secret ballot. Have you any sheets of blank paper, Mr. Billing?

BILLING: Yes—I have some here; both blue and white.

ASLAKSEN: Splendid. That will expedite matters. We'll just cut it into slips— There! (*To the meeting*) Blue stands for no, and white for yes. I shall collect the votes myself.

(THE MAYOR *leaves the room.* ASLAKSEN *and a couple of others circulate about the room with the pieces of paper in hats.*)

A GENTLEMAN (*To* HOVSTAD): What can be the matter with the doctor? I don't know what to make of it!

HOVSTAD: He's a dreadfully impetuous man, you know!

ANOTHER GENTLEMAN (*To* BILLING): You've been a guest there; tell me—does the fellow drink?

BILLING: Strike me dead—I don't know how to answer that. I know there's always plenty of hot toddy in the house!

A THIRD GENTLEMAN: He strikes me as unbalanced.

FIRST GENTLEMAN: Is there any insanity in the family, I wonder?

BILLING: I don't know—I shouldn't be surprised.

A FOURTH GENTLEMAN: It's pure malice, if you ask me. He's got a chip on his shoulder about something.

BILLING: I remember one day he mentioned wanting a raise in salary—but I know he didn't get it.

ALL THE GENTLEMEN (*Together*): Then that must be it, of course!

THE DRUNKEN MAN (*In the crowd*): Give me a blue one! And I want a white one, too!

SEVERAL PEOPLE: There's that drunk again! Throw him out!

MORTEN KIIL (*Comes up to* STOCKMANN): Well, Stockmann! Look where your monkey-tricks have led to!

DR. STOCKMANN: I've simply done my duty.

MORTEN KIIL: What was that you said about the Milldale Tanneries?

DR. STOCKMANN: You heard; I said they generated filth.

MORTEN KIIL: You mean mine too?

DR. STOCKMANN: Yours is among the worst.

MORTEN KIIL: And are you going to print that in the papers?

DR. STOCKMANN: I shall keep nothing back.

MORTEN KIIL: It'll cost you dear—I warn you! *(He goes out.)*

A FAT GENTLEMAN *(Goes up to HORSTER without bowing to the ladies)*: I see you lend your house to enemies of the People, Captain.

HORSTER: I've a right to use my property as I see fit, sir.

THE GENTLEMAN: Very good. Then I shall follow your example.

HORSTER: What do you mean by that?

THE GENTLEMAN: You'll hear from me tomorrow. *(Turns away and goes out.)*

PETRA: Captain Horster—wasn't that the owner of your ship?

HORSTER: Mr. Vik, yes.

ASLAKSEN *(His hands full of slips of paper, mounts the platform and rings)*: Allow me to announce the result of the vote, gentlemen. All the voters, with one exception—

A YOUNG GENTLEMAN: That must have been the drunk!

ASLAKSEN: With the exception of one intoxicated person this meeting unanimously declares Dr. Tomas Stockmann to be an enemy of the People. *(Cheers and applause)* Three cheers for our deeply loved and honorable community! *(Cheers)* And three cheers for our able and energetic Mayor who has so loyally set family prejudice aside! *(Cheers)* The meeting is adjourned. *(He steps down from the platform.)*

BILLING: Let's have three cheers for the chairman!

ALL: Three cheers for Aslaksen!

DR. STOCKMAN: Give me my hat and coat, Petra. Captain—have you room for any passengers on your trip to the New World?

HORSTER: There'll always be room for you and yours, Dr. Stockmann.

DR. STOCKMANN *(As PETRA helps him with his coat)*: Thanks. Come, Katrine! Come, boys! *(He gives his wife his arm.)*

MRS. STOCKMANN *(In a low voice)*: Let's go out the back way, Tomas, dear.

DR. STOCKMANN: No back ways for us, Katrine. *(Raises his voice)* You'll hear more from the enemy of the People before he finally shakes the dust off his feet! I'm not as forbearing as a certain person I could mention; I can't bring myself to say "I forgive you, for you know not what you do."

ASLAKSEN: That comparison is blasphemous, Doctor Stockmann!

BILLING: Strike me—! If that isn't too much for a decent man to stand!

A COARSE VOICE: And he actually threatens us, too!

ANGRY SHOUTS: Let's smash in his windows! Duck him in the fjord!

A MAN (*In the crowd*): Blow your horn, Evensen! Go on, man! Blow!

(*Horn-blowing, whistles and catcalls; wild shouts.* DR. STOCK-MANN *and his family go towards the door—*CAPTAIN HORSTER *clears the way for them.*)

ALL (*Yelling after them as they go out*): Enemy of the People! Enemy of the People! Enemy of the People!

BILLING: Strike me dead! I wouldn't want to drink toddy at the Stockmanns' house tonight!

(*The people throng towards the door; the shouting is taken up outside; from the street cries of "Enemy of the People! Enemy of the People!" are heard.*)

CURTAIN

ACT FIVE

SCENE: DR. STOCKMANN'S *study. The walls are lined with bookshelves and glass cabinets containing various medicines. In the back wall is the door to the living room. Two windows in the wall right, with all the panes smashed in. In the center of the room is the doctor's desk covered with books and papers. The room is in disorder. It is morning.* DR. STOCKMANN *in a dressing-gown and slippers and with a skull-cap on his head is stooping down and raking under one of the cabinets with an umbrella; he succeeds in raking out a stone.*

DR. STOCKMANN *(Calling through the open door)*: Here's another one, Katrine!

MRS. STOCKMANN *(From the living room)*: You'll find a lot more, I expect.

DR. STOCKMANN *(Adds the stone to a pile on the table)*: I'm going to keep these stones, Katrine; they're precious relics. I want Morten and Ejlif to have them constantly before their eyes—and I'll leave them as a heritage. *(Raking about under the book-case)* By the way, hasn't—what the devil *is* that girl's name—hasn't she been to the glazier yet?

MRS. STOCKMANN *(Coming in)*: Yes; but he wasn't sure he could come today.

DR. STOCKMANN: I suppose he doesn't dare.

MRS. STOCKMANN: That's what Randina thinks; she thinks he's afraid of the neighbors. *(Talks to someone in the living room)* What is it, Randina? Oh, thanks. *(Goes out and returns immediately)* A letter for you, dear.

DR. STOCKMANN: Let's see. *(Opens the letter and reads)* Well —it's not surprising!

MRS. STOCKMANN: Who is it from?

DR. STOCKMANN: The landlord. He's giving us notice.

MRS. STOCKMANN: Not really! He's such a nice man, too—!

DR. STOCKMANN *(Glancing at the letter)*: He daren't do otherwise, he says. He's very sorry; but he daren't do otherwise —public opinion—he has to earn his living—he's afraid of offending certain influential men—and so on.

MRS. STOCKMANN: That just shows you, Tomas.

DR. STOCKMANN: Oh, yes; it shows me right enough. They're all cowards in this town; no one dares do anything for fear of offending someone else. *(Flings the letter on the table)* Well—what do we care, Katrine; we're off to the New World—

MRS. STOCKMANN: You really think that's a wise decision, Tomas?

DR. STOCKMANN: You don't expect me to stay here, do you? After
being spat on? After being branded as an enemy of the People
and having my windows smashed? And, look, Katrine! Somebody actually tore a hole in my black trousers!

MRS. STOCKMANN: Oh, Tomas! And they're your best ones too!

DR. STOCKMANN: Yes! Well—you should never wear your best
trousers when you go out to fight for truth and freedom! But I
don't care so much about the trousers—you can always patch
them up for me. What I can't stomach is having that mob attack
me as though they were my equals!

MRS. STOCKMANN: I know, Tomas; they've behaved abominably
to you here. But does that necessarily mean we have to leave the
country altogether?

DR. STOCKMANN: It'd be just as bad in all the other towns; the
mob is just as insolent-minded there as here. Well—to Hell with
it! Let the mongrels yap; that's not the worst of it. The worst of it
is that all over the country men are nothing but abject slaves to
the party-bosses. Not that the so-called Free West is apt to be
much better; I daresay enlightened public opinion, the solid majority and all the rest of the trash is just as rampant there—but at
least it's on a bigger scale; they may kill a man, but they don't put
him to slow torture; they don't clamp a free soul into a strait
jacket. And, at a pinch, there's room to get away. (*Walks up and
down*) If only I knew of some primeval forest, some little South-
Sea island that was going cheap—

MRS. STOCKMANN: But—what about the boys, Tomas?

DR. STOCKMANN (*Comes to a standstill*): What an amazing
woman you are, Katrine! You wouldn't really want the boys to
grow up in a society like ours, would you? You must have seen
last night that half the population of this town is raving
mad—and if the other half hasn't lost its wits, it's only because
they're such block-heads that they have no wits to lose!

MRS. STOCKMANN: Dear Tomas—you say such reckless things!

DR. STOCKMANN: Well—isn't it true? They turn every idea
upside-down; they make a hotch-potch out of right and wrong;
they take lies for truth and truth for lies. But the craziest thing of
all is to see a lot of grownup men calling themselves Liberals,

parading about pretending to themselves and others that they're friends of freedom! You must admit that's pretty silly!

MRS. STOCKMANN: Yes; I suppose it is, but—(PETRA *enters from the living room*) Home from school already, Petra?

PETRA: I've been dismissed.

MRS. STOCKMANN: Dismissed!

DR. STOCKMANN: You too!

PETRA: Mrs. Busk gave me my notice—so I thought I'd better leave at once.

DR. STOCKMANN: You were quite right!

MRS. STOCKMANN: Fancy Mrs. Busk doing a thing like that! How disgraceful of her!

PETRA: It wasn't disgraceful of her, Mother. I could see how upset she was. But she didn't dare do otherwise, she said. So—I'm dismissed.

DR. STOCKMANN (*Laughs and rubs his hands*): She didn't dare do otherwise—just like the rest! This is delightful!

MRS. STOCKMANN: I suppose—after that dreadful scene last night—

PETRA: It wasn't only that. Father—listen to this!

DR. STOCKMANN: Well?

PETRA: Mrs. Busk showed me at least three letters she'd received this morning—

DR. STOCKMANN: Anonymous, of course?

PETRA: Yes.

DR. STOCKMANN: They never dare sign their names, Katrine!

PETRA: Two of them warned her that a certain gentleman—a frequent visitor at our house, so he said—had been talking at the club last night, and telling everyone that my views on certain subjects were decidedly advanced—

DR. STOCKMANN: I hope you didn't deny it!

PETRA: Of course not! Mrs. Busk has fairly advanced views too—that is, in private; but since I'd been publicly accused, she dared not keep me on.

MRS. STOCKMANN: A frequent visitor—just think of it! You see, Tomas—that's what comes of all your hospitality!

DR. STOCKMANN: We won't stay in this pig sty any longer. Get packed as soon as you can, Katrine. We'll leave this place at once—the sooner the better!

MRS. STOCKMANN: Be quiet a moment; I thought I heard some-one in the hall. See who it is, Petra.

PETRA *(Opens the hall door)*: Oh, it's you, Captain Horster! Do come in.

HORSTER *(From the hall)*: Good morning. I thought I'd just come over and see how you were getting on.

DR. STOCKMANN *(Shaking his hand)*: Thanks; that's very kind of you.

MRS. STOCKMANN: And thank you, Captain Horster, for helping us last night.

PETRA: How did you ever manage to get home?

HORSTER: It wasn't bad—I'm a pretty hefty man, you know. And, anyway—there was more noise than action!

DR. STOCKMANN: Isn't it amazing what cowards those people are? Come here—I want to show you something. Here are all the stones they threw in at us last night. Just look at them! There aren't more than two decent stones among the lot; most of them are pebbles—a lot of gravel! And yet they stood out there shouting and yelling that they were going to kill me! But as for really doing it—oh, no! Nothing as positive as that!

HORSTER: Well—for once—I should think you'd have been grate-ful, Doctor!

DR. STOCKMANN: Oh, I am—of course! But it's tragic all the same; I sometimes think—supposing a really serious struggle of na-tional proportions were involved; you can be sure enlightened public opinion would instantly take to its heels and run away, and the great solid majority would scatter like a herd of fright-ened sheep; that's the depressing part of it—it makes me sick to think of. But, damn it—why should I care what they do! They've called me an enemy of the People, so I might as well *be* an enemy of the People!

MRS. STOCKMANN: You'll never be that, Tomas.

DR. STOCKMANN: I wouldn't be too sure, Katrine. One ugly word can act as an irritant sometimes—and that damned expression—! I can't get rid of it; it's dug its way into the pit of my stomach— I feel it gnawing away there like a bitter acid. All the magnesia tablets in the world won't make it stop!

PETRA: They're not worth taking seriously, Father.

HORSTER: Some day they'll change their minds, Doctor—you'll see.

MRS. STOCKMANN: Yes, Tomas; I'm sure of that.

DR. STOCKMANN: They may—when it's too late. Well—serve them right! Let them wallow in their filth and cry their hearts out with remorse at having driven a patriot into exile. When do you sail, Captain?

HORSTER: Hm—that's really what I wanted to talk to you about—

DR. STOCKMANN: Oh? Is anything the matter with the ship?

HORSTER: No, nothing; except—I shan't be with her.

PETRA: You surely haven't been dismissed?

HORSTER (With a smile): But I have, you see.

PETRA: You, too.

MRS. STOCKMANN: That just shows you, Tomas.

DR. STOCKMANN: And all for the sake of truth! If I'd thought anything like this could happen—!

HORSTER: You mustn't be upset. Some other company will take me on.

DR. STOCKMANN: And to think that a man like Vik—! A man of means—who can afford to be completely independent—! How disgusting!

HORSTER: He's not such a bad man, really. He told me himself he'd like to keep me on—only he didn't dare—

DR. STOCKMANN: He didn't dare! Of course not!

HORSTER: He said it wasn't always easy—when you're a member of a party—

DR. STOCKMANN: He hit the nail on the head that time! A party—! A sausage-machine—that's what a party's like! All the brains are ground up together and reduced to hash; and that's why the world is filled with a lot of brainless, empty-headed numskulls!

MRS. STOCKMANN: Tomas! Please!

PETRA (To HORSTER): If you hadn't seen us home, this mightn't have happened.

HORSTER: I don't regret it.

PETRA (*Holds out her hand to him*): Thank you!

HORSTER: But I wanted to tell you this: if you're really bent on going—there's another way it could be—

MRS. STOCKMANN: Hush! I thought I heard a knock.

PETRA: I believe it's Uncle.

DR. STOCKMANN: Aha! (*Calls*) Come in!

MRS. STOCKMANN: Now, Tomas—promise me, please—!

(THE MAYOR *enters from the hall*.)

THE MAYOR (*In the doorway*): Oh, you're busy. Then I'd better—

DR. STOCKMANN: No, no. Come in.

THE MAYOR: I wanted to speak to you alone.

MRS. STOCKMANN: We'll go into the living room.

HORSTER: I'll come back later, then.

DR. STOCKMANN: No, Captain Horster—don't go away. I'm anxious to hear more about—

HORSTER: Very well; I'll wait.

(*He follows* MRS. STOCKMANN *and* PETRA *into the living room.* THE MAYOR *says nothing, but glances at the windows*.)

DR. STOCKMANN: A bit draughty, isn't it? Better put on your hat.

THE MAYOR: Thanks—if I may. (*Does so*) I think I caught cold last night. I felt a sudden chill—

DR. STOCKMANN: Really? I thought it was a bit on the warm side!

THE MAYOR: I regret I was unable to prevent that most unfortunate business.

DR. STOCKMANN: Is there anything special you want to say to me?

THE MAYOR (*Producing a large envelope*): The management of the Baths sends you this document.

DR. STOCKMANN: My dismissal, I suppose.

THE MAYOR: Yes—as of today. We regret this decision but, frankly, we didn't dare do otherwise. Out of respect for public opinion, you understand.

DR. STOCKMANN: Didn't dare do otherwise. I seem to have heard those words before, today.

THE MAYOR: I think you should face the fact that from now on you won't be able to count on any practice here.

DR. STOCKMANN: To hell with my practice! But why are you so sure of that?

THE MAYOR: The Home-owners Association is circulating a petition urging all respectable citizens to refrain from calling on your services. Of course everyone will sign it—they wouldn't dare do otherwise.

DR. STOCKMANN: I don't doubt that. What else?

THE MAYOR: If you take my advice, you'll leave town for a while.

DR. STOCKMANN: Yes; I've already given serious thought to that.

THE MAYOR: You're wise. Then—after six months or so—when you've had time to think things over, you might perhaps feel ready to write us a few words of apology, admitting your mistake—

DR. STOCKMANN: And then I might be re-instated, do you think?

THE MAYOR: You might; it's by no means impossible.

DR. STOCKMANN: But what about public opinion? Aren't you forgetting that?

THE MAYOR: Public opinion has a way of changing; and, quite frankly, it would be greatly to our advantage to have a signed statement from you to that effect.

DR. STOCKMANN: Yes—I dare say it would be most convenient! I've already told you how I feel about that kind of crookedness.

THE MAYOR: You were in a very different position then. At that time you imagined you had the whole town at your back—

DR. STOCKMANN: And now, it seems, I have the whole town *on* my back! (*Flaring up*) But I don't care if the devil himself were on my back, I'll never consent to—! Never, I tell you; never!

THE MAYOR: As a family man you have no right to take this stand, Tomas. You simply have no right!

DR. STOCKMANN: I have no right, have I? There's only one thing in this world a free man has no right to do; you don't know what that is, do you?

THE MAYOR: No, I don't.

DR. STOCKMANN: Of course not; then I'll tell you. A free man has no right to wallow in filth. A free man has no right to debase himself to the point of wanting to spit in his own face!

THE MAYOR: That might sound quite convincing if there were no other explanation for your pig-headedness; but of course we know there is—

DR. STOCKMANN: What do you mean?

THE MAYOR: You know quite well what I mean. However as your brother, and as a man of some experience, I advise you not to put too much faith in certain hopes and prospects that may prove disappointing.

DR. STOCKMANN: What on earth are you getting at?

THE MAYOR: Don't try to tell me you're unaware of the terms of old Morten Kiil's will!

DR. STOCKMANN: I only know he's left what little he has to a home for indigent workmen. It's no business of mine.

THE MAYOR: To begin with, "what little he has" amounts to a considerable sum. Morten Kiil is a very wealthy man.

DR. STOCKMANN: I had no idea of that—

THE MAYOR: No? Are you sure? Perhaps you had no idea either that a large part of his fortune is to be placed in a trust fund for your children; and that during your lifetime you and your wife are to enjoy the income from this trust. Did he never tell you that?

DR. STOCKMANN: He never breathed a word of it! In fact he does nothing but complain how poor he is, and grumble about taxes. Peter—are you quite sure of this?

THE MAYOR: Quite sure. My information is most reliable.

DR. STOCKMANN: But—good heavens! Then the children are provided for—and Katrine too! I must tell her this at once— (*Calls*) Katrine, Katrine!

THE MAYOR (*Holding him back*): No, wait! Don't tell her yet.

MRS. STOCKMANN (*Opens the door*): What is it, dear?

DR. STOCKMANN: It's nothing; never mind.

(MRS. STOCKMANN *closes the door again*.)

DR. STOCKMANN (*Pacing up and down*): To think of it—provided for! All of them provided for—and for life too. How wonderful to feel one is provided for!

THE MAYOR: But that's just what you're not, you see. Morten Kiil can change his will whenever he sees fit.

DR. STOCKMANN: Oh, but he won't, Peter! The old badger's much too pleased with me for unmasking you and your precious friends.

THE MAYOR (*Starts and looks at him intently*): I see! That puts things in quite a different light.

DR. STOCKMANN: What things?

THE MAYOR: So it was all a put-up job! Those violent attacks you made on the leading men of the town—all in the name of truth, of course—were actually nothing but—!

DR. STOCKMANN: But what?

THE MAYOR: —nothing but a kind of sop to that vindictive old miser Morten Kiil. That was his reward for leaving all that money to you in his will!

DR. STOCKMANN: Peter—upon my word you are the lowest of the low!

THE MAYOR: I shall have no further dealings with you; your dismissal is irrevocable. We are well armed against you now. (*He goes out.*)

DR. STOCKMANN: Of all the filthy—! (*Calls*) Katrine! Have this floor scrubbed at once! Tell the girl—what the devil's her—*you* know—the girl with the smutty nose—to bring her pail and scrub-brush!

MRS. STOCKMANN (*In the doorway*): Tomas, Tomas! Hush!

PETRA (*Also in the doorway*): Father; Grandfather's here. He wants to know if he can speak to you alone.

DR. STOCKMANN: Of course he can. (*By the door*) Come in, sir. (MORTEN KIIL *enters.* STOCKMANN *closes the door behind him.*)

DR. STOCKMANN: Well, what is it? Won't you sit down?

MORTEN KIIL: No thanks. (*He looks round*) Well, Stockmann—things look very cozy here.

DR. STOCKMANN: Yes, don't they?

MORTEN KIIL: Very cozy indeed; a nice lot of fresh air too; plenty of that oxygen you talked so much about. Your moral fiber must be flourishing.

DR. STOCKMANN: It is.

MORTEN KIIL: Yes, to be sure. (*Tapping his breast pocket*) But do you know what I have here?

DR. STOCKMANN: Plenty of moral fiber too, I hope.

MORTEN KIIL: Something much better than that, I can assure you.

(Takes out a large wallet, opens it, and shows STOCKMANN *a bundle of papers.)*

DR. STOCKMANN *(Looks at him in amazement)*: Shares? Shares in the Baths?

MORTEN KIIL: They were easy enough to get today.

DR. STOCKMANN: Do you mean to say you've bought up—?

MORTEN KIIL: All I could lay my hands on!

DR. STOCKMANN: But, my dear sir—you know the present situation at the Baths—!

MORTEN KIIL: If you behave like a sensible man, you'll soon set that right again.

DR. STOCKMANN: You know I've tried to do everything I can —but these people are all lunatics!

MORTEN KIIL: You said last night that the worst filth came from my tannery. Now supposing that were true—it means that my father and my grandfather before me, and I myself for many years, have been poisoning the town—like three demons of destruction. You don't expect me to accept that accusation calmly, do you?

DR. STOCKMANN: I'm afraid you'll have to.

MORTEN KIIL: No thank you; my good name and reputation mean too much to me. People call me "the badger," so I'm told; and a badger's a kind of a pig, they tell me. But I intend to prove them wrong. While I live and after I die, my name shall be kept spotless.

DR. STOCKMANN: How are you going to manage that?

MORTEN KIIL: *You* are going to manage that for me, Stockmann. You are going to clear my name for me.

DR. STOCKMANN: I!

MORTEN KIIL: Do you know what money I used to buy these shares? No, of course you don't—but now I'm going to tell you. I used all the money Katrine, Petra and the boys were to inherit from me. For, in spite of everything, I have managed to save quite a bit, you see.

DR. STOCKMANN *(Flaring up)*: Do you mean to say you used Katrine's money to do this!

MORTEN KIIL: Yes—I've invested every penny of it in the Baths.

Now let's see how much of a madman you really are, Stockmann.
Now if you keep on spreading this story that a lot of filthy animals
seep into the water from my tannery, you'll just be flaying pieces
of skin off Katrine, and off Petra too—to say nothing of the boys,
of course. No decent father would dream of doing that—unless
he were a madman.

DR. STOCKMANN (*Pacing up and down*): But I am a madman; I *am*
a madman, don't you see?

MORTEN KIIL: Sacrifice your wife and children? You couldn't be as
stark raving mad as that!

DR. STOCKMANN (*Stopping in front of him*): Why in God's name
didn't you talk to me before buying all this rubbish?

MORTEN KIIL: What's done is done; it's too late now.

DR. STOCKMANN (*Walking about restlessly*): If only I weren't so
absolutely certain—! But I'm absolutely positive I'm right.

MORTEN KIIL (*Weighing the wallet in his hand*): If you persist in
this lunacy, these things won't be worth much, will they? (*Puts
the wallet back in his pocket.*)

DR. STOCKMANN: Damn it! Surely there must be some scientific
way of purifying the water—some sort of disinfectant—

MORTEN KIIL: To kill those animals, you mean?

DR. STOCKMANN: Yes—or at least to make them harmless.

MORTEN KIIL: You might try rat-poison.

DR. STOCKMANN: Oh! Don't talk nonsense!—And since everyone
says it's merely an illusion on my part—why not let it be an illusion then! Let them have their way! Ignorant, damnable mongrels that they are! They've called me an enemy of the
People—torn the clothes off my back—

MORTEN KIIL: And smashed in all your windows!

DR. STOCKMANN: And one has a duty toward one's family, after
all. I must talk it over with Katrine. She's better at these things
than I am.

MORTEN KIIL: A good idea; she'll give you sensible advice.

DR. STOCKMANN (*Turns on him angrily*): How could you behave
in this fantastic manner? Gambling with Katrine's money; putting me through this agony—this torment! What kind of a devil
are you!

MORTEN KIIL: If I'm a devil, perhaps I'd better go. But I want your decision—either yes or no—by two o'clock. If the answer's "no," I'll make these over to charity at once—this very day.

DR. STOCKMANN: And what will Katrine get?

MORTEN KIIL: Not a damn penny! (*The door to the hall opens;* HOVSTAD *and* ASLAKSEN *are seen outside*) I certainly never expected to meet them here!

DR. STOCKMANN (*Staring at them*): What does this mean? How dare you come to see me?

HOVSTAD: We have our reasons.

ASLAKSEN: We've something to discuss with you.

MORTEN KIIL (*In a whisper*): Yes or no—by two o'clock.

ASLAKSEN (*With a glance at* HOVSTAD): Aha!
(MORTEN KIIL *goes out.*)

DR. STOCKMANN: Well, what do you want? Be quick about it.

HOVSTAD: It's natural you should resent the attitude we were forced to take last night—

DR. STOCKMANN: So that's what you call an attitude, is it? A fine attitude! Behaving like a couple of cowards—a couple of old women—!

HOVSTAD: Call it what you like; but, you see, we have no alternative—

DR. STOCKMANN: You didn't dare do otherwise, I suppose!

HOVSTAD: If that's how you choose to put it.

ASLAKSEN: You should have given us some inkling, Dr. Stockmann. The slightest hint to Mr. Hovstad or to me—

DR. STOCKMANN: Hint? What about?

ASLAKSEN: About your real motive in this matter.

DR. STOCKMANN: I don't know what you mean.

ASLAKSEN (*Nods confidentially*): Of course you do, Dr. Stockmann.

HOVSTAD: Why make a mystery of it now?

DR. STOCKMANN (*Looks from one to the other*): What the devil's all this about—?

ASLAKSEN: You know your father-in-law's been all over town buying up shares in the Baths—isn't that so?

DR. STOCKMANN: Yes, he has—but what of that?

ASLAKSEN: It might have been wiser to choose somebody else to do it for you; the connection is a bit too obvious.

HOVSTAD: And wouldn't it have been more prudent if you hadn't mixed yourself up personally in this affair? The attack on the Baths should have been made by someone else. Why didn't you take me into your confidence, Dr. Stockmann?

DR. STOCKMANN (*Staring straight in front of him; a light seems to dawn on him, and he says as though thunderstruck*): This is incredible! Can such things be!

ASLAKSEN (*Smiling*): Well—obviously! But they should be handled with more delicacy, it seems to me.

HOVSTAD: And it was unwise to attempt it single-handed; it's always easier to avoid responsibility for a matter of this sort, if you have others working with you.

DR. STOCKMANN (*Calmly*): Come to the point, gentlemen. What is it you want?

ASLAKSEN: Perhaps Mr. Hovstad had better—

HOVSTAD: No; you explain it, Aslaksen.

ASLAKSEN: It's simply this: Now that we know how matters really stand, we feel safe in venturing to place *The People's Monitor* at your disposal.

DR. STOCKMANN: You feel safe, do you? What about public opinion? Aren't you afraid of raising a storm of protest?

HOVSTAD: We are prepared to weather it.

ASLAKSEN: And, before long, you can make a sudden change of tactics, Doctor. As soon as the charges made against the Baths have the desired effect—

DR. STOCKMANN: As soon as my father-in-law and I have bought up the shares at an attractive price, I suppose you mean—?

HOVSTAD: It's mainly for scientific reasons, I presume, that you wish to gain control of the establishment—?

DR. STOCKMANN: That goes without saying; and of course it was for scientific reasons too that I persuaded the old badger to become my partner in this plan. We'll patch up the pipes a bit, make a few little adjustments at the Beach —and it won't cost the town a penny. What do you think? That ought to do the trick!

HOVSTAD: I should think so—provided you have the *Monitor* to back you up.

ASLAKSEN: In a free community the Press is all-powerful, Doctor Stockmann.

DR. STOCKMANN: Unquestionably! And so is public opinion too. I suppose you'll answer for the Home-owners Association, Mr. Aslaksen?

ASLAKSEN: The Home-owners Association, and the Temperance Society too; you may depend on that.

DR. STOCKMANN: Now, tell me, gentlemen—I'm almost ashamed to mention such a thing—what is your price?

HOVSTAD: I beg you to believe, Doctor, that we'd be only too happy to give you our support for nothing. But, unfortunately, the status of *The People's Monitor* is somewhat precarious; it's not as financially successful as it deserves to be. And it would seem a pity, just now when there's so much to be done in the field of general politics, to have to close our doors.

DR. STOCKMANN: I understand; I realize that would be very hard for a friend of the People, like yourself. (*Flaring up*) But *I'm* the People's enemy! An enemy of the People—have you forgotten that? (*Striding about the room*) Where's my stick? Where the devil is my stick?

HOVSTAD: What do you mean?

ASLAKSEN: You surely don't intend—?

DR. STOCKMANN (*Comes to a halt*): And what if I refuse to give you a penny of those shares? You must remember we rich people don't like parting with our money!

HOVSTAD: I advise *you* to remember that this business can be presented in a very ugly light.

DR. STOCKMANN: Yes; and you're just the man to do it! If I don't come to the rescue of your *Monitor*, I've no doubt you'll see to that. You'll hound me, won't you? You'll bait me—you'll slaughter me as a dog slaughters a hare!

HOVSTAD: That's the law of nature; every animal for himself, you know.

ASLAKEN: We all have to take our food where we can find it.

DR. STOCKMANN: Then go out into the gutter, where you belong, and find it there! (*Striding about the room*) I'll show you who the strongest animal is here! (*Finds his umbrella and brandishes it at them*) Now—get out!

HOVSTAD: You wouldn't dare attack us—!

ASLAKSEN: Be careful with that umbrella—!

DR. STOCKMANN: Out of the window with you, Mr. Hovstad!

HOVSTAD (*By the hall door*): Have you gone raving mad?

DR. STOCKMANN: Out of the window, Mr. Aslaksen! Jump, I tell you—and be quick about it!

ASLAKSEN (*Running round the desk*): Moderation, Doctor Stockmann—moderation! I'm not a strong man, you know; I can't stand things like this—(*Screams*) Help! Help!

(MRS. STOCKMANN, HORSTER *and* PETRA *enter from the living room*.)

MRS. STOCKMANN: Good gracious, Tomas! What are you doing?

DR. STOCKMANN (*Brandishing the umbrella*): Go on—jump, I tell you! Into the gutter where you belong!

HOVSTAD: You're a witness to this, Captain Horster! An unprovoked assault—! (*Rushes out to the hall.*)

ASLAKSEN (*Bewildered*): I must look up the law on matters of this sort—! (*He escapes through the door to the living room.*)

MRS. STOCKMANN (*Clinging to the doctor*): Tomas—for heaven's sake control yourself!

DR. STOCKMANN (*Throws down the umbrella*): They both got away—damn them!

MRS. STOCKMANN: But what did they want, Tomas, dear?

DR. STOCKMANN: I'll tell you presently; I've other things to attend to now. (*Goes to his desk and writes something on a visiting-card*) Look, Katrine! I want you to see what I've written here.

MRS. STOCKMANN: Three large "No's"—what can that mean?

DR. STOCKMANN: I'll tell you that presently too. (*Giving* PETRA *the card*): Here, Petra; tell Smudgy-face to run over to the badger and give him this. And hurry! (PETRA *goes out with the card*) I never expected to have so many visits from the devil's em-

issaries as I've had today! But I know how to deal with them; I'll
sharpen my pen against them till it becomes a goad; I'll dip it in
gall and venom; I'll hurl my entire ink-pot at their brazen heads!

MRS. STOCKMANN: But, Tomas—aren't we going away?

(PETRA *returns*)

DR. STOCKMANN: Well?

PETRA: She's gone with it.

DR. STOCKMANN: Splendid! —Did you say going away? No, I'll be
damned if we are, Katrine—we're going to stay right here!

MRS. STOCKMANN: Here in the town?

DR. STOCKMANN: Here in the town. The battle-field is here, and
here the battle must be fought, and here I shall win the victory!
As soon as you've patched my trousers I'll be off and try to find a
place for us to live. We can't get through the winter without a
roof over our heads!

HORSTER: Will my roof do?

DR. STOCKMANN: You really mean it?

HORSTER: Of course. I've such a lot of room, and I'm hardly ever
home myself.

MRS. STOCKMANN: Oh, Captain Horster—that is kind of you!

PETRA: Thanks!

DR. STOCKMANN (*Shaking his hand*): Thanks—and thanks again!
That's a great load off my mind. Now I can set to work in earnest.
Oh, there's such a lot to do, Katrine! And I'll have all my time to
myself—that's just as well; for, I forgot to tell you—I've been dismissed—

MRS. STOCKMANN (*Sighing*): Yes—I expected that!

DR. STOCKMANN: —and now they want to take away my practice,
too! Well—let them! There are always the poor people—those
that can't afford to pay; they're really the ones that need me
most, you see. But, by God, they're going to hear from me! I'll
harangue them every single day—"in season and out of season,"
as somebody or other put it.

MRS. STOCKMANN: Haven't you done enough talking, Tomas,
dear?

DR. STOCKMANN: Don't be absurd, Katrine! Do you think I'd
allow public opinion, and the solid majority, and all the rest of it

to drive me from the field? No, thank you! Besides, my aim is perfectly simple and straightforward. I just want to din into the heads of these poor misguided mongrels, that these so-called Liberals are freedom's bitterest enemies—that party programs do nothing but stifle living truths—that justice and morality are being turned upside-down by expediency and greed—until eventually life itself will scarcely be worth living! Surely I ought to be able to make the people see that, Captain Horster? Don't you think so?

HORSTER: Perhaps; I don't know much about such things myself.

DR. STOCKMANN: It's all quite simple—let me explain it to you! First, the party-bosses have got to be wiped out; they're just like wolves, you see—like ravening wolves! They batten on the small-fry. In order to keep themselves alive they devour literally hundreds of them every single year. Take Hovstad and Aslaksen, for instance—think of the small-fry they devour! Or if they don't devour them, they debase them and corrupt them till all they're good for is to become Home-owners or subscribers to *The People's Monitor!* (*Sits on the edge of the table*) Come here, Katrine! Just look at that radiant, gallant sunshine! And doesn't the air smell fresh and clear this morning?

MRS. STOCKMANN: If only we could live on air and sunshine, Tomas, dear!

DR. STOCKMANN: Oh, but we can—with a little help from you! You'll scrimp and save away and we shall manage splendidly. That's the least of my worries. One thing does worry me though; where am I to find a decent freedom-loving man to carry on the work after I'm gone?

PETRA: Don't start worrying about that, Father; you've still got lots of time ahead of you! —Why, look; here are the boys!

(EJLIF *and* MORTEN *enter from the living room.*)

MRS. STOCKMANN: What's happened? It's not a holiday today!

MORTEN: We got into a fight with some of the other boys—

EJLIF: No, we didn't! They got into a fight with us!

MORTEN: And Mr. Rörlund said we'd better stay home for a few days.

DR. STOCKMANN (*Snapping his fingers and jumping down from*

the table): That gives me an idea! Yes, by heaven, that gives me
an idea! You shan't set foot in that blasted school again!

THE BOYS: Not go to school!

MRS. STOCKMANN: But, Tomas—

DR. STOCKMANN: Never again, I say! I'll start teaching you myself; or, better still—you shan't be taught a blessed thing—

MORTEN: Hurrah!

DR. STOCKMANN: The only thing I'll teach you, is to become decent freedom-loving men. —You'll help me, Petra, won't you?

PETRA: I'd love to, Father.

DR. STOCKMANN: We'll have the school in the very room where
they branded me an enemy of the People. But we'll have to have
more pupils—I want a dozen boys at least.

MRS. STOCKMANN: You'll never get them to come, Tomas; not in
this town.

DR. STOCKMANN: Wait and see. (*To the boys*) You must know a
few street-urchins—some regular guttersnipes—?

MORTEN: Oh, yes, Father! I know lots of them!

DR. STOCKMANN: Then find a few good specimens and bring them
to me. I'm going to experiment with a few mongrels for a change;
there's plenty of good raw-material there.

MORTEN: What are we to do, Father, when we grow up to be decent freedom-loving men?

DR. STOCKMANN: Drive the wolves away to the Far West, my
boys!

MRS. STOCKMANN: But suppose it's the wolves who drive you
away, Tomas, dear?

DR. STOCKMANN: Drive *me* away! Are you stark raving mad,
Katrine? I'm the strongest man in the town! Don't you know
that?

MRS. STOCKMANN: The strongest—? You mean, *now*?

DR. STOCKMANN: Yes! I'll even go so far as to say that I'm one of
the strongest men in the whole world!

MORTEN: Are you really, Father?

DR. STOCKMANN (*Dropping his voice*): Hush! You mustn't say a
word about it yet; I've made a great discovery, you see.

MRS. STOCKMANN: Not another, Tomas, dear!

DR. STOCKMANN: Another, yes—another! (*Gathers them round him and speaks in a confidential tone*) And I'll tell you what it is: the strongest man in the world is the man who stands alone.

MRS. STOCKMANN: (*Smiles and shakes her head*): Oh, Tomas, dear—!

PETRA: (*Grasps his hands and says with eyes full of faith*): Father!

CURTAIN

The Wild Duck

A PLAY IN FIVE ACTS

1884

CHARACTERS

WERLE, *a wholesale merchant and manufacturer*

GREGERS WERLE, *his son*

OLD EKDAL

HJALMAR EKDAL, *his son, a photographer*

GINA EKDAL, *Hjalmar's wife*

HEDVIG, *their daughter, a girl of fourteen*

MRS. SÖRBY, *Werle's housekeeper*

RELLING, *a doctor*

MOLVIK, *a former student of theology*

GRAABERG, *Werle's bookkeeper*

PETTERSEN, *Werle's servant*

JENSEN, *a hired waiter*

A FAT GENTLEMAN

A BALD GENTLEMAN

A NEARSIGHTED GENTLEMAN

SIX OTHER GENTLEMEN, *guests at Werle's party*

SEVERAL HIRED WAITERS

The first act takes place in Werle's house, the four following acts at Hjalmar Ekdal's.

ACT
ONE

SCENE: *In* WERLE'S *house. A study richly and comfortably furnished; bookcases and upholstered furniture; a desk covered with papers and documents stands in the center of the room; several lamps with green shades give a subdued light. In the back wall double doors stand open, with portieres drawn back. Beyond them is seen a large elegantly furnished room, brightly lighted with lamps and branched candlesticks. A small baize door down right leads to* WERLE'S *office. Down left a fireplace with a brightly burning coal fire, and above this a double door to the dining room.*

WERLE'S *servant* PETTERSEN, *in livery, and* JENSEN, *a hired waiter in black, are straightening up the room. In the large room beyond, two or three other waiters move about tidying up and lighting more candles. From the dining room comes the hum of conversation, laughter, the sound of many voices; a glass is tapped with a knife; silence follows, then a toast is proposed. Shouts of "Bravo!" and then again the buzz of conversation.*

PETTERSEN (*As he lights a lamp on the mantlepiece and replaces the shade*): Hear that, Jensen? The old boy's on his feet again toasting Mrs. Sörby. Listen to him holding forth!

JENSEN (*Pushing forward an armchair*): Is it true what people say? That he's sweet on her, I mean?

PETTERSEN: Hell! How should I know!

JENSEN: I'll bet he was quite a chaser in his day!

PETTERSEN: I shouldn't wonder.

JENSEN: He's giving this party for his son, I hear.

PETTERSEN: Yes; he got home yesterday.

JENSEN: I never even knew Werle had a son.

PETTERSEN: He has a son all right. But he spends most of his time up at the Works, in Höjdal; he hasn't been back once; not in all the years I've worked here.

A WAITER (*In the doorway of the inner room*): Pettersen! There's an old fellow out here—says he wants—

PETTERSEN (*Muttering*): What is it *now!*

(OLD EKDAL *appears from the right in the inner room. He wears a threadbare overcoat with a turned-up collar; has on woollen mittens and carries a stick and an old fur cap. There is a brown paper parcel under his arm. He wears a dirty reddish-brown wig and has a small gray mustache.*)

PETTERSEN (*Going towards him*): What the devil are *you* doing here?

EKDAL (*In the doorway*): Got to get into the office, Pettersen.

PETTERSEN: The office was closed an hour ago—

EKDAL: I know—the porter told me. But Graaberg's still there, isn't he? Let me slip in this way, Pettersen—there's a good fellow! (*Points to the baize door*) Not the first time I've used this door, eh?

PETTERSEN: All right. (*Opens the door*) But when you leave, go out the other way—don't come back through here. We have company, you know.

EKDAL: Oh, yes—I know; I know. Hm! Thanks, Pettersen. Thanks, old man. You're a good friend. (*Mutters under his breath*) Ass! (*He goes into the office;* PETTERSEN *closes the door after him.*)

JENSEN: Does *he* belong to the office?

PETTERSEN: No! He just does a bit of copying now and then—when they're extra busy. Takes it home with him. Poor old Ekdal! Quite a swell in his day, he was.

JENSEN: He still has a way with him—

PETTERSEN: Yes, indeed! A military man he was. A lieutenant, no less.

JENSEN: A lieutenant! *Him?*

PETTERSEN: It's a fact. Then he went into business—something to do with timber, I believe. They say he once played Mr. Werle a very dirty trick. They were running the Höjdal Works

together—they were partners then, you see. Oh, I know old
Ekdal well. Many's the time we've drunk a bottle of ale at Mrs.
Eriksen's; we've downed many a glass of bitters there together
he and I.

JENSEN: Shouldn't think there was much chance of a treat from
him!

PETTERSEN: Don't be a fool, Jensen! I'm the one who does the
treating. It's as well to be kind to a gent like that who's come
down in the world.

JENSEN: What happened? Did he go bankrupt?

PETTERSEN: Worse than that; he went to jail.

JENSEN: To jail!

PETTERSEN: Some kind of penitentiary, at any rate. (*Listens*) Sh!
They're getting up from table.

(*The dining-room door is flung open from within by a couple of
waiters.* MRS. SÖRBY *comes out talking to two gentlemen.*
WERLE *and the other guests follow gradually. Finally*
HJALMAR EKDAL *and* GREGERS WERLE *appear.*)

MRS. SÖRBY (*In passing*): You can serve the coffee in the music
room, Pettersen.

PETTERSEN: Very well, Madam. (*She and the two gentlemen go
into the inner room and off right.* PETTERSEN *and* JENSEN *go
out the same way.*)

FAT GENTLEMAN (*To* BALD GENTLEMAN): Phew! That was hard
work! Quite a meal!

BALD GENTLEMAN: With a little good will it's quite amazing what
one can put away in three hours!

FAT GENTLEMAN: Oh, my dear fellow—I'm thinking of the after-
math!

A THIRD GENTLEMAN: They say coffee and liqueurs are being
served in the music room.

FAT GENTLEMAN: Splendid! Perhaps Mrs. Sörby will play a tune
for us.

BALD GENTLEMAN: If we aren't careful she may play us the wrong
kind of tune someday!

FAT GENTLEMAN: Don't worry about Bertha! She's not the kind
to go back on old friends!

WERLE (*In a low tone, dejectedly*): I don't think anyone noticed—did they, Gregers?

GREGERS (*Looks at him*): Noticed what?

WERLE: Then you didn't notice either?

GREGERS: No. What do you mean?

WERLE: We were thirteen at table.

GREGERS: Really? Were we?

WERLE (*With a glance towards* HJALMAR EKDAL): As a rule we're never more than twelve. (*To the others*) This way, gentlemen! (WERLE *and the others go out through the inner room to the right. Only* HJALMAR *and* GREGERS *remain.*)

HJALMAR (*Who has overheard*): Gregers—you shouldn't have invited me.

GREGERS: Don't be absurd! Not invite my best and only friend—? The party was given for me, wasn't it?

HJALMAR: Your father didn't approve, I'm afraid. I'm never asked to the house, you know.

GREGERS: So I gather. But I had to see you and have a talk. I'll be going away again soon—We've drifted so far apart since the old days at school. Do you realize it's sixteen or seventeen years since we last met?

HJALMAR: Is it really as long as that?

GREGERS: It is indeed! Well—how have you been? You're looking well. You've put on weight, I think; you've grown quite stout.

HJALMAR: I wouldn't exactly call it stout. I'm no longer a boy—if that's what you mean. I've filled out a bit—that's only natural.

GREGERS: Yes, of course. Well—outwardly you seem in splendid shape.

HJALMAR (*In a gloomy tone*): But inwardly—that's another story! I don't have to tell you all that I've been through. You know all about *that* catastrophe!

GREGERS: Yes. What's happened to your father? What's he doing now?

HJALMAR: Don't speak of it! The poor, miserable old man! I look after him, of course; he lives with me. He has no one else to turn to. But it's too painful to talk about—Tell me about yourself. Have you been getting on well—up at the Works?

GREGERS: I've been living in splendid isolation. I've had plenty of time for contemplation, I can tell you. Let's sit here and be comfortable. (*He sits down in an armchair by the fire, and pulls* HJALMAR *down to another one beside him.*)

HJALMAR (*Sentimentally*): As a matter of fact, Gregers, I'm very grateful that you asked me here today. It proves that you no longer have anything against me.

GREGERS (*Surprised*): Why on earth should you think I had anything against you?

HJALMAR: You had at first, you know.

GREGERS: At first? How do you mean?

HJALMAR: Directly after the—catastrophe. It was understandable enough. It was only by a miracle that your father escaped being dragged into all that ghastly business.

GREGERS: But that's no reason why I should have had anything against *you*. What put that into your head?

HJALMAR: I happen to know you did, Gregers. Your father told me so himself.

GREGERS: *Father* did? Well! Hm—Was that why I never heard from you? Why you never wrote to me?

HJALMAR: Of course.

GREGERS: You never even told me you'd decided to take up photography.

HJALMAR: I know. Your father advised me not to write to you at all.

GREGERS (*Gazes straight before him*): Well—well! Perhaps he was wise in that—But, tell me—are you happy in your work? Does it appeal to you, I mean?

HJALMAR (*With a sigh*): Yes—more or less; I really can't complain. It all seemed very strange to me at first. I found myself in such totally different circumstances, you see. Father had lost absolutely everything—he was completely ruined. And then there was all the scandal—the disgrace—

GREGERS (*Moved*): Yes, yes. I understand.

HJALMAR: I naturally had to give up my studies—I was forced to leave the university. We hadn't a penny left—nothing but debts—mostly to your father, I believe.

GREGERS: Hm.

HJALMAR: I thought it best to break off all my former friendships—sever all my old connections. In fact it was your father who advised me to do so; and since he seemed to want to help me—

GREGERS: Father did?

HJALMAR: You must be aware of that. Where was *I* to get the money to learn photography, furnish a studio, and buy all the necessary equipment? It takes quite a bit of capital to make a start, you know.

GREGERS: You mean—*Father* provided that?

HJALMAR: Of course; didn't you know? I understood him to say he'd written you about it.

GREGERS: No—he never mentioned it. He must have forgotten, I suppose. Actually, we've never exchanged anything but business letters. So it was *Father* who—!

HJALMAR: Yes, it was. He didn't want it generally known, he said—but it was he. He also made it possible for me to marry. Didn't you know that either?

GREGERS: No—I didn't. (*Shakes him by the arm*) My dear Hjalmar—I can't tell you how glad I am about all this. But I feel guilty, too. I've misjudged Father all these years—in some ways, anyhow. I thought he had no heart—no feelings. This proves me wrong. It's funny—one would almost think he was trying to atone for something—

HJALMAR: Atone?

GREGERS: Yes—it's as though he were suffering from a sense of guilt; I don't know *what* to call it. But I'm certainly delighted to hear all this about him. So you're married, are you? You're a braver man that I am! How does it feel? Are you content?

HJALMAR: Yes—I'm very happy, thank you. She's a thoroughly good wife—and very capable, as well. And, after all—she's not *entirely* without education.

GREGERS (*Rather surprised*): No—I don't suppose she is—

HJALMAR: Life's the best education, when you come right down to it. And, being so much with me, she— And I've a couple of very brilliant friends who drop in almost every day. She's learning—Gina's learning! You'd never recognize her.

GREGERS: Gina?

HJALMAR: Yes; Gina's her name—don't you remember?

GREGERS: *Whose* name is Gina? I don't know what you're—

HJALMAR: You must remember Gina! She worked here for a while.

GREGERS (*Looks at him*): You don't mean Gina Hansen?

HJALMAR: Gina Hansen, yes—of course.

GREGERS: —who kept house for us those last few years—when Mother was so ill?

HJALMAR: Yes, that's the one. But—my dear fellow—your father wrote you all about it; I'm *positive* he did!

GREGERS (*Who has risen*): He wrote and told me you were married, but not that— (*Walks about the room*) Wait, though! On second thought—I think he may have—His letters were always so very brief. (*Sinks down on the arm of the chair*) Tell me, Hjalmar—this is most interesting—how did you happen to meet this Gina—your wife, I mean?

HJALMAR: It was all quite simple. Gina didn't stay here long, you know. Things were very upset here at the time—what with your mother's illness; it was all too much for Gina, so she left. It was the year before your mother died, I think; or the same year, perhaps—I'm not quite sure.

GREGERS: It was the same year; I was away—up at the Works. And then what happened?

HJALMAR: Gina went home to her mother—Mrs. Hansen; an honest, hard-working woman who ran a little restaurant. They had a room to rent—a nice, comfortable room—

GREGERS: And I suppose you were lucky enough to acquire it?

HJALMAR: Yes. It was your father who recommended it. And, of course, there I got to know Gina very well.

GREGERS: And then you got engaged?

HJALMAR: Yes. It doesn't take young people long to fall in love—hm—

GREGERS (*Rises and paces about*): Tell me—was it *after* you became engaged that Father—I mean—was it after that, that you took up photography?

HJALMAR: Yes; I had to work at something; I was anxious to have a home of my own, you see. Your father and I agreed that a photographer's career would be practical and easy. And Gina thought so too—especially as she'd done a bit of retouching herself and knew quite a lot about it.

GREGERS: So it worked out very neatly, didn't it?

HJALMAR (*Rises, pleased*): Yes—wasn't it amazing? It really worked out very neatly!

GREGERS: No doubt of that! My father seems to have played the part of Divine Providence where you're concerned!

HJALMAR: He came to the rescue of his old friend's son. That shows what a kind heart he has!

(MRS. SÖRBY *enters arm in arm with* WERLE.)

MRS. SÖRBY: It's no use arguing, dear Mr. Werle! You mustn't stay in those bright lights another moment. It's bad for you!

WERLE (*Lets go of her arm and passes his hand over his eyes*): You know—I believe you're right.

(PETTERSEN *and* JENSEN *carry round trays of refreshments.*)

MRS. SÖRBY (*To the guests in the inner room*): Do come in here, gentlemen, and have some punch.

FAT GENTLEMAN (*Comes up to* MRS. SÖRBY): It can't be true! No smoking? You surely don't mean to deprive us of that precious prerogative!

MRS. SÖRBY: I'm afraid it can't be helped, Your Excellency! Smoking is not allowed in Mr. Werle's sanctum.

BALD GENTLEMAN: My dear lady! And when did you inaugurate this harsh decree?

MRS. SÖRBY: After our last dinner party, Mr. Balle. Several of our guests quite overstepped the mark.

BALD GENTLEMAN: Isn't it ever permitted to overstep the mark, dear Madam Bertha! Not even by an inch or two?

MRS. SÖRBY: Never! Under any circumstances, Mr. Balle.
(*Most of the guests are now gathered in the study; servants hand round glasses of punch.*)

WERLE (*To* HJALMAR, *who is standing apart beside a table*): What are you so engrossed in, Ekdal?

HJALMAR: I was just looking at this album, Mr. Werle.

BALD GENTLEMAN (*Who is wandering about*): Ah, photographs! Of course—that's your line, isn't it?

FAT GENTLEMAN (*In an armchair*): I do hope you've brought some of your own!

HJALMAR: No, I'm afraid I haven't.

FAT GENTLEMAN: Too bad! It's good for the digestion to look at pictures after dinner.

BALD GENTLEMAN: And it provides entertainment, too.

NEARSIGHTED GENTLEMAN: All such contributions thankfully received!

MRS. SÖRBY: In other words, gentlemen, you mean a guest should sing for his supper!

FAT GENTLEMAN: Certainly, Mrs. Sörby—especially when the supper is so excellent!

BALD GENTLEMAN: Still—when it involves one's livelihood—

MRS. SÖRBY: Of course! I quite agree! (*They go on laughing and joking.*)

GREGERS (*Softly*): You ought to join in the conversation, Hjalmar.

HJALMAR (*Squirming*): What have *I* got to talk about?

FAT GENTLEMAN: Werle—I claim that Tokay is a comparatively mild wine; don't you agree?

WERLE (*By the mantlepiece*): Yes, I suppose so. I'll vouch for that Tokay you had today, at any rate. It's quite an exceptional vintage; an unusually good year—but I needn't tell *you* that!

FAT GENTLEMAN: I admit it had a most delicate bouquet.

HJALMAR (*Diffidently*): Is there a difference in the years, then?

FAT GENTLEMAN (*Laughing*): Come now! What a question!

WERLE (*Smiles, to* HJALMAR): Fine wines are lost on you it seems!

BALD GENTLEMAN: Wines are like photographs, Mr. Ekdal—they both need sunshine. Or am I mistaken?

HJALMAR: No—light is certainly important.

MRS. SÖRBY: What about court chamberlains? I hear they thrive on sunshine too!

BALD GENTLEMAN: Such sarcasm! Is that kind?

NEARSIGHTED GENTLEMAN: Mrs. Sörby will have her joke, you know!

FAT GENTLEMAN: Yes! And at our expense! (*Wags his finger at her*) Oh, Madam Bertha! Madam Bertha!

MRS. SÖRBY: Joking apart, however, Mr. Ekdal—wines differ

greatly according to the year. Old vintages are nearly always best.

NEARSIGHTED GENTLEMAN: Am *I* an old vintage, Mrs. Sörby?

MRS. SÖRBY: Far from it, Excellency!

BALD GENTLEMAN: There! You see? How about me, dear Mrs. Sörby—?

FAT GENTLEMAN: And me! What would *my* vintage be?

MRS. SÖRBY: A most sweet vintage, Excellency! (*She sips her glass of punch. The men all laugh and flirt with her.*)

WERLE: Trust Mrs. Sörby to find a way out—when she wants to! Fill up your glasses, gentlemen! See to it, Pettersen—! Drink with me, Gregers, won't you? (GREGERS *doesn't move*) And you, Ekdal—won't you join us? There was no opportunity to drink with you at dinner.

(GRAABERG, *the bookkeeper, sticks his head in at the baize door.*)

GRAABERG: Excuse me, sir. I'm afraid I can't get out—

WERLE: Have they locked you in again?

GRAABERG: I'm afraid so, sir—Flakstad went off with the keys.

WERLE: Never mind—come through this way.

GRAABERG: But—I'm not alone, sir; there are two of us, sir.

WERLE: It doesn't matter; come along! The two of you! (GRAABERG *and* OLD EKDAL *come out of the office.*)

WERLE (*Involuntarily*): Ugh!

(*The laughter and talk among the guests breaks off suddenly.* HJALMAR *starts at the sight of his father, puts down his glass and turns towards the fireplace.*)

EKDAL (*Without looking up, makes little bows to right and left as he passes through, murmuring*): Excuse me. Came in the wrong way. Door was locked. Door locked. Excuse me (*He and* GRAABERG *go into the inner room and off right.*)

WERLE (*Between his teeth*): That blasted Graaberg!

GREGERS (*Stares open-mouthed; to* HJALMAR): Surely—that couldn't have been—!

FAT GENTLEMAN: What's going on? Who *was* that?

GREGERS: Nobody; just the bookkeeper, and someone with him.

NEARSIGHTED GENTLEMAN (*To* HJALMAR): Who *was* that man? Did you know him?

HJALMAR: No—I don't know—I didn't notice—

FAT GENTLEMAN (*Rising*): What the devil's happening? (*He joins another group, who are talking under their breath*.)

MRS. SÖRBY (*To* PETTERSEN *in a whisper*): Give him something to take home with him; something nice—you understand?

PETTERSEN (*Nods*): I'll see to it. (*Goes out*.)

GREGERS (*Softly, with emotion, to* HJALMAR): It really was he, then!

HJALMAR: Yes.

GREGERS: And you actually stood there and said you d o ʀ c w him!

HJALMAR (*In a vehement whisper*): But how could I—!

GREGERS: —acknowledge your own father?

HJALMAR (*Miserably*): If you were in *my* place, you—
(*The conversation among the guests, which has been carried on in a low tone, now swells into forced joviality*.)

BALD GENTLEMAN (*In a friendly manner approaches* HJALMAR *and* GREGERS): Aha! Reminiscing about old days at college, eh? Don't you smoke, Mr. Ekdal? May I give you a light? Oh—but of course!—it's not allowed!

HJALMAR: Thank you—I don't think I—

FAT GENTLEMAN: How about reciting a poem for us, Mr. Ekdal? You used to be so good at it.

HJALMAR: I'm afraid I don't remember any.

FAT GENTLEMAN: What a pity! Well—what can we find to do, Balle? (*They move away and go into the other room*.)

HJALMAR (*Gloomily*): I'm going, Gregers. When a man's been through what I've been through, you see— Say goodbye to your father for me.

GREGERS: Yes—of course. Do you think you'll go straight home?

HJALMAR: Yes—why do you ask?

GREGERS: I thought I might drop in a little later.

HJALMAR: No, don't do that—don't come to my place, Gregers; it's too sad and depressing there. Especially on top of all this splendour! We'll arrange to meet somewhere in town.

MRS. SÖRBY (*Comes over to them and speaks in a low voice*): Are you going, Ekdal?

HJALMAR: Yes.

MRS. SÖRBY: Remember me to Gina.

HJALMAR: Thanks.

MRS. SÖRBY: Tell her I'll drop in one of these days.

HJALMAR: Thanks—I will. (*To* GREGERS) Don't come with me. I'll slip out without being seen. (*He strolls across the room, into the inner room, and out to the right.*)

MRS. SÖRBY (*In a low voice to* PETTERSEN, *who has returned*): Did you give the old man something?

PETTERSEN: A nice bottle of brandy, Madam.

MRS. SÖRBY: You might have thought of something better than that!

PETTERSEN: Oh, no, Mrs. Sörby! He'd rather have that than any-thing!

FAT GENTLEMAN (*In the doorway, with a sheet of music in his hand*): How about playing a duet, Mrs. Sörby?

MRS. SÖRBY: Yes! That would be delightful!

GUESTS: Bravo! Bravo! (*She joins the guests in the inner room and they all go out to the right.* GREGERS *remains standing by the fireplace.* WERLE *pretends to be looking for something on the desk and seems to want* GREGERS *to go;* GREGERS *doesn't move,* WERLE *goes towards the door.*)

GREGERS: Can you spare a moment, Father?

WERLE: Yes; what is it?

GREGERS: I'd like to talk to you.

WERLE: Can't it wait till we're alone?

GREGERS: No, it can't; we may never be alone again, you see.

WERLE (*Comes towards him*): And what does *that* mean? (*During the following the sound of a piano is heard in the distance, from the music room.*)

GREGERS: Why has that family been allowed to go downhill like that?

WERLE: You're referring to the Ekdals, I presume.

GREGERS: Yes; I'm referring to the Ekdals. There was a time when you and Lieutenant Ekdal were close friends.

WERLE: Yes; too close for comfort—I've suffered for it for years. That friendship almost cost me my good name.

GREGERS: Was he the only guilty one? You're sure of that?

WERLE: What do you mean?

GREGERS: You were in that big timber deal together, weren't you?

WERLE: Ekdal was in charge of the entire transaction. He surveyed the land—he drew up the maps. How was I to know that they were fraudulent! He deliberately encroached on property belonging to the Government; he felled all that timber—acres of it!—belonging to the State. Lieutenant Ekdal acted entirely on his own responsibility. I never for a moment realized what he was up to.

GREGERS: Perhaps he didn't quite realize it himself.

WERLE: That may be. The fact remains that he was found guilty, and I was acquitted.

GREGERS: Yes; I know nothing was ever proved against you.

WERLE: An acquittal is an acquittal. But what makes you bring up that distressing business? God knows it turned my hair gray long before its time. Is that the kind of thing you've spent all these years brooding about up there? I assure you here in town it's been forgotten long ago—at least as far as *I'm* concerned.

GREGERS: But what about the Ekdals?

WERLE: What do you expect me to do for them? Ekdal came out of prison a broken man; he was beyond all help. There are certain people in this world who, given the slightest blow, dive straight to the bottom and never come up again. Believe me, Gregers, I did everything I could—short of exposing myself to suspicion and endless gossip—

GREGERS: Suspicion? Yes—I see.

WERLE: I've arranged for Ekdal to do some odd jobs for the office—copying and so forth—and I pay him ten times what the work is worth—

GREGERS (*Without looking at him*): I don't doubt *that* for a moment.

WERLE: Why do you laugh? Do you think I'm not telling you the truth? I admit there's no record of it on the books; I never enter payments of that sort.

GREGERS (*With a cold smile*): You're very wise.

WERLE (*Taken aback*): What do you mean?

GREGERS (*Summoning up his courage*): How about the money you gave Hjalmar Ekdal to learn photography? Is *that* entered on the books?

WERLE: Entered—how? I don't—

GREGERS: I know now it was you who paid for his tuition; I also know that it was you who set him up in business.

WERLE: And you call that doing nothing for the Ekdals! Those people have cost me plenty, I assure you!

GREGERS: And are *those* expenses entered on the books?

WERLE: Why do you ask me that?

GREGERS: I have my reasons. Now, tell me: when you evinced this sudden interest in your old friend's son—it was just before his marriage, wasn't it?

WERLE: Good heavens! You don't expect me—after all, it's years ago—!

GREGERS: You wrote me a letter at that time—a business letter, naturally—and you mentioned briefly, in a postscript, that Hjalmar Ekdal had married a Miss Hansen.

WERLE: Quite right. That was her name.

GREGERS: But you omitted the fact that this Miss Hansen was *Gina* Hansen—our former housekeeper.

WERLE (*With a slightly forced laugh of derision*): It never occurred to me you were so interested in our former housekeeper.

GREGERS: You're right; I wasn't. But— (*Lowers his voice*) I happen to know there were others in this house who were; *extremely* interested.

WERLE: What do you mean by that? (*Flaring up*) You're not referring to *me*, by any chance?

GREGERS (*Softly but firmly*): But I *am* referring to you.

WERLE: How *dare* you! How dare you presume to—! I'll teach that photographer fellow—ungrateful wretch! Spreading lies about me—!

GREGERS: Hjalmar hasn't said a single word about it. I'm certain he hasn't the faintest suspicion of such a thing.

WERLE: Then where did you get it from? Who put such ideas into your head?

GREGERS: It was poor Mother; it was she who told me about it; the very last time I ever saw her.

WERLE: Your mother! Yes—of course. I might have known. You and she—! You always held together. She turned you against me from the start.

GREGERS: That's not true; it was because of all she suffered—all she had to bear; till she broke down and went utterly to pieces.

WERLE: Nonsense! She had no more to bear, and she suffered no more, than the majority of women. But it's impossible to deal with sickly, hysterical people—I've learned that to my cost!—How could you harbor these suspicions—how could you bring yourself to rake up all these malicious rumors against your own father, Gregers? I don't understand it. I should think at your age you could apply yourself to something more constructive.

GREGERS: It's about time, isn't it?

WERLE: It would do you good; I'm sure you'd feel much happier. What do you expect to accomplish up there at the Works, slaving away year after year at a routine office job? Refusing to accept a penny above the regular wages? It's sheer madness!

GREGERS: Yes; well—I'm not so sure of that.

WERLE: I understand your reasons well enough; you don't want to owe me anything; you want to be completely independent—Now, it so happens an excellent opportunity has opened up; one that would give you complete independence—full authority.

GREGERS: Indeed? What kind of opportunity?

WERLE: In my last letter—when I said it was essential for you to come back home at once—

GREGERS: Yes; what had you in mind? I've been waiting all day for you to tell me.

WERLE: What I had in mind was this: I propose to offer you a partnership.

GREGERS: In *your* firm? A partnership with *you*?

WERLE: It needn't be too *close* a partnership; we wouldn't necessarily have to work *together*. You could handle the business here, and I would move up to the Works.

GREGERS: To the Works? *You*?

WERLE: Yes; I no longer have the strength I used to have. It's time I started to let down a bit, you see. And I have to be careful of my

eyes—they've been bad lately; I've had a lot of trouble with
them.

GREGERS: That's nothing new; they've always troubled you.

WERLE: But not as they do now. There are other circumstances,
too, that make it advisable for me to move up there—for a while,
at any rate.

GREGERS: I certainly never expected anything like this.

WERLE: We've never been close—I know that, Gregers; but, after
all, we *are* father and son. There must be some way we can come
to an understanding.

GREGERS: In the eyes of the world, I suppose you mean.

WERLE: Well—at least that would be something, wouldn't it?
Think it over, Gregers. I'm sure we can manage it. Don't you
agree?

GREGERS (*Looks at him coldly*): What's your real motive in all this?

WERLE: My motive?

GREGERS: You're depending on me for something. You plan to
make use of me somehow.

WERLE: It's only natural for a father to depend upon his son.

GREGERS: Yes—so they say.

WERLE: I'm most anxious that you should stay home with me a little while. I'm very lonely, Gregers. All my life I've been a lonely
man—and one feels it more as one gets older. I need someone
near me—someone who—

GREGERS: You have Mrs. Sörby, haven't you?

WERLE: That's true—I have; and I don't know what I'd do without
her. She's good-natured and intelligent; and she's so cheerful
too—that means a lot to me.

GREGERS: Then what more do you want?

WERLE: But it's an awkward situation—for her, I mean. I'm afraid
it can't go on much longer. It puts her in a false position—there
might be talk. And that kind of thing doesn't do a man any good
either.

GREGERS: I think you can afford to risk it! As long as you go on giving the dinner parties you can give.

WERLE: But what about *her*, Gregers? I'm afraid she may find it
impossible to accept the situation any longer. And even if her af-

fection for me prompted her to stay—at the risk of talk and scandal and all the rest of it—would I be justified in—? You, with your high sense of integrity, tell me—?

GREGERS: You're thinking of marrying her, aren't you? Why not say so?

WERLE: And supposing I were? What then?

GREGERS: What then? Exactly!

WERLE: Would you be unalterably opposed to it?

GREGERS: By no means. Not at all.

WERLE: I wasn't sure. I thought perhaps—devotion to your mother's memory—

GREGERS: I'm not hysterical, you know.

WERLE: Well—whatever you may or may not be—you've taken a great weight off my mind. I'm delighted to know I can depend on your support.

GREGERS (*Looks at him intently*): Of course! *That's* how you plan to use me!

WERLE: Use you, indeed! What an expression!

GREGERS: Don't let's be fussy in our choice of words—not when we're alone, at any rate. (*With a short laugh*) Yes! Now I see! That's why it was so absolutely essential for me to come back here. We are to play the "Happy Family" in Mrs. Sörby's honor! The devoted father and the loving son! A touching picture! A new experience, indeed!

WERLE: Don't take that tone with me!

GREGERS: When was there ever a "Happy Family" in this house I'd like to know? Never—so far as *I* remember! But your plans require something of the sort. It'll make such a good impression—won't it? The beloved son rushing home to attend his dear old father's wedding! And what of all those ugly rumors about the miseries and torments the first wife had to bear? It'd be the end of them, wouldn't it? They'd be wiped out once and for all—and by her own son too!

WERLE: I don't think there's a man living you hate as much as you hate me.

GREGERS (*Softly*): I've seen you at close range.

WERLE: You've seen me through your mother's eyes. (*Lowers his voice a little*) You should remember that those eyes were—shall we say "clouded," now and then?

GREGERS (*Trembling*): I know what you're implying. But who was responsible for mother's tragic weakness? It was you, and all your—! The last of them being that woman you palmed off on Hjalmar Ekdal when you no longer—! Pah!

WERLE (*Shrugs his shoulders*): I hear your mother in every word you say.

GREGERS (*Takes no notice of him*): Yes! And he's there now—with that noble, trusting, childlike mind of his—living under the same roof with that degraded creature—quite unaware that what he calls his home is built on nothing but a lie! (*Comes a step nearer*) When I look back on all the wicked things you've done, I feel as though I were gazing at some ghastly battlefield—strewn with shattered corpses!

WERLE: I'm afraid the gulf between us is too wide to bridge.

GREGERS (*Bowing stiffly*): I share that opinion, so I shall take my hat and go.

WERLE: Go? Leave the house, you mean?

GREGERS: Yes. My purpose in life is clear to me at last.

WERLE: What purpose, may I ask?

GREGERS: You'd only laugh if I told you.

WERLE: I don't know, Gregers; a lonely man doesn't laugh so easily.

GREGERS (*Points toward the inner room*): Look, Father! Your distinguished guests are playing blindman's buff with Mrs. Sörby—Good night and goodbye.

(*He goes out by the back to the right. Sounds of laughter and gay conversation from the guests, who are now seen in the inner room.*)

WERLE (*Mutters contemptuously*): Ha—! He's not hysterical, eh? Poor fellow!

CURTAIN

ACT
TWO

SCENE: HJALMAR EKDAL'S *studio. It is a good-sized room evidently on the top floor of the building. On the right a large studio window is let into the sloping roof; it is half covered by a blue curtain. In the right-hand corner at the back is the hall door. Farther downstage on the same side is a door leading to the sitting room. Two doors on the opposite side and between them an iron stove. At the back a wide double door with sliding panels. The studio is plainly but comfortably fitted out and furnished. Between the doors on the right, standing out a little from the wall, a sofa with a table and some chairs; on the table a lighted lamp with a shade; beside the stove an old armchair. Photographic instruments and equipment of different kinds lying about the room. Against the back wall, to the left of the double doors, stands a bookcase containing a few books, boxes and bottles of chemicals, instruments, tools and other objects. Photographs and small articles such as camel's hair brushes, paper and so forth, lie on the table.*

    GINA EKDAL *sits on a chair by the table sewing.* HEDVIG *is sitting on the sofa, with her hands shading her eyes and her thumbs in her ears, reading a book.*

GINA (*Glances at her a couple of times as if in secret anxiety*): Hedvig!

HEDVIG (*Doesn't hear her.*)

GINA (*Louder*): Hedvig!

HEDVIG (*Takes away her hands and looks up*): Yes, Mother?

GINA: You mustn't go on reading any longer, Hedvig dear.

HEDVIG: Oh, just a *little* longer, Mother! A *tiny* bit longer— please!

GINA: No; put your book down now—there's a good girl. Your father'd be angry. *He* never reads of an evening, you know.

HEDVIG (*Closes the book*): But Father doesn't care much for reading.

GINA (*Lays aside her sewing and takes up a pencil and a little account book from the table*): How much was the butter today—do you remember?

HEDVIG: One sixty-five.

GINA: That's right. (*Marks it down*) We certainly use enough butter in this house! Then there was the sausage, and the cheese—let's see— (*Puts it down*) —and then the ham— (*Adding up*) that comes to nearly—

HEDVIG: And don't forget the beer—

GINA: Oh, yes—of course. (*Puts it down*) It mounts up all right! Well—it can't be helped!

HEDVIG: But since Father was out to dinner, we saved a bit on that.

GINA: Yes, that's true. And I took in eight fifty for those photographs.

HEDVIG: Did you? As much as that!

GINA: Yes; eight fifty exactly.

(*A pause.* GINA *picks up her sewing again.* HEDVIG *takes a pencil and a piece of paper and starts to draw, shading her eyes with her left hand.*)

HEDVIG: It's fun to think of Father at Mr. Werle's; at that grand dinner party—isn't it?

GINA: But it wasn't really Mr. Werle who invited him—it was his son. (*After a pause*) We don't have nothing to do with Mr. Werle.

HEDVIG: I do hope Father'll come home soon; I'm looking forward to it. He promised he'd ask Mrs. Sörby to give him something nice for me.

GINA: They've plenty of good things to spare in *that* house!

HEDVIG (*Goes on drawing*): I'm beginning to be a bit hungry, too.

(OLD EKDAL *comes in by the hall door. He has a paper parcel under his arm, and another parcel in his coat pocket.*)

GINA: Why Grandfather! How late you are today!

EKDAL: They'd locked the office. Had to wait in Graaberg's room. Then had to go through—hm.

HEDVIG: Grandfather—did they give you some more copying to do?

EKDAL: All of this—look!

GINA: Good!

HEDVIG: And you've got a parcel in your pocket, too.

EKDAL: Never mind that! That's nothing. (*Puts his stick away in a corner*) This'll keep me busy quite a while, Gina—eh? (*Opens one of the sliding panels in the back wall a little*) Hush! (*Peeps inside the opening for a moment and slides the panel closed again*) He-he! They've all gone to sleep together. And she's gone into her basket of her own accord. He-he!

HEDVIG: You're sure she's not cold in that basket, Grandfather?

EKDAL: What nonsense! Cold? In all that straw? (*He goes towards the farthest door on the left*) Are there any matches in there?

GINA: On the chest of drawers.

(EKDAL *goes into his room.*)

HEDVIG: I'm glad Grandfather got all that copying to do.

GINA: Yes, poor old Grandfather. At least it'll mean a little pocket money for him.

HEDVIG: And it'll keep him from hanging round that horrid bar at Mrs. Eriksen's.

GINA: That's true, too.

HEDVIG: Do you suppose they're still sitting at the dinner table, Mother?

GINA: Lord knows; I shouldn't wonder.

HEDVIG: I expect Father's having some lovely things to eat! He'll be in an awfully jolly mood when he gets home. Don't you think so, Mother?

GINA: Yes. But I wish we could tell him that room was rented.

HEDVIG: Oh, we shan't need that this evening.

GINA: It'd be a real help, you know. And we don't use it.

HEDVIG: No—I meant we won't need it this evening, because he'll be in a good mood anyway. The news about the room'll come in handy another time.

GINA (*Looks up at her*): You like having a bit of good news to tell your father, don't you?

HEDVIG: It makes things pleasanter.

GINA (*Thinks this over*): There's something in that.

(OLD EKDAL *comes in again and starts towards the door down left.*)

GINA (*Half turning in her chair*): Do you want anything in the kitchen, Grandfather?

EKDAL: I just want— No! Don't get up! (*Goes out.*)

GINA: I hope he won't go messing about the stove. (*Waits a moment*) Better go and see what he's up to, Hedvig.

(EKDAL *comes in again carrying a small jug of steaming hot water.*)

HEDVIG: Did you go to get hot water, Grandfather?

EKDAL: I did—yes. Need it for something. Got to do some writing; ink's as thick as porridge—hm.

GINA: But you'll eat your supper first—won't you, Grandfather? It's in there ready for you.

EKDAL: Can't be bothered with supper, Gina. Busy, I tell you. Don't want anyone coming in my room—not anyone—hm.

(*He goes into his room.* GINA *and* HEDVIG *look at each other.*)

GINA (*Softly*): Wonder where he got the money.

HEDVIG: From Graaberg, I suppose.

GINA: No! Graaberg always sends *me* his money.

HEDVIG: Then he got it on credit, I expect.

GINA: Poor Grandfather, who'd give *him* credit?

(HJALMAR EKDAL, *wearing an overcoat and a gray felt hat, comes in from the hall door.*)

GINA (*Throws down her sewing and rises*): Why, Hjalmar! Are you back so soon?

HEDVIG (*Jumps up at the same time*): Fancy your being back already, Father!

HJALMAR (*Taking off his hat*): Most of the guests were leaving.

HEDVIG: So early?

HJALMAR: Well—it was an early dinner, after all. (*Starts to take off his overcoat.*)

GINA: Let me help you.

HEDVIG: Me too! (*They help him off with his coat;* GINA *hangs it up on a hook on the back wall.*)

HEDVIG: Were there a lot of people, Father?

HJALMAR: No, not many; about twelve or fourteen, I should think.

GINA: I suppose you had a chance to talk to all of them?

HJALMAR: Yes, of course. Though I must say Gregers took up most of my time.

GINA: Is he just as plain as ever?

HJALMAR: I can't say he's particularly handsome—Isn't the old man home yet?

HEDVIG: Yes; Grandfather's in his room. He's busy writing.

HJALMAR: Did he say anything?

GINA: What about?

HJALMAR: Then he didn't mention—? I heard something about his being with Graaberg, you see. I'll just look in on him a minute.

GINA: No—I don't think I'd do that—

HJALMAR: Why not? Did he say he didn't want to see me?

GINA: He doesn't want to see *anyone* this evening—

HEDVIG (*Signaling*): Hm—hm!

GINA (*Not noticing*): He fetched himself some hot water from the kitchen.

HJALMAR: You mean he's—?

GINA: Yes—I suppose so.

HJALMAR: Ah, well! Poor old man! My poor old father! Let him be—If it makes him a little happier—!

(OLD EKDAL, *in a dressing gown and smoking a pipe, comes in from his room.*)

EKDAL: Home, are you? Thought I heard your voice.

HJALMAR: I just got back.

EKDAL: You didn't see me, did you?

HJALMAR: No; but someone told me you'd passed through—; so I thought I'd come on after you.

EKDAL: Hm. Nice of you, Hjalmar— Who were all those people?

HJALMAR: Oh, I don't know—just people. There was Court Chamberlain Balle; and then there was Flor—and Kaspersen—they're court chamberlains too—honorary, of course. I don't remember all the others—but I know most of them had titles of some sort.

EKDAL: Titled people, eh? D'you hear that, Gina?

GINA: Yes. They're very grand over there these days.

HEDVIG: What did all these titled people do, Father? Did they sing—or give recitations?

HJALMAR: No; they just talked a lot of rubbish. They tried to persuade me to recite something—but, of course, I wouldn't hear of that.

EKDAL: Wouldn't hear of that, eh?

GINA: Oh—perhaps you should have, Hjalmar.

HJALMAR: Certainly not. One shouldn't cater to every Tom, Dick and Harry. (*Paces about the room*) I don't intend to, anyhow.

EKDAL: No; Hjalmar's not that kind.

HJALMAR: I see no reason why *I* should be expected to entertain the guests, on the rare occasions when I go into Society. That's up to those other fellows; they spend their lives going from one dinner table to another, gorging and guzzling day in and day out. It's only right they should do something to earn all that good food they eat.

GINA: I hope you didn't tell them that!

HJALMAR (*Humming*): Hm–hm–hm— I think I made my position clear.

EKDAL: To all those titled people, eh?

HJALMAR: Why not? (*Casually*) We also had a slight argument about Tokay.

EKDAL: Tokay! There's a fine wine!

HJALMAR: Yes—it *can* be. It's all according to the year, of course; vintages differ. It depends on the amount of sunshine the grapes have.

GINA: Hjalmar—I believe there's nothing you don't know!

EKDAL: They surely didn't dispute that?

HJALMAR: Oh—they tried to; but they were reminded that there was a difference in the vintage of court chamberlains too; their quality also varies according to the year—so they were told.

GINA: The things you think up, Hjalmar!

EKDAL: He-he! You really gave it to them, eh?

HJALMAR: Straight in their silly faces!

EKDAL: Hear that, Gina? All those titled people! Straight in their silly faces!

GINA: Straight in their silly faces! Fancy!

HJALMAR: I wouldn't want this to go any further, mind you. It's not right to repeat things like that; and it was all perfectly amicable, of course. They're nice friendly fellows; I wouldn't want to hurt their feelings.

EKDAL: But—straight in their silly faces, eh?

HEDVIG (*Ingratiatingly*): It's nice to see you in a dinner jacket, Father. It's so becoming to you!

HJALMAR: It is, isn't it? This one fits beautifully—almost as if it had been made for me— A little tight in the armholes, perhaps. Here—help me, Hedvig. (*Takes off the dinner jacket*) I'll put on my old house coat. Where is it, Gina?

GINA: Here it is. (*Brings him the coat and helps him on with it.*)

HJALMAR: There we are! See that Molvik gets his jacket back first thing in the morning.

GINA (*Laying it away*): I'll see to it.

HJALMAR (*Stretching himself*): Ah! That feels more comfortable! And, you know—I really think a loose, casual coat like this suits my figure even better. What do *you* think, Hedvig?

HEDVIG: Yes, Father—I believe you're right!

HJALMAR: Now—I'll tie my necktie in a loose knot, with flowing ends— There! See?

HEDVIG: That looks lovely with your mustache, and your long curly hair!

HJALMAR: I don't think I'd call it *curly;* wavy, perhaps.

HEDVIG: Yes. They're too big for curls.

HJALMAR: *Wavy*—definitely.

HEDVIG (*After a pause, tugs at his coat*): Father!

HJALMAR: Well—what is it?

HEDVIG: Oh! *You* know what it is!

HJALMAR: No, I don't—

HEDVIG (*Half laughing, half whimpering*): Father—please don't tease me any longer!

HJALMAR: I don't know what you mean.

HEDVIG (*Shaking him*): Of course you do! Oh, please, Father! Aren't you going to give them to me? All those nice things you promised to bring home?

HJALMAR: Good Lord!—I forgot about them!

HEDVIG: You're only teasing me! It's mean of you! Where are they?

HJALMAR: No, honestly—I really *did* forget. But, wait! I've brought you something else. (*He goes and looks in the pockets of the dinner jacket.*)

HEDVIG (*Jumps up and down, clapping her hands*): Oh, Mother, Mother!

GINA: You see; if you're just patient—

HJALMAR (*With a piece of paper*): Look—here it is.

HEDVIG: This? But it's just a piece of paper.

HJALMAR: It's the bill of fare, that's what it is—the entire bill of fare. Do you see—it says here: menu? That means bill of fare.

HEDVIG: Is that really all you brought?

HJALMAR: I told you—I forgot. But you just take it from me—all these fancy dishes are greatly overrated. Now you sit at the table and study the bill of fare, and I'll tell you what all the dishes taste like. Won't that be fun?

HEDVIG (*Gulping down her tears*): Thanks.

(*She sits down, but doesn't read the menu.* GINA *signals to her;* HJALMAR *sees her.*)

HJALMAR (*Pacing up and down the room*): The head of the family is expected to think of everything—it's quite amazing! If by chance he forgets the slightest thing, he's immediately surrounded by glum faces. Well—one has to get used to it, I suppose. (*Stops by the stove near the old man*) Have you taken a look in there this evening, Father?

EKDAL: You bet I have! She's in her basket!

HJALMAR: No! Is she really? Then she's beginning to get used to it.

EKDAL: Told you she would, didn't I? But there are still a couple of little things—

HJALMAR: A few improvements—yes.

EKDAL: They *must* be done, you know.

HJALMAR: Yes—let's just go over them. We'll sit here on the sofa.

EKDAL: All right. Hm. First I'll fill my pipe. Got to clean it, too. Hm. (*Goes into his room.*)

GINA (*Smiles, to* HJALMAR): His pipe, indeed!

HJALMAR: Leave him alone, Gina—never mind! Poor wretched old man!—About those improvements—yes. I think I'll have a go at them tomorrow.

GINA: You won't have time tomorrow, Hjalmar.

HEDVIG: Oh yes he will, Mother!

GINA: Those prints have got to be retouched; they've sent for them several times, you know.

HJALMAR: Oh do stop nagging me about those prints! I'll get them done. Anything happen today? Any new orders?

GINA: No; I'm afraid not. I have those two sittings for tomorrow, though.

HJALMAR: And that's all, eh? Of course—if no one makes the smallest effort—

GINA: But what more can I do? I've advertised in several papers—all we could afford.

HJALMAR: Advertising! A lot of good *that* does! And what about the room? I suppose nothing's happened about that either?

GINA: Not yet, no.

HJALMAR: What else can one expect? Rooms don't rent themselves! Everything requires a little effort, Gina!

HEDVIG (*Going towards him*): Would you like me to fetch your flute, Father?

HJALMAR: No thanks. No flute for me; no pleasures of any sort for *me*. (*Pacing about*) All I have to look forward to is *work*. As long as my strength holds out, I suppose I'll have to keep on working—!

GINA: Hjalmar dear—I didn't mean—

HEDVIG: Let me get you a nice bottle of beer, Father.

HJALMAR: No; not for me. I require nothing— (*Stops*) Beer? —Beer did you say?

HEDVIG (*Cheerfully*): Yes, Father. Nice, cool beer.

HJALMAR: Oh, very well—if you insist; you might bring in a bottle.

GINA: Yes, do. That would be very nice.

(HEDVIG *runs towards the kitchen door.*)

HJALMAR (*By the stove, stops her, puts his arm round her and draws her to him*): Hedvig! Hedvig!

HEDVIG (*With tears of joy*): Dear, *darling* Father!

HJALMAR: No—don't call me that. I sat there at the rich man's table—stuffing myself at that festive board—and I couldn't even—!

GINA (*Sitting at the table*): Oh, don't talk nonsense, Hjalmar!

HJALMAR: No—it's not nonsense! But don't be too hard on me. You know how much I love you—

HEDVIG (*Throws her arms round him*): And we love you too, Father! More than we can ever say!

HJALMAR: And remember—if I'm difficult at times—it's because I have so many problems—so many cares. There, there! (*Dries his eyes*) No! No beer at a time like this—give me my flute. (HEDVIG *runs to the bookshelf and fetches it*.) Thanks! There! That's right—my flute in my hand, and you two at my side—! (HEDVIG *sits at the table near* GINA; HJALMAR *walks up and down and starts to play with gusto; it is a Bohemian peasant dance; his tempo is slow and plaintive and his attack highly sentimental. He breaks off in the middle of the tune, gives his left hand to* GINA *and says emotionally*) Our rooms may be poor and humble, Gina—but they're home all the same. And I can say from the bottom of my heart: it's good to be here!

(*He starts to play again; soon after there is a knock at the hall door*.)

GINA (*Rises*): Just a minute, Hjalmar. I think there's someone at the door.

HJALMAR (*Puts the flute back on the shelf*): What can it be? How tiresome!

(GINA *goes and opens the door*.)

GREGERS: Excuse me—

GINA (*Takes a step back*): Oh!

GREGERS: Does Mr. Ekdal, the photographer, live here?

GINA: Yes, he does.

HJALMAR (*Going towards the door*): Gregers! So you came after all. Well—come in then.

GREGERS (*Coming in*): I said I'd come to see you.

HJALMAR: Yes, but this evening—? Did you leave the party?

GREGERS: Both the party and my father's house— Good evening; do you recognize me, Mrs. Ekdal?

GINA: It's not hard to recognize young Mr. Werle.

GREGERS: That's true—I'm very like my mother; you remember her, I expect?

HJALMAR: Left your father's house you say?

GREGERS: Yes; I've gone to a hotel.

HJALMAR: Have you really? Well—since you're here, sit down; take off your things.

GREGERS: Thanks. (*He takes off his overcoat. He has changed his clothes and now wears a plain tweed suit.*)

HJALMAR: Here—sit on the sofa. Make yourself at home.
(GREGERS *sits on the sofa*, HJALMAR *on a chair by the table*.)

GREGERS (*Looking round*): So this is your home, Hjalmar. This is where you live.

HJALMAR: Yes; this is the studio, of course—

GINA: But it's such a nice large room—we nearly always sit here.

HJALMAR: We had a better place before; but this has great advantages; there's a lot of extra space—

GINA: And there's another room we can rent out—just down the passage.

GREGERS: Oh—you have lodgers then?

HJALMAR: Well—not just now. They're not so easy to find, you know; you have to keep your wits about you. (*To* HEDVIG) We might have that beer now. (HEDVIG *nods and goes out to the kitchen*.)

GREGERS: Is that your daughter?

HJALMAR: That's Hedvig, yes.

GREGERS: Is she your only child?

HJALMAR: Yes; she's the only one. She's our greatest joy, and— (*Lowers his voice*) our greatest sorrow too.

GREGERS: How do you mean?

HJALMAR: She's in danger of losing her eyesight, you see.

GREGERS: Of going blind!

HJALMAR: Yes; so far her eyes are not too seriously affected, and they may continue to be all right for a while; but eventually, the doctor says, it's bound to come.

GREGERS: What a dreadful thing! Has he any idea what caused it?

HJALMAR (*Sighs*): It may be hereditary, he thinks.

GREGERS (*With a slight start*): Hereditary?

GINA: Hjalmar's mother's eyes were bad, you see.

HJALMAR: So Father says; I don't remember her.

GREGERS: Poor child!—How does she take it?

HJALMAR: We naturally haven't told her anything about it; she suspects nothing. She's like a gay, carefree little bird, twittering away as it flutters towards the inevitable darkness. (*Overcome*) It's a terrible grief for me; it's heartbreaking to think of, Gregers. (HEDVIG *brings in a tray with beer and glasses and puts it on the table*.)

HJALMAR (*Stroking her hair*): Thank you, Hedvig, thank you! (HEDVIG *puts her arm round his neck and whispers in his ear*.)

HJALMAR: No—no sandwiches now. (*Looks at* GREGERS) Unless you'd like one, Gregers?

GREGERS (*With a gesture of refusal*): No—no thank you.

HJALMAR (*Still melancholy*): You might bring a few anyway—especially if there's a nice crusty piece of bread. And don't spare the butter, will you?

(HEDVIG *nods gaily and goes out to the kitchen*.)

GREGERS (*Who has been following her with his eyes*): She seems so strong and healthy otherwise.

GINA: There's nothing wrong with her apart from that, thank goodness.

GREGERS: She'll grow up to look like you—don't you think so, Mrs. Ekdal? How old is she now?

GINA: Nearly fourteen; her birthday's the day after tomorrow.

GREGERS: Tall for her age, isn't she?

GINA: She's shot up very fast in the past year.

GREGERS: It makes one feel old to see the youngsters growing up. How long is it now since you were married?

GINA: Let's see—we've been married nearly fifteen years.

GREGERS: Really! Is it as long as that?

GINA (*Becoming attentive; looks at him*): It is indeed.

HJALMAR: That's right. Fifteen years—all but a few months (*Changing the subject*) They must have been long years for you, Gregers—up there at the Works.

GREGERS: They seemed long at the time; yet in looking back at them, they went by very quickly.

(OLD EKDAL *comes in from his room, without his pipe, but wearing his old military cap; his walk is a bit unsteady.*)

EKDAL: All right, Hjalmar my boy—I'm ready now to talk about those—hm. What was it we were supposed to talk about?

HJALMAR (*Goes to him*): Father—we have a visitor; Gregers Werle—I don't know if you remember him—

EKDAL (*Looks at* GREGERS, *who has risen*): Werle? The son is it? What does he want with me?

HJALMAR: Nothing; he came to see me, Father.

EKDAL: Oh. Then there's nothing wrong?

HJALMAR: Of course not.

EKDAL (*Waves his arms*): Not that I'm afraid, you know—but—

GREGERS (*Goes over to him*): I bring you greetings from your old hunting grounds, Lieutenant Ekdal.

EKDAL: Hunting grounds?

GREGERS: Yes—up by the Höjdal Works; remember?

EKDAL: Oh, up there. I was well known in those parts once.

GREGERS: You were a mighty hunter in those days.

EKDAL: I was; that's true enough! You're looking at my cap, I see. I ask no one's permission to wear it in the house. As long as I don't walk about the streets in it—

(HEDVIG *brings in a plate of sandwiches and sets it on the table.*)

HJALMAR: Sit down, Father; have a glass of beer. Help yourself, Gregers.

(EKDAL *mutters something and stumbles over to the sofa,* GREGERS *sits on the chair nearest to him, and* HJALMAR *on the other side of* GREGERS. GINA *sits slightly away from the table with her sewing;* HEDVIG *stands by her father.*)

GREGERS: Do you remember, Lieutenant Ekdal, how Hjalmar and I used to come up and visit you—in the summer, and at Christmas?

EKDAL: Did you? No—I don't remember that. Yes—I was a mighty hunter in my day. Shot bears too. Nine of them.

GREGERS (*Looks at him sympathetically*): I suppose you don't go hunting any more.

EKDAL: I wouldn't say that, my friend. I still get a bit of hunting now and then. Not *that* kind, of course. For the forest, you see—the forest—! (*Drinks*) Is the forest up there just as fine as ever?

GREGERS: Not as fine as it was in your time. It's been thinned out quite a bit.

EKDAL: Thinned out, eh? (*Softly, as though afraid*) That's a dangerous business. That brings trouble. The forest takes revenge, you see.

HJALMAR (*Filling his glass*): Have a little more, Father.

GREGERS: It must be hard on a man like you—a man used to the open—to live in a stuffy town, cooped up in a little room—

EKDAL (*Laughs and glances at* HJALMAR): Oh, it's really not so bad here. No. Not bad at all.

GREGERS: But don't you miss the open spaces—the cool sweep of the wind through the trees—and all the animals and birds—?

EKDAL (*Smiles*): Let's show it to him, Hjalmar.

HJALMAR (*Hastily, with some embarrassment*): No—not this evening, Father.

GREGERS: What is it he wants to show me?

HJALMAR: Oh, nothing—you can see it some other time.

GREGERS (*Goes on talking to the old man*): Do you know what I was thinking, Lieutenant Ekdal? Why don't you come up to the Works with me? I expect to be going back there soon. They'll have plenty of copying for you to do up there, I'm sure. This is no place for you. You've nothing here to cheer you up—or keep you interested.

EKDAL (*Looks at him in amazement*): Nothing here to keep me—!

GREGERS: You have Hjalmar here I know; but he has his own work to attend to. And a man like you—accustomed to an active outdoor life—

EKDAL (*Thumps the table*): Hjalmar—he's *got* to see it!

HJALMAR: This is a bad time, Father. It's dark, remember—

EKDAL: Nonsense! There's the moonlight, isn't there? (*Rises*) I tell you he *must* see it! Let me get by. Hjalmar—come and help me!

HEDVIG: Yes—*do,* Father!

HJALMAR (*Rising*): Oh—very well.

GREGERS (*To* GINA): What can it be?

GINA: It's nothing very wonderful—!

(EKDAL *and* HJALMAR *have gone to the back wall and each opens his side of the sliding door.* HEDVIG *helps the old man;* GREGERS *remains standing by the sofa;* GINA *continues sewing undisturbed. Through the opening one sees a large, deep, irregularly shaped attic, filled with nooks and corners; a couple of stovepipes run through it from the rooms below. There are skylights through which the moon shines brightly on parts of the big room—while other parts are in deep shadow.*)

EKDAL (*To* GREGERS): Come closer, if you like.

GREGERS (*Going over to them*): What is it I'm supposed to see?

EKDAL: Take a good look now! Hm.

HJALMAR (*Somewhat embarrassed*): All this belongs to Father— you realize that, of course.

GREGERS (*At the opening peers into the attic*): Oh! I *see*, Lieutenant Ekdal—you keep poultry!

EKDAL: I should say we *do* keep poultry! They've gone to roost now—but you should see our hens by daylight!

HEDVIG: And then there's—

EKDAL: Sh! Not a word about that yet!

GREGERS: And I see doves there, too.

EKDAL: Yes! There are doves there right enough! Their nesting boxes are up under the eaves. Doves like to roost high, you know.

HJALMAR: They're not a common variety, by any means; at least not all of them.

EKDAL: Common! No indeed! We have tumblers—and a pair of pouters too. And now—look here! You see that hutch over by the wall?

GREGERS: What's that used for?

EKDAL: That, Sir, is where the rabbits sleep at night.

GREGERS: Then you have rabbits, too?

EKDAL: I should damn well say we *do* have rabbits! He wants to know if we have rabbits, Hjalmar! Hm. But just you wait! We're coming to the *real* thing now! Out of the way, Hedvig! Now you stand here—that's it. And look down there— Do you see a basket there with straw in it?

GREGERS: Yes—and isn't there a bird there, too?

EKDAL: Hm. "A bird," he says—!

GREGERS: It's a duck, isn't it?

EKDAL (*Annoyed*): Yes—it's a duck; that's clear!

HJALMAR: But what *kind* of a duck do you think?

HEDVIG: It's not just an *ordinary* duck, you know—

EKDAL: Sh!

GREGERS: And it doesn't look like a Muscovy duck, either.

EKDAL: No—it's no Muscovy duck, dear Mr. Werle. It happens to be a *wild* duck, you see.

GREGERS: A wild duck! Is it really?

EKDAL: That's what it is! That "bird," as you called it, that is the wild duck. It's our wild duck, Sir.

HEDVIG: *My* wild duck. It belongs to me.

GREGERS: How does it manage in there? Is it all right?

EKDAL: It has its own trough of water, of course, to splash about in.

HJALMAR: And we change the water every other day.

GINA (*Turning towards* HJALMAR): It's getting to be freezing in here, Hjalmar dear.

HJALMAR: Let's close her up, then. Anyway—they don't like to be disturbed at night. Go on, Hedvig—close her up! (HJALMAR *and* HEDVIG *close the sliding doors.*)

EKDAL: You'll be able to see her better some other time. (*Sits in the armchair by the stove*) Remarkable creatures those wild ducks, I can tell you!

GREGERS: How did you manage to catch it, Lieutenant Ekdal?

EKDAL: I didn't catch it myself. There's a certain man here in town, you see—we have him to thank for that.

GREGERS (*With a slight start*): That man wasn't my father, by any chance?

EKDAL: Your father—that's it; he's the man. Hm.

HJALMAR: Strange that you should guess that, Gregers!

GREGERS: You were telling me how much you owed to Father—in many different ways, you said; so I thought, perhaps—

GINA: But Mr. Werle didn't actually give us the duck himself—

EKDAL: Still, Gina—Haakon Werle is the man we have to thank for her. (*To* GREGERS) He was out shooting in a boat. He fired at her and brought her down. But his sight isn't too good now, you see—and so he only winged her. Hm.

GREGERS: But she was wounded, I suppose?

HJALMAR: Oh yes—she had some shot in her.

HEDVIG: Her wing was broken, poor thing; she couldn't fly.

GREGERS: Did she dive to the bottom then?

EKDAL (*Sleepily, with thickened speech*): Course she did! Always do that—wild ducks do. Make straight for the bottom—as far as they can go. Then they get trapped down there among the slimy roots and tangled reeds—and they never come up again.

GREGERS: But *your* wild duck came up again, Lieutenant Ekdal.

EKDAL: Had an amazingly clever dog, your father had. That dog—he dived down after her and brought her back.

GREGERS (*Turning to* HJALMAR): And then they gave her to you?

HJALMAR: No; not at once. First they took her to your father's house; but she started to pine away—so Pettersen was told to put an end to her—

EKDAL (*Half asleep*): That ass Pettersen—hm—

HJALMAR (*Lowers his voice*): And that's how we happened to get hold of her. Father knows Pettersen quite well, so when he heard about the wild duck he persuaded him to let *us* have her.

GREGERS: And the attic seems to agree with her, does it? She's doing well in there?

HJALMAR: Remarkably well—amazing, isn't it? She's grown quite plump, and she doesn't seem to miss her freedom. She's been there some time now, and I suppose she's forgotten all about it; that's what counts, you know.

GREGERS: I expect you're right; as long as she's kept away from the sky and the water—and has nothing to remind her— But I must be going now. Your father's gone to sleep, I think.

HJALMAR: Don't go on that account—

GREGERS: Oh, by the way—did you say you had an extra room? A room to rent, I mean?

HJALMAR: Yes, we have. Do you know anyone who—?

GREGERS: Would you let me have it?

HJALMAR: You?

GINA: Oh no, Mr. Werle, you—

GREGERS: If so, I'll move in first thing tomorrow morning.

HJALMAR: We'd be delighted!

GINA: But, Mr. Werle—it's not *your* kind of room—*really* it's not!

HJALMAR: What are you talking about, Gina?

GINA: I mean—it wouldn't be big enough, or light enough—

GREGERS: That doesn't matter, Mrs. Ekdal.

HJALMAR: It seems like a very nice room to me! And not badly furnished either.

GINA: How about those two fellows underneath?

GREGERS: What fellows?

GINA: There's one that says he's been a tutor—

HJALMAR: That's Molvik—Mr. Molvik—a B.A.

GINA: And the other one calls himself a doctor; his name's Relling.

GREGERS: Relling? I think I know him slightly. He had a practice up at Höjdal for a while.

GINA: Well—they're a no-good, rowdy lot! Out till all hours every night—drinking themselves silly—

GREGERS: I shan't mind them; I'll soon get used to it. I'll try to be as adaptable as the wild duck—

GINA: All the same—you'd better sleep on it.

GREGERS: You don't seem very anxious to have me as a lodger, Mrs. Ekdal.

GINA: Who, *me?* Why do you say that?

HJALMAR: I must say, Gina—you're being very odd about it. (*To* GREGERS) You plan to stay in town then—for the present?

GREGERS: That's what I've decided, yes.

HJALMAR: Not at your father's house, though? What do you plan to do?

GREGERS: I only wish I knew. When one has the misfortune to bear the name of "Gregers," followed by the name of "Werle"—a pretty hideous combination, don't you think?

HJALMAR: I don't think so at all.

GREGERS: Pah! I'd feel like spitting on a man with a name like that! But since I'm doomed to go on being Gregers Werle in this world—

HJALMAR (*Laughs*): Ha! Ha! Well—if you weren't Gregers Werle, what would you choose to be?

GREGERS: I think I'd choose to be a clever dog.

GINA: A dog!

HEDVIG (*Involuntarily*): Oh, no!

GREGERS: Yes, a very clever dog; the kind that plunges after wild ducks when they dive to the bottom, and get trapped down in the mud.

HJALMAR: That's beyond me, Gregers! What *are* you driving at?

GREGERS: Just nonsense; never mind. I'll move in early tomorrow morning then. (*To* GINA) I won't be any trouble; I'm used to doing things myself. (*To* HJALMAR) We'll discuss details tomorrow— Good night, Mrs. Ekdal. (*Nods to* HEDVIG) Good night!

GINA: Good night, Mr. Werle.

HEDVIG: Good night.

HJALMAR (*Who has lighted a candle*): Wait; I'll see you out. The stairs are rather dark.

(GREGERS *and* HJALMAR *go out by the hall door*.)

GINA (*Sits with her sewing in her lap gazing before her*): What a queer thing to say—that he'd like to be a dog.

HEDVIG: You know, Mother—I think he really meant something quite different.

GINA: What else *could* he have meant?

HEDVIG: I don't know; but it's almost as though everything he said *really* meant something different.

GINA: Do you think so? Well—it seems very queer to me.

HJALMAR (*Comes back*): The lamp down in the hall was still alight. (*Blows out the candle and puts it down*) Ah! Now, perhaps we can have a bite to eat! (*Starts to eat the sandwiches*) You see, Gina, what happens when you keep your wits about you—?

GINA: What do you mean—"wits about you"?

HJALMAR: We rented the room, didn't we? And to an old friend like Gregers, too.

GINA: I don't know what to think of that.

HEDVIG: It'll be fun, Mother—you'll see!

HJALMAR: You really are amazing! I thought you were so hipped on renting it—and now you behave as if you didn't want to.

GINA: If it had only been to someone else— What will Mr. Werle say I wonder.

HJALMAR: Old Werle? It's no business of his.

GINA: I expect they've been quarreling again; otherwise young Werle would never have left home. You know they've never been able to get on together.

HJALMAR: That may be, but still—

GINA: You never know; Mr. Werle may think it's all your doing.

HJALMAR: Well—let him! Mr. Werle's done a lot for me—God knows I'm the first one to admit it—but he can't expect me to go on kowtowing to him for ever!

GINA: But—Hjalmar dear—he might take it out on Grandfather; he might tell Graaberg not to give him any more copying to do.

HJALMAR: I could almost say: I wish he would! You don't seem to understand how humiliating it is for a man like me to see his old father treated like a servant. But some day the pendulum will swing the other way; it won't be long now—I feel it! (*Takes another sandwich*) I have a sacred duty in life, and I intend to perform it to the full!

HEDVIG: You will, Father! I know you will!

GINA: Hush! Don't wake him!

HJALMAR (*Lowers his voice*): To the *full*, I say! There'll come a day when— That's another reason why I'm glad we've rented the room, you see. It'll make me a bit more independent. A man needs independence if he's to face the task *I* have to face. (*By the armchair; with emotion*) Poor white-haired old man!—Don't you be afraid—lean on your Hjalmar; his shoulders are broad. They're strong, at any rate. One of these fine days you'll wake up to see—(*To* GINA) Don't you believe me?

GINA (*Rising*): Yes, of course I do. But let's get him to bed.

HJALMAR: Yes—very well.

(*They lift up the old man carefully.*)

CURTAIN

ACT
THREE

SCENE: HJALMAR EKDAL'S *studio. It is morning; daylight streams through the large window in the slanting roof, and the curtain is drawn back.* HJALMAR *sits at the table busy retouching a photograph; several others lie before him. After a few moments* GINA *comes in through the hall door, wearing a hat and coat and with a basket on her arm.*

HJALMAR: Back already, Gina?

GINA: Yes; I've no time for dawdling.

HJALMAR: Did you look in at Gregers?

GINA: I certainly did! You should just see the mess in there! He's made a good start, he has!

HJALMAR: Why? What's he done?

GINA: Used to doing things for himself, says he! So he lights the stove, but leaves the damper shut: the whole room's filled with smoke. The smell in there's enough to—

HJALMAR: Oh, dear!

GINA: But that isn't the worst of it: he decides to put the fire *out* again; so what does he do but take the pitcher from his washstand and empty every blessed drop of water right into the stove! The floor's a mess!

HJALMAR: What a nuisance.

GINA: I got the porter's wife to come and clean it up for him—the pig! But it'll be afternoon before the place is fit to live in.

HJALMAR: What's Gregers doing now?

GINA: He went out for a bit.

HJALMAR: While you were gone, I stopped in to see him too.

GINA: I know; you've asked him to lunch, I hear.

HJALMAR: Not *lunch* exactly—more of a snack, you know. After all, it's his first day here—I didn't know what else to do. You must have something in the house.

GINA: I'll have to try and find something, I suppose.

HJALMAR: Don't be *too* skimpy, though. Relling and Molvik are coming too, I think. I ran into Relling on the stairs, and I couldn't very well—

GINA: Oh dear! Do we have to have *them* too?

HJALMAR: Good heavens—one more or less—what difference does it make?

EKDAL (*Opens his door and looks in*): Look here, Hjalmar— (*Sees* GINA) Oh.

GINA: Anything you want, Grandfather?

EKDAL: No, no. It doesn't matter. Hm! (*Goes into his room again.*)

GINA (*Picking up her basket*): Don't let him go out will you? Keep an eye on him.

HJALMAR: All right, all right—I will. Oh, Gina; some herring salad might be just the thing: Relling and Molvik were on a bit of a spree last night.

GINA: Just so long as they don't get here before I'm ready.

HJALMAR: Of course they won't. Just take your time.

GINA: Very well; meanwhile you can get a bit of work done.

HJALMAR: Work! I *am* working, aren't I? What more can I do?

GINA: I just meant—the sooner you get it done, the sooner it'll be over with. (*She takes the basket and goes out to the kitchen.* HJALMAR *sits for a few moments working reluctantly on the photograph.*)

EKDAL (*Peeps in, looks round the studio, and says softly*): Are you busy, Hjalmar?

HJALMAR: Slaving away at these blasted pictures—!

EKDAL: Well—never mind; as long as you're busy—Hm!
(*He goes into his room again but leaves the door open.*)

HJALMAR (*Goes on working for some time in silence, then lays down his brush and goes over to the open door*): Are *you* busy, Father?

EKDAL (*In a low growl, from his room*): If *you're* busy then *I'm* busy too. Hm.

HJALMAR: Yes; very well. (*Goes back to his work.*)

EKDAL (*Presently, coming to the door again*): Hm. Hjalmar, I'm not as busy as all *that*, you know.

HJALMAR: I thought you were writing.

EKDAL: To hell with it! It's not a matter of life and death, after all. It won't hurt Graaberg to wait a day or two.

HJALMAR: No; and you're not his slave, either.

EKDAL: There's that job in there, you see—

HJALMAR: Just what *I* was thinking of. Would you like to go in? I'll open up for you.

EKDAL: It mightn't be a bad idea.

HJALMAR (*Rises*): Then we'd have it all done, wouldn't we?

EKDAL: And we've got to finish it before tomorrow morning. It *is* tomorrow, isn't it? Hm?

HJALMAR: Of course, it's tomorrow.

(HJALMAR *and* EKDAL *each pull open a side of the sliding door. Inside the attic the morning sun pours through the skylights; some doves are flying about, others sit cooing on their perches; the clucking of hens can be heard farther back in the attic.*)

HJALMAR: There! Now you can get to work, Father.

EKDAL (*Goes into the attic*): Aren't you coming too?

HJALMAR: Well, you know—Yes! I believe I— (*Sees* GINA *at the kitchen door*) No, no! I can't—haven't time! Too much work to do! How about our new invention, though? (*He pulls a cord and a curtain drops inside the opening; the lower part consists of an old piece of sailcloth, the upper part of a piece of fishing net. The floor of the attic is now concealed*) There! Now perhaps I can have a little peace!

GINA: Must he go messing about in there again?

HJALMAR: Would you rather he'd run off to Mrs. Eriksen's? (*Sits down*) What is it you want? I thought you said—

GINA: I wanted to ask—will it be all right to lay the table for lunch in here?

HJALMAR: Why not? There aren't any appointments, are there?

GINA: Just that engaged couple; you know—the two that want to be photographed together.

HJALMAR: Why the devil can't they be photographed together some *other* day?

GINA: It's all right, Hjalmar dear. I told them to come in the late afternoon; you'll be taking your nap by then.

HJALMAR: That's good; we'll eat in here then.

GINA: Very well; but there's no hurry—you can go on using the table for a good while yet.

HJALMAR: I'm using it—don't worry! I'm using it for all I'm worth!

GINA: Then, later on—you'll be free, you see. (*She goes into the kitchen. A short pause.*)

EKDAL: (*In the doorway of the attic, behind the net*): Hjalmar!

HJALMAR: Well?

EKDAL: Afraid we'll have to move that water trough—

HJALMAR: I said so all along.

EKDAL: Hm-hm-hm. (*Goes away from the door again. HJALMAR goes on working a little, then glances towards the attic and starts to rise. HEDVIG comes in from the kitchen.*)

HJALMAR (*Sits down again hurriedly*): What do you want?

HEDVIG: Just to be with you, Father.

HJALMAR: What are you snooping about in here for? Were you told to keep an eye on me?

HEDVIG: Of course not.

HJALMAR: What's your mother up to now?

HEDVIG: She's busy making the herring salad. (*Goes over to the table*) Father—isn't there anything I can do to help?

HJALMAR: No, no. I'll carry on alone as long as my strength holds out. Never you fear, Hedvig; while your father keeps his health—

HEDVIG: Father! I won't have you say such awful things! (*She wanders about the room a little, stops by the doorway, and looks into the attic.*)

HJALMAR: What's he doing? Can you see?

HEDVIG: Making a new runway to the water trough, I think.

HJALMAR: He'll never manage that alone! And here I have to sit—*chained* to this—!

HEDVIG (*Goes to him*): Give me the brush, Father. I do it quite well, you know.

HJALMAR: Nonsense! You'd only hurt your eyes.

HEDVIG: No, I wouldn't—really! Please give me the brush.

HJALMAR (*Rises*): It'll only take a minute—

HEDVIG: What's the harm, then? (*Takes the brush*) There! (*Sits down*) I'll use this one as a model.

HJALMAR: Don't strain your eyes, do you hear? And remember, I'm not responsible; you're doing this on your own responsibility you understand!

HEDVIG (*Starts retouching*): Of course.

HJALMAR: You're very good at it. I'll only be a minute. (*He slips through the side of the curtain into the attic.* HEDVIG *sits at her work.* HJALMAR *and* EKDAL *are heard arguing.*)

HJALMAR (*Appears behind the net*): Hedvig—would you hand me those pincers on the shelf; and the chisel, too. (*Turning back to the attic*) You'll see, Father— Now just let me show you what I mean! (HEDVIG *has fetched the tools from the shelf and hands them in to him.*) Thanks. It's a good thing I got here when I did! (*Goes away from the opening; they can be heard carpentering and talking inside.* HEDVIG *stands watching them. A moment later there's a knock at the hall door; she doesn't hear it.*)

GREGERS (*Bareheaded and without an overcoat comes in and stops near the door*): Hm—!

HEDVIG (*Turns and goes toward him*): Good morning. Do come in.

GREGERS: Thanks. (*Looks toward the attic*) Have you workmen in the house?

HEDVIG: No; it's only Father and Grandfather. I'll call them.

GREGERS: No, don't. I'd rather wait a little. (*Sits down on the sofa.*)

HEDVIG: It's so untidy here— (*Starts clearing away the photographs.*)

GREGERS: Never mind—don't bother! Are those the prints that need retouching?

HEDVIG: Yes; I was just helping Father with them.

GREGERS: Don't let me disturb you.

HEDVIG: No—you won't. (*She gathers the things together and sits down to work;* GREGERS *watches her in silence.*)

GREGERS: Did the wild duck sleep well last night?

HEDVIG: Yes, thank you; I think so.

GREGERS (*Turning and looking towards the attic*): How different
   it looks by day; quite different than by moonlight.

HEDVIG: Yes—it changes all the time. In the morning it's not a bit
   the same as it is in the afternoon; and it looks quite different on
   rainy days from the way it looks when the sun shines.

GREGERS: You've noticed that, have you?

HEDVIG: Of course; how could I help it?

GREGERS: Do you spend much time in there with the wild duck?

HEDVIG: I go in whenever I can manage it—

GREGERS: I expect you're pretty busy. You go to school, I suppose?

HEDVIG: No—not any more; Father's afraid I'll hurt my eyes.

GREGERS: Does he give you lessons himself then?

HEDVIG: He promised to; but so far he hasn't had time.

GREGERS: Is there nobody else who could help you with your
   studies?

HEDVIG: There's Mr. Molvik; but he's not always—

GREGERS: Sober, you mean?

HEDVIG: Yes—I suppose that's it.

GREGERS: Then you've a good deal of spare time, haven't you? I
   should think it must be a world all to itself in there.

HEDVIG: Oh, it is! And it's full of the most wonderful things too!

GREGERS: Is it really?

HEDVIG: Yes. There are great big cupboards filled with books; and
   lots of them have pictures in them.

GREGERS: Aha!

HEDVIG: And there's an old desk with drawers and pigeonholes;
   and a great big clock with figures that used to pop in and out. But
   the clock's stopped—so they don't work any more.

GREGERS: Time has ceased to exist in the wild duck's world.

HEDVIG: And there's an old paintbox too—and lots of other things;
   and all the books, of course.

GREGERS: And you read the books, I suppose?

HEDVIG: Whenever I can I do. But most of them are in English,
   and I don't understand English, you see. Still—I look at the pictures. There's one very large book—*Harrison's History of*

London it's called—it must be a hundred years old, I should think. That has lots of pictures in it. On the front page there's a picture of death holding an hourglass—and he has a lady with him. That one's horrid, I think. But there are heaps of others; pictures of churches, and castles, and streets, and great ships sailing on the sea.

GREGERS: Where did all these wonderful things come from?

HEDVIG: An old sea captain lived here once, and he must have brought them home with him. They used to call him "The Flying Dutchman"; and that was funny, because he wasn't Dutch at all, you know.

GREGERS: Wasn't he?

HEDVIG: No. Then he went away, and never came back—and the things just stayed here.

GREGERS: Tell me—when you sit in there looking at those pictures—don't you ever long to travel, and see something of the world yourself?

HEDVIG: Oh, no! I want to stay home always and help Father and Mother.

GREGERS: To retouch photographs?

HEDVIG: No—not only that. Do you know what I'd *really* like to do? I'd like to learn engraving; then I could make pictures like the ones in all those books.

GREGERS: Hm. What does your father say to that?

HEDVIG: He doesn't like the idea at all; Father's funny in some ways. He keeps talking about my learning basket weaving and wickerwork! I don't think that'd be much fun, do you?

GREGERS: No—I shouldn't think so.

HEDVIG: Still—in a way he's right; he says if I'd learned basketwork I could have made the wild duck its new basket.

GREGERS: That's true enough; you'd have been the logical one to do it, after all.

HEDVIG: Yes—because it's *my* wild duck, you see.

GREGERS: Of course it is.

HEDVIG: Yes, it belongs to me. But when Father and Grandfather want it, I don't mind lending it to them, you know.

GREGERS: What do they do with it?

HEDVIG: Oh, they look after it, and build things for it; all that sort of thing.

GREGERS: I'm not surprised; she's the most important creature in there!

HEDVIG: Indeed she is! After all, she's a *real* wild bird. And it must be so sad for her to be there all by herself.

GREGERS: She has no family, like the rabbits—

HEDVIG: No. And the hens, too; lots of them were hatched at the same time and were little chicks together. But she has no one belonging to her, poor thing. She's a complete stranger; no one knows where she came from—no one knows anything about her.

GREGERS: And then, too—she was rescued from the boundless deep, remember!

HEDVIG (*Glances at him swiftly and represses a smile*): What makes you call it the boundless deep?

GREGERS: What would you have me call it?

HEDVIG: Most people would say "from under the water" or "from the bottom of the sea."

GREGERS: But *I* prefer the boundless deep.

HEDVIG: It sounds funny to hear somebody else say that.

GREGERS: Why? What do you mean?

HEDVIG: Nothing. You'd only laugh at me.

GREGERS: Of course I wouldn't. Tell me—what made you smile? Go on!

HEDVIG: It's just that whenever I think of that place in there—suddenly—unexpectedly, you know—I think of it as the boundless deep. It *feels* like that, somehow. You must think me awfully silly!

GREGERS: No—don't say that!

HEDVIG: After all—it's only an old attic.

GREGERS (*Looks at her intently*): Are you so sure?

HEDVIG (*Astonished*): That it's an attic?

GREGERS: Yes. How can you be so certain?

(HEDVIG *is silent and looks at him open-mouthed.* GINA *comes in from the kitchen with a tablecloth.*)

GREGERS (*Rising*): I'm afraid I came too early.

GINA: You have to be somewhere, I suppose. We're nearly ready now. Clear off the table, Hedvig.

(HEDVIG *obeys; she and* GINA *lay the table during the following.* GREGERS *sits in the armchair looking through a photograph album.*)

GREGERS: I hear you've done quite a bit of retouching, Mrs. Ekdal.

GINA (*With a sidelong glance*): Yes, I have.

GREGERS: A lucky coincidence, wasn't it?

GINA: Why lucky?

GREGERS: Since Hjalmar's a photographer, I mean.

HEDVIG: And Mother can take pictures too.

GINA: I more or less *had* to take it up.

GREGERS: Then I suppose it's you who really runs the business?

GINA: When Hjalmar has too many other things to do, I—

GREGERS: I dare say his father takes up a good deal of his time.

GINA: Yes; and this is no fit job for Hjalmar anyway—wasting his time taking pictures of a lot of silly people!

GREGERS: I quite agree; but once having chosen it as his profession—

GINA: He's no *ordinary* photographer, mind you! I'm sure you understand that, Mr. Werle.

GREGERS: Yes, of course, but still—

(*A shot is heard from the attic.*)

GREGERS (*Starting up*): What's that?

GINA: There they go—at that shooting again!

GREGERS: Do you mean to say they shoot in there?

HEDVIG: They're out hunting, you see.

GREGERS: What! (*Goes to the door of the attic*) Are you out hunting, Hjalmar?

HJALMAR (*From inside the net*): Oh, you've come. I didn't know. I was so taken up with— (*To* HEDVIG) Why didn't you call us? (*Comes into the studio.*)

GREGERS: Do you mean to tell me you go shooting in the attic?

HJALMAR (*Showing a double-barreled pistol*): Only with this old thing.

GINA: You and Grandfather'll get into trouble one of these days—fooling with that gun.

HJALMAR (*Irritably*): How often have I told you—this weapon is a *pistol*.

GINA: I don't see that that makes it any better.

GREGERS: Well, Hjalmar—so you've become a hunter too!

HJALMAR: We do a little rabbit shooting now and then. It pleases the old man, you know.

GINA: Men are a queer lot! Must have their divergence!

HJALMAR (*Angrily*): Diversion—I suppose you mean!

GINA: That's what I said, isn't it?

HJALMAR: Well— ! Hm. (*To* GREGERS) It works out very well; the attic's so high up, no one can hear the shooting. (*Lays the pistol on the top shelf of the bookcase*) Mind you don't touch the pistol, Hedvig. One of the barrels is still loaded; remember that.

GREGERS (*Peering through the net*): You have a rifle too, I see.

HJALMAR: It's an old gun of father's. But there's something wrong with the lock—it won't fire any more. It's fun to have it, though; we take it apart, grease it, give it a good cleaning—and then put it together again. That is—*Father* does; he likes puttering about with things like that.

HEDVIG (*Beside* GREGERS): Look! You can see the wild duck clearly now.

GREGERS: Yes—I was just looking at her. She seems to drag her wing a bit.

HJALMAR: That's not strange; that's the broken wing, you see.

GREGERS: And she's lame in one foot, isn't she?

HJALMAR: Yes—perhaps a little.

HEDVIG: That's the foot the dog caught hold of.

HJALMAR: But she's all right otherwise; it's quite amazing —considering she had a charge of shot in her, and the dog grabbed her with his teeth—

GREGERS (*With a glance at* HEDVIG): —and she was down in the boundless deep, as well.

HEDVIG (*Smiling*): Yes.

GINA (*Goes on laying the table*): That blessed wild duck! She gets enough fuss made over her!

HJALMAR: Hm— Will lunch be ready soon?

GINA: Yes, in a minute. Now, Hedvig—come and help me.
(GINA *and* HEDVIG *go out into the kitchen.*)

HJALMAR (*In a low voice*): I wouldn't stand there watching Father;
he doesn't like it. (GREGERS *moves away from the attic door*) I'd
better close up before the others come. (*Claps his hands to drive
the birds back*) Shoo! Get back there! (*Draws up the net and
pulls the door panels together*) These contraptions are all my
own invention. It's rather fun to fiddle about with things like
that. Gina doesn't like the hens and rabbits to get into the studio,
so it's important to keep all this in running order.

GREGERS: Yes, I see—It's your wife who really runs the business
then?

HJALMAR: I leave the routine part of it to her. It gives me a chance
to work on more important things; I use the sitting room, you
see.

GREGERS: What kind of things?

HJALMAR: I'm surprised you haven't asked me that before. But
you haven't heard about the invention, I suppose?

GREGERS: Invention? No.

HJALMAR: You haven't, eh? Of course—I know you've been living
in the wilds—

GREGERS: Have you invented something?

HJALMAR: I haven't quite solved it yet; but I'm working on it constantly. I didn't become a photographer in order to spend my life
taking commonplace pictures of commonplace people—I need
hardly tell you that.

GREGERS: Just what your wife was saying.

HJALMAR: When I chose the photographic medium, I swore to
myself that I would raise it to the level of a science and an art
combined; so I set to work on this invention.

GREGERS: What kind of an invention is it? What does it consist of?

HJALMAR: My dear fellow, you mustn't try to pin me down to details yet; these things take time, you know. And, believe me, it's
not a question of self-glorification—I'm not working on it for my
own sake, I assure you! I have a fixed purpose in life—a sacred
duty; and I consider this work part of it.

GREGERS: What is this "purpose in life" you speak of?

HJALMAR: Are you forgetting that white-haired old man in there?

GREGERS: Your poor father—yes. What exactly do you plan to do for him?

HJALMAR: I plan to give him back his self-respect by restoring the name of Ekdal to its former dignity and honor.

GREGERS: I see.

HJALMAR: Yes—I shall rescue him! Poor, broken old man! Do you know that from the moment the trouble started—from the very beginning—he went all to pieces, and he seemed unable to recover. In those terrible days—all during the trial—he was so changed, I hardly knew him—That pistol over there—the one we use to shoot rabbits with—that played its part in the Ekdal tragedy too!

GREGERS: The pistol! Really?

HJALMAR: Oh, yes! When he was found guilty, and they sentenced him to prison—he stood with that pistol in his hand—

GREGERS: You mean—he was going to—?

HJALMAR: Yes. But his courage failed him; he dared not use it. That shows you how broken and demoralized he was. Imagine! He, a soldier! A great hunter with nine bears to his credit. A man directly descended from two Lieutenant Colonels—in successive generations, naturally—and yet his courage failed him! Can you understand that, Gregers?

GREGERS: Yes; I understand that very well.

HJALMAR: I don't. But that pistol was to turn up again in the Ekdal Saga. When I thought of him in his prison clothes—under lock and key—in that gloomy prison cell—! Those were agonizing days for me! I kept all the shades down in my room. I'd look out now and then, and I couldn't understand how the sun could still be shining. I couldn't understand how people could still be walking through the streets—laughing and chatting about trivial things. It seemed to me as though the world had come to a standstill—as though life itself were under an eclipse.

GREGERS: I felt like that when Mother died.

HJALMAR: And there came a moment when Hjalmar Ekdal seized that pistol and aimed it at his own breast.

GREGERS: You, too, thought of—!

HJALMAR: Yes.

GREGERS: But you didn't fire?

HJALMAR: No—I didn't fire. By a supreme effort I conquered the temptation—and I went on living. It takes courage to choose life under such circumstances, I can tell you.

GREGERS: That depends on how you look at it.

HJALMAR: No, my dear fellow—it's indisputable. And I'm glad I managed to find the necessary strength, for now I shall be able to finish my invention. And when it's ready, Dr. Relling thinks —and I agree with him—that Father may get permission to wear his uniform again. I shall demand that as my sole reward.

GREGERS: Does that mean so much to him—?

HJALMAR: It's his dearest wish. Oh, Gregers—my heart bleeds for him! Whenever we have a little family celebration—Gina's and my wedding anniversary, whatever it may be—in comes the old man wearing the lieutenant's uniform he wore in happier days. But if there's a knock at the door, or if he hears someone in the hall—back he runs to his room as fast as his poor old legs will carry him; for he dare not be caught wearing it in public. It breaks my heart to see him!

GREGERS: When do you expect to finish the invention?

HJALMAR: Good heavens—that's impossible to say! An invention is not a matter of routine, you know. It depends on inspiration—on a sudden intuition—on factors beyond one's immediate control.

GREGERS: But you're making progress with it?

HJALMAR: Of course I'm making progress! I wrestle with it every day—my mind is full of it. Every afternoon, as soon as I've had lunch, I lock myself in the sitting room in there, where I can work in peace. But it's no use *hounding* me about it; as Relling says, that does more harm than good!

GREGERS: What about all this business in the attic? Don't you find that distracting? Doesn't it waste a great deal of your time?

HJALMAR: On the contrary! You mustn't think that for a moment! I must have *some* relaxation, after all; something to relieve the strain of incessant concentration. And, anyhow, inspiration is quite unpredictable; when it comes it comes—that's all!

GREGERS: You know, Hjalmar—I think you and the wild duck have quite a lot in common.

HJALMAR: The wild duck! What on earth do you mean?

GREGERS: You dived to the bottom too, and got yourself trapped down there.

HJALMAR: You mean that I was wounded too—by the blow that almost killed my father?

GREGERS: No, not exactly. It's not that you're wounded, Hjalmar; but you've lost your way in a poisonous swamp. You've become infected with an insidious disease, and you've sunk to the bottom to die in the dark.

HJALMAR: Die in the dark? I? Really, Gregers—how can you talk such nonsense!

GREGERS: But don't worry—I'll bring you back. I have a purpose in life too, you see. One I discovered yesterday.

HJALMAR: That's all very well—but kindly leave *me* out of it! I assure you that—apart from a perfectly justifiable melancholy —I'm as content and happy as any man could be.

GREGERS: That's part of the illness, you see. It's all part of the poison.

HJALMAR: My dear Gregers—please don't go on about illnesses and poisons any more! I dislike that kind of talk. In my house no one ever speaks to me about unpleasant things.

GREGERS: That I can well believe.

HJALMAR: I dislike it and it's bad for me— And I don't care what you say—there are no swamps or poisons here! My surroundings may be modest—my home may be humble; but I'm an inventor and the breadwinner of a family, and I assure you this exalts me above any petty material concerns— Ah! Here comes lunch! (GINA *and* HEDVIG *enter bringing bottles of beer, a decanter of brandy, glasses, etc. At the same time* RELLING *and* MOLVIK *enter from the hall, both without hats or overcoats;* MOLVIK *is dressed in black.*)

GINA (*Placing dishes on the table*): You're just in time!

RELLING: Molvik got a whiff of herring salad and there was no holding him!

HJALMAR: I'd like you to meet Mr. Molvik, Gregers; and doctor—oh, but you know Dr. Relling, don't you?

GREGERS: Slightly, yes.

RELLING: Mr. Werle Junior, of course. We had a few little skir-
mishes up at the Höjdal Works. Did you just move in?

GREGERS: This morning.

RELLING: Molvik and I live just below you; so if you should happen to need a doctor or a clergyman, you won't have far to go.

GREGERS: I might have to take you up on that: we were thirteen at
table yesterday.

HJALMAR: I do wish you'd stop talking about unpleasant things!

RELLING: Your time hasn't come yet, Hjalmar! No need to worry!

HJALMAR: For the sake of my family I hope you're right. But let's
sit down now—and eat, drink and be merry!

GREGERS: Shouldn't we wait for your father?

HJALMAR: No; he'll have lunch in his own room presently. Come
on! (*The men seat themselves at table and start eating and drinking.* GINA *and* HEDVIG *go in and out waiting on them.*)

RELLING: Molvik was drunk as a Lord yesterday, Mrs. Ekdal.

GINA: Was he? Again?

RELLING: Didn't you hear him when I brought him home last
night?

GINA: Can't say I did.

RELLING: Just as well; last night he was downright disgusting.

GINA: Is that true, Molvik?

MOLVIK: Let us draw a veil over last night's proceedings; they
have no connection with my better self.

RELLING: He becomes like one possessed; then he insists on
dragging me out with him. He's daemonic—that's what it is.

GREGERS: Daemonic?

RELLING: Yes; Molvik is daemonic.

GREGERS: Hm.

RELLING: And people with daemonic natures can't be expected to
go through life on an even keel, you know. They're obliged to
run amok now and then—they *have* to— Are you still slaving
away at those horrible grimy Works?

GREGERS: I have been until now.

RELLING: Did you ever get anyone to honor that claim you made
such a fuss about up there?

GREGERS: Claim? (*Understands him*) Oh, I see.

HJALMAR: Claim? What sort of a claim, Gregers?

GREGERS: Nothing. A lot of nonsense.

RELLING: Not at all! He carried on a regular crusade! He went from house to house preaching about something—what was it you called it?—the Claim of the Ideal?

GREGERS: I was young then.

RELLING: Yes! You were young all right! But did you ever get anyone to honor it? You hadn't while I was there, as I remember.

GREGERS: And not since, either.

RELLING: Have you perhaps learned to compromise a little?

GREGERS: Compromise? Never in dealing with a man who really *is* a man.

HJALMAR: No! I should hope not!— More butter, Gina.

RELLING: And a bit of pork for Molvik.

MOLVIK: Ugh! Not *pork*!

(*There's a knock at the attic door.*)

HJALMAR: Father wants to come out; open up for him, Hedvig. (HEDVIG *goes and slides the door open a little way;* EKDAL *comes in carrying a fresh rabbit skin;* HEDVIG *closes the door after him.*)

EKDAL: Good morning, gentlemen! Good hunting today! Shot a big one!

HJALMAR: And you skinned it without waiting for me—!

EKDAL: Salted it, too. Good *tender* meat, is rabbit meat. And sweet; tastes like sugar. Enjoy your lunch, gentlemen! (*Goes into his room.*)

MOLVIK (*Getting up*): Excuse me— I can't— I must get downstairs at once—

RELLING: Take some soda water, man!

MOLVIK: Ugh—Ugh! (*Hurries out by the hall door.*)

RELLING (*To* HJALMAR): Let's drink a toast to the old hunter.

HJALMAR (*Clinks glasses with him*): To the gallant old sportsman on the brink of the grave.

RELLING: To the old gray-haired— (*Drinks*) By the way, is his hair gray or white?

HJALMAR: A little of both, I think. As a matter of fact, he hasn't much hair left.

RELLING: Well—you can get on just as well in a wig! You know—you really are a lucky man, Hjalmar; you have a definite purpose in life to strive for—

HJALMAR: And, believe me, I *am* striving for it—!

RELLING: And there's your good, capable wife—padding about so quietly in her old felt slippers, making everything cozy and comfortable for you—

HJALMAR: Yes, Gina— (*Nods to her*) You're a good companion on life's journey, Gina dear.

GINA: Don't go making a fool of me!

RELLING: And then, there's your Hedvig, Hjalmar—

HJALMAR (*Moved*): Yes—best of all, my child! My Hedvig! Come here to me, my darling! (*Strokes her hair*) What day is it tomorrow, eh?

HEDVIG (*Shakes him*): Don't say anything about that, Father.

HJALMAR: It cuts me to the heart to think how meager it will be; just a little ceremony in the attic—

HEDVIG: But I like that best of all!

RELLING: Just you wait till the invention's finished, Hedvig!

HJALMAR: Yes!— *Then* you'll see! Your future will be taken care of; you shall live in comfort all your life—I shall make sure of that! I shall demand—well—something or other on your behalf. It will be the poor inventor's sole request.

HEDVIG (*In a whisper, her arms round his neck*): Dear, darling Father!

RELLING (*To* GREGERS): Isn't it pleasant for a change to sit here with this happy family—eating delicious food at a well-spread table?

HJALMAR: It's a joy to share a meal with such good friends!

GREGERS: Personally—I don't like the smell of poison.

RELLING: Poison?

HJALMAR: Oh, don't start *that* again!

GINA: I'd have you know, Mr. Werle, there's no smell of poison here; I air this room out every single day!

GREGERS: No amount of airing can ever get rid of the stench I mean.

HJALMAR: Stench!

GINA: Well—I must say—!

RELLING: Perhaps you brought the stench with *you*, from those mines of yours up there!

GREGERS: You *would* call what I have to bring a stench! That would be like you, Dr. Relling.

RELLING: Now listen, Mr. Werle Junior—! Unless I'm very much mistaken you're still obsessed by that blasted *Claim of the Ideal* of yours. I'll bet you have a copy on you now—hidden in some pocket.

GREGERS: You're wrong. I have it hidden in my heart.

RELLING: Well—wherever it is don't produce it here! Not while *I*'m around at any rate.

GREGERS: And what if I produce it all the same?

RELLING: Then I give you fair warning, I shall kick you downstairs head first.

HJALMAR (*Rising*): Why, Relling!

GREGERS: All right! Why don't you try it—!

GINA (*Coming between them*): Dr. Relling! Please! That's enough of that—! But I'd like to tell *you* something, Mr. Werle. After that filthy mess you made with your stove in there, you've no business to come talking about stenches and poisons to *me*! (*There's a knock at the hall door.*)

HEDVIG: Mother, there's someone at the door.

HJALMAR: What *is* this! Now we're to be overrun with visitors, I suppose!

GINA: Never mind—I'll go. (*She goes and opens the door, starts and draws back*) Ah!— Oh, no!

(WERLE, *wearing a fur coat, steps into the room.*)

WERLE: I beg your pardon; I'm told my son is living here.

GINA (*With a gasp*): Why—yes.

HJALMAR (*Goes towards him*): Won't you do us the honor, Mr. Werle—

WERLE: Thank you; I merely wish to see my son.

GREGERS: I'm here; what is it?

WERLE: May we go to your room?

GREGERS: My room? Yes—very well—

GINA: Oh! But it's in no fit state—!

WERLE: Out here in the hall will do; but I'd like to speak to you alone.

HJALMAR: You can have this room to yourselves, Mr. Werle. Come, Relling—we'll go in here. (HJALMAR *and* RELLING *go into the sitting room;* GINA *takes* HEDVIG *with her into the kitchen*.)

GREGERS (*After a short pause*): Well? Now that we're alone, what is it?

WERLE: I gather from something you said last night—and your moving here to the Ekdals seems to confirm it—that you're bent on causing me some mischief.

GREGERS: I intend to open Hjalmar Ekdal's eyes; he must be made to see his position in its true light.

WERLE: I suppose this is the "purpose in life" you spoke of yesterday?

GREGERS: You've left me no other.

WERLE: Why hold *me* responsible for your warped mind, Gregers?

GREGERS: I hold you responsible for the fact that my whole *life* has been warped. I'm not referring now to what happened to my mother— But I have you to thank for the burden of guilt that weighs on my conscience.

WERLE: So it's your conscience that torments you, is it?

GREGERS: I knew you were laying a trap for old Lieutenant Ekdal, and I should have been man enough to face you with it. I should at least have warned him. I guessed what you were up to.

WERLE: Then why didn't you speak out?

GREGERS: I was too much of a coward; I didn't dare. At that time, I was so dreadfully afraid of you. I went on being afraid of you for years.

WERLE: But you're no longer afraid now, it seems.

GREGERS: No—thank God. I know the wrong done to old Ekdal—by me and others—can never be undone. But I can at least save Hjalmar. I can prevent his life from being ruined by a mass of lies.

WERLE: What good do you think that would do? You don't imagine you'd be doing him a service?

GREGERS: I know I would.

WERLE: And Hjalmar Ekdal will agree with you, you think? You actually believe he's man enough to *thank* you for it?

GREGERS: I know he is.

WERLE: Hm—we'll see.

GREGERS: Besides—if I'm to go on living—I must try to find a cure for my sick conscience.

WERLE: You'll never find a cure; your conscience has been sick, as you choose to call it, ever since you were a little child. That's a legacy from your mother, Gregers; that's all she had to leave you.

GREGERS (*With a scornful smile*): You haven't got over it yet, have you? You expected her to bring you a fortune when you married her—you've never recovered from the shock of having been mistaken!

WERLE: Let's stick to the point, shall we? You still insist on guiding young Ekdal back to, what is in your opinion, the right path?

GREGERS: That is my intention.

WERLE: Then I might have spared myself this visit; for I suppose it's no good asking whether you'll change your mind and come back home again?

GREGERS: No.

WERLE: And you won't consider joining the firm either?

GREGERS: No.

WERLE: Very well. But, since I'm marrying again, I'll arrange to have your part of the estate transferred to you at once.

GREGERS: No—I don't want it.

WERLE: You don't want it?

GREGERS: My conscience won't allow me to accept it.

WERLE (*After a pause*): Are you going up to the Works again?

GREGERS: No; I've resigned from your employ.

WERLE: What do you plan to do?

GREGERS: I only want to fulfill my purpose in life—that's all.

WERLE: But what do you propose to live on?

GREGERS: I've saved up a little money from my wages.

WERLE: How long will *that* last!

GREGERS: Long enough for me, I expect.

WERLE: What does that mean?

GREGERS: I'll answer no more questions.

WERLE: Very well then, Gregers. Goodbye.

GREGERS: Goodbye.

(WERLE *goes out by the hall door.*)

HJALMAR (*Sticks his head round the sitting-room door*): Has he gone?

GREGERS: Yes.

(HJALMAR *and* RELLING *come in.* GINA *and* HEDVIG *come from the kitchen.*)

RELLING: That certainly put an end to the lunch party, didn't it!

GREGERS: Put on your things, Hjalmar. I want you to come for a long walk with me.

HJALMAR: All right, I'd be glad to. What did your father want? Was it anything to do with me?

GREGERS: Come along. We've got to have a talk. I'll go and get my coat. (*Goes out by the hall door.*)

GINA (*To* HJALMAR): I wouldn't go with him if I were you.

RELLING: No, don't! Stay where you are.

HJALMAR (*Getting his hat and overcoat*): What! When an old friend wants to pour out his heart to me in private—!

RELLING: But, damn it! Can't you see the fellow's mad? He's a crackpot—a lunatic!

GINA: You hear that, Hjalmar? His mother was a bit queer too at times.

HJALMAR: All the more reason his friend should keep a watchful eye on him. (*To* GINA) Be sure to have dinner ready in good time. Goodbye for the present. (*He goes out by the hall door.*)

RELLING: Too bad that fellow didn't fall right into Hell down one of the Höjdal mine shafts!

GINA: Good gracious! What makes you say that?

RELLING (*Mutters*): I have my reasons.

GINA: Do you think young Werle's really mad?

RELLING: No, worse luck; I don't suppose he's any madder than most people. But he's a sick man all the same.

GINA: What do you think's the matter with him?

RELLING: Well—I'll tell you, Mrs. Ekdal: I'd say he had integrity-
fever—a particularly bad case of it.

GINA: Integrity-fever?

HEDVIG: Is that a kind of illness?

RELLING: Yes; it's a national disease, but it only breaks out sporad-
ically. (*Nods to* GINA) Thanks for lunch. (*He goes out by the hall
door*.)

GINA (*Pacing restlessly up and down*): Ugh! That Gregers Werle!
He's always been a troublemaker.

HEDVIG (*Stands by the table, gives her mother a searching look*):
Mother; this all seems very strange.

CURTAIN

ACT
FOUR

SCENE: HJALMAR EKDAL'S *studio*. *A photograph has just been
taken; a camera covered with its cloth, a pedestal, two chairs and a
console table stand forward in the room. It is late afternoon, the
sun is setting; during the act dusk falls.* GINA *stands at the hall
door with a slide and a wet photographic plate in her hand; she is
talking to somebody outside.*

GINA: Without fail! Don't worry, I never break a promise. I'll have
the first dozen ready for you Monday—Good afternoon. (*Someone is heard going down the stairs.* GINA *closes the door, slips
the plate into the slide and puts it into the camera.*)

HEDVIG (*Comes in from the kitchen*): Have they gone?

GINA (*Tidying up*): Yes, thank God I got rid of them at last.

HEDVIG: It's funny Father isn't back yet.

GINA: You're sure he's not in Relling's room?

HEDVIG: No, he's not there; I just ran down the back stairs to see.

GINA: And his dinner's getting cold too.

HEDVIG: It's funny—Father's never late for dinner.

GINA: He'll be here soon—you'll see.

HEDVIG: I wish he'd come: things seem so queer today.

GINA (*Calls out*): Here he is now!

(HJALMAR EKDAL *comes in by the hall door*.)

HEDVIG (*Runs to him*): We thought you'd *never* come back, Father!

GINA (*Gives him a sidelong look*): You were out a long time, Hjalmar.

HJALMAR (*Doesn't look at her*): A fairly long time, yes.

GINA: Did you have something to eat with Werle?

HJALMAR (*Hanging up his coat*): No.

GINA (*Going towards the kitchen*): I'll bring your dinner at once, then.

HJALMAR: Never mind about dinner. I don't want anything to eat.

HEDVIG (*Goes nearer to him*): Don't you feel well, Father?

HJALMAR: Well? Yes—well enough. We had a very tiring walk, Gregers and I.

GINA: You shouldn't have gone with him, Hjalmar. You know you're not used to long walks.

HJALMAR: There are many things one has to get used to in this world. (*He wanders about the room*) Has anyone been here while I was out?

GINA: Only that engaged couple.

HJALMAR: No new orders, I suppose?

GINA: No, not today.

HEDVIG: But tomorrow there are sure to be some, Father!

HJALMAR: Let's hope so. For tomorrow I mean to set to work in earnest.

HEDVIG: Tomorrow! Have you forgotten what day it is tomorrow, Father?

HJALMAR: Ah, yes—of course. The day after tomorrow, then. I intend to take personal charge of everything. From now on I shall do all the work myself.

GINA: Why should you bother to do that, Hjalmar? You know it only makes you miserable. I can take the pictures well enough; and that sets you free to work on your invention.

HEDVIG: And then there's the wild duck, Father—and all the hens and rabbits—

HJALMAR: I won't hear another word about that childish nonsense! From tomorrow on I shall never set foot in there again.

HEDVIG: But, Father, tomorrow you promised we'd have our celebration—

HJALMAR: Hm. Yes, that's true. From the day *after* tomorrow, then. As for that wild duck, I'd like to wring its neck!

HEDVIG (*Cries out*): The wild duck!

GINA: I never heard of such a thing!

HEDVIG (*Shakes him*): But, Father! It's *my* wild duck! You can't—!

HJALMAR: That's the only thing that stops me. I haven't the heart to do it, Hedvig—for your sake. But I ought to do it, I'm convinced of that. No creature that has been in that man's hands should be allowed to stay under my roof.

GINA: Good Lord—what if Grandfather did get it from poor old Pettersen—

HJALMAR: One has certain moral obligations; there are laws—one might call them the laws of the Ideal. A man may jeopardize his soul by failing to obey them.

HEDVIG: But the poor wild duck, Father! Think of the wild duck!

HJALMAR: I told you—I intend to spare it for your sake. Not a hair of its head—I mean—it shall be spared. I've other things to deal with—far more important things than that. Now that it's dusk, Hedvig, you'd better run along and take your walk as usual.

HEDVIG: Must I, Father? I don't much feel like going out.

HJALMAR: I think you'd better go. You seem to be blinking your eyes a lot—it's this foul air in here. It's bad for you.

HEDVIG: Very well. I'll go by the back stairs. My hat and coat—? They must be in my room. But, Father—promise me you won't hurt the wild duck while I'm gone?

HJALMAR: Not a feather on it shall be harmed, I promise you. (*Clasps her to him*) You and I, Hedvig—we two—! Run along now.

(HEDVIG *nods to her parents and goes out through the kitchen*.)

HJALMAR (*Walks about the room with downcast eyes*): Gina.

GINA: Yes?

HJALMAR: From tomorrow on—from the day *after* tomorrow, rather—I wish to take charge of the household accounts myself.

GINA: You want to look after the accounts as well?

HJALMAR: I intend to check all the receipts at any rate.

GINA: Lord knows *that* won't take you very long.

HJALMAR: I wonder. It seems to me our money stretches a surprisingly long way. (*Stops and looks at her*) How do you manage it?

GINA: It's because Hedvig and I use so very little, I suppose.

HJALMAR: What about Father's work for Mr. Werle? Is it true that he gets very generously paid for it?

GINA: I don't know how generous it is. I don't know what other people get, you see.

HJALMAR: Well—how much *do* they pay him? Tell me!

GINA: It varies; he gets enough to cover his expenses here, and maybe a little pocket money besides.

HJALMAR: Enough to cover his expenses! Why have you never told me this?

GINA: I didn't like to; I knew it made you happy to think he owed everything to you.

HJALMAR: And instead he owes it all to Mr. Werle!

GINA: Well, God knows, Mr. Werle can afford it.

HJALMAR: Light the lamp!

GINA (*Lighting the lamp*): Anyway—how do we know it *does* come from Mr. Werle? It might be Graaberg who—

HJALMAR: Don't try to evade matters by dragging Graaberg into this!

GINA: Well, I mean—I only thought—

HJALMAR: Hm!

GINA: I didn't get Grandfather that copying to do; it was Bertha—in the days when she still used to come and see us—

HJALMAR: Why is your voice trembling?

GINA (*Putting on the lamp shade*): My voice—?

HJALMAR: Yes; and your hands are shaking too. Don't tell me I'm mistaken!

GINA (*Firmly*): What's he been saying about me, Hjalmar? You might just as well come out with it.

HJALMAR: Is it true—*can* it be true, that—that there was something between you and Werle, while you were in service there?

GINA: No. It wasn't true then, at any rate. Mr. Werle wouldn't leave me alone, *that's* true enough. His wife got suspicious, and fussed and fumed and made a lot of scenes; made my life miserable, she did. And then I gave my notice.

HJALMAR: And after that?

GINA: Then I went home, and Mother—well, she wasn't the kind of woman you took her for, Hjalmar; she kept on at me all the time—you see Mr. Werle had become a widower by then.

HJALMAR: Well?

GINA: I suppose I'd better tell you; he gave me no peace until I let him have his way.

HJALMAR (*Clasps his hands together*): So this is the mother of my child! How could you hide this from me!

GINA: It was wrong of me, I know; I should have told you long ago.

HJALMAR: You should have told me at the very start; then I'd have known what kind of woman I was dealing with.

GINA: But if you'd known—would you have married me?

HJALMAR: What do you think? Of course not!

GINA: That's why I couldn't bring myself to tell you. I'd grown so fond of you, you see. I'd have been so miserable—I couldn't bear the thought of it.

HJALMAR (*Paces about*): So this is my Hedvig's mother! And to think that I owe all I possess— (*Kicks a chair*) my home and everything that's in it, to a man who was your former lover! To that damned scoundrel Werle!

GINA: Hjalmar, do you regret these years we've been together?

HJALMAR (*Stands in front of her*): Tell me! Haven't your days been filled with remorse at the thought of the web of deceit you've spun around me? Answer me! Hasn't it been a constant source of agony and shame to you?

GINA: Hjalmar dear—I've had so much to do. My days have been so full—what with the house and all—

HJALMAR: So you've never even given a moment's thought to your past life!

GINA: It's a long time ago—to tell you the truth I'd almost forgotten the whole stupid business.

HJALMAR: It's this crude, sluggish content that I find so shocking—so revolting! Not a twinge of remorse—incredible!

GINA: I'd like you to tell *me* something, Hjalmar; what would have become of you if you hadn't found a wife like me?

HJALMAR: Like you—!

GINA: Yes. You know I was always more practical and more efficient than you were; I suppose that's only natural—I'm a couple of years older, after all.

HJALMAR: What would have become of *me*?

GINA: You were getting into some pretty wild habits when you first met me. You can't deny that, can you?

HJALMAR: Wild habits! That's what you call them, do you? But how could *you* understand what a man goes through when he's on the brink of despair, as I was! Especially a man with my ardent, sensitive nature.

GINA: Maybe that's true. Anyway—I don't hold it against you; you made a real good husband once we got married and settled down— And things were beginning to be so cozy and comfortable here. Hedvig and I were thinking we might even start spending a bit more on ourselves—get ourselves a few clothes, perhaps—and a little extra food.

HJALMAR: In this swamp of deceit, you could actually think of things like that!

GINA: Oh, God! I wish that awful man had never set foot inside this house!

HJALMAR: I was happy here too; I loved my home. But it was all a delusion! How I shall ever find the necessary inspiration now to bring my invention to fruition, heaven knows! It will die with me, I expect. And it will be your fault—it will be your past, Gina, that will have killed it.

GINA (*On the verge of tears*): You mustn't say that, Hjalmar! Please don't say things like that! All I've ever wanted was to serve you—to do the best I could for you. You must know that!

HJALMAR: What's become of the poor breadwinner's dream now! As I lay in there on the sofa, incessantly brooding over my invention, I realized only too well that the effort of creation was fast sapping my strength. I had a premonition: I knew that the day when I finally held the patent in my hand—I knew that day would be my last! I saw you in my dream—the proud widow of the inventor—sad, but prosperous and grateful.

GINA (*Drying her tears*): Hjalmar, you *mustn't* say such things! God forbid that I should ever be a widow.

HJALMAR: It makes no difference now one way or the other. The dream is over now—all over!

(GREGERS WERLE *opens the hall door cautiously and looks in.*)

GREGERS: May I come in?

HJALMAR: Yes; come in.

GREGERS (*Comes forward, his face beaming with joy, and holds out both his hands to them*): Well, my dear friends—! (*Looks from one to the other and says to* HJALMAR *in a whisper*) Perhaps you haven't had your talk yet?

HJALMAR (*Loudly*): Yes—we have.

GREGERS: You *have?*

HJALMAR: I've just been through the bitterest moments of my life.

GREGERS: But, surely, the most uplifting too?

HJALMAR: Anyway—we've got it over with; at least for the time being.

GREGERS (*In great surprise*): But—I don't understand—

HJALMAR: What don't you understand?

GREGERS: This crisis was to have been a turning point; the basis for a whole new way of life. No more falsehood and deception, but a union based on confidence and truth—

HJALMAR: Yes, I know; I know all that.

GREGERS: I expected to find you both radiant—transfigured. But you seem sad and gloomy—

GINA: Yes—well. (*Takes off the lamp shade*)

GREGERS: I don't expect you to understand me, Mrs. Ekdal. It's only natural that you should need time to— But *you,* Hjalmar? You must feel like a man newly dedicated to higher things.

HJALMAR: Yes, of course I do. To some extent—that is.

GREGERS: Surely there can be no greater joy than to forgive a poor erring creature; to rehabilitate her through love and understanding.

HJALMAR: It's not so easy to recover from the bitter experience I've just lived through!

GREGERS: Perhaps not for an *ordinary* man; but for a man like *you*—

HJALMAR: Yes—I realize that. But don't *hound* me about it, Gregers. These things take time, you know.

GREGERS: There's a lot of the wild duck in you, Hjalmar. (RELLING *enters through the hall door*.)

RELLING: Well, well! So we're on the subject of the wild duck again!

HJALMAR: Yes: Mr. Werle's poor wounded victim—

GREGERS: Mr. Werle? Were you talking about *him?*

HJALMAR: Him—and *us;* yes.

RELLING (*To* GREGERS *in an undertone*): You damned interfering fool!

HJALMAR: What did you say?

RELLING: Nothing. I was just expressing my feelings about this quack here. (*To* GREGERS) Why don't you get out before you ruin both their lives?

GREGERS: Their lives won't be ruined, I assure you, Dr. Relling. I needn't speak of Hjalmar—we know him. But I feel sure that, fundamentally, she too possesses the necessary qualities of decency and loyalty—

GINA (*Almost in tears*): Then why couldn't you have let me be?

RELLING: May I ask you, Mr. Werle Junior, what you think you're doing in this house?

GREGERS: Laying the foundations of a true marriage.

RELLING: I see; so you think the Ekdals' marriage wasn't good enough?

GREGERS: I suppose it was as good as the majority of marriages—unfortunately! But it certainly was never based on truth.

HJALMAR (*To* RELLING): I'm afraid you've never given much thought to the Ideal.

RELLING: Rubbish, my friend! Tell me, Mr. Werle—roughly speaking—how many true marriages have you encountered in your life?

GREGERS: Hardly any—now I come to think of it.

RELLING: Neither have I.

GREGERS: But I've seen all too many of the other kind. And I know only too well how harmful such marriages can be to both people concerned.

HJALMAR: A man's spiritual integrity can be totally destroyed—that's the appalling part of it!

RELLING: I've never actually been married—so perhaps I'm not competent to judge. But one thing I *do* know: the child is part of the marriage too; and I advise you to leave the child alone.

HJALMAR: Hedvig!—My poor Hedvig!

RELLING: Yes; you'd better damn well leave Hedvig out of this! You two are grown-up people; if you want to make a mess of your lives, that's up to you. But I warn you to be careful about Hedvig. You might cause her irreparable harm.

HJALMAR: Harm?

RELLING: Yes. Or she might try to harm herself—and others too.

GINA: What makes you think that, Relling?

HJALMAR: You mean—? There's no immediate danger to her eyesight, is there?

RELLING: I'm not talking about her eyesight! Hedvig's at a difficult age. Heaven knows *what* she might get into her head.

GINA: You're right—she's had some queer ideas of late. She's taken to messing about with the kitchen stove, for instance. Playing at "house-on-fire" she calls it. I've been afraid she might really set fire to the place one of these days.

RELLING: There, you see! I knew it.

GREGERS (*To* RELLING): But how do you explain that kind of thing?

RELLING (*Curtly*): Adolescence—Mr. Werle Junior.

HJALMAR: As long as she has her father—! As long as I'm this side of the grave—!

(*There's a knock at the door.*)

GINA: Hush, Hjalmar; there's someone in the hall. (*Calls out*) Come in!

(MRS. SÖRBY *enters; she wears a hat and a warm coat.*)

MRS. SÖRBY: Good evening!

GINA (*Goes towards her*): Why, Bertha! Is it you?

MRS. SÖRBY: Yes. I hope I'm not disturbing you?

HJALMAR: Good heavens, no! How could an emissary from *that* house—!

MRS. SÖRBY (*To* GINA): Actually—I'd hoped to find you alone, at this time of day. I just ran over to have a little chat with you, and say good-bye.

GINA: Good-bye? Are you going away?

MRS. SÖRBY: Early tomorrow morning—up to Höjdal. Mr. Werle left this afternoon. (*To* GREGERS, *casually*) He told me to say goodbye to you for him.

GINA: Well—fancy!

HJALMAR: So Mr. Werle's gone, has he? And you're going after him?

MRS. SÖRBY: Yes. What do you say to that, Ekdal?

HJALMAR: I say: be careful!

GREGERS: Let me explain; my father is going to marry Mrs. Sörby.

HJALMAR: Marry her!

GINA: Oh, Bertha! So it's really happened at last!

RELLING (*With a slight quiver in his voice*): This surely can't be true?

MRS. SÖRBY: Yes, dear Dr. Relling, it's true enough.

RELLING: You're really going to marry again?

MRS. SÖRBY: It looks like it! Mr. Werle got a special license, and we're to have a very quiet wedding, up at the Works.

GREGERS: Then let me be a dutiful stepson, and wish you happiness.

MRS. SÖRBY: Thanks very much—if you really mean it. I hope it will bring happiness to both of us.

RELLING: I don't see why it shouldn't. Mr. Werle never gets drunk, as far as I know—and, unlike the late-lamented horse doctor, he's not in the habit of beating his wives either.

MRS. SÖRBY: Oh, let poor Sörby rest in peace. He had his good points too.

RELLING: But I expect Mr. Werle has even better ones.

MRS. SÖRBY: At least he hasn't wasted all that was best in him; when a man does that, he must face the consequences.

RELLING: Tonight I shall go out with Molvik.

MRS. SÖRBY: Don't do that, Relling. Please—for my sake!

RELLING: What else is there to do? (*To* HJALMAR) If you feel like joining us, Hjalmar—come along!

GINA: No, thank you. Hjalmar doesn't go to places of *that* sort!

HJALMAR (*In an angry undertone*): Oh, do be quiet!

RELLING: Goodbye Mrs.—Werle. (*Goes out by the hall door*.)

GREGERS (*To* MRS. SÖRBY): You seem to be on very intimate terms with Dr. Relling.

MRS. SÖRBY: We've known each other for many years. At one time it looked as though something might have come of it.

GREGERS: It's just as well for you it didn't.

MRS. SÖRBY: Yes, you're right. But then, I've never been one to act on impulse. A woman can't afford to throw herself away.

GREGERS: Aren't you afraid I might say something to my father about this former friendship?

MRS. SÖRBY: I've naturally told him all about it.

GREGERS: Oh?

MRS. SÖRBY: Yes; I've told him everything that anyone could possibly find to say against me. The moment I realized what was in his mind, I made a point of doing so.

GREGERS: Then you're more than usually frank, it seems to me.

MRS. SÖRBY: I've always been frank. I think for a woman it's the best policy

HJALMAR: What do you say to that, Gina?

GINA: We can't all be alike. Some women are one way, and some another.

MRS. SÖRBY: You know, Gina—I believe my way is best. And Mr. Werle has no secrets from me either. He can sit and talk to me quite openly—just like a child. It's the first time he's ever been able to do that. It's all wrong that a man of his type—full of health and vigor—should have had to spend the best years of his life listening to interminable lectures on his sins! And mostly imaginary sins too—as far as I can make out.

GINA: Lord knows *that*'s true enough!

GREGERS: If you ladies intend to pursue this topic, I think I'd better go.

MRS. SÖRBY: No—you needn't go; I shan't say any more. I just wanted you to know that my dealings have been honorable and aboveboard from the start. I dare say many people will envy me and think me very lucky—and in a way I am. But I shall give as good as I get, I promise you. I shall never fail him. And now that he'll soon be helpless, I'll be able to repay him by serving him and caring for him always. I can do that better than anyone else, I think.

HJALMAR: What do you mean—helpless?

GREGERS (*To* MRS. SÖRBY): Don't say anything about that here.

MRS. SÖRBY: It's no use trying to hide it any longer; he's going blind.

HJALMAR (*With a start*): Blind? He's going blind you say? That's very strange.

GINA: Lots of people do, unfortunately.

MRS. SÖRBY: You can imagine what that means to a man in his position. I shall simply have to use my eyes for both of us, and do the best I can— But I really can't stay any longer—I have so much to do— By the way, I was to give you a message, Mr. Ekdal: If there's anything Werle can ever do for you, just mention it to Graaberg.

GREGERS: An offer that Hjalmar Ekdal will most certainly refuse.

MRS. SÖRBY: Really? He didn't used to be so—

GINA: No, Bertha. Hjalmar doesn't need anything from Mr. Werle now.

HJALMAR (*Slowly and forcefully*): Be so good as to give my regards to your future husband, and tell him I intend to call on Mr. Graaberg very shortly—

GREGERS: What! You don't mean you—?

HJALMAR: —call on Mr. Graaberg, I say, and demand a full accounting of the money I owe to his employer. I intend to pay this debt of honor—ha-ha-ha! debt of honor is a good name for it!—but no more of that—I intend to pay it in full with interest at 5 per cent.

GINA: But, Hjalmar dear—where will we ever get the money?

HJALMAR: You may tell your fiancé that I am forging ahead with my invention. Tell him that I am sustained in this laborious task by the desire to rid myself once and for all of this painful debt

That is my chief motive in pursuing the work on my invention so relentlessly. I plan to devote the profits to freeing myself from all obligation to your future husband.

MRS. SÖRBY: What has been happening here?

HJALMAR: You may well ask!

MRS. SÖRBY: Well—I'll say good-bye. There were a couple of other things I wanted to talk to you about, Gina—but they must wait till some other time—Goodbye.

(HJALMAR *and* GREGERS *bow silently;* GINA *takes* MRS. SÖRBY *to the door.*)

HJALMAR: Not beyond the threshold, Gina!

(MRS. SÖRBY *goes out;* GINA *closes the door after her.*)

HJALMAR: There, Gregers! That burden of debt is off my mind!

GREGERS: It soon will be, at any rate.

HJALMAR: I think my behavior might be described as suitably correct?

GREGERS: Your behavior was admirable, as I knew it would be.

HJALMAR: There are times when one cannot possibly disregard the claim of the Ideal. But it will be a long hard struggle. It's not easy for a man without a penny to his name, and with a family to support, to pay off a long-standing debt of this sort—on which, one might say, the dust of oblivion has settled. But it must be faced; my integrity as a human being demands it.

GREGERS (*Puts his hands on* HJALMAR'S *shoulders*): My dear Hjalmar—wasn't it a good thing that I came?

HJALMAR: Ye-es.

GREGERS: Don't you feel happier, now that you see your position clearly?

HJALMAR (*Somewhat impatiently*): Yes—of course I do. But there's one thing that offends my sense of justice.

GREGERS: What thing?

HJALMAR: It's just that—but perhaps I shouldn't speak of your father in this way—

GREGERS: Say anything you like as far as I'm concerned.

HJALMAR: It shocks me to think that he has succeeded where I have failed. His marriage will be a *true* marriage, you see.

GREGERS: How can you say a thing like that!

HJALMAR: But it's so, isn't it? Your father's marriage to Mrs. Sörby is based on truth and mutual confidence. They've kept nothing back; they hold no secrets from each other. They've reached a complete agreement. It's as though they'd each confessed their sins and given each other absolution.

GREGERS: Well—what then?

HJALMAR: That's the whole point—don't you see? You said yourself that no true marriage could exist unless these problems had been faced and cleared away.

GREGERS: But this is quite different, Hjalmar. You surely don't compare yourself—or Gina here—with *those* two—? You know quite well what I mean.

HJALMAR: All the same—there's something about this that offends my sense of justice. If things like this are allowed to happen, there's obviously no such thing as a Divine Power ruling the Universe!

GINA: Hjalmar! For God's sake don't say such things!

GREGERS: Hm. Don't let's embark on that subject.

HJALMAR: Yet—now I come to think of it—it's possible to see the hand of Destiny at work in this: He's going blind.

GINA: But perhaps that isn't true.

HJALMAR: I'm positive it's true; if there *is* such a thing as Divine Justice it *must* be true. Look at all the unsuspecting people he's hoodwinked in his time—!

GREGERS: A great many, unfortunately.

HJALMAR: And now he's being made to pay for it by going blind himself: it's retribution.

GINA: You frighten me when you say such dreadful things.

HJALMAR: It's sometimes salutary to examine the darker sides of life.

(HEDVIG, *in her hat and coat, comes in by the hall door. She is breathless and excited.*)

GINA: Back already?

HEDVIG: Yes; I didn't want to stay out any longer. And it was just as well, because I met someone at the front door as I came in—

HJALMAR: That Mrs. Sörby, I suppose.

HEDVIG: That's right.

HJALMAR (*Pacing up and down*): I hope that's the last time you'll ever lay eyes on *her*.

(*A pause.* HEDVIG *glances from one to the other as if trying to gauge their mood.*)

HEDVIG (*Coaxingly, going up to* HJALMAR): Father.

HJALMAR: Well—what is it?

HEDVIG: Mrs. Sörby brought me something.

HJALMAR: Something for you?

HEDVIG: Yes—it's something for tomorrow.

GINA: Bertha always has some little present for you on your birth-day.

HJALMAR: What is it?

HEDVIG: Oh, we're not supposed to see it yet. Mother's to bring it in to me early tomorrow morning.

HJALMAR: What *is* this? A conspiracy behind my back?

HEDVIG (*Rapidly*): No, of course not! You can see it if you like! Look—it's this great big letter. (*She takes it out of her coat pocket.*)

HJALMAR: So there's a letter too.

HEDVIG: That's all she gave me; the rest'll come later, I suppose. But, just think—a letter! It's the first one I've ever had. And there's "Miss" written on the envelope. (*Reads*) "Miss Hedvig Ekdal." Just think of it—that's *me*!

HJALMAR: Let me see that letter.

HEDVIG (*Hands it to him*): There you are.

HJALMAR: This is Mr. Werle's handwriting.

GINA: Are you sure, Hjalmar?

HJALMAR: Look for yourself.

GINA: I don't know about such things.

HJALMAR: May I open it, and read it, Hedvig?

HEDVIG: Of course, Father, if you want to.

GINA: Not this evening, Hjalmar; we're supposed to save it till to-morrow.

HEDVIG (*Softly*): Oh, let him read it, Mother. I'm sure it's some-thing nice. Father will be pleased and things will be all right again.

HJALMAR: I may open it then?

HEDVIG: Yes, Father, do! It'll be such fun to see what's in it!

HJALMAR: Very well. (*He opens the envelope, takes out a paper, reads it through, and seems bewildered*) What does this mean—?

GINA: What does it say?

HEDVIG: Do tell us, Father dear!

HJALMAR: Be quiet. (*Reads it through again; he turns pale but speaks with self-control*) It's a deed of gift.

HEDVIG: Really? What do I get?

HJALMAR: Here—read it yourself. (HEDVIG *takes it and goes over to the lamp to read it.*)

HJALMAR (*In an undertone, clenching his hands*): The eyes! The eyes—and now, *this*!

HEDVIG: But—isn't this for Grandfather?

HJALMAR (*Takes the paper from her*): Gina—what do you make of it?

GINA: I wouldn't understand anything about it. Just tell me what it is.

HJALMAR: It's a letter to Hedvig from Mr. Werle, informing her that in the future her grandfather need trouble himself no further with any copying work; but, instead—he may draw on Mr. Werle's office for a hundred crowns a month.

GREGERS: Aha!

HEDVIG: A hundred crowns, Mother! That's what I thought it said!

GINA: That's nice for Grandfather.

HJALMAR: —a hundred crowns a month as long as he may need it; which means as long as he lives, of course.

GINA: Poor old man—so he's provided for at least.

HJALMAR: Wait. There's more to come. You probably didn't read this, Hedvig. Afterwards the gift reverts to you.

HEDVIG: To me! All that money to *me*!

HJALMAR: For the rest of your life you will receive a hundred crowns a month, he writes. Do you hear that, Gina?

GINA: Yes, I hear it.

HEDVIG: All that money, Father! Think of it! (*Shakes him*) Father, Father—aren't you glad?

HJALMAR (*Shakes her off*): Glad! (*Paces up and down*) God! What

perspectives—what vistas all this opens up to me! So—it's
Hedvig! Why should he shower gifts on her!

GINA: Well, I suppose—it's Hedvig's birthday after all—

HEDVIG: But it will all belong to you, Father! You know I'll give it
all to you and Mother!

HJALMAR: To your mother, yes! Of course—that's as it should be!

GREGERS: Hjalmar—this is a trap he's laid for you.

HJALMAR: Another one of his traps, you think?

GREGERS: He said to me only this morning: Hjalmar Ekdal is not
the man you take him for.

HJALMAR: Not the man—!

GREGERS: You'll soon find out, he said.

HJALMAR: So he wants to show you he can bribe me—

HEDVIG: Mother, what does all this mean?

GINA: Go and take off your things.

(HEDVIG *goes out through the kitchen, on the verge of tears*.)

GREGERS: Well, Hjalmar—? Was *he* right about you, or am I?

HJALMAR (*Slowly tears the paper in two and lays the pieces on the
table*): There is my answer.

GREGERS: Just what I expected.

HJALMAR (*Goes over to* GINA *who is standing by the stove and
says in a low voice*): I want no more lies, I warn you, Gina. If
things were really over between you and Werle when you became "fond of me"—as you choose to put it—why did he make it
possible for us to marry?

GINA: He perhaps thought he'd be able to come and go as he liked,
here in our house.

HJALMAR: Was that all? Mightn't he have been afraid? Wasn't it
something to do with your condition at the time?

GINA: I don't know what you mean.

HJALMAR: I must know— Has your child the right to live under
my roof?

GINA (*Draws herself up; her eyes flash*): You ask *me* that!

HJALMAR: Answer me! Does Hedvig belong to me—or—? Well?

GINA (*Looks at him coldly and defiantly*): I don't know.

HJALMAR (*Trembling slightly*): You don't know?

GINA: No. How should I? A creature like *me*—?

HJALMAR (*Quietly, turning away from her*): Then I have nothing more to do in this house.

GREGERS: Consider what you're doing, Hjalmar!

HJALMAR (*Putting on his overcoat*): What is there to consider? For a man like me there can be no alternative.

GREGERS: There are many things to be considered. You three must stay together. How else can you start afresh in a spirit of forgiveness and self-sacrifice?

HJALMAR: I don't want to. Never, never! My hat! (*Takes his hat*) My home is nothing but a mass of ruins! (*Bursts into tears*) Gregers! I have no child!

HEDVIG (*Who has opened the kitchen door*): Father! What are you saying! (*Runs to him*) Father!

GINA: There, you see!

HJALMAR: Don't touch me, Hedvig! Keep away from me—I can't bear to look at you! Oh! Those eyes—! Good-bye. (*Starts towards the door.*)

HEDVIG (*Clings to him, screaming*): No! No! Don't leave me!

GINA (*Cries out*): The poor child, Hjalmar! Look at the child!

HJALMAR: I won't! I can't! I must get out of here—away from this! (*He tears himself away from* HEDVIG *and goes out through the hall door.*)

HEDVIG (*Her eyes full of despair*): He's going away from us, Mother! He's going away! He'll never come back—never!

GINA: Don't cry, Hedvig. Father will come back—you'll see.

HEDVIG (*Flings herself down on the sofa sobbing*): No he won't! He won't! He'll never come home to us any more!

GREGERS: I meant it all for the best, Mrs. Ekdal. You do believe that, don't you?

GINA: Yes—I suppose so. But God forgive you all the same.

HEDVIG: I shall die if he doesn't come back, Mother—I shall die! What have I done to him? Go and find him, Mother, and bring him home again!

GINA: Yes, darling—yes! Try and be calm now. I'll go and look for him. (*Puts on her outdoor things*) Perhaps he's down at Relling's. Don't cry any more—promise!

HEDVIG (*Sobbing convulsively*): I won't—I won't! I promise! If only he'll come back!

GREGERS: You don't think it would be better to let him fight it out alone?

GINA: Let him do that later! We must get the child quieted down first. (*Goes out by the hall door.*)

HEDVIG (*Sits up and dries her tears*): Please! What is it all about? You've got to tell me! Why doesn't Father want me any more?

GREGERS: You must wait till you're grown-up before asking about that.

HEDVIG: But I can't wait till I'm grown-up and go on being misera-ble like this!—I think I know what it's all about—Perhaps I'm not really Father's child.

GREGERS (*Uneasily*): How could *that* be?

HEDVIG: Mother may have picked me up somewhere; and Fa-ther's just discovered it. I've read about things like that.

GREGERS: But even if that were so—

HEDVIG: I don't see why he should stop being fond of me on that account; I should think he'd love me even more. The wild duck came to us as a present too—and I love it very dearly all the same.

GREGERS (*Switches the conversation*): The wild duck—yes! Let's talk about the wild duck for a while.

HEDVIG: Poor wild duck. He can't bear to look at her either any more. Just think—he said he'd like to wring her neck!

GREGERS: But I'm sure he'd never do it!

HEDVIG: He said he'd like to! I thought it was horrid of him. I say a prayer for the wild duck every night. I ask God to protect it from death and everything that's evil.

GREGERS (*Looking at her*): Do you say your prayers every night?

HEDVIG: Yes, I do.

GREGERS: Who taught you to do that?

HEDVIG: I taught myself. Father was terribly ill once—they had to put leeches on his chest. He kept saying death was staring him in the face.

GREGERS: Well?

HEDVIG: So that night when I went to bed, I said a prayer for him. And I've kept on with it ever since.

GREGERS: And now you pray for the wild duck too?

HEDVIG: Yes, I thought I'd better; she was so very weak at first, you know.

GREGERS: Do you say your prayers in the morning too?

HEDVIG: No—of course not!

GREGERS: Why not? Aren't morning prayers any good?

HEDVIG: Well—in the morning it's light, you see; there's nothing to be afraid of then.

GREGERS: And this wild duck you're so fond of— You say your father wanted to wring its neck?

HEDVIG: He said he'd *like* to—but that he'd spare her for my sake. That was kind of him, I thought.

GREGERS (*Coming a little nearer*): What if you were to offer up the wild duck as a sacrifice? For *his* sake?

HEDVIG (*Rises*): The wild duck!

GREGERS: Yes. Supposing you were to sacrifice to him the thing you love most dearly in the world?

HEDVIG: Would that do any good—do you think?

GREGERS: Try it, Hedvig.

HEDVIG (*Softly, with shining eyes*): Very well—I *will*.

GREGERS: Do you think you'll really have the courage?

HEDVIG: The wild duck! I'll ask Grandfather to shoot it for me.

GREGERS: Yes, do that. But don't say a word to your mother about it.

HEDVIG: Why not?

GREGERS: She doesn't understand us.

HEDVIG: The wild duck! I'll try and do it the first thing in the morning.

(GINA *comes in from the hall door*.)

HEDVIG (*Goes to her*): Did you find him, Mother?

GINA: No. But he went to fetch Relling, and they went out together.

GREGERS: Are you sure?

GINA: The porter's wife told me—she saw them. Molvik was with them too, she said.

GREGERS: That's strange! I should have thought he'd want to fight
    things out alone—!

GINA (*Taking off her things*): Men are queer creatures! God knows
    where Relling's dragged him off to. I ran over to Mrs.
    Eriksen's—but they weren't there.

HEDVIG (*Fighting back her tears*): What if he *never* comes back to
    us, Mother!

GREGERS: He'll come back. I'll send him word tomorrow. You'll
    see—he'll come. Go to sleep now, Hedvig—and don't worry.
    Good night. (*He goes out by the hall door.*)

HEDVIG (*Sobbing, throws herself into her mother's arms*):
    Mother! Mother!

GINA (*Pats her shoulder and sighs*): Ah, yes! Relling was right.
    That's what happens when people come around with all this
    crazy talk of claims and idols!

                                                              CURTAIN

ACT
FIVE

SCENE: HJALMAR EKDAL's *studio. Cold gray morning light;
patches of snow lie on the large panes of the studio window.*

GINA *enters from the kitchen wearing an apron with a bib and
carrying a broom and a duster; she goes towards the sitting-room
door. At the same moment* HEDVIG *comes in quickly from the hall.*

GINA (*Stops*): Well?

HEDVIG: Mother—you know, I think he's down at Relling's—

GINA: There, you see!

HEDVIG: —Because the porter's wife says there were two people
    with Relling when he came home last night.

GINA: Just what I thought.

HEDVIG: But what good does it do, if he won't come up to us?

GINA: At least I can go down and have a talk with him.

(OLD EKDAL *in his slippers and a dressing gown, and smoking his pipe, appears at the door of his room.*)

EKDAL: Oh, Hjalmar— Isn't Hjalmar home?

GINA: No, he's gone out.

EKDAL: What—so early? And in all this snow? Well—never mind. I'll take my morning walk alone.

(*He slides open the attic door;* HEDVIG *helps him; he goes in; she closes it after him.*)

HEDVIG: Mother—what will poor Grandfather do, when he hears that Father's going to leave us?

GINA: Nonsense! Grandfather mustn't know anything about it. Thank God he was out yesterday—during all the rumpus.

HEDVIG: Yes, but—

(GREGERS *comes in from the hall.*)

GREGERS: Well? Any news of him?

GINA: They say he's down at Relling's

GREGERS: Relling's! Did he *really* go out with those two?

GINA: It looks like it.

GREGERS: How could he! When it was so important for him to be alone—to collect his thoughts in solitude!

GINA: Yes. That's what he should have done.

(RELLING *comes in from the hall.*)

HEDVIG (*Going to him*): Is Father down with you?

GINA (*Simultaneously*): Is he down there?

RELLING: Yes, of course he is.

HEDVIG: You might have let us know!

RELLING: Yes—I'm a swine, I know. But I had that other swine on my hands—our daemonic friend, I mean. And I got so tired, I fell into a stupor—

GINA: What has Hjalmar got to say today?

RELLING: Nothing whatever.

HEDVIG: Hasn't he said anything at all?

RELLING: Not a blessed word.

GREGERS: Well—that's understandable enough.

GINA: Then what's he doing?

RELLING: Lying on the sofa snoring.

GINA: Is he? He's a great one for snoring, Hjalmar is.

GREGERS: You mean—he's actually *asleep*?

RELLING: He certainly appears to be.

GREGERS: I expect it's only natural; after the spiritual crisis he's been through—

GINA: And then, he's not used to gadding about at night.

HEDVIG: It'll do him good to get some sleep, Mother.

GINA: That's what I think. We'd better not wake him up too early. Thanks, Relling. I'll see about getting the house cleaned up a bit—come and help me, Hedvig.

(GINA *and* HEDVIG *go into the sitting room.*)

GREGERS (*Turning to* RELLING): How would you explain this spiritual upheaval that Hjalmar Ekdal's going through?

RELLING: Damned if I saw anything resembling a spiritual upheaval—!

GREGERS: Come now! At a turning point like this? When he's about to start on a whole new way of life—? You must realize that a man of Hjalmar's character—

RELLING: Did you say *character*? Hjalmar? If he ever possessed a vestige of that rare attribute, it was crushed in him, I assure you—thoroughly extirpated—while he was still a child.

GREGERS: That seems hardly likely—considering the loving care with which he was brought up.

RELLING: By those doting, hysterical maiden aunts of his, you mean?

GREGERS: Let me tell you they were women who never lost sight of the Ideal—now, I suppose, you'll start jeering again!

RELLING: No—I'm in no mood for that. I happen to know a lot about these ladies; he's often waxed eloquent on the subject of his two "soul-mothers"—as he calls them! Hjalmar has had the great misfortune of always being looked on as a shining light in his own particular circle—

GREGERS: And don't you think he is? Deep down—I mean?

RELLING: I've certainly never noticed it. That his father should have thought so—that's understandable enough; the old lieutenant's always been somewhat of an ass.

GREGERS: He's a man who has never lost his childlike nature —that's what you fail to understand.

RELLING: All right—have it your own way! Then, when our dear sweet Hjalmar went to college, his fellow students looked on him as the great hope of the Future, too. He was handsome enough—the scoundrel! Pink and white—the kind the girls all go for. And then he had a facile mind, and a romantic voice which he used to good effect declaiming other people's poetry, and other people's thoughts—

GREGERS (*Indignantly*): It can't be Hjalmar Ekdal you're talking about like this—?

RELLING: Yes—with your permission. This is the truth about that idol of yours to whom you bow the knee.

GREGERS: It never occurred to me I could be quite *that* blind.

RELLING: You are though—pretty nearly. You're a sick man too, you see.

GREGERS: You're right about that, at least.

RELLING: Yes. Yours is a complicated case. First you've got that blasted Integrity-Fever to contend with; then—what's worse—you live in a constant delirium of hero worship; it's absolutely necessary for you to look up to and adore something outside yourself.

GREGERS: It would inevitably have to be something outside myself.

RELLING: But you make such ridiculous mistakes about these imaginary paragons of yours! Why do you persist in presenting your Claim of the Ideal to people who are totally insolvent?

GREGERS: Why do you spend so much time with Hjalmar Ekdal, if this is your opinion of him?

RELLING: I'm a doctor of sorts, you know—God help me! I feel obliged to look after the sick people who live under the same roof with me.

GREGERS: So you think Hjalmar Ekdal is sick too?

RELLING: Most people are sick, unfortunately.

GREGERS: May I ask what cure you're using in Hjalmar's case?

RELLING: My usual one. I try to discover the Basic Lie—the pet illusion—that makes life possible; and then I foster it.

GREGERS: The basic lie? Surely—I misunderstood—?

RELLING: No, no; that's what I said: the Basic Lie that makes life possible.

GREGERS: And what "basic lie" do you suppose Hjalmar to be suffering from?

RELLING: I don't betray secrets like that to quacks. You've made enough mess of the case for me already. But my method is infallible; I've used it on Molvik too; I've convinced him he's daemonic—that did the trick for him.

GREGERS: You mean—he's *not* daemonic?

RELLING: What the Hell does it mean: to be daemonic? It's a lot of nonsense I invented to make life possible for him. Without that the poor harmless wretch would have gone under years ago—in an agony of despair and self-contempt. And what about the old lieutenant? But that's different: he discovered the cure for himself, you see.

GREGERS: Lieutenant Ekdal? What do you mean?

RELLING: Just think of it! The mighty bear hunter shooting rabbits in the attic. And there's no happier hunter in the world than that old man fooling about in there in all that rubbish. He's saved four or five withered old Christmas trees, and to him they're just as beautiful and green and fresh as the whole of the great Höjdal forest. To him the rooster and the hens are wild birds in the tree-tops; and the rabbits that lope about the attic floor are the bears he used to grapple with out in the wilds, when he was young and vigorous.

GREGERS: Poor old Lieutenant Ekdal; he's gone a long way from the ideals of his youth.

RELLING: While I think of it, Mr. Werle Junior—I wish you'd stop using that foreign word: ideals. We have a perfectly good one of our own: lies.

GREGERS: You seem to think the two things are related!

RELLING: They are: they're as alike as typhoid and malignant fever.

GREGERS: I shall never give up until I've rescued Hjalmar from your clutches, Dr. Relling.

RELLING: So much the worse for *him.* Rob the average man of his basic lie and you rob him of his happiness as well. (*To* HEDVIG *who comes in from the sitting room*) And now, little wild-duck mother, I'll just run down and see how your father's getting on; I expect he's lying there meditating on that wonderful invention. (*He goes out through the hall door.*)

GREGERS (*Going up to* HEDVIG): You haven't done it yet, have you? I can see it in your face.

HEDVIG: What? Oh, you mean—about the wild duck? No.

GREGERS: When it actually came to the point, I suppose your courage failed you.

HEDVIG: No—it wasn't that. But when I woke up this morning and remembered what we'd talked about, it seemed queer to me somehow.

GREGERS: Queer?

HEDVIG: Yes; I don't know— Last night, right at the time, I thought it was a very beautiful idea; but I didn't think so much of it—after I'd slept on it, you see.

GREGERS: I see that growing up in the atmosphere of this house has unfortunately had its effect on you.

HEDVIG: I don't care about that—if only Father would come back to us—

GREGERS: If only your eyes had been opened to the true values in life; if you only had the joyous, courageous spirit of self-sacrifice, you'd see how quickly your father would come back to you—But I still have faith in you, Hedvig—don't forget that. (*He goes out into the hall.*)

(HEDVIG *paces about the room; she is about to go into the kitchen when a knock is heard at the attic door;* HEDVIG *goes over and opens it a little way;* OLD EKDAL *comes out. She slides the door closed again.*)

EKDAL: Hm. Not much fun going for your morning walk alone.

HEDVIG: Didn't you feel like going hunting, Grandfather?

EKDAL: Weather's not right for hunting; it's so dark you can hardly see.

HEDVIG: Do you ever feel like shooting anything besides the rabbits?

EKDAL: Why? Aren't the rabbits good enough?

HEDVIG: Yes, of course; but, what about the wild duck?

EKDAL: Ho-ho! You're afraid I'll shoot your wild duck, are you? I'd never do that. Never.

HEDVIG: No. I don't suppose you could, could you? It's very difficult to shoot wild ducks, they say.

EKDAL: What do you mean I *couldn't*? I should rather think I *could*!

HEDVIG: How would you go about it, Grandfather?—Not with *my* wild duck, of course; I mean with others?

EKDAL: I'd shoot at the breast, you see; that's the surest place. And then you must always shoot *against* the feathers, you understand—not *with* them.

HEDVIG: And then do they die, Grandfather?

EKDAL: They die all right—if you shoot properly. I'll go in and brush up a bit. Hm—you see—hm. (*Goes into his room.*) (HEDVIG *waits a moment or two, glances towards the sitting room door, goes over to the bookcase, stands on tiptoe, takes the double-barreled pistol down from the shelf and looks at it.* GINA *carrying her broom and duster comes in from the sitting room.* HEDVIG *puts down the pistol hastily without being seen.*)

GINA: Don't stand there messing about with your father's things, Hedvig.

HEDVIG (*Going away from the bookcase*): I was just trying to tidy up a bit.

GINA: You'd better go in the kitchen and see if the coffee's keeping hot. I'll take a tray down to him when I go.

(HEDVIG *goes out;* GINA *begins sweeping and cleaning up the studio. After a while the hall door opens cautiously and* HJALMAR EKDAL *looks in; he wears his overcoat but no hat; he is unwashed and his hair is dishevelled and unkempt. His eyes are dull and heavy.*)

GINA (*Stands with the broom in her hand and looks at him*): Well now, Hjalmar—you came back after all.

HJALMAR (*Comes in and answers in a gloomy voice*): I've come back—but only to go away again immediately.

GINA: Yes—I suppose so. But, my goodness! What a state you're in!

HJALMAR: A state?

GINA: And it's your good overcoat too! That's done for, I'm afraid!

HEDVIG (*At the kitchen door*): Mother, shall I—? (*Sees* HJALMAR, *gives a cry of joy and runs towards him*) Father, Father!

HJALMAR (*Turns away with a gesture of repulsion*): Keep away from me! (*To* GINA) Keep her away, I tell you!

GINA (*In an undertone*): Go into the sitting room, Hedvig. (HEDVIG *silently obeys.*)

HJALMAR (*Making a show of being busy opens the table drawer*): I want my books—I'll need them with me. Where are my books?

GINA: What books?

HJALMAR: My scientific books, of course— All those technical periodicals I need for my invention.

GINA (*Looking in the bookcase*): Are they these things—without a binding?

HJALMAR: Yes—naturally.

GINA (*Lays a pile of magazines on the table*): Don't you want Hedvig to cut the pages for you?

HJALMAR: I want no pages cut for me.

(*A short pause.*)

GINA: So you still intend to leave us, Hjalmar?

HJALMAR (*Rummaging among the books*): I should think that was obvious.

GINA: Well, well!

HJALMAR: I don't intend to stay here to be stabbed through the heart each hour of the day!

GINA: God forgive you for believing all those dreadful things about me!

HJALMAR: Then prove—!

GINA: I think you're the one who ought to prove!

HJALMAR: After a past like yours? There are certain claims—I'm tempted to call them claims of the Ideal—

GINA: What about Grandfather? What's going to happen to him—poor old man?

HJALMAR: I know my duty. The poor helpless old man shall go with me. I'll go out presently and make arrangements—Hm. (*Hesitating*) Did anyone find my hat on the stairs?

GINA: No. Have you lost your hat?

HJALMAR: I naturally had it on when I came in last night; there's no doubt about that. But this morning I couldn't find it.

GINA: Dear Lord! Where on earth did you go with those two good-for-nothings?

HJALMAR: Don't bother me with trifles. I'm in no mood to remember details.

GINA: I do hope you haven't caught cold, Hjalmar! (*Goes out into the kitchen.*)

HJALMAR (*Mutters to himself in a low angry tone as he empties the table drawer*): You're a scoundrel, Relling; an infamous, treacherous scoundrel! I wish to God someone would wring your neck! (*He lays aside some old letters, catches sight of the torn document from the day before, picks it up and examines the two pieces; puts it down hurriedly as* GINA *enters.*)

GINA (*Puts a tray with coffee, etc. down on the table*): You might like a drop of something hot. And there's some bread and butter and a bit of that smoked tongue.

HJALMAR (*Glancing at the tray*): Smoked tongue, you say? No! Nothing under this roof! I haven't eaten a morsel of food for nearly twenty-four hours, that's true enough— but never mind! My notes! And the preliminary chapters of my autobiography! What has become of my diary—and all my important papers? (*Opens the door to the sitting room but draws back*) There she is again!

GINA: The poor child has to be somewhere!

HJALMAR: Come out. (*He stands aside.* HEDVIG, *terrified, comes into the studio.* HJALMAR, *his hand on the door knob, says to* GINA) During these last few moments in my former home I wish to be spared all contact with intruders— (*Goes into the sitting room.*)

HEDVIG (*Runs to her mother and says softly in a trembling voice*): Does he mean me?

GINA: Stay in the kitchen, Hedvig; or, no—perhaps you'd better go to your own room. (*Speaks to* HJALMAR *as she goes in to him*) Wait a minute, Hjalmar. Don't rummage about in all the drawers; *I* know where everything is.

HEDVIG (*Stands motionless for a moment, confused and terrified; she bites her lips to prevent herself from crying. Then she clenches her hands convulsively and says softly*): The wild duck! (*She steals over and takes the pistol from the shelf, slides open the attic door a little way, creeps in, and draws the door closed after her.* HJALMAR *and* GINA *begin to argue in the sitting room.*)

HJALMAR (*Comes in with some notebooks and old loose sheets of paper and lays them on the table*): What's the good of that portmanteau! That won't hold anything—I've *hundreds* of things to take with me!

GINA (*Follows him carrying the portmanteau*): Why not leave everything here for the time being, and just take a clean shirt and a pair of extra underdrawers?

HJALMAR: Phew! These exhausting preparations—! (*He pulls off his overcoat and throws it on the sofa.*)

GINA: Look! Your coffee's getting cold!

HJALMAR: Hm. (*Drinks a gulp without thinking and then another.*)

GINA (*Dusting the backs of the chairs*): You'll have a hard time finding a big enough place for all those rabbits.

HJALMAR: Good God! You don't expect me to drag all those rabbits with me!

GINA: Grandfather could never get along without his rabbits.

HJALMAR: He'll just have to get used to it. After all *I'm* sacrificing far more important things than rabbits!

GINA (*Dusting the bookcase*): I'd better pack your flute, hadn't I?

HJALMAR: No. No flute for me. But I shall need my pistol.

GINA: Are you going to take that gun along?

HJALMAR: My loaded pistol—yes.

GINA (*Looks for it*): It isn't here. He must have taken it in there with him.

HJALMAR: Is he in the attic?

GINA: Of course he is.

HJALMAR: Hm. Poor lonely old man. (*He takes some bread and butter and smoked tongue, eats it, and finishes his cup of coffee.*)

GINA: If we hadn't rented that room, you could have moved in there.

HJALMAR: And go on living under the same roof as—! Never! Never!

GINA: I suppose you couldn't manage in the sitting room for a day or two? You could have it all to yourself; I'd see to that.

HJALMAR: No! I can't breathe inside these walls!

GINA: Why not down with Relling and Molvik, then?

HJALMAR: Never mention their names to me again! The very thought of them is enough to take away my appetite—No—I shall simply have to go out into the storm; go from house to house, seeking shelter for my old father and myself.

GINA: But you have no hat, Hjalmar! You've gone and lost it, you know.

HJALMAR: Those two scoundrels! Vicious, infamous brutes! I'll have to pick up a hat somewhere on the way. (*Takes some more bread and tongue*) Something'll have to be done about it; I've no desire to risk my life. (*Looks for something on the tray.*)

GINA: What are you looking for?

HJALMAR: Butter.

GINA: I'll get you some at once. (*She goes out into the kitchen.*)

HJALMAR (*Shouting after her*): Oh, never mind; dry bread is good enough for me.

GINA (*Bringing in a dish of butter*): There you are; it's freshly churned.

(*She pours him a fresh cup of coffee; he sits on the sofa, spreads more butter on the already-buttered bread, and eats and drinks for a while in silence.*)

HJALMAR: Would it be possible for me, without being annoyed by anyone—anyone at all—to stay in the sitting room in there, just for a day or two?

GINA: Why, of course. I only wish you would.

HJALMAR: I don't see how I can possibly get Father moved in such a hurry.

GINA: No. And then, you ought to prepare him too. Tell him you don't want to live here with us any more.

HJALMAR (*Pushing away his coffee cup*): Yes, there is that. It's awful to think of having to broach this difficult subject with him. I must have a breathing spell—a chance to think things out. I can't cope with all these problems in a single day!

GINA: Of course not; and it's such awful weather too.

HJALMAR (*Touching* WERLE'S *letter*): I see that paper is still hanging about.

GINA: Yes. *I* haven't touched it.

HJALMAR: Well—it's no concern of mine—

GINA: *I* certainly never thought of using it.

HJALMAR: Still—there's no sense in throwing it away; in all the commotion of my moving, it might easily—

GINA: I'll take good care of it, Hjalmar.

HJALMAR: In the first place, the gift was made to Father; it's really up to him to decide whether he'll make use of it or not.

GINA (*Sighs*): Yes—poor old Father—

HJALMAR: Just as a matter of precaution, I think—have you any paste?

GINA (*Goes to the bookcase*): There's a pot of paste right here.

HJALMAR: And a brush?

GINA: Here's a brush too. (*Brings him the things.*)

HJALMAR (*Takes a pair of scissors*): Just a strip of paper on the back— Far be it for me to lay hands on other people's property—especially when it belongs to a penniless old man. And to—that other one as well. There! Leave it there for now, and when it's dry, put it away. I never want to lay eyes on that document again. Never!

(GREGERS WERLE *comes in from the hall.*)

GREGERS (*Somewhat surprised*): Oh—you're sitting in here, are you?

HJALMAR (*Rises hurriedly*): I just sat down for a moment; out of sheer exhaustion.

GREGERS: You seem to have had breakfast too.

HJALMAR: The body has its claims too, you know—occasionally.

GREGERS: Well—what have you decided?

HJALMAR: For a man like me there can be only one possible decision. I was busy gathering a few of my most important things together; but it's bound to take a little time.

GINA (*With a touch of impatience*): Which shall I do? Get the room ready, or pack your bag for you?

HJALMAR (*With an irritated look at* GREGERS): Pack the bag! —and get the room ready too!

GINA (*Picks up the portmanteau*): Very well; I'll just put in the shirt and those other things we spoke of. (*She goes into the sitting room and closes the door after her.*)

GREGERS (*After a short pause*): It never occurred to me that things would come to this. Is it really necessary for you to leave your home?

HJALMAR (*Wandering about restlessly*): What would you have me do? I wasn't made to bear unhappiness, Gregers. I need security; I must be surrounded by peace and comfort.

GREGERS: But you could find all that here, couldn't you? Why not try it? You have a splendid opportunity now to start afresh; why not begin again from here? And there's your invention to consider too; don't forget that.

HJALMAR: My invention! Don't even speak of that. That's a very doubtful proposition, I'm afraid.

GREGERS: Really? What do you mean?

HJALMAR: What on earth do you expect me to invent? Other people have invented practically everything already. It gets more difficult every day—

GREGERS: But I thought you'd worked so hard on it.

HJALMAR: It's all that damned Relling's fault!

GREGERS: Relling?

HJALMAR: Yes. He kept on telling me I had great inventive talent—that I would undoubtedly discover something to revolutionize photography.

GREGERS: I see! So it was Relling!

HJALMAR: But it's been a source of great happiness to me. Not so much the invention itself, but the fact that Hedvig had such faith in it. She believed in it as only a child can believe—unreservedly, whole heartedly—At least, I was fool enough to *think* she did.

GREGERS: Hedvig couldn't possibly deceive you—you *must* know that.

HJALMAR: I know nothing any more! She's the obstacle, you see. Hedvig's the one who's plunged my whole life into darkness.

GREGERS: Hedvig! Are you talking about *Hedvig*? How could she possibly plunge your life into darkness?

HJALMAR (*Without answering*): I've loved that child more than anything on earth. Each time I came back to this humble room, she would run to meet me—and it was such a joy to see her blinking up at me with those sweet little eyes of hers so full of happiness. I loved her with all my heart—fool that I was! And I imagined that she loved me just as deeply in return.

GREGERS: You *imagined* it, you say?

HJALMAR: What else *can* I say now? I can get nothing out of Gina. Besides—she's totally unaware of the part the Ideal plays in this whole business. But I must open my heart to you, Gregers: I'm tormented by the thought that perhaps Hedvig never really cared for me at all.

GREGERS: And supposing she were to give you a great proof of her love? (*Listens*) What's that? It sounded like the wild duck—

HJALMAR: Yes—it's the wild duck quacking; Father's in the attic.

GREGERS: Is he! (*His face lights up with joy*) You'll see—you may soon have proof of how much your poor misunderstood Hedvig loves you.

HJALMAR: What proof could she possibly give me? I'd never dare believe any assurances of hers.

GREGERS: I'm positive Hedvig doesn't even know the meaning of deceit.

HJALMAR: I wouldn't count too much on that, Gregers. Heaven knows what Gina and Mrs. Sörby have sat here scheming and plotting. And Hedvig's no fool—she has sharp ears. That gift may not have been such a surprise to her after all. As a matter of fact, I thought I noticed something in her manner—

GREGERS: What's got into you, Hjalmar? What makes you say such things?

HJALMAR: I've had my eyes opened—that's all. You'll see—this deed of gift may be only the beginning; Mrs. Sörby has always had a great fondness for Hedvig, and now she's in a position to do anything she wants to for the child. They could snatch her away from me whenever they chose to do so.

GREGERS: Nonsense! Hedvig would never consent to leave you.

HJALMAR: Don't be so sure. Just think of all *they* have to offer her! And *I* who have loved her so deeply—! My greatest happiness would have been to take her hand and lead her through life, as one might lead a frightened child through a dark, empty room. But—I'm convinced of it now!—the poor photographer up in his garret has never meant anything to her at all. She was just being shrewd; trying to keep on the good side of him until something better came along.

GREGERS: Come, Hjalmar—you know you don't believe that yourself.

HJALMAR: I don't know *what* to believe—that's the dreadful part of it—and I shall *never* know. You rely too much on the Ideal, my dear Gregers—otherwise you couldn't possibly doubt the truth of what I say. If those others were to come—laden with all their riches—and call out to the child: Leave him! You'll have a better life with us—

GREGERS: Yes? What then?

HJALMAR: And if I were to ask her: Hedvig, are you willing to give up that better life for me? (*With a scornful laugh*) You'd find out soon enough what her answer would be!

(*A pistol shot is heard in the attic.*)

GREGERS (*Loudly and joyfully*): Hjalmar!

HJALMAR: There! He's at his shooting again!

GINA (*Comes in*): Oh, Hjalmar—I wish Grandfather wouldn't bang away in there all by himself!

HJALMAR: I think I'll just look in—

GREGERS (*Eagerly, with emotion*): Wait, Hjalmar. Do you know what that was?

HJALMAR: Of course I do.

GREGERS: No you don't; but *I* know. That was the proof!

HJALMAR: What proof?

GREGERS: That was the child's sacrifice to you. She's persuaded your father to shoot the wild duck.

HJALMAR: The wild duck!

GINA: Good gracious!

HJALMAR: What's the point of that?

GREGERS: She's sacrificed the thing she loved best in the world to *you*. She thought, if she did that, you'd come to love her again, you see.

HJALMAR (*Tenderly, with emotion*): Poor child!

GINA: The things she thinks of!

GREGERS: All she wants is your love, Hjalmar. She can't live without it.

GINA (*Fighting back her tears*): You see, Hjalmar!

HJALMAR: Where is she, Gina?

GINA (*Sniffs*): She's in the kitchen, I suppose—poor little thing!

HJALMAR (*Tears open the kitchen door and says*): Hedvig, come! Come to me, Hedvig! (*Looks round*) No—she's not in here.

GINA: Then she must be in her room.

HJALMAR (*From outside*): She's not here either. (*Comes in again*) She must have gone out.

GINA: Well—you wouldn't have her anywhere about the house.

HJALMAR: I hope she'll come home soon—so that I can tell her— Everything's going to be all right now, Gregers. I believe we'll be able to start a new life after all.

GREGERS (*Quietly*): Thanks to the child; I knew it would be so. (OLD EKDAL *appears at the door of his room; he is in full uniform and is busy buckling on his sword.*)

HJALMAR (*In astonishment*): Why, Father! Were you in there?

GINA: Don't tell me you've been shooting in your room?

EKDAL (*Approaching, resentfully*): So you go hunting by yourself now, do you, Hjalmar?

HJALMAR (*Anxious and bewildered*): I thought you were in the attic; wasn't it you who fired that shot in there?

EKDAL: Fired a shot? I? Hm.

GREGERS (*Calls out to* HJALMAR): She's shot the wild duck herself!

HJALMAR: What can it mean! (*Rushes to the attic door, tears it open, looks in, and cries out*) Hedvig!

GINA (*Runs to the door*): God! What's happened?

HJALMAR (*Goes into the attic*): She's lying on the floor!

GREGERS: What! Hedvig? (*Goes in to* HJALMAR.)

GINA (*Simultaneously*): Hedvig! (*Inside the attic*) No, no, no!

EKDAL: Ho-ho! Is she going shooting too?

    (HJALMAR, GINA *and* GREGERS *carry* HEDVIG *into the studio; her right hand hangs down with the pistol still clasped tightly in its fingers*.)

HJALMAR (*Distracted*): The pistol must have gone off—she's wounded herself! Call for help! Help!

GINA (*Rushes out into the hall and calls down the stairs*): Relling! Relling! Dr. Relling! Come quickly!

    (HJALMAR *and* GREGERS *lay* HEDVIG *down on the sofa*.)

EKDAL (*Quietly*): The forest takes revenge.

HJALMAR (*On his knees beside her*): She's beginning to come to. She's coming to—yes, yes.

GINA (*Who has come in again*): Where is she wounded? I don't see anything—

    (RELLING *comes in hurriedly followed by* MOLVIK; *the latter without his waistcoat and necktie, and with his coat open*.)

RELLING: What's happening here?

GINA: They say Hedvig has shot herself.

HJALMAR: Quickly! Help us!

RELLING: Shot herself! (*He pushes the table aside and starts to examine her*.)

HJALMAR (*Still kneeling, looks up at him anxiously*): It can't be serious, can it? Eh, Relling? She's hardly bleeding at all; it can't be serious?

RELLING: How did it happen?

HJALMAR: We don't know—!

GINA: She wanted to shoot the wild duck.

RELLING: The wild duck?

HJALMAR: The pistol must have gone off.

RELLING: Hm. I see.

EKDAL: The forest takes revenge. But I'm not afraid! Not I! (*Goes into the attic and slides the door shut after him.*)

HJALMAR: Relling—why don't you say something?

RELLING: The bullet entered the breast.

HJALMAR: Yes—but she's coming to—

RELLING: Can't you see that Hedvig's dead?

GINA (*Bursts into tears*): My child! My little child!

GREGERS (*Huskily*): In the boundless deep—

HJALMAR (*Jumps up*): She must live, she *must!* For God's sake, Relling—if only for a moment. Just long enough for me to tell her how deeply I've loved her all the time!

RELLING: The bullet pierced her heart. Internal hemorrhage. Death must have been instantaneous.

HJALMAR: Oh, God! And I drove her from me like a dog! She died for love of me: she crept into the attic, filled with grief and terror, and died for love of me! (*Sobs*) Never to be able to tell her! Never to be able to atone! (*Clenches his fists and looks upwards shouting*) You, up there—! If you *are* there—! Why have you done this thing to me!

GINA: Hush, hush! You mustn't go on like that! We didn't deserve to keep her, I suppose.

MOLVIK: The child is not dead; it sleepeth.

RELLING: Rubbish.

HJALMAR (*Becomes calm, goes over to the sofa, folds his arms, and looks down at* HEDVIG): She's so stiff—so still.

RELLING (*Tries to loosen the hand holding the pistol*): She's holding it so tightly—so very tightly—

GINA: No, Relling—don't force her fingers. Let the gun be.

HJALMAR: She shall take it with her.

GINA: Yes; let her. But the child mustn't lie here—on show like this. She shall go to her own room. Help me, Hjalemar. (HJALMAR *and* GINA *carry* HEDVIG *between them.*)

HJALMAR (*As they carry her*): Gina, Gina! How can you ever bear it!

GINA: We must try and help each other. At least *now* she belongs to both of us.

MOLVIK (*Stretching out his arms and muttering*): Blessed be the

Lord; to earth thou shalt return; to earth thou shalt return—

RELLING (*In a whisper*): Shut up, you fool—you're drunk. (HJALMAR *and* GINA *carry the body out through the kitchen door.* RELLING *shuts it after them.* MOLVIK *slinks out into the hall.*)

RELLING (*Goes over to* GREGERS *and says*): No one will ever make me believe this was an accident.

GREGERS (*Who has been standing horrified, his face twitching*): How could this dreadful thing have happened. No one will ever know.

RELLING: The front of her dress was burned. She must have aimed the pistol at her heart and fired.

GREGERS: Hedvig has not died in vain. Didn't you see? His sorrow brought out all that is noblest in him.

RELLING: Most people are noble in the presence of death. One wonders how long this nobility of his will last.

GREGERS: Why shouldn't it last? Why shouldn't it increase and grow stronger with the years?

RELLING: The years! Before this year is out, little Hedvig will be no more to him than a theme on which to exercise his eloquence!

GREGERS: How dare you say that of Hjalmar Ekdal!

RELLING: We'll talk of this again when this year's grass has withered on her grave. You'll see: He'll be spouting about "the child snatched from her father's loving arms by an untimely death"; he'll be wallowing in a sea of self-pity and maudlin sentimentality. You wait. You'll see.

GREGERS: All I can say is—if *you* are right and *I* am wrong, then life is not worth living.

RELLING: Life would be quite pleasant all the same—if it were not for certain lunatics, certain fanatics, who hammer at our doors, insisting on some nonsense they call the Claim of the Ideal.

GREGERS (*Gazing before him*): Then I'm glad my fate is what it is.

RELLING: And what *is* it, may I ask?

GREGERS (*Starts to go*): To be thirteenth at table.

RELLING: The Hell it is. I wish I could believe it!

CURTAIN

Rosmersholm

A PLAY IN FOUR ACTS

1886

CHARACTERS

JOHANNES ROSMER, *owner of Rosmersholm; a former clergyman*

REBEKKA WEST, *a member of the household*

PROFESSOR KROLL, *Rosmer's brother-in-law*

ULRIK BRENDEL

PEDER MORTENSGAARD*

MRS. HELSETH, *housekeeper at Rosmersholm*

> *The action takes place at Rosmersholm, an old estate in the
> neighborhood of a small town on a fjord on the west coast of
> Norway.*

*For stage purposes, often PETER.

ACT
ONE

SCENE: *Sitting-room at Rosmersholm; spacious, old-fashioned, and comfortable. In front, on the right, a stove decked with fresh birch branches and wild flowers. Farther back, on the same side, a door. In the back wall, folding doors opening into the hall. To the left, a window, and before it a stand with flowers and plants. Beside the stove a table with a sofa and easy chairs. On the walls, old and more recent portraits of clergymen, officers and government officials in uniform. The window is open; so are the door into the hall and the house door beyond. Outside can be seen an avenue of fine old trees, leading up to the house. It is a summer evening, after sunset.* REBEKKA WEST *is sitting in an easy chair by the window, and crocheting a large white woolen shawl, which is nearly finished. She now and then looks out expectantly through the leaves of the plants.* MRS. HELSETH *presently enters.*

MRS. HELSETH: I suppose I had better start laying the table for supper, Miss?

REBEKKA: Yes, do. Mr. Rosmer should be back in a few minutes.

MRS. HELSETH: Aren't you sitting in a draught there, Miss?

REBEKKA: Yes, there is a little draught. You might just close the window.

(MRS. HELSETH *shuts the door into the hall, and then comes to the window.*)

MRS. HELSETH (*About to shut the window, looks out*): Isn't that Mr. Rosmer out there now?

REBEKKA (*Hastily*): Where? (*Rises*) Yes, so it is. (*Stands behind the curtain*) Stand back a little. Don't let him see us.

MRS. HELSETH (*Draws back from window*): You see, Miss?—He's beginning to use the path by the mill again.

REBEKKA: He used it the day before yesterday too. (*Peeps out between the curtains and the windowframe*) But I wonder whether—

MRS. HELSETH: Will he bring himself to cross the foot-bridge, do you think?

REBEKKA: That's just what I want to see. (*After a pause*) No, he's turning back. Today, again! He's going by the upper road. (*Leaves the window*) A long way round.

MRS. HELSETH: Well—Good Lord!—you can't blame him for not wanting to cross that bridge, Miss. When you think of what happened there—

REBEKKA (*Folding up her work*): They certainly cling to their dead at Rosmersholm.

MRS. HELSETH: Do you know what *I* think, Miss? I think it's the dead that cling to Rosmersholm.

REBEKKA (*Looks at her*): How do you mean—the dead?

MRS. HELSETH: It's as if they kept trying to come back; as if they couldn't quite free themselves from those they've left behind.

REBEKKA: What an idea! What put that into your head?

MRS. HELSETH: That would account for the White Horse, you see.

REBEKKA: What is all this about a White Horse, Mrs. Helseth?

MRS. HELSETH: It's no use talking to you about it, Miss; you don't believe such things.

REBEKKA: Do *you* believe them?

MRS. HELSETH (*Goes and shuts the window*): You'd only make fun of me, Miss. (*Looks out*) Look! Isn't that Mr. Rosmer on the path again—?

REBEKKA (*Looks out*): Let me see. (*Goes to the window*) No. Why—it's Professor Kroll!

MRS. HELSETH: Yes, so it is.

REBEKKA: What a funny thing! He seems to be coming here.

MRS. HELSETH: He makes no bones about going over the foot-bridge—even if she was his own sister! Well, I suppose I'd better lay the table, Miss

(*She goes out.* REBEKKA *stands at the window for a short time; then smiles and nods to someone outside. It begins to grow dark.*)

REBEKKA (*Goes to the door*): Oh, Mrs. Helseth! You'd better prepare a little something extra; something the Professor's specially fond of.

MRS. HELSETH (*Outside*): Very well, Miss; I'll see to it.

REBEKKA (*Opens the door to the hall*): Well—what a surprise! Welcome, my dear Professor!

KROLL (*In the hall, laying down his stick*): Many thanks. I hope I'm not disturbing you?

REBEKKA: You! How can you say such things!

KROLL (*Comes in*): Charming as ever! (*Looks around*) Is Rosmer up in his room?

REBEKKA: No, he's out for a walk. He's been gone a bit longer than usual; but he's sure to be here any minute. (*Indicating the sofa*) Won't you sit down till he comes?

KROLL (*Laying down his hat*): Many thanks. (*Sits down and looks about him*) What nice things you've done to the old place! It's all so cheerful—flowers everywhere!

REBEKKA: Mr. Rosmer's very fond of flowers.

KROLL: And you are too, I suppose.

REBEKKA: Yes, I am; I find them very soothing. We had to do without them though—until quite recently.

KROLL (*Nods sadly*): I know; on account of poor Beata. Their scent seemed to overpower her.

REBEKKA: Their colors, too. They upset her terribly.

KROLL: Yes, I remember. (*In a lighter tone*) Well—how are things going out here?

REBEKKA: Oh, quietly and peacefully as usual; the days slip by—one day just like the last. But what about you? I hope Mrs. Kroll is well?

KROLL: Oh, my dear Miss West, I'd rather not talk about my affairs. In family life one has to expect complications—especially in times like these.

REBEKKA (*Sits in an armchair by the sofa*): You haven't been to see us once, all during the holidays. Why haven't you? Tell me

KROLL: I didn't want to make a nuisance of myself.

REBEKKA: I can't tell you how we've missed you—

KROLL: Besides—I've been away—

REBEKKA: But only for a couple of weeks. I hear you've been attending a lot of meetings— You've been going in for politics—?

KROLL (*Nods*): Yes, what do you say to that? Who would ever have thought I'd become a political firebrand in my old age?

REBEKKA (*Smiling*): Well, you have always been a bit of a firebrand, Professor Kroll.

KROLL: In private life, perhaps—for my own amusement. But this is a serious matter. Do you ever read any of these radical newspapers, by any chance?

REBEKKA: I must admit, my dear Professor, that I—

KROLL: As far as you're concerned, my dear Miss West, there's no reason why you shouldn't—

REBEKKA: No, that's what I feel. I like to know what's going on—to keep up with the times—

KROLL: Certainly. And one naturally doesn't expect a woman to take an active part in this controversy—one might almost call it a civil war—that is raging all about us. Then you're no doubt familiar with the disgraceful way these gentlemen of "the people" have seen fit to treat me? The infamous abuse they've dared to heap upon me?

REBEKKA: I must say you gave as good as you got!

KROLL: I did indeed. And I'm proud of it. Now that I've tasted blood they'll soon find out I'm not the man to turn the other cheek—(*Breaks off*) But why should we discuss this painful subject?

REBEKKA: No, dear Professor, don't let us talk about it.

KROLL: I'd rather talk about you; how are you getting on at Rosmersholm, now that our poor Beata—?

REBEKKA: Thank you, well enough. It seems so empty here without her; one can't help feeling very sad—we miss her in so many ways. But, apart from that—

KROLL: Do you plan to go on staying here?—permanently, I mean?

REBEKKA: I really haven't given it much thought. I've grown so accustomed to this place— It's almost as if I, too, belonged here.

KROLL: But you *do!* You *do* belong here!

REBEKKA: And as long as Mr. Rosmer needs me—as long as I can be of any help or comfort to him—I feel I should remain.

KROLL (*Looks at her much moved*): It's a very wonderful thing, Miss West, for a woman to give up the best years of her life to others, as you have.

REBEKKA: What else had I to live for?

KROLL: Your devotion to your foster-father was admirable. It must have been very hard for you; half-paralyzed and unreasonable as he was—

REBEKKA: You mustn't think Dr. West was always so unreasonable—at least, not during the first years in Finmark. It was those terrible sea voyages that undermined his health. It wasn't until afterwards, when we moved down here—those last two years before his death—that things became so difficult.

KROLL: And presumably the years that followed were more difficult still—

REBEKKA: How can you say that! I was devoted to Beata—Poor darling! She had such need of tenderness and care.

KROLL: How kind you are to speak of her with so much understanding.

REBEKKA (*Moves a little nearer*): Dear Professor, you reassure me! You couldn't say that with such sincerity if you had any resentment in your heart towards me.

KROLL: Resentment! Why should you think that?

REBEKKA: Well, mightn't it be natural that you should resent a stranger presiding over things at Rosmersholm?

KROLL: What on earth—!

REBEKKA: But you have no such feeling, have you? (*Takes his hand*) Thank you, my dear Professor; many, many thanks!

KROLL: What on earth put that into your head?

REBEKKA: You've been to see us so seldom lately—I began to be a little frightened.

KROLL: Then you were totally mistaken, my dear Miss West. And, after all, things haven't really changed; you were in full charge here long before poor Beata died.

REBEKKA: Yes—but that was only a kind of stewardship on her behalf—

KROLL: All the same—For my part, Miss West—I should be only

too happy to see you— But perhaps I shouldn't mention such a thing.

REBEKKA: What do you mean?

KROLL: I'd be only too happy to see you take poor Beata's place.

REBEKKA: I have the only place I want, Professor.

KROLL: For all practical purposes, yes; but not as far as—

REBEKKA (*Interrupting gravely*): Shame on you, Professor Kroll. You shouldn't joke about such things!

KROLL: I dare say our good Rosmer feels he's had more than enough of married life. But still—

REBEKKA: Don't be so absurd, Professor!

KROLL: But still—Tell me—how old are you now, Miss West?—if you'll forgive the question!

REBEKKA: I'm ashamed to admit, Professor, I'm past twenty-nine—I'm in my thirtieth year.

KROLL: And Rosmer—how old is he? Let me see: he is five years younger than I am, so that would make him forty-three. That seems to me most suitable.

REBEKKA (*Rises*): No doubt—yes; very suitable indeed! You'll stay for supper, won't you?

KROLL: Yes, thank you; I'd like to very much. There's a matter I must discuss with Rosmer. And from now on, Miss West, I shall resume my former practice of coming out more often; we can't have you getting your head full of foolish notions!

REBEKKA: Yes—do that! I wish you would! (*Shakes both his hands*) Again—many thanks! How kind and good you are!

KROLL (*Gruffly*): Am I? That's not what I hear at home! (JOHANNES ROSMER *enters by the door on the right.*)

REBEKKA: Mr. Rosmer! Just look who's here!

ROSMER: Mrs. Helseth told me. (PROFESSOR KROLL *has risen;* ROSMER *takes his hand; with quiet emotion*) Welcome back to this house, my dear Kroll. (*Lays his hands on* KROLL'S *shoulders and looks into his eyes*) My dear, dear friend! I was certain things would straighten out between us.

KROLL: My dear fellow—don't tell me you've been imagining things too?

REBEKKA (*To* ROSMER): Isn't it wonderful, Rosmer? It was all imagination!

ROSMER: Is that really true? Then what made you stay away from me?

KROLL (*Gravely, in a low voice*): I didn't want to be a constant reminder of those unhappy years—and of poor Beata's tragic death.

ROSMER: How good of you! But then—you always were considerate. Still—it wasn't necessary to stay away on that account—Let's sit here on the sofa. (*They sit down*) No, I assure you, the thought of Beata isn't painful to me. She seems so close to us. We speak of her every day.

KROLL: Do you really?

REBEKKA (*Lighting the lamp*): Yes, indeed we do.

ROSMER: It's natural enough. We were both so devoted to her. And Rebek—Miss West and I did everything in our power to help her— We're confident of that; there's no room for self-reproach. That's why we can think of her with a sense of peace—a quiet tenderness.

KROLL: What splendid people you are! That settles it—I shall come out and see you every single day!

REBEKKA (*Seats herself in an arm-chair*): Be sure and keep your word!

ROSMER (*With some hesitation*): You know—I regret even this short interruption in our friendship. Ever since we've known each other you've been my chief adviser—since my student days, in fact.

KROLL: Yes—I've always been proud of it. But is there anything in particular—?

ROSMER: There are a number of things I'm most anxious to discuss with you. I'd like to talk to you quite frankly—heart to heart.

REBEKKA: It would do you good, wouldn't it, Mr. Rosmer? It must be such a comfort—between old friends—

KROLL: And I've a great deal to discuss with you. You know, of course, I've begun to take an active part in politics?

ROSMER: I know. How did that come about?

KROLL: I was forced into it—I had no choice. It's no longer possible to stand by idly looking on. Now that the radical party has, so unfortunately, come into power, it is high time that something was done about it. I have persuaded some of our friends in town to band together—to take some constructive action. I tell you it is high time!

REBEKKA (*With a faint smile*): Perhaps it might even be a little late?

KROLL: Oh, unquestionably, we should have stemmed the tide long ago—that would have been far better! But who could possibly foresee what was to happen? Not I, certainly! (*Rises and walks up and down*) But I can tell you my eyes are open now. You'd never believe it—but this seditious element has actually gained a foothold in the school!

ROSMER: The school? You surely don't mean *your* school?

KROLL: Yes, I tell you! What do you say to that? And it has come to my knowledge that for the past six months the senior boys—a considerable number of them at any rate—have been members of a secret society and subscribe to Mortensgaard's paper.

REBEKKA: What! *The Beacon?*

KROLL: Yes; nice mental sustenance for future government officials, is it not? But the most distressing thing is, that it's the most gifted students who have taken part in this conspiracy against me. The only ones who seem to have kept away from it are the dunces—at the bottom of the class.

REBEKKA: Does this really affect you so very deeply, Professor Kroll?

KROLL: Does it affect me? To see the work of a lifetime thwarted and undermined? (*Lower*) Still—all this might be endurable, perhaps. There's something worse, however. (*Looks around*) You're sure no one can hear us?

REBEKKA: No, no; of course not.

KROLL: Then, listen to this: the spirit of revolt has actually crept into my own house—into my own quiet home; the harmony of my family life has been utterly destroyed.

ROSMER (*Rises*): What do you mean? Into your home—!

REBEKKA (*Goes over to the Professor*): What can have happened, dear Professor?

KROLL: You wouldn't believe it, would you, that my own children—? In short—I find that Lauritz is the ringleader of this conspiracy; and my daughter Hilda has embroidered a red portfolio to keep *The Beacon* in.

ROSMER: —Your own home? It seems impossible!

KROLL: Yes—doesn't it? The very home of duty and obedience—where, at my insistence, order and decency have always reigned supreme—

REBEKKA: How does your wife take all this?

KROLL: That's the most astonishing thing about it. My wife, who has always shared my opinion on all subjects—has undeviatingly upheld my principles—seems inclined to take the children's point of view in this affair. She tells me I'm to blame—that I'm too harsh with them. Yet, surely there are times when discipline— Well, you see how my house is divided against itself. I naturally say as little about it as possible. Such things are best kept quiet. (*Wanders about the room*) Ah, well, well, well. (*Stands at window with hands behind his back and looks out.*)

REBEKKA (*Comes up close to* ROSMER, *and says rapidly and in a low voice, so that the Professor does not hear her*): Tell him!

ROSMER (*Also in a low voice*): Not this evening.

REBEKKA (*As before*): Yes! Tell him *now!* (*Goes to the table and busies herself with the lamp.*)

KROLL (*Comes forward*): Well, my dear Rosmer, now you know how the spirit of the times has cast its shadow over me—over my domestic as well as my official life. I could hardly be expected not to resist this dangerous and destructive force—this anarchy. I shall fight it with every weapon I can lay my hands on. I shall fight it by word and deed.

ROSMER: What do you expect to gain by that?

KROLL: I shall at least have done my duty as a citizen. And I hold it the duty of every right-thinking man with an atom of patriotism to do likewise. This was my main reason for wanting to talk to you this evening.

ROSMER: But, my dear Kroll, how do you mean—? How could I possibly—?

KROLL: You must stand by your old friends. You must join our ranks—march with us to battle!

REBEKKA: Professor Kroll, you know how Mr. Rosmer dislikes that sort of thing.

KROLL: Then he must get over his dislike. You've let yourself get out of touch with things, Rosmer. You bury yourself away out here, delving into the past, absorbed in your genealogical research—oh, far be it from me to scoff at such things—but this is no time to indulge in these pursuits. You have no conception of what is happening throughout the country. There is scarcely an established principle that hasn't been attacked; the whole order of Society is threatened! It will be a colossal task to set things right again.

ROSMER: Yes—I quite agree. But that sort of work isn't at all in my line.

REBEKKA: Besides, I think Mr. Rosmer has gradually acquired a wider view on life.

KROLL (*With surprise*): A wider view?

REBEKKA: Well—freer, if you like; less prejudiced.

KROLL: What does this mean? Rosmer, you are surely not so weak as to be taken in by any temporary advantage these anarchists have won?

ROSMER: As you know, I've very little understanding of politics, dear Kroll. But it does seem clear that in the past few years, men have at last begun to think for themselves—as individuals.

KROLL: And you immediately assume this to be to their advantage? You are mistaken, I assure you. I don't think you quite realize what these ideas are, that the radicals are spreading among the people—not only in the city, but out here in the country too. You should make some inquiries! You'd find them based on the brand of wisdom proclaimed in the pages of *The Beacon*.

REBEKKA: Yes; Mortensgaard certainly has great influence.

KROLL: It's inconceivable! A man with such a record—who was dismissed from his position as schoolteacher on moral grounds—to set himself up as a leader of the people! And he succeeds too! He actually succeeds! He is about to enlarge his paper, I understand. He's on the lookout for a capable assistant.

REBEKKA: I'm surprised you and your friends don't start a paper of your own.

KROLL: That is precisely what we intend to do. Only today we purchased the *County News*. Financial backing is no problem to us, of course, but— (*Turns to* ROSMER) —and now I come to the real purpose of my visit— Where are we to find an editor? That is the vital question. Tell me, Rosmer—don't you feel it your duty, for the good of the cause, to undertake this task?

ROSMER (*Almost in consternation*): I!

REBEKKA: You can't be serious!

KROLL: I can well understand your dislike of public meetings, and all that they imply. But this position would enable you to keep in the background—or rather—

ROSMER: No, no!— Please don't ask me to do this.

KROLL: I'd have no objection to trying my own hand at it. But that's out of the question—I'm burdened with too many duties as it is; while you have ample leisure—there's nothing to prevent you from undertaking it. We'd naturally give you all the help we could.

ROSMER: I can't do it, Kroll. I'm not suited to it.

KROLL: That's what you said when your father procured you the ministry here—

ROSMER: And I was right. That's why I resigned it.

KROLL: If you're as good an editor as you were a clergyman, we shan't complain!

ROSMER: Once and for all, my dear Kroll, I cannot do it.

KROLL: Well—but you'll lend us your name, at any rate?

ROSMER: My name?

KROLL: Yes, the mere name, Johannes Rosmer, will be a great help to the paper. We are all of us looked upon as hopeless reactionaries. I believe I myself am supposed to be a desperate fanatic! This will make it difficult for us to reach the people—poor misguided wretches that they are! You, on the other hand, have always kept aloof. Everyone knows and appreciates your integrity, your humanity, your fine mind and unimpeachable honor. Then, too, you are esteemed and respected as a former clergyman. And think of what the name "Rosmer" stands for in this part of the country!

ROSMER: No doubt—

KROLL (*Pointing to the portraits on the walls*): Rosmers of Rosmersholm—clergymen and soldiers, high-ranking officials; worthy, honorable gentlemen all!—A family that for nearly two centuries has held its place as the first in the district. (*Lays his hand on* ROSMER'S *shoulder*) You owe it to yourself, Rosmer, to all the traditions of your race, to defend those things that have always been held most precious in our society. (*Turns round*) Don't you agree with me, Miss West?

REBEKKA (*Laughing softly, as if to herself*): I'm afraid it all strikes me as utterly ludicrous—

KROLL: Ludicrous?

REBEKKA: Yes, ludicrous. I think I'd better tell you—

ROSMER (*Quickly*): No, no—don't! Not just now!

KROLL (*Looks from one to the other*): But, my dear friends, what does this mean—? (*Interrupting himself*) H'm!

(MRS. HELSETH *appears in doorway*.)

MRS. HELSETH: There's a man at the kitchen-door; he says he wants to see you, Sir.

ROSMER (*Relieved*): Well—show him in.

MRS. HELSETH: In *here*, Sir?

ROSMER: Yes, of course.

MRS. HELSETH: But he doesn't look like the sort you'd bring into the drawing room.

REBEKKA: What *does* he look like, Mrs. Helseth?

MRS. HELSETH: He's not much to look at, Miss, and that's a fact.

ROSMER: Did he give his name?

MRS. HELSETH: I think he said he was called Hekman—or something of the sort.

ROSMER: I know no one of that name.

MRS. HELSETH: And then he said something about Uldrik, too.

ROSMER (*In surprise*): Ulrik Hetman! Was that it?

MRS. HELSETH: That's it—Hetman.

KROLL: I seem to have heard that name—

REBEKKA: It's the name that strange man used to write under—

ROSMER (*To* KROLL): It's Ulrik Brendel's pen name.

KROLL: Quite right! That scoundrel Brendel!

REBEKKA: He's still alive, then.

ROSMER: I heard he had joined a troupe of actors.

KROLL: When I last heard of him, he was in the workhouse.

ROSMER: Ask him to come in, Mrs. Helseth.

MRS. HELSETH: Very well. (*She goes out*.)

KROLL: You're not going to let a man like that into your house?

ROSMER: He was once my tutor.

KROLL: I know. And I know too that he filled your head with a lot of revolutionary notions and that your father showed him the door—with a horsewhip.

ROSMER (*With a touch of bitterness*): Yes. Father was a martinet at home as well as in his regiment.

KROLL: You should be forever grateful to him for that, my dear Rosmer— Well!

(MRS. HELSETH *opens the door on the right for* ULRIK BRENDEL, *and then withdraws, shutting the door behind him. He is a handsome man, with gray hair and beard; somewhat gaunt but active and well set up. He is dressed like a common tramp: threadbare frock-coat; worn-out shoes; no shirt visible. He wears an old pair of black gloves, and carries a soft, greasy felt hat under his arm, and a walking-stick in his hand.*)

BRENDEL (*Hesitates at first, then goes quickly up to* KROLL, *and holds out his hand*): Good evening, Johannes!

KROLL: I beg your pardon—

BRENDEL: I'll be bound you never expected to see me again! And within these hated walls, too?

KROLL: I beg your pardon— (*Pointing*) Over there—

BRENDEL (*Turns*): Oh, of course! There you are! Johannes—my own beloved boy—!

ROSMER (*Takes his hand*): My dear old teacher.

BRENDEL: I couldn't pass by Rosmersholm without paying you a flying visit—in spite of certain painful memories!

ROSMER: You are heartily welcome here now—I assure you.

BRENDEL: And who is this charming lady—? (*Bows*) Mrs. Rosmer, no doubt.

ROSMER: Miss West.

BRENDEL: A near relation, I expect. And yonder stranger—? A brother of the cloth, I see.

ROSMER: Professor Kroll.

BRENDEL: Kroll? Kroll? Wait a bit— Weren't you a student of philology in your young days?

KROLL: Of course I was.

BRENDEL: Why, *Donnerwetter*—then I must have known you!

KROLL: I beg your pardon.

BRENDEL: Of course! You were—

KROLL: I beg your pardon—

BRENDEL: Yes! You were one of those paragons of virtue that got me kicked out of the Debating Club!

KROLL: It's very possible. But I acknowledge no closer acquaintance.

BRENDEL: Well, well! *Nach Belieben, Herr Doktor*. It's all one to me. Ulrik Brendel remains Ulrik Brendel just the same!

REBEKKA: I suppose you're on your way to town, Mr. Brendel?

BRENDEL: You have hit it, most charming lady. At certain intervals, I am constrained to strike a blow for existence. It goes against the grain; but—*enfin*—imperious necessity—

ROSMER: Oh, but my dear Mr. Brendel, mayn't I be allowed to help you. In one way or another, I am sure—

BRENDEL: To propose such a thing to me! You surely wouldn't wish to desecrate our friendship? Never, my dear Johannes; never!

ROSMER: But what do you plan to do in town? I'm afraid you won't find it easy to—

BRENDEL: Leave that to me, my boy. The die is cast. You see before you a man about to embark on a great campaign—greater and more intensive than all my previous excursions put together. (*To* KROLL) May I be so bold as to ask the *Herr Professor*—*unter uns*—have you such a thing as a reasonably clean, respectable and commodious Assembly Hall in your esteemed city?

KROLL: There is the Workers Union Hall—that is the largest.

BRENDEL: And has the *Herr Professor* any official influence in this, no doubt worthy, organization?

KROLL: I have nothing whatever to do with it.

REBEKKA (*To* BRENDEL): You should apply to Peder Mortensgaard.

BRENDEL: Pardon, Madame—what sort of an idiot is he?

ROSMER: What makes you suppose that he's an idiot?

BRENDEL: The name has such a distinctly plebian sound.

KROLL: I never expected *that* answer.

BRENDEL: However I will conquer my reluctance; there's no alternative. When a man finds himself at a turning point in his career, as I do—So be it. I will get in touch with this person—open direct negotiations with him—

ROSMER: Are you really at a turning point in your career—in all seriousness?

BRENDEL: Doesn't my own boy know that wherever I am and whatever I do, it's always in all seriousness? I'm about to put on a new man—to discard this modest reserve I have hitherto maintained.

ROSMER: How so?

BRENDEL: I intend to take hold of life with a strong hand—Go forward. Mount upward. We live in a tempestuous, an equinoctial age—I am about to lay my mite on the altar of Emancipation.

KROLL: So, you too—?

BRENDEL (*To them all*): Is the public in these parts at all familiar with my infrequent writings?

KROLL: No; I must honestly admit that—

REBEKKA: I've read some of them. My foster-father had them in his library.

BRENDEL: Then you wasted your time, fair lady. They're all so much trash, let me tell you.

REBEKKA: Indeed?

BRENDEL: Those that you've read, yes. My really significant works no man or woman knows. No one—except myself.

REBEKKA: Why is that?

BRENDEL: For the simple reason that I have never written them.

ROSMER: But my dear Mr. Brendel—

BRENDEL: You know I've always been a bit of a sybarite, my dear Johannes; a *Feinschmecker*. I like to enjoy things in solitude; then I enjoy them doubly—tenfold. Glorious dreams come to me—intoxicating thoughts—bold, lofty, unique ideas, that carry me aloft on powerful pinions; these I transform into poems, visions, pictures—all in the abstract, you understand.

ROSMER: Yes, yes.

BRENDEL: The joys, the ecstasy I have reveled in, Johannes! The

mysterious bliss of creation—in the abstract, as I said before. I
have been showered with applause, gratitude and fame; I have
been crowned with laurel-wreaths; all these tributes I have gar-
nered with joyous, tremulous hands. In my secret imaginings I
have been satiated with delight—with a rapture so intense, so
intoxicating—

KROLL: H'm.

ROSMER: But you've never written down any of these things?

BRENDEL: Not a word. The vulgar business of writing has always
nauseated me—filled me with disgust. Besides, why should I
profane my own ideals, when I can enjoy them by myself in all
their purity? But now they must be offered up. I assure you I feel
as a mother must when she delivers her young daughters into
their bridegrooms' arms. Nevertheless—they must be offered
up—offered upon the altar of Freedom. I will start with a series
of carefully planned lectures—all over the country—

REBEKKA (*With animation*): How splendid of you, Mr. Brendel!
You'll be giving the most precious thing you have.

ROSMER: The only thing.

REBEKKA (*Looking significantly at* ROSMER): There aren't many
people who'd do that—who'd have the courage to do that!

ROSMER (*Returning the look*): Who knows?

BRENDEL: I see my audience is touched. That puts new heart into
me—strengthens my will. So now I will proceed to action. Just
one thing more. (*To the Professor*) Tell me, *Herr Preceptor*— is
there a Temperance Society in town? A Total Abstinence Society? But of course there must be!

KROLL: I am the president, at your service.

BRENDEL: Of course! One only has to look at you! Then—be prepared! I may come and join up for a week or so.

KROLL: I beg your pardon—we do not accept members by the
week.

BRENDEL: *A la bonne heure, Herr Pedagogue*. Ulrik Brendel has
never been one to force his way into such Societies. (*Turns*) But I
dare not prolong my stay in this house, so rich in memories. I
must get to town and select a suitable lodging. There is a decent
hotel in the place, I hope.

REBEKKA: You'll have a hot drink before you go?

BRENDEL: What sort of a hot drink, gracious lady?

REBEKKA: A cup of tea, or—

BRENDEL: I thank my bountiful hostess—but I dislike taking advantage of private hospitality. (*Waves his hand*) Farewell, gentlefolk all! (*Goes toward door but turns again*) Oh, I almost forgot, Johannes—Pastor Rosmer—would you do your former teacher a favor, for old time's sake?

ROSMER: I should be delighted.

BRENDEL: Then, could you lend me a dress shirt—just for a day or two?

ROSMER: Is that all?

BRENDEL: You see, I happen to be traveling on foot—just for the time being. They're sending my trunk after me.

ROSMER· I see. But are you sure there's nothing else?

BRENDEL: Yes—come to think of it—if you could spare me a light overcoat—

ROSMER: Of course I can.

BRENDEL: And perhaps a respectable pair of shoes as well—?

ROSMER: I'll see to it. As soon as we know your address, we'll send them off to you.

BRENDEL: I wouldn't dream of putting you to so much trouble! Give me the bagatelles now—I'll take them with me.

ROSMER: Very well. Just come upstairs with me.

REBEKKA: No, let me go. Mrs. Helseth and I will see to it.

BRENDEL: I could never allow this distinguished lady—!

REBEKKA: Oh, nonsense, Mr. Brendel! Come along. (*She goes out.*)

ROSMER (*Detaining him*): There must be something else I can do for you?

BRENDEL: No; I can't think of a thing. But, of course—damnation take it! It just occurred to me; I wonder if you happen to have eight crowns on you, Johannes?

ROSMER: Let me see. (*Opens his purse*) Here are two ten-crown notes.

BRENDEL: Never mind—they'll do. I can always get change in town. Meanwhile—many thanks. Don't forget—that was two

tens you lent me. Good night, my own dear boy. Good night,
honored Sir! (*Goes out right.*)

(ROSMER *takes leave of him, and shuts the door behind him.*)

KROLL: Merciful Heaven!—so this is that Ulrik Brendel people
once expected such great things of.

ROSMER (*Quietly*): At least he's had the courage to live life in his
own way. It seems to me that's something to his credit.

KROLL: What do you mean? A life like his! Don't tell me he still has
the power to influence you?

ROSMER: Far from it. My mind is quite clear now, on all points.

KROLL: I wish I could believe that, Rosmer. You're easily swayed,
you know.

ROSMER: Sit down. I've got to talk to you.

KROLL: Very well. (*They seat themselves on the sofa.*)

ROSMER (*After a slight pause*): Our life here must strike you as
very comfortable and pleasant.

KROLL: Yes, indeed; it's comfortable and pleasant now—and
peaceful, too. You have found a home, Rosmer—and I have lost
one.

ROSMER: My dear friend, don't say that. The wound will heal in
time.

KROLL: Never. The sting can never be removed. Things can never
be the same.

ROSMER: Now listen to me, Kroll. We have been close friends for a
great many years. Does it seem to you conceivable that anything
could ever break our friendship?

KROLL: I can think of nothing that could ever come between us.
What makes you ask that question?

ROSMER: I ask it because I know how intolerant you are of any op-
position to your way of seeing things.

KROLL: That may be; but you and I have always agreed—at least
on essentials.

ROSMER (*In a low voice*): I'm afraid that's no longer true.

KROLL (*Tries to jump up*): What's that you say?

ROSMER (*Holds him back*): No, please sit still!

KROLL: What does this mean? I don't understand you. Explain
yourself.

ROSMER: It's as though my spirit had grown young again. I see things now with different eyes—with *youthful* eyes, Kroll; that's why I no longer agree with you, but with—

KROLL: With whom? Tell me!

ROSMER: With your children.

KROLL: With my children?

ROSMER: With Lauritz and Hilda—yes.

KROLL (*Bows his head*): A traitor! Johannes Rosmer a traitor!

ROSMER: I should have been happy—completely happy—in being what you call a traitor! But the thought of you saddened me. I knew it would be a great grief to you.

KROLL: I shall never get over it, Rosmer. (*Looks gloomily at him*) That you should be willing to share in this work of destruction—bring ruin on our unhappy country!

ROSMER: I intend to work for Freedom.

KROLL: Oh, yes—I know! That's what these false prophets call it—that's what their wretched followers call it too. But what sort of freedom can come from Anarchy, I ask you? From this spirit of evil that is spreading poison throughout our entire society?

ROSMER: I'm not wedded to this spirit of evil, as you call it, and I belong to neither party. I want to bring men together regardless of which side they may be on. I want them to unite for the common good. I intend to devote my whole life and all my strength to this one end: the creation of a true democracy.

KROLL: Haven't we democracy enough already! It's my opinion that we are all of us rapidly being dragged down into the mud where, hitherto, only the common people have seemed to prosper.

ROSMER: For that very reason I have faith in the true purpose of Democracy.

KROLL: What purpose?

ROSMER: That of giving all men a sense of their own nobility.

KROLL: All men—!

ROSMER: As many as possible, at any rate.

KROLL: By what means, may I ask?

ROSMER: By freeing their thoughts and purifying their aim

KROLL: You're a dreamer, Rosmer. And you think *you* can do this?

ROSMER: No, my dear friend; but I can at least open their eyes. They must do it for themselves.

KROLL: And you think they can?

ROSMER: Yes.

KROLL: By their own strength?

ROSMER: It must be by their own strength. There is no other.

KROLL (*Rises*): A strange way for a clergyman to talk!

ROSMER: I am no longer a clergyman.

KROLL: But what about your faith? The faith you were brought up in?

ROSMER: I no longer believe in it.

KROLL: You no longer—!

ROSMER: I've given it up. I *had* to give it up, Kroll.

KROLL: I see. I suppose one thing leads to another. So this was why you resigned your position in the church?

ROSMER: Yes. When it finally dawned on me that this was no temporary aberration—but, rather, a deep conviction that I neither could nor would shake off—then I left the church.

KROLL: To think that all this time, we, your friends, had no suspicion of what was going on inside you. Rosmer, Rosmer, how could you bring yourself to hide the truth from us!

ROSMER: I felt it concerned no one but myself. And I didn't want to cause you and my other friends unnecessary grief. I intended to go on living here just as before, quietly, serenely, happily. Reading, studying; steeping myself in all the books that had hitherto been closed to me. I wanted to become thoroughly familiar with this great world of truth and freedom that was suddenly revealed to me.

KROLL: Every word proves what you are—a traitor! But why did you change your mind? What made you decide to admit your guilt? And why just now?

ROSMER: You yourself forced me to it, Kroll.

KROLL: *I* did?

ROSMER: I was shocked to hear of your violence on the platform; to read your bitter speeches; the scurrilous attacks, the cruel, contemptuous scorn you heaped on your opponents. How could *you* be like that, Kroll? Then I realized I had an imperative duty to perform. Men are becoming evil in this struggle. We must get back to peace, and joy and mutual understanding. That's why I've made up my mind to declare my beliefs openly—to try my strength. Couldn't you—on your side—join in this work, and help me?

KROLL: Never! I shall never make peace with the destroyers of society.

ROSMER: Then if we must fight, let us, at least, use honorable weapons.

KROLL: Any man who goes against my fundamental principles I shall refuse to recognize; nor do I owe him any consideration.

ROSMER: Does that include me, as well?

KROLL: It is you who have broken with me, Rosmer; our friendship is at an end.

ROSMER: You *can't* mean that?

KROLL: Not *mean* it! This is an end to all your former friendships; now you must take the consequences.

(REBEKKA WEST *enters, and opens the door wide.*)

REBEKKA: He's gone. He is on his way to his great sacrifice! And now we can go to supper. Come, Professor.

KROLL (*Takes up his hat*): Good night, Miss West. I have nothing more to do here.

REBEKKA (*Eagerly*): What does he mean? (*Shuts the door and comes forward*) Did you tell him?

ROSMER: Yes. He knows now.

KROLL: We shan't let you go, Rosmer. You'll come back to us again.

ROSMER: I shall never go back to your opinions.

KROLL: Time will tell. You are not a man to stand alone.

ROSMER: But I shan't be alone; there are two of us to share the loneliness.

KROLL: You mean—? (*A suspicion crosses his face*) I see! Just what Beata said—!

ROSMER: Beata—?

KROLL (*Shaking off the thought*): No, no, forgive me; that was vile.

ROSMER: Why? What do you mean?

KROLL: Never mind! Forgive me! Good-bye. (*Goes toward door*.)

ROSMER (*Follows him*): Kroll! Our friendship can't end like this. I'll come and see you tomorrow.

KROLL (*In the hall, turns*): You shall never set foot in my house again. (*Takes up his stick and goes out.*)

(ROSMER *stands for a moment in the doorway; then shuts the door and walks up to the table.*)

ROSMER: It can't be helped, Rebekka. We'll face it together—like the loyal friends we are.

REBEKKA: What do you suppose he meant by "that was vile"?

ROSMER: Don't give it a thought, my dear. He himself didn't believe what he was saying. I'll go and talk to him tomorrow. Good night.

REBEKKA: Are you going up already, just as usual? I thought perhaps—after what had happened—

ROSMER: No—I'll go up, as usual. I can't tell you how relieved I feel now that it's over. You see—I'm quite calm about it all, Rebekka, dear. And you must take it calmly too. Good night.

REBEKKA: Good night, dear Rosmer; sleep well!

(ROSMER *goes out by the hall door, and his steps are heard ascending the staircase;* REBEKKA *goes and pulls a bell-rope. Shortly after,* MRS. HELSETH *enters.*)

REBEKKA: You might as well clear the table, Mrs. Helseth. Mr. Rosmer doesn't care for anything, and Professor Kroll's gone home.

MRS. HELSETH: Gone home? Is anything the matter with him?

REBEKKA (*Takes up work*): He said he felt a storm coming on—

MRS. HELSETH: That's queer. There's not a cloud in the sky this evening.

REBEKKA: I hope he won't run into that White Horse. I've a feeling the ghosts may be quite busy for a while.

MRS. HELSETH: Good gracious, Miss! Don't say such dreadful things.

REBEKKA: Well, well—who knows?

MRS. HELSETH (*Softly*): You mean you think someone's going to be taken from us, Miss?

REBEKKA: Of course not! Why should I think that? But there are all sorts of white horses in this world, Mrs. Helseth—Well, good night. I'm going to my room.

MRS. HELSETH: Good night, Miss.

(REBEKKA *goes out with her work.*)

MRS. HELSETH (*Turns the lamp down, shaking her head and muttering to herself*): Lord, Lord! That Miss West! What queer things she does say!

CURTAIN

ACT TWO

SCENE: JOHANNES ROSMER'S *study. Entrance door on the left. At the back, a doorway with a curtain drawn aside, leading into* ROSMER'S *bedroom. On the right a window, and in front of it a writing table covered with books and papers. Bookshelves and bookcases round the room. The furniture is simple. On the left, an old-fashioned sofa, with a table in front of it.*

JOHANNES ROSMER, *in a smoking-jacket, is sitting in a high-backed chair at the writing table. He is cutting and turning over the leaves of a pamphlet, and reading a little here and there. There is a knock at the door.*

ROSMER (*Without moving*): Come in.

REBEKKA (*Enters; she is wearing a dressing-gown*): Good morning.

ROSMER (*Turning the leaves of the pamphlet*): Good morning, dear. Is there anything you want?

REBEKKA: I just wanted to know if you had slept well.

ROSMER: Yes, I had a good restful night—no dreams; what about you?

REBEKKA: I slept well; at least toward morning—

ROSMER: I don't know when I've ever felt so light-hearted! It was good to get that off my chest at last.

REBEKKA: You should have done it long ago.

ROSMER: I can't imagine why I was such a coward.

REBEKKA: Well, it wasn't exactly cowardice—

ROSMER: Oh yes, it was; it was partly cowardice, at any rate—I realize that now.

REBEKKA: That makes it all the braver. (*Sits on a chair at writing table, close to him*) Rosmer, I want to tell you something I did last night—I hope you won't object—

ROSMER: Object? You know I never—

REBEKKA: You may think it was unwise of me—

ROSMER: Well—tell me.

REBEKKA: I gave Ulrik Brendel a note to Mortensgaard, before he left.

ROSMER (*A little doubtful*): Did you, Rebekka? What did you say?

REBEKKA: I told him he'd be doing you a favor if he were to keep an eye on Brendel; help him in any way he could.

ROSMER: Oh, you shouldn't have done that, dear. I'm afraid it will do more harm than good. And Mortensgaard is not the sort of man I choose to have dealings with. You know all about that former unpleasantness between us.

REBEKKA: But wouldn't it be as well to be on good terms with him again?

ROSMER: I? With Mortensgaard? What for?

REBEKKA: I thought it might be to your advantage—now that your old friends have turned against you.

ROSMER (*Looks at her and shakes his head*): You surely don't believe that Kroll or any of the others would try to take revenge on me? That they'd ever think of—?

REBEKKA: You never know what people will do in the first heat of anger. After the way the Professor took it—it seemed to me—

ROSMER: You should know him better than that. Kroll is a thoroughly honorable man. I'll go in and see him after lunch. I'd like to talk to all of them. You'll see—things will come out all right. (MRS. HELSETH *appears at door*.)

REBEKKA (*Rises*): What is it, Mrs. Helseth?

MRS. HELSETH: Professor Kroll is downstairs in the hall.

ROSMER (*Rises hastily*): Kroll!

REBEKKA: The Professor! Fancy!

MRS. HELSETH: He wants to know if he may come up and talk to Mr. Rosmer.

ROSMER (*To* REBEKKA): What did I tell you?—of course he may. (*Goes to door and calls downstairs*) Come up, dear friend! I am delighted to see you.

(ROSMER *holds the door open for him;* MRS. HELSETH *exits.* REBEKKA *closes the curtain to the alcove and tidies up here and there. Enter* KROLL, *hat in hand.*)

ROSMER (*With quiet emotion*): I was sure we hadn't said good-bye for good.

KROLL: I see things in quite a different light today.

ROSMER: I was sure you would, Kroll; now that you've had time to think things over—

KROLL: You misunderstand me. (*Lays his hat on table beside sofa*) It is of the utmost importance that I speak to you, alone.

ROSMER: But, why shouldn't Miss West—?

REBEKKA: No, no, Mr. Rosmer. I'll go.

KROLL (*Looks at her from head to foot*): I must ask Miss West's pardon for coming at such an early hour—for taking her unawares, before she has had time to—

REBEKKA (*Surprised*): How do you mean? Do you see anything wrong in my wearing a dressing gown about the house?

KROLL: Heaven forbid! Who am I to know what may now be customary at Rosmersholm?

ROSMER: Why, Kroll—you are not yourself today!

REBEKKA: My respects, Professor Kroll! (*Goes out.*)

KROLL: With your permission— (*Sits.*)

ROSMER: Yes, do sit down, let's talk things over amicably. (*Sits opposite the Professor.*)

KROLL: I haven't closed my eyes since yesterday. All night long I lay there turning things over in my mind.

ROSMER: And what have you to say today?

KROLL: It will be a long story, Rosmer. As a kind of preliminary—let me give you news of Ulrik Brendel.

ROSMER: Has he called on you?

KROLL: No. He took up quarters in a disreputable tavern, in the lowest possible company. There he started drinking and playing host to the others till his money ran out. In the end he turned on them; abused them as a pack of thieves and blackguards—in which he was undoubtedly quite right—whereupon they beat him up and pitched him into the gutter.

ROSMER: So he's incorrigible, after all.

KROLL: He had pawned the overcoat, but I hear that has been redeemed for him. Can you guess by whom?

ROSMER: By you, perhaps?

KROLL: No. By the noble Mr. Mortensgaard.

ROSMER: Indeed!

KROLL: Yes. It seems Mr. Brendel's first visit was to the "plebian idiot."

ROSMER: That was a lucky thing for him.

KROLL: To be sure it was. (*Leans across the table towards* ROSMER) This brings me to a matter I feel it my duty to warn you about, for our old—or rather for our former—friendship's sake.

ROSMER: What matter, my dear Kroll?

KROLL: I warn you; there are things going on behind your back in this house.

ROSMER: What makes you think that? Is it Reb—is it Miss West you're referring to?

KROLL: Precisely. Oh, it's not surprising. All this time she's been given such a free hand here. But still—

ROSMER: You're quite mistaken in this, Kroll. She and I are completely honest with each other—on all subjects.

KROLL: Then has she informed you that she has started a correspondence with the editor of *The Beacon?*

ROSMER: You mean those few words she gave to Ulrik Brendel?

KROLL: Oh, so you know about it. And you mean to say that you approve of her associating with this cheap journalist—this scandalmonger who never ceases to hold me up to ridicule?

ROSMER: My dear Kroll, I don't suppose it occurred to her to look at it from that angle. And, besides, she's a free agent—just as I am.

KROLL: I see. It's all part of this new line of conduct, I presume. Miss West undoubtedly shares your present point of view?

ROSMER: Yes, she does. We've worked towards it together—in loyal friendship.

KROLL (*Looks at him and slowly shakes his head*): You're a blind, deluded man, Rosmer!

ROSMER: I? Why should you call me that?

KROLL: Because I dare not—*will* not think the worst. No, no! Let me finish! You really do value my friendship, don't you, Rosmer? And my respect?

ROSMER: Surely that question should require no answer.

KROLL: Very well. But there are other questions that do require an answer—a full explanation on your part. Are you willing to submit to a sort of cross-examination—?

ROSMER: Cross-examination?

KROLL: Yes. Will you allow me to inquire frankly into various matters that it may pain you to be reminded of? You see—this apostasy of yours—this emancipation, as you prefer to call it—is bound up with many other things, that for your own sake you must explain to me.

ROSMER: Ask me anything you like, my dear Kroll. I have nothing to hide.

KROLL: Then tell me—what do you think was the real—the basic—reason for Beata's suicide?

ROSMER: Have you doubts on that score? You can hardly expect to find a reasonable explanation for the actions of a poor demented invalid.

KROLL: But are you quite certain Beata was completely irresponsible? Remember, the doctors were by no means convinced of that.

ROSMER: If the doctors had ever seen her as I so often saw her—day after day, night after night—they would have had no doubts.

KROLL: I had no doubts either, then.

ROSMER: No, unfortunately there wasn't the slightest room for doubt. Those paroxysms of morbid passion she was seized with! How could I respond to them—they appalled me; I told you all about it at the time. And then the constant reproaches she heaped upon herself in those last years; without basis—without reason.

KROLL: After she found out she could never have children; yes—I know.

ROSMER: She suffered untold agonies of mind—tormented herself incessantly—over something entirely out of her control. No normal human being would behave like that.

KROLL: Tell me—do you remember having any books in the house at that time, dealing with marital relations? From the so-called modern point of view, I mean?

ROSMER: Yes—I believe Miss West once lent me such a book; she inherited Doctor West's library, you know. But, my dear Kroll, you don't suppose for a moment we were careless enough to let it fall into poor Beata's hands? I give you my solemn word, we were both entirely blameless in this matter. It was her own sick brain that drove Beata to the verge of madness.

KROLL: I can tell you one thing, at any rate; Beata—poor, tormented creature that she was—put an end to her own life in order to bring happiness to yours; to set you free to live—after your own heart.

ROSMER (*Starts half up from chair*): What do you mean by that?

KROLL: Listen to me quietly, Rosmer! I must speak about it now. Not long before she died she came to see me twice and poured out all her sorrow and despair.

ROSMER: On this same subject?

KROLL: No. The first time she kept insisting you were about to break with the Faith—to leave the church.

ROSMER (*Eagerly*): That's quite impossible—utterly impossible! You're mistaken, I assure you!

KROLL: What makes you think that?

ROSMER: Because as long as Beata lived I'd come to no decision. I was in a turmoil—that is true—wrestling with doubts; but I never said a word to anyone; I fought it out alone and in the utmost secrecy. I don't think even Rebekka—

KROLL: Rebekka?

ROSMER: Well—Miss West then; I call her Rebekka for convenience' sake.

KROLL: So I have noticed.

ROSMER: It's quite inconceivable that Beata could ever have suspected such a thing. And if she had, why didn't she mention it to me? She never did—she never said a single word.

KROLL: Poor thing—she begged and implored me to talk to you.

ROSMER: Why didn't you, then?

KROLL: Because I thought she was unbalanced! I took that for granted at the time. To accuse a man like you of such a thing! The second time she came—it was about a month later—she seemed much calmer. But just as she was leaving, she turned to me and said: "It won't be long now before the White Horse appears at Rosmersholm."

ROSMER: The White Horse, yes—she often spoke of that.

KROLL: I tried to steer her away from such sad thoughts—but she continued; "I haven't long to live. Rosmer must marry Rebekka at once."

ROSMER (*Almost speechless*): What are you saying? I marry—?

KROLL: That was a Thursday afternoon— The following Saturday evening she threw herself from the bridge into the mill-race.

ROSMER: And you never warned us—!

KROLL: You know she was always saying she hadn't long to live.

ROSMER: I know; but still—you should have warned us!

KROLL: I thought of it, but by then it was too late.

ROSMER: But after it happened—why didn't you? Why haven't you told me this before?

KROLL: I didn't want to add to your grief—what good would it have done? In any case, at the time I took everything she said for the hysterical ravings of an unsound mind. Until yesterday evening I believed that firmly—

ROSMER: And now?

KROLL: Didn't Beata see quite clearly when she declared you were about to desert the faith you were brought up in?

ROSMER (*Looks fixedly straight before him*): That I *cannot* understand! It's quite imcomprehensible—

KROLL: Incomprehensible or not—there it is. And now—what about her other accusation, Rosmer? How much truth is there in that?

ROSMER: Was that an accusation?

KROLL: Perhaps you did not notice the way she worded it. She had to go, she said—why?—Well? Answer me!

ROSMER: So that I might marry Rebekka—

KROLL: That is not exactly the way she put it. Beata expressed it differently. She said: "I haven't long to live; Johannes must marry Rebekka at once."

ROSMER (*Looks at him for a moment; then rises*): Now I understand you, Kroll!

KROLL: Well? And what is your answer?

ROSMER (*Still quiet and self-restrained*): To something so unheard of—? The only right answer would be to show you the door.

KROLL (*Rises*): Well and good.

ROSMER (*Stands in front of him*): Wait a minute, Kroll! For well over a year—ever since Beata left us—Rebekka West and I have lived here alone at Rosmersholm. All that time you have been aware of Beata's accusation against us. Yet I've never noticed the slightest sign of disapproval on your part.

KROLL: Until yesterday evening I had no idea you were an atheist; and that the woman sharing your home was a free-thinker.

ROSMER: I see; you don't believe there can be purity of mind among free-thinkers? You don't believe there's such a thing as an instinctive sense of morality?

KROLL: I have no great faith in any morality that is not founded on the teachings of the church.

ROSMER: And does this apply to Rebekka and me as well? To our relationship?

KROLL: Consideration for you cannot alter my opinion that there is very little separation between free-thought and—

ROSMER: And?

KROLL: Free love—since you force me to put it into words.

ROSMER (*In a low voice*): Aren't you ashamed to say such a thing to me! You, who have known me since I was a boy?

KROLL: All the more reason for me to say it. I know how easily you are influenced by those around you. And this Rebekka of yours—well, this Miss West then—what do we really know about her? Next to nothing! In short, Rosmer—I refuse to give you up. I urge you to try and save yourself while there's still time.

ROSMER: In what way—Save myself?

(MRS. HELSETH *peeps in at the door*.)

ROSMER: What do you want?

MRS. HELSETH: I'm to ask Miss West to come downstairs.

ROSMER: Miss West is not up here.

MRS. HELSETH: Isn't she? (*Looks around room*) That's strange. (*Goes*.)

ROSMER: You were saying—

KROLL: Listen to me. What went on here in secret while Beata was alive—what may be going on here now, I shall inquire into no further. Your marriage was a most unhappy one; that may serve to excuse you, to some extent—

ROSMER: How little you really know me—!

KROLL: Don't interrupt me. What I mean is this; if your relationship with Miss West is to continue, at least keep your new opinions, your tragic fall from faith—for which she is undoubtedly to blame—keep these things to yourself! No! Let me speak! Let me speak! If the worst comes to the worst then for heaven's sake, think and believe and do whatever you like, but be discreet about it. It's a purely personal matter! It's not necessary to shout it from the house-tops.

ROSMER: Perhaps not. But it is necessary for me to free myself from a false and ambiguous position.

KROLL: It's your duty to uphold the traditions of your race, Rosmer! Remember that! For countless generations Rosmersholm has been a stronghold of discipline and order—of all those precious things that are most revered and highly respected in our Society. The whole district has always taken its stamp from Rosmersholm. It would cause the most deplorable, the most irreparable confusion, if it became known that you of all people had broken away from what might be called the Rosmer Way of Life.

ROSMER: That's not the way I see things, Kroll. It seems to me my duty is to spread a little light and happiness here, where former Rosmers spread only gloom and despotism.

KROLL (*Looks at him sternly*): That indeed would be a worthy mission for the last of the Rosmers to perform! No. Leave such

things alone—they are not for you. You were born to live the
quiet life of a scholar.

ROSMER: Perhaps. But all the same, I feel compelled to take part
in the present crisis.

KROLL: You realize it will mean a life and death struggle with all
your former friends?

ROSMER (*Quietly*): I can't believe they are all as fanatical as you.

KROLL: You are a simple-hearted soul, Rosmer; a naive soul. You
have no conception of the powerful storm that will sweep over
you.

(MRS. HELSETH *looks in at the door*.)

MRS. HELSETH: Miss West would like to know—

ROSMER: What is it?

MRS. HELSETH: There's a man downstairs who wants a few words
with you, Sir.

ROSMER: Is it the one who was here yesterday?

MRS. HELSETH: No; it's that Mortensgaard.

ROSMER: Mortensgaard!

KROLL: Aha! I see. So it's already come to this!

ROSMER: Why should he want to see me? Why didn't you send
him away?

MRS. HELSETH: Miss West told me to ask if he might come upstairs a minute.

ROSMER: Tell him I'm busy—

KROLL (*To* MRS. HELSETH): No! No! By all means let him come
up, Mrs. Helseth. (MRS. HELSETH *goes;* KROLL *takes up hat*) I
shall leave the field to him—for the moment. But the main battle
has yet to be fought.

ROSMER: I give you my word of honor, Kroll—I have nothing
whatever to do with Mortensgaard.

KROLL: I no longer believe anything you say, Rosmer. I can no
longer take your word on any subject. It's war to the death now.
We shall make every effort to disarm you.

ROSMER: That you should have sunk so low, Kroll!

KROLL: You dare say that to me! A man who—! Remember Beata?

ROSMER: Are you going to harp on that again?

KROLL: No. I shall leave you to solve the mystery of Beata's death after your own conscience—if you still possess anything of the sort.

(PEDER MORTENSGAARD *enters slowly and quietly by the door left. He is a small, wiry man with thin reddish hair and beard.*)

KROLL (*With a look of hatred*): I never thought I'd live to see *The Beacon* burning at Rosmersholm! (*Buttons his coat*) That settles it! I no longer have any doubt which course to take.

MORTENSGAARD (*Deferentially*): *The Beacon* may always be relied upon to light the Professor home.

KROLL: Yes; your good will has been apparent for some time. There is, to be sure, a commandment about bearing false-witness against your neighbor—

MORTENSGAARD: There is no need for Professor Kroll to teach me the commandments.

KROLL: Not even the seventh?

ROSMER: Kroll—!

MORTENSGAARD: Were that necessary, it would surely be the Pastor's business.

KROLL (*With covert sarcasm*): The Pastor's? Oh, of course! Pastor Rosmer is unquestionably the man for that— Good luck to your conference, gentlemen! (*Goes out, slams door behind him.*)

ROSMER (*Keeps eyes fixed on closed door and says to himself*): So be it, then. (*Turns*) Now, Mr. Mortensgaard; what brings you here?

MORTENSGAARD· I really came to see Miss West. I wanted to thank her for the nice note she sent me yesterday.

ROSMER: Yes, I know she wrote to you. Did you get a chance to talk to her?

MORTENSGAARD: Yes, for a little while. (*With a faint smile*) I understand there has been a certain change of views at Rosmersholm.

ROSMER: Yes. My views have changed on many subjects. On all subjects, perhaps.

MORTENSGAARD: So Miss West told me. She suggested that I come up and talk things over with you.

ROSMER: Talk what over, Mr. Mortensgaard?

MORTENSGAARD: I should like to make an announcement in *The*

Beacon. May I say that your views have changed, and that you are now ready to support the cause of progress—the cause of Freedom?

ROSMER: Announce it, by all means. In fact I urge you to do so.

MORTENSGAARD: It will be in tomorrow morning. It will cause quite a sensation: Pastor Rosmer of Rosmersholm stands ready to guide people toward the Light—in this sense too.

ROSMER: I don't quite understand you.

MORTENSGAARD: It's always a good thing for us to gain the approval of men like you—men well-known for their strict Christian principles; the moral support it gives our Cause is much needed—and invaluable.

ROSMER (*With some surprise*): Then, you don't know—? Didn't Miss West tell you about that, too?

MORTENSGAARD: About what, Pastor Rosmer? Miss West seemed in a great hurry; she said I'd better come upstairs and hear the rest from you.

ROSMER: I'd better tell you myself, then. You see—I've freed myself in every way: I no longer have any connection with the church, or with its doctrines; they no longer concern me in the least.

MORTENSGAARD (*Looks at him in amazement*): What! If the skies were to fall I couldn't be more—! Pastor Rosmer! Is this true?

ROSMER: Yes. So, you see—I am now in full accord with you. In this too I share the opinions you have held for many years. And this too you may announce tomorrow in *The Beacon*.

MORTENSGAARD: No. Forgive me, my dear Pastor, but I don't think it would be wise to touch on that side of the question.

ROSMER: How do you mean?

MORTENSGAARD: Not at first—at all events.

ROSMER: I don't quite understand—

MORTENSGAARD: Let me explain; you naturally don't know the circumstances as well as I do. Since you've come over to the cause of freedom—and I gather from Miss West you intend to take an active part in the Progressive movement—I presume you would wish to help the cause to the fullest possible extent.

ROSMER: Yes, I'm most anxious to do so.

MORTENSGAARD: Then I think I should point out, that if your defection from the church is publicly announced, it will prove a serious handicap to you from the start.

ROSMER: You think so?

MORTENSGAARD: Undoubtedly. You could accomplish very little—particularly in this part of the country. We've a great many free-thinkers in our ranks already—too many, I was about to say. What the party lacks is the Christian element, Pastor Rosmer—something that commands respect. That is our greatest need. So—in matters that do not directly concern the general public—it would seem wiser to be discreet. That's my opinion, at any rate.

ROSMER: In other words, if I make known my break with the church, you dare not have anything to do with me?

MORTENSGAARD (*Shaking his head*): I shouldn't like to risk it, Pastor Rosmer. In recent years I have made it a point never to lend support to anything or anyone antagonistic to the church.

ROSMER: Have you, yourself, returned to the fold, then?

MORTENSGAARD: That is a purely personal matter.

ROSMER: So that's it. Now I understand you.

MORTENSGAARD: You should understand, Pastor Rosmer, that my hands are tied more than most people's.

ROSMER: How so?

MORTENSGAARD: I am a marked man, you should know that.

ROSMER: Indeed?

MORTENSGAARD: A marked man, yes. Surely you've not forgotten? You were mainly responsible for that.

ROSMER: If I'd seen things then as I do now, I should have shown more understanding.

MORTENSGAARD: I dare say, but it's too late now. You branded me for good—branded me for life—I don't suppose you quite realize what that means. You soon may, though.

ROSMER: I?

MORTENSGAARD: Yes. You surely don't think Professor Kroll and his set will ever forgive a desertion like yours? They say the *County News* will be most sanguinary in future. You may find yourself a marked man, too.

ROSMER: They can't possibly harm me in personal matters, Mr. Mortensgaard. My private life has always been beyond reproach.

MORTENSGAARD (*With a sly smile*): That's a bold statement, Mr. Rosmer.

ROSMER: Perhaps, but I feel I have the right to make it.

MORTENSGAARD: Even if you were to examine your own conduct as thoroughly as you once examined mine?

ROSMER: Your tone is very curious. What are you hinting at? Anything definite?

MORTENSGAARD: Yes, quite definite. It's only a little thing. But it could prove quite nasty, if the wrong people were to get wind of it.

ROSMER: Then be good enough to tell me what it is.

MORTENSGAARD: Can't you guess that for yourself?

ROSMER: Certainly not. I've no idea.

MORTENSGAARD: Then I suppose I'd better tell you. I have a rather curious letter in my possession—one that was written here at Rosmersholm.

ROSMER: Miss West's letter, you mean? Is there anything curious about that?

MORTENSGAARD: No, there's nothing curious about that one. But I once received another letter from this house.

ROSMER: Was that from Miss West too?

MORTENSGAARD: No, Pastor Rosmer.

ROSMER: From whom do you mean then? Tell me!

MORTENSGAARD: From the late Mrs. Rosmer.

ROSMER: From my wife! You received a letter from my wife?

MORTENSGAARD: Yes, I did.

ROSMER: When?

MORTENSGAARD: Not long before Mrs. Rosmer died—about a year and a half ago, perhaps. That is the letter I find curious.

ROSMER: I suppose you know my wife's mind was affected at that time.

MORTENSGAARD: Yes, I know many people thought so. But the letter gave no indication of anything like that. No—when I called the letter "curious," I meant it in quite a different sense.

ROSMER: What on earth could my poor wife have written to you about?

MORTENSGAARD: She begins by saying something to the effect that she is living in great fear and anguish. There are so many malicious people in this neighborhood, she writes, whose only thought is to do you every possible harm.

ROSMER: Me?

MORTENSGAARD: That's what she says. Then comes the most curious part of all. Shall I go on?

ROSMER: Of course! By all means.

MORTENSGAARD: Your late wife then begs me to be magnanimous. She knows, she says, that it was you who had me dismissed from my position as a teacher and she humbly implores me not to take revenge.

ROSMER: What did she mean? In what way take revenge?

MORTENSGAARD: She says in the letter, that if I should hear scandalous rumors about certain things at Rosmersholm, I must discount them; that they are slanders spread by evil-minded people to do you injury.

ROSMER: Is all this in the letter?

MORTENSGAARD: You're welcome to read it yourself, Pastor Rosmer, at your convenience.

ROSMER: But I don't understand—! What scandalous rumors could she have been referring to?

MORTENSGAARD: First that you had deserted the Faith. She denied this absolutely—then. And next—h'm—

ROSMER: Well?

MORTENSGAARD: Next she writes—and this is rather confused—that to her knowledge there has been no breach of morals at Rosmersholm; that she has never been wronged in any way. And if rumors of that sort should reach me, she begs me to say nothing of the matter in *The Beacon*.

ROSMER: No name is mentioned?

MORTENSGAARD: None.

ROSMER: Who brought you this letter?

MORTENSGAARD: I promised not to say. It was brought to me one evening, after dark.

ROSMER: If you had made inquiries at the time, you would have found out that my poor wife was not fully responsible for her actions.

MORTENSGAARD: I did make inquiries, Pastor Rosmer. But that was not the impression I received.

ROSMER: Indeed? And what made you choose this particular moment to tell me about this letter?

MORTENSGAARD: I felt I should warn you to be exceedingly cautious, Pastor Rosmer.

ROSMER: In my personal life, you mean?

MORTENSGAARD: Yes; you're no longer entirely your own master. Remember—you've ceased to be a neutral.

ROSMER: Then you are quite convinced I have something to conceal?

MORTENSGAARD: There's no reason why a man of liberal views shouldn't be able to live his life to the full—live it exactly as he chooses; however I repeat, this is a time for caution. If certain rumors were to get about concerning you—rumors that might offend current prejudices, shall we say?—the whole Liberal Movement might be seriously affected. Good-bye, Pastor Rosmer.

ROSMER: Good-bye.

MORTENSGAARD: I'll go straight back to the office. This is important news; I'll have it in *The Beacon* by tomorrow.

ROSMER: Be sure to include everything.

MORTENSGAARD: Don't worry! I shall include everything that respectable people need to know. (*He bows and goes out.* ROSMER *remains standing in doorway while he goes down the stairs. The outer door is heard to close.*)

ROSMER (*In doorway, calls softly*): Rebekka, Re— H'm. (*Aloud*) Mrs. Helseth—isn't Miss West down there?

MRS. HELSETH (*From the hall below*): No; she's not here, Sir. (*The curtain in the background is drawn aside.* REBEKKA *appears in doorway.*)

REBEKKA: Rosmer!

ROSMER (*Turns*): Rebekka! What are you doing there? Have you been in my room all the time?

REBEKKA (*Goes up to him*): Yes, Rosmer. I was listening.

ROSMER: How could you do such a thing, Rebekka!

REBEKKA: I had to. He was so disgusting when he said that about my dressing-gown—

ROSMER: Then you were in there when Kroll—?

REBEKKA: Yes, I had to know what he meant by all those things he said—

ROSMER: I would have told you.

REBEKKA: You'd scarcely have told me everything. And certainly not in his words.

ROSMER: You heard the whole conversation, then?

REBEKKA: Most of it, I think. I had to go downstairs a moment when Mortensgaard came.

ROSMER: Then you came up again?

REBEKKA: Don't be angry with me; please, Rosmer, dear!

ROSMER: You're perfectly free to do whatever seems right to you, you know that. What do you make of it all, Rebekka—? Oh, I don't know when I've ever needed you as much as I do now!

REBEKKA: After all, we knew this would have to come some day; we've been prepared for it.

ROSMER: But, not for this.

REBEKKA: Why not for this?

ROSMER: I knew of course that sooner or later our friendship would be misunderstood—would be dragged down into the mud. Not by Kroll—I never expected that of him—but by all those others; those coarse-grained, insensitive people who are blind to everything but evil. I had good reason to guard our relationship so jealously. It was a dangerous secret.

REBEKKA: Why should we care what all those people think! We know we've done no wrong.

ROSMER: No wrong, you say? I? Yes, until today I was convinced of that. But now, Rebekka—?

REBEKKA: What?

ROSMER: How am I to explain Beata's dreadful accusation?

REBEKKA (*Vehemently*): Don't talk about Beata— Don't *think* about Beata any more! You were just beginning to escape from her—she's dead!

ROSMER: After what I've heard, she seems in a ghastly sort of way to be alive again.

REBEKKA: Not that, Rosmer! Please—not that!

ROSMER: Yes, I tell you. Somehow we must get to the bottom of it all. How could she possibly have misinterpreted things in such a hideous way?

REBEKKA: She was on the verge of madness! Surely you're not beginning to doubt that?

ROSMER: That's just it—I no longer feel quite sure; besides—even if she was—

REBEKKA: Even if she was—?

ROSMER: I mean—if her sick mind was on the borderline, what was it that gave the final impetus—that drove her to actual madness?

REBEKKA: What possible good can it do, to torment yourself with questions that have no answers?

ROSMER: I cannot help it, Rebekka. Much as I'd like to, I can't shake off these doubts.

REBEKKA: Don't you see how dangerous it is to keep on dwelling on this one morbid subject?

ROSMER (*Walks about restlessly in thought*): I must have given myself away somehow. She must have noticed how much happier I was after you came to live with us.

REBEKKA: Well—even if she did—?

ROSMER: She must have noticed how many things we had in common; how we were drawn together by our interest in the same books—in all the new ideas and theories. Yet I can't understand it! I was so careful to spare her feelings. I went out of my way, it seems to me, to keep her from knowing just how many interests we shared. Isn't that so, Rebekka?

REBEKKA: Yes, it is.

ROSMER: And you did the same. Yet in spite of that—! Oh, it's awful to think of! All that time she must have been watching us, observing us, noticing everything in silence; and her morbid love of me made her see it all in a false light.

REBEKKA (*Clenching her hands*): I should never have come to Rosmersholm!

ROSMER: The agony she must have gone through in silence! The sordid images her sick brain must have conjured up! Did she never say anything to you? Give any indication of her feelings, that might have warned you?

REBEKKA (*As if startled*): Do you think I'd have stayed here a moment longer if she had?

ROSMER: No, no, of course not— Oh, how she must have struggled, Rebekka—and all alone! To be so desperate, and quite alone! And then, the final triumph—the heart-breaking, silent accusation—of the mill-race. (*Throws himself into the chair by the writing-table, puts his elbows on the table and buries his face in his hands.*)

REBEKKA (*Approaches him cautiously from behind*): Tell me something, Rosmer. If it were in your power to call Beata back—to you—to Rosmersholm—would you do it?

ROSMER: How do I know what I would do, or wouldn't do? I can't tear my thoughts away from this one thing—this one irrevocable thing.

REBEKKA: You were just beginning to live, Rosmer. You *had* begun to live. You had freed yourself—in every way. You were feeling so buoyant, so happy—

ROSMER: It's true—I was. And now, to have to face all this!

REBEKKA (*Behind him, rests her arms on the back of his chair*): We were so happy sitting downstairs in the old room together, in the twilight—don't you remember? Talking over our new plans; helping one another to see life with new eyes. You wanted to take part in life, at last—to be really *alive* in life—you used to say. You wanted to go from house to house spreading the word of freedom, winning over men's hearts and minds, awakening in them a sense of the nobility of life—of their *own* nobility; you wanted to create a noble race of men—

ROSMER: Noble—and happy, yes.

REBEKKA: Yes—happy, too.

ROSMER: For minds are ennobled through happiness, Rebekka.

REBEKKA: Don't you think—through suffering, too. Great suffering, I mean?

ROSMER: Yes; if one can live through it, conquer it, and go beyond it.

REBEKKA: That's what *you* must do.

ROSMER (*Shakes his head gloomily*): I shall never quite get over this. There'll always be a doubt—a question in my mind. I'll never again experience the joy that fills life with such sweetness.

REBEKKA (*Bends over his chair-back and says more softly*): What joy do you mean, Rosmer?

ROSMER (*Looking up at her*): Peaceful joy— The confidence of innocence.

REBEKKA (*Recoils a step*): Ah! Innocence; yes.

(*A short pause.*)

ROSMER (*With elbow on table, leaning his head on his hand, and looking straight before him*): And how cleverly she worked the whole thing out. How systematically she put it all together! First she began to doubt the soundness of my faith— At that time how could she have suspected that? But she did suspect it; and later she became convinced of it. And then, of course, it was easy enough for her to believe in the possibility of all the rest. (*Sits up in his chair and runs his hands through his hair*) All these wild imaginings! I shall never get rid of them. I feel it. I know it. Suddenly, at any moment, they'll come sweeping through my mind—bringing back the thought of the dead.

REBEKKA: Like the White Horse of Rosmersholm.

ROSMER: Yes—just like that. Sweeping through the darkness—through the silence.

REBEKKA: And because of this wretched hallucination, you'd be willing to give up being alive in life!

ROSMER: It's hard—it's hard, Rebekka. But I have no choice. How can I ever recover from all this?

REBEKKA (*Behind his chair*): You must take up new interests; you must enter into new relationships—

ROSMER (*Surprised looks up*): New relationships?

REBEKKA: Yes—with the world at large. You must live, work, *act*—instead of sitting here brooding over insoluble enigmas.

ROSMER (*Rises*): New relationships? (*Walks across the floor, stops at the door and then comes back*) One question occurs to me, Rebekka; has it never occurred to you?

REBEKKA (*Scarcely breathing*): Tell me—what it is.

ROSMER: What future is there for our relationship—after today?

REBEKKA: I believe our friendship will endure—in spite of everything.

ROSMER: That's not quite what I meant. The thing that first brought us together and that unites us so closely—our faith in the possibility of a pure comradeship between a man and a woman—

REBEKKA: What of that—?

ROSMER: A relationship such as ours, I mean—shouldn't that presuppose a happy, peaceful life—?

REBEKKA: Well—?

ROSMER: But the life I face is one of struggle, unrest and violent agitation. For I intend to live my life, Rebekka! I will not be crushed by these gloomy speculations. I refuse to have a way of life imposed upon me, either by the living or by—anyone else.

REBEKKA: No! That must not happen, Rosmer. You must be free in every way!

ROSMER: Then—can you guess my thoughts? Can you guess them, Rebekka? There's only one way that I can free myself—rid myself of these haunting memories—this loathsome, tragic past.

REBEKKA: What way is that?

ROSMER: It must be stamped out, and replaced by something alive and real—

REBEKKA (*Groping for the chair-back*): Alive and real—? You mean—?

ROSMER (*Comes nearer*): If I were to ask you—? Oh, Rebekka! Will you be my wife?

REBEKKA (*For a moment, speechless, then cries out with joy*): Your wife! Your—! I!

ROSMER: Yes, let us truly belong to one another—let us be as one. The empty place must remain empty no longer.

REBEKKA: I—take Beata's place—?

ROSMER: Then it will be as though she'd never been.

REBEKKA (*Softly, trembling*): You believe that, Rosmer?

ROSMER: It must be so! It must! I refuse to live my life chained to a

corpse; help me to free myself, Rebekka! Together we will conquer all memories of the past; in freedom, in joy, in passion. You
shall be to me my first, my only, wife.

REBEKKA (*With self-control*): You must never speak of this again! I
can never be your wife.

ROSMER: Never! You mean—you could never come to love me?
But we love each other already, Rebekka! Our friendship has already turned to love.

REBEKKA (*Puts her hands over her ears as if in terror*): No, no!
Don't talk like that! Don't say such things!

ROSMER (*Seizes her arm*): But it has! Our relationship is full of
promise. You must feel that too—you must, Rebekka!

REBEKKA (*Once more firm and calm*): Listen to me. If you speak of
this again—I shall go away from Rosmersholm. I mean it.

ROSMER: You! Go away! But that's impossible.

REBEKKA: It's still more impossible that I should ever be your
wife. I can't be. I can never marry you.

ROSMER (*Looks at her in surprise*): You *can't* be? You say that so
strangely. Why can't you be?

REBEKKA (*Seizes both his hands*): For your sake, as well as
mine—don't ask me why. (*Lets go his hands*) Don't ask me,
Rosmer. (*Goes towards door.*)

ROSMER: From now on I shall never cease to ask that
question—why?

REBEKKA (*Turns and looks at him*): Then it's all over.

ROSMER: Between us, you mean?

REBEKKA: Yes.

ROSMER: It will never be over between us; and you will never go
away from Rosmersholm.

REBEKKA (*With her hand on the door handle*): Perhaps not. But if
you ask that question again, it will be over all the same.

ROSMER: How do you mean?

REBEKKA: Because then I shall go, the way Beata went. I've
warned you, Rosmer—

ROSMER: Rebekka—?

REBEKKA (*In the doorway, nods slowly*): I've warned you. (*She
goes out.*)

ROSMER (*Stares thunderstruck at the door, and says to himself*):
What does this mean?

CURTAIN

ACT THREE

SCENE: *The sitting-room at Rosmersholm. The window and the hall door are open. A bright sunny morning.* REBEKKA WEST, *dressed as in the first act, stands at the window, watering and arranging the flowers. Her crochet work lies in the arm-chair.* MRS. HELSETH *moves about the room, dusting the furniture with a feather duster.*

REBEKKA (*After a short silence*): It's strange that Mr. Rosmer should stay upstairs so late today.

MRS. HELSETH: He often does. He'll be down soon, I expect.

REBEKKA: Have you seen him yet this morning?

MRS. HELSETH: I caught a glimpse of him when I took his coffee up; he was in his bedroom, dressing.

REBEKKA: He didn't seem to feel well yesterday, that's why I asked.

MRS. HELSETH: No; he didn't look well. I was wondering if there was anything wrong between him and his brother-in-law.

REBEKKA: What do you think it could be?

MRS. HELSETH: I really couldn't say. Perhaps it's that Mortensgaard that's made trouble between them.

REBEKKA: It's possible. Do you know anything about this Peder Mortensgaard?

MRS. HELSETH: No indeed, Miss. How could you think that? A person like him!

REBEKKA: You mean because of that newspaper of his?

MRS. HELSETH: Not just because of that; but you must have heard about him, Miss. He had a child by a married woman whose husband had deserted her.

REBEKKA: Yes, I've heard it mentioned. But that must have been long before I came here.

MRS. HELSETH: Lord, yes! He was quite young at the time; and she should have known better. He wanted to marry her too; but of course that was impossible. He paid dearly for it, they say. But he's gone up in the world since then. Plenty of people run after him now.

REBEKKA: Yes, I hear most of the poor people go to him when they're in any trouble.

MRS. HELSETH: Oh, not just the poor people, Miss. There've been others too—

REBEKKA (*Looks at her furtively*): Really?

MRS. HELSETH (*By the sofa, dusting away vigorously*): Oh, yes, Miss. Perhaps the very last people you'd ever dream of.

REBEKKA (*Busy with the flowers*): That's just one of your ideas, Mrs. Helseth. You can't be sure about a thing like that.

MRS. HELSETH: That's what you think, Miss. But I am sure all the same. I may as well tell you—I once took a letter to Mortensgaard myself.

REBEKKA (*Turning*): *You* did?

MRS. HELSETH: Yes indeed I did. And what's more, that letter was written here at Rosmersholm.

REBEKKA: Really, Mrs. Helseth?

MRS. HELSETH: Yes indeed, Miss. And it was written on fine note paper, too; and sealed with fine red sealing wax.

REBEKKA: And you were asked to deliver it? Then, my dear Mrs. Helseth, it's not very hard to guess who wrote it.

MRS. HELSETH: Well?

REBEKKA: It was poor Mrs. Rosmer, I suppose—

MRS. HELSETH: I never said so, Miss.

REBEKKA: What was in the letter? But, of course, you couldn't very well know that.

MRS. HELSETH: Suppose I did know, all the same?

REBEKKA: You mean she told you?

MRS. HELSETH: No, not exactly. But after Mortensgaard had read it, he began asking me questions—kept on and on at me; it wasn't hard to guess what it was all about.

REBEKKA: What do you think it was? Dear, darling Mrs. Helseth, do tell me!

MRS. HELSETH: Certainly not, Miss. Not for the world!

REBEKKA: But surely you can tell *me!* After all, we're such good friends.

MRS. HELSETH: The good Lord preserve me from telling you anything about that, Miss. No! All I can say is that it was a horrible thing they'd got the poor sick lady to believe.

REBEKKA: Who got her to believe it?

MRS. HELSETH: Wicked people, Miss West. Wicked people.

REBEKKA: Wicked—?

MRS. HELSETH: Yes, and I say it again; real wicked people!

REBEKKA: Who do you suppose it could have been?

MRS. HELSETH: Oh, I know well enough what I think. But Lord forbid I should say anything. To be sure, there's a certain lady in town who—hm!

REBEKKA: You mean Mrs. Kroll, don't you?

MRS. HELSETH: She's a fine one, she is, with her airs and graces! She was always on her high horse with me. And I don't think she's ever had any too much love for you, either.

REBEKKA: Do you think Mrs. Rosmer was in her right mind when she wrote that letter?

MRS. HELSETH: A person's mind is a queer thing, Miss; not *clear* out of her mind, I wouldn't say.

REBEKKA: She seemed to go all to pieces when she found out she could never have children; that's when she first showed signs of madness.

MRS. HELSETH: Yes, that was a dreadful blow to her, poor lady.

REBEKKA (*Takes up her crochet work and sits in the chair by the window*): Still—it may have been the best thing for Mr. Rosmer.

MRS. HELSETH: What, Miss?

REBEKKA: That there were no children. Don't you think so?

MRS. HELSETH: I don't quite know what to say to that.

REBEKKA: I think it was. He could never have put up with a house full of children; they'd have disturbed him with their crying.

MRS. HELSETH: But children don't cry at Rosmersholm, Miss.

REBEKKA (*Looks at her*): Don't cry?

MRS. HELSETH: No. As long as people can remember, children have never been known to cry in this house.

REBEKKA: How very strange.

MRS. HELSETH: Yes, isn't it? It runs in the family. And then there's another strange thing. When they grow up, they never laugh. Never—as long as they live.

REBEKKA: Why, how queer—

MRS. HELSETH: Do you ever remember hearing or seeing Pastor Rosmer laugh, Miss?

REBEKKA: No—I don't believe I ever have, come to think of it. You're right, Mrs. Helseth. But then nobody laughs much in this part of the country, it seems to me.

MRS. HELSETH: No, they don't. It began at Rosmersholm, they say. And I suppose it spread round about, like one of those contagions.

REBEKKA: You're a very wise woman, Mrs. Helseth.

MRS. HELSETH: Don't you go making fun of me, Miss! (*Listens*) Hush—here's the Pastor coming down. He doesn't like to see me dusting. (*She goes out.*)

(JOHANNES ROSMER, *with hat and stick in his hand, enters from the hall.*)

ROSMER: Good morning, Rebekka.

REBEKKA: Good morning, dear. (*A moment after—crocheting*) Are you going out?

ROSMER: Yes.

REBEKKA: It's such beautiful weather.

ROSMER: You didn't come in to see me this morning.

REBEKKA: No, I didn't. Not today.

ROSMER: Aren't you going to in the future?

REBEKKA: I don't know yet, dear.

ROSMER: Has anything come for me?

REBEKKA: The *County News* came, yes.

ROSMER: The *County News?*

REBEKKA: There it is—on the table.

ROSMER (*Puts down his hat and cane*): Is there anything in it—?

REBEKKA: Yes.

ROSMER: Why didn't you send it up?

REBEKKA: I thought you'd see it soon enough.

ROSMER: Indeed? (*Takes the paper and reads, standing by the table*) Good heavens! " . . . We feel it our duty to issue a solemn warning against unprincipled renegades." (*Looks at her*) They call me a renegade, Rebekka.

REBEKKA: They mention no names.

ROSMER: It's obvious enough. (*Reads on*) "Men who secretly betray the cause of righteousness . . ." "Brazen Judases who seize the opportunity to proclaim their apostasy as soon as they feel it will work to their advantage."— " . . . wanton defamation of a name honored through generations."—" . . . in expectation of suitable rewards from the party momentarily in power." (*Lays down the paper on the table*) How dare they—? Men who have known me intimately for years! They know there's not a word of truth in all this—they themselves can't possibly believe it— Yet they write it all the same.

REBEKKA: That's not all of it.

ROSMER (*Takes up the paper again*): "Inexperience and lack of judgment the only excuse"—"pernicious influence—possibly extending to certain matters which, for the present, we prefer not to make public." (*Looks at her*) What do they mean by that?

REBEKKA: It is aimed at me—obviously.

ROSMER (*Lays down the paper*): It's an outrage—the work of thoroughly dishonorable men.

REBEKKA: Yes, I don't think they need throw stones at Mortensgaard!

ROSMER (*Walks about the room*): This has got to stop. If this kind of thing continues, all that is best in human nature will be destroyed. It must be stopped. It must! If only I could find some way to bring a little light into all this hideous darkness—how happy I should be!

REBEKKA (*Rises*): Yes, that would be a cause worth living for!

ROSMER: If I could only make them see themselves! Make them

repent and feel ashamed! If I could only make them see that they must work together for the common good—in charity and tolerance!

REBEKKA: Try it, Rosmer, try! You could do it—I *know* you could!

ROSMER: I believe it might be possible. And then—how glorious life would be! Instead of all this hideous discord—universal aspiration. A common goal. Each man in his own way contributing his best to further progress and enlightenment. Happiness for all—through all. (*Happens to look out of the window, shudders and says sadly*) But it could never come through me, Rebekka.

REBEKKA: Why not through you?

ROSMER: Nor could I ever have a share in it.

REBEKKA: Stop doubting yourself, Rosmer!

ROSMER: There can be no happiness where there is guilt.

REBEKKA (*Looks straight before her*): Stop talking about guilt—!

ROSMER: You know nothing about guilt, Rebekka. But I—

REBEKKA: You least of all.

ROSMER (*Points out the window*): The mill-race.

REBEKKA: Oh, Rosmer—!

(MRS. HELSETH *looks in at the door.*)

MRS. HELSETH: Miss West!

REBEKKA: Not just now, Mrs. Helseth—presently!

MRS. HELSETH: Just one word, Miss.

(REBEKKA *goes to the door.* MRS. HELSETH *tells her something. They whisper together for a few moments.* MRS. HELSETH *nods and goes out.*)

ROSMER (*Uneasily*): Was it anything for me?

REBEKKA: No, just household matters. Why don't you go out into the fresh air, dear Rosmer. Take a good, long walk.

ROSMER (*Takes up his hat*): Very well. Let's go together.

REBEKKA: I can't just now. You go alone. Throw off these gloomy thoughts. Promise me that.

ROSMER: I'm afraid I'll never be able to do that.

REBEKKA: But this is a mere delusion, Rosmer! You must not let it gain a hold on you—

ROSMER: It's no mere delusion. I brooded over it all night. Perhaps Beata was right after all.

REBEKKA: In what?

ROSMER: When she suspected me of being in love with you.

REBEKKA: Ah! I see.

ROSMER (*Lays his hat on the table*): I keep asking myself—weren't we deceiving ourselves when we called our feeling friendship?

REBEKKA: Should we have called it—?

ROSMER: Love— Yes. Even while Beata was alive, it was always you I thought of—you I longed for. It was with you that I found peace and happiness. Thinking back—it seems to me we fell in love from the very first—as two children might; sweetly, mysteriously—untroubled by dreams of passion or desire. Don't you think that's true, Rebekka? Tell me.

REBEKKA (*Struggling with herself*): I don't know what to answer.

ROSMER: And we imagined this communion was merely friend-ship, when all the time it was a spiritual marriage. That is why I say I'm guilty. I had no right to it. No right—for Beata's sake.

REBEKKA: No right to happiness? Is that what you believe, Rosmer?

ROSMER: She watched us with the eyes of love—and judged us ac-cordingly. What else could she have done? That judgment was inevitable.

REBEKKA: But since she was wrong, why should you blame your-self?

ROSMER: She killed herself for love of me. That fact remains. I shall never get over that, Rebekka.

REBEKKA: You *must* get over it. You've devoted your life to a great cause—you must think only of that.

ROSMER (*Shakes his head*): It can never be accomplished. Not by me. Not now that I know.

REBEKKA: Why not by you?

ROSMER: Because no victory was ever truly won by guilty men.

REBEKKA (*Vehemently*): Oh, all these doubts, these fears, these scruples! They're all ancestral relics come to haunt you. It's like this myth about the dead returning in the shape of galloping white horses—it's all part of the same thing!

ROSMER: That may be so—but if I can't escape these things, what difference does it make? And what I say is true, Rebekka; only a happy man—a blameless man—can bring a cause to lasting victory.

REBEKKA: Does happiness mean so much to you, Rosmer?

ROSMER: —Yes, it does.

REBEKKA: And yet you don't know how to laugh!

ROSMER: In spite of that, I have a great capacity for happiness.

REBEKKA: You must go for your walk now, dear. A good long walk. Do you hear? There—here is your hat. And here is your stick.

ROSMER (*Takes them from her*): Thanks. You're sure you won't come with me?

REBEKKA: No, I can't just now.

ROSMER: Very well; you're always with me, anyhow.

(*He goes out by the entrance door.* REBEKKA *waits a moment, cautiously watching his departure from behind the open door; then she goes to the door on right.*)

REBEKKA (*Opens the door and says in a low tone*): Mrs. Helseth! You may show him in, now. (*Goes toward the window; a moment after* PROFESSOR KROLL *enters. He bows silently and formally, and keeps his hat in his hand.*)

KROLL: Has he gone?

REBEKKA: Yes.

KROLL: Does he usually stay out for some time?

REBEKKA: Yes, usually. But one can't count on him today. So if you prefer not to see him—

KROLL: No; it's you I want to see; and quite alone.

REBEKKA: Then we had better not waste time. Sit down, Professor. (*Sits in the easy chair by window;* KROLL *sits on chair beside her.*)

KROLL: I don't suppose you quite realize, Miss West, how deeply this change in Johannes Rosmer has affected me.

REBEKKA: We expected that would be so—at first.

KROLL: Only at first?

REBEKKA: Rosmer was so confident that sooner or later you would join him.

KROLL: I?

REBEKKA: Yes, you—and all his other friends as well.

KROLL: There you see! That only goes to show how faulty his judgment has become, where men and practical matters are concerned.

REBEKKA: Well, after all—since he's chosen to be free—to stand completely on his own—

KROLL: But wait—you see, I don't believe that for a moment.

REBEKKA: Oh. Then what do you believe?

KROLL: I believe *you* are at the bottom of it all.

REBEKKA: Your wife put that into your head, Professor.

KROLL: Never mind who put it into my head; the fact remains that I have a strong suspicion—an exceedingly strong suspicion—the more I think things over, and piece together what I know of your behavior ever since you came here.

REBEKKA (*Looks at him*): I seem to recall a time when you felt an exceedingly strong faith in me, dear Professor. I might almost call it a *warm* faith.

KROLL (*In a subdued voice*): Whom could you not bewitch, if you set your mind to it?

REBEKKA: You think I set my mind to—?

KROLL: Yes, I do. I'm no longer such a fool as to imagine you had any feelings in the matter. You simply wanted to worm your way in here—to become firmly entrenched at Rosmersholm; and I was to help you do it. I see through your little game quite clearly now.

REBEKKA: You seem to forget that it was Beata who begged and implored me to come and live out here.

KROLL: Yes, when you had bewitched her too. For surely one could never call her feeling for you friendship? It was worship—idolatry. It developed into a kind of—I don't know what to call it—a kind of frenzied passion—Yes that's the only word for it.

REBEKKA: Be so good as to remember your sister's condition. So far as I am concerned, I don't think anyone can accuse me of being hysterical.

KROLL: No, that's true enough; and that makes you doubly dangerous to those you wish to get into your power. It's easy enough for you; you weigh each action with cold deliberation and accurately calculate each consequence; you're able to do this because you have no heart.

REBEKKA: Are you so sure of that?

KROLL: Yes; now I'm quite convinced of it. Otherwise how could you have lived here year after year pursuing your aim so ruthlessly? Well—you've succeeded in your purpose; you've gained full power over him and over everything around him. And in order to do this, you didn't hesitate to rob him of his happiness.

REBEKKA: That is not true. I did no such thing—you, yourself, did that!

KROLL: *I* did!

REBEKKA: Yes, when you led him to imagine he was responsible for Beata's tragic death.

KROLL: Has that really affected him so deeply?

REBEKKA: Well, naturally. A mind as sensitive as his—

KROLL: I thought a so-called emancipated man would be above such scruples— But I'm not surprised—in fact I anticipated something of the sort. Look at his ancestors—these men that stare out at us from all these portraits; the heritage they've handed down to him in an unbroken line through generations is not so easily discounted.

REBEKKA (*Looks down thoughtfully*): It's true; Johannes Rosmer's family roots go deep.

KROLL: Yes, and you should have taken that into account; especially if you had any real affection for him. But such a thing would be difficult for you to grasp. Your background is so entirely different.

REBEKKA: What do you mean by background?

KROLL: I am speaking of your origin—your family background, Miss West.

REBEKKA: Oh, I see! It's true I come of very humble people; but still—

KROLL: I am not referring to rank or social position. I was thinking of your moral background.

REBEKKA: Moral—? In what sense?

KROLL: The circumstances of your birth.

REBEKKA: What do you mean by that?

KROLL: I mention it only because I feel it accounts for your whole conduct.

REBEKKA: I don't understand this. I demand an explanation!

KROLL: I shouldn't have thought an explanation would be necessary. If you didn't know the facts, doesn't it seem rather odd that you should have let Dr. West adopt you?

REBEKKA (*Rises*): Ah! Now I understand.

KROLL: —and that you should have taken his name? Your mother's name was Gamvik.

REBEKKA (*Walks across the room*): My father's name was Gamvik, Professor Kroll.

KROLL: Your mother's work must have kept her in constant touch with the doctor of the district—

REBEKKA: Yes, it did.

KROLL: And at your mother's death he immediately adopts you and takes you to live with him. He treats you with the greatest harshness, yet you make no attempt to get away. You're well aware that he won't leave you a penny—actually, all he left you was a trunk full of books—and yet you stay on; you put up with him and nurse him to the end.

REBEKKA (*Stands by the table, looking scornfully at him*): And because I did all this, you assume there must be something improper—something immoral about my birth?

KROLL: I believe your care of him was the result of involuntary filial instinct. As a matter of fact I attribute your entire conduct to the circumstances of your birth.

REBEKKA (*Vehemently*): But there is not a word of truth in what you say! And I can prove it! Dr. West didn't come to Finmark till after I was born.

KROLL: I beg your pardon, Miss West, I've made inquiries. He was there the year before.

REBEKKA: You're wrong! You're utterly wrong, I tell you!

KROLL: The day before yesterday you told me yourself that you were twenty-nine—in your thirtieth year, you said.

REBEKKA: Really! Did I say that?

KROLL: Yes, you did. And I calculate from that—

REBEKKA: Stop! You needn't. You might as well know—I'm a year older than I say I am.

KROLL (*Smiles incredulously*): Indeed! You surprise me! What motive have you for that?

REBEKKA: After I'd passed twenty-five I felt I was getting a little old for an unmarried woman, so I began to lie about my age.

KROLL: I should have thought an emancipated woman like you would be above such conventions!

REBEKKA: I know it was absurd and idiotic of me—but there you are! It's one of those silly ideas one clings to in spite of oneself.

KROLL: Be that as it may; but that still does not refute my theory; for Dr. West paid a brief visit to Finmark the year before his appointment there.

REBEKKA (*With a vehement outburst*): That's not true!

KROLL: Not true, Miss West?

REBEKKA: No. My mother never mentioned such a thing.

KROLL: She didn't—eh?

REBEKKA: No, never. Nor Dr. West either; he never said a word about it.

KROLL: Mightn't that have been because they both had good reason to wish to skip a year, just as you have done? Perhaps it runs in the family, Miss West.

REBEKKA (*Walks about clenching and wringing her hands*): What you say is quite impossible. You simply want to trick me into believing it! But it's not true—it can't be true! It can't! It can't—!

KROLL (*Rises*): My dear Miss West—why in Heaven's name are you so upset about it? You quite terrify me! What am I to think—to believe—?

REBEKKA: Nothing! You must think and believe nothing.

KROLL: Then you really must explain this agitation. Why should this matter—this possibility—affect you in this way?

REBEKKA (*Controlling herself*): It is perfectly simple, Professor Kroll. I don't choose to be considered illegitimate.

KROLL: I see! Well—I suppose I shall have to be satisfied with that explanation—at least for the time being. But then, am I to conclude that you still have certain prejudices on this point too?

REBEKKA: Yes, I suppose I have.

KROLL: I don't think this so-called Emancipation of yours goes very deep! You've steeped yourself in a lot of new ideas and new opinions. You've picked up a lot of theories out of books—theories that claim to overthrow certain irrefutable and unassailable principles—principles that form the bulwark of our Society. But this has been no more than a superficial, intellectual exercise, Miss West. It has never really been absorbed into your bloodstream.

REBEKKA (*Thoughtfully*): Perhaps you are right.

KROLL: Just put yourself to the test—you'll see! And if this is true of you, how much truer must it be of Johannes Rosmer. For him all this is sheer, unmitigated madness—it's running blindfold to destruction! Do you suppose a man of his sensitive retiring nature could bear to be an outcast—to be persecuted by all his former friends—exposed to ruthless attacks from all the best elements in the community? Of course not! He's not the man to endure that.

REBEKKA: He must endure it! It's too late for him to turn back now.

KROLL: No, it's not too late—not by any means; it's still possible to hush the matter up—or it can be attributed to a mere temporary aberration, however deplorable. But one thing is essential.

REBEKKA: What might that be?

KROLL: You must persuade him to legalize this relationship, Miss West.

REBEKKA: His relationship with me?

KROLL: Yes. You must insist on his doing that.

REBEKKA: You still cling to the belief that our relationship requires to be legalized, as you call it?

KROLL: I prefer not to examine the situation too closely. But I seem to have noticed that the usual cause for lightly disregarding the so-called conventions is—

REBEKKA: A relationship between man and woman, you mean?

KROLL: Frankly—yes. That is my opinion.

REBEKKA (*Wanders across the room and looks out the window*): I might almost say—I wish you were right, Professor Kroll.

KROLL: What do you mean? You say that very strangely.

REBEKKA: Oh, never mind—don't let's discuss it any more. Listen! Here he comes.

KROLL: So soon! I must go, then.

REBEKKA (*Goes towards him*): No—please stay. There's something I want you to hear.

KROLL: Not just now. I don't think I could bear to see him.

REBEKKA: Please—I beg you! You'll regret it later, if you don't. It's the last time I shall ever ask anything of you.

KROLL (*Looks at her in surprise and puts down his hat*): Very well, Miss West—if you insist.

(*A short silence. Then* JOHANNES ROSMER *enters from the hall.*)

ROSMER (*Sees the Professor and stops in the doorway*): What! You here!

REBEKKA: He would have preferred not to meet you, dearest.

KROLL (*Involuntarily*): "Dearest!"

REBEKKA: Yes, Professor; Rosmer and I sometimes call each other "dearest." That's another result of our relationship.

KROLL: Was this what you wanted me to hear?

REBEKKA: That—and a good deal more.

ROSMER (*Comes forward*): What is the purpose of this visit?

KROLL: I wanted to make one last effort to stop you—to win you back.

ROSMER (*Points to the newspaper*): After what's printed there?

KROLL: I did not write it.

ROSMER: Did you take any steps to prevent it?

KROLL: I should not have felt justified in doing that. It was not in my power, in any case.

REBEKKA (*Tears the paper into shreds, crushes up the pieces and throws them behind the stove*): There! Now it's out of sight; let it be out of mind, too. There'll be no more of that sort of thing, Rosmer.

KROLL: If you use your influence, you can make sure of that!

REBEKKA: Come and sit down, Rosmer. Let's all sit down. I'm going to tell you everything.

ROSMER (*Seats himself mechanically*): What has come over you, Rebekka? Why this peculiar calm? What is it?

REBEKKA: It's the calm of decision. (*Seats herself*) Sit down—you too, Professor.

(KROLL *seats himself.*)

ROSMER: Decision? What decision?

REBEKKA: I've come to a decision, Rosmer. I'm going to give you back what to you makes life worth living: your confidence of innocence.

ROSMER: What are you talking about!

REBEKKA: Just listen to me—then you'll know.

ROSMER: Well?

REBEKKA: When I first came here from Finmark—with Dr. West—I felt as if a great, new, wonderful world was opening up before me. Doctor West had taught me many things—in fact, all the scattered knowledge I had of life in those days, I'd learned from him. (*With a struggle and in a scarcely audible voice*) And then—

KROLL: And then?

ROSMER: But, Rebekka—I already know all this.

REBEKKA (*Mastering herself*): Yes, of course; I suppose you do.

KROLL (*Looks hard at her*): Perhaps I had better go.

REBEKKA: No, stay where you are, Professor. (*To* ROSMER) So, you see—I wanted to be a part of this new world; I wanted to belong to it—to share in all these new ideas. One day Professor Kroll was telling me of the great influence Ulrik Brendel had over you, when you were still a boy; I suddenly thought it might be possible for me to carry on his work.

ROSMER: You came here with a hidden purpose—?

REBEKKA: I wanted us to join hands and work for this new Freedom; we were to be in the very front ranks and march on side by side; forward—always forward. But I soon found there was a gloomy, insurmountable barrier standing in your way.

ROSMER: Barrier? What barrier?

REBEKKA: I knew there could be no freedom for you unless you could break loose—get out into the clear bright sunshine. I saw you pining away here; defeated—stultified by your disastrous marriage.

ROSMER: You've never before spoken of my marriage in such terms.

REBEKKA: No—I did not dare; I didn't want to frighten you.

KROLL (*Nods to* ROSMER): Do you hear that?

REBEKKA (*Goes on*): I could see where your salvation lay—your only salvation. And so I set to work.

ROSMER: Set to work? How?

KROLL: Do you mean by that—?

REBEKKA: Yes, Rosmer— (*Rises*) No! Stay where you are! You too, Professor Kroll. Now you must know the truth. It wasn't you, Rosmer. You are entirely innocent. It was *I* who worked on Beata and deliberately lured her into madness.

ROSMER (*Springs up*): Rebekka!

KROLL (*Rises from sofa*): —into madness!

REBEKKA: Yes, the madness that led her to the mill-race. That is the truth. Now you know all about it.

ROSMER (*As if stunned*): I don't understand— What is it she's saying? I don't understand a word—!

KROLL: But I'm beginning to.

ROSMER: But what did you do? What could you possibly have said to her? There was nothing to tell—absolutely nothing!

REBEKKA: She was given to understand that you were gradually working yourself free from all your former beliefs and prejudices.

ROSMER: Yes, but that was not true at the time.

REBEKKA: I knew it soon would be.

KROLL (*Nods to* ROSMER): Aha!

ROSMER: Well? And what else? I must know everything.

REBEKKA: Shortly after that—I begged and implored her to let me go away from Rosmersholm.

ROSMER: What made you want to go—then?

REBEKKA: I didn't want to. I wanted to stay here. But I led her to believe it would be wisest for me to go—for all our sakes—before it was too late. I hinted that if I were to remain here, something—anything—might happen.

ROSMER: You actually did all this!

REBEKKA: Yes, Rosmer.

ROSMER: So that is what you meant by "setting to work"!

REBEKKA (*In a broken voice*): That's what I meant—yes.

ROSMER (*After a pause*): Have you confessed everything now, Rebekka?

REBEKKA: Yes.

KROLL: No, not quite.

REBEKKA (*Looks at him in fear*): What more could there be?

KROLL: Didn't you finally persuade Beata that it was necessary —not merely that it would be wisest—but that it was definitely necessary for you to go away as soon as possible—for yours and Rosmer's sake? Well? Didn't you?

REBEKKA (*Low and indistinctly*): I may have—Yes, perhaps.

ROSMER (*Sinks into armchair by window*): And she was deceived by all these lies! Poor, wretched, bewildered little thing—she actually believed them; firmly believed them! (*Looks up at* REBEKKA) Oh! Why didn't she come to me! But she didn't—she never said a word. You persuaded her not to, didn't you, Rebekka? I see it in your face.

REBEKKA: She had become obsessed by the fact that she was childless—and never could have children; because of that she felt she had no right here. She was convinced it was her duty to efface herself—her duty to you, I mean.

ROSMER: And you did nothing to dissuade her from that thought?

REBEKKA: No.

KROLL: Perhaps you confirmed her in it? Answer me! Didn't you?

REBEKKA: I dare say that's how she understood it.

ROSMER: She always gave way to you in everything; you dominated her completely. And then—she *did* efface herself! (*Springs up*) How could you play this horrible game, Rebekka?

REBEKKA: I had to choose between your life and hers.

KROLL (*Severely and impressively*): What right had you to make such a choice!

REBEKKA (*Vehemently*): You seem to think I acted with shrewd deliberation—that I was cold and calm about it all; but I was a very different person then. And, anyway—most people's minds are divided, it seems to me. I wanted Beata out of the way—somehow; but at the same time it never occurred to me that the thing would really happen. A voice inside me kept crying out "Stop! No further!"—but I couldn't resist the impulse to go on. And I went on—step by step—in spite of myself. I thought: a little further—just a little further; a tiny step more—and then another; I couldn't stop! And suddenly—there it was! That's the way these things happen, you see. (*A short silence.*)

ROSMER (*To* REBEKKA): What will become of you now? After this?

REBEKKA: I don't know. It doesn't greatly matter.

KROLL: Not a single word of remorse! I dare say you feel none?

REBEKKA (*Coldly putting aside his question*): You must excuse me, Professor Kroll—that concerns no one but myself. I shall deal with that in my own way.

KROLL (*To* ROSMER): So this is the woman you've been sharing your life with—in the closest intimacy! (*Looks round at the portraits*) I wonder what all these good souls would say, if they could see us now!

ROSMER: Are you going back to town?

KROLL (*Takes up his hat*): Yes. The sooner, the better.

ROSMER (*Does the same*): Then I'll go with you.

KROLL: You will! There—you see! I was sure we hadn't really lost you.

ROSMER: Come, Kroll! Let us go. (*Both go out through the hall without looking at* REBEKKA.)

(*After a moment* REBEKKA *goes cautiously to the window and looks out through the flowers.*)

REBEKKA (*Speaks to herself under her breath*): And still he won't venture over the bridge—he's taking the upper-road again. He never will cross by the mill-race. Never. (*Leaves the window*) Ah, well! (*Goes and pulls bell-rope—a moment after,* MRS. HELSETH *enters.*)

MRS. HELSETH: Yes, Miss?

REBEKKA: Mrs. Helseth, would you be so kind as to have my trunk brought down from the attic?

MRS. HELSETH: Your trunk, Miss?

REBEKKA: Yes, you know, the brown sealskin trunk.

MRS. HELSETH: I know the one, Miss. Are you going on a journey?

REBEKKA: Yes, Mrs. Helseth—I'm going on a journey.

MRS. HELSETH: You mean—at once?

REBEKKA: As soon as I've packed.

MRS. HELSETH: Well—I must say! You'll be back soon, won't you, Miss?

REBEKKA: I'm never coming back, Mrs. Helseth.

MRS. HELSETH: *Never*, Miss! But how shall we manage at Rosmersholm without you? And just when the poor master was beginning to be happy and comfortable, too!

REBEKKA: I had a bad fright today, Mrs. Helseth.

MRS. HELSETH: Good gracious, Miss! How?

REBEKKA: I thought I caught a glimpse of the white horses.

MRS. HELSETH: The white horses! In broad daylight!

REBEKKA: I expect they're around both day and night—the white horses of Rosmersholm. (*With a change of tone*) And now—would you see to the trunk, Mrs. Helseth?

MRS. HELSETH: Yes, of course, Miss; the trunk.

(*They both go out by the door right.*)

CURTAIN

ACT FOUR

SCENE: *The sitting-room at Rosmersholm. Late evening. A lighted lamp, with a lamp-shade, on the table.* REBEKKA WEST *stands by the table, packing some small articles in a handbag. Her cloak, hat and the white crocheted shawl are hanging over the back of the sofa.*

MRS. HELSETH *enters from the door right.*

MRS. HELSETH (*Speaks in a low voice and appears ill at ease*): All your things are down now, Miss. They're in the kitchen hallway.

REBEKKA: Thank you. You've ordered the carriage?

MRS. HELSETH: Yes. What time will you want it, Miss? The coachman wants to know.

REBEKKA: About eleven o'clock, I should think. The steamer sails at midnight.

MRS. HELSETH (*Hesitates a little*): But what about Mr. Rosmer? Supposing he's not back by then?

REBEKKA: I'll have to leave all the same. If I don't see him, say I'll write to him—a long letter, tell him.

MRS. HELSETH: Letters may be all very well— But, poor Miss West— Don't you think you should try and have another talk with him?

REBEKKA: Perhaps. And yet—perhaps I'd better not.

MRS. HELSETH: To think I should live to see this! I certainly never thought a thing like this would happen!

REBEKKA: What *did* you think then, Mrs. Helseth?

MRS. HELSETH: I thought Pastor Rosmer would be more dependable.

REBEKKA: Dependable?

MRS. HELSETH: That's what I said, Miss.

REBEKKA: But, my dear Mrs. Helseth, what do you mean by that?

MRS. HELSETH: I mean what's right and proper, Miss. He shouldn't be allowed to get out of it like this.

REBEKKA (*Looks at her*): Listen to me, Mrs. Helseth—I want you to be quite honest with me; why do you think I am going away?

MRS. HELSETH: I suppose it can't be helped, Miss. But it's not right of Pastor Rosmer all the same. There was some excuse for Mortensgaard; her husband was still alive, you see—so they couldn't marry, however much they wanted to. But in Pastor Rosmer's case—!

REBEKKA (*With a faint smile*): Did you actually believe such a thing of Pastor Rosmer and me?

MRS. HELSETH: No, never, Miss! That is, I mean—not until today.

REBEKKA: And what made you change your mind?

MRS. HELSETH: I'm told the papers are saying dreadful things about the Pastor—

REBEKKA: Aha!

MRS. HELSETH: I wouldn't put anything past a man who would take up Mortensgaard's religion!

REBEKKA: I see. But what about me? What have you to say of me?

MRS. HELSETH: Lord bless me, Miss—I can't think you're to blame. We're all of us human—and it's not easy for a single woman to be always on her guard.

REBEKKA: That is very true, Mrs. Helseth—We are all of us human—Did you hear something?

MRS. HELSETH (*In a low voice*): I thought—I do believe he's coming, Miss.

REBEKKA (*Starts*): In that case—? (*Resolutely*) Well—so be it (ROSMER *enters from hall.*)

ROSMER (*Sees handbag, etc.—turns to* REBEKKA *and asks*): What does this mean?

REBEKKA: I am going.

ROSMER: At once?

REBEKKA: Yes. (*To* MRS. HELSETH) Eleven o'clock then.

MRS. HELSETH: Very well, Miss. (*Goes out by the door right.*)

ROSMER (*After a short pause*): Where are you going, Rebekka?

REBEKKA: North; by the steamer.

ROSMER: Why North?

REBEKKA: That's where I came from.

ROSMER: What do you plan to do?

REBEKKA: I don't know. I just want to put an end to the whole business.

ROSMER: Put an end to it?

REBEKKA: Rosmersholm has crushed me.

ROSMER (*His attention aroused*): How can you say that?

REBEKKA: Crushed me utterly—completely. When I came here I had a healthy, fearless spirit—but I've had to bow before an alien law. I no longer have the courage to face anything.

ROSMER: Why not? What law do you mean?

REBEKKA: Don't let's talk about it, Rosmer. What happened between you and Kroll?

ROSMER: We have made peace.

REBEKKA: I see. So that is how it ended.

ROSMER: All our old friends were gathered at his house. They convinced me that the kind of work I had in mind was not for me. And anyway—the rehabilitation of mankind—! How hopeless it all seems! I shall give up all thought of that.

REBEKKA: Perhaps it's for the best.

ROSMER: Have you come to think that too?

REBEKKA: These past few days I've come to think it; yes.

ROSMER: You're lying.

REBEKKA: Lying—!

ROSMER: Yes, you're lying. You never really had faith in me. You never really believed I would succeed.

REBEKKA: I believed we might succeed together.

ROSMER: That's not true, either. You believed yourself destined for great things; you believed you could use me as an instrument—as a means to serve your ends. That's what you believed.

REBEKKA: Listen to me, Rosmer—

ROSMER (*Seats himself listlessly on the sofa*): Oh, what is the use? I know the truth now. I've been nothing but clay in your hands.

REBEKKA: You *must* listen to me, Rosmer. We must talk this thing through. It'll be the last time we'll ever talk together. (*Sits in chair close to sofa*) I was going to write you all about it— once I'd got away—but perhaps it's best that I should tell you now.

ROSMER: Have you still more to confess?

REBEKKA: Yes. The most vital thing of all.

ROSMER: Vital—?

REBEKKA: Something you've never suspected for a moment—and yet it's the key to all the rest.

ROSMER (*Shakes his head*): I don't understand.

REBEKKA: It is true that I did everything to worm my way in here—I had a feeling it would be to my advantage whichever way things went.

ROSMER: And you succeeded in your purpose.

REBEKKA: In those days I believe I could have succeeded in absolutely anything—my spirit was still free and fearless then. I had no scruples; no personal ties stood in my way. Then I began to be possessed by the thing that was to crush me—the thing that broke my spirit and warped my life forever.

ROSMER: Why can't you speak plainly?

REBEKKA: I became possessed by a wild, uncontrollable passion, Rosmer—

ROSMER: Passion? You—! For what? For whom?

REBEKKA: For you.

ROSMER (*Tries to spring up*): What—?

REBEKKA (*Stops him*): No—stay where you are! Let me go on.

ROSMER: You mean to tell me you loved me—in that way?

REBEKKA: At that time I called it love. Yes, I thought it was love, then. But now I know it wasn't. It was what I just said: a wild, uncontrollable passion.

ROSMER (*With difficulty*): Can this be true, Rebekka? Is it possible that you're really speaking of *yourself*?

REBEKKA: It's hard for you to believe it of me, isn't it?

ROSMER: So this was the cause—this was the reason—that you "set to work" as you call it?

REBEKKA: It swept over me like a storm at sea—like one of those winter-storms we have up in the North. It seizes hold of you and carries you off with it—wherever it will. Resistance is impossible.

ROSMER: And you let this storm carry poor Beata to her death.

REBEKKA: Yes. It was a death-struggle between us at that time, you see.

ROSMER: You were certainly the strongest; stronger than Beata and me together.

REBEKKA: I knew you well enough to realize that I had no hope of reaching you until you were a free man—not only in spirit, but in fact.

ROSMER: But I don't understand you, Rebekka. You—your whole conduct—is incomprehensible to me. I am free now—both in spirit and in fact. You have reached the very goal you aimed at from the first. And yet—in spite of that—

REBEKKA: I have never been further from my goal than I am now.

ROSMER: And yet in spite of that, I say—yesterday when I asked you, begged you, to be my wife—you cried out, as if in terror, that that could never be!

REBEKKA: I cried out in despair, Rosmer.

ROSMER: But why?

REBEKKA: Because Rosmersholm has robbed me of my strength. My spirit that was once so fearless has become warped and crippled here—as though its wings had been clipped. I no longer have any daring, Rosmer—I've lost the power of action.

ROSMER: How did this happen to you?

REBEKKA: Through living with you.

ROSMER: But how? How?

REBEKKA: When I found myself alone with you—and you began to be yourself again—

ROSMER: Yes, yes?

REBEKKA: —For you were never quite yourself while Beata was alive—

ROSMER: No—I'm afraid that's true.

REBEKKA: Then I was able to live here with you in peace, in solitude; you confided your thoughts to me without reserve; I became aware of your slightest mood—of all the tenderness and delicacy of your nature; and gradually—little by little—a great change came over me. At first it was almost imperceptible—but it grew and grew—until at last it dominated my whole being.

ROSMER: What *is* all this, Rebekka!

REBEKKA: And all that other thing—that evil, sensual thing —seemed to fade into the distance. All violent passion subsided—conquered by silence. My mind was filled with peace. My spirit became still; it was like the stillness on one of our northern birdcliffs under the midnight sun.

ROSMER: Tell me more about this, Rebekka. Everything you know about it—tell me!

REBEKKA: There's not much more to tell. Only this: I knew then that love had come to me; real love; love that asks nothing for itself—that is content with life together—just as we have known it.

ROSMER: If I'd only had an inkling of all this—!

REBEKKA: It's perhaps best as it is. Yesterday when you asked me to be your wife—I cried out with joy—

ROSMER: Yes, you did, didn't you, Rebekka? It sounded so to me.

REBEKKA: For a moment—yes! For a moment I forgot myself! It was my former fearless spirit trying to assert itself—struggling

for freedom. But it no longer has any power—no power to endure.

ROSMER: How do you account for this change in you?

REBEKKA: My will has become infected by the Rosmer view on
life—your view on life at any rate.

ROSMER: Infected?

REBEKKA: Yes! It has grown weak and sickly. It's become a slave to
laws that it despised before. Living with you, Rosmer, has ex-
alted and purified my spirit—

ROSMER: How I wish I could believe that, Rebekka—!

REBEKKA: You *can* believe it. The Rosmer view on life
exalts—but—but—!

ROSMER: Well?

REBEKKA: —it kills happiness!

ROSMER: You really think that?

REBEKKA: I know it does, for me.

ROSMER: How can you be so sure? If I were to ask you again, now,
Rebekka—if I were to beg you—to entreat you—

REBEKKA: My dearest—you must never speak of this again!
There's something—in my past—that makes it quite impossible!

ROSMER: Something beyond what you've already told me?

REBEKKA: Yes. It has to do with something else—something quite
different.

ROSMER: I've sometimes thought—isn't it strange, Rebekka?
—I've sometimes thought I knew.

REBEKKA: And yet—? In spite of that—?

ROSMER: I never really believed it. I used to speculate on it
sometimes—play with it—in my thoughts—

REBEKKA: I'll tell you about it—if you want me to—

ROSMER: No—not a word! Whatever it may be—I can forget it.

REBEKKA: But I can't, you see.

ROSMER: Rebekka—!

REBEKKA: That's what's so dreadful, Rosmer! Happiness is here;
I've only to stretch out my hand to seize it. But now I've
changed, and this—thing in my past, stands in the way.

ROSMER: Your past is dead, Rebekka. It can no longer touch
you—it no longer has any claim on you, as you are now.

REBEKKA: You know those are just phrases! What about innocence? Can I ever find that again?

ROSMER (*Wearily*): Innocence—!

REBEKKA: Innocence, yes. Happiness and joy cannot exist without it—you said that yourself, Rosmer. That was the truth you wanted to instill in those noble men you dreamed of—

ROSMER: Don't remind me of that, Rebekka. It was an immature dream, a nebulous fancy—I no longer believe in it myself. Nobility cannot be imposed upon us from without.

REBEKKA (*Quietly*): Not even by love, Rosmer? Quiet, unselfish love?

ROSMER (*Thoughtfully*): Yes—what a great power that could be! How glorious—if only it existed! But does it? If I were only sure—if I could only convince myself of that.

REBEKKA: You don't believe me, Rosmer?

ROSMER: How can I believe you fully—when I think of all these incredible things you've concealed from me for years? And now—this new approach—how do I know what secret purpose lies behind it? Is there something you wish to gain by it? Be honest with me! You know I'll do anything in my power to give you what you want.

REBEKKA (*Wringing her hands*): Oh these doubts—these morbid doubts! Rosmer, Rosmer!

ROSMER: I know! But what can I do? I'll never be able to get rid of them. How can I ever be quite certain of your love?

REBEKKA: But you must know in your heart how truly changed I am—and that this change has come to me through you—because of you!

ROSMER: I no longer believe in my power to change others, Rebekka. I no longer believe in myself in any way. I have no faith in myself, and I have no faith in you.

REBEKKA (*Looks at him sadly*): How will you be able to endure life, Rosmer?

ROSMER: I don't know. I can't imagine how. I don't think I will be able to endure it. I can think of nothing in this world worth living for.

REBEKKA: Still—life renews itself continually. Let's cling to it, Rosmer. We shall leave it soon enough.

ROSMER (*Jumps up restlessly*): Then give me back my faith. My faith in your love, Rebekka! My faith in you! Give me proof! I must have proof!

REBEKKA: Proof! How can I give you proof?

ROSMER: You must! I can't endure this desolation—this dreadful emptiness—this—this—

(*A loud knock at the hall door.*)

REBEKKA (*Starts from her chair*): What was that?

(*The door opens.* ULRIK BRENDEL *enters. He wears a dress shirt, a black coat and a good pair of high shoes, with his trousers tucked into them. Otherwise he is dressed as in the first act. He looks excited.*)

ROSMER: Oh—it's you, Mr. Brendel!

BRENDEL: Johannes, my boy—hail and farewell!

ROSMER: Where are you going so late at night?

BRENDEL: Downhill.

ROSMER: How do you mean?

BRENDEL: I am going home, beloved pupil. I am homesick for the great Nothingness.

ROSMER: Something has happened to you, Mr. Brendel; what is it?

BRENDEL: So, you notice the change in me, eh? I'm not surprised! When last I entered these halls, I was a prosperous man—full of self-confidence—

ROSMER: I don't quite understand—

BRENDEL: But tonight you see me a deposed monarch, squatting on the ash-heap that was once my palace.

ROSMER: If there's anything I can do to help you—

BRENDEL: You have managed to retain your good child-like heart, Johannes. Could you oblige me with a loan?

ROSMER: Of course! Gladly.

BRENDEL: Could you spare me an ideal or two?

ROSMER: What did you say?

BRENDEL: A couple of cast-off ideals? You'd be doing a good deed,

I assure you. For I'm broke, my boy. Cleaned out. Stripped.

REBEKKA: Didn't you give your lecture, Mr. Brendel?

BRENDEL: No, entrancing lady. Only think! Just as I stood there ready to empty my horn of plenty, I made the painful discovery that I was bankrupt.

REBEKKA: But what about all those unwritten works of yours?

BRENDEL: I've sat for twenty-five years like a miser on his money-bags. And yesterday—when I went to open them, intending to pour forth the treasure—I found there was none! The Teeth of Time had ground it into dust. It all amounted to *nichts* and nothing!

ROSMER: Are you quite sure of that?

BRENDEL: There is no room for doubt, my boy. The President convinced me.

ROSMER: The President?

BRENDEL: Well—his Excellency, then. *Ganz nach Belieben.*

ROSMER: But whom do you mean?

BRENDEL: Peder Mortensgaard, of course.

ROSMER: What!

BRENDEL (*Mysteriously*): Hush! Peder Mortensgaard is Lord and Master of the Future. Never have I stood in a more august presence. Peder Mortensgaard has divine power; he is omnipotent; he can do anything he wills!

ROSMER: You don't really believe that!

BRENDEL: Yes, my boy! For Peder Mortensgaard never *wills* more than he can do. Peder Mortensgaard is capable of living without ideals. And that, you see, is the secret of action and success. It is the sum of worldly wisdom. *Basta!*

ROSMER (*In a low voice*): I understand now why you're leaving poorer than you came.

BRENDEL: *Bien!* So just take a *Beispiel* from your old teacher. Throw out everything he tried to impress upon your mind. Don't build your house on shifting sand. And be wary—be very sure—before you build too many hopes on this charming creature who fills your life with sweetness.

REBEKKA: Is that meant for me?

BRENDEL: Yes, my fascinating mermaid.

REBEKKA: Why shouldn't he build hopes on me?

BRENDEL (*Comes a step nearer*): It seems my former pupil has chosen to fight for a great cause.

REBEKKA: Well—?

BRENDEL: His Victory is certain, but—remember this—on one irrevocable condition.

REBEKKA: What condition?

BRENDEL (*Taking her gently by the wrist*): That the woman who loves him, will gladly go out into the kitchen and hack off her sweet, rosy, little finger—here—right at the middle joint. Item: that the aforesaid loving woman will—with equal gladness—chop off her incomparable, exquisite, left ear. (*Lets her go, and turns to* ROSMER) Farewell, my victorious Johannes.

ROSMER: Are you going now? In the dark? In the middle of the night?

BRENDEL: The dark is best. Peace be with you. (*He goes. There is a short silence in the room.*)

REBEKKA (*Breathes heavily*): It's so close in here—it's stifling! (*Goes to the window, opens it, and remains standing by it.*)

ROSMER (*Sits down in arm-chair by stove*): There's nothing else to do, Rebekka—I see that now. You'll have to go away.

REBEKKA: Yes, I see no choice.

ROSMER: Let's make the most of these last moments. Come over here and sit with me.

REBEKKA (*Goes and sits on the sofa*): What have you to say to me, Rosmer?

ROSMER: First I want to tell you this; you needn't have any anxiety about your future.

REBEKKA (*Smiles*): Ha—my future!

ROSMER: I took care of that long ago. Whatever happens, you will be looked after.

REBEKKA: You thought of that too—my dearest!

ROSMER: I should think you'd have known that.

REBEKKA: It's a long time since I've concerned myself with things of that sort.

ROSMER: I suppose you thought things could never change between us.

REBEKKA: Yes, I did.

ROSMER: So did I. But if I were to go—

REBEKKA: You will live longer than I will, Rosmer—

ROSMER: This wretched life of mine! At least I have the power to end it when I chose.

REBEKKA: What do you mean? You'd never think of—?

ROSMER: Would that be so strange? I've allowed myself to be defeated—miserably, ignominiously defeated. I turned my back on the work I had to do; I surrendered—gave up the fight before it had actually begun!

REBEKKA: You must take it up again, Rosmer! You'll win—you'll see! You have the power to change men's spirits; to fill their minds with hope and aspiration—to bring nobility into their lives. Try! Don't give up the fight!

ROSMER: I no longer have faith, Rebekka!

REBEKKA: But you've already proved your power. You've changed my spirit. As long as I live I can never go back to being what I was.

ROSMER: If I could only believe that.

REBEKKA (*Pressing her hands together*): Oh, Rosmer! Do you know of nothing—nothing, that could make you believe that?

ROSMER (*Starts as if in fear*): Don't ask me that, Rebekka! This must go no further! Don't say another word!

REBEKKA: But it must go further! Tell me! Do you know of anything that could remove this doubt? I can think of nothing.

ROSMER: It's best that you shouldn't—best for us both.

REBEKKA: No! I won't be put off with that. Do you know of anything that would absolve me in your eyes? If you do—I have the right to know it.

ROSMER (*As if impelled against his will to speak*): Very well—let's see. You say you're filled with a great love—a pure, transcendent love. That through me your spirit has been changed—your life transformed. Is this really true, Rebekka? You're sure of that? Shall we put it to the test?

REBEKKA: I am ready to do that.

ROSMER: At any time?

REBEKKA: Now, if you like. The sooner the better.

ROSMER: Then would you be willing, Rebekka—now—this evening—for my sake—to— (*Breaks off*) Oh—no, no!

REBEKKA: Yes, Rosmer—yes! Tell me, and you'll see!

ROSMER: Have you the courage to—are you willing to—gladly, as Ulrik Brendel said—for my sake, now tonight—gladly—to go the same way Beata went?

REBEKKA (*Rises slowly from the sofa; almost voiceless*): Rosmer!

ROSMER: That question will go on haunting me after you're gone; I shan't be able to get away from it. Over and over again I shall come back to it. I can picture it so clearly: You're standing out on the bridge, right in the very center. Now you're leaning far out over the railing, as though hypnotized by the rushing stream below. But then—you turn away. You dare not do—what she did.

REBEKKA: And supposing I *did* dare? Dared to do it—gladly? What then?

ROSMER: I should *have* to believe you then. My faith would be restored to me; faith in my vision of life—faith in my power to make men see that vision.

REBEKKA (*Takes up her shawl slowly, and puts it over her head; says with composure*): You shall have your faith again.

ROSMER: Have you the courage, have you the will—to do this, Rebekka?

REBEKKA: You'll know that tomorrow—or later—when they find my body.

ROSMER (*Puts his hand to his forehead*): There's a ghastly fascination about this—

REBEKKA: For I don't want to be left down there—any longer than necessary. You must see that they find me.

ROSMER (*Springs up*): This is sheer madness! Go—or stay, if you will! I'll believe anything you tell me—just as I always have.

REBEKKA: These are just words, Rosmer! This time, there can be no escape in cowardice. After today—how can you ever believe in me again?

ROSMER: But I don't want to see you fail, Rebekka.

REBEKKA: I shall not fail.

ROSMER: You won't be able to help it. You'd never have the courage Beata had.

REBEKKA: Don't you think so?

ROSMER: No—never. You're not like Beata. You're not under the spell of madness.

REBEKKA: No. But I've fallen under another spell—the spell of Rosmersholm; and now I know that if I've sinned, then I must pay the penalty.

ROSMER (*Looks at her fixedly*): Is that what you've come to believe, Rebekka?

REBEKKA: Yes.

ROSMER (*With resolution*): Well, I still believe that man is a free spirit. There is no judge above us; we must each judge ourselves.

REBEKKA (*Misunderstanding him*): That's true, too. My going will save what's best in you.

ROSMER: There's nothing left in me to save.

REBEKKA: Oh, yes there is! But as for me—I should be nothing but a kind of sea-troll, clinging to the ship on which you must sail forward—pulling it back. I must go overboard. Why should I stay on in this world dragging out a stunted life? Pondering and brooding over a happiness that my past forbids me to enjoy? No—I must get out of the game.

ROSMER: If you go—then I go with you.

REBEKKA (*Smiles almost imperceptibly, looks at him, and says more softly*): Yes, you come too—you shall be witness—

ROSMER: I will go with you, I say.

REBEKKA: As far as the bridge, yes. You know you never dare set foot on it.

ROSMER: You've noticed that?

REBEKKA (*Sadly and brokenly*): Yes; that's how I knew my love was hopeless.

ROSMER: I lay my hand upon your head, Rebekka—and take you in marriage as my true wife.

REBEKKA (*Takes both his hands, and bows her head towards his breast*): Thank you, Rosmer. (*Lets him go*) Now I can go—gladly!

ROSMER: Man and wife should go together.

REBEKKA: Only as far as the bridge, Rosmer.

ROSMER: Out onto the bridge too; I have the courage now. However far you go—I shall go with you.

REBEKKA: Are you quite certain, Rosmer? Is this the best way for you?

ROSMER: I'm quite certain it's the only way.

REBEKKA: What if you were deceiving yourself? Supposing this were only a delusion— One of those White Horses that prey on Rosmersholm?

ROSMER: It may be so. The White Horses! We Rosmers can never escape them!

REBEKKA: Then stay, Rosmer!

ROSMER: The husband belongs with his wife, as the wife with her husband.

REBEKKA: Tell me this first: Is it you who go with me? Or is it I who go with you?

ROSMER: We shall never know the answer to that question, Rebekka.

REBEKKA: I should so like to know—

ROSMER: We go together, Rebekka. I with you, and you with me.

REBEKKA: Yes—I believe that's true—

ROSMER: For now we two are *one*.

REBEKKA: Yes, now we are *one*. Come! Let us go—gladly!

(*They go out hand in hand through the hall, and are seen to turn to the left. The door remains open. The room stands empty for a little while. Then the door to the right is opened by* MRS. HELSETH.)

MRS. HELSETH: Miss West—the carriage is— (*Looks around*) No one here? They must have gone out together—at this time of night too! (*Goes out into hall, looks round, and comes in again*) They're not out on the bench. Ah, well—(*Goes to the window and looks out*) Lord bless me! What's that white thing out there—! It's them—out on the bridge, and in each other's arms! (*Shrieks aloud*) Ah! Over the railing—both of them—down into the mill-race! Help! Help! (*Her knees tremble; she leans on the chair-back, shaking all over; she can scarcely get the words out*) No! No one can help them now. It's the dead wife—the dead wife has taken them.

CURTAIN

The Lady from the Sea

A PLAY IN FIVE ACTS

1888

CHARACTERS

DOCTOR WANGEL, *district physician*

ELLIDA WANGEL, *his second wife*

BOLETTE

HILDE, *a young girl*

his daughters by his former marriage

ARNHOLM, *a schoolmaster*

LYNGSTRAND

BALLESTED

A STRANGER

Young townspeople, tourists, etc.
The action takes place in the summertime, in a small town beside a fjord in Northern Norway.

ACT ONE

SCENE: *Stage left.* WANGEL'S *house, with a large veranda; surrounded front and side by a garden. Below the veranda a flagstaff. In the garden, stage right, an arbor with tables and chairs. In the background a hedge with a small gate. Beyond the hedge a road along the shore, lined with trees. Through the trees a glimpse of the fjord with high mountain peaks in the distance. It is a warm, sparkling summer morning.*

BALLESTED, *a middle-aged man wearing an old velvet jacket and a broad-brimmed artist's hat, stands at the foot of the flagstaff, arranging the rope. The flag lies on the ground. A little way from him stands an easel with a canvas on it. On a campstool beside it are brushes, palette and a paint box.*

BOLETTE *comes out onto the veranda through the door from the garden room, which stands open. She carries a large vase of flowers, which she places on the table.*

BOLETTE: Were you able to fix it, Ballested?

BALLESTED: Yes indeed, Miss Bolette—it was simple enough. I hope you don't mind my asking, Miss—are you expecting company today?

BOLETTE: Yes, we are. Professor Arnholm's coming; he arrived in town last night.

BALLESTED: Arnholm. You mean that man who used to be your tutor?

BOLETTE: That's the one.

BALLESTED: So he's come back for a visit, has he?

BOLETTE: That's why we want to raise the flag—to welcome him.

BALLESTED: Of course, of course! I see!

(BOLETTE *goes into the house again. A moment later*
LYNGSTRAND *enters on the road from the right. He stops at the
sight of the easel and the painting materials and looks at them
with interest. He is a spare, delicate young man, poorly but
neatly dressed.*)

LYNGSTRAND (*From the other side of the hedge*): Good morning!

BALLESTED (*Turning*): What's that? Oh! Good morning! (*Hoists
the flag*) There! Up she goes! (*He ties off the rope and busies himself at the easel*) I say good morning to you, Sir, though I don't
believe I've had the pleasure—

LYNGSTRAND: You're a painter, are you?

BALLESTED: Correct. Any objections?

LYNGSTRAND: Well—I mean—you must be a painter; I can see
that you are. Would it be all right if I came in a moment?

BALLESTED: Want to have a look?

LYNGSTRAND: I'd like to very much.

BALLESTED: There's not much to see yet—it's just a start. But
come in if you like—you're very welcome.

LYNGSTRAND: Thanks—then I will. (*He comes through the garden gate.*)

BALLESTED (*Painting*): I'm trying to catch that bit of the fjord—in
between those islands.

LYNGSTRAND: Oh, yes—I see.

BALLESTED: Of course I still have to put the figure in. But it's so
hard to find models around here.

LYNGSTRAND: Oh—there's to be a figure, is there?

BALLESTED: Yes—a dying mermaid. I'm going to put her here in
the foreground—stretched out by that rock.

LYNGSTRAND: Why is she dying?

BALLESTED: Well, you see—she strayed inland and lost her way;
and she can't get back to the sea again. So she's pining away here
in the shallows.

LYNGSTRAND: Oh, I see.

BALLESTED: I got the idea from Mrs. Wangel—the lady who lives
here, you know.

LYNGSTRAND: What will you call the picture when it's finished?

BALLESTED: I thought of calling it "The Mermaid's End."

LYNGSTRAND: Splendid. It should be a fine piece of work.

BALLESTED: Are you a fellow artist by any chance?

LYNGSTRAND: A painter, you mean?

BALLESTED: Yes.

LYNGSTRAND: No; no, I'm not. But I'm going to be a sculptor. My name is Lyngstrand—Hans Lyngstrand.

BALLESTED: A sculptor, eh? Well—that's a great art too; a fine, distinguished art. Haven't I passed you on the street now and then? How long have you been here?

LYNGSTRAND: About two weeks. I hope to spend the summer here—if I can manage it.

BALLESTED: A nice holiday by the seaside, eh?

LYNGSTRAND: I thought it might benefit my health.

BALLESTED: Not an invalid, I hope?

LYNGSTRAND: A bit on the delicate side—nothing serious. It's my lungs; I have difficulty in breathing.

BALLESTED: That's nothing much! Still—it might be wise to see a doctor.

LYNGSTRAND: I thought of consulting Dr. Wangel—someday when he's not too busy.

BALLESTED: A good idea. (*Looks off left*) Here comes another steamer—packed with people, too. It's amazing what a lot of tourists we've had these past few years.

LYNGSTRAND: It seems like a very busy place.

BALLESTED: It gets worse every summer. Too many visitors! I'm afraid our little town may lose its charm.

LYNGSTRAND: Were you born here?

BALLESTED: No; no, I wasn't. But through the years I've become thoroughly accla—acclimatized. I've become attached to the place. Time and habit, I suppose.

LYNGSTRAND: Have you lived here long?

BALLESTED: Around seventeen or eighteen years. I first came here with Skive's company—a theatrical troupe, you know. There were financial difficulties, and the company disbanded.

LYNGSTRAND: And you stayed on here?

BALLESTED: Yes, I stayed on, and I can't say I've regretted it. You see, I was a scenic artist in those days.

(BOLETTE *comes out of the house carrying a rocking chair,
which she places on the veranda*.)

BOLETTE (*Calls back into the house*): Hilde—bring Father's footstool, will you? You know—the embroidered one.

LYNGSTRAND (*Goes to the veranda and greets her*): Good morning, Miss Wangel!

BOLETTE (*At the balustrade*): Well! If it isn't Mr. Lyngstrand!
How do you do! Excuse me a moment; I just have to—(*Goes into
the house*.)

BALLESTED: I see you know the Wangels.

LYNGSTRAND: Not really. I've been introduced to the young ladies; and I had a nice talk with Mrs. Wangel at the last band concert. She said I might come and call on them.

BALLESTED: You should get to know them better; it'd be a good
connection.

LYNGSTRAND: I had thought of dropping in—just to pay my respects, you know—if a suitable opportunity arose—

BALLESTED: "Suitable opportunity"! What nonsense—! (*Looks
off left*) Damn it all! (*Gathers his things together*) The steamer's
docked already. I'd better get to the hotel. Someone might need
my services. I'm an expert hairdresser too, you know.

LYNGSTRAND: You must be very versatile.

BALLESTED: In a small place like this you have to learn to
accla—acclimatize yourself to various professions. If you ever
need anything in the hair-goods line—just ask for Ballested the
dancing master.

LYNGSTRAND: Dancing master—?

BALLESTED: Or leader of the brass band if you prefer. By the
way—we're giving a concert tonight up at Prospect Park!
Well—goodbye! Goodbye!

(*He picks up his painting materials and goes out through the gate
and off left.* HILDE *comes out of the house carrying the footstool.* BOLETTE *brings more flowers.* LYNGSTRAND *greets*
HILDE *from the garden.*)

HILDE (*At the railing. Does not return his greeting*): Bolette told
me you'd screwed up enough courage to come inside the gate
today.

LYNGSTRAND: I hope you don't mind—I did take the liberty—

HILDE: Been for your morning walk?

LYNGSTRAND: I can't say I've walked very far—

HILDE: Been for a swim?

LYNGSTRAND: I went in for a few minutes. I saw your mother down at the beach. She was just going into her bathhouse.

HILDE: Who was?

LYNGSTRAND: Your mother.

HILDE: Well, well! (*She places the footstool in front of the rocking chair*.)

BOLETTE (*Changing the subject*): Did you see Father's boat by any chance?

LYNGSTRAND: There was a sailboat heading in for shore.

BOLETTE: That must have been Father. He had to visit a patient on one of the islands. (*She arranges a couple of things on the table*.)

LYNGSTRAND (*Steps up onto the lowest step of the veranda*): What a lot of lovely flowers!

BOLETTE: Yes—they're pretty, aren't they?

LYNGSTRAND: Beautiful! Is it some sort of celebration?

BOLETTE: It is indeed!

LYNGSTRAND: I thought it must be! Your father's birthday perhaps?

BOLETTE (*Warningly, to* HILDE): Hm-hm!

HILDE (*Pays no attention*): No—Mother's.

LYNGSTRAND: Oh! Your mother's!

BOLETTE (*In a low angry tone*): Stop it, Hilde!

HILDE (*Likewise*): Leave me alone, will you! (*To* LYNGSTRAND) Isn't it about time for your lunch?

LYNGSTRAND (*Backs down the step*): Yes, I ought to eat something, I suppose.

HILDE: You must be living in the lap of luxury down at the hotel!

LYNGSTRAND: Oh—I don't live there any more; it was too expensive.

HILDE: Then where do you live now?

LYNGSTRAND: I'm boarding at Mrs. Jensen's.

HILDE: Mrs. Jensen? Which one?

LYNGSTRAND: You know—the midwife.

HILDE: Well! I must say—! Excuse me, Mr. Lyngstrand—I've really too much to do—I can't stand here—

LYNGSTRAND: Oh—I oughtn't to have said that.

HILDE: What?

LYNGSTRAND: Well—what I just said.

HILDE (*Gives him a withering look*): I don't know what you're talking about.

LYNGSTRAND: No; of course not. Well—I'll say good-bye for the present.

BOLETTE (*Comes forward to the top of the steps*): Good-bye, Mr. Lyngstrand. You really must forgive us—we're very busy today. Perhaps some other time—when you've nothing better to do—you'll stop in and see Father and—well—all the rest of the family.

LYNGSTRAND: Thank you. I'd like to very much. (*He bows and goes out by the garden gate. He turns and bows again before disappearing off left.*)

HILDE (*Under her breath*): Adieu, Monsieur! Give my love to Mother Jensen!

BOLETTE (*Softly, shaking her by the arm*): Hilde—! You dreadful child! He might hear you!

HILDE: Well—let him!

BOLETTE (*Looking off right*): Here comes Father.
(DR. WANGEL *enters on the path from the right. He has on traveling clothes and carries a small bag.*)

WANGEL: Well, little girls! Here I am home again! (*He comes through the gate.*)

BOLETTE (*Runs down into the garden to meet him*): It's wonderful to have you back!

HILDE (*Also runs to meet him*): All through for the day, Father?

WANGEL: Not quite; I'll have to go down to the office presently—just for a little while. Any news of Arnholm?

BOLETTE: He got in last night. We asked at the hotel.

WANGEL: You haven't seen him yet?

BOLETTE: No, not yet. He's sure to come and see us this morning, though.

WANGEL: Yes—I expect so.

HILDE (*Tugging at his arm*): Look, Father! Look over there!

WANGEL (*Turns and looks up at the veranda*): Well! Doesn't it look festive!

BOLETTE: We've done a fine job, haven't we?

WANGEL: You certainly have! Where is—? Are we alone here?

HILDE: Yes. She went—

BOLETTE (*Breaking in*): Mother went for a swim.

WANGEL (*Looks tenderly at* BOLETTE *and pats her head. With some hesitation*): It's lovely, children. But—you won't leave it like this all day, will you? I mean—the flag flying and all?

HILDE: Of course, Father! What do you suppose!

WANGEL: Well—it's just that—

BOLETTE (*Nodding and smiling at him*): Don't you see, Father! It's in honor of Arnholm! He's an old friend, and he hasn't been here for years—it's only natural!

HILDE (*Smiling and tugging at his arm*): After all—he was Bolette's tutor, Father!

WANGEL: You're full of mischief, both of you!—Still—it's understandable enough—her memory is very dear to us. All the same— Here, Hilde (*Gives her his bag*)—this goes to the office—I don't quite like it, children; it's the wrong way to go about it. The fact that every year the three of us—Well, what can one say! I suppose it can't be otherwise.

HILDE (*About to go off left through the garden with her father's bag, stops and turning points off stage*): Look! Someone's coming up the road. Do you suppose it's the professor?

BOLETTE (*Looking off*): That old man? You're crazy! That can't be Mr. Arnholm!

WANGEL: Wait, children—I believe—Yes! Of course it's he!

BOLETTE (*Staring, in amazement*): Why—so it is!

(ARNHOLM, *smartly dressed, wearing gold spectacles and carrying a light cane, appears on the road coming from the left. He looks tired, as though overworked. He bows in a friendly way and comes into the garden through the gate.*)

WANGEL (*Goes to meet him*): Welcome my dear Arnholm! Welcome to your old haunts again!

ARNHOLM: My dear Doctor! Many thanks! It's good to see you!
(*They shake hands and come back through the garden*) And are
these—? The children! (*Gives them his hands*) I never would
have known them!

WANGEL: I'm sure you wouldn't!

ARNHOLM: Bolette, perhaps. Yes—I think I'd have known her.

WANGEL: I doubt it. It's eight or nine years since you last saw her.
Many things have changed since then.

ARNHOLM: Oh, I don't know— The trees have grown a bit, of
course; and that summerhouse is new—

WANGEL: I didn't mean just outwardly—

ARNHOLM: And, of course, now you have a couple of marriageable
young ladies on your hands.

WANGEL: A couple! Come now! One, perhaps—

HILDE (*Under her breath*): *Dear* Father!

WANGEL: It's cooler on the veranda; you'll be more comfortable
there.

ARNHOLM: Thank you, dear Doctor.
(*They go up the steps to the veranda.* WANGEL *gives* ARNHOLM
the rocking chair.)

WANGEL: Do sit down, you look quite tired after your journey.

ARNHOLM: Not really. Now that I'm here I'll soon—

BOLETTE (*To* WANGEL): Shall I fetch some lemonade, Father?
We'd better have it inside. It's getting warm out here.

WANGEL: Lemonade would be very nice, I think; and perhaps a
little cognac too.

BOLETTE: Cognac, Father?

WANGEL: Just a drop—for those of us who want it!

BOLETTE: Very well. Hilde—take Father's bag down to the office.
(BOLETTE *goes into the house and closes the door after her.*
HILDE *takes the bag and goes off left through the garden.*)

ARNHOLM (*Who has followed* BOLETTE *with his eyes*): A charming girl! Both charming girls, Doctor.

WANGEL (*Sitting down*): They are, aren't they?

ARNHOLM: I can't get over Bolette. Hilde too, for that matter.
But, what about you, dear Doctor? What are your plans? Do you
intend to go on living here?

WANGEL: Yes, I suppose so. I was born and raised here, you see. And I've known great happiness here too. You remember my first wife, Arnholm? I was not allowed to keep her long. Her death was a great sorrow to us all.

ARNHOLM: I remember her well.

WANGEL: But I've been very fortunate in my second wife. She's made me very happy too. All in all, fate has been most kind to me.

ARNHOLM: Have you children by this marriage?

WANGEL: About two and a half years ago we had a little boy. We lost him when he was only five months old.

ARNHOLM: Isn't your wife home today?

WANGEL: She should be here any moment now. She went down to bathe. She never misses a day this time of year—no matter what the weather is.

ARNHOLM: She's quite well I hope?

WANGEL: Yes, I think so; though she's been a little nervous, on and off, these past few years; I can't quite make out what's wrong with her. But as long as she can get into the sea—! That seems to keep her well and happy.

ARNHOLM: She was always like that, as I remember.

WANGEL (*With a scarcely perceptible smile*): Of course—you knew her, didn't you? When you were teaching up at Skjoldvik?

ARNHOLM: That's right. I was living at the parsonage; she often used to visit there. And I nearly always caught a glimpse of her when I went to see her father at the lighthouse.

WANGEL: Those years at the lighthouse seem to have made a great impression on her. It's only natural, I suppose. The people round here don't understand her. They call her "The Lady from the Sea."

ARNHOLM: Do they?

WANGEL: Yes. That's why— Do talk to her about the old days, Arnholm; I've a feeling it would do her good.

ARNHOLM (*Looks at him doubtfully*): Are you sure? What makes you think so?

WANGEL: I'm certain of it.

ELLIDA'S VOICE (*Off stage in the garden*): Wangel! Are you there?

WANGEL (*Rising*): Yes, dear. I'm here.

(ELLIDA WANGEL, *wrapped in a large light cloak, enters through the trees by the summerhouse. Her wet hair hangs down over her shoulders.* ARNHOLM *rises.*)

WANGEL (*Smiles and holds out his hands to her*): Here comes the mermaid!

ELLIDA (*Goes quickly to the veranda and grasps his hands*): When did you get back? Thank heaven you're home again!

WANGEL: Just now—a few moments ago. (*Indicates* ARNHOLM) Here's an old friend waiting to see you.

ELLIDA: So you got here at last! Do forgive me for not being here to welcome you!

ARNHOLM: Don't mention it! No need to stand on ceremony with me!

WANGEL: How was the water? Cool and bracing?

ELLIDA: Flat and tepid! The water's never bracing here! It's not like the open sea. Here in the fjords the water always strikes me as unhealthy.

ARNHOLM: Unhealthy?

ELLIDA: Yes, unhealthy. And I believe it has an unhealthy effect on people too.

WANGEL (*Smiling*): A fine recommendation for a health resort!

ARNHOLM: Do you know what I think, Mrs. Wangel? I think there's a strange bond between you and the open sea—and everything connected with it.

ELLIDA: Perhaps. I've often thought that might be true— Well! Aren't you pleased? Look at all these decorations in your honor! The girls *have* been busy!

WANGEL (*Embarrassed*): Hm— (*Looks at his watch*) I think I'd better—

ARNHOLM: You mean—? All this is for me?

ELLIDA: Well—of course! We're not usually this festive. Uh! It's stifling here! (*Goes down in the garden*) Let's go and sit in the arbor. There's sometimes a little breeze out there. (*She settles herself in the arbor.*)

ARNHOLM (*Joins her*): It seems delightfully cool to me.

ELLIDA: You're used to city air. They say Christiania is dreadful in the summer.

WANGEL (*Who has also come down into the garden*): Ellida dear—will you look after our friend for a little while?

ELLIDA: Have you business to attend to?

WANGEL: I must just look in at the office. And then I'll change my clothes. I shan't be long—

ARNHOLM (*Sits down in the arbor*): Take your time, my dear Doctor. I'm sure we'll find plenty to talk about.

WANGEL: I'm sure you will. Well—goodbye for now! (*He goes off through the garden left.*)

ELLIDA (*After a short pause*): It's quite pleasant here.

ARNHOLM: I find it *very* pleasant!

ELLIDA: They call this my summerhouse— I had it built, you see. Or rather Wangel did—to please me.

ARNHOLM: Is this where you usually sit?

ELLIDA: Yes, nearly always—in the daytime.

ARNHOLM: And, I suppose, the children keep you company?

ELLIDA: No—they usually stick to the veranda.

ARNHOLM: And Wangel?

ELLIDA: He divides his time between us. Sometimes he sits with me—sometimes with the girls.

ARNHOLM: Was that arrangement your idea?

ELLIDA: I think we all prefer it. We can always call across to each other—if, by chance, we've anything to say.

ARNHOLM (*After a reflective pause*): The first time I got to know you—up at Skjoldvik, I mean— How long ago that seems—!

ELLIDA: It's a good ten years ago.

ARNHOLM: Just about—yes. I can see you so clearly—standing by the Lighthouse. "The Heathen" our old priest used to call you; he said that when your father had you christened he gave you the name of a ship—not the name of a Christian!

ELLIDA: What did you start to say?

ARNHOLM: At that time the last thing I would have thought possible was to meet you here again as Mrs. Wangel.

ELLIDA: That was before Wangel was— The children's mother was still living then. Their real mother, I mean.

ARNHOLM: Yes, I know. But even if things had been different—even if he'd had no ties—I still would never have expected this.

ELLIDA: Neither would I. Not at that time.

ARNHOLM: Wangel is such a fine man—so honorable and kind—

ELLIDA (*Warmly*): Yes! Indeed he is!

ARNHOLM: But I can't help wondering what you could possibly have in common. You're such different kinds of people, it seems to me.

ELLIDA: You're right. We are.

ARNHOLM: Then—how did it happen? Tell me.

ELLIDA: Don't ask me about it, Arnholm. I don't think I can explain it. And even if I could—I don't believe you'd understand.

ARNHOLM: Hm. (*In a lower tone*) Does your husband know—? Have you ever told him how I felt about you at that time?

ELLIDA: Of course not! I've never mentioned it.

ARNHOLM: I'm glad. I should feel embarrassed if I thought—

ELLIDA: Well, you needn't. I told him what was true: that I was very fond of you, and that in those days you were the best and truest friend I had.

ARNHOLM: Thank you. I've often wondered—why did you never write to me after I went away?

ELLIDA: I thought it would make it easier for you—since I couldn't share your feelings.

ARNHOLM: Perhaps so.

ELLIDA: Why did *you* never write?

ARNHOLM (*Looks at her with a half-reproachful smile*): I couldn't take the initiative—you might have misunderstood my motives. You'd refused me with such finality—I didn't want to seem importunate.

ELLIDA: Yes—I see. But how is it you've remained single all these years?

ARNHOLM: I had no desire to marry. I preferred to stay true to my memories.

ELLIDA: Nonsense! It's high time you forgot them! You should have been happily married long ago.

ARNHOLM: I'm getting old, it's true! I'm nearly thirty-eight!

ELLIDA: You see! You'd better hurry up! (*Is silent a moment, then speaks in a low serious tone*) I'd like to tell you something, Arnholm—something I couldn't possibly have told you then.

ARNHOLM: What is it?

ELLIDA: When you asked me to marry you—I *had* to refuse you. I had no choice.

ARNHOLM: I understand. All you felt for me was friendship.

ELLIDA: But what you don't understand is this: At that particular time my heart, my mind—all of me—belonged to someone else.

ARNHOLM: At that particular time, you say?

ELLIDA: Yes. Precisely.

ARNHOLM: But that's impossible! Surely you're mistaken. You scarcely knew Wangel then.

ELLIDA: I'm not speaking of Wangel.

ARNHOLM: Not of—? But who else was there? I don't remember a single soul at Skjoldvik who could have meant anything to you.

ELLIDA: It would seem so, wouldn't it? It was all such madness!

ARNHOLM: Won't you tell me about it?

ELLIDA: No; there's no need. But I was not free at that time—I did want you to know that.

ARNHOLM: You mean—if you had been free—?

ELLIDA: Well?

ARNHOLM: —your answer to me would have been different?

ELLIDA: It's hard to say; my answer to Wangel was different, wasn't it?

ARNHOLM: But—I don't understand; what's the point in telling me this now—?

ELLIDA (*Rises and moves about in restless agitation*): I must confide in someone! No—stay where you are!

ARNHOLM: You mean—your husband doesn't know—?

ELLIDA: I told him when he first asked me to marry him that at one time I had been bound to someone else. He never tried to find out any more about it, and since then we've neither of us men-

tioned it. It was sheer madness in any case. And then, it all
ended so abruptly. In a way—that is.

ARNHOLM (*Rises*): Only in a way? Not entirely?

ELLIDA: Yes, yes—entirely, my dear Arnholm. I know what you
must be thinking—but it's nothing like that, I assure you. It's
hard to understand—I couldn't possibly explain it. You'd either
think me ill—or raving mad—

ARNHOLM: Ellida—Mrs. Wangel—you must tell me the whole
story! I insist!

ELLIDA: Very well—I'll try. But you're such a sane, well-balanced
man— You'd never be able to realize what— (*Looks off stage
and breaks off suddenly*) Wait! Someone's coming. Some other
time. (LYNGSTRAND *appears from the road left and enters the
garden. He wears a flower in his buttonhole and carries a large
bouquet wrapped in paper and tied with silk ribbons. He stops,
hesitating by the veranda steps.*)

ELLIDA (*From the arbor*): Are you looking for the girls, Mr.
Lyngstrand?

LYNGSTRAND (*Turning*): Oh—you're there, Mrs. Wangel. (*Bows
and goes towards her*) No—as a matter of fact I wasn't. I was
looking for you. You did give me leave to call on you, and—

ELLIDA: Of course I did. You're always welcome here.

LYNGSTRAND: Thanks. This seemed a good opportunity—since
you're celebrating here today—

ELLIDA: So you know about it, do you?

LYNGSTRAND: Yes, indeed. That's why— May I offer you these
flowers, Mrs. Wangel?

ELLIDA (*Smiles*): How lovely, Mr. Lyngstrand! How kind of you!
But here's Professor Arnholm—you should give them to him.
You see, it's in his honor—

LYNGSTRAND (*Looks from one to the other puzzled*): I'm sorry—I
don't know this gentleman. It's just—I meant them as a birthday
present, Mrs. Wangel.

ELLIDA: Birthday? You're mistaken, Mr. Lyngstrand. It's nobody's birthday here today.

LYNGSTRAND: Oh yes, it is! (*With a quiet smile*) I know all about it;
but I didn't realize it was such a secret.

ELLIDA: Know all about what, Mr. Lyngstrand?

LYNGSTRAND: About your birthday—that today is your birthday, Mrs. Wangel!

ELLIDA: *My* birthday?

ARNHOLM (*Looks at her inquiringly*): Today? Surely not.

ELLIDA (*To* LYNGSTRAND): Whatever made you think that?

LYNGSTRAND: It was something Miss Hilde said. You see, I was here a little while ago, and I couldn't help asking about all the flowers—and why the flag was flying—

ELLIDA: Yes? Well?

LYNGSTRAND: And Miss Hilde said: "It's because of Mother's birthday."

ELLIDA: Ah—I see!

ARNHOLM (*Exchanges a glance with* ELLIDA): Well—since the young man's found out about it, Mrs. Wangel—

ELLIDA: Of course—since you've found out about it—

LYNGSTRAND (*Offers the bouquet again*): May I offer my congratulations—

ELLIDA (*Takes the flowers*): Many, many thanks. Do sit down a moment, Mr. Lyngstrand. (ELLIDA, ARNHOLM *and* LYNGSTRAND *sit down in the arbor*) This business of my birthday—was to have been kept secret, Mr. Arnholm.

ARNHOLM: So I see. We outsiders weren't supposed to know about it!

ELLIDA (*Lays the bouquet on the table*): That's right. Outsiders weren't supposed to know.

LYNGSTRAND: I won't say a word to anyone—I promise.

ELLIDA: Oh—it's not as important as all that. But tell me about yourself. I think you're looking better than you did.

LYNGSTRAND: I'm getting along very nicely, thank you. And next year—if I can manage to go South—

ELLIDA: The girls told me that's what you hope to do—

LYNGSTRAND: Yes. I have a patron in Bergen who is interested in helping me. He's promised to send me there.

ELLIDA: How did you run across him?

LYNGSTRAND: It was a great bit of luck. I happened to be employed on one of his ships, you see—

ELLIDA: Really? Did you want to be a sailor?

LYNGSTRAND: No; far from it! But when my mother died Father didn't want me hanging about the house—so he sent me to sea. On the voyage home we were shipwrecked in the English Channel. It was the best thing that could have happened to me.

ARNHOLM: How do you mean?

LYNGSTRAND: I was in the icy water for hours before they rescued me—and this trouble started in my chest. I was forbidden to go to sea again. It was a great bit of luck for me!

ARNHOLM: Is that the way you look at it?

LYNGSTRAND: Yes, of course. After all—this lung condition isn't dangerous; and now I'll be able to become a sculptor—I always dreamed of that. Modeling in clay is wonderful; to feel it taking shape under one's fingers!

ELLIDA: What do you want to model? Mermen and mermaids? Vikings, perhaps?

LYNGSTRAND: No—nothing like that. As soon as I can manage it, I plan to start on a big piece of work—a group, as they call it.

ELLIDA: I see. What sort of a group?

LYNGSTRAND: I want to try and express something I once experienced.

ARNHOLM: A good idea. Stick to the things you really know.

ELLIDA: But what is it to be?

LYNGSTRAND: The main figure is that of a young woman—a sailor's wife. She's sleeping, but it's a restless sleep—tormented by dreams. I believe I can make it quite clear that she's dreaming.

ARNHOLM: Is that all?

LYNGSTRAND: Oh, no. There's to be another figure—a sort of phantom, you might call it. It's her husband; she's been unfaithful to him while he was away—and now he's drowned.

ARNHOLM: You mean he—?

ELLIDA: Drowned?

LYNGSTRAND: Yes—drowned at sea. But the strange thing is that he's come home all the same. It's the middle of the night, and he stands there by the bed looking down at her. The water is dripping from his hair and from his clothes. He should look as though he'd just been hauled out of the sea.

ELLIDA (*Leans back in her chair*): What a strange idea! (*Closes her eyes*) I can see it vividly.

ARNHOLM: But my dear Mr.—Mr.—I thought you said it was something you'd experienced?

LYNGSTRAND: So I have—in a way.

ARNHOLM: Seen a dead man come to—?

LYNGSTRAND: I didn't mean I'd actually experienced it- -not literally, that is. But still—

ELLIDA (*With eager animation*): Tell me more about it! I'd like to understand it thoroughly.

ARNHOLM (*Smiles*): Quite in your line, isn't it? Anything to do with the magic of the sea!

ELLIDA: How did it happen, Mr. Lyngstrand?

LYNGSTRAND: Well, you see—we were sailing from a town called Halifax, and we had to leave our boatswain behind—laid up in a hospital. We took on an American instead. This new boatswain—

ELLIDA: The American?

LYNGSTRAND: Yes. One day he borrowed a whole lot of old newspapers from the captain; he wanted to learn Norwegian he said. He was always poring over them.

ELLIDA: Well?

LYNGSTRAND: One night there was a violent storm. All hands were on deck—all except the boatswain and me. He'd sprained his ankle and couldn't walk; I was sick and lying in my bunk. He sat there in the fo'c'sle, poring over one of the old newspapers as usual—

ELLIDA: Yes? Yes?

LYNGSTRAND: Suddenly he let out a kind of roar; I looked at him and his face was as white as chalk. Then he crumpled the paper in his hands and tore it into a thousand pieces. But he did it quietly; quite quietly.

ELLIDA Did he speak? Did he say anything?

LYNGSTRAND: Not at first. But after a while he said, as if to himself: "Married. Married another man while I was away."

ELLIDA (*Closes her eyes and says half to herself*): He said that, did he?

LYNGSTRAND: Yes. And the strange thing is, he said it in perfect Norwegian. I remember thinking what a gift for languages he must have had.

ELLIDA: And after that? What happened then?

LYNGSTRAND: The strangest thing of all. I'll never be able to forget it. He added—and he said this very quietly too—:"She's mine and she always will be. I shall go back and find her. Even were I to drown I should rise up from the bottom of the sea to claim her; and she would have to follow me."

ELLIDA (*Pours herself a glass of water. Her hand trembles*): Pah! It's stifling here today!

LYNGSTRAND: And there was such intensity—such power—in the way he said this, I felt sure he was actually capable of doing it.

ELLIDA: What became of him? Do you know?

LYNGSTRAND: He's dead, Mrs. Wangel. I'm sure of that.

ELLIDA (*Rapidly*): What makes you think so?

LYNGSTRAND: It was just after this that we were wrecked in the Channel. I got off in the longboat with the captain and five others. The mate and another man went in the dinghy—and the American went with them.

ELLIDA: And nothing's been heard of them since?

LYNGSTRAND: Not a word, Mrs. Wangel. That's why I'd so much like to translate this story into a work of art; the unfaithful wife, and her husband who comes back from the depths of the sea to take revenge. I see them both so clearly.

ELLIDA: So do I. (*She rises*) Come— Shall we go inside? Or we might join Wangel. It's stifling here. (*She goes out of the arbor.*)

LYNGSTRAND (*Who has also risen*): I'm afraid I must be going. I only looked in for a moment to wish you a happy birthday.

ELLIDA: Well—if you must— (*Shakes hands with him*) Goodbye, and thanks for the flowers.

(LYNGSTRAND *bows and goes out through the gate and off left.*)

ARNHOLM (*Rises and joins* ELLIDA): I'm afraid this has upset you, Mrs. Wangel.

ELLIDA: Yes, in a way—although—

ARNHOLM: Still—it's no more than might have been expected.

ELLIDA (*Looks at him bewildered*): Expected?

ARNHOLM: So it seems to me.

ELLIDA: Expect someone to come back from the dead?

ARNHOLM: What do you mean? Don't tell me it's that absurd story—!

ELLIDA: Not so absurd, perhaps.

ARNHOLM: Is that what has upset you? This nonsense about a dead man? I thought of course—

ELLIDA: What did you think?

ARNHOLM: I thought you were just pretending to be moved by that because you were upset about this birthday celebration. It surely must distress you to find that your husband and his children still live in a world of memories in which you have no share.

ELLIDA: Oh, no. That can't be helped. Wangel doesn't belong to me alone; I've no right to expect it.

ARNHOLM: I think you have.

ELLIDA: I haven't; that's the point. I have my memories too. A life of memories in which *they* can have no share.

ARNHOLM: You! (*In a low voice*) Are you implying—? Don't you—Don't you really love your husband?

ELLIDA: Yes! I do! I've grown to love him with all my heart. That's what makes it all so dreadful—so confusing—so unthinkable!

ARNHOLM: Tell me what's troubling you. You *must* confide in me!

ELLIDA: I can't—I can't! Not now. Some other time, perhaps.

BOLETTE (*Comes out onto the veranda and down into the garden*): Here comes Father—he's back from the office. Couldn't we all go and sit inside?

ELLIDA: Yes, let's.

WANGEL (*Enters with* HILDE *round the house from the left; he has changed his clothes*): Now I'm a free man again! How about a nice cool drink?

ELLIDA: Just a moment. (*She goes back to the arbor and fetches the bouquet.*)

HILDE: What lovely flowers! Where did you get them?

ELLIDA: From Mr. Lyngstrand, Hilde dear.

HILDE (*With a start*): Lyngstrand!

BOLETTE (*Uneasily*): Was he here again?

ELLIDA (*With a half smile*): Yes, he came back to bring these. They're a birthday present.

BOLETTE (*With a glance at* HILDE): Oh—!

HILDE (*Mutters*): The little beast!

WANGEL (*In acute embarrassment, to* ELLIDA): You see, darling—it's just that—

ELLIDA: Come along, girls! Let's put my flowers in water with the others. (*She goes onto the veranda.*)

BOLETTE (*Softly to* HILDE): You see? She's really very kind.

HILDE (*Angrily. Under her breath*): It's all put on! She's playing up to Father!

WANGEL (*Who has followed* ELLIDA *to the veranda; presses her hand*): Thank you! Thank you, my dear!

ELLIDA (*Arranging the flowers*): Nonsense! It's only right that I should join you in celebrating—Mother's birthday!

ARNHOLM: Hm— (*He joins* WANGEL *and* ELLIDA. BOLETTE *and* HILDE *remain in the garden.*)

CURTAIN

ACT TWO

SCENE: *In Prospect Park; a wooded height behind the town. A cairn of stones stands in the background supporting a weather vane. Large stones for seats are placed round the vane and in the foreground. Far below in the background one sees the outer fjord, with islands and jutting promontories. The open sea is not visible. It is twilight on a clear summer night. The sky is tinged with orange over the mountain peaks in the far distance. The sound of singing is heard faintly from the lower slopes on the right.*

Young people from the town, ladies and gentlemen come in couples from the right, pass the vane conversing familiarly and go out to the left. Shortly afterwards BALLESTED *appears, acting as guide to a party of foreign tourists. He is loaded with the ladies' shawls and satchels.*

BALLESTED (*Points upward with his stick*): Sehen Sie, meine Herrschaften—over there *liegt eine andere* height. *Das willen wir* also *besteigen, und so herunter*— (*He continues in English and leads the party out to the right.*)

(HILDE *comes quickly up the slope on the right and looks backward. Presently* BOLETTE *comes up the same way.*)

BOLETTE: Hilde! Why do you insist on running away from Lyngstrand?

HILDE: That snail's pace drives me mad. Look at him! Look at him creeping up the hill!

BOLETTE: He's very ill, remember.

HILDE: Do you think it's really serious?

BOLETTE: I'm sure it is.

HILDE: Father examined him today. I wonder what he thought.

BOLETTE: He told me. It's hardening of the lungs or something. Father says he hasn't long to live.

HILDE: Is that what he said? I thought as much!

BOLETTE: Now don't go saying anything to *him!*

HILDE: Of course not! (*Drops her voice*) Look at little Hans crawling up the slope! Wouldn't you know he'd have a name like Hans? He looks just like it!

BOLETTE (*In a whisper*): Now behave yourself! I warn you! (LYNGSTRAND *enters from the right carrying a parasol.*)

LYNGSTRAND: I'm so sorry! I can't seem to keep up with you.

HILDE: You've taken to using a parasol I see.

LYNGSTRAND: It's your mother's. I'd forgotten my stick, so she lent me this instead.

BOLETTE: Are Father and the others still down there?

LYNGSTRAND: Yes; your father went into the restaurant a moment, and the others are outside listening to the music. They're coming up here a little later on your mother said.

HILDE (*Stands and stares at him*): You're quite exhausted, aren't you?

LYNGSTRAND: I am a little tired. I'd better sit down for a bit. (*Sits on a rock downstage right*.)

HILDE (*Stands in front of him*): There's to be a dance tonight down by the bandstand. Have you heard?

LYNGSTRAND: I heard it mentioned, yes.

HILDE: Do you like dancing?

BOLETTE (*Who is picking wild flowers*): Hilde! Do let Mr. Lyngstrand get his breath!

LYNGSTRAND: I don't know. I think I might like it very much.

HILDE: Haven't you ever learned?

LYNGSTRAND: As a matter of fact I haven't, but that isn't what I meant. I'm not allowed to—on account of my chest, you know.

HILDE: Oh yes! That "weakness" as you call it.

LYNGSTRAND: Yes—that's it.

HILDE: It must make you very unhappy, doesn't it?

LYNGSTRAND: No, not really. (*Smiles*) I think it's due to that that people are so very kind to me.

HILDE: And, besides—it isn't really serious.

LYNGSTRAND: Not in the least. Your father didn't seem to think so either.

HILDE: All you need's that trip abroad—and then you'll be quite well again.

LYNGSTRAND: Quite well! I'm sure of that.

BOLETTE (*Brings him the flowers*): Here's a boutonniere for you, Mr. Lyngstrand.

LYNGSTRAND: Oh, thank you, Miss Bolette! How very kind of you.

HILDE (*Looking down off right*): Here they come now.

BOLETTE (*Also looking down*): I wonder if they know the path. No! They're going the wrong way.

LYNGSTRAND (*Rises*): I'll run down to the turn and call them back.

HILDE: You'll have to give a good shout or they won't hear you.

BOLETTE: Don't go! You'll get so tired again.

LYNGSTRAND: Going downhill's easy! (*He goes off right*.)

HILDE: "Downhill" says he! (*Watches him*) He's actually running!

He forgets he'll have to climb all the way up again!

BOLETTE: Poor thing—

HILDE: If Lyngstrand proposed to you, would you accept him?

BOLETTE: Are you crazy?!

HILDE: I mean—if he didn't have this "weakness" in his chest? And if he weren't going to die so soon? Would you?

BOLETTE: I think I'll let you have him.

HILDE: No thank you! He can't even support himself. He hasn't a penny to his name.

BOLETTE: Why are you so interested in him, then?

HILDE: It's this "weakness" of his. It fascinates me.

BOLETTE: But you're not a bit sorry for him, are you?

HILDE: No, I'm not. But it intrigues me.

BOLETTE: What do you mean?

HILDE: It's fun to watch him; to make him say it isn't serious. I like to hear him tell about his plans; about going abroad and becoming a great sculptor. He's so confident—so pleased with everything. And all the time I know nothing will ever come of it; nothing can possibly come of it—because he won't live long enough. It's absolutely thrilling!

BOLETTE: Thrilling!

HILDE: Yes, thrilling! Why shouldn't I say so? I find it absolutely thrilling!

BOLETTE: What a beast you are, Hilde!

HILDE: That's what I want to be. Out of spite! (*Looks down*) Here they come at last! Look at Arnholm—he doesn't like climbing either! (*Turns around*) By the way—do you know what I noticed while we were having lunch?

BOLETTE: No—what?

HILDE: His hair's beginning to fall out! He's quite bald on top.

BOLETTE: What nonsense! That's not true!

HILDE: Oh yes it is! And he has awful wrinkles round his eyes. How could you ever have been in love with him, Bolette!

BOLETTE (*Smiling*): It does seem funny, doesn't it? I remember once crying my heart out because he said Bolette was an ugly name.

HILDE: You didn't! (*Looks down again*) Look! Just look at this!

Arnholm and the Lady from the Sea! She seems very taken up with him. Do you suppose there's anything between them?

BOLETTE: You ought to be ashamed, Hilde—saying a thing like that! Just as we were getting along so well—

HILDE: Don't fool yourself, my girl! We'll never get along. She's not our sort—and she doesn't like us either. God knows what Father ever saw in her. I wouldn't be surprised if she went mad one of these days.

BOLETTE: Mad! Whatever put that into your head?

HILDE: It's quite possible, you know. After all, her mother died a lunatic—I know that for a fact.

BOLETTE: Where do you pick up such things? For God's sake keep your mouth shut! Try and behave—for Father's sake, Hilde! Do you hear?

(WANGEL, ELLIDA, ARNHOLM and LYNGSTRAND *come up the path from the right*.)

ELLIDA (*Pointing towards the background*): It's right out there!

ARNHOLM: Of course. It must be.

ELLIDA: That's where the sea is.

BOLETTE (*To* ARNHOLM): It's pretty up here, isn't it?

ARNHOLM: Beautiful! A glorious view!

WANGEL: Did you never come up here before?

ARNHOLM: No never. It was inaccessible in my time; there wasn't even a path, as I remember.

WANGEL: That's true—it was a wilderness then. All this has been developed in the last few years.

BOLETTE: The view's even finer over there. They call that Pilot's Peak.

WANGEL: How about going there, Ellida?

ELLIDA (*Sits down on a rock stage right*): You others go if you like. I think I'll stay here for a while.

WANGEL: Then I'll stay with you. The girls will show you around, Arnholm, if you care to see the sights.

BOLETTE: Would you like to, Mr. Arnholm?

ARNHOLM: I'd be delighted. Is there a path all the way to the top?

BOLETTE: Yes, a nice wide one.

HILDE: People can even walk arm in arm on it!

ARNHOLM (*Jokingly*): Can they indeed, Miss Hilde! (*To* BO-
LETTE) Let's see if she's right, shall we?

BOLETTE (*Repressing a smile*): If you like.
(*They go off left arm in arm.*)

HILDE (*To* LYNGSTRAND): Shall we go too—?

LYNGSTRAND: Arm-in-arm—?

HILDE: Why not? I've no objection.

LYNGSTRAND (*Takes her arm and laughs delightedly*): This *is* fun,
isn't it?

HILDE: Fun?

LYNGSTRAND: It's almost as if we were engaged!

HILDE: Don't tell me it's the first time you've given your arm to a
lady, Mr. Lyngstrand! (*They go out left.*)

WANGEL (*Stands upstage beside the landmark*): It's nice to be
alone for a little while, Ellida.

ELLIDA: Yes. Come here and sit beside me.

WANGEL: How peaceful it is. Now we can talk.

ELLIDA: What about?

WANGEL: About you. About us. We can't go on like this, Ellida.

ELLIDA: How do you mean?

WANGEL: We must have faith in one another. We must be
close—as we used to be.

ELLIDA: I wish that were possible—but I'm afraid it's not.

WANGEL: I believe I understand. From certain things you've
said—I think I know what's wrong.

ELLIDA: You don't. You can't! Don't say you understand.

WANGEL: But I do. I know how honest, how loyal you are—

ELLIDA: Loyal—yes. That's true, I think—

WANGEL: The only relationship that could make you happy—that
could make you feel secure—must be complete and perfect.

ELLIDA (*Looks at him intently*): Well?

WANGEL: Being a man's second wife is hard for you, Ellida.

ELLIDA: What makes you say that—just now?

WANGEL: I've often suspected it, and what happened today convinced me I was right. I know you were upset by that birthday
celebration the children had arranged. You blamed me for it too,
I think—and perhaps in a way you're right. It's hard for a man to

wipe out old memories—at least it is for me. That's not my nature.

ELLIDA: I know. I know that very well.

WANGEL: But you're mistaken all the same. You know, Ellida —I believe the thought of the children's mother has become almost an obsession with you. You think of her as still alive; you feel her invisible presence in our midst; and you're tormented because you imagine I divide my love equally between you. You've come to see something almost immoral in our relationship; that's why you can no longer bring yourself to live with me as my wife.

ELLIDA: Is that how you see it, Wangel? You've come to that conclusion?

WANGEL: Yes, I have. Today it all became quite clear to me.

ELLIDA: Quite clear, you say. No! You mustn't believe that.

WANGEL: Oh, I know there's more to it than that.

ELLIDA: What more?

WANGEL: I know you find these surroundings unendurable. The mountains weigh on you and crush your spirit. The light is not intense enough, nor the horizon wide enough. The air here is not potent or bracing enough for you.

ELLIDA: It's true. Day and night, winter and summer, I can never shake off this longing for the sea. I'm homesick for it.

WANGEL: I know, Ellida dear. (*Lays his hand on her head*) That's why I've decided to take my poor sick child back home again.

ELLIDA: What do you mean?

WANGEL: We'll move away from here.

ELLIDA: Move away!

WANGEL: Yes; to the open sea—where you can have the sort of home you long for.

ELLIDA: That's impossible! You mustn't think of that. You could never be happy anywhere but here.

WANGEL: That's as it may be. Besides—do you think I could ever be happy without you?

ELLIDA: But I'm here—and I shall go on being here. You know I'm yours, Wangel.

WANGEL: Are you mine, Ellida?

ELLIDA: As for going away—you mustn't talk about that any more. Your work is here; your life is here. This place means everything to you!

WANGEL: We're moving all the same. My mind's made up, Ellida.

ELLIDA: What would we gain by it?

WANGEL: You would regain your health and peace of mind.

ELLIDA: I wonder. And you? You must think of yourself. What would *you* gain by it?

WANGEL: I would regain you, my darling.

ELLIDA: You wouldn't, Wangel! You wouldn't! That's what's so pitiful—so heartbreaking!

WANGEL: We shall find out; for I insist on getting you away from here—the sooner the better. My mind's made up, I tell you!

ELLIDA: No! I won't have it! In that case—God help me—I'd rather tell you everything.

WANGEL: I wish you would, Ellida.

ELLIDA: I won't have your life made miserable on my account. And I assure you it would do no good.

WANGEL: Now tell me everything. You've promised!

ELLIDA: I'll try. I don't know if I can put it into words. Sit here beside me. (*They sit down on a rock.*)

WANGEL: Well, Ellida?

ELLIDA: Do you remember that day you came and asked me to be your wife? You spoke of your first marriage—very honestly and simply. You told me how happy it had been.

WANGEL: Yes. So it was.

ELLIDA: I know, dear. I only mention it because I want you to remember that I was honest with you too. I told you then about another man; a man I'd been engaged to—in a way.

WANGEL: In a way—?

ELLIDA: Yes. In a way. It lasted such a little while, you see. He had to leave—and shortly after that, I broke it off. I told you all about it.

WANGEL: Why do you speak of him now, Ellida? It had nothing to do with me. I've never even asked you who he was.

ELLIDA: That's true, you haven't. You've always spared my feelings.

WANGEL (*Smiles*): And, after all—it wasn't very difficult to guess his name.

ELLIDA: His name?

WANGEL: Yes. There weren't many to choose from up at Skjoldvik. There was actually only one man who—

ELLIDA: You think it was Arnholm, I suppose.

WANGEL: Well—wasn't it?

ELLIDA: No.

WANGEL: Not Arnholm? Then—I can't imagine—

ELLIDA: Do you remember one year late in the fall, a large American ship came into Skjoldvik harbor for repairs?

WANGEL: I remember very well; the captain was found murdered in his cabin. They wanted a post-mortem—they sent for me.

ELLIDA: Yes—so they did.

WANGEL: The second mate had killed him—so they said.

ELLIDA: But no one knew for certain. It was never proved against him.

WANGEL: There wasn't much doubt about it. Why else should he have drowned himself?

ELLIDA: He didn't drown himself. He sailed on another ship bound for the North.

WANGEL (*Amazed*): How do you know that?

ELLIDA (*With an effort*): Because he's the man I was engaged to.

WANGEL: What are you saying! That's impossible!

ELLIDA: All the same it's true. He was the man.

WANGEL: But how could you have done such a thing, Ellida? Become engaged to a man like that—an utter stranger! What was his name?

ELLIDA: He called himself Freeman then. But later, in his letters, he used the name of Johnston—Alfred Johnston.

WANGEL: Where was he from?

ELLIDA: He said he came from Finmark. But he was born in Finland and came across the border as a child—with his father, I think he said.

WANGEL: He was a Quinn, then.

ELLIDA: I believe that's what they're called.

WANGEL: What else do you know about him?

ELLIDA: Just that he went to sea when he was still a boy. He'd made many long voyages.

WANGEL: Nothing else?

ELLIDA: No. We didn't talk much about that sort of thing.

WANGEL: What did you talk about?

ELLIDA: Mostly about the sea.

WANGEL: Ah—! The sea!

ELLIDA: About storms and calms. Dark nights on the Ocean—and bright sunny days as well. But mostly about whales and porpoises, and the seals that bask on the reefs in the warm sunshine. And we talked about the sea birds too—the gulls and eagles. It was strange—as we talked I always felt that he was part of all these things.

WANGEL: How about you—?

ELLIDA: I felt somehow as though I were part of them too.

WANGEL: I see. And so you became engaged to him.

ELLIDA: Yes. He said I had to.

WANGEL: Had to? Had you no will of your own?

ELLIDA: Not while he was there. Then—afterwards—it all seemed so incredible.

WANGEL: Did you see him often?

ELLIDA: Not very often. He came out to have a look at the lighthouse—that's how I got to know him. After that we used to meet occasionally. But when the thing about the captain happened, he had to go away.

WANGEL: Tell me about that.

ELLIDA: Very early one morning—just before dawn—I got a note from him. He told me to come to him at Bratthammer—you know, the headland between Skjoldvik and the lighthouse.

WANGEL: Yes—I know it well.

ELLIDA: I was to come at once, he said. He had to talk to me.

WANGEL: And you went?

ELLIDA: I had to—I couldn't help it. Then he told me that during the night he'd stabbed the captain.

WANGEL: He told you that himself? He actually admitted it?

ELLIDA: Yes. But he'd only done what was right, he said.

WANGEL: What did he mean—right? What reason did he give?

ELLIDA: He wouldn't say. He said it would be wrong for me to hear about such things.

WANGEL: And you believed him?

ELLIDA: It never occurred to me not to. Still—he had to get away. And just as he was about to say good-bye to me—you'll never believe what he did then.

WANGEL: Tell me!

ELLIDA: He took a key ring from his pocket; then he took from his finger a ring he used to wear. I had a small ring on my finger; he slipped it off, put both rings onto the key ring—and said: "Now together we will be wedded to the sea."

WANGEL: Wedded—?

ELLIDA: That's what he said. Then, with all his might, he threw the key ring with our two rings on it far out into the deep water.

WANGEL: And you, Ellida? You agreed to this?

ELLIDA: Yes—can you believe it? I felt at the time as though it had to be. But then, thank God, he went away!

WANGEL: And once he'd gone—?

ELLIDA: I soon came to my senses then. I saw how utterly absurd—how meaningless it had all been.

WANGEL: But you said something about letters. Did you hear from him?

ELLIDA: Yes, I heard from him. Only a few lines the first time—from Archangel. He just said he was going to America. He told me where to write to him.

WANGEL: And did you write?

ELLIDA: At once. I simply said that it was all over between us. That he must no longer think of me—just as I would never think of him.

WANGEL: And he wrote again in spite of that?

ELLIDA: Yes, he wrote again.

WANGEL: What was his answer?

ELLIDA: He didn't refer to what I'd said. It was as though I'd never broken off with him. He told me quite calmly that I must wait for him. When he was ready for me he would let me know, and then I was to go to him at once.

WANGEL: He wouldn't release you then?

ELLIDA: No. Of course, I wrote again. I repeated what I'd said, almost word for word—but in even stronger terms.

WANGEL: And then did he give in?

ELLIDA: Oh no, far from it. He wrote quite calmly as before. Not a word about my breaking off with him. Then I realized it was useless, and I never wrote to him again.

WANGEL: And you didn't hear from him either?

ELLIDA: Yes. I had three more letters from him after that. The first was from California. The second was from China. The last letter I had was from Australia. He said he was going to the gold mines. I've not heard from him since.

WANGEL: He seems to have had great power over you, Ellida.

ELLIDA: Yes. He was a terrifying man!

WANGEL: Don't think about it any more. Never, dearest Ellida! Promise me that. Once we get you away from the fjords, out by the open sea, the tang of the salt air will cure you—

ELLIDA: Don't even think of that, Wangel! Don't even speak of it! It wouldn't be any use. It wouldn't help me to escape.

WANGEL: Escape from what? What do you mean, my dearest?

ELLIDA: My fear of him. The strange power he has over me—

WANGEL: But you escaped from that long ago—when you broke off with him. It's all over long ago.

ELLIDA (*Jumps up*): But it's not over, you see!

WANGEL: Not over!

ELLIDA: No! It isn't over—and I'm afraid it never will be!

WANGEL (*In a choked voice*): You've never been able to forget this man?

ELLIDA: I had forgotten him. And then, suddenly, it was as if he had come back again.

WANGEL: How long ago was that?

ELLIDA: About three years ago—a little more, perhaps. It was while I was carrying the child.

WANGEL: During that time! I see! That explains many things, Ellida.

ELLIDA: You're wrong, believe me! There *can* be no explanation for this thing that's taken hold of me.

WANGEL (*Looks at her sorrowfully*): To think that all these years you've loved another man!

ELLIDA: That's not true. I love no one but you.

WANGEL (*In a low voice*): Yet for a long time now, you've refused to be a wife to me. Why is that, Ellida?

ELLIDA: The thought of that strange man fills me with terror.

WANGEL: Terror?

ELLIDA: Yes, terror. I think only the Ocean could fill one with such an overwhelming dread. You see, Wangel—

(*The young people from the town come back from the left, bow, and go out right.* ARNHOLM, BOLETTE, HILDE, *and* LYNGSTRAND *follow them.*)

BOLETTE (*As they pass by*): You're still here, are you?

ELLIDA: It's been so cool and pleasant.

ARNHOLM: We're going down to dance.

WANGEL: Good. We'll join you later.

HILDE: Good-bye for now.

ELLIDA: Mr. Lyngstrand—wait a minute, will you?

(LYNGSTRAND *waits.* ARNHOLM, BOLETTE *and* HILDE *go off right.*)

ELLIDA (*To* LYNGSTRAND): Are you going to dance too?

LYNGSTRAND: No, Mrs. Wangel. I think I'd better not.

ELLIDA: That's right. You're wise. That weakness in your lungs—you haven't quite recovered yet.

LYNGSTRAND: Not quite—that's true.

ELLIDA (*With some hesitation*): How long ago is it since you were on that voyage—?

LYNGSTRAND: When this lung trouble began, you mean?

ELLIDA: Yes. When you were shipwrecked—

LYNGSTRAND: Let's see—a little over three years, it must have been.

ELLIDA: Three years.

LYNGSTRAND: Yes—just about. We left America in February and ran into the equinoctial gales. The wreck happened in March.

ELLIDA (*Looks at* WANGEL): You see—that was the time—

WANGEL: But, Ellida dear—?

ELLIDA: Don't let us keep you, Mr. Lyngstrand. Go and join the others. But don't dance, will you?

LYNGSTRAND: No. I'll just look on. (*He goes out right.*)

WANGEL: Why did you ask about that voyage, Ellida?

ELLIDA: Johnston was on that voyage. I'm certain of it.

WANGEL: What makes you think that?

ELLIDA (*Without answering*): That's when he found out I'd married someone else. That's when it first came over me.

WANGEL: The terror?

ELLIDA: Yes. At times—quite suddenly—he seems to stand before me. He stands a little to one side. He never looks at me. He just stands there.

WANGEL: How does he appear to you, Ellida?

ELLIDA: Just as he did last time I saw him.

WANGEL: Ten years ago?

ELLIDA: Yes, at Bratthammer. The thing I see most clearly is a bluish-white pearl—a scarfpin he always wore. It's like the eye of a dead fish. It seems to glare at me.

WANGEL: Ellida! For God's sake—! You're really ill, my darling. More ill than you know.

ELLIDA: Yes. Help me, Wangel! Help me if you can. I'm afraid this will destroy me.

WANGEL: And you've lived with this for three whole years. Lived with this secret torment. Why didn't you confide in me?

ELLIDA: I couldn't—don't you see? Not until now—not till it became necessary for your own sake. If I'd confided this much to you—I should have had to tell you about the most ghastly thing of all—ah! It's unspeakable!

WANGEL: Unspeakable—?

ELLIDA: Don't ask about it, Wangel! One more thing, and then I've done: the child's eyes. How can we ever solve that mystery?

WANGEL: That was just your imagination, Ellida dear. The child's eyes were completely normal.

ELLIDA: That's not true! How could you fail to see it? His eyes changed color with the sea. They were blue and calm on sunny days—just like the water. And in a storm they became dark and troubled. You may not have seen it, but I did.

WANGEL (*Humoring her*): Well—supposing it were so? What then?

ELLIDA (*Softly—closer to him*): I've seen eyes like that before.

WANGEL: When? Where?

ELLIDA: Ten years ago. At Bratthammer.

WANGEL (*Steps back*): What do you—?

ELLIDA (*Trembling. In a whisper*): The child had his eyes. The strange man's eyes.

WANGEL (*Cries out involuntarily*): Ellida—!

ELLIDA (*Clasps her head in her hands in despair*): Now perhaps you understand why I cannot—why I *dare* not live with you as your wife! (*She turns suddenly and runs off down the hill to the right.*)

WANGEL (*Hurries after her, calling*): Ellida—Ellida! My poor, tragic Ellida!

                                                                            CURTAIN

ACT THREE

SCENE: *A remote corner of* DR. WANGEL's *garden. It is a damp swampy place, overshadowed by large old trees. To the right is seen the edge of a stagnant pond. A low open fence separates the garden from the footpath and the fjord in the background. In the far distance beyond the fjord, a mountain range rises into peaks. It is late afternoon, almost evening.*

  BOLETTE *sits on a stone bench stage left sewing. A couple of books and a sewing basket lie beside her on the bench.* HILDE *and* LYNGSTRAND, *with fishing rods, stand at the edge of the pond.*

HILDE: Look! There's a great big one! Do stand still!

LYNGSTRAND (*Looking*): Where?

HILDE: There! Can't you see? And, look over there! God's truth—there's another one! (*Looks off through the trees*) Drat it! Here he comes—just in time to frighten them away!

BOLETTE· Who is it?

HILDE: Your dear tutor, my pet!

BOLETTE: What do you mean, my—?

HILDE: God knows he was never *mine!*

(ARNHOLM *enters from among the trees, right.*)

ARNHOLM: Don't tell me that pond has fish in it!

HILDE: Just the same old carp.

ARNHOLM: Are they still alive?

HILDE: They're tough old boys, they are! But it won't be long now! Some of them are about to meet their death!

ARNHOLM: I should think you'd have better luck in the fjord.

LYNGSTRAND: But there's something so mysterious about the pond!

HILDE: The pond is much more thrilling. Have you been in for a swim?

ARNHOLM: I just came from the bathhouse.

HILDE: You stay inside the ropes, I suppose.

ARNHOLM: Yes. I'm no great swimmer, I'm afraid.

HILDE: Can you swim on your back?

ARNHOLM: No.

HILDE: I can. (*To* LYNGSTRAND) Let's try over there on the other side.

(*They skirt the pond and go off right.*)

ARNHOLM (*Going closer to* BOLETTE): All by yourself, Bolette?

BOLETTE: I nearly always am.

ARNHOLM: Isn't your mother here?

BOLETTE: No. She went for a walk with Father.

ARNHOLM: How is she this afternoon?

BOLETTE: I really don't know. I forgot to ask.

ARNHOLM: What are your books?

BOLETTE: One's a book on plants; and the other's a geography.

ARNHOLM: Do you like that kind of reading?

BOLETTE: Yes, when I've time for it— My household duties come first, of course.

ARNHOLM: Doesn't your mother—your stepmother, I mean—help look after the house?

BOLETTE: No—that's my responsibility. I had to look after it during the two years Father was alone—and I've kept on ever since.

ARNHOLM: Then you're just as fond of reading as you used to be?

BOLETTE: Oh, yes. I read all the useful books I can lay my hands on. One should know something about the world, it seems to me. We're so isolated here—so cut off from everything.

ARNHOLM: You mustn't say that, Bolette dear.

BOLETTE: I can't help it. It's true. We live very much like those old carp there in the pond. In the fjord close by, great shoals of free fish sweep in and out, but the poor tame domestic fish know nothing about that; and they'll never be able to join in.

ARNHOLM: They probably wouldn't last long if they could.

BOLETTE: I don't see that that would matter much.

ARNHOLM: Besides this place is no longer isolated; not in the summer at all events. People from all over the world meet here—visitors are always passing through . It's become a kind of crossroads.

BOLETTE: You can afford to joke, seeing that you're a visitor yourself.

ARNHOLM: But I'm not joking!

BOLETTE: "Visitors from all over the world," "crossroads"—that's the sort of talk you hear in town; they're always saying things like that.

ARNHOLM: Yes—I must confess I've heard them!

BOLETTE: But there's not a word of truth in it! At least, it doesn't affect those of us who live here permanently. What difference does it make if "people from all over the world" pass through on their way to see the midnight sun? We never see it—there's no midnight sun for us! No! We're just stuck here in our carp pond!

ARNHOLM (*Sits beside her*): Bolette, dear—tell me—is there anything you really long to do?

BOLETTE: Yes—perhaps.

ARNHOLM: What is it?

BOLETTE: I long to get away from here.

ARNHOLM: That more than anything?

BOLETTE: I'd like the opportunity to study. I'd like to find out about all kinds of things.

ARNHOLM: I remember—when I was your tutor—your father often spoke of sending you to college.

BOLETTE: Poor Father! He says so many things—but when it actually comes to the point he— Father hasn't got much strength of character, you know.

ARNHOLM: You're right about that, I'm afraid. But have you never discussed this with him? Have you never told him how you felt?

BOLETTE: As a matter of fact, I haven't.

ARNHOLM: You ought to—before it's too late, Bolette. Why haven't you told him?

BOLETTE: I suppose it's because I have no strength of character either. I take after him in that.

ARNHOLM: Aren't you being a bit unfair to yourself?

BOLETTE: No, I don't think so. Besides—Father has so little time for me. I don't think he particularly wants to think about my future. He seems to shy away from it. He's so completely taken up with Ellida, you see.

ARNHOLM: With—? How do you mean?

BOLETTE: He and my stepmother— (*Breaking off*) Father and Mother are completely engrossed in one another.

ARNHOLM: All the more reason for you to get away from here.

BOLETTE: But I couldn't leave Father; I don't think I have the right.

ARNHOLM: You'll have to leave him sometime, Bolette dear; why put it off?

BOLETTE: Of course, I realize I'll have to leave him sometime. And I suppose I should think a little more about myself—try to get a job, or something. When Father goes I'll have no one to depend on. But poor Father—I dread the thought of leaving him.

ARNHOLM: Dread—?

BOLETTE: Yes. I dread it for his sake.

ARNHOLM: But what about your stepmother? She'd be here with him.

BOLETTE: That's true enough. But she's not like Mother was. She's not capable of taking hold of things. There's so much she doesn't see—or doesn't want to see. Perhaps she just doesn't want to bother. I don't know which it is.

ARNHOLM: Hm—I think I understand.

BOLETTE: Poor Father—he's so weak in lots of ways. You may

have noticed it yourself. He hasn't enough work to fill up all his time. And she's certainly no help to him. That's partly his own fault, I suppose.

ARNHOLM: In what way?

BOLETTE: Father wants to be surrounded by cheerful, happy faces. The house must be filled with joy and sunshine, he always says. So I'm afraid he very often allows her to take medicine that's harmful to her in the long run.

ARNHOLM: You really think so?

BOLETTE: I can't think otherwise; she's so very queer at times. (*Vehemently*) It does seem hard though, doesn't it, that I should have to stay home here! Especially as it doesn't really help Father at all. And, after all, I have a duty towards myself as well.

ARNHOLM: We must explore this whole matter very thoroughly, Bolette.

BOLETTE: Oh, what's the use! I suppose I'm destined to spend the rest of my days here in my carp pond!

ARNHOLM: Nonsense! That's entirely up to you.

BOLETTE: You really mean that?

ARNHOLM: Most definitely. Your future lies in your own hands.

BOLETTE: If only that were true—! You'd really be willing to put in a good word for me with Father?

ARNHOLM: That too, of course. But the main thing is that I should talk to you quite frankly—straight from the heart. (*Looks off left*) Sh! Don't let them notice anything. We'll go on talking presently. (ELLIDA *enters from the left. She wears no hat but has a scarf over her head and shoulders.*)

ELLIDA (*With nervous agitation*): It's nice here! It's lovely here!

ARNHOLM (*Rising*): Have you been for a walk?

ELLIDA: Yes; we had a wonderful walk—Wangel and I. Now we're going for a sail.

BOLETTE: Won't you sit down?

ELLIDA: No thanks. I don't feel like sitting down.

BOLETTE (*Moves over on the bench*): There's plenty of room here.

ELLIDA (*Walking about*): No, no! I can't sit down—I can't!

ARNHOLM: You seem much better; that walk has done you good.

ELLIDA: Yes! I feel marvellous! And I feel so happy! So safe. So safe and— (*Looks off left*) There's a big steamer coming in. What could it be?

BOLETTE (*Rises and looks off*): It must be the English ship.

ARNHOLM: They're dropping anchor by the buoy. Does she usually stop here?

BOLETTE: Only for half an hour; then she goes on farther up the fjord.

ELLIDA: And tomorrow out to sea again—out to the open sea. Right across the sea! Oh, to be able to sail on her! If one only could!

ARNHOLM: You've never been on a long sea voyage, have you, Mrs. Wangel?

ELLIDA: Never. Never in all my life. Only a few little trips in among the fjords.

BOLETTE (*With a sigh*): No! We have to stick to dry land, I'm afraid.

ARNHOLM: After all—that's where we belong.

ELLIDA: I don't believe that for a moment.

ARNHOLM: Why? We're surely land creatures, are we not?

ELLIDA: I don't believe it. I believe that if we had grown accustomed to live at sea—even in the sea, perhaps—we'd be much better people. Better and happier.

ARNHOLM: You really believe that?

ELLIDA: I'm convinced of it. I've discussed it with Wangel many times—

ARNHOLM: And what does *he* think?

ELLIDA: He thinks there might be something in it.

ARNHOLM (*Joking*): It's possible. But what's done is done. We chose the wrong path and became land beasts instead of sea beasts. I'm afraid it's too late to change it now!

ELLIDA: That's unfortunately true. I believe that people are instinctively aware of it; in an obscure way it weighs on them; fills them with sorrow—with a kind of anguish. Believe me—it's at the root of all our melancholy. I'm certain of it.

ARNHOLM: But, my dear Mrs. Wangel—I don't think the majority of people are so melancholy. On the contrary, it seems to me that most of them accept life cheerfully and easily—with a deep, uncomplicated sense of joy.

ELLIDA: That's not so—I assure you. It's merely a surface joy—the sort of joy one feels during the summer, when the days are long and bright. Underneath there's always the knowledge of the dark days to come. And that knowledge clouds our joy—like the clouds that sail over the fjord; one moment it's bathed in sunshine, then suddenly—

BOLETTE: Come now! Don't think such gloomy thoughts! Just now you were so gay and cheerful.

ELLIDA: It's true, I was. All this—it's so stupid of me. (*Looks round uneasily*) Why doesn't Wangel come? He promised me he would—and now there's no sign of him. Perhaps he's forgotten. Dear Mr. Arnholm, go and find him for me, will you?

ARNHOLM: Of course I will.

ELLIDA: Tell him to come to me at once. I can't see him any more—

ARNHOLM: Can't see him—?

ELLIDA: You wouldn't understand. When he's away from me I often can't remember what he looks like. It's as though I'd lost him— It's a dreadful feeling. Please go and find him!
(*She wanders over towards the pond.*)

BOLETTE (*To* ARNHOLM): I'll go with you. You might not know—

ARNHOLM: There's no need. I'll manage—

BOLETTE (*Under her breath*): I'm worried. I'm afraid he went aboard the steamer.

ARNHOLM: Why afraid?

BOLETTE: He usually goes to see if he can find any acquaintances among the passengers. And there's a refreshment bar on board—

ARNHOLM: Oh. We'd better go then.
(*He and* BOLETTE *go off left.* ELLIDA *stands a while gazing into the pond. From time to time she mutters a few broken phrases to herself. A stranger in traveling clothes enters from the left along the footpath beyond the fence. He has bushy reddish hair, and*

has a beard. He wears a Scotch cap and carries a traveling satchel slung across his shoulder by a strap.)

THE STRANGER (*Walks slowly along the fence and looks into the garden. He catches sight of* ELLIDA. *He stops and looks at her searchingly, intently; then says in a low voice*): Good evening, Ellida!

ELLIDA (*Turns round and cries out*): Ah, my dear—there you are at last!

STRANGER: Yes—at last.

ELLIDA (*Looks at him with astonishment and apprehension*): Who are you? Are you looking for someone?

STRANGER: You know I am, Ellida.

ELLIDA (*With a start*): What's this? You called me by my first name! Who are you looking for?

STRANGER: For you, of course.

ELLIDA (*Shaken*): Ah—! (*Stares at him, staggers backwards with a half-smothered cry*) The eyes! The eyes!

STRANGER: I see you begin to recognize me. I knew you at once, Ellida.

ELLIDA: The eyes! Don't look at me like that! I'll call for help!

STRANGER: Sh! Don't be frightened. I won't harm you.

ELLIDA (*Covers her eyes with her hands*): Don't look at me like that, I say!

STRANGER (*Leans his arms on the garden fence*): I came in on the English steamer.

ELLIDA (*Gives him a frightened look*): What do you want with me?

STRANGER: I promised to come as soon as I could—

ELLIDA: Go away! Go away again! You must never come here any more! I wrote you that everything was over between us! Everything! You know I did!

STRANGER (*Unperturbed; without answering her*): I wanted to come to you before. But I couldn't. At last I was able to manage it. And here I am.

ELLIDA: What do you want with me? What are you thinking of? What have you come for?

STRANGER: I've come to take you away with me, of course.

ELLIDA: Take me away! Is that why you've come?

STRANGER: Yes—naturally.

ELLIDA: But I'm married—surely you must know—

STRANGER: Yes—I know.

ELLIDA: And yet—in spite of that—you've come!

STRANGER: In spite of that.

ELLIDA (*Hides her head in her hands*): Oh, this is dreadful—! The Terror! Terror!

STRANGER: Don't you want to come with me?

ELLIDA (*Beside herself*): Don't look at me like that!

STRANGER: Don't you want to come with me, I asked you?

ELLIDA: No, no! I don't want to! Never! Never! I don't want to go with you, I tell you! I don't want to, and I can't. (*Lower*) I dare not, either.

STRANGER (*Climbs over the fence and comes into the garden*): Very well, Ellida. But I've one thing to say to you before I leave.

ELLIDA (*Tries to escape but cannot. She stands as though paralyzed with fear, leaning against a tree trunk by the pond*): Don't touch me! Don't come near me! Stay where you are! Don't touch me, I say!

STRANGER (*Cautiously takes a few steps towards her*): You mustn't be afraid of me, Ellida.

ELLIDA (*Puts her hands in front of her eyes*): Don't look at me like that!

STRANGER: Don't be afraid. Don't be afraid.

(DR. WANGEL *comes through the garden from the left. He speaks as he comes through the trees.*)

WANGEL: You've been waiting a long time—I'm sorry, darling!

ELLIDA (*Rushes to him and clings to his arm as she cries out*): Oh, Wangel! Save me! Save me—if you can!

WANGEL: Ellida! In God's name—

ELLIDA: Save me! He's here, Wangel! Don't you see?

WANGEL (*Looks at the* STRANGER): Who is this man? (*Goes towards him*) Who are you? What are you doing in this garden?

STRANGER (*Indicates* ELLIDA): I came to talk to her.

WANGEL: Indeed. Then I suppose it was you who—? (*To* ELLIDA) They told me at the house a strange man had been asking for you.

STRANGER: Yes, it was I.

WANGEL: Why do you want to see my wife? (*Turns*) Do you know him, Ellida?

ELLIDA (*Softly, wringing her hands*): Do I know him! Yes! I know him!

WANGEL: Well?

ELLIDA: It is he, Wangel! It is he! The man I told you of—!

WANGEL: What's that you say? (*Turns*) Are you Johnston? Are you the man who—?

STRANGER: Call me Johnston if you like. That's not my name though.

WANGEL: Isn't it?

STRANGER: Not any more.

WANGEL: Why do you wish to see my wife? What do you want of her? You know of course that the lighthouse keeper's daughter married long ago. And you must know who her husband is.

STRANGER: I've known that for three years or more.

ELLIDA (*Intently*): How did you hear of it?

STRANGER: I was on my way home—home to you. I came across an old newspaper—a local paper from this part of the country. In it I found the announcement of your marriage.

ELLIDA (*Gazing in front of her*): My marriage— So that was how—

STRANGER: It seemed very strange to me, Ellida. For the ceremony of the rings—that was a marriage too.

ELLIDA (*Buries her face in her hand*): Ah—!

WANGEL: How dare you—!

STRANGER: Had you forgotten that?

ELLIDA (*Feeling his gaze on her*): Don't look at me like that!

WANGEL (*Confronting him*): Kindly address yourself to me. Since you know the circumstances, what possible reason can you have for coming here?

STRANGER: I promised Ellida I would come to her as soon as possible.

WANGEL: Ellida—! What! Again!

STRANGER: And Ellida promised faithfully to wait for me.

WANGEL: How dare you call my wife by her first name! It's unendurable!

STRANGER: Perhaps. But she belongs to me.

WANGEL: To you! Of all the—!

ELLIDA (*Shrinking behind* WANGEL): Ah—! He'll never let me go!

WANGEL: You say she belongs to you!

STRANGER: Did she tell you the story of the rings? My ring and hers?

WANGEL: Of course she did. What of it? She broke off with you—you're well aware of that. You received her letters, didn't you?

STRANGER: The ceremony of the rings was a valid marriage ceremony—Ellida and I were fully agreed on that.

ELLIDA: No, no! I won't have it—do you hear? I never want to see you again—I want nothing more to do with you!

WANGEL: Are you insane? You don't expect to base any claim whatever on that nonsense!

STRANGER: No. In your sense of the word, I have no claim on her.

WANGEL: Then what do you plan to do? You don't imagine you can take her away by force—against her will!

STRANGER: What would be the good of that? She must come of her own free will, if she's to come at all.

ELLIDA (*Starts and cries out*): My own free will—!

WANGEL: You don't suppose—!

ELLIDA (*To herself*): My own free will—!

WANGEL: You're behaving like a madman! Go away—leave us alone! We've nothing more to say to you.

STRANGER (*Looks at his watch*): I must get back to the ship—it's almost time. (*A step nearer*) Well, Ellida— I've kept my part of the bargain. (*Closer still*) I've kept my word to you.

ELLIDA (*Imploringly, shrinking away*): Oh—! Don't touch me!

STRANGER: I give you till tomorrow night to think it over.

WANGEL: What is there to think over? Now get out of here!

STRANGER (*Still to* ELLIDA): I have to go up the fjord now with the steamer. I'll be back tomorrow night, then I'll see you again. Wait for me here in the garden. I prefer to settle this matter with you alone. You understand?

ELLIDA (*Softly, in a trembling voice*): You hear that, Wangel?

WANGEL: Don't worry, dearest. I shall prevent this visit.

STRANGER: Goodbye for now, Ellida. Tomorrow night, then.

ELLIDA (*In a tone of entreaty*): No, no! Not tomorrow night! Never again!

STRANGER: And if by then you've decided to come with me—

ELLIDA: Don't look at me like that!

STRANGER: See that you're ready for the journey.

WANGEL: Go back to the house, Ellida.

ELLIDA: I can't. Help me! Save me, Wangel!

STRANGER: But just remember, if you don't come with me tomorrow—then it will be over.

ELLIDA (*Looks at him, trembling*): Over? Forever?

STRANGER (*With a nod*): Forever. I shall never come back here. You'll not see me any more, and you won't hear from me either. I shall be dead to you, Ellida. Gone forever.

ELLIDA (*Breathes uneasily*): Ah—!

STRANGER: Think it over carefully. Good-bye. (*He climbs over the fence, stops, and says*) Be ready for the journey tomorrow night, Ellida. I shall come for you. (*He goes slowly and calmly along the footpath and off right.*)

ELLIDA (*Looks after him a moment*): Of my own free will, he said! Think of it. He said I was to go with him of my own free will.

WANGEL: Keep calm, my darling. He's gone now. You'll never see him again.

ELLIDA: How can you say that? He'll be here tomorrow night.

WANGEL: Let him come. He won't see you—I'll take good care of that.

ELLIDA (*Shakes her head*): You won't be able to prevent him.

WANGEL: Of course I shall. Rely on me.

ELLIDA (*Musing—without listening to him*): And after he's been here tomorrow night—? And after he's sailed away over the ocean—?

WANGEL: What then?

ELLIDA: I wonder, will he never—never come back again?

WANGEL: You can be certain of that, Ellida dear. What should he do here? He heard you say you would have nothing more to do with him. The matter's ended.

ELLIDA (*To herself*): Then it's tomorrow night—or never.

WANGEL: And even if he should come here again—

ELLIDA: What then?

WANGEL: I'll know what to do. I'll make sure that he does no further harm.

ELLIDA: How can you—?

WANGEL: I'll know what to do, I tell you! Unless he leaves you alone, he'll have to answer for the murder of the captain.

ELLIDA: No, no! Not that! We know nothing about that murder! Absolutely nothing!

WANGEL: But he confessed to you himself!

ELLIDA: No! I won't have it! If you say anything about that I shall deny it. He must never be caged in. His home is on the sea. He belongs there!

WANGEL (*Looks at her and says slowly*): Ellida—oh, Ellida!

ELLIDA (*Clings to him passionately*): My dear, my faithful one—save me from that man!

WANGEL (*Gently disengaging himself*): Come, my darling. Come with me!

(LYNGSTRAND *and* HILDE, *both with fishing rods, enter along the pond from the right.*)

LYNGSTRAND (*Goes quickly to* ELLIDA): Mrs. Wangel—I've something remarkable to tell you!

WANGEL: Well—what is it?

LYNGSTRAND: Can you believe it—we've just seen the American!

WANGEL: The American?

HILDE: I saw him too.

LYNGSTRAND: He came from the footpath along the garden, and went aboard the English steamer.

WANGEL: Where did you know this man?

LYNGSTRAND: We were at sea together once. I was certain he'd been drowned. And there he was as large as life!

WANGEL: What more do you know about him?

LYNGSTRAND: Nothing much. Only I expect he came back to take revenge. His wife was unfaithful to him while he was at sea—

WANGEL: What's that you say?

HILDE: Mr. Lyngstrand plans to use the story for a statue.

WANGEL: What are you talking about?

ELLIDA: I'll tell you about it later.

(ARNHOLM *and* BOLETTE *come along the footpath from the left outside the fence.*)

BOLETTE (*Calls to them in the garden*): Do come and see! The English steamer's sailing up the fjord.

(*A large steamer glides slowly past in the distance.*)

LYNGSTRAND (*To* HILDE, *near the garden fence*): Tonight he'll suddenly appear before her.

HILDE (*Nodding*): You really think so? Before his faithless wife!

LYNGSTRAND: On the stroke of midnight—yes!

HILDE: How absolutely thrilling!

ELLIDA (*Gazing after the ship*): So—tomorrow—

WANGEL: And then—never again.

ELLIDA (*Softly and tremulously*): Oh, Wangel—save me from myself.

WANGEL (*Looks at her anxiously*): Ellida—I'm afraid. What's happened to you?

ELLIDA: I'm bewitched, Wangel.

WANGEL: Bewitched?

ELLIDA: That man is like the sea.

(*She goes slowly through the garden out to the left, in deep thought.* WANGEL *walks beside her uneasily, observing her intently.*)

CURTAIN

ACT
FOUR

SCENE: *The garden room at* DR. WANGEL'S. *Doors right and left. In the back wall between the two windows a glass door leading out to the veranda; it stands open. A part of the garden is seen below. A sofa and table downstage left. To the right a piano and farther upstage a large flower stand. Stage center a round table with chairs round it. On the table a rose bush in bloom and other plants in pots about the room. It is late morning.*

BOLETTE *is seated on the sofa by the table, left, working on a piece of embroidery.* LYNGSTRAND *sits on a chair at the upper end of the table.* BALLESTED *is seated in the garden painting.* HILDE *stands beside him looking on.*

LYNGSTRAND: (*Sits for a while in silence, leaning his arms on the table watching* BOLETTE *work*): That work must be very difficult, Miss Wangel.

BOLETTE: It's not really so difficult; as long as you count correctly.

LYNGSTRAND: Do you have to count too?

BOLETTE: Yes—the stitches. Look—do you see?

LYNGSTRAND: Oh, of course! My goodness! It's quite an art, isn't it? Do you draw the design as well?

BOLETTE: No—I follow a pattern.

LYNGSTRAND: Oh—you need a pattern, do you?

BOLETTE: Yes.

LYNGSTRAND: Then it's not really an art after all.

BOLETTE: No; it's more of a knack, I suppose.

LYNGSTRAND: Still—you might perhaps learn to acquire an art.

BOLETTE: Even without talent?

LYNGSTRAND: Yes, you might. If you were to spend some time with a real artist—

BOLETTE: You think I could learn from him?

LYNGSTRAND: Perhaps "learn" is the wrong word for it. But you might absorb it by degrees—through a kind of miracle, Miss Wangel.

BOLETTE: What a strange idea!

LYNGSTRAND (*After a pause*): Have you given much thought to—? Have you thought at all—deeply and seriously I mean—about marriage, Miss Wangel?

BOLETTE (*Glances at him*): About—? Why, no.

LYNGSTRAND: I have.

BOLETTE: Really? Have you?

LYNGSTRAND: Yes, indeed. I often think a great deal about serious things; and particularly about marriage. And I've read a great many books about it too. I believe one should look upon marriage as a kind of miracle. The woman gradually undergoes a change; she comes to resemble her husband more and more.

BOLETTE: Acquires his interests, you mean?

LYNGSTRAND: Yes—that's it!

BOLETTE: And what about his gifts? His skills? His talents?

LYNGSTRAND: Who knows—? She might also—

BOLETTE: You believe a wife might gradually absorb her husband's knowledge? Her husband's way of thinking?

LYNGSTRAND: That too—yes. By degrees, of course. Through a kind of miracle. But this sort of thing could only happen in a *real* marriage—one founded on true love, and mutual happiness.

BOLETTE: I suppose it's never occurred to you that the husband too might undergo a change? Might come to resemble his wife, I mean?

LYNGSTRAND: The husband—? No. I've never thought of that.

BOLETTE: Why shouldn't it work both ways?

LYNGSTRAND: Well, you see—a man has a vocation—a fixed purpose in life. In that lies his strength. He has his work to live for.

BOLETTE: All men? Without exception?

LYNGSTRAND: No, perhaps not. I was thinking mainly of artists, you see.

BOLETTE: Do you think it's right for an artist to get married?

LYNGSTRAND: Most certainly. That is, if he finds someone he really loves—

BOLETTE: Even so—isn't it best for him to live for his art alone?

LYNGSTRAND: But marriage needn't interfere with that.

BOLETTE: Then what happens to her?

LYNGSTRAND: Her? Whom do you mean?

BOLETTE: The woman he marries, of course. What does *she* have to live for?

LYNGSTRAND: She must live for his art too. I should think that would be happiness enough for any woman.

BOLETTE: Hm—I'm not so sure—

LYNGSTRAND: Yes—believe me, Miss Wangel. It's not only a question of the honor and glory she would enjoy through him—that's the least part of it, perhaps. But to be able to help him to create—and to make his work easier for him; to take care of him and serve him, and make life comfortable for him. That would be a great joy for a woman, I should think.

BOLETTE: I've never heard of anything so selfish!

LYNGSTRAND: Selfish! You surely don't think *me* selfish, do you? You wouldn't say that if you really knew me! (*Leans closer towards her*) Miss Wangel—when I'm gone—and I shan't be here much longer—

BOLETTE (*Looks at him with compassion*): Don't think sad thoughts like that!

LYNGSTRAND: I don't see anything particularly sad about it.

BOLETTE: What do you mean?

LYNGSTRAND: I'll be leaving in a month. Home first, for a bit—and then off to the South.

BOLETTE: Oh, yes—I see. Of course.

LYNGSTRAND: Will you think of me, now and then, Miss Wangel?

BOLETTE: Yes; gladly.

LYNGSTRAND (*Happily*): You promise?

BOLETTE: Yes, I promise.

LYNGSTRAND: Your solemn word, Miss Wangel?

BOLETTE: My solemn word. (*In a different tone*) But—what possible difference can all this make? It can never lead to anything!

LYNGSTRAND: Don't say that—please! To know that you're here at home thinking of me—would make me very happy!

BOLETTE: And, after that? What then?

LYNGSTRAND: What then—? Well—I don't know exactly—

BOLETTE: No more do I. There are so many things against it. Everything in the world is against it, it seems to me.

LYNGSTRAND: Perhaps a miracle will happen—an unexpected turn of fate. Something of that sort. I'm a very lucky man, you know.

BOLETTE (*With animation*): Yes! You believe that, don't you?

LYNGSTRAND: I'm utterly convinced of it. You'll see—when I come back home again, in a few years, I'll be completely cured, and I'll be rich and famous!

BOLETTE: Yes. We must hope for that.

LYNGSTRAND: You can depend on it! Just so long as you keep on sending me faithful, loving thoughts. And you've given me your word—

BOLETTE: Yes, you have my word. (*Shakes her head*) But it won't lead to anything all the same.

LYNGSTRAND: Oh, yes it will! It'll be a great help to *me;* in my work, you know.

BOLETTE: You really mean that?

LYNGSTRAND: With all my heart. And think how exciting it'll be for you! Even though you have to stay in this remote, provincial place—you'll know that you're helping to create my master-piece!

BOLETTE: I see. But you—on your side?

LYNGSTRAND: I?

BOLETTE (*Looks out towards the garden*): Sh! Talk of something else. Here's Mr. Arnholm.

(ARNHOLM *is seen in the garden left. He stops and talks to* BALLESTED *and* HILDE.)

LYNGSTRAND: You're fond of your old tutor, aren't you, Miss Bolette?

BOLETTE: Fond of him?

LYNGSTRAND: Yes. I mean—you like him, don't you?

BOLETTE: Of course I do. He's such a wonderful friend—and I value his advice. He's so kind and understanding.

LYNGSTRAND: It seems odd that he's never married.

BOLETTE: Why odd?

LYNGSTRAND: He's quite well off they say.

BOLETTE: Yes—so I've heard. He's never found anyone who'd have him, I suppose. In his case I can see it might be difficult.

LYNGSTRAND: Why so?

BOLETTE: Well, the trouble is—he's been tutor to nearly all the young girls he's ever known.

LYNGSTRAND: What difference would that make?

BOLETTE: Good Heavens! One would never think of marrying one's tutor!

LYNGSTRAND: Why shouldn't a young girl fall in love with her tutor? Is that impossible?

BOLETTE: Yes, quite. After she's grown up, I mean.

LYNGSTRAND: How very strange!

BOLETTE: Sh!

(*All during the above,* BALLESTED *has been collecting his things; he exits through the garden right.* HILDE *helps him.* ARNHOLM *comes onto the veranda and enters the room.*)

ARNHOLM: Good morning, dear Bolette. Good morning, Mr.—Mr.—Hm!

(*He looks annoyed and nods coldly to* LYNGSTRAND, *who rises and bows.*)

BOLETTE (*Rises and goes to* ARNHOLM): Good morning, Mr. Arnholm.

ARNHOLM: How's everything today?

BOLETTE: Fine, thank you.

ARNHOLM: Has your stepmother gone for her daily swim, as usual?

BOLETTE: No. She's up in her room.

ARNHOLM: Isn't she feeling well?

BOLETTE: I don't know. She's locked herself in.

ARNHOLM: Hm—has she?

LYNGSTRAND: I noticed yesterday she seemed upset; about that American, I mean.

ARNHOLM: What do you know of that?

LYNGSTRAND: I told Mrs. Wangel he was still alive; that I'd seen him on the path beyond the garden.

ARNHOLM: Oh—I see.

BOLETTE (*To* ARNHOLM): You and Father stayed up very late last night.

ARNHOLM: Fairly late—yes. We had quite a serious talk.

BOLETTE: Did you put in a good word for me?

ARNHOLM: No, Bolette dear. I didn't get a chance. He was too absorbed in other things.

BOLETTE (*With a sigh*): I'm afraid he always is!

ARNHOLM (*Gives her a significant look*): But in a little while, we'll continue yesterday's conversation—you and I. Where is your father now? He hasn't gone out, has he?

BOLETTE: I think he went to the office. I'll go and fetch him.

ARNHOLM: No never mind. I'll go and talk to him down there.

BOLETTE (*Hears something off left*): Wait a minute, Mr. Arnholm. I think I hear him on the stairs. He went up to see her, I expect. (DR. WANGEL *comes in through the door left*.)

WANGEL (*Gives* ARNHOLM *his hand*): Arnholm! You're here already. It's good of you to come so early. There are still several things I want to talk to you about.

BOLETTE (*To* LYNGSTRAND): Let's join Hilde in the garden, shall we?

LYNGSTRAND: Yes, Miss Wangel, I'll be glad to. (*They go out into the garden through the trees in the background*.)

ARNHOLM (*Who has followed them with his eyes, then turns to* WANGEL): Who is that young man? Do you know anything about him?

WANGEL: No. Nothing much.

ARNHOLM: He's always hanging about the girls. Do you think that's wise?

WANGEL: Is he? I hadn't noticed.

ARNHOLM: Don't you think you ought to keep an eye on him?

WANGEL: Yes—I suppose I should. But what's a poor man to do? The girls are so used to looking after themselves—they resent interference. They won't take anything from me; nor from Ellida either.

ARNHOLM: Won't they listen to her either?

WANGEL: No. And I can't very well ask her to bother about these things; she's not equipped for that. (*Breaking off*) But that's not what we're here to talk about. Tell me—the matter we discussed last night—have you given any further thought to it?

ARNHOLM: Ever since I left you, I've thought of nothing else.

WANGEL: Then what ought I to do?

ARNHOLM: Surely you're a better judge of that than I am? After all, you're a physician.

WANGEL: You don't know how hard it is for a physician to treat someone he loves. And this is no ordinary illness. It's no case for an ordinary doctor—or for ordinary remedies.

ARNHOLM: How does she seem today?

WANGEL: I was just up to see her—she seemed to me quite calm. But under that reserve there's something that eludes me. And then she's so capricious—so unpredictable. Her mood changes constantly.

ARNHOLM: Part of her morbid condition, I suppose.

WANGEL: Not entirely. She was born like that, to some extent. She's a sea creature—that's where the trouble lies.

ARNHOLM: What precisely do you mean by that?

WANGEL: Have you never noticed that people who live by the sea are different from the rest of us? Their lives seem to reflect the ocean—with its waves and changing tides; it's as though their thoughts and feelings were controlled by it. And they can never be transplanted—I ought to have remembered that. It was wrong of me to drag Ellida away from there, and bring her inland.

ARNHOLM: You've really come to look at it like that?

WANGEL: Yes, I feel it more and more. I should have known it from the first—I *did* know it, I think. But I refused to face it. I was so very much in love with her, you see. I thought only of myself. I was unpardonably selfish!

ARNHOLM: Any man is apt to be selfish at a time like that—it's only natural. I don't think it's inherent in you, Doctor.

WANGEL: Oh, yes it is! I've been selfish all these years. I'm much older than she is, and I should have realized she needed guidance; I should have given her almost a father's care—helped her to develop spiritually and intellectually, and I've done nothing of the kind. I've been selfish and lazy; but, you see, I loved her so much just as she was. Then, gradually, she grew worse and worse, and I could think of nothing to do about it. (*Lower*) At last, in desperation, I wrote to you and asked you to come here.

ARNHOLM: Was *that* why you wrote to me?

WANGEL: Yes. But don't let anybody know that.

ARNHOLM: Why me? I don't understand why you should send for me?

WANGEL: There's no reason why you should; I was on the wrong track, you see. Ellida had been in love with you once, I thought—and perhaps still had a secret fondness for you. I thought it might do her good to talk to you again. That she might enjoy reminiscing about home—sharing old memories.

ARNHOLM: So when you wrote that there was someone here who missed me—and longed to see me—it was your wife you referred to?

WANGEL: Of course; who else?

ARNHOLM: Nothing—it's just that I didn't understand you.

WANGEL: No; how could you? I was on the wrong track, I tell you.

ARNHOLM: And you call yourself selfish!

WANGEL: I felt so guilty; it seemed to me I had so much to atone for. I was ready to do anything that might ease her mind a little.

ARNHOLM: About this strange man—and the power he evidently has over her—what explanation can you find for that?

WANGEL: I don't know. There are certain things about it that defy all explanation.

ARNHOLM: Do you think there's an element there beyond all explanation? Something that could never, under any circumstances, be explained?

WANGEL: It seems so—at the moment.

ARNHOLM: Do you believe there *are* such things?

WANGEL: I neither believe nor disbelieve. I just don't know. I can only suspend judgment.

ARNHOLM: Tell me something: that strange, uncanny conviction of hers, that the child's eyes were—

WANGEL: I don't believe a word of that! I simply won't believe it! That was pure imagination on her part—nothing else.

ARNHOLM: Did you notice the man's eyes when you saw him yesterday?

WANGEL: Yes, of course I did.

ARNHOLM: And you saw no resemblance?

WANGEL (*Evasively*): I don't quite know how to answer that. When I saw him it was growing dark. And I'd heard so much about the likeness from Ellida—I couldn't trust my judgment.

ARNHOLM: No—perhaps not. But about the other question: the fact that this restlessness—this sense of terror—came over her at the very time the man was on his homeward voyage?

WANGEL: I believe that's something she started to build up in her imagination two days ago, when Lyngstrand first told her about this man. When she heard that this Johnston, or Freeman, or whatever you want to call him, was on his way home three years ago in March—she hypnotized herself into believing there was a definite connection; that this mental state of hers dates from that very moment. Actually, of course, it came over her gradually. It didn't happen all at once.

ARNHOLM: But wasn't that about the time it started?

WANGEL: By no means. There had been definite symptoms long before that. She did happen to have a particularly violent attack three years ago in March, I must admit—

ARNHOLM: Ah! Then—you see!

WANGEL: But I felt that her physical condition at the time might well account for that. You see—it was just then that we—

ARNHOLM: Yes—one could interpret it both ways.

WANGEL (*Wringing his hands*): It's so dreadful not to be able to help her! To be utterly powerless! Not to be able to find some remedy—!

ARNHOLM: Would it do any good to move away from here? She

might be happier somewhere else; somewhere that would remind her of her home, perhaps.

WANGEL: Do you think I haven't thought of that? I suggested moving back to Skjoldvik—but she wouldn't hear of it.

ARNHOLM: Why not?

WANGEL: It wouldn't do any good, she said. She may be right in that.

ARNHOLM: What makes you think so?

WANGEL: In any case—on thinking the matter over—I doubt if I could manage it. It wouldn't be quite fair to the girls to ask them to live in such an out-of-the-way place. They must have the opportunity of meeting a few people now and then—of marrying and settling down some day.

ARNHOLM: Marrying? You've already given thought to that?

WANGEL: Well, naturally! I have to! —And yet, on the other hand, when I think of poor Ellida, I—! Oh, my dear Arnholm—I don't know what to do!

ARNHOLM: I don't think you need be too concerned about Bolette— (*Breaks off*) That reminds me; I wonder where she—where they went? (*Goes to the open door and looks out.*)

WANGEL (*Over by the piano*): I'd be ready to make any sacrifice for them—all three of them. But what? I don't know what to do! (ELLIDA *enters from the door left.*)

ELLIDA (*Rapidly, to* WANGEL): You won't go out this morning, will you?

WANGEL: Of course not. I'll stay home with you. (*Points to* ARNHOLM *who comes towards them*) You haven't said good morning to our friend here.

ELLIDA (*Turns*): Oh, I didn't see you, Mr. Arnholm. (*Gives him her hand*) Good morning.

ARNHOLM: Good morning, Mrs. Wangel. Aren't you going for your swim today?

ELLIDA: No, not today—I couldn't! Won't you sit down a moment?

ARNHOLM: Thank you—not just now. (*Looks at* WANGEL) I promised the girls to join them in the garden.

ELLIDA: I hope you'll find them there. I never know where they're off to.

WANGEL: I expect they're by the pond.

ARNHOLM: I'll track them down! (*He nods, crosses the veranda down into the garden and off right.*)

ELLIDA: What's the time, Wangel?

WANGEL (*Looks at his watch*): Just past eleven.

ELLIDA: Just past eleven. And at eleven—half-past eleven to-night, the steamer will be here. If only it were over!

WANGEL (*Goes closer to her*): Ellida dear—there's one thing I'd like to ask you.

ELLIDA: Yes? What's that?

WANGEL: The day before yesterday, when we were talking up at Prospect Heights, you told me there had been times during the past three years when you thought this man appeared to you.

ELLIDA: He did. You must believe me when I tell you that.

WANGEL: How did he look?

ELLIDA: How did he look—?

WANGEL: Yes—what did he look like at these times?

ELLIDA: But you know what he looks like, Wangel; you saw him yourself yesterday.

WANGEL: And was that how he looked each time you thought you saw him?

ELLIDA: Yes, of course.

WANGEL: Exactly as he looked in real life yesterday?

ELLIDA: Exactly—yes.

WANGEL: Then how did you fail to recognize him?

ELLIDA (*With a start*): Did I—?

WANGEL: Yes. You said yourself at first you had no idea who he was.

ELLIDA (*Impressed*): I believe you're right! What a strange thing, Wangel. To think of my not knowing him at once.

WANGEL: You only recognized him by his eyes, you said.

ELLIDA: Yes—his eyes! His eyes!

WANGEL: Yet in our talk the other day you said when he appeared to you he always looked just as he did ten years ago—that day you parted.

ELLIDA: Did I say that?

WANGEL: Yes, you did.

ELLIDA: Then he can't have changed, I suppose.

WANGEL: He must have. For you described him quite differently the night before last as we were walking home. Ten years ago he was clean shaven you said. His clothes were quite different too. And that scarfpin you spoke of—the one with the pearl—yesterday he wore nothing of that sort.

ELLIDA: That's true; he didn't.

WANGEL (*Looks at her intently*): Think hard, Ellida dear. Perhaps you no longer remember exactly how he looked, when you said good-bye to him at Bratthammer?

ELLIDA: I don't remember very clearly. Today I don't seem able to remember it at all. Isn't that strange!

WANGEL: Perhaps not so very strange. You've just seen him as he really is; reality has blotted out the imaginary picture you had of him in your mind, and now that's no longer clear to you.

ELLIDA: You think so, Wangel?

WANGEL: Yes. Reality has blotted out illusion. It's a good thing that he came.

ELLIDA: Good! You think it's good?

WANGEL: It may be your salvation.

ELLIDA (*Sits down on the sofa*): Wangel—come here and sit by me. I want you to know all my thoughts.

WANGEL: Yes—Ellida dear. (*He sits down on a chair on the other side of the table.*)

ELLIDA: You know—it was actually a great misfortune, for us both, that we of all people should have come together.

WANGEL (*With a start*): What are you saying!

ELLIDA: Yes, it was. How could it be otherwise? When you think of how it happened—it could lead to nothing but unhappiness.

WANGEL: "How it happened"? What do you mean?

ELLIDA: Listen to me, Wangel—it's no good lying to ourselves—or to each other—any more.

WANGEL: We surely don't do that!

ELLIDA: Oh yes, we do; we conceal the truth at any rate. And the truth—the plain unvarnished truth is this: You came up to Skjoldvik and you bought me, Wangel.

WANGEL: Bought! How can you say such things!

ELLIDA: I was as much to blame as you were. I accepted the bargain; I consented to sell myself to you.

WANGEL: Ellida—how have you the heart to call it that!

ELLIDA: What else is there to call it? You wanted to find a new wife; you could no longer bear your loneliness—

WANGEL: I wanted to find a new mother for my children, too.

ELLIDA: Yes—that may have entered into it; though you never bothered to find out if I was fit to be a mother to them. You saw me a few times, talked to me once or twice, took a fancy to me and—

WANGEL: If it pleases you to call it that—!

ELLIDA: And I on my side—I was helpless, I had no one to turn to, I was utterly alone—it seemed only natural to accept you: you offered me security.

WANGEL: That isn't how I looked on it, Ellida. I asked you in all honesty if you would come and share with me, and with my children, what little I possessed.

ELLIDA: I know you did. All the same I shouldn't have accepted. No matter how little or how much you had to offer—I shouldn't have accepted! I should never have sold myself to you! Hard work—even abject poverty—anything would have been better; anything as long as it was of my own free will—by my own choice.

WANGEL (*Rises*): Then—to you—these years we've lived together have been wasted?

ELLIDA: No! You mustn't think that, Wangel! I've had a good life here with you. You've given me everything anyone could wish for. But I didn't come to you of my own free will, you see.

WANGEL (*Looks at her*): Not of your own free will!

ELLIDA: No. It was not of my own free will I married you.

WANGEL: That's the expression he used yesterday!

ELLIDA: And it's the key to everything; it explains everything; I see things clearly now.

WANGEL: What do you see?

ELLIDA: I see that our life together has never really been a marriage.

WANGEL (*Bitterly*): The life we lead together now is certainly no marriage—that's true enough.

ELLIDA: It never has been—never. Perhaps the first one might have been.

WANGEL: "First one"? What do you mean?

ELLIDA: Mine—with him.

WANGEL (*Looks at her in amazement*): It's impossible for me to understand you.

ELLIDA: Oh, my dear—don't let's lie to each other any more; and don't let's lie to ourselves!

WANGEL: Very well. What then?

ELLIDA: You see—there's no escaping it. A promise, given of one's own free will, is just as binding as a marriage.

WANGEL: But, what on earth—!

ELLIDA (*Rises impetuously*): You must let me leave you, Wangel!

WANGEL: Ellida—! Ellida—!

ELLIDA: Yes—you must! Believe me—sooner or later it will have to happen. We never really belonged together, you and I.

WANGEL (*Controlling his emotion*): Has it really come to this?

ELLIDA: It was inevitable. It had to.

WANGEL: You've never really belonged to me—in spite of our years together!

ELLIDA: Oh, Wangel! If I could only love you as I want to love you—as you deserve to be loved! But I know now that I never shall.

WANGEL: Then you want a divorce, I suppose. A formal, legal divorce—

ELLIDA: I wish I could make you understand me. I care nothing about formalities. Surely this is not a question of externals. Can't we simply agree to release one another—of our own free will?

WANGEL (*Bitterly. Nods slowly*): Cancel the bargain?

ELLIDA (*Eagerly*): Precisely—cancel the bargain!

WANGEL: And after that, Ellida? Afterwards? Have you thought of what will happen to us then? What will life hold for us? I mean for you, as well as me.

ELLIDA: It makes no difference. We must simply take life as it comes. Only one thing matters, Wangel: I beg you and implore you—let me go! Give me back my freedom!

WANGEL: You're asking a terrible thing of me, Ellida. Give me a little time! We must discuss this further. Give yourself time to think things over—to be absolutely certain of what you want to do!

ELLIDA: There's no time for thinking. You must set me free today.

WANGEL: Today! Why must it be today!

ELLIDA: Because tonight he will be here.

WANGEL: He! The stranger? What has he to do with this?

ELLIDA: When I see him tonight, I must be free to choose.

WANGEL: What do you mean to do?

ELLIDA: I can't take refuge in belonging to another man. I must be in a position to choose freely. Otherwise my decision will be worthless.

WANGEL: "Choose" you say! How can you speak of choice in such a case?

ELLIDA: I must be free to choose—one way or the other. Either to let him go away alone—or to go with him.

WANGEL: Go with him! Do you understand what that would mean, Ellida? You'd be putting your whole future in his hands!

ELLIDA: I once put my whole future in your hands—without giving it a thought.

WANGEL: That may be. But this man—! You know nothing about him! He's a total stranger to you!

ELLIDA: I knew even less about you, perhaps. Yet I went with you all the same.

WANGEL: At least you had some idea of the kind of life you'd have with me; but in this case—! Think of what you're doing! You don't know who he is—or what he is!

ELLIDA: That's true. That's what makes it so terrifying!

WANGEL: Terrifying indeed!

ELLIDA: And for that very reason I feel I have no right to run away from it.

WANGEL: Because it's terrifying?

ELLIDA: Yes—precisely.

WANGEL: Ellida—what do you actually mean by "terrifying"?

ELLIDA: I mean something that is frightening—yet fascinating too.

WANGEL: Fascinating?

ELLIDA: Above all, fascinating—perhaps.

WANGEL: You are like the sea, Ellida.

ELLIDA: That's terrifying too.

WANGEL: Yes—frightening and fascinating, just as you are.

ELLIDA: Is that how you think of me, Wangel?

WANGEL: I've never really known you—not fully, at any rate. I see that now.

ELLIDA: Then set me free! Release me, Wangel! You're right—you've never known me. I'm not the person you thought I was. We can part now, of our own free will—with perfect understanding.

WANGEL: I realize it might be best for us to part; but, all the same, I can't bring myself to do it! To me it is you who are "terrifying," Ellida—and, above all, fascinating!

ELLIDA: I don't know how you can say that.

WANGEL: We must try and live through this day prudently and calmly. I dare not release you and let you go today. For your own sake, Ellida—I dare not! I have both a duty and a right. I intend to use them to protect you.

ELLIDA: Protect me? What against? There's no question here of force or violence. No one is threatening me, Wangel. It's not as simple as all that. The struggle lies within me—in my mind. The struggle between the terror and the fascination. You can't help me in that.

WANGEL: I can! I can give you strength, and help you to resist.

ELLIDA: Yes—if to resist were really what I wanted.

WANGEL: But—isn't it, Ellida?

ELLIDA: I don't know! Can't you see—! That's just what I don't know myself.

WANGEL: Tonight will decide everything, Ellida.

ELLIDA: Tonight! Just think—so soon! It's a question of my life—

WANGEL: And then tomorrow—

ELLIDA: Tomorrow! Perhaps, by then, I shall have betrayed my destiny—the life I was truly meant for.

WANGEL: Your destiny—?

ELLIDA: Yes. A life of truth and joy and freedom—lost to me forever. And to him too, perhaps.

WANGEL (*In a lower tone, seizing her by the wrists*): Ellida—do you love this man?

ELLIDA: Love—? How do I know! I only know he is both terrifying and fascinating to me, and that—

WANGEL: Yes?

ELLIDA (*Tears herself away*): —and that I've a feeling I belong with him.

WANGEL (*Bows his head*): I begin to understand.

ELLIDA: What possible help have you to offer? What remedy is there to suggest?

WANGEL (*Looks at her sadly*): Tomorrow—when he's gone and you are out of danger, I promise to release you and let you go. Then we will cancel the bargain.

ELLIDA: But, Wangel—! Tomorrow—that will be too late—!

WANGEL (*Glancing towards the garden*): The children! At least for the present—they must be spared!

(ARNHOLM, BOLETTE, HILDE *and* LYNGSTRAND *are seen in the garden*. LYNGSTRAND *takes leave of them and goes out to the left. The others enter the room.*)

ARNHOLM: We've been making all sorts of plans—

HILDE: We're going to sail up the fjord this evening and—

BOLETTE: No, Hilde! Don't tell!

WANGEL: We've been making a few plans too.

ARNHOLM: Really? Have you?

WANGEL: Yes. Ellida's going away tomorrow; she's decided to go to Skjoldvik for a while.

BOLETTE: She's going away—?

ARNHOLM: That strikes me as a very sensible idea, Mrs. Wangel.

WANGEL: Ellida wants to go home again; home to the sea.

HILDE (*Rushing wildly to* ELLIDA): You're going away? You're leaving us?

ELLIDA (*Startled*): Why, Hilde! What's the matter?

HILDE (*Controls herself*): Nothing. Nothing at all. (*Mutters as she turns away*) Go! For all I care!

BOLETTE: Father! Are you going to Skjoldvik too?—I believe you are! I can see it in your face!

WANGEL: No—of course not! I may go up for a visit now and then—

BOLETTE: But you'll come home to us—?

WANGEL: Yes—I'll come home to you—

BOLETTE: Just now and then, I suppose!

WANGEL: My dear child, it can't be helped. (*He walks away.*)

ARNHOLM (*To* BOLETTE *in a whisper*): We'll talk about this later. (*He goes over and joins* WANGEL. *They stand in the doorway talking in low tones.*)

ELLIDA (*Softly to* BOLETTE): What was the matter with Hilde? She seemed dreadfully upset!

BOLETTE: You don't know—you haven't noticed, I suppose, what Hilde's always longed for?

ELLIDA: Longed for?

BOLETTE: Yes. Ever since you first came to this house.

ELLIDA: No. What could that be?

BOLETTE: A word of tenderness from you; a word of love.

ELLIDA: Ah—! Is it possible—? Could I be needed here? (*She stands motionless, her hands clasped to her head, a prey to conflicting thoughts and emotions.* WANGEL *and* ARNHOLM *come forward talking in low tones.* BOLETTE *goes and looks off into the room right. Then throws the door wide open.*)

BOLETTE: Dinner's ready, Father dear—if you—

WANGEL (*With forced composure*): Splendid, Bolette! Arnholm—come along! We must drink a toast—a parting toast to "the Lady from the Sea." (*They go towards the door right.*)

CURTAIN

ACT FIVE

SCENE: *The remote corner of* DR. WANGEL'S *garden by the carp pond. Deepening summer twilight.* ARNHOLM, BOLETTE, LYNGSTRAND *and* HILDE *in a boat are punting along the shore from the left.*

HILDE: Here's a good place! Let's jump ashore.

ARNHOLM: No, no! Don't try that! Please!

LYNGSTRAND: I'm afraid I'm no good at jumping, Miss Hilde.

HILDE: How about you, Arnholm? Are you good at jumping?

ARNHOLM: I'd rather not attempt it.

BOLETTE: We'd much better land at the steps by the bathhouse.
   (*They punt off towards the right. At the same moment* BALLESTED *appears on the footpath from the right, carrying some music and a French horn. He greets those in the boat, turns and talks to them. The answers are heard farther and farther off.*)

BALLESTED: What's that you say? Yes, that's right—in honor of the English steamer. It's her last trip of the season. You'd better hurry if you want to hear the music. (*Shouts*) What? (*Shakes his head*) I can't hear you!
   (ELLIDA, *with a scarf over her head, comes in from the left followed by* DR. WANGEL.)

WANGEL: There's ample time, Ellida dear, I assure you.

ELLIDA: No, no. You're wrong! He might be here any moment.

BALLESTED (*Outside the garden fence*): Good evening, Doctor! Good evening, Mrs. Wangel!

WANGEL (*Becomes aware of him*): Oh—good evening, Ballested. There's to be another concert tonight is there?

BALLESTED: Yes. The brass band is to perform. At this time of year there's no lack of entertainment. We're playing in honor of the English steamer.

ELLIDA: Has she been sighted yet?

BALLESTED: No, not yet. But she creeps in between those islands, and before you know it she's lying at the pier.

ELLIDA: Yes—that's true.

WANGEL (*Partly to* ELLIDA): Her last trip of the season. She won't be back again this year.

BALLESTED: A sad thought, Doctor, isn't it? That's why we want to honor her, you see. Well, well! The happy summer days are nearly over. We shall soon be icebound: "Trapped in an icy prison," as the old melodrama puts it.

ELLIDA: "Trapped in an icy prison" —yes.

BALLESTED: A depressing thought. We've basked in the golden summer months like happy children! It'll be hard to reconcile ourselves to the dark days ahead. At first—that is. People learn to alcli—acli—acclimatize themselves, Mrs. Wangel. They do indeed! (*He bows and goes out left.*)

ELLIDA (*Looking out over the fjord*): This dreadful suspense! The agony of this last half hour of waiting.

WANGEL: You still insist on talking to him yourself?

ELLIDA: I must talk to him myself. I must be free to choose.

WANGEL: You have no choice, Ellida. You won't be allowed to choose. I won't allow it.

ELLIDA: No one can prevent my choosing, Wangel. If I should choose to go with him, you can prevent my leaving; you can keep me here by force, against my will—that's true enough. But you can't control my mind. If I feel I should and must choose him instead of you, you may forbid it—but the choice would still remain; and nothing you can do would alter it.

WANGEL: You're right; I've no way of controlling that.

ELLIDA: And then—I have no real reason to resist. What is there here at home to hold me back? I have no roots in this house, Wangel. The children are not mine; they never have been mine—not in their hearts, I mean. When I go away—if I go away, that is—either tonight with him, or tomorrow to

Skjoldvik—I shall have no keys to hand over, no instructions of any sort or kind to give. I have no roots in your house, I tell you. I've never been anything but an outsider here.

WANGEL: That was the way you wanted it.

ELLIDA: Not really. I had no wishes one way or the other; I simply left things as they were when I arrived. That was the way *you* wanted it—you, and no one else.

WANGEL: I did what I thought was best for you, Ellida.

ELLIDA: I know, Wangel—I know only too well! And now all that has to be paid for. I have no real ties here—no anchor; nothing to give me the help and strength I need. We have no common treasure—of memories shared—of experiences cherished through the years. There's no compelling force to hold me here.

WANGEL: I understand, Ellida. And tomorrow, I promise to give you back your freedom; you shall live your own life from then on.

ELLIDA: "My own life" you call it! I'm afraid I betrayed that when I married you. (*Clenches her hands in fear and agitation*) And now—tonight—in half an hour—he will be here. The man I failed; the man I should have felt irrevocably bound to—as he felt bound to me. He'll give me one last chance tonight to start afresh; to find my life again—that terrifying, fascinating life! Of my own free will, how can I let it go?

WANGEL: For this very reason I must insist on acting for you. As your husband, and as your doctor too.

ELLIDA: Yes, Wangel—I know you're right. I've often thought what peace and safety I should find if I could only cling to you—you must know that! If I could defy once and for all these terrifying, fascinating powers. But I can't! I can't bring myself to do it!

WANGEL: Come, Ellida—let's walk a little while.

ELLIDA: I should like to—but I dare not. This is where he said I was to wait.

WANGEL: Come along; you've still plenty of time.

ELLIDA: Are you sure?

WANGEL: Ample time, I tell you.

ELLIDA: Let's walk a little then.

(They go off downstage right. At the same time ARNHOLM *and* BOLETTE *enter along the upper back of the pond.)*

BOLETTE *(Catching sight of the others as they go out)*: Look over there—!

ARNHOLM *(Softly)*: Sh! Let them go.

BOLETTE: What's been happening between them lately?

ARNHOLM: Why? Have you noticed something?

BOLETTE: Have I noticed—!

ARNHOLM: Anything in particular, I mean?

BOLETTE: All kinds of things! What about you?

ARNHOLM: Well—I don't know—

BOLETTE: Oh yes, you do. Only you won't admit it.

ARNHOLM: I think it'll be a good thing for your stepmother to take this little trip.

BOLETTE: You think so?

ARNHOLM: It might be a good thing for all concerned for her to get away from time to time.

BOLETTE: If she goes home to Skjoldvik, she'll probably never come back again.

ARNHOLM: What makes you say that, Bolette dear?

BOLETTE: I'm certain of it. You wait and see! She won't come back. Not while Hilde and I are home at any rate.

ARNHOLM: You can get away if you really want to. You can study to your heart's content, become familiar with all the things you long to know about—live a fuller, happier life. What do you say to that?

BOLETTE *(Claps her hands)*: It sounds too wonderful! Oh—but it's quite impossible. Since Father can't see his way to—I've no one else to turn to.

ARNHOLM: Perhaps you'll allow your old—well—let's say your former tutor—to lend a helping hand.

BOLETTE: You, Mr. Arnholm? You mean you'd really—?

ARNHOLM: Stand by you? Of course—with all my heart! You can depend on me. What do you say? Do you consent?

BOLETTE: Do I consent! I'd do anything to get away from here—to see the world—to study and improve myself—do all the things

I've dreamed of, and that always seemed impossible—!

ARNHOLM: All this can come true—if you really want it.

BOLETTE: It would be almost too much happiness! You say you'll really help me? But—would it be right to accept this from a stranger?

ARNHOLM: Surely you can accept it from *me*, Bolette. You know you can accept anything from me.

BOLETTE (*Seizes his hands*): Yes, I really believe I can! I don't know why it is, but— (*In an outburst of emotion*) I'm so happy! I feel like laughing—and I feel like crying too! So—after all—I'll have a chance to live! I was beginning to be so afraid that life would pass me by.

ARNHOLM: You need never be afraid of that, Bolette dear. Now—tell me frankly—you're quite free, aren't you? You've no ties here at home?

BOLETTE: Ties? No—none at all.

ARNHOLM: You're sure?

BOLETTE: Yes, quite. That is—of course I'm tied to Father, in a way—and Hilde too, but—

ARNHOLM: Sooner or later you'll have to leave your father—and Hilde will have a life of her own someday; all that's just a question of time. But, apart from that, you say you have no ties? You're not engaged in any way?

BOLETTE: No. As far as that goes, I'm quite free to leave.

ARNHOLM: Then you shall come with me, Bolette dear.

BOLETTE: It's too wonderful to think of!

ARNHOLM: You trust me, don't you?

BOLETTE: Of course I do!

ARNHOLM: And you've no doubts—you're quite willing to place your future in my hands?

BOLETTE: Of course! Why shouldn't I? How can you ask? You're my old tutor, aren't you? Or my old-time tutor, perhaps I should say.

ARNHOLM: That's not the point—we needn't dwell on that. But since you're free—and have no ties of any sort—do you think you could—? Do you think you could see your way to—? Well—I'd like to ask you to join your life to mine, Bolette.

BOLETTE: Good heavens! What are you saying?

ARNHOLM: Will you join your life to mine, Bolette? Will you marry me?

BOLETTE (*Half to herself*): It's impossible! Utterly impossible!

ARNHOLM: Why should it be impossible—?

BOLETTE: Mr. Arnholm! You can't mean what you say! (*Looks at him*) Or— Perhaps— Was this what you had in mind when you offered me your help?

ARNHOLM: Bolette—listen to me a moment! This comes as a surprise, I realize that—

BOLETTE: Indeed it does! What else could you expect? A thing like that—coming from you—!

ARNHOLM: You're right. Of course you didn't know—how could you—that I came here for your sake.

BOLETTE: For my sake!

ARNHOLM: Yes, Bolette. This spring I had a letter from your father. I got the impression, from certain things he said, that your feelings for me were—well—a good deal warmer than mere friendship.

BOLETTE: How could Father write a thing like that!

ARNHOLM: It was all a mistake; that wasn't at all what he meant, you see. But I didn't know that at the time. So I built up in my imagination the picture of a young girl whose thoughts were full of me, and who waited eagerly for my return—No! Don't interrupt me, Bolette, please! Now, when a man is past the first flush of youth, as they call it, such a belief—or illusion if you prefer—makes a very strong impression. I started to think of you with tenderness and gratitude, and made up my mind to come and tell you that I shared your feelings—the feelings I imagined you had for me.

BOLETTE: Well—now you know it isn't true. You were mistaken!

ARNHOLM: That may be; but, all the same—it's too late now to change the picture of you I've built up in my heart. Can't you understand that, Bolette?

BOLETTE: How can such a thing be possible? I should never have believed it!

ARNHOLM: But now that you know it *is* possible—what do you say, Bolette? Won't you consent to be my wife?

BOLETTE: It seems quite inconceivable to me, Mr. Arnholm. After all—you were my tutor. I can't think of you in any other way.

ARNHOLM: Well—if you really feel you can't— However—this will in no way affect our friendship.

BOLETTE: How do you mean?

ARNHOLM: My offer stands, of course. I'll see that you get away from here; I'll help you to go on with your studies, and in the future I shall guarantee your security and independence; I promise you that. You can depend on me as a true and faithful friend.

BOLETTE: But, Mr. Arnholm—you've made all that impossible!

ARNHOLM: Is that impossible too?

BOLETTE: Of course! After what you've said to me—and after what I answered you— I couldn't possibly accept these things. I can take nothing from you now!

ARNHOLM: I see. Then you'd rather stay here and let "life pass you by"?

BOLETTE: That's such a dreadful thought!

ARNHOLM: You say you want to see something of the world; you long to take part in an active life; yet now that the opportunity is offered to you, you refuse it. How can you resign yourself to this meager, cooped-up life—knowing what infinite possibilities are open to you? Think seriously, Bolette.

BOLETTE: Yes, Mr. Arnholm; I know you're right.

ARNHOLM: And then, when your father is no longer with you, you'll be alone in the world—without any protection. You might find yourself obliged to marry some other man; a man whom you—quite conceivably—might not be able to care for, any more than you care for me.

BOLETTE: Everything you say is quite true, Mr. Arnholm; but—all the same—! —And yet, perhaps—

ARNHOLM: Well, Bolette?

BOLETTE: Perhaps it might not be so utterly impossible, after all—

ARNHOLM: You mean you might be willing to—? Or, at least, you'll accept my help—my friendship?

BOLETTE: No, no! That I could never do! That would be quite out of the question. But I might consent to—

ARNHOLM: Oh, Bolette! Will you—?

BOLETTE: Yes— I believe—I think I will.

ARNHOLM: You'll be my wife?

BOLETTE: Yes, if you'll still have me.

ARNHOLM: If I'll still have you—! (*Seizes her hand*) Thank you, thank you, Bolette dear! And as for the things you said—don't worry about them. Those doubts of yours don't trouble me. I shall know how to win your heart—you'll see. Oh, Bolette! How I shall cherish you!

BOLETTE: But you *will* take me away from here? You promised I should have a free and happy life.

ARNHOLM: Yes, and I'll keep my word.

BOLETTE: And you will allow me to go on with my studies?

ARNHOLM: I'll be your tutor, as I was before. Do you remember the last year you were my pupil—?

BOLETTE: I can't believe it! To be free—to have a chance to see the world! And not to have to think about the future; not to have to worry about money any more!

ARNHOLM: No; you needn't waste a thought on that. That, in it-self, is something, isn't it?

BOLETTE: My goodness, yes! It is indeed!

ARNHOLM: We shall get on splendidly, Bolette! We'll have such a happy, peaceful life together.

BOLETTE: Yes. I'm beginning to think—perhaps we might make a go of it. (*Looks off right and disengages herself hastily*) Please don't say anything to anybody yet!

ARNHOLM: What is it dear?

BOLETTE: Poor thing! (*Points*) Just look at him!

ARNHOLM: Is it your father—?

BOLETTE: No; it's that young sculptor. He's over there with Hilde.

ARNHOLM: Oh, Lyngstrand. What of him?

BOLETTE: Well—you know how ill he is; how delicate.

ARNHOLM: It's probably all put on.

BOLETTE: Oh, no—it's real enough. He hasn't long to live. But perhaps in a way it's best for him.

ARNHOLM: What makes you say that?

BOLETTE: Because—well—because I don't think his work will ever come to much—Let's go before they come.

ARNHOLM: Yes—let's, Bolette dear.

(HILDE *and* LYNGSTRAND *appear beside the pond.*)

HILDE: Hi! Hi there! Won't you condescend to wait for us?

ARNHOLM: We'll go on ahead.

(*He and* BOLETTE *go off left.*)

LYNGSTRAND (*Laughs quietly*): It's delightful—have you noticed? Everybody seems to be walking about in pairs these days.

HILDE (*Looking after them*): I'm willing to bet he's making love to her.

LYNGSTRAND: Really? What makes you think so?

HILDE: It's easy enough to tell—if you keep your eyes open.

LYNGSTRAND: But she won't have him; I'm sure of that.

HILDE: No. She thinks he's too old; and she's afraid he's going bald.

LYNGSTRAND: It's not because of that. She wouldn't have him anyway.

HILDE: How can you possibly know?

LYNGSTRAND: Because she's promised to think of someone else.

HILDE: Only to think about them?

LYNGSTRAND: While he's away—yes.

HILDE: I suppose you mean yourself. So she's to think about you, is she?

LYNGSTRAND: Possibly.

HILDE: Did she promise?

LYNGSTRAND: Yes, she did. She promised. But for heaven's sake don't tell her that you know.

HILDE: Don't worry. I'm as silent as the grave.

LYNGSTRAND: It was awfully nice of her I thought.

HILDE: Then, when you come home again, you'll get engaged I suppose. Do you intend to marry her?

LYNGSTRAND: No; I'm afraid that won't work out. I couldn't think of marrying for several years—not till my reputation is established; and by that time she'd probably be too old for me.

HILDE: Yet you expect her to go on thinking of you all the same!

LYNGSTRAND: Why not? It would be tremendously helpful to me as an artist. And what difference can it make to her? She has no vocation in life, you see. Still—I must say it was nice of her.

HILDE: You really believe, if Bolette went on thinking about you, it would make a difference in your work?

LYNGSTRAND: Yes, I believe it would. The fact that a young attractive woman was thinking of me—dreaming of me in secret— It would be positively—I don't know how to put it into words.

HILDE: Do you by any chance mean *thrilling?* Positively thrilling?

LYNGSTRAND: Yes—that's it! Thrilling! At least I think that's what I mean. (*Looks at her a moment*) You're so clever, Miss Hilde; really extraordinarily clever. By the time I come home again, you'll be about the same age your sister is now, won't you? And perhaps you'll have grown to look quite like her; and you may grow more like her in disposition too. You'll perhaps be a sort of combination of yourself and her—

HILDE: Would you like that?

LYNGSTRAND: I'm not quite sure. I rather think I would. But—for the moment—I prefer you as you are. Just exactly as you are.

HILDE: You like me like this, do you?

LYNGSTRAND: I like you very much like this.

HILDE: Hm. Tell me—as an artist—do you think I'm right to wear light colors?

LYNGSTRAND: Yes, I do indeed.

HILDE: You think they're becoming to me?

LYNGSTRAND: Most becoming.

HILDE: But, tell me—you who are an artist—how do you think I'd look in black?

LYNGSTRAND: Black isn't exactly right for summer. However I'm sure you'd look very well in it; especially with your figure.

HILDE: In black from head to toe—a black ruffle—black gloves—and a long black veil.

LYNGSTRAND: If I saw you dressed like that, Miss Hilde, I'd wish to be a painter. I'd paint a splendid picture of a beautiful young widow.

HILDE: Or a young girl grieving for her lost lover perhaps.

LYNGSTRAND: That would be even better. But you surely wouldn't want to dress like that?

HILDE: I don't know; it might be awfully thrilling.

LYNGSTRAND: Thrilling?

HILDE: Anyhow—it's thrilling to think about. (*Suddenly points off left*) Oh, look!

LYNGSTRAND: The English steamer! She's already docked! (WANGEL *and* ELLIDA *appear by the pond.*)

WANGEL: My dear Ellida, you're mistaken I assure you. (*Sees the others*) Oh—you're here, are you? She's not been sighted yet, has she, Mr. Lyngstrand?

LYNGSTRAND: You mean the English steamer?

WANGEL: Yes—of course!

LYNGSTRAND: She's already at the pier.

ELLIDA: Ah—! I was right!

WANGEL: So—she's come!

LYNGSTRAND: Like a thief in the night, Doctor. She crept in without a sound.

WANGEL: I expect Hilde would like to hear the music. Take her down to the pier, will you? You'd better hurry!

LYNGSTRAND: We were just going there, Doctor.

WANGEL: We may perhaps join you later. We'll be there in a little while.

HILDE (*To* LYNGSTRAND *in a whisper*): Another pair for you! (*She and* LYNGSTRAND *go off through the garden left. The sound of a brass band is heard in the distance through the following.*)

ELLIDA: He's come! He's here—I feel it!

WANGEL: Go into the house, Ellida; let me talk to him alone.

ELLIDA: No—that's impossible! Quite impossible, I tell you! (*Gives a cry*) Ah! There he is!
(*The* STRANGER *enters from the left, and stops on the path outside the garden fence.*)

STRANGER (*Bows*): Good evening. I told you I'd come back to-night, Ellida.

ELLIDA: Yes— This is the moment.

STRANGER: Are you ready for the journey? Or are you not?

WANGEL: No! Of course she isn't! You can see that for yourself.

STRANGER: I'm not speaking of traveling clothes, or trunks
—nothing of that sort. There's everything she needs on board.
I've engaged a cabin for her too. (*To* ELLIDA) Are you ready to
come with me, Ellida? Of your own free will?

ELLIDA (*Imploringly*): I beg of you, don't tempt me! Don't ask me
that!

(*A steamer bell is heard in the distance.*)

STRANGER: That's the first warning. You must decide now—yes or
no!

ELLIDA: Decide! My whole life depends on this decision! I'll never
have another chance to choose.

STRANGER: Never! Another half hour, and it will be too late.

ELLIDA: Why are you so ruthless? Why do you refuse to let me go?

STRANGER: We belong together; you know that.

ELLIDA: You mean—because we promised?

STRANGER: Men and women are not bound by promises. I refuse
to let you go because I can't.

ELLIDA (*Softly, tremulously*): Why didn't you come back before?

WANGEL: Ellida!

ELLIDA (*In an outburst*): What is this thing that beckons me and
tempts me—and drags me towards the unknown? It has all the
power and seduction of the sea!

(*The* STRANGER *climbs over the garden fence.*)

ELLIDA (*Shrinking behind* WANGEL): What is it! What do you
want?

STRANGER: You will choose me, Ellida! I know it. I can hear it in
your voice.

WANGEL: My wife has no choice to make. I'm here to choose for
her, and to protect her—yes, protect her! I warn you to get out!
Get out of this country—and stay out! You know you're wanted
here.

ELLIDA: Wangel! Not that!

STRANGER: What will you do to me?

WANGEL: I shall have you arrested immediately as the criminal
you are. You won't have a chance to get away. I know all about
that murder up at Skjoldvik.

ELLIDA: Wangel—how can you—!

STRANGER: I was prepared for that. (*Takes a revolver out of his breast pocket*) That's why I brought this with me.

ELLIDA (*Flings herself in front of* WANGEL): No! Not him! Rather kill me!

STRANGER: Don't be afraid. I won't harm either of you. I intend to live and die as a free man. I brought this for myself.

ELLIDA (*With increasing agitation*): Wangel! I must tell you this again—and I want him to hear it. I know you have the power to keep me here by force, and you intend to use it. But you can't control my mind. You can't prevent my thoughts, my longings and desires, from reaching out into that mysterious world of the unknown to which I belong, and that you have barred against me.

WANGEL: I understand, Ellida. I see you slipping further and further away from me. And I'm afraid this craving for a vague shadowy world of unreality will gradually destroy your mind—until it is blotted out in darkness.

ELLIDA: I feel it too, Wangel. It's like dark silent wings hovering over me.

WANGEL: Pray God it may not come to that. There's only one possible way of saving you; I can think of nothing else to do. Ellida! Here and now I release you from our bargain. You're free! I set you free. Now you can choose.

ELLIDA (*Looks at him for a moment as though speechless*): Is this true? Really true? You say this from your heart?

WANGEL: From my heart, Ellida.

ELLIDA: You'd really do this? You'd dare to do it?

WANGEL: Yes, I dare. Because I love you.

ELLIDA (*Softly and tremulously*): Have I become so close to you? So very dear?

WANGEL: Our years of marriage have made you so.

ELLIDA: And I never saw it! How blind I've been!

WANGEL: Your thoughts were filled with other things, Ellida. Now—I've released you. You're no longer bound to me by anything. Your life is yours again. You must act on your own responsibility; you're free to choose!

ELLIDA (*Puts her hands to her head and gazes fixedly towards*

WANGEL): Free to choose!— My own responsibility!— This changes everything!

(*The steamer bell rings again.*)

STRANGER: That's the last bell, Ellida. We must go.

ELLIDA (*Turns toward him, looks at him fixedly, and says in a determined voice*): I can never go with you after this.

STRANGER: Not go with me!

ELLIDA (*Clings to* WANGEL): Now I can never leave you.

WANGEL: Ellida—Ellida!

STRANGER: Is it all over then?

ELLIDA: All over.

STRANGER: What is it here that's stronger than my will?

ELLIDA: Your will can never touch me any more. You're like a dead man to me now. A dead seaman who came home out of the sea—and now goes back to it. You no longer terrify me—nor fascinate me either.

STRANGER: Goodbye, Mrs. Wangel! (*He vaults over the fence*) I've lived through many shipwrecks—I shall doubtless live through this one. I shall not think of you again.

(*He goes out to the left.*)

WANGEL (*Looks at her a while*): Ellida—your mind is like the sea; it ebbs and flows. What made you change?

ELLIDA: Don't you see? Everything changed—was bound to change—when you set me free to choose.

WANGEL: The unknown—it no longer fascinates you then?

ELLIDA: It neither frightens me nor fascinates me any more. I was free to gaze into it—to plunge into it if need be. I was free to choose it—and so I was able to reject it.

WANGEL: Gradually I begin to understand you. You see things in images—in symbols. I believe now, your longing for the sea—the fascination this strange man held for you—was only the expression of a growing need for freedom on your part.

ELLIDA: I've no way of knowing if that's true. But you've been a good doctor to me, Wangel. You found—and dared to use—the only remedy. The one thing that could save me.

WANGEL: In matters of life and death, we doctors have to dare! —Are you coming back to me, Ellida?

ELLIDA: Yes, my very dear—my faithful Wangel! I'm coming back to you. And this time—of my own free will.

WANGEL (*Looks at her tenderly*): Ellida! Ellida! We'll live wholly for each other from now on—

ELLIDA: And we'll share our memories; yours—as well as mine.

WANGEL: Yes, my darling!

ELLIDA: And we'll care for our two children—

WANGEL: Ours! You call them ours!

ELLIDA: I know they're not mine yet—but I shall try and win them.

WANGEL: Ours—! (*Kisses her hands rapidly and joyfully*) That one word makes me so happy.

(HILDE, BALLESTED, LYNGSTRAND, ARNHOLM *and* BOLETTE *come from the left into the garden. At the same time a number of young townspeople and summer visitors pass along the footpath.*)

HILDE (*Aside to* LYNGSTRAND): You'd think they were in love with each other, wouldn't you?

BALLESTED (*Who has overheard*): It's still summertime, you know.

ARNHOLM (*Glancing toward* WANGEL *and* ELLIDA): The English steamer's under way.

BOLETTE (*Going to the fence*): You can see her best from here.

LYNGSTRAND: Her last trip of the season.

BALLESTED: Yes. We shall soon be icebound. "Trapped in an icy prison," as the old melodrama says. A sad thought, Mrs. Wangel. And you're leaving too, I hear. You're off to Skjoldvik in the morning.

WANGEL: She's not going after all. We've changed our minds, you see.

ARNHOLM (*Looks from one to the other*): Really! Have you?

BOLETTE (*Coming forward*): Father—is this true?

HILDE (*Going to* ELLIDA): You're staying with us?

ELLIDA: Yes—if you'll have me, Hilde dear.

HILDE (*Struggling between tears and joy*): Have you! Heavens! How can you ask—!

ARNHOLM: This is quite a surprise, Mrs. Wangel.

ELLIDA: Well, you see, Mr. Arnholm— Do you remember the conversation we had yesterday?— Once you've decided to become a land creature, it's hard to find your way back to the sea again—

BALLESTED: That's like my mermaid, isn't it?

ELLIDA: Yes—very like.

BALLESTED: Only, of course, the mermaid dies of it. People on the other hand, are usually able to acclam—acclimatize themselves. I assure you, Mrs. Wangel—they do acclimatize themselves!

ELLIDA: Especially if they're free to choose.

WANGEL: And if they're allowed to act on their own responsibility, Ellida.

ELLIDA (*Quickly gives him her hand*): That's it—precisely!

(*The great steamer glides noiselessly down the fjord. The music is heard close inshore.*)

CURTAIN

Hedda Gabler

A PLAY IN FOUR ACTS

1890

CHARACTERS

JÖRGEN TESMAN,* *holder of a scholarship for research in the History of Civilization*

MRS. HEDDA GABLER TESMAN, *his wife*

MISS JULIANE TESMAN, *his aunt*

MRS. THEA RYSING ELVSTED

JUDGE BRACK

EJLERT LÖVBORG

BERTE, *maid at the Tesmans'*

The action takes place in Tesman's villa on the west side of the city (Oslo).

she likes to rise in horseback. w/ guns
different classes - slippers.
body language - rude.

*In performance, the form GEORGE is always used.

ACT
ONE

SCENE: *A large handsomely furnished drawing room, decorated in dark colors. In the back wall a wide opening with portieres that are drawn back. This opening leads to a smaller room decorated in the same style as the drawing room. In the right-hand wall of the front room is a folding door leading to the hall. In the wall opposite, on the left, a glass door, its hangings also drawn back. Through the panes can be seen part of a veranda and trees covered in autumn foliage. Standing well forward is an oval table, with a cover on it and surrounded by chairs. By the wall on the right stands a wide stove of dark porcelain, a high-backed arm-chair, an upholstered footstool and two tabourets. A small sofa fits into the right-hand corner with a small round table in front of it. Down left, standing slightly away from the wall, another sofa. Above the glass door, a piano. On either side of the opening in the back wall two étagères with terra-cotta and majolica ornaments. Against the back wall of the inner room a sofa, a table, and a couple of chairs. Above the sofa hangs the portrait of a handsome elderly man in the uniform of a general. Over the table a hanging lamp with an opalescent glass shade. A number of bouquets of flowers are arranged about the drawing room, in vases and glasses. Others lie on the various tables. The floors in both rooms are covered with thick carpets. It is morning. The sun shines through the glass door.*

MISS JULIANE TESMAN, *wearing a hat and carrying a parasol, enters from the hall followed by* BERTE, *who carries a bouquet wrapped in paper.* MISS TESMAN *is a good and pleasant-looking lady of about sixty-five. Simply but nicely dressed in a gray tailor-made.* BERTE *is a maid getting on in years, plain and rather countrified in appearance.*

MISS TESMAN (*Stops just inside the door, listens, and says softly*): Good gracious! They're not even up—I do believe!

BERTE (*Also speaks softly*): That's what I told you, Miss Juliane. The steamer got in so late last night; and the young mistress had such a lot of unpacking to do before she could get to bed.

MISS TESMAN: Well—let them sleep as long as they like. But when they do get up, they'll certainly need a breath of fresh air. (*She goes to the glass door and opens it wide.*)

BERTE (*At the table, uncertain what to do with the bouquet in her hand*): There's not a bit of room left anywhere. I'll just put them down here, Miss Juliane. (*Puts the bouquet down on the piano.*)

MISS TESMAN: So now you have a new mistress, Berte. Heaven knows it was hard enough for me to part with you.

BERTE (*On the verge of tears*): Don't think it wasn't hard for me too, Miss Juliane; after all those happy years I spent with you and Miss Rina.

MISS TESMAN: We'll just have to make the best of it, Berte. Master Jörgen needs you—he really does. You've looked after him ever since he was a little boy.

BERTE: That's true, Miss Juliane; but I can't help worrying about Miss Rina lying there helpless, poor thing; how *will* she manage? That new maid will never learn to take proper care of an invalid!

MISS TESMAN: I'll soon be able to train her; and until then, I'll do most of the work myself—so don't you worry about my poor sister, Berte.

BERTE: But, there's something else, Miss Juliane—you see, I'm so afraid I won't be able to please the young mistress.

MISS TESMAN: Well—there may be one or two things, just at first—

BERTE: She'll be very particular, I expect—

MISS TESMAN: That's only natural—after all, she's General Gabler's daughter. She was used to being spoiled when her father was alive. Do you remember how we used to see her galloping by? How smart she looked in her riding clothes!

BERTE: Indeed I do remember, Miss Juliane! Who would ever have thought that she and Master Jörgen would make a match of it!

MISS TESMAN: God moves in mysterious ways—! But, by the way, Berte—before I forget—you mustn't say Master Jörgen any more—it's Doctor Tesman!

BERTE: I know, Miss Juliane. That was one of the very first things the young mistress told me last night. So it's really true, Miss Juliane?

MISS TESMAN: Yes, it is indeed! He was made a doctor by one of the foreign universities while he was abroad. It was a great surprise to me; I knew nothing about it until he told me last night on the pier.

BERTE: Well—he's clever enough for anything, he is! But I never thought he'd go in for doctoring people!

MISS TESMAN: It's not *that* kind of a doctor, Berte! (*Nods significantly*) But later on, you may have to call him something even grander!

BERTE: Really, Miss Juliane? Now what could that be?

MISS TESMAN (*Smiles*): Wouldn't you like to know! (*Moved*) I wonder what my poor brother would say if he could see what a great man his little boy has become. (*Looking around*) But, what's this, Berte? Why have you taken all the covers off the furniture?

BERTE: The young mistress told me to. She said she couldn't bear them.

MISS TESMAN: Perhaps she intends to use this as the living room?

BERTE: I think maybe she does, Miss Juliane; though Master Jörgen—I mean the Doctor—said nothing about it.

(JÖRGEN TESMAN *enters the inner room from right, singing gaily. He carries an unstrapped empty suitcase. He is a young-looking man of thirty-three, medium height. Rather plump, a pleasant, round, open face. Blond hair and beard, wears spectacles. Rather carelessly dressed in comfortable lounging clothes.*)

MISS TESMAN: Good morning—good morning, my dear Jörgen!

TESMAN (*At the opening between the rooms*): Aunt Juliane! Dear Aunt Juliane! (*Goes to her and shakes her warmly by the hand*) Way out here—so early in the morning—eh?

MISS TESMAN: I had to come and see how you were getting on.

TESMAN: In spite of going to bed so late?

MISS TESMAN: My dear boy—as if that mattered to me!

TESMAN: You got home all right from the pier—eh?

MISS TESMAN: Quite all right, dear, thank you. Judge Brack was kind enough to see me safely to my door.

TESMAN: We were so sorry we couldn't give you a lift—but Hedda had such a fearful lot of luggage—

MISS TESMAN: Yes—she did seem to have quite a bit!

BERTE (*To* TESMAN): Should I ask the Mistress if there's anything I can do for her, sir?

TESMAN: No thank you, Berte—there's no need. She said she'd ring if she wanted anything.

BERTE (*Starting right*): Very good, sir.

TESMAN (*Indicates suitcase*): You might just take that suitcase with you.

BERTE (*Taking it*): Yes, sir. I'll put it in the attic. (*She goes out by the hall door.*)

TESMAN: Do you know, Aunt Juliane—I had that whole suitcase full of notes? It's unbelievable how much I found in all the archives I examined; curious old details no one had any idea existed.

MISS TESMAN: You don't seem to have wasted your time on your wedding trip!

TESMAN: Indeed I haven't—But do take off your hat, Aunt Juliane—let me help you—eh?

MISS TESMAN (*While he does so*): How sweet of you! This is just like the old days when you were still with us!

TESMAN (*He turns the hat round in his hands, looking at it admiringly from all sides*): That's a very elegant hat you've treated yourself to.

MISS TESMAN: I bought that on Hedda's account.

TESMAN: On Hedda's account—eh?

MISS TESMAN: Yes—I didn't want her to feel ashamed of her old aunt—in case we should happen to go out together.

TESMAN (*Patting her cheek*): What a dear you are, Aunt Juliane—always thinking of everything! (*Puts the hat down on a chair near the table*) And now let's sit down here on the sofa and have a cozy little chat till Hedda comes. (*They sit down. She leans her parasol in the corner of the sofa.*)

MISS TESMAN (*Takes both his hands and gazes at him*): I can't tell
you what a joy it is to have you home again, Jörgen.

TESMAN: And it's a joy for me to see you again, dear Aunt Juliane.
You've been as good as a father and mother to me—I can never
forget that!

MISS TESMAN: I know, dear—you'll always have a place in your
heart for your poor old aunts.

TESMAN: How *is* Aunt Rina—eh? Isn't she feeling a little better?

MISS TESMAN: No, dear. I'm afraid she'll never be any better,
poor thing! But I pray God I may keep her with me a little
longer—for now that I haven't you to look after any more, I don't
know what will become of me when she goes.

TESMAN (*Pats her on the back*): There, there, there!

MISS TESMAN (*With a sudden change of tone*): You know, I can't
get used to thinking of you as a married man, Jörgen. And to
think that you should have been the one to carry off Hedda
Gabler—the fascinating Hedda Gabler—who was always surrounded by so many admirers!

TESMAN (*Hums a little and smiles complacently*): Yes—I wouldn't
be surprised if some of my friends were a bit jealous of me—eh?

MISS TESMAN: And then this wonderful wedding trip! Five—
nearly six months!

TESMAN: Of course you must remember the trip was also of great
value to me in my research work. I can't begin to tell you all the
archives I've been through—and the many books I've read!

MISS TESMAN: I can well believe it! (*More confidentially, lowering
her voice*) But, Jörgen dear, are you sure you've nothing
—well—nothing *special* to tell me?

TESMAN: About our trip?

MISS TESMAN: Yes.

TESMAN: I can't think of anything I didn't write you about. I had a
doctor's degree conferred on me—but I told you that last night.

MISS TESMAN: Yes, yes—you told me about that. But what I mean
is—haven't you any—well—any expectations?

TESMAN: Expectations?

MISS TESMAN: Yes, Jörgen. Surely you can talk frankly to your
old aunt?

TESMAN: Well, of course I have expectations!

MISS TESMAN: Well?

TESMAN: I have every expectation of becoming a professor one of these days!

MISS TESMAN: A professor—yes, yes, I know dear—but—

TESMAN: In fact, I'm certain of it. But you know that just as well as I do, Aunt Juliane.

MISS TESMAN (*Chuckling*): Of course I do, dear—you're quite right. (*Changing the subject*) But we were talking about your journey—it must have cost a great deal of money, Jörgen!

TESMAN: Well, you see, the scholarship I had was pretty ample—that went a good way.

MISS TESMAN: Still—I don't see how it could have been ample enough for two—especially traveling with a lady—they say that makes it ever so much more expensive.

TESMAN: It does make it a bit more expensive—but Hedda simply had to have this trip—she really had to—it was the fashionable thing to do.

MISS TESMAN: I know—nowadays it seems a wedding has to be followed by a wedding trip. But tell me, Jörgen—have you been over the house yet?

TESMAN: I have indeed! I've been up since daybreak!

MISS TESMAN: What do you think of it?

TESMAN: It's splendid—simply splendid! But it seems awfully big—what on earth shall we do with all those empty rooms?

MISS TESMAN (*Laughingly*): Oh, my dear Jörgen—I expect you'll find plenty of use for them—a little later on.

TESMAN: Yes, you're right, Aunt Juliane—as I get more and more books—eh?

MISS TESMAN: Of course, my dear boy—it was your books I was thinking of!

TESMAN: I'm especially pleased for Hedda's sake. She had her heart set on this house—it belonged to Secretary Falk, you know—even before we were engaged, she used to say it was the one place she'd really like to live in.

MISS TESMAN: But I'm afraid you'll find all this very expensive,
my dear Jörgen—very expensive!

TESMAN (*Looks at her a little despondently*): Yes, I suppose so.
How much do you really think it will cost? I mean approximately—eh?

MISS TESMAN: That's impossible to say until we've seen all the
bills.

TESMAN: Judge Brack wrote Hedda that he'd been able to secure
very favorable terms for me.

MISS TESMAN: But you mustn't worry about it, my dear boy—for
one thing, I've given security for all the furniture and the carpets.

TESMAN: Security? You, dear Aunt Juliane? What sort of security?

MISS TESMAN: A mortgage on our annuity.

TESMAN (*Jumps up*): What!

MISS TESMAN: I didn't know what else to do.

TESMAN (*Standing before her*): You must be mad, Aunt
Juliane—quite mad. That annuity is all that you and Aunt Rina
have to live on!

MISS TESMAN: Don't get so excited about it! It's only a matter of
form, Judge Brack says. He was kind enough to arrange the
whole matter for me.

TESMAN: That's all very well—but still—!

MISS TESMAN: And from now on you'll have your own salary to depend on—and even if we should have to help out a little, just at
first—it would only be the greatest pleasure to us!

TESMAN: Isn't that just like you, Aunt Juliane! Always making sac-
rifices for me.

MISS TESMAN (*Rises and places her hands on his shoulders*): The
only happiness I have in the world is making things easier for
you, my dear boy. We've been through some bad times, I
admit—but now we've reached the goal and we've nothing to
fear.

TESMAN (*Sits down beside her again*): Yes—it's amazing how
everything's turned out for the best!

MISS TESMAN: Now there's no one to stand in your way—even your most dangerous rival has fallen. Well, he made his bed—let him lie on it, poor misguided creature.

TESMAN: Has there been any news of Ejlert—since I went away, I mean?

MISS TESMAN: They say he's supposed to have published a new book.

TESMAN: Ejlert Lövborg! A new book? Recently—eh?

MISS TESMAN: That's what they say—but I shouldn't think any book of his would be worth much. It'll be a very different story when *your* new book appears. What's it to be about, Jörgen?

TESMAN: It will deal with the Domestic Industries of Brabant during the Middle Ages.

MISS TESMAN: Fancy being able to write about such things!

TESMAN: Of course it'll be some time before the book is ready—I still have to arrange and classify all my notes, you see.

MISS TESMAN: Yes—collecting and arranging—no one can compete with you in that! You're not your father's son for nothing!

TESMAN: I can't wait to begin! Especially now that I have my own comfortable home to work in.

MISS TESMAN: And best of all—you have your wife! The wife you longed for!

TESMAN (*Embracing her*): Yes, you're right, Aunt Juliane —Hedda! She's the most wonderful part of it all! (*Looks toward opening between the rooms*) But here she comes—eh? (HEDDA *enters from the left through the inner room. She is a woman of twenty-nine. Her face and figure show breeding and distinction. Her complexion is pale and opaque. Her eyes are steel-gray and express a cold, unruffled repose. Her hair is an agreeable medium-brown, but not especially abundant. She wears a tasteful, somewhat loose-fitting negligee.*)

MISS TESMAN (*Goes to meet* HEDDA): Good morning, Hedda dear—and welcome home!

HEDDA (*Gives her her hand*): Good morning, my dear Miss Tesman. What an early visitor you are—how kind of you!

MISS TESMAN (*Seems slightly embarrassed*): Not at all. And did the bride sleep well in her new home?

HEDDA: Thank you—fairly well.

TESMAN (*Laughing*): Fairly well! I like that, Hedda! You were sleeping like a log when I got up!

HEDDA: Yes—fortunately. You know, Miss Tesman, one has to adapt oneself gradually to new surroundings. (*Glancing toward the left*) Good heavens—what a nuisance! That maid's opened the window and let in a whole flood of sunshine!

MISS TESMAN (*Starts towards door*): Well—we'll just close it then!

HEDDA: No, no—don't do that! Jörgen, dear, just draw the curtains, will you? It'll give a softer light.

TESMAN (*At the door*): There, Hedda! Now you have both shade and fresh air!

HEDDA: Heaven knows we need some fresh air, with all these stacks of flowers! But do sit down, my dear Miss Tesman.

MISS TESMAN: No—many thanks! Now that I know everything's all right here, I must be getting home to my poor sister.

TESMAN: Do give her my best love, Aunt Juliane—and tell her I'll drop in and see her later in the day.

MISS TESMAN: Yes, dear, I'll do that. . . . Oh! I'd almost forgotten (*Feeling in the pocket of her dress*) I've brought something for you!

TESMAN: What can that be, Aunt Juliane—eh?

MISS TESMAN (*Produces a flat parcel wrapped in newspaper and presents him with it*): Look, dear!

TESMAN (*Opens the parcel*): Oh, Aunt Juliane! You really kept them for me! Isn't that touching, Hedda—eh?

HEDDA (*By the* étagère *on the right*): Well, what is it, dear?

TESMAN: My slippers, Hedda! My old bedroom slippers!

HEDDA: Oh, yes—I remember. You often spoke of them on our journey.

TESMAN: I can't tell you how I've missed them! (*Goes up to her*) Do have a look at them, Hedda—

HEDDA (*Going toward stove*): I'm really not very interested, Jörgen—

TESMAN (*Following her*): Dear Aunt Rina embroidered them for me during her illness. They have so many memories for me—

HEDDA (*At the table*): Scarcely for me, Jörgen.

MISS TESMAN: Of course not, Jörgen! They mean nothing to Hedda.

TESMAN: I only thought, now that she's one of the family—

HEDDA (*Interrupting*): We shall never get on with this servant, Jörgen!

MISS TESMAN: Not get on with Berte?

TESMAN: Hedda dear, what do you mean?

HEDDA: (*Pointing*): Look! She's left her old hat lying about on the table.

TESMAN (*Flustered—dropping the slippers on the floor*): Why— Hedda—!

HEDDA: Just imagine if someone were to come in and see it!

TESMAN: But, Hedda! That's Aunt Juliane's hat!

HEDDA: Oh! Is it?

MISS TESMAN (*Picks up the hat*): Yes, indeed it is! And what's more it's not old—little Mrs. Tesman!

HEDDA: I really didn't look at it very closely, Miss Tesman.

MISS TESMAN (*Puts on the hat*): This is the very first time I've worn it!

TESMAN: And it's a lovely hat, too—quite a beauty!

MISS TESMAN: Oh, it isn't as beautiful as all that. (*Looking round*) Where's my parasol? (*Takes it*) Ah—here it is! (*Mutters*) For this is mine too—not Berte's.

TESMAN: A new hat and a new parasol—just think, Hedda!

HEDDA: Most handsome and lovely, I'm sure!

TESMAN: Yes—isn't it, eh? But do take a good look at Hedda —see how lovely *she* is!

MISS TESMAN: Hedda was always lovely, my dear boy—that's nothing new. (*She nods and goes toward the right.*)

TESMAN (*Following her*): But don't you think she's looking especially well? I think she's filled out a bit while we've been away.

HEDDA (*Crossing the room*): Oh, do be quiet . . . !

MISS TESMAN (*Who has stopped and turned toward them*): Filled out?

TESMAN: Of course, you can't notice it so much in that loose dress—but I have certain opportunities—

HEDDA (*Stands at the glass door—impatiently*): You have no opportunities at all, Jörgen—

TESMAN: I think it must have been the mountain air in the Tyrol—

HEDDA (*Curtly interrupting*): I'm exactly as I was when we left!

TESMAN: That's what you say—but I don't agree with you! What do you think, Aunt Juliane?

MISS TESMAN (*Gazing at her with folded hands*): Hedda is lovely—lovely! (*Goes to her, takes her face in her hands and gently kisses the top of her head*) God bless and keep you, Hedda Tesman, for Jörgen's sake!

HEDDA (*Quietly freeing herself*): Please! Oh, please let me go!

MISS TESMAN (*With quiet emotion*): I shan't let a day pass without coming to see you!

TESMAN: That's right, Aunt Juliane!

MISS TESMAN: Good-bye, dearest Hedda—good-bye!

(*She goes out by the hall door.* TESMAN *sees her out. The door remains half open.* TESMAN *can be heard repeating his greetings to* AUNT RINA *and his thanks for the bedroom slippers. Meanwhile,* HEDDA *paces about the room, raises her arms and clenches her hands as though in desperation. She flings back the curtains of the glass door and stands gazing out. In a moment* TESMAN *returns and closes the door behind him.*)

TESMAN (*Picking up the slippers from the floor*): What are you looking at, Hedda?

HEDDA (*Once more calm and controlled*): I'm just looking at the leaves—they're so yellow—so withered.

TESMAN (*Wraps up the slippers and puts them on the table*): Well, we're well into September now.

HEDDA (*Again restless*): God, yes! September—September already!

TESMAN: Didn't you think Aunt Juliane was a little strange? Almost solemn, I thought. What do you suppose was the matter with her—eh?

HEDDA: Well, you see, I scarcely know her. Isn't she always like that?

TESMAN: No, not as she was today.

HEDDA (*Leaving the glass door*): Perhaps she was annoyed about the hat.

TESMAN: Oh, not specially—perhaps just for a moment—

HEDDA (*Crosses over toward the fireplace*): Such a peculiar way to behave—flinging one's hat about in the drawing room—one doesn't do that sort of thing.

TESMAN: I'm sure Aunt Juliane won't do it again.

HEDDA: I shall manage to make my peace with her. When you see her this afternoon, Jörgen, you might ask her to come and spend the evening here.

TESMAN: Yes, I will, Hedda. And there's another thing you could do that would give her so much pleasure.

HEDDA: Well—what's that?

TESMAN: If you could only be a little more affectionate with her—just for my sake—eh?

HEDDA: I shall try to call her Aunt—but that's really all I can do.

TESMAN: Very well. I just thought, now that you belong to the family—

HEDDA: I really don't see why, Jörgen— (*She goes up toward the center opening.*)

TESMAN (*After a short pause*): Is there anything the matter with you, Hedda, eh?

HEDDA: No, nothing. I'm just looking at my old piano. It doesn't seem to fit in with the rest of the furniture.

TESMAN: The first time I draw my salary, we'll see about exchanging it.

HEDDA: Exchange it! Why exchange it? I don't want to part with it. Why couldn't we put it in the inner room and get a new one for here? That is, of course, when we can afford it.

TESMAN (*Slightly taken back*): Yes, I suppose we could do that.

HEDDA (*Takes up the bouquet from the piano*): These flowers weren't here last night when we arrived.

TESMAN: I expect Aunt Juliane brought them for you.

HEDDA (*Examines the bouquet*): Here's a card. (*Takes out a card and reads it*) "Shall return later in the day." Can you guess who it's from?

TESMAN: No. Tell me.

HEDDA: From Mrs. Elvsted.

TESMAN: Really! Sheriff Elvsted's wife. The former Miss Rysing.

HEDDA: Exactly. The girl with that irritating mass of hair—she was always showing off. I've heard she was an old flame of yours, Jörgen?

TESMAN (*Laughs*): Oh, that didn't last long, and it was before I met you, Hedda. Fancy her being in town.

HEDDA: Funny that she should call on us. I haven't seen her for years. Not since we were at school together.

TESMAN: I haven't seen her, either, for ever so long. I wonder how she can stand living in that remote, dreary place.

HEDDA: I wonder! (*After a moment's thought, says suddenly*) Tell me, Jörgen, doesn't Ejlert Lövborg live somewhere near there?

TESMAN: Yes, I believe he does. Somewhere in that neighborhood.

BERTE (*Enters by the hall door*): That lady, ma'am, who left some flowers a little while ago is back again. (*Pointing*) The flowers you have in your hand, ma'am.

HEDDA: Oh, is she? Very well, ask her to come in.

(BERTE *opens the door for* MRS. ELVSTED *and exits.* MRS. ELVSTED *is a fragile woman with soft, pretty features. Her large, round, light-blue eyes are slightly prominent and have a timid, questioning look. Her hair is unusually fair, almost white-gold and extremely thick and wavy. She is a couple of years younger than* HEDDA. *She wears a dark visiting dress, in good taste but not in the latest fashion.*)

HEDDA (*Graciously goes to meet her*): How do you do, my dear Mrs. Elvsted? How delightful to see you again after all these years.

MRS. ELVSTED (*Nervously, trying to control herself*): Yes, it's a very long time since we met.

TESMAN (*Gives her his hand*): And we haven't met for a long time, either, eh?

HEDDA: Thank you for your lovely flowers.

MRS. ELVSTED: Oh, don't mention it. I would have come to see you yesterday, but I heard you were away.

TESMAN: Have you just arrived in town, eh?

MRS. ELVSTED: Yes, I got here yesterday morning. I was so upset not to find you at home.

HEDDA: Upset! But why, my dear Mrs. Elvsted?

TESMAN: But, my dear Mrs. Rysing—eh, Mrs. Elvsted, I mean—

HEDDA: I hope you're not in any trouble.

MRS. ELVSTED: Well, yes, I am, and I know no one else in town that I could possibly turn to—

HEDDA (*Puts the bouquet down on the table*): Come, let's sit down here on the sofa—

MRS. ELVSTED: I'm really too nervous to sit down.

HEDDA: Of course you're not. Come along now— (*She draws* MRS. ELVSTED *down to the sofa and sits beside her*.)

TESMAN: Well, Mrs. Elvsted?

HEDDA: Has anything gone wrong at home?

MRS. ELVSTED: Well, eh—yes, and no. I do hope you won't misunderstand me.

HEDDA: Perhaps you'd better tell us all about it, Mrs. Elvsted.

TESMAN: I suppose that's what you've come for, eh?

MRS. ELVSTED: Yes, of course. Well, first of all—But perhaps you've already heard— Ejlert Lövborg is in town, too.

HEDDA: Lövborg!

TESMAN: What! Ejlert Lövborg has come back! Think of that, Hedda!

HEDDA: Good heavens, yes, I heard it!

MRS. ELVSTED: He's been here for a week. A whole week. I'm so afraid he'll get into trouble—

HEDDA: But, my dear Mrs. Elvsted, why should you be so worried about him?

MRS. ELVSTED (*Gives her a startled look and speaks hurriedly*): Well, you see—he's the children's tutor.

HEDDA: Your children's?

MRS. ELVSTED: No. My husband's. I have none.

HEDDA: Oh, your stepchildren's then?

MRS. ELVSTED: Yes.

TESMAN (*With some hesitation*): Was he—I don't quite know how to put it—was he dependable enough to fill such a position, eh?

MRS. ELVSTED: For the last two years his conduct has been irreproachable.

TESMAN: Has it, really? Think of that, Hedda!

HEDDA: Yes, yes, yes! I heard it.

MRS. ELVSTED: Irreproachable in every respect, I assure you, but still I know how dangerous it is for him to be here in town all alone, and he has quite a lot of money with him. I can't help being worried to death about him.

TESMAN: But why did he *come* here? Why didn't he stay where he was? With you and your husband, eh?

MRS. ELVSTED: After his book was published he felt too restless to stay on with us.

TESMAN: Oh, yes, of course. Aunt Juliane told me he had published a new book.

MRS. ELVSTED: Yes, a wonderful book. A sort of outline of civilization. It came out a couple of weeks ago. It's sold marvelously. Made quite a sensation.

TESMAN: Has it really? Then I suppose it's something he wrote some time ago—during his better years.

MRS. ELVSTED: No, no. He's written it all since he's been with us.

TESMAN: Well, isn't that splendid, Hedda? Think of that!

MRS. ELVSTED: Yes, if only he'll keep it up.

HEDDA: Have you seen him here in town?

MRS. ELVSTED: Not yet. I had great trouble finding out his address, but this morning I got it at last.

HEDDA (*Gives her a searching look*): But doesn't it seem rather odd of your husband to—

MRS. ELVSTED (*With a nervous start*): Of my husband—what?

HEDDA: Well—to send you on such an errand. Why didn't he come himself to look after his friend?

MRS. ELVSTED: Oh, no. My husband is much too busy. And besides, I had some shopping to do.

HEDDA (*With a slight smile*): Oh, I see!

MRS. ELVSTED (*Rising quickly and uneasily*): I implore you, Mr.

Tesman, be good to Ejlert Lövborg if he should come to see
you. I'm sure he will. You were such great friends in the old
days, and after all, you're both interested in the same studies.
You specialize in the same subjects—as far as I can understand.

TESMAN: Yes, we used to, at any rate.

MRS. ELVSTED: That's why I'd be so grateful if you too would
—well—keep an eye on him. You will do that, won't you, Mr.
Tesman?

TESMAN: I'd be delighted to, Mrs. Rysing.

HEDDA: Elvsted!

TESMAN: I'd be delighted to do anything in my power to help
Ejlert. You can rely on me.

MRS. ELVSTED (*Presses his hands*): Oh, how very kind of you! I
can't thank you enough . . . (*Frightened*) You see, my husband
is so very fond of him.

HEDDA (*Rises*): Yes—I see. I think you should write to him,
Jörgen. He may not care to come of his own accord.

TESMAN: Perhaps that would be the right thing to do, Hedda, eh?

HEDDA: Yes. The sooner the better. Why not at once?

MRS. ELVSTED (*Imploringly*): Oh, yes, please do!

TESMAN: I'll write him this minute. Have you his address, Mrs.
Ry—Elvsted?

MRS. ELVSTED (*Takes a slip of paper from her pocket and gives it
to him*): Here it is.

TESMAN: Splendid. Then I'll go in. (*Looks around*) Oh—I mustn't
forget my slippers. Ah! Here they are. (*Takes the parcel and
starts to go.*)

HEDDA: Mind you write him a nice friendly letter, Jörgen, and a
good long one, too.

TESMAN: I most certainly will.

MRS. ELVSTED: But don't let him know that I suggested it!

TESMAN: Of course not! That goes without saying, eh? (*He goes out
right, through the inner room.*)

HEDDA (*Smilingly goes to* MRS. ELVSTED *and says in a low voice*):
There! Now we've killed two birds with one stone.

MRS. ELVSTED: What do you mean?

HEDDA: Couldn't you see that I wanted to get rid of him?

MRS. ELVSTED: Yes, to write the letter.

HEDDA: And so that I could talk to you alone.

MRS. ELVSTED (*Bewildered*): About the same thing?

HEDDA: Precisely.

MRS. ELVSTED (*Apprehensively*): But there's nothing else to tell, Mrs. Tesman. Absolutely nothing.

HEDDA: Of course there is. I can see that. There's a great *deal* more to tell. Come along. Sit down. We'll have a nice friendly talk. (*She forces* MRS. ELVSTED *down into the armchair by the stove and seats herself on one of the tabourets.*)

MRS. ELVSTED (*Anxiously looking at her watch*): But, really, Mrs. Tesman, I was just thinking of going—

HEDDA: Oh, you can't be in such a hurry. Come along, now—I want to know all about your life at home.

MRS. ELVSTED: I prefer not to speak about that.

HEDDA: But to me, dear! After all, we went to school together.

MRS. ELVSTED: Yes, but you were in a higher class, and I was always so dreadfully afraid of you then.

HEDDA: Afraid of me!

MRS. ELVSTED: Yes, dreadfully. When we met on the stairs you always used to pull my hair.

HEDDA: Did I, really!

MRS. ELVSTED: Yes. And once you said you were going to burn it all off.

HEDDA: I was just teasing you, of course!

MRS. ELVSTED: I was so silly in those days, and afterwards we drifted so far apart. We lived in such different worlds. . . .

HEDDA: Well, then we must drift together again. At school we always called each other by our first names. Why shouldn't we now?

MRS. ELVSTED: I think you're mistaken—

HEDDA: Of course not. I remember it distinctly. We were *great* friends! (*Draws her stool near to* MRS. ELVSTED *and kisses her on the cheek*) So you must call me Hedda.

MRS. ELVSTED (*Pressing her hands and patting them*): You're so kind and understanding. I'm not used to kindness.

HEDDA: And I shall call you my darling little Thora.

MRS. ELVSTED: My name is Thea.

HEDDA: Yes, yes, of course, I meant Thea! (*Looking at her compassionately*) So my darling little Thea—you mean they're not kind to you at home?

MRS. ELVSTED: If only I had a home! But I haven't. I never had one.

HEDDA (*Gives her a quick look*): I suspected something of the sort.

MRS. ELVSTED (*Gazing helplessly before her*): Ah!

HEDDA: Tell me, Thea—I'm a little vague about it. When you first went to the Elvsteds', you were engaged as housekeeper, weren't you?

MRS. ELVSTED: I was supposed to go as governess, but Mrs. Elvsted—the first Mrs. Elvsted, that is—was an invalid, and rarely left her room, so I had to take charge of the house as well.

HEDDA: And, eventually, you became mistress of the house?

MRS. ELVSTED (*Sadly*): Yes, I did.

HEDDA: How long ago was that?

MRS. ELVSTED: That I married him?

HEDDA: Yes.

MRS. ELVSTED: Five years ago.

HEDDA: Yes, that's right.

MRS. ELVSTED: Oh, those five years, especially the last two or three of them— If only you knew, Mrs. Tesman!

HEDDA (*Slaps her lightly on the hand*): Mrs. Tesman! Thea!

MRS. ELVSTED: I'll try—You have no idea, Hedda—

HEDDA (*Casually*): Ejlert Lövborg's lived near you about three years, hasn't he?

MRS. ELVSTED (*Looks at her doubtfully*): Ejlert Lövborg? Why, yes, he has.

HEDDA: Had you met him before, here in town?

MRS. ELVSTED: No, not really—I knew him by name, of course.

HEDDA: But I suppose up there you saw a good deal of him.

MRS. ELVSTED: Yes, he came to our house every day. He gave the children lessons, you see. I had so much to do; I couldn't manage that, as well.

HEDDA: No. Of course not. And I suppose your husband's away from home a good deal.

MRS. ELVSTED: Yes. Being sheriff, he often has to travel about his district.

HEDDA (*Leans against the arm of the chair*): Now, my dear darling little Thea, I want you to tell me everything—exactly as it is.

MRS. ELVSTED: Well, then you must question me.

HEDDA: Tell me—what sort of a man is your husband, Thea? To live with, I mean. Is he kind to you?

MRS. ELVSTED (*Evasively*): He probably thinks he is.

HEDDA: But isn't he much too old for you, dear? There must be at least twenty years between you.

MRS. ELVSTED (*Irritably*): Yes, that makes it all the harder. We haven't a thought in common. Nothing, in fact.

HEDDA: But, I suppose he's fond of you in his own way.

MRS. ELVSTED: Oh, I don't know. I think he finds me useful. And then it doesn't cost much to keep me. I'm not expensive.

HEDDA: That's stupid of you.

MRS. ELVSTED (*Shakes her head*): It couldn't be otherwise. Not with him. I don't believe he really cares about anyone but himself. And perhaps a little for the children.

HEDDA: And for Ejlert Lövborg, Thea?

MRS. ELVSTED (*Looking at her*): Ejlert Lövborg? What makes you say that?

HEDDA: Well, it's obvious!— After all, he's sent you all this way into town, simply to look for him!— (*With the trace of a smile*) Wasn't that what you told Jörgen?

MRS. ELVSTED (*With a nervous twitch*): Yes, I suppose I did. (*Vehemently but in a low voice*) Oh, I might as well tell you the truth. It's bound to come out sooner or later.

HEDDA: What—?

MRS. ELVSTED: Well, then—my husband knew nothing about my coming here.

HEDDA: Your husband didn't know!

MRS. ELVSTED: No, of course not. He was away himself at the time. I couldn't stand it any longer, Hedda. I simply couldn't. I felt so alone, so deserted—

HEDDA: Yes, yes—well?

MRS. ELVSTED: So I packed a few of my things—just those I

needed most—I didn't say a word to anyone. I simply left the
house.

HEDDA: Just like that!

MRS. ELVSTED: Yes, and took the next train to town.

HEDDA: But, Thea, my darling! How did you dare do such a thing?

MRS. ELVSTED (*Rises and walks about the room*): What else could
I possibly do?

HEDDA: But what will your husband say when you go home again?

MRS. ELVSTED (*At the table, looks at her*): Back to him!

HEDDA: Well, of course.

MRS. ELVSTED: I shall never go back to him again.

HEDDA (*Rises and goes toward her*): You mean you've actually left
your home for *good*?

MRS. ELVSTED: I saw nothing else to do.

HEDDA: But to leave like that, so openly—

MRS. ELVSTED: You can't very well *hide* a thing like that!

HEDDA: But what will people say about you, Thea?

MRS. ELVSTED: They can say whatever they like. (*Sits on the sofa
wearily and sadly*) I only did what I had to do.

HEDDA (*After a short silence*): What are your plans now?

MRS. ELVSTED: I don't know yet. All I know is that I must live
near Ejlert Lövborg, if I'm to live at all.

HEDDA (*Takes a chair from the table, sits down near* MRS.
ELVSTED *and strokes her hands*): Tell me, Thea—how did this
friendship start between you and Ejlert Lövborg?

MRS. ELVSTED: It grew gradually. I began to have a sort of power
over him.

HEDDA: Really?

MRS. ELVSTED: Yes. After a while he gave up his old habits. Oh,
not because I asked him to—I never would have dared do that.
But I suppose he realized how unhappy they made me, and so he
dropped them.

HEDDA (*Concealing a scornful smile*): So, my darling little Thea,
you've actually reformed him!

MRS. ELVSTED: Well, *he* says so, at any rate, and in return he's
made a human being out of me. Taught me to think and understand so many things.

HEDDA: Did he give you lessons, too, then?

MRS. ELVSTED: Not lessons, exactly, but he talked to me, explained so much to me—and the most wonderful thing of all was
when he finally allowed me to share in his work. Allowed me to
help him.

HEDDA: He did, did he?

MRS. ELVSTED: Yes. He wanted me to be a part of everything he
wrote.

HEDDA: Like two good comrades!

MRS. ELVSTED (*Brightly*): Comrades! Why, Hedda, that's exactly
what *he* says! I ought to be so happy, but somehow I'm not. I'm
so afraid it may not last.

HEDDA: You're not very sure of him, then?

MRS. ELVSTED (*Gloomily*): I sometimes feel a shadow between
Lövborg and me—a woman's shadow.

HEDDA (*Looks at her intently*): Who could that be?

MRS. ELVSTED: I don't know. Someone he knew long ago. Someone he's never been able to forget.

HEDDA: Has he told you anything about her?

MRS. ELVSTED: He spoke of her once—quite vaguely.

HEDDA: What did he say?

MRS. ELVSTED: He said that when they parted she threatened to
shoot him.

HEDDA (*With cold composure*): What nonsense! No one does that
sort of thing here!

MRS. ELVSTED: I know. That's why I think it must have been that
red-haired cabaret singer he was once—

HEDDA: Very likely.

MRS. ELVSTED: They say she used to go about with loaded pistols.

HEDDA: Then of course it must have been she.

MRS. ELVSTED (*Wringing her hands*): But, Hedda, they say she's
here now—in town, again! I'm so worried I don't know what to
do!

HEDDA (*With a glance toward inner room*): Sh! Here comes
Tesman. Not a word to him. All this is between us.

MRS. ELVSTED (*Jumps up*): Yes, yes, of course.

(JÖRGEN TESMAN, *a letter in his hand, enters from the right
through the inner room.*)

TESMAN: Well, here is the letter signed and sealed!

HEDDA: Splendid! Mrs. Elvsted was just leaving, Jörgen. Wait a minute! I'll go with you as far as the garden gate.

TESMAN: Do you think Berte could post this for me, dear?

HEDDA (*Takes the letter*): I'll tell her to.

(BERTE *enters from the hall*.)

BERTE: Judge Brack wishes to know if you will see him, ma'am.

HEDDA: Yes. Show him in. And post this letter, will you?

BERTE (*Taking the letter*): Certainly, ma'am.

(*She opens the door for* JUDGE BRACK *and goes out. The* JUDGE *is a man of forty-five. Thick-set but well-built and supple in his movements. His face is rounded and his profile aristocratic. His short hair is still almost black and carefully dressed. His eyes are bright and sparkling. His eyebrows thick. His mustache also thick with short-cut ends. He wears a smart walking suit, slightly youthful for his age. He uses an eyeglass, which he lets drop from time to time.*)

BRACK (*Bowing, hat in hand*): May one venture to call so early in the day?

HEDDA: Of course one may.

TESMAN (*Shakes hands with him*): You know you're always welcome. (*Introduces him.*) Judge Brack, Miss Rysing.

HEDDA: Ah!

BRACK (*Bows*): Delighted.

HEDDA (*Looks at him and laughs*): What fun to have a look at you by daylight, Judge.

BRACK: Do you find me—altered?

HEDDA: A little younger, I think.

BRACK (*Laughs and goes down to fireplace*): I thank you, most heartily.

TESMAN: But what do you say to Hedda, eh? Doesn't she look flourishing? She's positively—

HEDDA: For heaven's sake, leave me out of it, Jörgen! You'd far better thank Judge Brack for all the trouble he's taken.

BRACK: Oh, don't mention it. It was a pleasure, I assure you.

HEDDA: Yes, you're a loyal soul; but I mustn't keep Mrs. Elvsted waiting. Excuse me, Judge. I'll be back directly. (*Exchange of greetings.* MRS. ELVSTED *and* HEDDA *go out through the hall door.*)

BRACK: Well, I hope your wife's pleased with everything.

TESMAN: We really can't thank you enough. Of course she wants to rearrange things a bit, and she talks of buying a few additional trifles.

BRACK: Is that so?

TESMAN: But you needn't bother about that. Hedda will see to that herself. Why don't we sit down, eh?

BRACK (*Sits at table*): Thanks. Just for a moment— There's something I must talk to you about, my dear Tesman.

TESMAN: Yes, the expenses, eh? (*Sits down*) I suppose it's time we got down to business.

BRACK: Oh, that's not so very pressing. Though perhaps it would have been wiser to be a bit more economical.

TESMAN: But that would have been out of the question. You know Hedda, Judge. After all, she's been used to a certain standard of living—

BRACK: Yes, that's just the trouble.

TESMAN: Fortunately, it won't be long before I receive my appointment.

BRACK: Well, you see—such things sometimes hang fire.

TESMAN: Have you heard anything further, eh?

BRACK: Nothing really definite. (*Interrupts himself*) But, by the way, I have one bit of news for you.

TESMAN: Well?

BRACK: Your old friend Ejlert Lövborg is back in town.

TESMAN: I've heard that already.

BRACK: Really? Who told you?

TESMAN: That lady who went out with Hedda.

BRACK: Oh, yes, what was her name? I didn't quite catch it.

TESMAN: Mrs. Elvsted.

BRACK: Oh, yes, the sheriff's wife. Of course. Lövborg's been living near them these past few years.

TESMAN: And, just think, I'm delighted to hear he's quite a reformed character.

BRACK: Yes, so they say.

TESMAN: And he's published a new book, eh?

BRACK: Indeed he has.

TESMAN: I hear it's made quite a sensation.

BRACK: A most unusual sensation.

TESMAN: Think of that. I'm delighted to hear it. A man of such extraordinary gifts. I felt so sorry to think he'd gone completely to wrack and ruin!

BRACK: Well—everybody thought so.

TESMAN: I wonder what he'll do now—how on earth will he manage to make a living?

(*During these last words* HEDDA *has re-entered by the hall door.*)

HEDDA: (*Tc* BRACK *with a scornful laugh*): Isn't that just like Tesman, Judge? Always worrying about how people are going to make their living.

TESMAN: We were just talking about Ejlert Lövborg, dear.

HEDDA (*Giving him a quick glance. Seats herself in the armchair by the stove and asks casually*): What's the matter with him?

TESMAN: That money he inherited—he's undoubtedly squandered that long ago. And he can't very well write a new book every year, eh? So why shouldn't I wonder what's to become of him?

BRACK: Perhaps I can give you some information on the subject.

TESMAN: Indeed?

BRACK: You must remember that his relatives have a great deal of influence.

TESMAN: But they washed their hands of him long ago.

BRACK: At one time he was considered the hope of the family.

TESMAN: At one time, perhaps. But he soon put an end to that.

HEDDA: Who knows? (*With a slight smile*) I hear they've quite reformed him up at the Elvsteds'.

BRACK: And then there's his new book, of course.

TESMAN: Yes, that's true. Let's hope things will turn out well for him. I've just written him a note. I asked him to come and see me this evening, Hedda dear.

BRACK: But you're coming to my stag party this evening. You promised me last night on the pier.

HEDDA: Had you forgotten, Tesman?

TESMAN: Yes, I really had.

BRACK: In any case, I think you can be pretty sure he won't come.

TESMAN: Why shouldn't he?

BRACK (*With a slight hesitation, rises and leans against the back of the chair*): My dear Tesman, and you, too, Mrs. Tesman, I think it's only right that I should inform you of something that—

TESMAN: That concerns Ejlert, eh?

BRACK: Yes, you as well as him.

TESMAN (*Jumps up anxiously*): But, my dear Judge, what is it?

BRACK: I think you should be prepared to find your appointment deferred—rather longer than you desired or expected.

TESMAN: Has anything happened to prevent it, eh?

BRACK: The nomination may depend on the result of a competition.

TESMAN: A competition! Think of that, Hedda. But who would my competitor be? Surely not—?

BRACK: Yes. Ejlert Lövborg. Precisely. (HEDDA *leans further back in the armchair with an ejaculation.*)

TESMAN: No, no! It's impossible! It's utterly inconceivable, eh?

BRACK: It may come to that, all the same.

TESMAN: But, Judge Brack, this would be incredibly unfair to me. (*Waving his arms*) Just think, I'm a married man! We married on these prospects, Hedda and I. Think of the money we've spent, and we've borrowed from Aunt Juliane, too! Why, they practically promised me the appointment, eh?

BRACK: Don't get so excited. You'll probably get the appointment all the same, only you'll have to compete for it.

HEDDA (*Sits motionless in the armchair*): Just think, Jörgen, it will have quite a sporting interest.

TESMAN: Dearest Hedda, how can you be so indifferent about it?

HEDDA (*As before*): Indifferent! I'm not in the least indifferent. I can hardly wait to see which of you will win.

BRACK: In any case, I thought it better to warn you, Mrs. Tesman! Perhaps under the circumstances, you'd better go easy on those "additional trifles" you're thinking of buying.

HEDDA: I don't see how this could possibly make any difference, my dear Judge.

BRACK: Really? Then I've no more to say. Good-bye. I'll call for you later on my way back from my afternoon walk.

TESMAN: Yes, yes—I'm so upset—my head's in a whirl!

HEDDA (*Still reclining, holds out her hand to him*): I shall hope to see you later, Judge.

BRACK: Thank you, Mrs. Tesman. Good-bye.

TESMAN (*Accompanies him to the door*): Good-bye, my dear Judge. You really must excuse me—
(JUDGE *goes out by the hall door*.)

TESMAN (*Pacing the room*): Oh, Hedda, Hedda, one should never rush into adventures, eh?

HEDDA (*Looks at him and smiles*): Do you do that, Jörgen?

TESMAN: What else can you call it? To get married and settle down on mere expectations, eh?

HEDDA: You may be right.

TESMAN: Well, at least we have our lovely home, Hedda, eh? The home we both dreamt of.

HEDDA (*Rises slowly and wearily*): I'd counted on doing a lot of entertaining. That was part of the agreement, I thought. We were to keep open house.

TESMAN: I'd been so looking forward to it, Hedda dear. To see you, a brilliant hostess, surrounded by distinguished guests— Well, we'll just have to make the best of it for the time being, dear— Be happy in one another— We can always invite Aunt Juliane in now and then. But I wanted it to be so different for you, Hedda. So very different.

HEDDA: I suppose this means I'll have to do without my butler.

TESMAN: Yes, I'm afraid a butler is quite out of the question!

HEDDA: You promised me a saddle-horse, remember? I suppose *that's* out of the question, too?

TESMAN: I'm afraid so, Hedda.

HEDDA (*Walks about the room*): Well, at least I have one thing to amuse myself with.

TESMAN (*Beaming*): Thank heaven for that. What is it, Hedda, eh?

HEDDA (*At center opening—looks at him with suppressed scorn*): My pistols, Jörgen.

TESMAN: Your pistols!

HEDDA (*With cold eyes*): General Gabler's pistols. (*She goes out through the inner room to the left*.)

TESMAN (*Rushes to the center opening and calls after her*): Oh, Hedda, darling, please don't touch those dangerous things. For my sake, Hedda, eh?

CURTAIN

ACT TWO

SCENE: *The room at the Tesmans' as in the first act. Only the piano has been removed and replaced by an elegant little writing table with bookshelves. A smaller table has been placed by the sofa left. Most of the bouquets have been removed.* MRS. ELVSTED'S *bouquet stands on the large table downstage. It is afternoon.*

HEDDA, *dressed to receive callers, is alone in the room. She stands by the open glass door loading a pistol. The matching pistol lies in an open pistol case on the writing table.*

HEDDA (*Looks down into the garden and calls out*): Welcome back, Judge!

BRACK (*Is heard calling below at a distance*): Thank you, Mrs. Tesman.

HEDDA (*Raises the pistol and takes aim*): Now, I'm going to shoot you, Judge!

BRACK (*From below*): No, no, don't aim at me like that!

HEDDA: That's what you get for sneaking in the back way. (*She fires.*)

BRACK (*Nearer*): Have you gone quite mad?

HEDDA: So sorry. Did I hit you by any chance?

BRACK (*Still from outside*): I wish you'd stop all this nonsense.

HEDDA: Come along, Judge, I'll let you pass.

(JUDGE BRACK, *dressed as for a men's party, comes in through the glass door. Over his arm he carries a light overcoat.*)

BRACK: So you're still fooling with those pistols. What are you shooting at?

HEDDA: Just killing time. Shooting up into the blue.

BRACK (*Gently takes the pistol out of her hand*): Allow me. (*Examines it*) Hm . . . I know this pistol . . . I've seen it before. (*Looks around*) Where's the case for it? Ah, here! (*Places the pistol in its case and closes it*) So that game is finished for today.

HEDDA: What in heaven's name am I to do with myself all day long!

BRACK: Haven't you had any visitors?

HEDDA (*Closing the glass door*): Not one. I suppose all our friends are still out of town.

BRACK: Isn't Tesman home?

HEDDA (*At the writing table, putting the pistol case away in a drawer*): No. He rushed off to his aunts' directly after lunch. He didn't expect you so early, Judge.

BRACK: Fancy my not thinking of that— That was stupid of me.

HEDDA (*Turns her head and looks at him*): Why stupid?

BRACK: Because I should have come even earlier.

HEDDA (*Crossing the room*): Then you'd have found no one to receive you, for I've been dressing ever since lunch.

BRACK: But isn't there a little crack in the door through which one might converse?

HEDDA: No. You forgot to provide one, Judge.

BRACK: Again stupid of me.

HEDDA: We must just sit here and wait until Tesman comes— He may not be back for some time.

BRACK: Never mind. I shan't be impatient.

(HEDDA *sits in the corner of the sofa.* BRACK *lays his overcoat over the back of the nearest chair and sits down, but keeps his hat in his hand. A short pause. They look at each other.*)

HEDDA: Well?

BRACK (*In the same tone*): Well?

HEDDA: I spoke first.

BRACK (*Slightly bending forward*): Let's have a really pleasant little talk, Mrs.—Hedda.

HEDDA (*Leaning farther back on the sofa*): It seems ages since our last one, doesn't it, Judge? Of course, I don't count the few words we had last night and this morning.

BRACK: I know—you mean a *real* talk. Just a "twosome."

HEDDA: Yes, that's it.

BRACK: Every single day I've wished you were home again.

HEDDA: I've wished that, too.

BRACK: You have? Really, Mrs. Hedda? And I thought you were having such a good time on your journey.

HEDDA: Ha!

BRACK: Tesman's letters led me to think so.

HEDDA: Oh, well, Tesman! You know Tesman, my dear Judge! His idea of bliss is grubbing about in a lot of dirty bookshops and making endless copies of antiquated manuscripts.

BRACK (*With a touch of malice*): Well, after all, that's his vocation in life, you know. Or a large part of it.

HEDDA: Yes, if it's one's vocation, I suppose that makes it different, but as for me! Oh, my dear Judge, I can't tell you how bored I've been!

BRACK (*Sympathetically*): Are you really serious?

HEDDA: Of course. Surely you can understand? How would *you* like to spend six whole months without meeting a soul you could really talk to?

BRACK: I shouldn't like it at all.

HEDDA: But the most unendurable thing of all was—

BRACK: What?

HEDDA: To be everlastingly with one and the same person.

BRACK (*With a nod of agreement*): Morning, noon, and night, at all possible times.

HEDDA: I said "everlastingly."

BRACK: But with our good Tesman, I should have thought one might—

HEDDA: Tesman is a specialist, my dear Judge.

BRACK: Undeniably.

HEDDA: And specialists are not amusing traveling companions—
Not for long, at any rate.

BRACK: Not even the specialist you happen to love?

HEDDA: Ugh! Don't use that revolting word!

BRACK (*Startled*): What? What's that, Mrs. Hedda?

HEDDA (*Half laughing, half in irritation*): Just you try it! Nothing
but the history of civilization morning, noon, and night.

BRACK: Everlastingly.

HEDDA: And then all this business about the domestic industries
of Brabant during the Middle Ages. That's the most maddening
part of it all.

BRACK (*Looks at her searchingly*): But, tell me, in that case, how
did it happen that you—?

HEDDA: Married Tesman, you mean? Is there anything so very
odd in that?

BRACK: Both yes and no, Mrs. Hedda.

HEDDA: I had danced myself tired, my dear Judge—and I wasn't
getting any younger. (*With a slight shudder*) But I won't talk
about that. I won't even think about it.

BRACK: You certainly have no cause.

HEDDA (*Watching him intently*): And one must admit that Jörgen
Tesman is a thoroughly worthy man.

BRACK: A worthy, dependable man. There can be no question of
that.

HEDDA: And I don't see anything especially—*funny* about him, do
you?

BRACK: Funny? No—o—not really. No, I wouldn't say that.

HEDDA: After all, he's a distinguished scholar. Who knows? He
may still go far.

BRACK (*Looks at her uncertainly*): I thought you believed like everyone else that some day he'd become a really famous man.

HEDDA (*In a tired voice*): Yes, so I did. And then since he was so
absolutely bent on supporting me, I really didn't see why I
shouldn't accept his offer.

BRACK: No, if you look at it from that point of view—

HEDDA: Well, that was more than some of my other admirers were
prepared to do, my dear Judge.

BRACK (*Laughs*): I can't answer for the others, of course. You know that, generally speaking, I have a great respect for the state of matrimony, but I confess, that as an individual—

HEDDA (*Jokingly*): I never had any hopes as far as you were concerned.

BRACK: All I ask of life is to know a few people intimately. A few nice people whom I can help and advise, in whose houses I can come and go as a trusted friend.

HEDDA: Of the—master of the house, you mean?

BRACK (*With a bow*): Well, preferably, of the mistress. But of the master, too, of course! I find such a triangular friendship, if I may call it so, a great convenience to all concerned.

HEDDA: Yes, God knows, a third person would have been welcome on our journey. Oh, those infernal tête-à-têtes!

BRACK: Cheer up! Your wedding trip is over now.

HEDDA (*Shaking her head*): Not by a long shot. No, we've only stopped at a station on the line.

BRACK: Then the thing to do is to jump out and stretch oneself a bit, Mrs. Hedda.

HEDDA: I never jump out.

BRACK: Why not?

HEDDA: There's always someone there waiting to—

BRACK (*Laughing*): Stare at your legs, you mean?

HEDDA: Precisely.

BRACK: Well, good heavens—

HEDDA (*With a gesture of distaste*): I don't like that sort of thing. I'd rather keep my seat and continue the tête-à-tête.

BRACK: But if a third person were to jump *in* and join the couple?

HEDDA: Ah! But *that's* quite a different thing!

BRACK: A trusted, understanding friend.

HEDDA: Gay and entertaining in a variety of ways?

BRACK: And not a bit of a specialist.

HEDDA (*With an audible sigh*): That would certainly be a great relief!

BRACK (*Hears the front door open and glances in that direction*): The triangle is completed.

HEDDA (*In a half-tone*): And on goes the train.

(JÖRGEN TESMAN *enters from the hall. He wears a gray walk-ing suit and a soft felt hat. He carries a great number of paperbound books under his arm and in his pockets.*)

TESMAN (*Goes up to the table beside the corner sofa*): Pooh! It's a warm job to carry all these books, Hedda. (*Puts them down*) I'm positively perspiring! (HEDDA *makes a scarcely audible ejacula-tion: "How charming, Jörgen!"* TESMAN *puts some of the books down on the table*) Oh, you're here already, Judge. Berte didn't tell me.

BRACK (*Rising*): I came in through the garden.

HEDDA: What are all those books, Jörgen?

TESMAN (*Thumbing through the books*): They're some new books on my special subject. I simply had to have them.

HEDDA: Your special subject, Jörgen?

BRACK: On his special subject, Mrs. Tesman. (*He and* HEDDA *ex-change a confidential smile.*)

HEDDA: Do you need still more books on your special subject, Jörgen?

TESMAN: One can never have too many, Hedda. One *must* keep up with all the new publications.

HEDDA: Yes, I suppose one must.

TESMAN (*Searching among the books*): Look, I got Ejlert Lövborg's new book, too. (*Offers it to her*) Would you care to have a look at it, Hedda, eh?

HEDDA: No, thank you— Well, perhaps a little later, Jörgen.

TESMAN: I glanced through it on my way home.

BRACK: What do you think of it? As a specialist, I mean.

TESMAN: He handles his subject with the greatest restraint. That is what struck me most— It's quite remarkable. He never wrote like that before. (*Gathers the books together*) I'll just take these into my study. I'm longing to cut the leaves. And then I suppose I'd better change, though we needn't go just yet, eh?

BRACK: Oh, no. There's not the slightest hurry.

TESMAN: Then I'll take my time. (*Starts to go out with the books but stops and turns at center opening*) Oh, by the way, Hedda, Aunt Juliane is afraid she can't come to see you this evening.

HEDDA: Oh? Why not? Is she still annoyed about the hat?

TESMAN: Of course not. That wouldn't be a bit like her! No, but you see, Aunt Rina's very ill.

HEDDA: She always is.

TESMAN: Yes, but today she's worse than ever, poor thing!

HEDDA: Then she'll need her sister with her. That's only natural. I shall have to try and bear it.

TESMAN: I can't tell you how delighted Aunt Juliane was to see you looking so well, so positively flourishing.

HEDDA (*In a half-tone, rising*): Oh, those eternal aunts!

TESMAN: What did you say, dear?

HEDDA (*Going to the glass door*): Nothing—nothing—nothing!

TESMAN: Very well, Hedda—eh? (*He goes out right, through the inner room.*)

BRACK: What was that you said about a hat?

HEDDA: Oh, it was just something that happened this morning. Miss Tesman had taken off her hat and put it down on the table. (*Looks at him and smiles*) And I pretended to think it was the servant's.

BRACK (*Shakes his head*): Why, my dear Mrs. Hedda. How could you do such a thing to that nice old lady?

HEDDA (*Walks nervously about the room*): My dear Judge, I really don't know. I suddenly get impulses like that and I simply can't control them. (*Flings herself down in the armchair by the stove*) I don't know how to explain it myself.

BRACK (*Behind the armchair*): You're not really happy. I think that's the explanation.

HEDDA (*Gazing straight before her*): I can't imagine why I should be—happy. Can you tell me?

BRACK: Well, to begin with; here you are, in the very house you always longed to live in.

HEDDA (*Looks up at him and laughs*): You really believe in that fairy tale?

BRACK: Wasn't it true, then?

HEDDA: I'll tell you how it happened: last summer I made use of Tesman to see me home from parties.

BRACK: Unfortunately, my way lay in a different direction.

HEDDA: Yes, you were going in a different direction then, weren't you, Judge?

BRACK (*Laughs*): Shame on you, Mrs. Hedda! And so you and Tesman—?

HEDDA: Well, one evening we happened to pass by this house. Tesman, poor thing, was turning and twisting and couldn't think of anything to say. I really felt sorry for the poor learned wretch.

BRACK (*Smiles skeptically*): Sorry! You!

HEDDA: Yes, I really did. I felt sorry for him. And so just to make conversation, to help him out a bit, I was foolish enough to say what a charming house this was, and how I should love to live in it.

BRACK: No more than that?

HEDDA: Not *that* evening.

BRACK: But afterwards?

HEDDA: Afterwards! Afterwards my foolishness was not without consequences, my dear Judge.

BRACK: Yes— Unfortunately, that happens all too often.

HEDDA: Thanks! So, you see it was this fictitious enthusiasm for Secretary Falk's Villa that really brought Tesman and me together. It was the immediate cause of our engagement, our wedding, our wedding journey, and all the rest of it. Well, my dear Judge, they say, as you make your bed, so you must lie.

BRACK: This is really priceless! So I suppose you didn't really care a rap about the house?

HEDDA: No, God knows, I didn't!

BRACK: Still, now that we've made it so attractive and comfortable for you—

HEDDA: To me it smells of lavender and dried rose leaves. What might be called the "Aunt Juliane atmosphere."

BRACK (*Laughs*): No. That's probably a legacy from the late Mrs. Falk.

HEDDA: Yes! Yes, you're right! There is a touch of decay about it. (*She clasps her hands behind her head, leans back in the chair and looks at him*) Oh, my dear Judge, my dear Judge! How incredibly I shall bore myself here!

BRACK: Why shouldn't you, too, find some sort of vocation in life, Mrs. Hedda?

HEDDA: A vocation—that would attract me?

BRACK: Preferably, yes.

HEDDA: God only knows what kind of a vocation that would be! I often wonder whether— (*Breaks off*) But that wouldn't be any good, either.

BRACK: What? Tell me.

HEDDA: I was wondering whether I could get Jörgen to go into politics.

BRACK (*Laughs*): Tesman? No, really! I'm afraid political life would be the last thing in the world for him.

HEDDA: I know you're probably right; but I could try and get him into it all the same.

BRACK: But what satisfaction would it be to you unless he were successful at it? Why should you want to drive him into it?

HEDDA: Because I'm *bored*, I tell you. (*After a pause*) So you think it quite out of the question for Jörgen ever to become—let's say—Secretary of State?

BRACK: Ha, ha! Mrs. Hedda. You must remember, apart from anything else, to become anything of that sort he'd have to be a fairly rich man.

HEDDA (*Rises impatiently*): There you are. Money! Always money! (*Crosses the room*) It's this genteel poverty that makes life so hideous, so utterly ludicrous.

BRACK: Now I should say the fault lies elsewhere.

HEDDA: Where then?

BRACK: I don't believe you've ever really been stirred by anything in life.

HEDDA: Anything serious, you mean?

BRACK: If you like. But I expect it will come.

HEDDA (*Tossing her head*): If you're thinking about that ridiculous professorship, that's Jörgen's own affair. I assure you I shan't give a thought to that!

BRACK: I dare say. But suppose you should suddenly find yourself faced with what's known in solemn language, as a grave responsibility— (*Smiling*) a *new* responsibility, Mrs. Hedda.

HEDDA (*Angrily*): Be quiet! Nothing of that sort will ever happen to me.

BRACK (*Cautiously*): We'll talk of this again a year from now, at the very latest.

HEDDA (*Curtly*): That sort of thing doesn't appeal to me, Judge. I'm not fitted for it. No responsibilities for me!

BRACK: What makes you think you're less fitted than the majority of women? Why should you deliberately turn away from duties—?

HEDDA (*At the glass door*): Be quiet, I tell you! I sometimes think there's only one thing in this world I'm really fitted for.

BRACK (*Nearer to her*): What's that, if I may ask?

HEDDA (*Looking out*): Boring myself to death! Now you know it. (*Turns, looks toward the inner room, and laughs*) Ah! I thought so—here comes the professor!

BRACK (*Softly, warningly*): Now, now! Mrs. Hedda!

(JÖRGEN TESMAN, *dressed for the party, his gloves and hat in his hands, enters from the right through the inner room.*)

TESMAN: Oh, Hedda, has any message come from Ejlert, eh?

HEDDA: No.

TESMAN: Then he'll be here presently, you'll see.

BRACK: You really think he'll come?

TESMAN: I'm almost sure of it. What you told us this morning was probably just a rumor.

BRACK: Do you think so?

TESMAN: At any rate, Aunt Juliane didn't believe for a moment that he would ever stand in my way again. Think of that!

BRACK: Well, then, there's nothing to worry about.

TESMAN (*Puts his hat and gloves down on a chair, right*): I'd like to wait for him as long as possible, though.

BRACK: We've plenty of time. My guests won't arrive before seven or half-past.

TESMAN: Meanwhile, we can keep Hedda company and see what happens, eh?

HEDDA (*Puts* BRACK'S *overcoat and hat on the corner sofa*): And if the worst comes to the worst, Mr. Lövborg can spend the evening with me.

BRACK: What do you mean by "the worst"?

HEDDA: I mean—if he refuses to go with you and Tesman.

TESMAN (*Looks at her dubiously*): But, Hedda dear, do you think it would be quite the thing for him to stay here with you, eh? Remember, Aunt Juliane isn't coming.

HEDDA: No, but Mrs. Elvsted is. We three can have a cup of tea together.

TESMAN: Oh, well, then it would be *quite* all right.

BRACK (*Smiling*): It might perhaps be the best thing for him, too.

HEDDA: Why the "best thing," Judge?

BRACK: Well, you know how rude you are about my stag parties, Mrs. Tesman. You always say they're only safe for men of the strictest principles.

HEDDA: I'm sure Mr. Lövborg's principles are strict enough now. A converted sinner—

(BERTE *appears at the hall door.*)

BERTE: There's a gentleman asking to see you, ma'am.

HEDDA: Oh, yes—show him in.

TESMAN (*Softly*): It must be Ejlert. Think of that!

(EJLERT LÖVBORG *enters from the hall. He is slim and lean. The same age as* TESMAN, *he looks older, as though worn out by life. Hair and beard dark-brown; a long, pale face, but with patches of color on the cheekbones; he wears a well-cut black visiting suit, obviously new. He carries dark gloves and a silk hat. He stands near the door and makes a rapid bow. He seems slightly embarrassed.* TESMAN *goes to him and shakes him by the hand*) Welcome, my dear Ejlert. So at last we meet again!

LÖVBORG (*Speaks in a hushed voice*): Thanks for your letter, Jörgen. (*Approaches* HEDDA) May I shake hands with you, too, Mrs. Tesman?

HEDDA (*Takes his hand*): How do you do, Mr. Lövborg, I'm delighted to see you. (*She motions with her hand*) I don't know if you two gentlemen—

LÖVBORG (*With a slight bow*): Judge Brack, I believe.

BRACK (*Bows likewise*): Yes, I've had the pleasure, some years ago.

TESMAN (*To* LÖVBORG, *with his hands on his shoulders*): And now, Ejlert, you must make yourself at home, mustn't he,

Hedda? I hear you're going to settle in town again, eh?

LÖVBORG: Yes, I am.

TESMAN: Well, that's splendid. I just got your new book, Ejlert, but I haven't had time to read it yet.

LÖVBORG: I wouldn't bother to, if I were you.

TESMAN: Why, what do you mean?

LÖVBORG: It's pretty thin stuff.

TESMAN: Just think! How can you say that?

BRACK: It's been enormously praised, I hear.

LÖVBORG: That was exactly what I wanted, so I put nothing in it that anyone could take exception to.

BRACK: Very wise of you.

TESMAN: But, my dear Ejlert—

LÖVBORG: You see, I'm determined to make a fresh start; to win a real position for myself.

TESMAN (*Slightly embarrassed*): Oh, so that's what you plan to do, eh?

LÖVBORG (*Smiles, puts down his hat, and takes a parcel wrapped in paper from his coat pocket*): But when this one appears, Jörgen Tesman, you'll have to read it, for this is a real book. Every ounce of my true self is in this.

TESMAN: Really! What's it about?

LÖVBORG: It's the sequel.

TESMAN: Sequel? Sequel of what?

LÖVBORG: Of the other book.

TESMAN: You mean, the new one?

LÖVBORG: Yes, of course.

TESMAN: But, my dear Ejlert, surely that comes right down to our time, doesn't it?

LÖVBORG: Yes, but this deals with the future.

TESMAN: With the future. But good heavens, we know nothing about the future!

LÖVBORG: There's a thing or two to be said about it all the same. (*Opens the parcel*) Look here—

TESMAN: That's not your handwriting.

LÖVBORG: No, I dictated it. (*Thumbs through the pages*) It falls into two sections. The first deals with the civilizing forces of the future and the second— (*turning to the pages toward the end*) forecasts the probable lines of development.

TESMAN: How remarkable! I should never have thought of writing anything of that sort.

HEDDA (*At the glass door, drumming on the pane*): No, I daresay not.

LÖVBORG (*Puts the manuscript back in its wrapping and lays it on the table*): I brought it with me; I thought I might read you a bit of it this evening.

TESMAN: That was very kind of you, Ejlert, but this evening— (*Glancing at* BRACK) I don't see how we can manage it—

LÖVBORG: Well, then, some other time. There's no hurry.

BRACK: The fact is, Mr. Lövborg, I'm giving a little party this evening to celebrate Tesman's return.

LÖVBORG (*Looking for his hat*): Oh, then I mustn't detain you.

BRACK: No, but wait. I'd be delighted if you would give me the pleasure of your company.

LÖVBORG (*Curtly and decisively*): I'm sorry. I can't. Thank you very much.

BRACK: Oh, nonsense! Do, come. We shall be quite a select little circle, and I can assure you, we shall have a "jolly time," as Mrs. Hed—Mrs. Tesman puts it.

LÖVBORG: I don't doubt that, but nevertheless—

BRACK: And you could bring your manuscript with you and read it to Tesman at my house. I could give you a room all to yourselves.

TESMAN: Yes, think of that, Ejlert. Why shouldn't you do that, eh?

HEDDA (*Interposing*): But, Jörgen dear, if Mr. Lövborg says he doesn't want to go, I'm sure Mr. Lövborg would much prefer to stay here and have supper with me.

LÖVBORG (*Looking at her*): With you, Mrs. Tesman?

HEDDA: Mrs. Elvsted will be here, too.

LÖVBORG: Oh— (*Casually*) I saw her for a moment today.

HEDDA: Oh, did you? Well, she's spending the evening here. So you see, you're almost obliged to stay, Mr. Lövborg. Otherwise, Mrs. Elvsted will have no one to see her home.

LÖVBORG: That's true. Many thanks. In that case, I will stay, Mrs. Tesman.

HEDDA: Splendid! I'll just give one or two orders to the servant. (*She goes to the hall door and rings.* BERTE *enters.* HEDDA *talks to her in a whisper and points to the inner room.* BERTE *nods and goes out.*)

TESMAN (*During the above, to* EJLERT LÖVBORG): Tell me, Ejlert, is it this new subject, the future, that you are going to lecture about?

LÖVBORG: Yes.

TESMAN: They told me at the bookstore that you were planning a series of lectures.

LÖVBORG: Yes, I am. I hope you've no objection.

TESMAN: No, of course not, but—

LÖVBORG: I can quite see that it might interfere with your plans.

TESMAN (*Depressed*): I can't very well expect you, out of consideration for *me*, to—

LÖVBORG: But, of course, I'll wait until you receive your appointment.

TESMAN: What! You'll wait! Then—then you're not going to compete with me, eh?

LÖVBORG: No. I only want people to realize that I *could* have—a sort of moral victory, if you like.

TESMAN: Why, bless my soul, then Aunt Juliane was right after all! I was sure of it. Hedda, just think, Ejlert is not going to stand in our way!

HEDDA (*Curtly*): Our way! Do please leave me out of it, Jörgen. (*She goes up toward the inner room where* BERTE *is arranging a tray with decanters and glasses on the table.* HEDDA *nods approvingly and comes forward again.* BERTE *goes out.*)

TESMAN (*During the above*): What do you say to this, Judge, eh?

BRACK: Well, I say a moral victory may be all very fine but—

TESMAN: Yes, certainly, but all the same—

HEDDA (*Looks at* TESMAN *with a cold smile*): You stand there looking absolutely thunderstruck, Jörgen.

TESMAN: Well, you know, I almost believe I am.

HEDDA (*Pointing to the inner room*): And now, gentlemen, won't you have a glass of cold punch before you go?

BRACK (*Looks at his watch*): A sort of stirrup cup, you mean. Yes, that's not a bad idea.

TESMAN: A capital idea, Hedda. Just the thing. Now that a heavy weight has been lifted off my mind—

HEDDA: You'll join them, Mr. Lövborg?

LÖVBORG (*With a gesture of refusal*): No, thank you, nothing for me.

BRACK: Why, surely, cold punch is not poison.

LÖVBORG: Perhaps not for everyone.

HEDDA: Well, then, you two go in and I'll sit here and keep Mr. Lövborg company.

TESMAN: Yes, do, Hedda, dear.

(TESMAN *and* BRACK *go into the inner room, sit down, drink punch, smoke cigarettes, and carry on an animated conversation during the following.* EJLERT LÖVBORG *remains standing by the stove.* HEDDA *goes to the writing table.*)

HEDDA (*In a raised voice*): Perhaps you'd like to look at some snapshots, Mr. Lövborg. You know, Tesman and I did some sightseeing in the Tyrol, on our way home. I'd so love to show you— (*She brings over an album which she lays on the table by the sofa, in the further corner of which she seats herself.* EJLERT LÖVBORG *approaches, then stops and stands looking at her. He then takes a chair and sits on her left with his back to the inner room. She opens the album*) Do you see this group of mountains, Mr. Lövborg? It's the Ortlar group— Oh, yes, Tesman has written the name underneath. "The Ortlar group near Meran."

LÖVBORG (*Who has never taken his eyes off her, says softly and slowly*): Hedda Gabler—

HEDDA (*Gives him a hasty look*): Sh!

LÖVBORG (*Repeats softly*): Hedda Gabler—

HEDDA (*Looking at the album*): That was my name in the old days, when you and I knew each other.

LÖVBORG: Then I must learn never to say Hedda Gabler again? Never as long as I live?

HEDDA (*Turning over the pages*): Yes, I'm afraid you must.

LÖVBORG (*In an indignant tone*): Hedda Gabler married! And married to Jörgen Tesman!

HEDDA: Such is life!

LÖVBORG: Oh, Hedda, Hedda, how could you throw yourself away like that?

HEDDA (*Looks at him sharply*): I won't have you say such things.

LÖVBORG: Why shouldn't I?

(TESMAN *comes into the room and goes toward the sofa.*)

HEDDA (*Hears him coming and says in a casual tone*): And this, Mr. Lövborg, is a view from the Ampezzo Valley. Just look at those peaks. (*Looks up at* TESMAN *affectionately*) Oh, Jörgen dear, what's the name of these curious peaks?

TESMAN: Let me see—oh, those are the Dolomites.

HEDDA: Oh, yes, those are the Dolomites, Mr. Lövborg.

TESMAN: Hedda dear, are you sure you wouldn't like me to bring some punch. For yourself, at any rate, eh?

HEDDA: Yes, I think I will have some, dear. And perhaps a few biscuits.

TESMAN: A cigarette?

HEDDA: No, I think not, dear.

TESMAN: Very well.

(*He goes into the inner room again and out to the right.* BRACK *sits in the inner room, occasionally keeping an eye on* HEDDA *and* LÖVBORG.)

LÖVBORG (*Softly as before*): Answer me, Hedda. How could you do it?

HEDDA (*Apparently absorbed in the album*): If you go on calling me Hedda, I won't talk to you.

LÖVBORG: Can't I say Hedda even when we're alone?

HEDDA: No. You may think it, but you mustn't say it.

LÖVBORG: I understand. It offends your love for Jörgen Tesman.

HEDDA (*Glances at him and smiles*): Love? How funny you are!

LÖVBORG: It's not love, then?

HEDDA: All the same, no unfaithfulness, remember.

LÖVBORG: Hedda, answer me just one thing.

HEDDA: Sh!

(TESMAN *comes from the inner room carrying a small tray.*)

TESMAN: Here you are! Doesn't this look tempting? (*He puts the tray down on the table.*)

HEDDA: Why do you bring it yourself, Jörgen?

TESMAN (*Filling the glasses*): I think it's such fun to wait on you, Hedda.

HEDDA: But you've poured out two glasses. Mr. Lövborg said he wouldn't have any.

TESMAN: I know. But Mrs. Elvsted will be here soon, won't she?

HEDDA: Oh, yes, of course, Mrs. Elvsted—

TESMAN: Had you forgotten her, eh?

HEDDA: Yes, you know we were so engrossed in these photographs. Oh, Jörgen dear, do you remember this little village?

TESMAN: Yes, of course I do. It's the one just below the Brenner Pass. Don't you remember? We spent the night there.

HEDDA: Oh, yes. And met that gay party of tourists.

TESMAN: Yes, that was the place. Just think, if only we could have had you with us, Ejlert, eh? (*He goes back to the inner room and sits down with* JUDGE BRACK.)

LÖVBORG: Answer me this one thing, Hedda.

HEDDA: Well?

LÖVBORG: Was there no love in your feeling for *me*, either? Not the slightest touch of love?

HEDDA: I wonder— To me it seems that we were just two good comrades, two thoroughly intimate friends. (*Smiles*) You especially were exceedingly frank!

LÖVBORG: It was you who made me so.

HEDDA: You know, as I look back on it all, I realize there was something very beautiful, something fascinating, something daring—yes, daring—in that secret intimacy, that comradeship no living soul suspected.

LÖVBORG: Yes, there was, wasn't there, Hedda? Do you remember when I used to come to your home in the afternoon and the General sat over at the window reading his paper, with his back toward us—

HEDDA: We two sat on the corner sofa—

LÖVBORG: Always the same illustrated paper before us—

HEDDA: For want of an album, yes!

LÖVBORG: Do you remember, Hedda, all those wild things I confessed to you? Things no one suspected at the time—my days and nights of passion and frenzy, of drinking and madness— How did you make me talk like that, Hedda? By what power?

HEDDA: Power?

LÖVBORG: Yes. How else can one explain it? And all those devious questions you used to ask—

HEDDA: Questions you understood so perfectly—

LÖVBORG: How could you bring yourself to ask such questions? So candidly, so boldly?

HEDDA: In a devious way, if you please.

LÖVBORG: Yes, but boldly, all the same.

HEDDA: How could you bring yourself to answer them, Mr. Lövborg?

LÖVBORG: That's just what I can't understand. There must have been love at the bottom of it. Perhaps you felt that by making me confess like that you were somehow washing away my sins.

HEDDA: No, not quite.

LÖVBORG: What was your motive, then?

HEDDA: Isn't it quite easy to understand, that a young girl, especially if it can be done in secret—

LÖVBORG: Well?

HEDDA: Should be tempted to investigate a forbidden world? A world she's supposed to know nothing about?

LÖVBORG: So that was it.

HEDDA: That had a lot to do with it, I think.

LÖVBORG: I see; we were both greedy for life. That made us comrades. But why did it end?

HEDDA: You were to blame for that!

LÖVBORG: You broke with me.

HEDDA: I realized the danger; you wanted to spoil our intimacy—to drag it down to reality. You talk of my boldness, my candor—why did you try to abuse them?

LÖVBORG (*Clenching his hands*): Why didn't you do as you said? Why didn't you shoot me?

HEDDA: Because . . . I have such a fear of scandal.

LÖVBORG: Yes, Hedda, you are a coward at heart.

HEDDA : A terrible coward. (*With a change of tone*) But after all, it was a lucky thing for you. You found ample consolation at the Elvsteds'.

LÖVBORG: I know Thea has confided in you.

HEDDA: And I suppose you've confided in her—about us?

LÖVBORG: Not a word. She's too stupid to understand that.

HEDDA: Stupid?

LÖVBORG: About that sort of thing—yes.

HEDDA: And I am a coward. (*Leans toward him, without looking him in the eye, says softly*) Now I'll confide something to you.

LÖVBORG (*Intensely*): Well?

HEDDA: My not daring to shoot you—

LÖVBORG: Yes?

HEDDA: That was not my greatest cowardice that evening.

LÖVBORG (*Looks at her a moment, understands, and whispers passionately*): Oh, Hedda, Hedda Gabler! I begin to understand the real meaning of our comradeship. You and I!— You see, it *was* your craving for life—

HEDDA (*Softly, with a keen look*): Be careful! Believe nothing of the sort. (*It has begun to get dark. The hall door is opened by* BERTE. HEDDA *closes the album with a bang and calls out smilingly*) At last! Thea darling!— (MRS. ELVSTED *enters from the hall. She is in evening dress. The door is closed behind her.* HEDDA, *still on the sofa, stretches out her arms toward her*) Darling little Thea, I thought you were never coming!

(*In passing,* MRS. ELVSTED *lightly greets the gentlemen in the inner room, then goes to the table and gives* HEDDA *her hand.* EJLERT LÖVBORG *rises. He and* MRS. ELVSTED *greet each other with a silent nod.*)

MRS. ELVSTED: Shouldn't I go and say good evening to your husband?

HEDDA (*Puts her arm around* MRS. ELVSTED *and leads her toward sofa*): No, we needn't bother about them. I expect they'll soon be off.

MRS. ELVSTED: Are they going out?

HEDDA: Yes. To a wild party!

MRS. ELVSTED (*Quickly. To* LÖVBORG): You're not going, are you?

LÖVBORG: No.

HEDDA: No. Mr. Lövborg is staying here with us.

(LÖVBORG *sits down again on the sofa.*)

MRS. ELVSTED (*Takes a chair and starts to sit beside him*): Oh,
how nice it is to be here!

HEDDA: No, no, little Thea, not there! You be a good girl and sit
here, next to me. I'll sit between you.

MRS. ELVSTED: Just as you like. (*She goes round the table and sits
on the sofa to* HEDDA'S *right.* LÖVBORG *sits down again.*)

LÖVBORG (*To* HEDDA, *after a short pause*): Isn't she lovely to
look at?

HEDDA (*Lightly stroking her hair*): Only to look at?

LÖVBORG: We're two real comrades, she and I. We have absolute
faith in each other. We can talk with perfect frankness.

HEDDA: Not in a devious way, Mr. Lövborg.

LÖVBORG: Well—

MRS. ELVSTED (*Softly, clinging to* HEDDA): Oh, I'm so happy,
Hedda! You know—he actually says I've inspired him in his
work.

HEDDA (*Looks at her and smiles*): Does he really, dear?

LÖVBORG: And then she has such courage, Mrs. Tesman.

MRS. ELVSTED: Good heavens, courage!

LÖVBORG: Tremendous courage where your comrade is concerned.

HEDDA: God, yes, courage! If one only had that!

LÖVBORG: What then?

HEDDA: Then life might perhaps be endurable, after all. . . .
(*With a sudden change of tone*) Now, my darling little Thea, you
must have a nice glass of cold punch.

MRS. ELVSTED: No, thank you. I never take anything like that.

HEDDA: Then how about you, Mr. Lövborg?

LÖVBORG: I don't either, thank you.

MRS. ELVSTED: No, he doesn't either.

HEDDA (*Looks at him intently*): But if I want you to.

LÖVBORG: It makes no difference.

HEDDA (*Laughs*): Poor me! Have I no power over you at all, then?

LÖVBORG: Not in that respect.

HEDDA: No, but seriously. I really think you ought to take it for
your own sake.

MRS. ELVSTED: Why, Hedda—

LÖVBORG: How do you mean?

HEDDA: People might begin to suspect that you weren't quite sure, quite confident of yourself.

MRS. ELVSTED (*Softly*): Don't, Hedda.

LÖVBORG: People may suspect whatever they like.

MRS. ELVSTED (*Happily*): Yes, let them.

HEDDA: You should have seen Judge Brack's face a moment ago. . . .

LÖVBORG: Indeed?

HEDDA: His contemptuous smile when you didn't dare join them in there.

LÖVBORG: Didn't dare! I simply preferred to stay here and talk to you.

MRS. ELVSTED: That's natural enough, Hedda.

HEDDA: That's not what Judge Brack thought. You should have seen him smile and look at Tesman when you didn't dare go to his ridiculous little party.

LÖVBORG: Didn't dare! You say I didn't dare!

HEDDA: No, *I* don't say it—but that's how Judge Brack looks at it.

LÖVBORG: Well, let him.

HEDDA: So you're not going with them?

LÖVBORG: No, I'm staying here with you and Thea.

MRS. ELVSTED: Yes, Hedda, of course, he is.

HEDDA (*Smiles and nods approvingly to* LÖVBORG): There, you see! Firm as a rock. Faithful to all good principles now and forever. That's how a man should be. (*Turns to* MRS. ELVSTED *and says with a caress*) What did I tell you this morning, Thea? Didn't I tell you not to be upset?

LÖVBORG (*Amazed*): Upset?

MRS. ELVSTED (*Terrified*): Hedda—! *Please*, Hedda.

HEDDA: You see? Now are you convinced? You haven't the slightest reason to be so anxious and worried. . . . There! Now we can all three enjoy ourselves.

LÖVBORG (*With a start*): What does all this mean, Mrs. Tesman?

MRS. ELVSTED: Oh, God! What are you doing, Hedda?

HEDDA: Be careful! That horrid Judge is watching you.

LÖVBORG: So you were anxious and worried on my account?

MRS. ELVSTED (*Softly, miserably*): Oh, Hedda, you've ruined everything.

LÖVBORG (*Looks at her intently for a moment. His face is distorted*): Well, my comrade! So that's all your faith amounts to!

MRS. ELVSTED (*Imploringly*): You *must* listen to me, Ejlert—

LÖVBORG (*Takes one of the glasses of punch, raises it, and says in a low, hoarse voice*): Your health, Thea! (*He empties the glass, puts it down, and takes the second one.*)

MRS. ELVSTED (*Softly*): Hedda, Hedda, how could you do this?

HEDDA: I do it? I? Are you crazy?

LÖVBORG: And your health, too, Mrs. Tesman. Thanks for the truth. Long live the truth! (*He empties the glass and is about to fill it again.*)

HEDDA (*Lays her hand on his arm*): There, there! No more for the present. You're going to the party, remember.

LÖVBORG (*Putting down the glass*): Now, Thea, be honest with me.

MRS. ELVSTED: Yes?

LÖVBORG: Did your husband know you came after me?

MRS. ELVSTED (*Wringing her hands*): Ejlert! . . .

LÖVBORG: It was arranged between you, wasn't it, that you should come to town and keep an eye on me. I dare say the old man suggested it himself. No doubt he needed my help in the office. Or perhaps it was at the card table he missed me.

MRS. ELVSTED (*Softly, in great distress*): Ejlert! Ejlert!

LÖVBORG (*Seizes the glass and is about to fill it*): Let's drink to the old sheriff, too!

HEDDA (*Preventing him*): No more now. Remember you're going to read your manuscript to Jörgen.

LÖVBORG (*Calmly, putting down the glass*): I'm behaving like a fool, Thea. Try and forgive me, my dear, dear comrade. You'll see—I'll prove to you—I'll prove to everyone, that I'm all right again. I'm back on my feet. Thanks to you, Thea.

MRS. ELVSTED (*Radiant*): Oh, thank God!

(*In the meantime* BRACK *has looked at his watch. He and* TESMAN *rise and come into the drawing room.*)

BRACK (*Takes up his hat and overcoat*): Well, Mrs. Tesman, it's time to go.

HEDDA: I suppose it is, Judge.

LÖVBORG (*Rising*): I've decided to join you, Judge.

MRS. ELVSTED (*Softly, imploringly*): Oh, Lövborg, don't!

HEDDA (*Pinching her arm*): Sh! They'll hear you.

LÖVBORG (*To* BRACK): Since you were kind enough to invite me.

BRACK: You've changed your mind?

LÖVBORG: Yes, if you don't mind.

BRACK: I'm delighted.

LÖVBORG (*Putting the manuscript in his pocket, to* TESMAN): I should like to show you one or two things before the manuscript goes to press.

TESMAN: Just think, how delightful! But, Hedda, dear, in that case, how is Mrs. Elvsted to get home?

HEDDA: Oh, we shall manage, somehow.

LÖVBORG (*Looking toward the ladies*): Mrs. Elvsted? Of course, I'll come back and fetch her. (*Comes nearer*) Around ten o'clock, Mrs. Tesman. Will that do?

HEDDA: That will be splendid, Mr. Lövborg.

TESMAN: Well, then, that's settled. But you mustn't expect me so early, Hedda.

HEDDA: Oh, you can stay as long as you like, Jörgen.

MRS. ELVSTED (*With suppressed anxiety*): Well, then, Mr. Lövborg, I'll wait here till you come.

LÖVBORG (*With his hat in his hand*): That's understood, Mrs. Elvsted.

BRACK: Well, gentlemen, shall we start? I hope we're going to have a very jolly time, as a certain fair lady puts it.

HEDDA: If only the fair lady could be there, unseen, Judge.

BRACK: Why unseen?

HEDDA: So as to share a little in your unbridled fun.

BRACK (*Laughs*): I shouldn't advise the fair lady to try it.

TESMAN (*Also laughing*): Come. You're a nice one, Hedda. Think of that!

BRACK: Well, good-bye. Good-bye, ladies!

LÖVBORG (*Bowing*): About ten o'clock then.

HEDDA: Yes, Mr. Lövborg!

(BRACK, LÖVBORG, *and* TESMAN *go out by the hall door. Simultaneously,* BERTE *comes in from the inner room with a lighted lamp which she puts on the drawing-room table; she goes out again through the inner room.*)

MRS. ELVSTED (*Who has risen and paces restlessly about the room*): Hedda, what will come of all this!

HEDDA: At ten o'clock he will be here, with vine leaves in his hair. Flushed and fearless!

MRS. ELVSTED: If I could only believe that—

HEDDA: And then, you see, he will have regained confidence in himself. He'll be a free man forever and ever.

MRS. ELVSTED: Pray God you may be right.

HEDDA: I am right! It will be as I say. (*Rises and approaches her*) Doubt him as much as you like. I believe in him. Now we shall see—

MRS. ELVSTED: You have some hidden reason for all this, Hedda.

HEDDA: Yes, I have. For once in my life I want the power to shape a human destiny.

MRS. ELVSTED: But surely, you have that!

HEDDA: I haven't. I never have had.

MRS. ELVSTED: But what about your husband?

HEDDA: Do you think he's worth bothering about! If you could only understand how poor I am; and that you should be allowed to be so rich!— (*She flings her arms round her passionately*) I think I shall have to burn your hair off, after all!

MRS. ELVSTED: Let me go! Let me go! I'm afraid of you, Hedda!

BERTE (*At the center opening*): Supper's ready, ma'am.

HEDDA: Very well, we're coming.

MRS. ELVSTED: No, no! I'd rather go home alone. Now—at once!

HEDDA: Nonsense! You'll do nothing of the sort, you silly little thing. You'll have some supper and a nice cup of tea and then at ten o'clock Ejlert Lövborg will be here with vine leaves in his hair— (*She almost drags* MRS. ELVSTED *toward the center opening.*)

CURTAIN

ACT
THREE

SCENE: *The room at the Tesmans'. The portieres of the center opening are closed as well as the curtains of the glass door. The shaded lamp on the table is turned low. In the stove, of which the door stands open, there has been a fire which is now nearly burnt out.*

MRS. ELVSTED, *wrapped in a large shawl, reclines in the armchair close to the stove with her feet on a footstool.* HEDDA *lies asleep on the sofa, covered with a rug.*

MRS. ELVSTED (*After a pause, suddenly straightens up in her chair and listens eagerly. Then she sinks back wearily and says softly and plaintively*): Not yet—Oh God!—Oh God!—Not yet—

(BERTE *slips cautiously in by the hall door. She has a letter in her hand.*)

MRS. ELVSTED (*Turns and whispers eagerly*): Did someone come?

BERTE (*Softly*): A girl just brought this letter, ma'am.

MRS. ELVSTED (*Quickly, stretching out her hand*): A letter! Give it to me!

BERTE: It's for Dr. Tesman, ma'am.

MRS. ELVSTED: Oh.

BERTE: Miss Tesman's maid brought it. I'll just put it on the table.

MRS. ELVSTED: Yes, do.

BERTE (*Puts down the letter*): I think I'd better put out the lamp, ma'am.

MRS. ELVSTED: You might as well—it must be nearly daylight.

BERTE (*Puts out the lamp*): It *is* daylight, ma'am.

MRS. ELVSTED: So it is! Broad daylight—and no one's come home yet!

BERTE: Lord bless you, ma'am—I thought something like this would happen.

MRS. ELVSTED: You did?

BERTE: Yes—when I saw them go off with a—certain gentleman, last night—we used to hear plenty about him in the old days.

MRS. ELVSTED: Sh! Not so loud! You'll wake Mrs. Tesman—

BERTE (*Looks toward the sofa and sighs*): Yes, you're right—let her sleep, poor thing. Shall I make up the fire, ma'am?

MRS. ELVSTED: Thank you—you needn't trouble—

BERTE: Very well, ma'am. (*She goes out softly by the hall door.*)

HEDDA (*Wakes at the closing of the door and looks up*): What —what was that?

MRS. ELVSTED: It was just the maid—

HEDDA (*Looks round her*): What are we doing in here? Oh yes! Now I remember! (*She sits up on the sofa, stretches herself, and rubs her eyes*) What's the time, Thea?

MRS. ELVSTED (*Looks at her watch*): It's past seven.

HEDDA: When did Jörgen get home?

MRS. ELVSTED: He hasn't come.

HEDDA: Not home yet?

MRS. ELVSTED (*Rising*): No one has come.

HEDDA: And we were fools enough to sit up half the night —watching and waiting!

MRS. ELVSTED (*Wringing her hands*): And waiting in such terrible anxiety!

HEDDA (*Yawns, and says with her hand in front of her mouth*): Well—we might have spared ourselves the trouble.

MRS. ELVSTED: Did you manage to get a little sleep?

HEDDA: Yes, I believe I slept quite well—didn't you?

MRS. ELVSTED: I couldn't, Hedda—I couldn't possibly!

HEDDA (*Rises and goes toward her*): There, there! There's nothing to worry about! It's easy to see what's happened.

MRS. ELVSTED: What—tell me!

HEDDA: Brack's party probably dragged on for hours—

MRS. ELVSTED: I expect that's true, but still—

HEDDA: —and probably Tesman didn't want to come home and wake me up in the middle of the night—perhaps he was in no condition to show himself, after the famous party.

MRS. ELVSTED: But where could he have gone?

HEDDA: To his aunts', of course!—I expect he went there to sleep it off. They always keep his old room ready for him.

MRS. ELVSTED: No, he can't be there. That letter just came for him, from Miss Tesman.

HEDDA: Letter? (*Looks at the address*) Oh, yes! It's from Aunt Juliane. Well—then I suppose he stayed at Judge Brack's. As for Ejlert Lövborg—he is sitting with vine leaves in his hair, reading his manuscript.

MRS. ELVSTED: You're talking nonsense, Hedda! You know you don't believe a word of it—

HEDDA: What a little ninny you are, Thea!

MRS. ELVSTED: Yes, I'm afraid I am—

HEDDA: And how dreadfully tired you look!

MRS. ELVSTED: I am—dreadfully tired.

HEDDA: Now you do exactly as I tell you! You go into my room—lie down on the bed—and get a little rest.

MRS. ELVSTED: No, no!—I'd never be able to sleep.

HEDDA: Of course you would.

MRS. ELVSTED: Besides, your husband should be back soon; I must find out at once—

HEDDA: I'll tell you the moment he arrives—

MRS. ELVSTED: You promise, Hedda?

HEDDA: Yes—you can count on me—Go on in now, and have a good sleep.

MRS. ELVSTED: Thanks—I will try. (*She goes out through the inner room.*)

(HEDDA *goes to the glass door and opens the curtains. Bright daylight streams into the room. She takes a small mirror from the writing table, looks at herself in it, and tidies her hair. Then she goes to the hall door and rings the bell. A few moments later* BERTE *appears at the hall door.*)

BERTE: Did you ring, ma'am?

HEDDA: Yes—do something to the fire—I'm absolutely frozen.

BERTE: Certainly, ma'am—I'll make it up at once. (*She rakes the embers together and puts on a piece of wood. She stops and listens*) That was the front door, ma'am.

HEDDA: See who it is—I'll look after the fire.

BERTE: It'll soon burn up, ma'am.

(*She goes out by the hall door.* HEDDA *kneels on the footstool and puts several pieces of wood in the stove. After a short pause* JÖRGEN TESMAN *comes in from the hall. He looks tired and rather serious. He tiptoes up toward the center opening and is about to slip through the curtains.*)

HEDDA (*At the stove, without looking up*): Good morning, Jörgen!

TESMAN (*Turns*): Hedda! (*Approaches her*) Good heavens—are you up so early, eh?

HEDDA: Yes, I'm up very early today, Jörgen.

TESMAN: And I was sure you'd still be sound asleep—think of that, Hedda!

HEDDA: Sh! Don't talk so loud. You'll wake Mrs. Elvsted.

TESMAN: Did Mrs. Elvsted stay here all night?

HEDDA: Naturally—since no one came to call for her.

TESMAN: No—I suppose not—

HEDDA (*Closes the stove door and rises*): Well—did you enjoy yourselves?

TESMAN: Were you worried about me, Hedda, eh?

HEDDA: That would never occur to me—I asked if you'd enjoyed yourselves?

TESMAN: Yes, we really did, Hedda. Especially at first—you see, Ejlert read me part of his book. We got there quite early, think of that—and Brack had all sorts of arrangements to make, so Ejlert read to me.

HEDDA (*Sits to the right of table*): Yes?—Well?

TESMAN (*Sits on a stool near the stove*): Hedda, you can't conceive what a book it will be! I believe it's one of the most remarkable things that has ever been written. Think of that!

HEDDA: I'm really not very interested, Jörgen.

TESMAN: I've something to confess, Hedda—after he'd finished reading, I had such a horrid feeling—

HEDDA: A horrid feeling, Jörgen?

TESMAN: Yes. I felt quite jealous of Ejlert, because he'd been able to write such a book. Just think, Hedda.

HEDDA: Yes, yes! I *am* thinking!

TESMAN: It's really appalling, that he, with all his great gifts, should be so utterly incorrigible!

HEDDA: Because he has more daring than any of the rest of you?

TESMAN: It's not that, Hedda—he's utterly incapable of moderation.

HEDDA: Well—tell me what happened.

TESMAN: There's only one word to describe it, Hedda—it was an orgy!

HEDDA: Did he have vine leaves in his hair?

TESMAN: Vine leaves? No, I didn't see any vine leaves—but he made a long incoherent speech in honor of the woman who had inspired him in his work—that was the phrase he used.

HEDDA: Did he mention her name?

TESMAN: No, he didn't. But I can't help thinking he meant Mrs. Elvsted—just you see!

HEDDA: Where did you part?

TESMAN: When the party finally broke up, there were only a few of us left—so we came away together. Brack came with us too—he wanted a breath of fresh air; and then we decided we had better take Ejlert home—he was in pretty bad shape, you see.

HEDDA: Yes, I dare say.

TESMAN: And then, the strangest thing happened, Hedda—the most tragic thing! I'm really almost ashamed to tell you about it—for Ejlert's sake—

HEDDA: Oh, do go on, Jörgen!

TESMAN: Well—as we were nearing town, you see—I happened to drop a little behind the others—only for a minute or two—think of that!

HEDDA: Yes, yes!—Well?

TESMAN: And then, as I hurried after them, what do you think I found on the sidewalk, eh?

HEDDA: How should I know?

TESMAN: You mustn't say a word about it to anyone, Hedda—do you hear? Promise me—for Ejlert's sake.

HEDDA: Yes, Jörgen!

TESMAN (*Takes a parcel wrapped in paper from his pocket*): Just think, dear—I found this.

HEDDA: Isn't that the parcel he had with him yesterday?

TESMAN: Yes. It's his precious, irreplaceable manuscript. He had lost it, and hadn't even noticed it. Isn't it tragic, Hedda, that—?

HEDDA: Why didn't you give it back to him at once?

TESMAN: I didn't dare trust him with it, in the condition he was in.

HEDDA: Did you tell any of the others you'd found it?

TESMAN: Certainly not! I didn't want them to know—for Ejlert's sake, you see.

HEDDA: Then no one knows that Ejlert Lövborg's manuscript is in your possession?

TESMAN: No—and no one must know it.

HEDDA: What did you say to him afterwards?

TESMAN: I didn't get a chance to talk to him again; he and two or three of the others gave us the slip and disappeared—think of that!

HEDDA: I suppose they took him home then.

TESMAN: Yes, I suppose they did—and Brack went home too.

HEDDA: And where have you been gallivanting ever since?

TESMAN: Someone suggested we should go back to his house and have an early breakfast there—or perhaps it should be called a late supper—eh? And now—as soon as I have had a little rest and poor Ejlert has had a chance to recover himself a bit—I must take this back to him.

HEDDA (*Stretching out her hand for the parcel*): No, Jörgen— don't give it back to him—not right away, I mean. Let me read it first.

TESMAN: No, dearest Hedda, I daren't do that. I really dare not.

HEDDA: You dare not, Jörgen?

TESMAN: Think of the state he'll be in when he wakes up and can't find his manuscript! There's no copy of it, Hedda—think of that! He told me so himself.

HEDDA (*Looks at him searchingly*): Tell me, Jörgen—would it be quite impossible to write such a thing over again?

TESMAN: Oh, I should think so, Hedda. You see, it's the inspiration—

HEDDA: Yes, of course—the inspiration. . . . I suppose it depends on that. (*Lightly*) By the way, Jörgen, here's a letter for you.

TESMAN: Just think—

HEDDA: (*Hands it to him*): It came just a little while ago.

TESMAN: It's from Aunt Juliane, Hedda! What can it be? (*He puts the parcel down on the other stool, opens the letter, glances through it, and jumps up*) Oh, Hedda—she says Aunt Rina is dying, poor thing.

HEDDA: Well—we were expecting that.

TESMAN: And that I must hurry, if I want to see her again—I'll just run over and see them at once.

HEDDA (*Suppressing a smile*): Will you run, Jörgen?

TESMAN: Oh, my dearest Hedda—if you could only bring yourself to come with me! Just think!

HEDDA (*Rising. Rejects the idea wearily*): No, no! Don't ask me to do that! I'll have nothing to do with sickness or death. I loathe anything ugly.

TESMAN: Well then, in that case— (*Rushing about*) My hat?—My overcoat?—Oh, in the hall. I do hope I won't be too late, Hedda—eh?

HEDDA: Well, after all—if you run, Jörgen—!
(BERTE *enters by the hall door*.)

BERTE: Judge Brack is here, sir—and wishes to know if you'll see him?

TESMAN: At this hour? No, no! I can't possibly—

HEDDA: But I'll see him. (*To* BERTE) Ask him to come in, Berte. (BERTE *goes. Rapidly, in a whisper*) Jörgen!— The manuscript! (*She snatches it up from the stool*.)

TESMAN: Yes, give it to me!

HEDDA: No, no. I'll keep it here till you come back. (*She goes over to the writing table and puts it in the bookcase.* TESMAN *in a frenzy of haste can't get his gloves on.* BRACK *enters from the hall.*)

HEDDA (*Nodding to him*): You're certainly an early bird, Judge.

BRACK: I am, aren't I? (*To* TESMAN) Where are you off to in such a hurry?

TESMAN: I must rush off to my aunts'. Just think, Aunt Rina is dying, poor thing.

BRACK: Dear me, is she? Then don't let me detain you; every moment may be precious.

TESMAN: Yes, I really must run—good-bye, good-bye, Hedda— (*He rushes out by the hall door*.)

HEDDA (*Approaching* BRACK): I hear the party was more than usually jolly last night, Judge.

BRACK: Yes, I've been up all night—haven't even changed my clothes.

HEDDA: So I see—

BRACK: What has Tesman told you of last night's adventures?

HEDDA: Oh, nothing much; some dreary tale about going to someone's house and having breakfast.

BRACK: Yes, I've heard about that breakfast party—but Ejlert Lövborg wasn't with them, was he?

HEDDA: No—he'd been escorted home.

BRACK: By Tesman, you mean?

HEDDA: No—by some of the others.

BRACK (*Smiling*): Jörgen Tesman is certainly a naïve creature, Mrs. Hedda.

HEDDA: Yes, God knows he is! But, you're very mysterious—what else happened last night?

BRACK: Oh, a number of things—

HEDDA: Do sit down, Judge, and tell me all about it! (*She sits to the left of the table.* BRACK *sits near her, at the long side of the table*)—Well?

BRACK: I had special reasons for keeping an eye on my guests —or rather some of my guests—last night.

HEDDA: One of them being Ejlert Lövborg, I suppose.

BRACK: Frankly—yes.

HEDDA: This sounds quite thrilling, Judge!

BRACK: Do you know where he and some of the others spent the rest of the night?

HEDDA: No. Do tell me—if it's not quite unmentionable!

BRACK: No. It's by no means unmentionable. Well—they turned up at an extremely gay party.

HEDDA: A *very* jolly party, Judge?

BRACK: An excessively jolly one!

HEDDA: Do go on!

BRACK: Lövborg, as well as the others, had been invited some time ago. I knew all about it. But he had refused the invitation, for he had become a reformed character, as you know—

HEDDA: At the Elvsteds', yes. But he went all the same?

BRACK: Well, you see, Mrs. Hedda, he became somewhat inspired at my place last night—

HEDDA: Yes. I heard he was . . . inspired.

BRACK: Rather violently inspired, in fact—and so, he changed his mind. We men are not always as high-principled as perhaps we should be.

HEDDA: I'm sure you are an exception, Judge. But to get back to Ejlert Lövborg—

BRACK: So—to make a long story short—ue did finally turn up at Mlle. Diana's residence.

HEDDA: Mlle. Diana?

BRACK: Yes, it was she who was giving the party—to a very select circle of her friends and admirers.

HEDDA: Is she that red-haired woman?

BRACK: Precisely.

HEDDA: A sort of . . . singer?

BRACK: Yes—in her leisure moments. She is also a mighty huntress—of men. You must have heard of her, Mrs. Hedda. In the days of his glory Ejlert Lövborg was one of her most enthusiastic protectors.

HEDDA: But how did all this end, Judge?

BRACK: In a none-too-friendly fashion, it seems. After greeting him most tenderly, Mlle. Diana finally proceeded to tear his hair out!

HEDDA: What? —Lövborg's?

BRACK: Yes. It seems he accused her, or her friends, of having robbed him. He kept insisting some valuable notebook had disappeared—as well as various other things. In short, he raised quite a terrific row.

HEDDA: What did all this lead to?

BRACK: It led to a general free-for-all, in which the women as well as the men took part. Fortunately the police at last appeared on the scene.

HEDDA: The police?

BRACK: Yes. I'm afraid it may prove an expensive amusement for Ejlert Lövborg—crazy lunatic that he is!

HEDDA: How?

BRACK: They say he made a violent resistance—half killed one policeman, and tore another one's coat off his back. So they marched him off to the police station.

HEDDA: Where did you hear all this?

BRACK: From the police themselves.

HEDDA (*Gazing straight before her*): So that's what happened! Then, after all, he had no vine leaves in his hair!

BRACK: Vine leaves, Mrs. Hedda?

HEDDA (*With a change of tone*): Tell me, Judge—why should you be so interested in spying on Lövborg in this way?

BRACK: In the first place—I am not entirely indifferent to the fact that during the investigation it will be known that he came directly from my house.

HEDDA: You mean, the case will go to court?

BRACK: Naturally. However—be that as it may. But I felt it my duty, as a friend of the family, to give you and Tesman a full account of his nocturnal exploits.

HEDDA: For what reason, Judge?

BRACK: Because I have a shrewd suspicion that he means to use you as a sort of . . . screen.

HEDDA: Whatever makes you think that?

BRACK: After all—we're not completely blind, Mrs. Hedda. You watch! This Mrs. Elvsted—she'll be in no great hurry to leave town.

HEDDA: Well—supposing there were something between them —there must be plenty of other places where they could meet.

BRACK: Not a single *home*. From now on, every respectable house will be closed to Ejlert Lövborg.

HEDDA: And mine ought to be too, you mean?

BRACK: Yes. I admit it would be more than painful to me if he should be welcome here. If this undesirable and superfluous person should be allowed to force his way into the—

HEDDA: —the Triangle?

BRACK: Precisely. It would simply mean that I should find myself homeless.

HEDDA (*Looks at him with a smile*): I see. So you want to be cock-of-the-walk, Judge. That is your aim.

BRACK (*Nods slowly and speaks in a low voice*): Yes—that is my aim; and for that I will fight with every weapon I can command.

HEDDA (*Her smile vanishing*): I wonder, Judge, now one comes to think of it, if you're not rather a dangerous person.

BRACK: Do you think so?

HEDDA: I'm beginning to think so. And I'm exceedingly glad that you have no sort of hold over me.

BRACK (*Laughs ambiguously*): Well, well, Mrs. Hedda—perhaps you're right. If I had, who knows what I might be capable of.

HEDDA: Come now! Come, Judge! That sounds almost like a threat.

BRACK (*Rising*): Not at all! For the Triangle, it seems to me, ought, if possible, to be based on mutual understanding.

HEDDA: There I entirely agree with you.

BRACK: Well—now I've said all I had to say—I'd better be off. Good-bye, Mrs. Hedda. (*Crossing toward the glass door.*)

HEDDA (*Rising*): Are you going through the garden, Judge?

BRACK: Yes, it's a short cut for me.

HEDDA: Yes—and then it's the back way, isn't it?

BRACK: Very true; I've no objection to back ways. They are rather intriguing at times.

HEDDA: When there's shooting going on, you mean?

BRACK (*At the glass door, laughingly*): People don't shoot their tame poultry, I fancy.

HEDDA (*Also laughing*): And certainly not the cock-of-the-walk, Judge! Good-bye!

(*They exchange laughing nods of farewell. He goes. She closes the glass door after him.* HEDDA, *now serious, stands looking out. She goes up and peeps through the portieres into the inner room. Then goes to the writing table, takes* LÖVBORG'S *parcel from the bookcase, and is about to examine it.* BERTE *is heard speaking loudly in the hall.* HEDDA *turns and listens. She hurriedly locks the parcel in the drawer and puts the key on the inkstand.* EJLERT LÖVBORG, *wearing his overcoat and carrying his hat in his hand, tears open the hall door. He looks somewhat confused and excited.*)

LÖVBORG (*Turns toward the hall*): I will go in, I tell you! (*He closes the door, turns, sees* HEDDA, *at once controls himself and bows.*)

HEDDA (*At the writing table*): Well, Mr. Lövborg! Isn't it rather late to call for Thea?

LÖVBORG: And rather early to call on you—forgive me.

HEDDA: How do you know Thea's still here?

LÖVBORG: They told me at her lodgings she'd been out all night.

HEDDA (*Goes to the table*): Did you notice anything odd in their manner when they told you that?

LÖVBORG (*Looks at her inquiringly*): Anything odd?

HEDDA: Didn't they seem to think it—a little—queer?

LÖVBORG (*Suddenly understanding*): Oh, of course! I see what you mean. I suppose I'm dragging her down with me— However, I didn't notice anything. I suppose Tesman isn't up yet?

HEDDA: No—I don't think so—

LÖVBORG: When did he get home?

HEDDA: Oh, very late.

LÖVBORG: Did he tell you anything?

HEDDA: He just said it had all been very jolly at Judge Brack's.

LÖVBORG: Nothing else?

HEDDA: No, I don't believe so. In any case, I was so dreadfully sleepy—

(MRS. ELVSTED *comes in through the portieres from the inner room. She goes to him.*)

MRS. ELVSTED: Ejlert! At last!

LÖVBORG: Yes—at last—and too late!

MRS. ELVSTED (*Looks at him anxiously*): What is too late?

LÖVBORG: Everything's too late now—it's all up with me.

MRS. ELVSTED: No, no! You mustn't say that!

LÖVBORG: You'll say the same when you hear—

MRS. ELVSTED: I don't want to hear anything!

HEDDA: Perhaps you'd rather talk to her alone? I'll leave you.

LÖVBORG: No! Stay, please—I beg of you!

MRS. ELVSTED: But I don't want to hear anything, I tell you.

LÖVBORG: I don't intend to talk about last night, Thea—

MRS. ELVSTED: No?

LÖVBORG: No. I just want to tell you that now we must part.

MRS. ELVSTED: Part?

HEDDA (*Involuntarily*): I knew it!

LÖVBORG: I no longer have any use for you, Thea.

MRS. ELVSTED: How can you say that! No more use for me? You'll let me go on helping you—we'll go on working together, Ejlert?

LÖVBORG: I shall do no more work, from now on.

MRS. ELVSTED (*Despairingly*): Then, what shall I have to live for?

LÖVBORG: You must try and live as though you'd never known me.

MRS. ELVSTED: But you know I can't do that!

LÖVBORG: You must try, Thea. You must go home again.

MRS. ELVSTED (*Protesting vehemently*): Never! I won't leave you! I won't allow you to drive me away. We must be together when the book appears.

HEDDA (*Whispers, in suspense*): Ah, yes—the book!

LÖVBORG (*Looks at her*): My book and Thea's—for that's what it is.

MRS. ELVSTED: Yes—that's true; I feel that. That's why we must be together when it's published. I want to see you showered with praise and honors—and, the joy! I want to share that with you too!

LÖVBORG: Our book will not be published, Thea.

MRS. ELVSTED: Not published?

LÖVBORG: No. It never can be.

MRS. ELVSTED (*Anxiously, with foreboding*): Lövborg—what have you done with the manuscript?

HEDDA (*Watches him intently*): Yes—the manuscript?

MRS. ELVSTED: Where is it?

LÖVBORG: Thea! Don't ask me about it!

MRS. ELVSTED: Yes—I must know—I have a right to know.

LÖVBORG: Very well, then!—I've torn it into a thousand pieces!

MRS. ELVSTED (*Cries out*): No—no!

HEDDA (*Involuntarily*): But that's not—

LÖVBORG (*Looks at her*): Not true, you think?

HEDDA (*Controlling herself*): Of course it must be—if you say so! But it sounds so utterly incredible!

LÖVBORG: It's true all the same.

MRS. ELVSTED (*Wringing her hands*): Torn his own work to pieces!—Oh, God, Hedda!

LÖVBORG: I've torn my life to pieces—why shouldn't I tear up my work as well!

MRS. ELVSTED: And you did this last night?

LÖVBORG: Yes. I tore it into a thousand pieces. I scattered them far out on the fjord. I watched them drift on the cool sea water—drift with the current and the wind. In a little while they'll sink, deeper and deeper—just as I shall, Thea.

MRS. ELVSTED: Lövborg—this thing you've done to the book—it's as though you'd killed a little child.

LÖVBORG: You're right—it was child-murder.

MRS. ELVSTED: Then—how could you?—it was my child too.

HEDDA (*Almost inaudibly*): The child—

MRS. ELVSTED (*Breathes heavily*): It's all over then—I'll go now, Hedda.

HEDDA: But you won't be leaving town?

MRS. ELVSTED: I don't know what I'll do—there's nothing but darkness before me. (*She goes out by the hall door.*)

HEDDA (*Stands waiting a moment*): Then—you're not going to see her home, Mr. Lövborg?

LÖVBORG: I?—Do you want people to see her with *me*?

HEDDA: Of course, I don't know what else may have happened last night—but is it so utterly irreparable?

LÖVBORG: It won't end with last night—I know that only too well; and the trouble is, that kind of life no longer appeals to me. I have no heart to start it again—she's somehow broken my courage—my defiant spirit!

HEDDA (*Gazes before her*): To think that that pretty little fool should have influenced a man's destiny! (*Looks at him*) Still, I don't see how you could be so heartless.

LÖVBORG: Don't say that!

HEDDA: What do you expect me to say! You've destroyed her whole purpose in life—isn't that being heartless?

LÖVBORG: Hedda—to you I can tell the truth.

HEDDA: The truth?

LÖVBORG: First, promise me—give me your word—that Thea will never know.

HEDDA: I give you my word.

LÖVBORG: Good. There was no truth in what I said just now—

HEDDA: You mean—about the manuscript?

LÖVBORG: Yes. I didn't tear it to pieces or scatter it on the fjord—

HEDDA: Where is it then?

LÖVBORG: But I have destroyed it, Hedda—utterly destroyed it!

HEDDA: I don't understand.

LÖVBORG: Just now, Thea said I had killed our child—

HEDDA: Yes—so she did—

LÖVBORG: One can do worse things to a child than kill it— I wanted to spare Thea the truth—

HEDDA: What do you mean?

LÖVBORG: I couldn't bring myself to tell her; I couldn't say to her: Thea, I spent last night in a frenzy of drinking—I took our child with me, dragged it round with me to all sorts of obscene and loathsome places—and I lost our child—lost it! God only knows what's become of it—or who's got hold of it!

HEDDA: But, when you come right down to it, this was only a book—

LÖVBORG: Thea's pure soul was in that book.

HEDDA: Yes—so I understand.

LÖVBORG: Then you must also understand why no future is possible for us.

HEDDA: What will you do now?

LÖVBORG: Nothing. I want to make an end of it. The sooner the better.

HEDDA (*Takes a step toward him*): If you do make an end of it,

Ejlert Lövborg—let it be beautiful!

LÖVBORG (*Smiles*): Beautiful! Shall I put vine leaves in my hair, as you wanted me to in the old days?

HEDDA: No—I don't believe in vine leaves any more. But—for once—let it be beautiful! Good-bye—you must go now—you mustn't come here any more.

LÖVBORG: Good-bye, Mrs. Tesman. Remember me to Jörgen Tesman. (*He's on the point of going.*)

HEDDA: No, wait!—I want you to take something of mine with you—as a token— (*She goes to the writing table, opens the drawer, and the pistol case. Goes back to* LÖVBORG, *carrying one of the pistols.*)

LÖVBORG (*Looks at her*): This? Is this the token?

HEDDA (*Nods slowly*): Do you remember it? It was aimed at you once.

LÖVBORG: You should have used it then.

HEDDA: Take it!—Use it now!

LÖVBORG (*Puts the pistol in his inner pocket*): Thanks.

HEDDA: But let it be—beautiful, Ejlert Lövborg! Promise me that!

LÖVBORG: Good-bye, Hedda Gabler.

(*He goes out by the hall door.* HEDDA *listens at the door a moment. Then she goes to the writing table and takes out the parcel with the manuscript, peeps inside the cover, half takes out a few sheets of paper and looks at them. Then she takes the parcel over to the armchair by the stove and sits down. She has the parcel in her lap. In a moment she opens the stove door, then opens the parcel.*)

HEDDA (*She throws part of the manuscript in the fire and whispers to herself*): Your child, Thea—your child and Ejlert Lövborg's. Darling little Thea, with the curly golden hair. (*Throws more of the manuscript into the stove*) I'm burning your child, Thea. (*Throws in the rest of the manuscript*) I'm burning it—burning it—

CURTAIN

ACT
FOUR

SCENE: *The same room at the* TESMANS'. *It is evening. The drawing room is dark. In the inner room the hanging lamp over the table is lighted. The curtains are drawn over the glass doors.* HEDDA, *dressed in black, paces back and forth in the dark room. Then she goes up into the inner room and off left. A few chords are heard on the piano. She appears again and returns to the drawing room.* BERTE *enters from the right, through the inner room, carrying a lighted lamp which she puts down on the table by the corner sofa in the drawing room. Her eyes are red with weeping and she has black ribbons on her cap. She goes out right, quietly and circumspectly.* HEDDA *goes to the glass door, pulls the curtains aside a little, and peers out into the darkness. After a moment* MISS TESMAN *comes in from the hall. She is in mourning and wears a hat and veil.* HEDDA *goes toward her and holds out her hand.*

MISS TESMAN: Well, Hedda, here I am, all dressed in black! My poor sister has found rest at last!

HEDDA: As you see, I have heard already. Tesman sent me a note.

MISS TESMAN: He promised he would. I wish Rina hadn't left us just now—this is not the time for Hedda's house to be a house of mourning.

HEDDA (*Changing the subject*): It is good to know she died peacefully, Miss Tesman.

MISS TESMAN: Yes, her end was so calm, so beautiful. And thank heaven, she had the joy of seeing Jörgen once more—and bidding him good-bye.—He is not home yet?

HEDDA: No. He wrote me he might be detained. But do sit down, Miss Tesman.

MISS TESMAN: No, thank you, my dearest Hedda. I should like
  nothing better, but I have so much to do. I must prepare my darling sister for her burial. She must look her very sweetest when
  they carry her to her grave.

HEDDA: Can I do anything to help?

MISS TESMAN: Oh, no, you mustn't think of that! This is no time
  for Hedda Tesman to take part in such sad work. Nor let her
  thoughts dwell on it either—

HEDDA: H'm—one's thoughts—!

MISS TESMAN (*Continuing the theme*): How strange life is! At
  home we shall be sewing a shroud; and soon I expect there will
  be sewing here, too—but of a different kind, thank God!

(JÖRGEN TESMAN *enters by the hall door*.)

HEDDA: Well! Here you are at last!

TESMAN: You here, Aunt Juliane? With Hedda? Think of that!

MISS TESMAN: I am just going, my dear boy. Did you get everything done?

TESMAN: I'm afraid I forgot half of it. I'll have to run over and see
  you in the morning. Today my brain's in a whirl! I can't keep my
  thoughts together.

MISS TESMAN: But, my dear Jörgen, you mustn't take it so much
  to heart.

TESMAN: How do you mean?

MISS TESMAN: We must be glad for her sake—glad that she has
  found rest at last.

TESMAN: Oh, yes, of course—you are thinking of Aunt Rina.

HEDDA: I'm afraid it will be very lonely for you now, Miss
  Tesman.

MISS TESMAN: It will be at first—but I won't let poor Rina's room
  stay empty for long.

TESMAN: Really? Who will you put in it—eh?

MISS TESMAN: One can always find some poor invalid who needs
  to be taken care of.

HEDDA: Would you really take such a burden on yourself again?

MISS TESMAN: A burden? Heaven forgive you, child, it has been
  no burden to me.

HEDDA: But it's different with a stranger!

MISS TESMAN: I simply must have someone to live for—and one soon makes friends with sick folks; and perhaps some day there may be something in this house to keep an old aunt busy.

HEDDA: Oh, please don't trouble about us!

TESMAN: Just think! What a wonderful time we three might have together if—

HEDDA: If—?

TESMAN (*Uneasy*): Nothing. Let's hope things will work out for the best—eh?

MISS TESMAN: Well, well, I daresay you two want to have a little talk. (*Smiling*) And perhaps Hedda may have something to tell you, Jörgen. Good-bye! I must go home to poor Rina. (*Turning at the door*) How strange it is to think that now Rina is with my poor brother, as well as with me.

TESMAN: Yes, think of that, Aunt Juliane! Eh?

(MISS TESMAN *goes out by the hall door.*)

HEDDA (*Gives* TESMAN *a cold, searching look*): Aunt Rina's death seems to affect you more than it does Aunt Juliane.

TESMAN: Oh, it's not that alone. It's Ejlert I am so terribly upset about.

HEDDA (*Quickly*): Have you heard anything new?

TESMAN: I called on him this afternoon. I wanted to tell him the manuscript was safe.

HEDDA: Did you see him?

TESMAN: No, he wasn't home. But later, I met Mrs. Elvsted and she said he had been here, early this morning.

HEDDA: Yes, directly after you had left.

TESMAN: And he said that he had torn his manuscript to pieces, eh?

HEDDA: That is what he said.

TESMAN: Good heavens, he must have gone completely mad! I suppose in that case you didn't dare give it back to him, Hedda.

HEDDA: No, he didn't get it.

TESMAN: But of course you told him that we had it?

HEDDA: No. Did you tell Mrs. Elvsted?

TESMAN: No, I thought I had better not. But you ought to have told him. Just think—he might do himself some injury. Give me

the manuscript. I'll run over with it at once. Where is it, Hedda?
Eh?

HEDDA (*Cold and motionless, leaning against the armchair*): I
haven't got it any longer.

TESMAN: Haven't got it? What in the world do you mean?

HEDDA: I've burnt it—every word of it.

TESMAN (*Starts up in terror*): Burnt! Burnt Ejlert's manuscript!

HEDDA: Don't shout so loud. The servant might hear you.

TESMAN: Burnt! Why, good God—! No, no, no! It's utterly impossible!

HEDDA: It's true, all the same.

TESMAN: Do you realize what you have done, Hedda? It is unlaw-
ful appropriation of lost property. Think of that! Just ask Judge
Brack, he will tell you what that means.

HEDDA: It would be wiser not to speak of it—either to Judge Brack
or to anyone else.

TESMAN: But how could you do anything so unheard of? What put
it into your head? What possessed you? Do answer me—

HEDDA (*Suppressing a scarcely perceptible smile*): I did it for your
sake, Jörgen!

TESMAN: For my sake!

HEDDA: This morning when you told me that he had read it to
you—

TESMAN: Yes, yes—what then?

HEDDA: You admitted that you were jealous of his work.

TESMAN: Of course, I didn't mean that literally.

HEDDA: All the same—I couldn't bear the thought of anyone putting you in the shade.

TESMAN (*In an outburst of mingled doubt and joy*): Hedda? Is this
true? But—but—I have never known you to show your love like
that before. Think of that!

HEDDA: Then—perhaps I'd better tell you that—just now—at this
time— (*Violently breaking off*) No, no; ask Aunt Juliane. She'll
tell you all about it.

TESMAN: Oh, I almost think I understand, Hedda. (*Clasping his
hands together*) Great heavens! Do you really mean it, eh?

HEDDA: Don't shout so loud. The servants will hear—

TESMAN (*Laughing with irrepressible joy*): The servants—? Why, how absurd you are, Hedda! It's only my dear old Berte! Why, I'll run out and tell her myself!

HEDDA (*Clenching her hands in despair*): Oh God, I shall die—I shall die of all this—!

TESMAN: Of what, Hedda? What is it? Eh?

HEDDA (*Coldly, controlling herself*): It's all so ludicrous—Jörgen!

TESMAN: Ludicrous! That I should be overjoyed at the news? Still, after all, perhaps I had better not tell Berte.

HEDDA: Why not that—with all the rest?

TESMAN: No, no, I won't tell her yet. But I must certainly tell Aunt Juliane. Oh, she will be so happy—so happy!

HEDDA: When she hears that I've burnt Ejlert Lövborg's manuscript—for your sake?

TESMAN: No, of course not—nobody must know about the manuscript. But I will certainly tell her how dearly you love me, Hedda. She must share that joy with me. I wonder, now, whether this sort of thing is usual in young wives? Eh?

HEDDA: Why not ask Aunt Juliane that, too?

TESMAN: I will, indeed, some time or other. (*Again agitated and concerned*) But the manuscript. Good God—the manuscript! I can't bear to think what poor Ejlert will do now! (MRS. ELVSTED, *dressed as on her first visit, wearing a hat and coat, comes in from the hall door.*)

MRS. ELVSTED (*Greets them hurriedly, and says in evident agitation*): Hedda, dear—please forgive my coming back so soon.

HEDDA: What is it, Thea? What has happened?

TESMAN: Is it something to do with Ejlert Lövborg, eh?

MRS. ELVSTED: Yes, I am terribly afraid he has met with some accident.

HEDDA (*Seizes her arm*): Ah!—You think so?

TESMAN: Why should you think that, Mrs. Elvsted?

MRS. ELVSTED: When I got back to my lodgings—I heard them talking about him. There are all sorts of strange rumors—

TESMAN: Yes, I've heard them too! And yet I can bear witness that he went straight home last night. Think of that!

HEDDA: What sort of things did they say?

MRS. ELVSTED: Oh, I couldn't quite make it out. Either they knew nothing definite or—in any case, they stopped talking the moment I came in, and I didn't dare question them.

TESMAN (*Moving about the room uneasily*): We must only hope you misunderstood them, Mrs. Elvsted.

MRS. ELVSTED: No, I am sure they were talking about him—they said something about a hospital or—

TESMAN: Hospital?

HEDDA: No, no! That's impossible!

MRS. ELVSTED: Oh, I am so terribly afraid for him. I finally went to his house to ask after him!

HEDDA: You went there yourself, Thea?

MRS. ELVSTED: What else could I do? I couldn't bear the suspense any longer.

TESMAN: But you didn't find him—eh?

MRS. ELVSTED: No. And the people there knew nothing about him. They said he hadn't been home since yesterday afternoon.

TESMAN: Yesterday! Just think—how could they say that?

MRS. ELVSTED: I am sure something terrible must have happened to him!

TESMAN: Hedda dear—supposing I run over and make some inquiries—?

HEDDA: No, no! Please don't mix yourself up in this affair.

(JUDGE BRACK, *hat in hand, enters by the hall door which* BERTE *opens and closes behind him. He looks grave and bows silently.*)

TESMAN: Oh, it's you, my dear Judge—eh?

BRACK: Yes, it's imperative that I see you at once.

TESMAN: I can see you have heard the news about Aunt Rina?

BRACK: Yes, that among other things.

TESMAN: Isn't it sad? Eh?

BRACK: Well, my dear Tesman, that depends on how you look at it.

TESMAN (*Looks at him doubtfully*): Has anything else happened?

BRACK: Yes.

HEDDA (*Intensely*): Anything sad, Judge?

BRACK: That, too, depends on how you look at it, Mrs. Tesman

MRS. ELVSTED (*In an involuntary outburst*): Oh! It's something about Ejlert Lövborg!

BRACK (*Glancing at her*): What makes you think that, Mrs. Elvsted? Perhaps you have already heard something—?

MRS. ELVSTED (*Confused*): No, no, nothing at all—but—

TESMAN: Well, for heaven's sake, tell us. What is it?

BRACK (*Shrugging his shoulders*): Well, I am sorry to say, Ejlert Lövborg has been taken to the hospital—they say he is dying.

MRS. ELVSTED (*Cries out*): Oh, God! God!

TESMAN: To the hospital!! And dying—

HEDDA (*Involuntarily*): So soon then—

MRS. ELVSTED (*Tearfully*): And we parted in anger, Hedda!

HEDDA (*In a whisper*): Thea—Thea—be careful!

MRS. ELVSTED (*Not heeding her*): I must go to him! I must see him alive!

BRACK: I'm afraid it is useless, Mrs. Elvsted. No one is allowed to see him.

MRS. ELVSTED: But at least tell me what happened to him? What is it?

TESMAN: He didn't try to kill himself—eh?

HEDDA: Yes—I am sure he did!

TESMAN: Hedda, how can you—?

BRACK (*Not taking his eyes off her*): Unfortunately, you have guessed quite correctly, Mrs. Tesman.

MRS. ELVSTED: Oh, how horrible!

TESMAN: Killed himself!—Think of that!

HEDDA: Shot himself!

BRACK: You are right again, Mrs. Tesman.

MRS. ELVSTED (*Trying to control herself*): When did it happen, Judge Brack?

BRACK: This afternoon—between three and four.

TESMAN: But, where did it happen? Eh?

BRACK (*With a slight hesitation*): Where? Well—I suppose at his lodgings.

MRS. ELVSTED: No, it couldn't have been there—for I was there myself between six and seven.

BRACK: Well, then, somewhere else—I don't know exactly. I only know that he was found—he had shot himself . . . through the heart.

MRS. ELVSTED: How horrible! That he should die like that!

HEDDA (*To* BRACK): Through the heart?

BRACK: Yes—as I told you.

HEDDA: Through the heart—

TESMAN: It's absolutely fatal, you say?

BRACK: Absolutely! Most likely it is already over.

MRS. ELVSTED: Over—all over—oh, Hedda!

TESMAN: You're quite positive of this? Who told you—eh?

BRACK (*Curtly*): One of the police.

HEDDA (*Loudly*): At last, a deed worth doing!

TESMAN (*Terrified*): Good heavens, what are you saying, Hedda?

HEDDA: I say, there is beauty in this.

BRACK: H'm, Mrs. Tesman—

TESMAN: Beauty! Think of that!

MRS. ELVSTED: Oh, Hedda, how can you talk of beauty in such a case?

HEDDA: Ejlert Lövborg has made up his own account with life. He had the courage to do—the one right thing.

MRS. ELVSTED: No; no! You mustn't believe that! He did it in delirium!

TESMAN: In despair.

HEDDA: No! No! He didn't—I'm sure of that!

MRS. ELVSTED: I tell you he must have been delirious—as he was when he tore up our manuscript!

BRACK (*With a start*): The manuscript? He tore up the manuscript?

MRS. ELVSTED: Yes. Last night.

TESMAN (*In a low whisper*): Oh, Hedda, we'll never get over this!

BRACK: H'm—how very extraordinary.

TESMAN (*Pacing the room*): To think of Ejlert dead! And his book destroyed too—his book that would have made him famous!

MRS. ELVSTED: If only there were some way of saving it—

TESMAN: Yes, if only there were!—There's nothing I wouldn't give—

MRS. ELVSTED: Perhaps there is a way, Mr. Tesman.

TESMAN: What do you mean?

MRS. ELVSTED (*Searches in the pocket of her dress*): Look! I have
kept all the notes he used to dictate from—

HEDDA (*Takes a step toward her*): Ah—!

TESMAN: You have, Mrs. Elvsted?—Eh?

MRS. ELVSTED: Yes. I took them with me when I left home
—they're here in my pocket—

TESMAN: Do let me see them!

MRS. ELVSTED (*Hands him a bundle of scraps of paper*): I'm afraid
they are dreadfully mixed up—

TESMAN: Perhaps, together, we might be able to sort them
out—just think!

MRS. ELVSTED: We could try at any rate—

TESMAN: We'll do it—we *must* do it—I'll devote my life to it!

HEDDA: You, Jörgen? Your life?

TESMAN: Or at least, all the time I can spare. My own work will
simply have to wait—I owe this to Ejlert's memory . . . you understand, Hedda, eh?

HEDDA: You may be right.

TESMAN: Now, my dear Mrs. Elvsted, we must pull ourselves
together—it is no good brooding over what has happened. Eh?
We must try and control our grief as much as possible—

MRS. ELVSTED: Yes, you're right, Mr. Tesman, I *will* try—

TESMAN: That's splendid! Now then, let's see—we must go
through the notes at once— Where shall we sit? Here? No, no,
we'd better go in there— Excuse me, Judge— Come along,
Mrs. Elvsted!

MRS. ELVSTED: Oh! If only it were possible—

(TESMAN *and* MRS. ELVSTED *go into the inner room. She takes
off her hat and coat. They sit at the table under the hanging lamp
and become absorbed in examining the papers.* HEDDA *goes toward the stove and sits down in the armchair. After a moment*
BRACK *joins her.*)

HEDDA (*In a low voice*): Oh, what a sense of freedom there is in
this act of Ejlert Lövborg's.

BRACK: Freedom, Mrs. Hedda? Of course, it is freedom for him.

HEDDA: I mean for me. It gives me a sense of freedom to know that

an act of deliberate courage is still possible in this world—an act
of spontaneous beauty.

BRACK (*Smiles*): H'm—my dear Mrs. Hedda—

HEDDA: Oh, I know what you are going to say. For you're a specialist, too, in a way—just like—well, you know.

BRACK (*Looks at her intently*): Ejlert Lövborg meant more to you
than you are willing to admit—even to yourself. Or am I mistaken?

HEDDA: I don't answer such questions. I know that Ejlert
Lövborg had the courage to live his life as he saw it—and to end
it in beauty. He had the strength and the will to break with
life—while still so young.

BRACK: It pains me to do so, Mrs. Hedda—but I fear I must rob
you of this beautiful illusion.

HEDDA: Illusion?

BRACK: It would soon be destroyed, in any case.

HEDDA: What do you mean?

BRACK: He did not shoot himself—of his own accord.

HEDDA: Not of his own—?

BRACK: No, the thing did not happen exactly as I told it.

HEDDA (*In suspense*): You've concealed something? What is it?

BRACK: For poor Mrs. Elvsted's sake, I slightly changed the facts.

HEDDA: What are the facts, then?   *Tension*

BRACK: First, that he is already dead.

HEDDA: At the hospital.

BRACK: Yes—without regaining consciousness.

HEDDA: What else have you concealed?

BRACK: That—the tragedy did not happen at his lodgings—

HEDDA: That makes no difference—

BRACK: Doesn't it? Not even if I tell you that Ejlert Lövborg was
found shot in—in Mademoiselle Diana's boudoir?

HEDDA (*Attempts to jump up but sinks back again*): That is impossible, Judge. He couldn't have gone there again today.

BRACK: He was there this afternoon. He went there to claim something he said they had taken from him—talked wildly about a lost
child—

HEDDA: Ah—that was why—

BRACK: I thought he must have meant the manuscript. But now I hear he destroyed that himself. So I suppose it must have been his pocketbook.

HEDDA: Yes—probably. So, he was found—there.

BRACK: Yes. With a discharged pistol in his breast pocket. He had wounded himself mortally.

HEDDA: Through the heart!—Yes!

BRACK: No—in the bowels.

HEDDA (*Looks at him with an expression of loathing*): How horrible! Everything I touch becomes ludicrous and despicable!—It's like a curse!

BRACK: There is something else, Mrs. Hedda—something rather ugly—

HEDDA: What is that?

BRACK: The pistol he carried—

HEDDA (*Breathless*): What of it?

BRACK: He must have stolen it.

HEDDA (*Leaps up*): That is not true! He didn't steal it!

BRACK: No other explanation is possible. He *must* have stolen it—hush!

(TESMAN *and* MRS. ELVSTED *have risen from the table in the inner room and come into the drawing room.*)

TESMAN (*His hands full of papers*): Hedda dear, it is almost impossible to see under that lamp. Just think!

HEDDA: Yes, I am thinking.

TESMAN: Do you think you'd let us use your desk, eh?

HEDDA: Of course—no, wait! Just let me clear it first.

TESMAN: Oh, you needn't trouble, Hedda. There's plenty of room.

HEDDA: No, no! Let me do as I say. I'll put all these things in on the piano.

(*She has taken something covered with sheet music from under the bookcase, puts some added pieces of music on it, and carries the whole lot into the inner room and off left.* TESMAN *arranges the scraps of paper on the writing table and moves the lamp from the corner table over to it. He and* MRS. ELVSTED *sit down and resume their work.* HEDDA *returns.*)

HEDDA (*Stands behind* MRS. ELVSTED'S *chair, gently ruffling her hair*): Well, darling little Thea—how are you getting on with Ejlert Lövborg's memorial?

MRS. ELVSTED (*Looks up at her with a disheartened expression*): I'm afraid it's all very difficult—

TESMAN: We *must* manage it. We've simply got to do it! And you know sorting out and arranging other people's papers—that's something I'm particularly good at—

(HEDDA *crosses to the stove and sits down on one of the stools.* BRACK *stands over her, leaning on the armchair.*)

HEDDA (*In a whisper*): What was that you said about the pistol?

BRACK (*Softly*): That he must have stolen it.

HEDDA: Why stolen?

BRACK: Because any other explanation ought to be out of the question, Mrs. Hedda.

HEDDA: Indeed?

BRACK (*Glancing at her*): Of course, Ejlert Lövborg was here this morning. Was he not?

HEDDA: Yes.

BRACK: Were you alone with him?

HEDDA: Yes—for a little while.

BRACK: Did you leave the room while he was here?

HEDDA: No.

BRACK: Try to remember. Are you *sure* you didn't leave the room—even for a moment?

HEDDA: I might have gone into the hall—just for a moment—

BRACK: And where was your pistol case?

HEDDA: It was put away in—

BRACK: Well, Mrs. Hedda?

HEDDA: It was over there on the desk.

BRACK: Have you looked since to see if both pistols are there?

HEDDA: No.

BRACK: Well, you needn't. I saw the pistol Lövborg had with him, and I recognized it at once as the one I had seen yesterday—and before that too.

HEDDA: Have you got it by any chance?

BRACK: No, the police have it.

HEDDA: What will the police do with it?

BRACK: Search until they find the owner.

HEDDA: Do you think they will succeed?

BRACK (*Bends over her and whispers*): No, Hedda Gabler, not so long as I keep silent.

HEDDA (*Gives him a frightened look*): And if you do *not* keep silent—what then?

BRACK (*Shrugs his shoulders*): One could always declare that the pistol was stolen.

HEDDA (*Firmly*): It would be better to die!

BRACK (*Smiling*): One *says* such things—but one doesn't *do* them.

HEDDA (*Without answering*): And if the pistol were not stolen and the police find the owner? What then?

BRACK: Well, Hedda—then—think of the scandal!

HEDDA: The scandal!

BRACK: The scandal, yes—of which you are so terrified. You'd naturally have to appear in court—both you and Mademoiselle Diana. She would have to explain how the thing happened—whether it was an accident or murder. Did he threaten to shoot her, and did the pistol go off then—or did she grab the pistol, shoot him, afterwards putting it back into his pocket. She might have done that, for she is a hefty woman, this—Mademoiselle Diana.

HEDDA: What have I to do with all this repulsive business?

BRACK: Nothing. But you will have to answer the question: Why did you give Ejlert Lövborg the pistol? And what conclusion will people draw from the fact that you did give it to him?

HEDDA (*Bowing her head*): That is true. I didn't think of that.

BRACK: Well, fortunately, there is no danger as long as I keep silent.

HEDDA (*Looks up at him*): That means you have me in your power, Judge! You have me at your beck and call from now on.

BRACK (*Whispers softly*): Dearest Hedda—believe me—I shall not abuse my advantage.

HEDDA: I am in your power, all the same. Subject to your commands and wishes. No longer free—not free! . . . (*Rises impetuously*) No, I won't endure that thought. Never!

BRACK (*Looks at her half mockingly*): People manage to get used to the inevitable.

HEDDA (*Returns his look*): Yes, perhaps. (*She crosses to the writing table. Suppressing an involuntary smile and imitating* TESMAN'S *intonations*) Well? How's it going, Jörgen, eh?

TESMAN: Heaven knows, dear. In any case, it will take months to do.

HEDDA (*As before*): Think of that! (*She runs her fingers softly through* MRS. ELVSTED'S *hair*) Doesn't it seem strange to you, Thea? Here you are working with Tesman—as you used to work with Ejlert Lövborg?

MRS. ELVSTED: If I could only inspire your husband in the same way!

HEDDA: Oh, no doubt that will come—in time.

TESMAN: You know, Hedda—I'm really beginning to feel something of the sort! Why don't you go and talk to Judge Brack again?

HEDDA: Is there nothing at all—I can do to help?

TESMAN: No, thank you. Not a thing. (*Turning his head*) You'll have to keep Hedda company from now on, my dear Judge.

BRACK (*With a glance at Hedda*): It will give me the greatest of pleasure!

HEDDA: Thanks. But this evening I feel a little tired. I'll go and lie down on the sofa for a little while.

TESMAN: Yes, do that dear—eh?

(HEDDA *goes into the inner room and closes the portieres after her. A short pause. Suddenly she is heard playing a wild dance tune on the piano.*)

MRS. ELVSTED (*Starts up from her chair*): Oh—what's that?

TESMAN (*Runs to the center opening*): Dearest Hedda, don't play dance music tonight! Think of Aunt Rina! And of poor Ejlert!

HEDDA (*Sticks her head out between the curtains*): And of Aunt Juliane. And of all the rest of them— Never mind— From now on, I promise to be quiet. (*She closes the curtains again.*)

TESMAN (*At the writing table*): I don't think it is good for her to see us at this distressing work; I have an idea, Mrs. Elvsted. You can move over to Aunt Juliane's and then I'll come over in the evenings and we'll work there. Eh?

Fact finder

Lovborg - Someone comes out w/ a theory.

MRS. ELVSTED: Perhaps that would be the best thing to do.

HEDDA (*From the inner room*): I can hear what you are saying, Tesman. What am I to do with all those long evenings— here—by myself?

TESMAN (*Turning over the papers*): Oh, I am sure Judge Brack will be kind enough to drop in and see you.

BRACK (*In the armchair, calls out gaily*): Every single evening, with the very greatest of pleasure, Mrs. Tesman! I'm sure we'll have a very jolly time together, we two.

HEDDA (*In a loud, clear voice*): Yes, that's what you hope, Judge, isn't it?—Now that you are cock-of-the-walk— *ho competition* (*A shot is heard within.* TESMAN, MRS. ELVSTED, *and* BRACK *leap to their feet.*)

TESMAN: Now she is playing with those pistols again.

(*He throws back the portieres and runs in, followed by* MRS. ELVSTED. HEDDA *lies stretched out on the sofa, dead. Confusion and cries.* BERTE, *alarmed, comes in from the right.*)

TESMAN (*Cries out, to* BRACK): Shot herself! Shot herself in the temple! Think of that!

BRACK (*Sinks into the armchair, half fainting*): Good God— but—people don't *do* such things!

                                                                CURTAIN

do your own thing business

Man can only be play-thing to her, but not under the control by of by them

ends it
beautiful
she has to do what she he couldn't do.

[people in society] — do what she society wants you to do.

Bea mother.

curtain — dramatize to her life. end of her life.

child — double shot need someone to live for — Tes

The Master Builder

A PLAY IN THREE ACTS

1892

CHARACTERS

MASTER BUILDER HALVARD SOLNESS

MRS. ALINE SOLNESS, *his wife*

DOCTOR HERDAL, *the family doctor*

KNUT BROVIK, *former architect now employed by Solness*

RAGNAR BROVIK, *his son, a draughtsman*

KAJA FOSLI, *his niece, a bookkeeper*

MISS HILDE WANGEL*

SOME LADIES

A CROWD IN THE GARDEN

The action takes place in the home of Master Builder Solness.

*Care should be taken to pronounce this name with an initial *v* and the word as a whole to rhyme roughly with *jungle*.

ACT
ONE

SCENE: *A plainly furnished workroom in the house of* MASTER
BUILDER SOLNESS.*In the left wall folding doors lead to the hall.
To the right is the door to the inner rooms. In the back wall an open
door leads to the draughtsmen's office. Downstage left a desk with
books, papers, and writing materials. Above the door a stove. In
the right-hand corner a sofa with a table and a couple of chairs. On
the table a water pitcher and glass. Downstage right a smaller
table with a rocking chair and an armchair. The work lights are lit
in the draughtsmen's office and there are lighted lamps on the corner table and the desk.*

In the draughtsmen's office KNUT BROVIK *and his son* RAGNAR
are seated working over plans and calculations. KAJA FOSLI *stands
at the desk in the front room writing in a ledger.* KNUT BROVIK *is a
thin old man with white hair and beard. He wears a somewhat
threadbare but well-brushed black coat. He wears glasses and a
white, rather discolored, neckcloth.* RAGNAR BROVIK *is a well-
dressed, light-haired man in his thirties, with a slight stoop.* KAJA
FOSLI *is a slight young girl just over twenty, carefully dressed and
delicate-looking. She wears a green eyeshade. All three go on
working for some time in silence.*

BROVIK (*Rises suddenly from the drawing table, as though in distress; he breathes heavily and laboriously as he comes forward
into the doorway*): It's no use! I can't bear it much longer!
KAJA (*Goes toward him*): Dear Uncle—you feel very ill this evening, don't you?
BROVIK: I get worse every day.

RAGNAR (*Has risen and comes forward*): Why don't you go home, Father—try and get some sleep?

BROVIK (*Impatiently*): Go to bed, I suppose!

KAJA: Then, take a little walk—

RAGNAR: Yes, do. I'll go with you.

BROVIK (*Insistently*): No I won't go till he gets back. I must have it out with him (*With suppressed bitterness*)—with the *Boss*. I must have it settled, once and for all.

KAJA (*Anxiously*): Oh, no, Uncle—please wait—

RAGNAR: Better wait, Father.

BROVIK (*Breathes painfully*): I haven't much time for waiting.

KAJA (*Listening*): Sh! I hear him on the stairs! (*All three go back to work. A short pause.*)

(HALVARD SOLNESS *comes in from the hall. He is a middle-aged man but strong and vigorous, with close-cropped curly hair, a dark moustache, and thick dark eyebrows. His gray-green jacket is buttoned and has a turned-up collar and broad lapels. He wears a soft gray felt hat and carries a couple of portfolios under his arm.*)

SOLNESS (*By the door, points towards the draughtsmen's office and asks in a whisper*): Have they gone?

KAJA (*Softly, shaking her head*): No. (*She takes off the eyeshade.*) (SOLNESS *crosses the room, throws his hat on a chair, puts the portfolios on the table by the sofa and comes back toward the desk.* KAJA *continues to write in the ledger but seems nervous and uneasy.*)

SOLNESS (*Out loud*): What are you entering there, Miss Fosli?

KAJA (*With a start*): It's just something that—

SOLNESS: Let me see, Miss Fosli— (*He bends over her, pretending to look in the ledger, and whispers*) Kaja!

KAJA (*Softly, still writing*): Yes?

SOLNESS: Why do you always take that shade off when I come in?

KAJA: Because I look so ugly with it on—

SOLNESS (*With a smile*) And you don't want to look ugly, Kaja?

KAJA (*Half glancing at him*): No—not when you are here.

SOLNESS (*Gently strokes her hair*): Poor, poor little Kaja!

KAJA (*Bending her head*): Sh! They'll hear you!

(SOLNESS *strolls across to the right, turns and pauses at the draughtsmen's office.*)

SOLNESS: Did anyone call while I was out?

RAGNAR: Yes—those young people who want to build at Lövstrand—

SOLNESS (*In a growling tone*): Oh, those two! Well, they'll just have to wait—I'm not quite clear about the plans yet.

RAGNAR: They're very eager to see some drawings as soon as possible—

SOLNESS (*As before*): Yes, yes—I know! They're all the same!

BROVIK: They're so looking forward to having a home of their own.

SOLNESS: I know—the same old story! So they grab the first thing that comes along—a mere roof over their heads—nothing to call a home! No, thank you! If that's all they want, let them go to somebody else. Tell them that the next time they come!

BROVIK (*Pushes his glasses up on his forehead and looks at him in amazement*): How do you mean—"somebody else"? Would you give up the commission?

SOLNESS (*Impatiently*): Well, why not? I'm not interested in building that sort of trash! Anyhow—I know nothing about these people.

BROVIK: Oh, they're reliable enough. Ragnar knows them quite well—he sees quite a lot of them—they're thoroughly respectable young people.

SOLNESS: Respectable! Respectable! That's not the point! Why can you never understand me? You don't see what I mean! (*Angrily*) I don't care to deal with a lot of strangers. Let them apply to whom they like as far as I'm concerned.

BROVIK (*Rising*): You really mean that?

SOLNESS (*Sulkily*): Why shouldn't I mean it? (*He walks about the room.*)

(BROVIK *exchanges a look with* RAGNAR, *who makes a gesture of warning; he then comes into the front room.*)

BROVIK: I'd like to have a talk with you, if I may.

SOLNESS: Of course.

BROVIK (*To* KAJA): Kaja—go in there for a few minutes.

KAJA (*Uneasily*): But, Uncle—

BROVIK: Do as I say, child—and close the door after you.
(KAJA *goes reluctantly into the draughtmen's office, and glancing anxiously and imploringly at* SOLNESS, *shuts the door*.)

BROVIK (*Lowers his voice*): I don't want the poor children to know how ill I am.

SOLNESS: It's true—you haven't looked well lately.

BROVIK: I get weaker every day.

SOLNESS: Why don't you sit down?

BROVIK: Thanks—may I?

SOLNESS (*Placing the armchair*): Here—sit here. Well?

BROVIK (*Has seated himself with difficulty*): Well, you see—it's about Ragnar. I'm worried about Ragnar—what's to become of him?

SOLNESS: Why should you be worried about him? He can work here for me as long as he likes.

BROVIK: But that's just what he doesn't like; he feels he can't stay here any longer.

SOLNESS: Why not? He does pretty well here, it seems to me. But, of course, if he wants more money—

BROVIK: No, no! That has nothing to do with it. (*Impatiently*) But he thinks it's time he did some work on his own account.

SOLNESS: Do you think Ragnar is capable enough for that?

BROVIK: That's just the point—I've begun to have doubts about the boy. After all, you've never given him a single word of encouragement. And yet—he must have talent—I can't help feeling that.

SOLNESS: But what does he know? He's had absolutely no experience—he's a good draughtsman—but is that enough?

BROVIK (*Looks at him with concealed hatred and speaks in a hoarse voice*): Experience! You hadn't had much experience either when you came to work for me; but you managed to make a name for yourself! (*Breathes with difficulty*) You pushed your way up—outstripping me and all the others!

SOLNESS: Well, you see, I was lucky.

BROVIK: Yes! You were lucky—that's true enough! All the more reason for you to be generous! I want to see Ragnar do some work on his own before I die. And then—I'd like to see them married, too.

SOLNESS (*Sharply*): Married? Is Kaja so very keen on that?

BROVIK: Not Kaja so much; but Ragnar speaks of it every day. (*Imploringly*) You must give him a chance! Help him to get some independent work! Let me see the boy do something on his own—

SOLNESS (*Peevishly*): What the hell do you expect me to do? Drag commissions down from the moon for him?

BROVIK: He has the chance of a commission now—quite a big piece of work.

SOLNESS (*Uneasily, startled*): Has he?

BROVIK: Yes, if you'd give your consent—

SOLNESS: What sort of work?

BROVIK (*With slight hesitation*): They might commission him to build that house at Lövstrand.

SOLNESS: That! I'm building that myself!

BROVIK: But it doesn't really interest you—

SOLNESS (*Flaring up*): Not interest me! How dare you say that?

BROVIK: You said so yourself just now.

SOLNESS: Never mind what I said. So they'd let Ragnar build their house, would they?

BROVIK: Well, you see, he's a friend of theirs—and, just for fun, he's made some drawings—worked out some plans and estimates—

SOLNESS: And are they pleased with these drawings of his?

BROVIK: If you'd look them over—give them your approval—

SOLNESS: Then they'd give Ragnar the commission?

BROVIK: They seemed delighted with his ideas—they found them different—new and original, they said.

SOLNESS: New and original, eh? Not the old-fashioned stuff I go in for, I suppose! (*With suppressed irritation*) So that's why they came while I was out; they wanted to see Ragnar!

BROVIK: No, no! They came to see you—they wanted to talk it over with you—find out if you would consider withdrawing from—

SOLNESS (*Angrily*): I—withdraw!

BROVIK: If you approved of Ragnar's drawings—

SOLNESS: I retire in favor of your son!

BROVIK: Withdraw from the agreement, they meant—

SOLNESS: It comes to the same thing! (*Laughs angrily*) So that's it, is it? Halvard Solness is to think about retiring now! He must make room for younger men—for the youngest of all, perhaps. He must make room—room—room!

BROVIK: God knows there's plenty of room for more than one single man—!

SOLNESS: I'm not so sure of that. But I tell you one thing—I shall never retire! I'll give way to no one! Never of my own free will. I'll never consent to that!

BROVIK (*Rises with difficulty*): I see.—Don't you realize that I'm a dying man? Am I never to see any work of Ragnar's doing? Would you deny me the joy of seeing my faith in Ragnar justified?

SOLNESS (*Turns away and mutters*): Don't say any more just now—

BROVIK: You must answer this one question! Am I to face death in such bitter poverty?

SOLNESS (*After a short struggle with himself he says in a low but firm voice*): You must face death as best you can.

BROVIK: Very well—so be it. (*Goes up-stage.*)

SOLNESS (*Following him, half in desperation*): Don't you understand—I can do nothing about it! I'm made that way—I can't change my nature!

BROVIK: No—I don't suppose you can. (*Reels and supports himself against the table*) May I have a glass of water?

SOLNESS: Of course. (*Fills a glass and hands it to him*) Here you are.

BROVIK: Thanks. (*Drinks and puts the glass down again.*)

SOLNESS (*Goes and opens the door of the draughtsmen's office*): Ragnar—you'd better take your father home.

(RAGNAR *rises quickly. He and* KAJA *come into the front room.*)

RAGNAR: What's the matter, Father?

BROVIK: Give me your arm— Now, let us go.

RAGNAR: Very well. Put your things on too, Kaja.

SOLNESS: No. Miss Fosli must stay a moment—there's a letter I want written.

BROVIK (*Looks at* SOLNESS): Good night. Sleep well—if you can.

SOLNESS: Good night.

(BROVIK *and* RAGNAR *go out by the hall door.* KAJA *goes to the desk.* SOLNESS *stands with bent head, to the right, by the arm-chair.*)

KAJA: Is there a letter?

SOLNESS (*Curtly*): No, of course not. (*Looks at her sternly*) Kaja!

KAJA (*Anxiously, in a low voice*): Yes?

SOLNESS (*With an imperious gesture*): Come here! At once!

KAJA (*Hesitantly*): Yes.

SOLNESS (*As before*): Nearer!

KAJA (*Obeying*)· What do you want of me?

SOLNESS (*Looks at her for a moment*): Is all this your doing?

KAJA: No, no! You mustn't think that!

SOLNESS: But it's true that you want to get married—isn't it?

KAJA (*Softly*): Ragnar and I have been engaged for four or five years—and so—

SOLNESS: And so you think it's about time you got married—is that it?

KAJA: Ragnar and Uncle are so insistent—I suppose I shall have to give in.

SOLNESS (*More gently*): But, Kaja—surely you must care for Ragnar a little bit, too?

KAJA: I cared a great deal for him once—before I came here to you.

SOLNESS: And now?

KAJA (*Passionately, clasping her hands and holding them out to-ward him*): Now there's only one person in the world I care about—you know that! I shall never care for anyone else!

SOLNESS: Yes—that's what you say! And yet you'd go away—leave me here to struggle on alone.

KAJA: But couldn't I stay here with you—even if Ragnar—?

SOLNESS (*Dismissing the idea*): No! That's out of the question! If Ragnar goes off and starts work on his own—he'll need you himself.

KAJA (*Wringing her hands*): Oh, I don't see how I *can* leave you! It's utterly impossible!

SOLNESS: Then get these foolish ideas out of Ragnar's head! By all means marry him if you like— (*In a different tone*) I mean . . . he has a good position here; for his own sake, try and persuade him not to give it up. For then—I'll be able to keep you here too, my dear little Kaja.

KAJA: Yes—yes—how wonderful that would be—if we could only manage it.

SOLNESS (*Takes her head in his hands and whispers*): I can't do without you—I must have you near me, Kaja—do you understand? I must have you near me—

KAJA (*With nervous exultation*): Oh, God!

SOLNESS (*Kisses her hair*): Kaja!—Kaja!

KAJA (*Sinks down at his feet*): You're so good to me! So incredibly good to me!

SOLNESS (*Vehemently*): Get up! For God's sake, get up! I hear someone coming! (*He helps her to her feet. She staggers over to the desk.*)

(MRS. SOLNESS *enters by the door on the right. She is thin and seems wasted with grief, but shows traces of bygone beauty. Blond ringlets. Dressed in good taste, wholly in black. Speaks somewhat slowly, in a plaintive voice.*)

MRS. SOLNESS (*In the doorway*): Halvard!

SOLNESS (*Turns*): Oh— Is that you, my dear?

MRS. SOLNESS (*With a glance at Kaja*): I hope I'm not disturbing you.

SOLNESS: Of course not—Miss Fosli has just a short letter to write—

MRS. SOLNESS: Yes—so I see.

SOLNESS: What did you want, Aline?

MRS. SOLNESS: I just wanted to tell you Dr. Herdal is in the drawing room—won't you come in and join us, Halvard?

SOLNESS (*Gives her a suspicious glance*): Hm . . . Has the doctor anything special to say to me?

MRS. SOLNESS: Nothing special, Halvard. He really came to call on me, but he thought he'd like to say how-do-you-do to you at the same time.

SOLNESS (*Laughs to himself*): Yes, I dare say—Well, just ask him to wait.

MRS. SOLNESS: Then you'll come in presently?

SOLNESS: Perhaps— Presently—presently, my dear—in a little while.

MRS. SOLNESS (*With another glance at* KAJA): You won't forget, Halvard? (*She withdraws, closing the door behind her.*)

KAJA (*Softly*): Oh dear! I'm afraid Mrs. Solness was annoyed with me—

SOLNESS: Not at all. No more than usual, at any rate. Still, I think you'd better go now, Kaja.

KAJA: Yes—I suppose I *must* go now.

SOLNESS (*Severely*): And mind you get this matter settled for me—do you hear?

KAJA: Oh, if it was only a question of *me*—

SOLNESS: I will have it settled, I say! By tomorrow at latest!

KAJA (*Anxiously*): If the worst comes to the worst—I'd gladly break off my engagement—

SOLNESS (*Angrily*): Break off your engagement! You must be mad!

KAJA (*Distractedly*): I *must* stay here with you. It's impossible for me to leave you—utterly impossible!

SOLNESS (*In a sudden outburst*): But—damn it—what about Ragnar, then? It's Ragnar that I—

KAJA (*Looks at him with eyes full of terror*): You mean . . . it's mostly because of Ragnar that you—?

SOLNESS (*Controlling himself*): No—no! Of course not! You don't understand me— Don't you see—it's you that I want, Kaja—you above everything. And because of that, you must persuade Ragnar to stay on here. There—there—now, run along home.

KAJA: Yes. Well—good night.

SOLNESS: Good night. (*As she starts to go*) Oh, by the way—did Ragnar leave those drawings of his here?

KAJA: I don't think he took them with him—

SOLNESS: Find them for me, will you? I might have a look at them, after all.

KAJA (*Happily*): Oh! *Would* you?

SOLNESS: Just for your sake, little Kaja—Hurry up now! Find them for me. Quickly!—Do you hear?

(KAJA *hurries into the draughtsmen's office, searches anxiously in the table drawer, finds a portfolio and brings it in with her*.)

KAJA: Here they are—

SOLNESS: Good. Just put them on the table.

KAJA (*Puts down the portfolio*): Good night—You *will* think kindly of me?

SOLNESS: You know I always do that—Good night, dear little Kaja. (*Glances to the door right*) Go now—Go!

(MRS. SOLNESS *and* DR. HERDAL *enter by the door on the right. He is a stoutish elderly man, with a round, self-satisfied face*.)

MRS. SOLNESS (*Still in the doorway*): Halvard, I really can't keep the doctor any longer.

SOLNESS: Bring him in here, then.

MRS. SOLNESS (*To* KAJA, *who is turning down the desk lamp*): Have you finished the letter, Miss Fosli?

KAJA (*Confused*): The letter—?

SOLNESS: Yes.—It was just a short one.

MRS. SOLNESS: It must have been very short.

SOLNESS: You may go now, Miss Fosli. And be sure to be here in good time in the morning.

KAJA: I will, Mr. Solness. Good night, Mrs. Solness. (*Exits to hall*.)

MRS. SOLNESS: How very lucky you were to find that young girl, Halvard.

SOLNESS: Yes. She's useful in many ways.

MRS. SOLNESS: So it seems.

HERDAL: Is she good at bookkeeping, too?

SOLNESS: Well—she's had a good deal of experience these last two years—and she's so good-natured and willing—anxious to help in every way.

MRS. SOLNESS: That must be very gratifying.

SOLNESS: It is—especially when you're not accustomed to that sort of thing.

MRS. SOLNESS (*In a tone of gentle remonstrance*): How can you say that, Halvard?

SOLNESS: I'm sorry, my dear Aline. I beg your pardon.

MRS. SOLNESS: Don't mention it. So—Doctor, you'll come back later and join us for a cup of tea?

HERDAL: I have just one more patient to see—then I'll be back.

MRS. SOLNESS: Thank you, Doctor. (*She goes out by the door on the right.*)

SOLNESS: Are you in a hurry, Doctor?

HERDAL: No, not at all.

SOLNESS: May I talk to you for a little while?

HERDAL: With the greatest of pleasure.

SOLNESS: Good—then, let's sit down. (*He motions the doctor to take the rocking chair and sits down himself in the armchair. He gives the doctor a searching look*) Tell me—did you notice anything about Aline?

HERDAL: Just now—while she was here?

SOLNESS: Yes. In her attitude toward me. Did you notice anything?

HERDAL (*Smiling*): Well—one could hardly help noticing that your wife—

SOLNESS: Yes?

HERDAL: That your wife doesn't seem to care much for this Miss Fosli.

SOLNESS: Oh, is that all! Yes—I've noticed that myself.

HERDAL: And I suppose that's not really very surprising, is it?

SOLNESS: What?

HERDAL: That she should resent your seeing so much of another woman.

SOLNESS: Perhaps you're right—and Aline too. But I'm afraid that can't be helped.

HERDAL: Couldn't you get a man for the job?

SOLNESS: You mean an ordinary clerk? No, that wouldn't do at all.

HERDAL: But, what if your wife—you know how nervous and delicate she is—what if this situation is too much of a strain for her?

SOLNESS: Even so—that can make no difference. I've strong reasons for keeping Kaja Fosli; no one else can take her place.

HERDAL: No one else?

SOLNESS (*Curtly*): No, no one!

HERDAL: Might I ask you a rather personal question, Mr. Solness?

SOLNESS: By all means.

HERDAL: One must admit that in some things women have an uncomfortably keen intuition—

SOLNESS: That's true, but—?

HERDAL: And, if your wife so thoroughly resents this Kaja Fosli—

SOLNESS: Well?

HERDAL: Is there really not the faintest reason for this instinctive dislike?

SOLNESS (*Looks at him and rises*): Aha!

HERDAL: Now don't be angry—be frank with me; isn't there?

SOLNESS (*With curt decision*): No.

HERDAL: None whatever, eh?

SOLNESS: Only her own suspicious nature.

HERDAL: I gather there have been quite a number of women in your life, Mr. Solness.

SOLNESS: That may be true—

HERDAL: And you were quite attached to some of them, no doubt?

SOLNESS: I don't deny it.

HERDAL: But in this case—there's nothing of that sort?

SOLNESS: Nothing at all—on my side.

HERDAL: But—on hers?

SOLNESS: I don't think you have the right to ask that question, Doctor.

HERDAL: Well—we were discussing your wife's intuition, you know—

SOLNESS: Yes—so we were. For that matter—Aline's intuition, as you call it, has been proved right more than once.

HERDAL: There! You see!

SOLNESS (*Sits down*): Dr. Herdal—I'd like to tell you a strange story—that is, if you'd care to hear it—

HERDAL: I like listening to strange stories.

SOLNESS: Very well. Perhaps you remember that I took Knut

Brovik and his son into my employ—when the old man's business failed—

HERDAL: Yes—I remember vaguely—

SOLNESS: They're useful fellows, you see—both highly gifted, each in his own way. But then, of course, young Ragnar got himself engaged—and decided he wanted to get married and start to build on his own account. They're all the same, these young people—

HERDAL (*Laughing*): They do have a bad habit of wanting to get married!

SOLNESS: But that didn't happen to suit me—I needed Ragnar myself—and the old man too; he's a first-class engineer; good at calculating bearing-strains, cubic contents—all that technical stuff, you know—

HERDAL: No doubt that's indispensable.

SOLNESS: Yes, it is; but Ragnar was determined to work on his own; nothing would dissuade him.

HERDAL: Then what made him stay on with you?

SOLNESS: I'll tell you how that happened. One day Kaja Fosli came here to the office. She came to see them on some errand or other—she had never been here before. When I saw how infatuated Ragnar was with her, it occurred to me that if I were to give her a job here, I might get him to stay on too—

HERDAL: That was logical enough—

SOLNESS: Yes, but wait a minute! I never said a word about it at the time. I just stood looking at her, and wished with all my might that I could persuade her to work here. I simply said a few friendly words to her, and then she went away.

HERDAL: Well?

SOLNESS: Well, the next day, toward evening—after old Brovik and Ragnar had gone home—she came here again, and behaved as if we'd come to some agreement.

HERDAL: Agreement? What about?

SOLNESS: About the very thing I'd had in mind the day before—though I had actually never said a word about it.

HERDAL: That was strange—

SOLNESS: Yes, wasn't it? It was as though she'd read my thoughts.

She asked what her duties were to be—when I wanted her to start work—and so on—

HERDAL: I suppose she thought she'd like a job here, so she could be near Ragnar.

SOLNESS: That's what I thought at first; but that wasn't it. No sooner had she started to work here, than she began to drift away from him.

HERDAL: Over to you, you mean?

SOLNESS: Exactly. She seemed to be constantly aware of me. Whenever I look at her—even when her back's turned—I can tell that she feels it; she trembles nervously whenever I come near her—

HERDAL: That's easily explained—

SOLNESS: Perhaps. But how did she know what I was thinking that first evening? Why did she behave as if I had asked her to come here, when actually I had only thought about it? I had wished it—had willed it, if you like, but silently; inwardly. How did she know? Can you explain that, Dr. Herdal?

HERDAL: No, I must confess I can't.

SOLNESS: No—you can't, can you? That's why I've never mentioned it— But it's become a damn nuisance to me in the long run; every day I have to keep up this pretense—and it's not fair to her, poor girl. (*Vehemently*) But there's nothing I can do about it. If she leaves me—then Ragnar will leave too.

HERDAL: Haven't you explained this to your wife?

SOLNESS: No.

HERDAL: Well—why on earth don't you?

SOLNESS (*Looks at him intently and says in a low voice*): Because—well—because I find a sort of salutary self-torture in allowing Aline to do me this injustice.

HERDAL (*Shakes his head*): I'm afraid I don't understand you, Mr. Solness.

SOLNESS: Yes—don't you see? It's like paying off part of a huge, immeasurable debt.

HERDAL: To your wife?

SOLNESS: Yes. It seems to relieve my mind. I feel I can breathe more freely for a while.

HERDAL: I don't understand you in the least.

SOLNESS: Very well—then let's not talk about it. (*He saunters across the room, comes back and stops beside the table. He looks at the doctor with a sly smile*) Well, Doctor? I suppose you think you've drawn me out very cleverly?

HERDAL (*With some irritation*): "Drawn you out"? Again I haven't the faintest idea what you mean, Mr. Solness.

SOLNESS: Oh, come! Why deny it? Do you suppose I haven't noticed it?

HERDAL: Noticed what?

SOLNESS (*Slowly, in a low voice*): The way you've been observing me of late.

HERDAL: Observing you? *I*? Why should I do that?

SOLNESS: Because you think that I'm— Damn it! Because you think the same of me that Aline does!

HERDAL: And what does *she* think of you?

SOLNESS (*Recovering his self-control*): Aline has begun to think that I'm—well—let's call it ill.

HERDAL: You? Ill? She's never mentioned such a thing to me. What does she think is the matter with you?

SOLNESS (*Leans over the back of the chair and says in a whisper*): Aline is convinced that I am mad. That's what she thinks.

HERDAL (*Rising*): But, my dear Mr. Solness—!

SOLNESS: I tell you it *is* so! And she's convinced you of it too! Don't think I haven't noticed it. I'm not fooled so easily, Dr. Herdal!

HERDAL (*Looks at him in amazement*): I give you my word, Mr. Solness, such a thought has never crossed my mind.

SOLNESS (*With an incredulous smile*): It hasn't—eh?

HERDAL: Never! Nor your wife's mind either—I could swear to that.

SOLNESS: I wouldn't do that if I were you. Who knows? Perhaps, in a way, she may be right.

HERDAL: Well, really—I must say!

SOLNESS (*Interrupting with a sweep of his hand*): Well, well—my dear Doctor—we won't discuss it any further. We must simply agree to differ. (*Changes to a tone of quiet amusement*) But I suppose, Doctor—

HERDAL: What?

SOLNESS: Since you don't believe that I'm ill—or crazy—or mad—or whatever you want to call it—

HERDAL: Well?

SOLNESS: I suppose you consider me a very happy man?

HERDAL: Would I be mistaken in that?

SOLNESS (*Laughs*): No, no! Of course not! God forbid! To be Halvard Solness—Solness the great Master Builder! What could be more delightful!

HERDAL: You've been an amazingly lucky man—I should think you'd admit that!

SOLNESS: I have indeed—I can't complain on that score.

HERDAL: Ever since the old house burned down—that was your first bit of luck.

SOLNESS (*Seriously*): It was Aline's old home—don't forget that.

HERDAL: Yes. It must have been a great grief to her.

SOLNESS: She never got over it—though that was twelve or thirteen years ago.

HERDAL: No—the consequences were too tragic.

SOLNESS: It was all too much for her.

HERDAL: Still—that fire is what started your career; you built your success on those ruins; you were just a poor boy from a country village, and now you're at the head of your profession. You must admit, luck was on your side, Mr. Solness.

SOLNESS (*Looks at him in embarrassment*): Yes— That's just why I'm so horribly afraid.

HERDAL: You afraid? Why? Because you've had the luck on your side?

SOLNESS: Yes—it fills me with terror. Some day that luck will turn, you see.

HERDAL: Nonsense! What should make the luck turn?

SOLNESS (*Firmly. With assurance*): The younger generation.

HERDAL: The younger generation? Oh, come now! You're not an old man yet! Your position here is more assured than ever.

SOLNESS: The luck will turn. I know it. I feel the day approaching. Some young man will suddenly shout: "Get out of my way!"; then all the others will crowd after him, clamoring, threatening:

"Make room! Make room! Make room!" You'll see, Doctor—one of these days the younger generation will come knocking at my door—

HERDAL (*Laughing*): Well, what if they do?

SOLNESS: What if they do? That will be the end of Master Builder Solness.

(*There is a knock at the door on the left.*)

SOLNESS (*With a start*): What is that? Didn't you hear?

HERDAL: Someone knocked at the door.

SOLNESS (*Loudly*): Come in!

(HILDE WANGEL *enters from the hall. She is of medium height, supple, and delicate of build. Somewhat sunburnt. She wears hiking clothes, carries a knapsack on her back, a plaid in a strap and an alpenstock.*)

HILDE (*Goes straight up to Solness, her eyes sparkling with happiness*): Good evening!

SOLNESS (*Looks at her doubtfully*): Good evening—

HILDE (*Laughs*): Don't tell me you don't recognize me!

SOLNESS: I'm sorry—but, just for the moment—

HERDAL (*Approaching*): But *I* recognize you, my dear young lady—

HILDE (*Pleased*): Oh! I remember you! You're the one who—

HERDAL: Of course! (*To* SOLNESS) We met up in the mountains last summer. (*To* HILDE) What became of the other ladies?

HILDE: They went on to the West Coast—

HERDAL: Didn't they approve of all the fun we had?

HILDE: Probably not!

HERDAL (*Shaking his finger at her*): You must admit—you did flirt with us a bit!

HILDE: What did you expect? I couldn't compete with all that knitting!

HERDAL (*Laughs*): No! Knitting's not much in your line!

SOLNESS: Have you just arrived in town?

HILDE: Just this moment.

HERDAL: All alone, Miss Wangel?

HILDE: All alone!

SOLNESS: Wangel? Is your name Wangel?

HILDE (*Looks at him with amused surprise*): Of course it is!

SOLNESS: Are you by any chance Dr. Wangel's daughter—from Lysanger?

HILDE (*As before*): Of course! Whose daughter did you think I was?

SOLNESS: Oh, then I suppose we met up there; that summer I built the tower on the old church.

HILDE (*More seriously*): Of course that's when we met!

SOLNESS: Well—that's a long time ago.

HILDE (*Looks at him intently*): It's exactly the ten years.

SOLNESS: You must have been a mere child then.

HILDE (*Carelessly*): I was about twelve or thirteen—

HERDAL: Is this your first trip to town, Miss Wangel?

HILDE: Yes, it is.

SOLNESS: And have you no friends here?

HILDE: Just you—and your wife, of course.

SOLNESS: Oh, so you know her too?

HILDE: Very slightly—we met quite briefly, at the sanatorium.

SOLNESS: Oh, up there?

HILDE: Yes. She asked me to come and see her if ever I came to town. (*Smiles*) Not that that was necessary, of course.

SOLNESS: Funny she should never have mentioned it.
    (HILDE *puts her stick down by the stove, takes off her knapsack and lays it and the plaid on the sofa.* DR. HERDAL *offers to help her.* SOLNESS *stands and gazes at her.*)

HILDE: Well—is it all right for me to stay the night here?

SOLNESS: I expect that can be managed—

HILDE: You see—I didn't bring any clothes with me—just what I have on. I have a change of underwear in my knapsack—but that'll have to go to the wash—it's very dirty.

SOLNESS: We'll take care of that—I'll just call my wife.

HERDAL: Meanwhile, I'll visit my patient.

SOLNESS: Yes, do. And you'll come back later?

HERDAL (*With a playful glance at* HILDE): Don't worry—I'll be back! (*Laughs*) You were right after all, Mr. Solness—

SOLNESS: How do you mean?

HERDAL: The younger generation did come knocking at your door!

SOLNESS (*Cheerfully*): In quite a different way though!

HERDAL: Oh, in a very different way! That's undeniable!

(DR. HERDAL *goes out by the hall door*. SOLNESS *opens the door on the right and calls through to the other room*.)

SOLNESS: Aline! Would you be kind enough to come in here a minute? There's a Miss Wangel here—a friend of yours.

MRS. SOLNESS (*Appears in the doorway*): Who did you say it was? (*Sees* HILDE) Oh, it's you, Miss Wangel. (*Goes to her and shakes hands*) So you did come to town, after all.

SOLNESS: Miss Wangel just arrived. She wants to know if she may stay the night here.

MRS. SOLNESS: Here with us? Of course—with pleasure.

SOLNESS: Just till she can get her clothes in order, you know.

MRS. SOLNESS: I'll help you as best I can—it's no more than my duty. Your trunk will be here presently, I suppose?

HILDE: Oh, I have no trunk!

MRS. SOLNESS: Well—everything will work out for the best, I dare say. If you'll just stay and talk to my husband for a while, I'll see about getting a room comfortable for you.

SOLNESS: Why not put her in one of the nurseries? They're all ready as it is—

MRS. SOLNESS: Yes—we have plenty of room there— (*To* HILDE) Sit down now and rest a little. (*She goes out right.*)

(HILDE *with her hands behind her back strolls about the room looking at various things*. SOLNESS *stands down front beside the table and follows her with his eyes*.)

HILDE (*Stops and looks at him*): Are there so many nurseries here?

SOLNESS: There are three nurseries in the house.

HILDE: You must have a great many children!

SOLNESS: No, we have no children. So you'll have to be the child here for the time being.

HILDE: Yes—for tonight. I shan't cry! I intend to sleep like a log!

SOLNESS: You must be very tired.

HILDE: Not a bit! No, it's not that; but it's such fun just to lie in bed and dream—

SOLNESS: Do you usually dream at night?

HILDE: Almost always.

SOLNESS: What do you dream about most?

HILDE: I won't tell you! Some other time, perhaps. (*She again strolls about the room, stops at the desk and examines some of the books and papers*.)

SOLNESS: Are you looking for something?

HILDE: No—I was just interested in all these things. (*Turns toward him*) Perhaps I shouldn't touch them?

SOLNESS: Go right ahead!

HILDE: Do you write in this great ledger?

SOLNESS: No. That's for the accountant.

HILDE: A woman?

SOLNESS (*Smiles*): Yes, of course.

HILDE: Does she work here every day?

SOLNESS: Yes.

HILDE: Is she married?

SOLNESS: No; she's single.

HILDE: Indeed!

SOLNESS: But she expects to marry soon.

HILDE: Well—that'll be nice for her.

SOLNESS: Yes—but not so nice for me—for then I'll have no one to help me.

HILDE: You're sure to find someone else just as good.

SOLNESS: How would you like to stay here—and write in the ledger?

HILDE: Not I, thank you! Nothing like that for me! (*She again strolls across the room and sits down in the rocking chair. SOLNESS joins her at the table*) There are better things than that to be done around here!— (*Looks at him with a smile*)—Don't you think so too?

SOLNESS: Unquestionably! I suppose you'll start by visiting all the shops and decking yourself out in the height of fashion.

HILDE (*Amused*): No—I think I'll leave the shops alone!

SOLNESS: Why?

HILDE: Well—you see—I'm all out of money!

SOLNESS: No trunk and no money—eh?

HILDE: Neither the one nor the other! But what does that matter now!

SOLNESS: You know—I really like you for that!

HILDE: Only for that?

SOLNESS: For that among other things— (*Sits in the armchair*) Is your father still alive?

HILDE: Yes—Father's alive.

SOLNESS: Do you plan to study here?

HILDE: No, that hadn't occurred to me.

SOLNESS: But I suppose you'll be here for some time?

HILDE: It depends how things turn out. (*She sits awhile looking at him, half seriously, half smiling. Then she takes off her hat and puts it on the table in front of her*) Master Builder?

SOLNESS: Yes?

HILDE: Have you a very bad memory?

SOLNESS: Bad memory? No—not that I know of—

HILDE: Well—aren't you going to talk to me about what happened up there?

SOLNESS (*Startled for a moment*): At Lysanger? (*Indifferently*) I don't see much to talk about in that.

HILDE (*Looks at him reproachfully*): How can you sit there and say such things!

SOLNESS: Well—suppose you talk to *me* about it.

HILDE: When the tower was finished—don't you remember all the excitement in the town?

SOLNESS: Yes—I shall never forget that day.

HILDE (*Smiles*): Oh, you won't, won't you? That's kind of you!

SOLNESS: Kind?

HILDE: There was a band in the churchyard and hundreds and hundreds of people—we schoolgirls were dressed all in white—and we all carried flags—

SOLNESS: Oh, yes! Those flags! I certainly remember them—

HILDE: And then you climbed up the scaffolding—right to the very top. You had a great wreath in your hand, and you hung it high up on the weather vane—

SOLNESS (*Curtly interrupting*): I used to do that in those days—it's an old custom, you know.

HILDE: It was wonderfully thrilling to stand below and look up at you. What if he were to fall over—he, the Master Builder himself!

SOLNESS (*As though trying to divert her from the subject*): That might easily have happened too; one of those little devils dressed in white, carried on so and kept screaming up at me—

HILDE (*Sparkling with pleasure*): —"Hurrah for Master Builder Solness!"

SOLNESS: —and then she kept brandishing her flag and waving it so wildly—the sight of it made me feel quite dizzy.

HILDE (*Seriously. In a low voice*): That particular little devil—that was I.

SOLNESS (*Staring at her intently*): Of course—I see that now. It must have been you.

HILDE: It was so wonderfully thrilling! It didn't seem possible to me that any Master Builder in the whole world could build such a tremendously high tower. And then to see you up there yourself—right at the very top—as large as life! And to know that you weren't in the least bit dizzy—that was what made one so—dizzy to think of!

SOLNESS: How could you be so sure that I was not—?

HILDE: You dizzy? Of course not! I knew that with my whole being! Besides—if you had been—you could never have stood up there and sung.

SOLNESS (*Looks at her in amazement*): Sung? Did *I* sing?

HILDE: Of course you did!

SOLNESS (*Shakes his head*): I've never sung a note in my life.

HILDE: Well—you sang then! It sounded like harps in the air.

SOLNESS (*Thoughtfully*): There's something very strange about all this.

HILDE (*Is silent awhile, looking at him; then says in a low voice*): But of course the *real* thing—happened afterwards.

SOLNESS: What "real" thing?

HILDE (*Sparkling with vivacity*): I surely needn't remind you of *that?*

SOLNESS: Please—*do* remind me a little of *that* too!

HILDE: Don't you remember, a great dinner was given for you at the Club—

SOLNESS: Yes. That must have been the same afternoon—for I left the next morning.

HILDE: And from the Club, you came on to our house—

SOLNESS: I believe you're right, Miss Wangel! It's amazing! You seem to remember every little detail—

HILDE: "Little details"—is that what you call them? I suppose it was a "little detail" too that I happened to be alone in the room when you came in?

SOLNESS: Oh? Were you alone?

HILDE (*Ignoring this*): You didn't call me a "little devil" then.

SOLNESS: No. I suppose not—

HILDE: You told me I looked lovely in my white dress. You said I looked like a little princess.

SOLNESS: I expect you did, Miss Wangel. And I remember feeling so free and buoyant that day—

HILDE: And then you said that when I grew up I was to be *your* princess—

SOLNESS (*Laughing a little*): Well—well! I said that too, did I?

HILDE: Yes, you did. And when I asked how long I'd have to wait, you said you'd come back again in ten years—and carry me off like a troll—to Spain, or some such place. And you promised to buy me a kingdom there.

SOLNESS (*As before*): There's nothing like a good dinner to make you feel generous! But—did I really say all that?

HILDE (*Laughing to herself*): Yes, you did. You even told me what the kingdom was to be called.

SOLNESS: Well—what?

HILDE: It was to be called the Kingdom of Orangia, you said.

SOLNESS: A very appetizing name!

HILDE: I didn't like it a bit! It sounded almost as if you were making fun of me.

SOLNESS: Of course I *couldn't* have been doing that.

HILDE: Well, I should hope not—considering what you did next.

SOLNESS: What in God's name did I do next?

HILDE: Don't tell me you've forgotten that too! I know better; you couldn't *help* remembering it.

SOLNESS: Won't you give me just a little hint? Well?

HILDE (*Looks at him intently*): You came and kissed me, Master Builder.

SOLNESS (*Rising, open-mouthed*): I did!

HILDE: Yes, you did. You took me in your arms and bent my head back and kissed me—many times.

SOLNESS: Now really—my dear Miss Wangel—!

HILDE: You surely don't intend to deny it?

SOLNESS: I most certainly *do* deny it!

HILDE (*Looks at him scornfully*): Oh, indeed! (*She goes slowly up to the stove and remains standing motionless, her face averted from him, her hands behind her back. Short pause.*)

SOLNESS (*Moves up behind her cautiously*): Miss Wangel—! (HILDE *is silent and doesn't move*) Now don't stand there like a statue. You must have dreamt these things— (*Lays his hand on her arm*) Now look here! (HILDE *moves her arm impatiently. A thought strikes him*) Or perhaps—wait a minute! There's some mystery behind all this—I must have thought about it. I must have willed it, wished it, longed to do it, and then— Perhaps that would explain it. (HILDE *is still silent*) Oh, very well then—damn it!—then I *did* do it, I suppose!

HILDE (*Turns her head a little but without looking at him*): Then you admit it now?

SOLNESS: Anything you like.

HILDE: You took me in your arms?

SOLNESS: Yes—

HILDE: Bent my head back?

SOLNESS: Very far back—

HILDE: And kissed me?

SOLNESS: Yes, I did.

HILDE: Many times?

SOLNESS: As many times as you like.

HILDE (*Turns toward him quickly. Once more her eyes are sparkling with happiness*): There, you see! I got it out of you at last!

SOLNESS (*With a slight smile*): Yes—how could I possibly have forgotten a thing like that.

HILDE (*Again a little sulkily, retreats from him*): Oh, you've probably kissed so many girls in your day!

SOLNESS: No—you mustn't think that of me!

(HILDE *sits down in the armchair.* SOLNESS *stands leaning against the rocking chair and watches her intently.*)

SOLNESS: Miss Wangel!

HILDE: Well?

SOLNESS: And then what happened? I mean—what came of all this between us two?

HILDE: Nothing came of it—you know that perfectly well—just then all the others came in, and then—isch!

SOLNESS: Of course—all the others came in. To think of my forgetting that too.

HILDE: I don't believe you've really forgotten anything. You're just a bit ashamed, that's all. You couldn't possibly forget a thing of that sort.

SOLNESS: No—one wouldn't think so.

HILDE (*Again sparkling with life*): I suppose, now, you'll tell me you've forgotten what date it was?

SOLNESS: What date?

HILDE: Yes—on what day of what month did you hang the wreath on the tower? Well? Tell me at once!

SOLNESS: I'm afraid I've forgotten the actual date—I remember it was ten years ago, some time in the autumn.

HILDE (*Nods her head slowly several times*): Yes, it *was* ten years ago—on the nineteenth of September.

SOLNESS: Yes, it must have been around that time. Fancy your remembering that too! But, wait a minute—isn't it—? Yes! It's the nineteenth of September today.

HILDE: Yes it is. And the ten years are up. And you didn't come as you had promised me.

SOLNESS: Promised? Threatened, I suppose you mean.

HILDE: Why? It didn't seem like a threat to me.

SOLNESS: Well, then—making a little fun of you, perhaps.

HILDE: Was that all you wanted? To make fun of me?

SOLNESS: I was just teasing you, I suppose—I don't remember anything about it—but it couldn't have been anything else; after all, at that time you were only a child.

HILDE: Don't be so sure! Perhaps I wasn't quite such a child either. Not quite such a callow little brat as you imagine.

SOLNESS (*With a searching look*): Did you really, in all seriousness, expect me to come back again?

HILDE (*Conceals a half-teasing smile*): Of course I did!

SOLNESS: You really expected me to come back to your home and carry you off with me?

HILDE: Just like a troll—yes!

SOLNESS: And make a princess of you?

HILDE: That's what you promised.

SOLNESS: And give you a kingdom as well?

HILDE (*Gazing at the ceiling*): Why not? Oh, perhaps not an ordinary, *everyday* sort of kingdom—

SOLNESS: But something else just as good?

HILDE: Oh, at *least* as good! (*Looks at him a moment*) I thought to myself—if he can build the highest church tower in the world, he must surely be able to raise some sort of a kingdom as well—

SOLNESS (*Shakes his head*): I can't quite make you out, Miss Wangel.

HILDE: Can't you? It all seems so simple to me.

SOLNESS: No, I can't make out whether you mean all you say—or whether you're just joking.

HILDE (*Smiles*): Making fun of you, perhaps—I too?

SOLNESS: Precisely—making fun of us both. (*Looks at her*) How long have you known that I was married?

HILDE: I've always known that. Why? What makes you ask?

SOLNESS (*Lightly*): Oh, nothing—it just occurred to me. (*Looks at her seriously and says in a low voice*) Why have you come here?

HILDE: I want my kingdom—the time is up!

SOLNESS (*Laughs involuntarily*): What an amazing girl you are!

HILDE (*Gaily*): Out with my kingdom, Master Builder. (*Raps the table with her fingers*) My kingdom on the table!

SOLNESS (*Pushing the rocking chair nearer and sitting down*): No, but seriously—why have you come? What do you really want to do here?

HILDE: Well, to begin with—I want to go round and look at all the things you've built.

SOLNESS: That'll give you plenty of exercise!

HILDE: Yes—I know you've built a tremendous lot!

SOLNESS: I have. Especially these last few years—

HILDE: Many church towers too? Immensely high ones?

SOLNESS: No, I don't build church towers any more. Nor churches either.

HILDE: Then what do you build now?

SOLNESS: Homes for human beings.

HILDE (*Thoughtfully*): Couldn't you build some sort of a—some sort of a church tower over those homes as well?

SOLNESS (*With a start*): What do you mean by that?

HILDE: I mean—something that soars—that points straight up into the free air—with the vane at a dizzy height!

SOLNESS (*Pondering*): How extraordinary that you should say that. That's what I've always longed to do.

HILDE (*Impatiently*): Well—why don't you *do* it then?

SOLNESS (*Shakes his head*): I don't think people would approve of it.

HILDE: Wouldn't they? How can they be so stupid!

SOLNESS (*In a lighter tone*): I'm building a home for myself, however—just over there—

HILDE: For yourself?

SOLNESS: Yes—it's almost finished—and there's a tower on that.

HILDE: A high tower?

SOLNESS: Yes.

HILDE: Very high?

SOLNESS: Much too high for a home—people are sure to say!

HILDE: I'll go out and see that tower first thing in the morning, Master Builder.

SOLNESS (*Sits resting his cheek on his hand and gazes at her*): What's your name, Miss Wangel—your first name, I mean?

HILDE: My name's Hilde, of course.

SOLNESS (*As before*): Hilde, eh?

HILDE: You must have known that! You called me Hilde yourself, that day when you—misbehaved.

SOLNESS: Did I really?

HILDE: Yes. Only then you said "little Hilde"—I didn't like that.

SOLNESS: So you didn't like that, Miss Hilde.

HILDE: Not at a time like that! *Princess* Hilde, however, would sound very well, I think.

SOLNESS: Princess Hilde of—what was to be the name of the king-dom?

HILDE: I'll have nothing more to do with that stupid kingdom! I'm determined to have quite a different one.

SOLNESS (*Leaning back in the chair, still gazing at her*): Isn't it strange! The more I think of it, the more it seems to me that all these years I've been tormented by—

HILDE: By what?

SOLNESS: By some half-forgotten experience that I kept trying to recapture. But I never could remember clearly what it was.

HILDE: You should have tied a knot in your handkerchief, Master Builder.

SOLNESS: Then I should have only tormented myself wondering what the knot was about.

HILDE: Yes! There are trolls of that sort in the world too!

SOLNESS (*Rises slowly*): What a good thing it is that you've come to me now.

HILDE (*Looks deep into his eyes*): Is it a good thing?

SOLNESS: Yes—don't you see? I've been so lonely here—gazing at everything so helplessly. (*In a lower voice*) I must tell you, Hilde—I've begun to be so afraid—so terribly afraid of the younger generation.

HILDE (*With a little snort of contempt*): The younger generation! Surely that's nothing to be afraid of!

SOLNESS: Oh, yes it is! That's why I've locked and barred myself in. (*Mysteriously*) I tell you one of these days the younger gener-ation will thunder at my door—they'll break through and over-whelm me!

HILDE: In that case, I think that you yourself should go out and open the door to the younger generation.

SOLNESS: Open the door?

HILDE: Of course! Let them come in to you—in friendship.

SOLNESS: No, no! Don't you see? The younger generation comes bringing retribution. It heralds the turn of fortune; it marches triumphantly, under a new banner.

HILDE (*Rises, looks at him, and says with quivering lips*): Can I be of use to you, Master Builder?

SOLNESS: You can indeed! For you too march under a new banner, it seems to me. Yes! Youth matched against youth!

(DR. HERDAL *comes in by the hall door*.)

HERDAL: Well! So you and Miss Wangel are still here.

SOLNESS: Yes—we found so much to talk about—

HILDE: Old things as well as new.

HERDAL: Did you really?

HILDE: It's been the greatest fun! Mr. Solness has the most remarkable memory. He remembers things so vividly—down to the tiniest detail!

(MRS. SOLNESS *enters by the door right*.)

MRS. SOLNESS: Your room is ready now, Miss Wangel.

HILDE: How very kind you are.

SOLNESS (*To* MRS. SOLNESS): The nursery?

MRS. SOLNESS: Yes, the middle one. Well—shall we go in to supper?

SOLNESS (*Nodding to* HILDE): Hilde shall sleep in the nursery, she shall!

MRS. SOLNESS (*Looks at him*): Hilde?

SOLNESS: Yes, Miss Wangel's name is Hilde. I knew her when she was a little girl.

MRS. SOLNESS: Did you really, Halvard? Come, let us go in. Supper is on the table.

(*She takes* DR. HERDAL'S *arm and goes out with him to the right.* HILDE *has meanwhile been collecting her belongings.*)

HILDE (*Softly and rapidly to* SOLNESS): Was that true what you said just now? Can I be of use to you?

SOLNESS (*Takes her things from her*): You are the one being I have needed most.

HILDE (*Looks at him with happy eyes full of wonder and clasps her hands*): But then—oh, how wonderful the world is!

SOLNESS (*Eagerly*): How do you mean?

HILDE: Why then—I *have* my kingdom!

SOLNESS (*Involuntarily*): Hilde!

HILDE (*Again with quivering lips*): Almost—I was going to say. (*She goes out to the right,* SOLNESS *following her.*)

CURTAIN

ACT
TWO

SCENE: *A small, prettily furnished drawing room in* SOLNESS'
*house. In the back, a glass door leading out to the veranda and gar-
den. The right-hand corner is cut off transversely by a large bay
window, in which are flower stands. The left-hand corner is simi-
larly cut off by a transverse wall, in which is a small door papered
like the wall. On each side, an ordinary door. In front, on the
right, a console table with a large mirror over it. Well-filled stands
of plants and flowers. In front, on the left, a sofa with a table and
chairs. Further back, a bookcase. Well forward in the room, in
front of the bay window, a small table and some chairs. It is early
in the day.*

SOLNESS *sits by the little table with* RAGNAR BROVIK'S *portfolio open in front of him. He is turning the drawings over and
closely examining some of them.* MRS. SOLNESS *moves about
noiselessly with a small watering pot, attending to her flowers. She
is dressed in black as before. Her hat, cloak, and gloves lie on a
chair near the mirror. Unobserved by her,* SOLNESS *now and then
follows her with his eyes. Neither of them speaks.*

KAJA FOSLI *enters quietly by the door on the left.*

SOLNESS (*Turns his head and says with casual indifference*):
Oh—it's you.

KAJA: I just wanted to let you know that I was here—

SOLNESS: Very well. Did Ragnar come too?

KAJA: No, not yet. He had to wait for the doctor. But he's coming
presently to find out—

SOLNESS: How is the old man feeling?

KAJA: Not at all well. He begs you to excuse him—he'll have to stay in bed today.

SOLNESS: Of course. Let him rest. But you'd better get to your work now—

KAJA: Yes. (*Pauses at the door*) Would you like to speak to Ragnar when he comes?

SOLNESS: No—I've nothing special to say to him.

(KAJA *goes out again to the left.* SOLNESS *remains seated, turning over the drawings.*)

MRS. SOLNESS (*Over beside the plants*): I expect he'll die now, as well.

SOLNESS (*Looks up at her*): As well as who?

MRS. SOLNESS (*Not answering him*): Yes—old Brovik is going to die too. You'll see, Halvard.

SOLNESS: My dear Aline, don't you think you should go out for a little walk?

MRS. SOLNESS: Yes, I suppose I should. (*She continues to attend to the flowers.*)

SOLNESS (*Bending over the drawings*): Is she still asleep?

MRS. SOLNESS (*Looking at him*): Miss Wangel? So it's Miss Wangel you're thinking about.

SOLNESS (*Indifferently*): I just happened to remember her.

MRS. SOLNESS: Miss Wangel was up long ago.

SOLNESS: Really. Was she?

MRS. SOLNESS: When I went in to see her, she was putting her things in order. (*She goes to the mirror and slowly begins to put on her hat.*)

SOLNESS (*After a short pause*): Well—we've found a use for one of our nurseries after all, Aline.

MRS. SOLNESS: So we have.

SOLNESS: It seems to me that's better than having them all empty.

MRS. SOLNESS: Yes, you're right—that emptiness is dreadful.

SOLNESS (*Closes the portfolio, rises and goes to her*): You'll see, Aline—from now on things are going to be much better—more cheerful. Life will be easier—especially for you.

MRS. SOLNESS (*Looks at him*): From now on?

SOLNESS: Yes, you'll see, Aline—

MRS. SOLNESS: Because *she* has come here? Is that what you mean?

SOLNESS (*Checking himself*): I mean—after we've moved into the new house.

MRS. SOLNESS (*Takes her coat*): Really, Halvard? Do you think things will be better then?

SOLNESS: Of course they will, Aline. I'm sure you must think so too.

MRS. SOLNESS: I think nothing at all about the new house.

SOLNESS (*Downcast*): It's hard for me to hear you talk like that, considering it's mostly for your sake that I built it. (*He offers to help her on with her coat.*)

MRS. SOLNESS (*Evading him*): I'm afraid you do far too much for my sake.

SOLNESS (*With a certain vehemence*): You mustn't say such things, Aline; I can't bear it!

MRS. SOLNESS: Then I won't say them, Halvard.

SOLNESS: But I stick to what I said—you'll see—things'll be much easier for you over there.

MRS. SOLNESS: Heavens! Easier for me!

SOLNESS (*Eagerly*): Yes, I tell you; you *must* see that! There'll be so many things to remind you of your old home.

MRS. SOLNESS: Father's and Mother's home—that was burned to the ground.

SOLNESS (*In a low voice*): Yes, poor Aline! I know what a great grief that was to you.

MRS. SOLNESS (*Breaking out in lamentation*): You can build as much as you like, Halvard—you'll never be able to build another real home for me.

SOLNESS (*Crosses the room*): Then for God's sake don't let's talk about it any more!

MRS. SOLNESS: We don't as a rule talk about it—you always carefully avoid the subject.

SOLNESS (*Stops suddenly and looks at her*): Avoid? Why should I avoid it?

MRS SOLNESS: Don't think I don't understand you, Halvard. I

know you want to spare me—you try to find excuses for me—as much as you possibly can.

SOLNESS (*Looks at her in astonishment*): For *you*, Aline? *I* find excuses for *you!*

MRS. SOLNESS: Yes, Halvard—for me; I know that only too well.

SOLNESS (*Involuntarily; to himself*): That too!

MRS. SOLNESS: As for the old house—it was meant to be, I suppose. But it's what came after the fire—the dreadful thing that followed! That's what I can never—!

SOLNESS (*Vehemently*): You must stop thinking about *that*, Aline!

MRS. SOLNESS: How can I help thinking about it! And for once I must speak about it too! I can't bear it any longer—I'll never be able to forgive myself!

SOLNESS (*Exclaiming*): Yourself—!

MRS. SOLNESS: Yes. I should have been strong, Halvard. I had my duties both to you and to the little ones. I shouldn't have let the horror overwhelm me—nor the grief at the loss of my old home. (*Wrings her hands*) Oh, Halvard, if I'd only had the strength!

SOLNESS (*Softly, much moved, comes toward her*): Aline —promise me that you will never think these thoughts again—promise me that!

MRS. SOLNESS: Promise! One can promise anything!

SOLNESS (*Clenches his hands and crosses the room*): Oh, this is all hopeless—hopeless! Can we never have any brightness in our home? Never a ray of sunlight?

MRS. SOLNESS: This is not a *home*, Halvard.

SOLNESS: No. You're right. (*Gloomily*) And I don't suppose it'll be any better in the new house either.

MRS. SOLNESS: No. It won't be any better. It'll be just as empty and desolate there, as it is here.

SOLNESS (*Vehemently*): Then why in God's name did we build it?—Can you tell me that?

MRS SOLNESS: That's a question only you can answer, Halvard.

SOLNESS (*With a suspicious glance at her*): What do you mean by *that*, Aline?

MRS SOLNESS: What do I mean?

SOLNESS: Yes—damn it! You said it so strangely. What are you trying to imply, Aline?

MRS. SOLNESS: Halvard—I assure you—

SOLNESS (*Comes closer*): I know what I know, Aline. I'm neither blind nor deaf—just remember that!

MRS. SOLNESS: What are you talking about, Halvard? What is it?

SOLNESS (*Stands in front of her*): You know perfectly well you manage to find a furtive hidden meaning in the most innocent word I happen to say!

MRS. SOLNESS: *I* do, Halvard! How can you say that!

SOLNESS (*Laughs*): It's natural enough, I suppose—when you're dealing with a sick man—

MRS. SOLNESS (*Anxiously*): Sick! Are you ill, Halvard?

SOLNESS (*Violently*): A half-mad man, then—a lunatic, if you prefer to call it that!

MRS. SOLNESS (*Feels blindly for a chair and sits down*): Halvard—for God's sake!

SOLNESS: But you're both wrong, do you hear? Both you and the doctor! I'm in no such state! (*He walks up and down the room. MRS. SOLNESS follows him anxiously with her eyes. Finally he goes up to her and says calmly*) As a matter of fact there's absolutely nothing wrong with me.

MRS. SOLNESS: No. There isn't, is there? But then, what is it that troubles you so?

SOLNESS: It's this terrible burden of debt—I sometimes feel I can't bear it any longer!

MRS. SOLNESS: Debt? But you owe no one anything, Halvard.

SOLNESS (*Softly. With emotion*): I owe a boundless debt to you—to you—to *you*, Aline.

MRS. SOLNESS (*Rises slowly*): What are you hiding from me, Halvard? Tell me the truth.

SOLNESS: I'm not hiding anything from you. I've never harmed you—never deliberately, never intentionally, that is—and yet I feel crushed by a terrible sense of guilt.

MRS. SOLNESS: Toward me?

SOLNESS: Yes—mostly toward you.

MRS. SOLNESS: Then you must be—ill—after all, Halvard.

SOLNESS (*Gloomily*): Yes. I suppose I must be—or not far from it. (*He looks toward the door on the right, which is opened at this moment*) Ah! Now it gets lighter!

(HILDE *comes in. She has made some alteration in her dress.*)

HILDE: Good morning, Master Builder!

SOLNESS (*Nods*): Did you sleep well?

HILDE: Splendidly! Like a child in a cradle! I lay there and stretched myself like—like a princess!

SOLNESS (*Smiles a little*): You were quite comfortable then?

HILDE: I was indeed!

SOLNESS: Did you have any dreams?

HILDE: Yes—but horrid ones!

SOLNESS: Really?

HILDE: Yes. I dreamt I was falling over a high steep precipice. Do you ever dream that sort of thing?

SOLNESS: Yes, now and then.

HILDE: It's wonderfully thrilling, though; you feel yourself falling further and further—down and down—

SOLNESS: I know! It makes your blood run cold.

HILDE: Do you draw your legs up under you when you're falling?

SOLNESS: As high as I possibly can.

HILDE: So do I!

MRS. SOLNESS (*Takes her gloves*): I'd better go into town now, Halvard. (*To* HILDE) I'll try and get some of the things you need, Miss Wangel.

HILDE (*Starts to throw her arms round her neck*): Dear, darling Mrs. Solness! You're really much too kind to me—incredibly kind!

MRS. SOLNESS (*Deprecatingly, freeing herself*): Not at all—it's no more than my duty. I'm only too glad to do it.

HILDE (*Offended, pouts*): There's really no reason why I shouldn't go myself—now that I look so respectable. What do you think?

MRS. SOLNESS: To tell you the truth, I'm afraid people might stare at you a little.

HILDE (*Contemptuously*): Is *that* all? That'd be fun!

SOLNESS (*With suppressed ill-humor*): Yes, but then people might think *you* were mad too.

HILDE: Mad? Why? Is the place so full of mad people?

SOLNESS (*Points to his own forehead*): Here is *one*, at any rate—

HILDE: You—Master Builder!

MRS. SOLNESS: Now really, my dear Halvard!

SOLNESS: You surely must have noticed it.

HILDE: No, I can't say I have— (*Thinks a moment and laughs a little*) Though there was *one* thing—

SOLNESS: Do you hear that, Aline?

MRS. SOLNESS: What thing, Miss Wangel?

HILDE: I won't tell you.

SOLNESS: Oh, yes—do!

HILDE: No, thanks—I'm not quite as mad as *that!*

MRS. SOLNESS: When you are alone, Miss Wangel's sure to tell you, Halvard.

SOLNESS: Oh—you think so?

MRS. SOLNESS: Of course. After all, she's such an old friend of yours—you've known her ever since she was a child, you tell me. (*She goes out by the door on the left.*)

HILDE (*After a short pause*): Your wife doesn't seem to like me very much.

SOLNESS: Why do you say that?

HILDE: Wasn't it pretty obvious?

SOLNESS (*Evasively*): It's just her manner—Aline's become very shy these past few years—

HILDE: Oh—has she really?

SOLNESS: But underneath she's an immensely kind, gentle, good-hearted creature—you'll see, when you know her better—

HILDE: Perhaps. But I wish she wouldn't talk so much about her duty.

SOLNESS: Her duty?

HILDE: Yes. Why did she have to say she'd get those things for me because it was her *duty?* I hate that ugly, horrid word!

SOLNESS: Why?

HILDE: I don't know—it sounds so cold and harsh and prickly: Duty, duty, duty! It *is* prickly! Don't you think so too?

SOLNESS: I've never thought about it.

HILDE: Well, it *is!* And if she's as kind as you say she is—why does she use a word like that?

SOLNESS: Well—what on earth should she have said?

HILDE: She could have said she'd *love* to do it, because she'd taken such a tremendous fancy to me. She could have said something like that—something warm and friendly—don't you see?

SOLNESS (*Looks at her*): That's what you'd have liked, is it?

HILDE: Yes, of course. (*She wanders about the room, stops at the bookcases and examines the books*) What a lot of books you have!

SOLNESS: Yes—I seem to have collected a good many—

HILDE: Do you read them all too?

SOLNESS: When I was young I used to try to. Do you read much?

HILDE: No, never! I've given it up—it all seems so irrelevant.

SOLNESS: That's just how I feel.

(HILDE *wanders about a little, stops at the small table, opens the portfolio and turns over the contents.*)

HILDE: Are these your drawings?

SOLNESS: No, they were done by a young man who's my assistant here.

HILDE: Then he's been studying with you, I suppose.

SOLNESS: He's learned something from me, I dare say.

HILDE: Then he must be very clever. (*Looks at a drawing*) Isn't he?

SOLNESS: He could be worse. He serves my purpose—

HILDE: I expect he's frightfully clever!

SOLNESS: Why? Do you see that in the drawings?

HILDE: What? These things! No! But if he's a pupil of yours—

SOLNESS: I've had lots of pupils in my time—but they haven't amounted to much.

HILDE: I can't think how you can be so stupid, Master Builder!

SOLNESS: Stupid? Why do you think me stupid?

HILDE: You must be—or you wouldn't waste your time teaching all these people—

SOLNESS: Why not?

HILDE: What for? You're the only one who should be allowed to build. You should build everything yourself, Master Builder—you alone!

SOLNESS (*Involuntarily*): Hilde!

HILDE: Well?

SOLNESS: Whatever put that idea into your head?

HILDE: Why? Am I so wrong?

SOLNESS: No—it's not that— But, do you know something, Hilde?

HILDE: What?

SOLNESS: I myself am obsessed by that very thought. I sit here alone, in silence, brooding over it incessantly.

HILDE: That's quite natural, it seems to me.

SOLNESS (*Gives her a somewhat searching look*): You'd probably already noticed it—

HILDE: No—I can't say I had.

SOLNESS: But, a few minutes ago—when you admitted to thinking me a little—queer—in just one thing, you said—

HILDE: Oh! I was thinking of something quite different.

SOLNESS: What was it?

HILDE: I won't tell you.

SOLNESS (*Crossing the room*): Just as you like. (*He stops at the bow window*) Come here, Hilde. I want to show you something.

HILDE (*Goes toward him*): What?

SOLNESS: Do you see—over there in the garden—?

HILDE: Yes?

SOLNESS: Just beyond the stone quarry—

HILDE: Oh—the new house, you mean?

SOLNESS: Yes—the one they're working on; it's nearly finished.

HILDE: It seems to have a very high tower—

SOLNESS: The scaffolding is still up.

HILDE: Is that your new house?

SOLNESS: Yes.

HILDE: The one you'll soon be moving into?

SOLNESS: Yes.

HILDE (*Looks at him*): Are there nurseries in that house too?

SOLNESS: Three—just as there are here.

HILDE: And no children.

SOLNESS: No—and there never will be.

HILDE (*With a half-smile*): Well? Wasn't I right?

SOLNESS: How?

HILDE: Aren't you a little—mad, after all?

SOLNESS: So that's what you were thinking of.

HILDE: Yes—all those empty nurseries I slept in.

SOLNESS (*Lowers his voice*): We *have* had children—Aline and I—

HILDE (*Breathlessly*): Have you?

SOLNESS: Two little boys. They were the same age—

HILDE: Twins, then.

SOLNESS: Yes, twins. It's eleven or twelve years ago—

HILDE (*Cautiously*): And are they both—? Did you lose them? Both of them?

SOLNESS (*With quiet emotion*): They only lived two weeks—not even that. Oh, Hilde—it's so good that you've come to me; now at last I have someone I can talk to!

HILDE: Can't you talk to—*her*, too?

SOLNESS: Not about this. Not as I want to—as I need to. (*Gloomily*) And there are so many *other* things I can never talk to her about!

HILDE (*In a subdued voice*): So *that* was all you meant, when you said you needed me!

SOLNESS: Chiefly, yes. Yesterday at least—today, I'm no longer sure— (*Breaking off*) Sit down, Hilde—sit there, so you can look out into the garden. (HILDE *seats herself in the corner of the sofa.* SOLNESS *draws up a chair*) Would you like to hear about it?

HILDE: Very much.

SOLNESS (*Sits down*): Good—then I'll tell you the whole story.

HILDE: I can see the garden from here—and I can see you, Master Builder—so tell me all about it— Begin!

SOLNESS (*Points through the window*): There used to be an old house where the new house stands—Aline and I spent the first years of our marriage there; it had belonged to her mother—and we inherited it, and the huge garden as well.

HILDE: Was there a tower on the old house, too?

SOLNESS: No—nothing like that! It looked like a large, ugly, gloomy wooden box from the outside; but inside it was comfortable enough.

HILDE: What happened? Did you tear it down?

SOLNESS: No. It burnt down.

HILDE: All of it?

SOLNESS: Yes.

HILDE: Was it a great loss to you?

SOLNESS: That depends on how you look at it. As a builder—that fire was the making of me—

HILDE: Was it? Then—

SOLNESS: It was just after the birth of the two little boys—

HILDE: The poor little twins, yes.

SOLNESS: They were so sturdy and healthy—and they were growing so fast—you could see a difference from day to day—

HILDE: Yes. Babies do grow quickly at first.

SOLNESS: It was such a pretty sight to see Aline lying there with the two of them in her arms. But then came the night of the fire—

HILDE (*With excitement*): What happened? Tell me! Was anyone burnt?

SOLNESS: No, not that. Everyone got out of the house safely—

HILDE: Well—what then?

SOLNESS: Well, you see—it was a terrible shock to Aline; all the shouts—the confusion—the flames—the sudden fear—She and the little boys were sound asleep; they got them out just in time; they had to drag them out of bed, and carry them just as they were, out into that bitter night—

HILDE: Was that why they—?

SOLNESS: No, they recovered from that. But later, Aline developed a fever, and it affected her milk; she would insist on nursing them herself—it was her duty, she said. And our two little boys, they—they—oh!

HILDE: They didn't get over that?

SOLNESS: No, they didn't get over that. That is how we lost them.

HILDE: How terrible for you.

SOLNESS: Hard enough for me; but ten times harder for Aline.

(*Clenching his hands in suppressed fury*) Why are such things allowed to happen in this world! (*Shortly and firmly*) From the day I lost them, I had no joy in building churches.

HILDE: Didn't you even like building the church tower in our town?

SOLNESS: No, I didn't like it. I remember how glad I was when that tower was finished.

HILDE: I remember that too.

SOLNESS: I shall never build anything of that sort again. Neither churches nor church towers.

HILDE (*Nods slowly*): Only houses for people to live in.

SOLNESS: Homes for human beings, Hilde.

HILDE: But homes with high towers—and spires soaring above them!

SOLNESS: If possible. (*In a lighter tone*) Well—as I told you—that fire was the making of me—as a builder, that is.

HILDE: Why don't you call yourself architect, like the others?

SOLNESS: My education wasn't thorough enough for that. What I know, I've mostly found out for myself.

HILDE: But you climbed to the top just the same!

SOLNESS: Thanks to the fire, yes. Most of the old garden I cut up into small building lots; I was free to try out my ideas—to build exactly as I chose. Then—nothing could stop me; success came with a rush.

HILDE (*Looks at him keenly*): What a happy man you must be, Master Builder.

SOLNESS (*Gloomily*): Happy! You sound like all the others!

HILDE: I should think you *must* be happy. If you could only stop thinking about the two little boys.

SOLNESS (*Slowly*): They're not so easy to forget, Hilde.

HILDE (*Somewhat uncertainly*): Not even after all these years?

SOLNESS (*Stares at her without answering*): So you think me a happy man—

HILDE: Well, *aren't* you? I mean—apart from that?

SOLNESS (*Still looking at her*): When I told you all that about the fire—

HILDE: Yes?

SOLNESS: Weren't you struck by one particular thing?

HILDE (*After thinking in vain for a moment*): No. What do you mean?

SOLNESS: Weren't you struck by the fact that it was solely because of that fire that I had the chance to build these homes for human beings? These comfortable, warm, cheerful homes where a mother and a father and a whole troop of children could enjoy life in peace and happiness—sharing the big things and the little things—and, best of all, *belonging* to each other, Hilde?

HILDE (*Ardently*): Well—isn't that a great happiness for you, to be able to build these beautiful homes?

SOLNESS: What about the price, Hilde? The terrible price I had to pay for that opportunity?

HILDE: But can't you *ever* get over that?

SOLNESS: No. In order to build these homes for others, I had to give up—give up forever—a real home of my own.

HILDE (*Cautiously*): But was that *really* necessary? "Forever," you say.

SOLNESS: Yes. That was the price of this happiness. This so-called "happiness" was not to be bought any cheaper.

HILDE (*As before*): But, couldn't you still—?

SOLNESS: No. Never. That's another consequence of the fire—and of Aline's illness afterwards.

HILDE (*Looks at him with an indefinable expression*): And yet you build all these nurseries!

SOLNESS (*Seriously*): Haven't you ever been attracted by the impossible, Hilde? Hasn't it ever called out to you—cast its spell over you?

HILDE (*Thinking*): The impossible! (*With sudden animation*) Of course! Do you feel that too?

SOLNESS: Yes.

HILDE: Then there must be a bit of a troll in you too.

SOLNESS: Why troll?

HILDE: What would *you* call that sort of thing?

SOLNESS (*Rises*): It may be so— (*Vehemently*) But how can I help becoming a troll—when things always work out as they do for me!

HILDE: How do you mean?

SOLNESS (*In a low voice, with inward emotion*): Listen to this carefully, Hilde: All that I have been able to achieve—everything I've built and created—all the beauty, security, comfort —magnificence too, if you like— (*Clenches his hands*) Oh, it's too terrible to think of—!

HILDE: What *is* it that's so terrible?

SOLNESS: All of this had to be paid for—not in money—but in human happiness. And I don't mean just *my* happiness either—but that of other people. Think of that, Hilde! That is the price my position as an artist has cost me—and others. And I have to look on, and watch the others paying that price for me day after day; over and over again forever!

HILDE (*Rises and looks at him steadily*): I suppose now you're thinking of—*her?*

SOLNESS: Mostly of Aline, yes. She, too, had a vocation in life, just as I had. (*His voice quivers*) But Aline's vocation had to be sacrificed, so that mine could force its way up to a sort of great victory. Her vocation had to be stunted, crushed—smashed to pieces! You see—Aline, too, had a talent for building.

HILDE: She? For building?

SOLNESS (*Shakes his head*): Oh, I don't mean houses and towers and spires—not *my* kind of building—

HILDE: What then?

SOLNESS: Aline had a gift for building up the souls of little children, Hilde. She could teach them to become beautiful and strong in mind and body; she could help them to grow up into fine, honorable human beings. That was her talent. But it's all been wasted—it's of no use to anyone now. It's like a smoldering heap of ruins.

HILDE: Well—even if this were true—

SOLNESS: It is! It is true—I know it!

HILDE: But it's surely not your fault!

SOLNESS (*Fixes his eyes on her*): I wonder. That is the great, the terrible question. It torments me day and night!

HILDE: But why?

SOLNESS: Well, you see—perhaps it *was* my fault in a way.

HILDE: You mean—the fire?

SOLNESS: Everything! The whole business! On the other hand—I may have had nothing to do with it.

HILDE (*Looks at him with a troubled expression*): If you talk like that, Master Builder, I'll begin to think you are—ill, after all.

SOLNESS: I dare say I'll never be quite sane on that subject. (RAGNAR BROVIK *cautiously opens the little door in the left-hand corner.* HILDE *steps forward.*)

RAGNAR (*As he sees* HILDE): Oh, excuse me, Mr. Solness—

SOLNESS: No, no! Don't go! Let's get it over with.

RAGNAR: I wish we could.

SOLNESS: Your father is no better, I hear.

RAGNAR: He's failing very rapidly now. That's why I must beg you to write a few encouraging words on one of my drawings; just something for Father to see before he—

SOLNESS (*Vehemently*): I don't want to hear any more about those drawings of yours!

RAGNAR: Have you looked at them?

SOLNESS: Yes, I have.

RAGNAR: And they're no good? And I suppose *I'm* no good either.

SOLNESS (*Evasively*): You stay on here with me, Ragnar. You can have everything your own way. You can marry Kaja—you'll have no worries—you may even be happy, too. But don't think of building on your own account.

RAGNAR: I'd better go home and tell Father what you say—I promised him I would. Is this what you want me to tell him, before he dies?

SOLNESS (*With a groan*): As far as I'm concerned—tell him what you like! Why tell him anything? (*With a sudden outburst*) There's nothing I can do about it, Ragnar.

RAGNAR: May I have the drawings to take with me?

SOLNESS: Yes, take them—take them by all means! They're there on the table.

RAGNAR (*Goes to the table*): Thanks.

HILDE (*Puts her hand on the portfolio*): No—leave them here!

SOLNESS: What for?

HILDE: Because I want to look at them, too.

SOLNESS: But, I thought you had—! (*To* RAGNAR) Well—just leave them, then.

RAGNAR: Very well.

SOLNESS: And now—hurry back to your father.

RAGNAR: Yes, I suppose I must.

SOLNESS (*As if in desperation*): And, Ragnar—don't ask me to do things that are beyond my power! Do you hear, Ragnar, you mustn't!

RAGNAR: No, no. I beg your pardon. (*He bows and goes out by the corner door.* HILDE *goes over and sits down on a chair near the mirror.*)

HILDE (*Looking at* SOLNESS *angrily*): That was a very ugly thing to do.

SOLNESS: You think so, too?

HILDE: Yes, it was disgusting! It was hard, and cruel, and wicked!

SOLNESS: You don't understand the facts.

HILDE: I don't care! You oughtn't to be like that!

SOLNESS: You said yourself, just now, that I alone should be allowed to build.

HILDE: I may say such things—it's not for you to say them.

SOLNESS: Who has a better right? I've paid a high enough price for my position.

HILDE: That precious domestic comfort of yours—I suppose you mean!

SOLNESS: And what about my peace of mind, Hilde?

HILDE (*Rising*): Peace of mind! Yes, I see! I understand— Poor Master Builder! You think that you—

SOLNESS (*With a quiet laugh*): Sit down again, Hilde. I want to tell you something funny.

HILDE (*Sits down; with intent interest*): Well?

SOLNESS: I know it sounds ludicrous! But the whole question revolves round a little crack in the chimney.

HILDE: A crack in the chimney?

SOLNESS: Yes—that's how it started. (*He moves a chair nearer* HILDE *and sits.*)

HILDE (*Impatiently, taps her knee*): Well—now for the crack in the chimney, Master Builder!

SOLNESS: A long time before the fire, I'd noticed that little crack in the flue. Whenever I went up to the attic, I looked to see if it was still there.

HILDE: And it *was?*

SOLNESS: Yes, for no one else knew about it.

HILDE: And you said nothing?

SOLNESS: No. Not a word.

HILDE: And you didn't think of repairing it?

SOLNESS: I thought of it—but never got down to it. Each time I decided to get to work, it was exactly as if a hand held me back. Not today, I thought—tomorrow; and I did nothing about it.

HILDE: What made you put it off like that?

SOLNESS: I became obsessed with an idea. (*Slowly, and in a low voice*) Through that little black crack in the chimney, I might perhaps force my way upward as a builder.

HILDE (*Looking straight in front of her*): That must have been thrilling!

SOLNESS: It was almost irresistible—quite irresistible. It all seemed so simple at the time. I wanted it to happen on a winter morning, just before noon. Aline and I were to be out driving in the sleigh. At home, the servants were to have built great fires in all the stoves—

HILDE: Of course, it was to have been very cold that day—

SOLNESS: Bitterly cold, yes. And they would naturally want Aline to be nice and warm when she came in—

HILDE: I suppose she's very chilly by nature—

SOLNESS: Yes, she is. And on the way home we were to have seen the smoke—

HILDE: Only the smoke?

SOLNESS: At first, yes. But by the time we got to the garden gate, the old wooden box was to be a roaring mass of flames. That's the way I wanted it to be.

HILDE: Oh, why—*why* couldn't it have happened so!

SOLNESS: You may well say that, Hilde.

HILDE: But, Master Builder—are you quite sure the fire *was* caused by that crack in the chimney?

SOLNESS: On the contrary—I'm quite sure the crack in the chimney had nothing to do with it.

HILDE: What!

SOLNESS: It was proved quite definitely that the fire broke out in a clothes closet, in an entirely different part of the house.

HILDE: Then what's all this nonsense about a crack in the chimney!

SOLNESS: May I go on talking to you a little longer, Hilde?

HILDE: Yes—if you'll try and talk sense!

SOLNESS: I'll try. (*He moves his chair nearer. In a confidential tone*) Don't you believe, Hilde, that there exist certain special, chosen people, who have been endowed with the power and faculty of *wishing* a thing, *desiring* a thing, *willing* a thing, so persistently, so—inexorably—that they make it happen? Don't you believe that?

HILDE (*With an indefinable expression in her eyes*): If that is true, we'll find out some day whether *I* am one of the chosen.

SOLNESS: It's not by our own power alone that we can accomplish such things; we must have the Helpers and Servers with us in order to succeed; and they never come of their own accord—we have to summon them; to call on them; inwardly—persistently.

HILDE: What *are* these Helpers and Servers?

SOLNESS: We'll discuss that some other time; let's go on talking about the fire now.

HILDE: Don't you think that fire would have happened—even if you hadn't wished for it?

SOLNESS: If old Knut Brovik had owned that house, it would never have burnt down so conveniently for him—I'm convinced of that. He doesn't know *how* to call for the Helpers—nor for the Servers either. (*Rises in unrest*) So you see, Hilde, perhaps I *am* to blame for the death of the two little boys; and perhaps it's my fault, too, that Aline never became what she could and should have been; what she most longed to be.

HILDE: No! It's the fault of the Helpers and Servers!

SOLNESS: But who *called* for the Helpers and Servers? I did! And they came, and obeyed my will. (*In increasing excitement*) And these good people call that "having luck on your side"! Do you know what that kind of luck feels like? It's as though I had an open wound here on my breast; and the Helpers and Servers flay pieces of skin off other people in order to heal my wound. But it goes on burning and throbbing—it never heals—never!

HILDE (*Looks at him attentively*): You *are* ill, Master Builder. I'm inclined to think you're *very* ill.

SOLNESS: Why not say mad? That's what you mean.

HILDE: No, I don't mean mentally.

SOLNESS: What *do* you mean then? Tell me!

HILDE: I wonder if you weren't born with a sickly conscience.

SOLNESS: A sickly conscience? What in the world is that!

HILDE: I mean that your conscience is too delicate and feeble; it won't face the hard things; it refuses to carry any burden that seems heavy!

SOLNESS (*Growls*): And what sort of a conscience *should* one have?

HILDE: I would prefer your conscience to be—thoroughly robust.

SOLNESS: Robust? I see. Is *your* conscience robust, may I ask?

HILDE: Yes, I think so. I've never noticed that it wasn't.

SOLNESS: I dare say it's never been put to the test.

HILDE (*With a quivering of the lips*): I don't know about that. It wasn't any too easy for me to leave Father—I'm so awfully fond of him—

SOLNESS: Oh, well! For a month or two—!

HILDE: I feel I shall never go home again.

SOLNESS: Never? Then why did you leave him?

HILDE (*Half seriously, half banteringly*): Have you forgotten again that the ten years are up?

SOLNESS: Nonsense! Was anything wrong at home?

HILDE (*Seriously*): No. But something within me urged and goaded me to come here—it was as though something beckoned to me and lured me on.

SOLNESS (*Eagerly*): That's it. That's *it*, Hilde! There's a troll in you, just as there is in me; and it's the troll in us that summons the powers outside us; and then, whether we like it or not, we're forced to give in.

HILDE: You know—I believe you're right, Master Builder.

SOLNESS (*Walks about the room*): Oh, what a lot of invisible devils there are in this world, Hilde!

HILDE: Devils, too?

SOLNESS (*Stops*): Good devils and bad devils. Blond devils and dark devils! If only we could be sure which kind had hold of us—then things would be simple enough! (*He paces about.*)

HILDE (*Follows him with her eyes*): Yes! Or if we had a vigorous, radiantly healthy conscience—and had the courage to follow our own will!

SOLNESS (*Stops beside the table*): I'm afraid most people are as weak as I am, in that respect.

HILDE: I shouldn't wonder.

SOLNESS (*Leaning against the table*): In the Sagas—have you read any of the old Sagas?

HILDE: Yes! When I used to read books—

SOLNESS: The Sagas tell about the Vikings who sailed to foreign lands, and plundered, and burned, and killed all the men—

HILDE: And captured the women—

SOLNESS: Carried them off with them—

HILDE: Took them home in their ships—

SOLNESS: And behaved to them—like the very worst of trolls!

HILDE (*Looks straight before her with a half-veiled expression*): I think that must have been thrilling!

SOLNESS (*With a short, deep laugh*): To carry off women?

HILDE: To *be* carried off.

SOLNESS (*Looks at her a moment*): Indeed.

HILDE (*As if breaking the thread of the conversation*): But what made you speak of these Vikings, Master Builder?

SOLNESS: What robust consciences *they* must have had! They went home again and could eat and drink, and were as happy as children. And as for the women! They must have liked those ruffians—they quite often refused to leave them! Can you understand that, Hilde?

HILDE: Of course! I understand those women perfectly.

SOLNESS: Oho! Perhaps you'd do the same yourself?

HILDE: Why not?

SOLNESS: Live of your own free will with a ruffian?

HILDE: Yes. If I loved him.

SOLNESS: But how *could* you love a man like that?

HILDE: Good Heavens, Master Builder! You know you don't *choose* whom you're going to love!

SOLNESS (*Looks meditatively at her*): No. I suppose the troll in you takes care of that

HILDE (*Half laughing*): Yes—and all those devils that you know so well! The blond ones, and the dark ones too!

SOLNESS (*Quietly and warmly*): I hope the devils will choose well for you, Hilde.

HILDE: They've already chosen for me—once and for all.

SOLNESS (*Looks at her earnestly*): Hilde, you're like a wild bird of the woods.

HILDE: Far from it! I don't hide away under the bushes.

SOLNESS: No. Perhaps you're more like a bird of prey.

HILDE: Perhaps. (*Very vehemently*) And why not a bird of prey? Why shouldn't I, too, go hunting? And carry off the prey I want—if I can get my claws into it—and conquer it.

SOLNESS: Hilde—do you know what you are?

HILDE: I suppose I'm some sort of strange bird—

SOLNESS: No. You're like the dawning day. When I look at you—I feel as though I were watching the sunrise.

HILDE: Tell me, Master Builder—are you sure you've never called *me* to you? Inwardly, you know?

SOLNESS (*Softly and slowly*): I'm almost sure I must have.

HILDE: What did you want of me?

SOLNESS: You are Youth, Hilde.

HILDE: Youth? That Youth you're so afraid of?

SOLNESS (*Nods slowly*): And that in my heart, I yearn toward so deeply—

    (HILDE *rises, goes to the little table, and fetches* RAGNAR'S *portfolio.*)

HILDE (*Holds out the portfolio to him*): What about these drawings, Master Builder—?

SOLNESS (*Shortly; waving them away*): Put those things away! I've seen enough of them!

HILDE: But you're going to write on them for him, you know.

SOLNESS: Write on them! Never!

HILDE: But the poor old man's dying! It would make them both so happy! And he might get the commission too.

SOLNESS: That's just exactly what he would get! He's made sure of that!

HILDE: Well—if that's true—it surely couldn't hurt you to tell a little lie for once?

SOLNESS: A lie? (*Raging*) Hilde—take those damn drawings away!

HILDE (*Draws the portfolio toward her*): All right, all right! Don't bite me! You talk of trolls—it seems to me you're behaving like a troll yourself! (*Looks round the room*) Where's the pen and ink?

SOLNESS: There isn't any here.

HILDE (*Goes toward the door*): That young lady must have some in the office—

SOLNESS: Stay where you are, Hilde! You want me to lie, you say. I suppose, for the old man's sake, I might do that; I broke him—destroyed him—

HILDE: Him, too?

SOLNESS: I needed room for myself. But this Ragnar must never be allowed to get ahead—

HILDE: Poor thing—there's not much hope of that—you say he has no talent.

SOLNESS (*Comes closer to her and whispers*): If Ragnar Brovik gets his chance, he'll break me—destroy me, as I did his father.

HILDE: Destroy you! You mean—he has the power for *that*?

SOLNESS: He has indeed! *He* is the younger generation waiting to thunder at my door—to make an end of Halvard Solness!

HILDE (*Looks at him with quiet reproach*): And you would bar him out! For shame, Master Builder!

SOLNESS: My struggle has cost me agony enough! And I'm afraid the Helpers and Servers won't obey me any longer.

HILDE: Then you'll just have to get on without them.

SOLNESS: It's hopeless, Hilde. Sooner or later the luck will turn. Retribution is inexorable.

HILDE (*In distress, putting her hands over her ears*): Don't talk like that! Do you want to kill me? Do you want to rob me of what means more to me than life!

SOLNESS: What is that?

HILDE: The need to see you great. To see you with a wreath in your hand—high, high up, upon a church tower! (*Calm again*) Now—get out your pencil, Master Builder— You must have a pencil in your pocket—

SOLNESS (*Takes one from his pocket*): Yes—here's one—

HILDE (*Lays the portfolio on the table*): Good. We'll just sit down here, Master Builder—

(SOLNESS *seats himself at the table.* HILDE *stands behind him, leaning over the back of the chair.*)

HILDE: —and we'll write on the drawings; something very nice—very kind—for this horrid Ruar—whatever his name is!

SOLNESS (*Writes a few words, turns his head and looks at her*): Tell me one thing, Hilde.

HILDE: Yes?

SOLNESS: If you were really waiting for me all these ten years—

HILDE: Well?

SOLNESS: Why didn't you write to me? Then I could have answered you.

HILDE (*Hastily*): No, no, no! That's just what I didn't want!

SOLNESS: Why not?

HILDE: I was afraid that might ruin everything— But we were writing on the drawings, Master Builder.

SOLNESS: So we were.

HILDE (*Bends forward and looks over his shoulder as he writes*): Kindly and generously. Oh, how I hate—how I hate this Roald—!

SOLNESS (*Writing*): Have you never really loved anyone, Hilde?

HILDE (*Harshly*): What? What did you say?

SOLNESS: Have you never loved anyone, I asked.

HILDE: Anyone else, I suppose you mean.

SOLNESS (*Looks up at her*): Anyone else, yes. Have you never? In all these ten years? Never?

HILDE: Oh, yes, now and then. When I was furious with you for not coming.

SOLNESS: Then you *have* cared for other people, too?

HILDE: Maybe a little—for a week or so— Good Heavens, Master Builder! You must know all about things like that!

SOLNESS: What have you come for, Hilde?

HILDE: Don't waste time talking! The poor old man might go and die in the meantime!

SOLNESS: Answer me, Hilde. What do you want of me?

HILDE: I want my kingdom.

SOLNESS: Hm—

(*He gives a rapid glance toward the door on the left, and then goes on writing on the drawings. At that moment* MRS. SOLNESS *enters; she has some packages in her hand.*)

MRS. SOLNESS: I've brought a few of the things myself, Miss Wangel. The large parcels will be sent later on.

HILDE: You're really much too kind to me!

MRS. SOLNESS: My simple duty—nothing else.

SOLNESS (*Reads over what he has written*): Aline?

MRS. SOLNESS: Yes, Halvard?

SOLNESS: Did you happen to notice whether she—whether the bookkeeper was out there?

MRS. SOLNESS: Of course she was there. She was at her desk—as she always is when *I* go through the room.

SOLNESS (*Puts the drawings in the portfolio. Rises*): Then I'll just give her these, and tell her that—

HILDE (*Takes the portfolio from him*): Oh, let me have that pleasure! (*Goes to the door, but turns*) What's her name?

SOLNESS: Miss Fosli.

HILDE: No, no! That sounds so formal! Her first name, I mean!

SOLNESS: Kaja—I believe.

HILDE (*Opens the door and calls out*): Kaja! Hurry! Come in here! The Master Builder wants to talk to you.

(KAJA *appears at the door.*)

KAJA (*Looks at him in alarm*): You want me—?

HILDE (*Handing her the portfolio*): Take these home, Kaja. The Master Builder has written on them now.

KAJA: At last!

SOLNESS: Give them to the old man as soon as possible—

KAJA: I'll go home with them at once—

SOLNESS: Yes, do. Now Ragnar will have his chance to build.

KAJA: May he come and thank you—?

SOLNESS (*Harshly*): I want no thanks! Tell him that from me.

KAJA: Yes—I will.

SOLNESS: And tell him, too, that I shall no longer need his services—nor yours either.

KAJA (*Softly—tremulously*): Nor mine—either?

SOLNESS: You'll have other things to think of now—a great deal to attend to—that's as it should be. Take the drawings home now, Miss Fosli. At once! Do you hear!

KAJA (*As before*): Yes, Mr. Solness. (*She goes out*.)

MRS. SOLNESS: Heavens! What deceitful eyes she has!

SOLNESS: She? That poor little creature?

MRS. SOLNESS: Oh, I can see what I can see, Halvard. So you're really dismissing them?

SOLNESS: Yes.

MRS. SOLNESS: Her, as well?

SOLNESS: Wasn't that what you wanted?

MRS. SOLNESS: But how will you get on without her?—No doubt you have someone in reserve, Halvard.

HILDE (*Playfully*) As for me—I'd be no good at a desk!

SOLNESS: Never mind, never mind, Aline. Everything will be all right— You just think about getting ready to move into your new home—as quickly as possible. This evening we'll hang up the wreath— (*Turns to* HILDE) at the very top of the tower. What do you say to *that*, Miss Hilde?

HILDE: It'll be wonderful to see you up there again—high up!

SOLNESS: Me!

MRS. SOLNESS: Whatever put that into your head, Miss Wangel! My husband—who always gets so dizzy!

HILDE: Dizzy! He!

MRS. SOLNESS: Oh, yes. I assure you.

HILDE: But I saw him myself at the top of a high church tower!

MRS. SOLNESS: Yes—I've heard rumors about that. But it's quite impossible.

SOLNESS (*Vehemently*): Impossible! Impossible! But I stood there all the same!

MRS. SOLNESS: How can you say that, Halvard. You know you

don't even dare go out on the second-story balcony here—You've always been like that!

SOLNESS: You may see something different this evening.

MRS. SOLNESS (*In alarm*): No, no! God forbid that I should ever see that! I'll send word to the doctor at once. He must prevent you.

SOLNESS: But, Aline—!

MRS. SOLNESS: For you are ill, Halvard—this proves it. Oh, God! Oh, God! (*She goes hastily out to the right.*)

HILDE (*Looks at him intently*): Is it so, or is it not?

SOLNESS: That I get dizzy?

HILDE: That my Master Builder *dare* not, *cannot* climb as high as he builds?

SOLNESS: Is that how you look at it?

HILDE: Yes.

SOLNESS: Is there no part of me that's safe from you, Hilde?

HILDE (*Looks toward the window*): Up there then—right up there!

SOLNESS (*Comes to her*): You could live in the topmost room of the tower, Hilde—you could live there like a princess.

HILDE (*Indefinably; half in jest, half in earnest*): That's what you promised—

SOLNESS: Did I really?

HILDE: You said I was to be a princess—that you'd give me a kingdom—and then you went and—

SOLNESS (*Cautiously*): Are you sure it wasn't all a dream—just something you imagined?

HILDE (*Sharply*): You mean that you didn't do it?

SOLNESS: I scarcely know myself. (*More softly*) But I *do* know one thing now—and that is—

HILDE: What? Tell me at once!

SOLNESS: That I *ought* to have done it!

HILDE (*Exclaims, with animation*): *You* could never be dizzy!

SOLNESS: Then, this evening we will hang up the wreath, Princess Hilde.

HILDE (*With a bitter curve of her lips*): Over your new home—yes!

SOLNESS: Over the new house—that will never be a home for me. (*He goes out through the garden door.*)

HILDE (*Looks straight in front of her with a faraway expression, and whispers to herself. The only words audible are*): —frightfully thrilling!

CURTAIN

ACT
THREE

SCENE: *The large broad veranda of* SOLNESS' *house. Part of the house, with outer door leading to the veranda, is seen to the left. A railing along the veranda to the right. At the back, from the end of the veranda, a flight of steps leads down to the garden below. Tall, old trees in the garden spread their branches over the veranda and toward the house. Far to the right, in among the trees, a glimpse is caught of the lower part of a new villa, with scaffolding round so much as is seen of the tower. In the background the garden is bounded by an old wooden fence. Outside the fence, a street with low tumbledown cottages.*

Evening sky with sunlit clouds.

On the veranda, a garden bench stands along the wall of the house, and in front of the bench a long table. On the other side of the table, an armchair and some stools. All the furniture is of wickerwork.

MRS. SOLNESS, *wrapped in a large white crepe shawl, sits resting in the armchair and gazes over to the right. Shortly after,* HILDE WANGEL *comes up the flight of steps from the garden. She*

is dressed as in the last act and wears a hat. She has in her bodice a
little nosegay of small common flowers.

MRS. SOLNESS (*Turning her head a little*): So you've been round
the garden, Miss Wangel?

HILDE: Yes. I've been exploring it—

MRS. SOLNESS: And found some flowers too, I see.

HILDE: There are such heaps of them—in among the bushes.

MRS. SOLNESS: Fancy! Are there really? Still? You see—I scarcely
ever go there.

HILDE (*Comes nearer*): Really? Don't you? I should have thought
you'd take a run down there every day.

MRS. SOLNESS (*With a faint smile*): I don't "run" anywhere. Not
any more, Miss Wangel.

HILDE: But you must go down there sometimes—there are such
lovely things to see there.

MRS. SOLNESS: It's all become so alien to me. I'm almost afraid to
see it again.

HILDE: Your own garden!

MRS. SOLNESS: I don't feel that it *is* mine any longer.

HILDE: How do you mean?

MRS. SOLNESS: No—it's no longer mine, Miss Wangel. It was different when Mother and Father were alive. But they've done
such dreadful things to the garden; they've divided it up and
built houses for a lot of strangers—people I don't know; and they
sit at their windows and stare at me.

HILDE (*Brightly*): Mrs. Solness?

MRS. SOLNESS: Yes?

HILDE: Do you mind if I stay here with you for a while?

MRS. SOLNESS: Of course not. I'd be delighted—if you'd care to.

HILDE (*Moves a stool over by the armchair and sits down*): Ah!
How nice it is to sit and sun oneself like a cat!

MRS. SOLNESS (*Lays her hand gently on the back of* HILDE'S
head): It's kind of you to want to sit here with me. I thought you
were on your way to join my husband.

HILDE: Why should I want to join him?

MRS. SOLNESS: I thought perhaps you were helping him with
something.

HILDE: No. Anyway—he's not at home just now. He's down there
with the workmen. He looked so ferocious, I didn't dare talk to
him!

MRS. SOLNESS: He's so kind and gentle underneath all that—

HILDE: He! Kind and gentle!

MRS. SOLNESS: You don't really know him yet, Miss Wangel.

HILDE (*Gives her an affectionate look*): Are you glad to be moving
into the new house?

MRS. SOLNESS: I suppose I should be glad—for it's what Halvard
wants—

HILDE: Oh, not just because of that!

MRS. SOLNESS: Oh, yes, Miss Wangel. After all, it's my duty to try
and please him. Still—there are times when it's very hard to
force one's mind to obedience.

HILDE: That must be very hard indeed.

MRS. SOLNESS: Yes, it is. Especially when one has as many faults
as I have—

HILDE: Or when one has suffered as much as you have—

MRS. SOLNESS: What do you know about that?

HILDE: Your husband told me.

MRS. SOLNESS: He seldom talks about such things to me.
Yes—I've been through a great deal in my life, Miss Wangel.

HILDE (*Nods sympathetically*): Poor Mrs. Solness! First the old
house burnt down—

MRS. SOLNESS (*With a sigh*): Yes. I lost everything I had.

HILDE: And what followed was even worse—

MRS. SOLNESS (*With a questioning look*): Worse?

HILDE: That must have been the worst of all.

MRS. SOLNESS: How do you mean?

HILDE: You lost the two little boys.

MRS. SOLNESS: Oh, the little boys—yes. Well, you see—that was
a thing apart. That was the will of the Almighty. One must bow
before His will—yes, and be thankful too.

HILDE: Are you able to do that?

MRS. SOLNESS: Not always, I'm afraid. Although I know that it's
my duty—still, I often fail in it.

HILDE: I think that's very natural.

MRS. SOLNESS: I have to keep reminding myself that it was a just punishment for me—

HILDE: Punishment? Why?

MRS. SOLNESS: Because I hadn't the strength to bear misfortune.

HILDE: But—I don't understand—

MRS. SOLNESS: No, no, Miss Wangel. Don't talk to me any more about the two little boys. We must be glad for them; they are at peace and happy now. No—it's the small losses in life that break one's heart. It's losing all the little things—things that might seem insignificant to other people.

HILDE (*Lays her arms on* MRS. SOLNESS' *knee and looks up at her affectionately*): Dear Mrs. Solness—what sort of things do you mean?

MRS. SOLNESS: As I say—just little things. The old family portraits were all burnt on the walls. The old silk dresses were burnt—they had been in the family for countless generations. All Mother's and Grandmother's lace—and all the jewels—they were burnt too. And then—all the dolls.

HILDE: The dolls?

MRS. SOLNESS (*Her voice choked with tears*): I had nine lovely dolls.

HILDE: And they were burnt too?

MRS. SOLNESS: All of them. Oh, it was hard—so hard for me.

HILDE: Were they dolls you'd played with as a little girl? Had you stored them away all those years?

MRS. SOLNESS: They were not stored away. The dolls and I went on living together.

HILDE: You mean, after you were grown up?

MRS. SOLNESS: Yes, long after that.

HILDE: And even after you were married, too?

MRS. SOLNESS: Oh, yes. As long as he knew nothing about it, it was— But they were all burnt up, poor things. No one thought of saving them. Oh, it's so tragic to think of. You mustn't laugh at me, Miss Wangel.

HILDE: I'm not laughing in the least.

MRS. SOLNESS: In a way, you see, there was life in them, too. I carried them under my heart. Like little unborn children. (DR.

HERDAL *comes out of the house and sees* MRS. SOLNESS *and*
HILDE.)

HERDAL: Are you sitting out here catching cold, Mrs. Solness?

MRS. SOLNESS: It's so pleasant and warm here today.

HERDAL: But is anything the matter! I had a note from you.

MRS. SOLNESS (*Rises*): Yes. There's something I must talk to you
about.

HERDAL: Very well. Then perhaps we had better go in. (*To*
HILDE) I see you're still dressed for mountain climbing Miss
Wangel.

HILDE: In full regalia! But I don't intend to go breaking my neck
today. We two will sit quietly here and look on.

HERDAL: What are we to look on at?

MRS. SOLNESS (*Softly to* HILDE, *in a frightened tone*): Hush,
hush! For God's sake! He's coming. Do try to get that idea out of
his head. And let us be friends, Miss Wangel. Don't you think
we can?

HILDE (*Throws her arms impetuously round* MRS. SOLNESS'
neck): Oh—if we only could!

MRS. SOLNESS (*Gently disengaging herself*): There, there! He's
coming, Doctor. Let me have a word with you.

HERDAL: Is it about him?

MRS. SOLNESS: Yes—of course it's about him. Do come in.
(*She and* DR. HERDAL *enter the house. Next moment* SOLNESS
*comes up from the garden by the flight of steps. A serious look
comes over* HILDE'S *face*.)

SOLNESS (*Glances at the house door that is closed cautiously from
within*): Have you noticed, Hilde? As soon as I come, she goes.

HILDE: I've noticed that as soon as you come you make her go.

SOLNESS: Perhaps. But I can't help it. (*Looks at her observantly*)
Are you cold, Hilde? You look as if you were cold.

HILDE: It's because I've just come up out of a tomb.

SOLNESS: What does *that* mean?

HILDE: I feel as if I'd been frozen through and through, Master
Builder.

SOLNESS (*Slowly*): I think I understand—

HILDE: Why did you come up here?

SOLNESS: I saw you from down below.

HILDE: Then you must have seen her too.

SOLNESS: I knew she'd go away at once if I came.

HILDE: Does it make you unhappy—her avoiding you like that?

SOLNESS: In a way it's almost a relief.

HILDE: Not to have her always before your eyes?

SOLNESS: Yes.

HILDE: Not to be constantly reminded of her grief at the loss of the two little boys?

SOLNESS: Yes. Mostly that.

(HILDE *crosses the veranda with her hands behind her back, and stands by the railing gazing out across the garden.*)

SOLNESS (*After a short pause*): Did you have a long talk with her? (HILDE *doesn't answer but stands there motionless*) Did you have a long talk, I asked. (HILDE *makes no reply*) What did she talk about, Hilde? (HILDE *still stands silent*) Poor Aline! I suppose it was about the little boys. (HILDE *shudders and nods rapidly several times*) She'll never get over it. Never in this world. (*He goes toward her*) Now you're standing there again like a statue; just as you did last night.

HILDE (*Turns and looks at him with great serious eyes*): I must go away.

SOLNESS (*Sharply*): Go away!

HILDE: Yes.

SOLNESS: No! I won't let you!

HILDE: What can I do here now?

SOLNESS: Just *be* here, Hilde!

HILDE (*Looks him up and down*): Yes, I dare say! You know it wouldn't stop at that.

SOLNESS (*Recklessly*): So much the better!

HILDE (*Vehemently*): I can't do any harm to one whom I *know*. I can't take anything that belongs to her.

SOLNESS: Who ever said you *would*?

HILDE: A stranger, yes! That's quite a different thing. Someone I'd never laid eyes on. But someone I've come close to—! No, no! Never that! No!

SOLNESS: But I've suggested nothing of that sort.

HILDE: Oh, Master Builder—you know well enough what would happen if I stayed. So I must go away.

SOLNESS: What'll become of *me* if you go away? What shall I have to live for then?

HILDE (*With an inscrutable look in her eyes*): There's no need to worry about *you*. You have your duties to her. Live for those duties.

SOLNESS: It's too late, Hilde. All these powers, these—these—

HILDE: Devils?

SOLNESS: Yes, devils! And the troll within me, too; they have drained the lifeblood out of her. (*Laughs bitterly*) They did it for my happiness. And now I'm chained alive to this dead woman. I! I who cannot bear to live without joy in life!

HILDE (*Goes round the table and sits down on the bench, her elbows on the table and her head in her hands. Sits and stares at him a moment*): What will you build next, Master Builder?

SOLNESS (*Shakes his head*): I don't think I'll build much more, Hilde.

HILDE: No cheerful, happy homes—for a mother and a father and a whole troop of children?

SOLNESS: I wonder—will there be any use for such homes from now on?

HILDE: Poor Master Builder! And for ten whole years you've dedicated your life to that alone!

SOLNESS: You're right there, Hilde.

HILDE (*In a sudden outburst*): Oh, how absurd it all is! How senseless!

SOLNESS: All—what?

HILDE: This business of not daring to grasp your own happiness—your own life! And all because someone you *know*, happens·to stand in the way.

SOLNESS: Someone you've no right to cast aside.

HILDE: I wonder. I wonder if that's *really* true. Perhaps, after all, one *has* the right—? And yet—somehow— Oh! To be able to sleep it all away! (*She stretches out her arms flat across the table and rests her head on them, closing her eyes.*)

SOLNESS (*Turns the armchair round and sits down at the table*):

Did you have a happy home up there with your father, Hilde?

HILDE (*Without moving, as though half asleep*): All I had was a cage.

SOLNESS: And you really don't want to go back there?

HILDE (*As before*): Wild birds can't live in cages.

SOLNESS: They must be free to hunt in the open air—

HILDE (*As before*): Birds of prey were meant for hunting.

SOLNESS (*Lets his eyes dwell on her*): Oh! To have the Viking spirit in life, Hilde!

HILDE (*In her usual voice, opens her eyes but still doesn't move*): And the other thing? Say what that was!

SOLNESS: A robust conscience.

(HILDE *sits erect on the bench, once more full of animation. Her eyes are happy and sparkling.*)

HILDE (*Nods to him*): I know what you're going to build next, Master Builder!

SOLNESS: Then you know more than I do, Hilde.

HILDE: Yes. Master Builders are so stupid.

SOLNESS: Well? What's it to be?

HILDE (*Nods again*): The castle.

SOLNESS: What castle?

HILDE: *My* castle, of course.

SOLNESS: So you want a castle now?

HILDE: You owe me a kingdom, don't you?

SOLNESS: That's what you *say*.

HILDE: All right. So you owe me this kingdom; and you can't have a kingdom without a castle, I should hope!

SOLNESS (*More and more animated*): No. They usually go together.

HILDE: Very well. Then build it for me at once!

SOLNESS (*Laughs*): Must you have it this very instant?

HILDE: Of course! For the ten years are up—and I'm not going to wait any longer. So—out with my castle, Master Builder!

SOLNESS: It's no joke to owe you anything, Hilde!

HILDE: You should have thought of that before—it's too late now. So— (*Raps on the table*) my castle on the table! It's my castle and I want it at once!

SOLNESS (*More seriously, leaning toward her with his arms on the table*): How do you see this castle of yours, Hilde?

HILDE (*Her expression becomes more and more veiled. She seems to be peering into her innermost being*): My castle must stand on a high hill—high, high up. It must have a clear view on all sides—so that I can see far, far around.

SOLNESS: I suppose it's to have a high tower?

HILDE: A tremendously high tower. And at the very top of the tower there must be a balcony. And I shall stand out on it—

SOLNESS (*Involuntarily clutches at his forehead*): How can you bear to stand at such a dizzy height—!

HILDE: Ah, but I shall! I shall stand up there and look down at all the others—at those who are building churches. And homes for a mother and father and a whole troop of children. And you shall come and look down at them too.

SOLNESS (*Softly*): Will the Master Builder be allowed to come up to the princess?

HILDE: If the Master Builder will.

SOLNESS (*More softly still*): Then I think he will come.

HILDE (*Nods*): Yes. The Master Builder will come.

SOLNESS: But he'll never build any more—poor Master Builder!

HILDE (*With animation*): Ah, but he will! We two will build together. We'll build the loveliest—the very loveliest thing in all the world.

SOLNESS (*Intently*): Hilde—tell me what that is!

HILDE (*Smiles at him, shakes her head a little and talks as though to a child*): Master builders are such very—very stupid people.

SOLNESS: Yes, I know they are. But tell me what it is—this loveliest thing in all the world that we two are to build together?

HILDE (*Is silent for a moment, then says with an indefinable expression in her eyes*): Castles-in-the-air.

SOLNESS: Castles-in-the-air?

HILDE (*Nodding*): Castles-in-the-air, yes. Do you know what sort of a thing a castle-in-the-air is?

SOLNESS: It's the loveliest thing in the world, you say.

HILDE (*Rises abruptly, and makes a gesture of repulsion with her hand*): The loveliest thing in the world! Castles-in-the-air

—they're so easy to take refuge in. And they're easy to build too—especially for builders who have a—dizzy conscience.

SOLNESS (*Rises*): From now on, we two will build together, Hilde

HILDE (*With a half-doubting smile*): A real castle-in-the-air?

SOLNESS: Yes. One on a firm foundation.

(RAGNAR BROVIK *comes out of the house. He carries a large green wreath, decked with flowers and ribbons.*)

HILDE (*In a burst of happiness*): The wreath! Oh, it'll be splendid!

SOLNESS (*In surprise*): Why have *you* brought the wreath, Ragnar?

RAGNAR: I promised the foreman I would.

SOLNESS (*With relief*): Then your father must be better?

RAGNAR: No.

SOLNESS: Wasn't he pleased with what I wrote?

RAGNAR: It came too late.

SOLNESS: Too late?

RAGNAR: He was unconscious by the time she brought it. He'd had a stroke.

SOLNESS: Then you must go home to him. You must stay with him, Ragnar.

RAGNAR: He doesn't need me any more.

SOLNESS: But, surely, you ought to *be* there!

RAGNAR: She's there with him—sitting by his bed.

SOLNESS (*Rather uncertainly*): Kaja?

RAGNAR (*With a dark look*): Yes, Kaja.

SOLNESS: Go home to them both, Ragnar. Give me the wreath.

RAGNAR (*Suppressing a mocking smile*): You don't mean that you're going to—

SOLNESS: I'll take it down to the men. (*Takes the wreath from him*) You go on home. We don't need you here today.

RAGNAR: No—I dare say you don't need me. But today I'm going to stay.

SOLNESS: Very well. As you like.

HILDE (*By the railing*): I'm going to stand here and watch you, Master Builder.

SOLNESS: *Watch* me?

HILDE: It'll be wonderfully thrilling!

SOLNESS (*In a low tone*): We'll discuss that later, Hilde. (*He takes the wreath and goes down the steps into the garden.*)

HILDE (*She watches him go, then turns to* RAGNAR): I should think you might at least have thanked him!

RAGNAR: Thanked him! Do you expect me to thank him?

HILDE: Yes, of course you should!

RAGNAR: It seems to me it's *you* I ought to thank.

HILDE: How can you say such a thing?

RAGNAR (*Without answering her*): But I warn you, Miss Wangel. You don't really know him yet.

HILDE (*Passionately*): No one knows him as *I* do—!

RAGNAR (*With a bitter laugh*): Thank him, indeed! When he's held me back year after year! When he's made my own father doubt me—made me doubt myself—and all because he wanted to—!

HILDE (*As though sensing something*): What? Tell me at once!

RAGNAR: Because he wanted to keep her with him.

HILDE (*With a start toward him*): That girl at the desk?

RAGNAR: Yes.

HILDE (*Clenching her hands, threateningly*): That's not true! You're telling lies about him!

RAGNAR: I didn't believe it either until today—when she told me herself.

HILDE (*As though beside herself*): What did she say? Tell me! At once! At once!

RAGNAR: She said—that he had taken possession of her whole being—her whole being, she said. That all her thoughts were for him alone. She said she could never leave him. That she must stay here where he is—

HILDE (*With flashing eyes*): She won't be allowed to!

RAGNAR (*As if feeling his way*): Who won't allow her?

HILDE (*Rapidly*): He won't permit it either!

RAGNAR: No—of course not. I understand everything now. From now on she'd only be in the way.

HILDE: You don't understand anything or you wouldn't talk like that. *I'll* tell you why he wanted her to stay here.

RAGNAR: Well—why?

HILDE: Because he wanted *you* to stay.

RAGNAR: Did he tell you that himself?

HILDE: No, but it's true! It *must* be true! (*Wildly*) I will— I *will* have it so!

RAGNAR: But the moment *you* came—he let her go.

HILDE: It was *you* that he let go! Why should he care about a strange girl like her!

RAGNAR (*After a moment's thought*): Could he have been afraid of me all these years?

HILDE: *He* afraid! I wouldn't be so conceited if I were you.

RAGNAR: He must have realized long ago that I had something in me. Besides—a coward—that's just what he is, you see.

HILDE: Yes! I'm likely to believe that!

RAGNAR: Well—in some ways he is a coward—the great Master Builder! Oh, he's not afraid of destroying other people's happiness—Father's and mine, for instance—but just ask him to climb up a miserable bit of scaffolding, and see what he says!

HILDE: You should have seen him at the top of a high tower as I once saw him.

RAGNAR: You saw *that?*

HILDE: Yes—indeed I did! He fastened the wreath to the church vane—and he looked so proud and free!

RAGNAR: He's supposed to have done that once—just once in his life, they say. It's become a sort of legend among us younger men. But no power on earth would induce him to do it again.

HILDE: He'll do it again today!

RAGNAR (*Scornfully*): Yes—I dare say!

HILDE: We shall see it!

RAGNAR: We'll neither of us ever see that.

HILDE (*With passionate vehemence*): I will see it! I *will* and I *must* see it!

RAGNAR: But he won't do it. He simply *dare* not do it. It's like an illness—don't you see?

(MRS. SOLNESS *comes out onto the veranda.*)

MRS. SOLNESS (*Looking round*): Isn't he here? Where did he go?

RAGNAR: Mr. Solness is down with the men.

HILDE: He took the wreath with him.

MRS. SOLNESS (*Terrified*): Took the wreath! Oh God! Brovik—go down to him. Try to get him to come up here.

RAGNAR: Shall I say you want him, Mrs. Solness?

MRS. SOLNESS: Yes, do—dear Brovik. No, no! Better not say *I* want him—tell him some people have just come and are asking to see him.

RAGNAR: Very well. I'll tell him, Mrs. Solness. (*He goes down the steps to the garden.*)

MRS. SOLNESS: Oh, I'm so anxious about him, Miss Wangel.

HILDE: What is there to be so afraid of?

MRS. SOLNESS: Surely you can understand? What if he really meant it? What if he were really to try and climb the scaffolding?

HILDE: Do you think he will?

MRS. SOLNESS: He's so unpredictable—it's impossible to tell. He might do anything!

HILDE: Then—perhaps you, too, think that he's—?

MRS. SOLNESS: I no longer know *what* to think of him, Miss Wangel. The doctor's just told me various things that —well—putting them together with several things I've heard him say—

HERDAL (*Comes out of the house*): Hasn't he come up yet?

MRS. SOLNESS: He'll be here soon, I think. They've just gone for him.

HERDAL (*Comes toward her*): You're wanted inside, Mrs. Solness—

MRS. SOLNESS: No, no. I'll stay on here and wait for Halvard.

HERDAL: But some ladies have come to call—

MRS. SOLNESS: Good Heavens—how tiresome! Just at this moment!

HERDAL: They insist on watching the ceremony.

MRS. SOLNESS: Then I suppose I'd better go in—after all, it's my duty—

HILDE: Why not ask them to go away?

MRS. SOLNESS: Oh, I can't very well do that. As long as they're here it's my duty to see them. But you stay out here, Miss Wangel, and talk to him when he comes.

HERDAL: Keep him up here as long as possible.

MRS. SOLNESS: Yes, do—dear Miss Wangel. Be firm with him. Make him give up that mad idea.

HILDE: Wouldn't it be best for you to do that?

MRS. SOLNESS: Yes—Heaven knows—that *is* my duty. But one has duties in so many directions that I—

HERDAL (*Looks toward the garden*)· Here he comes!

MRS. SOLNESS: Oh, dear! And I have to go in!

HERDAL (*To* HILDE): Don't say anything to him about my being here.

HILDE: I dare say I'll be able to find something else to talk to him about.

MRS. SOLNESS: And be sure and keep him here, Miss Wangel. I believe you can do it best.

MRS. SOLNESS *and* DR. HERDAL *go into the house.* HILDE *remains standing on the veranda.*)

SOLNESS (*Comes up the steps from the garden*): I hear someone wants to see me.

HILDE: It's only I, Master Builder.

SOLNESS: Oh, it's you, Hilde. I was afraid it might be Aline and the doctor.

HILDE: You're very easily frightened, I hear.

SOLNESS: Do you think so?

HILDE: Yes. I'm told you're afraid—afraid of climbing about—on scaffoldings, they say.

SOLNESS: Well—that's quite a special thing.

HILDE: Then you are afraid of it?

SOLNESS: Yes, I am.

HILDE: Afraid of falling down and killing yourself?

SOLNESS: No—not of that.

HILDE: Of what, then?

SOLNESS: I'm afraid of retribution, Hilde.

HILDE: Retribution? (*Shakes her head*) I don't understand that.

SOLNESS: Hilde—sit down a minute. I want to tell you something.

HILDE: I'm listening, Master Builder! (*She sits on a stool by the railing and looks at him expectantly.*)

SOLNESS (*Flings his hat on the table*): You know that I began by building churches—

HILDE (*Nods*): Yes. I know that very well!

SOLNESS: You see—I came from a pious home in a little country village. I suppose that's why I thought the finest thing I could devote my life to, was the building of churches.

HILDE: Yes. I see.

SOLNESS: And I think I may say that I built those humble little churches with such honest fervor that—that—

HILDE: Well?

SOLNESS: Well—that I think He should have been pleased with me.

HILDE: *He?* What *He?*

SOLNESS: He for whom they were built, of course. To whose honor and glory they were dedicated.

HILDE: And do you think He *wasn't* pleased with you?

SOLNESS: *He* pleased with *me?* How can you say that, Hilde? Didn't He give the troll in me full power? Didn't He give me mastery over all these—these—

HILDE: Devils?

SOLNESS: Yes—devils! Of both kinds! No. I soon found out that He wasn't pleased with me. (*Mysteriously*) That was really why He let the old house burn down.

HILDE: Was that the reason?

SOLNESS: Yes, don't you see? He wanted me to become a great master in my own sphere, so that I could go on building evermore glorious churches for Him. At first I didn't realize what He was up to—and then, suddenly, I saw it clearly.

HILDE: When was that?

SOLNESS: It was when I built the church tower at Lysanger.

HILDE: I thought so.

SOLNESS: I was up there alone in strange surroundings—I had plenty of time to think and meditate. And I suddenly understood why He had taken my little children from me. He didn't want me to become attached to anything; I was to be allowed no love or happiness, you understand. I was to be nothing but a Master Builder, and I was to devote my life solely to building for Him. But I soon put a stop to that!

HILDE: What did you do then?

SOLNESS: First I searched my own heart—put myself to the test—

HILDE: And then?

SOLNESS: Then I did the impossible. I no less than He.

HILDE: The impossible?

SOLNESS: I had never before been able to climb to a great height. But that day I did it.

HILDE: Yes, you did!

SOLNESS: And as I stood up there, high over everything, I said to Him: Listen to me, Almighty One! From now on I will be a free Master Builder; free in my sphere, just as You are in yours. I will never more build churches for You; only homes for human beings.

HILDE (*With great shining eyes*): That was the song that I heard in the air!

SOLNESS: Yes. But He won in the end.

HILDE: How do you mean?

SOLNESS: This building homes for human beings isn't worth a rap, Hilde!

HILDE: Is that how you feel now?

SOLNESS: Yes. Because now I see it. People have no use for these homes of theirs. Not to be happy in—no. And if I had such a home, I probably wouldn't have any use for it either. What does it all amount to—now that I look back on it? What have I ever built? What have I ever sacrificed for the chance of building? Nothing! Nothing! It all amounts to nothing!

HILDE: Then—will you never build anything any more, Master Builder?

SOLNESS: On the contrary—now I'm just going to begin!

HILDE: What will you build? What? Tell me at once!

SOLNESS: I believe there's just one possible dwelling place for human happiness—that's what I'm going to build now.

HILDE: Master Builder—you mean our castles-in-the-air?

SOLNESS: Castles-in-the-air, yes.

HILDE: I'm afraid you'd grow dizzy before you got halfway up.

SOLNESS: Not if I were to climb hand in hand with you, Hilde.

HILDE: With me alone? Will there be no others?

SOLNESS: What others?

HILDE (*With suppressed resentment*): That—Kaja—at the desk, for instance. Poor thing—don't you want to take her with you too?

SOLNESS: Aha! So *that* was what Aline was talking to you about.

HILDE: Is it so, or is it not?

SOLNESS: I won't answer that question! You must believe in me wholly and completely!

HILDE: For ten years I have believed in you so utterly—so utterly!

SOLNESS: You must go on believing in me!

HILDE: Then let me see you again free and high up!

SOLNESS (*Sadly*): I can't be like that every day, Hilde.

HILDE: You must be! I want you to be! (*Imploringly*) Just this once more, Master Builder! Do the impossible again!

SOLNESS (*Looks deep into her eyes*): If I try it, Hilde, I shall stand up there and talk to Him as I did before.

HILDE (*With growing excitement*): What will you say to Him?

SOLNESS: I shall say to Him: Listen to me, Almighty Lord—You may judge me as You will. But from now on I shall build only the loveliest thing in all the world—

HILDE (*Carried away*): Yes, yes, yes!

SOLNESS: I shall build it with a princess whom I love—

HILDE: Yes, tell Him that! Tell Him that!

SOLNESS: And then I'll say to Him: Now I shall go down and throw my arms round her and kiss her—

HILDE: —many times! Say that!

SOLNESS: —Many, many times, I'll say.

HILDE: —and then?

SOLNESS: Then I shall wave my hat—come down to earth again—and do as I told Him.

HILDE (*With outstretched arms*): Now I see you again as I did when there was a song in the air!

SOLNESS (*Looks at her with bowed head*): Hilde—how have you become what you are?

HILDE: How have you made me what I am?

SOLNESS (*Quickly and firmly*): The princess shall have her castle.

HILDE (*Joyfully, clapping her hands*): Master Builder! My lovely, lovely castle! *Our* castle-in-the-air!

SOLNESS: On a firm foundation.

(*A crowd of people has gathered in the street, dimly seen through the trees. The sound of a brass band is heard from beyond the new house.* MRS. SOLNESS, *wearing a fur piece round her neck,* DR. HERDAL, *carrying her white shawl over his arm, and several ladies come out on the veranda. At the same moment* RAGNAR *comes up from the garden.*)

MRS. SOLNESS (*To* RAGNAR): Are we to have music, too?

RAGNAR: Yes, it's the band from the builders' union. (*To* SOLNESS) I was to tell you—the foreman is ready to go up with the wreath.

SOLNESS (*Takes up his hat*): Very well; I'll go down to him.

MRS. SOLNESS (*Anxiously*): Need you go down there, Halvard?

SOLNESS (*Shortly*): I must be below with the men.

MRS. SOLNESS: But you'll stay down below—won't you, Halvard? You'll stay down with the men?

SOLNESS: Isn't that where I usually stay? On ordinary occasions? (*He goes down the steps to the garden.*)

MRS. SOLNESS (*At the parapet, calls after him*): And do tell the foreman to be careful! Promise me that, Halvard!

HERDAL (*To* MRS. SOLNESS): You see how right I was? He's forgotten all about that nonsense.

MRS. SOLNESS: Oh, what a relief! Twice workmen have fallen and been killed on the spot. (*Turns to* HILDE) Thank you, Miss Wangel, for being so firm with him. I'm sure I could never have managed him.

HERDAL (*Teasingly*): Just leave it to Miss Wangel! She can be firm with a man, when she puts her mind to it!

(MRS. SOLNESS *and* DR. HERDAL *join the ladies who stand on the steps looking out over the garden.* HILDE *remains standing in the foreground by the railing.* RAGNAR *goes over to her.*)

RAGNAR (*With suppressed laughter; in a whisper*): Miss Wangel—do you see all those young people down there in the street?

HILDE: Yes.

RAGNAR: Those are my fellow students. They're here to watch the Master!

HILDE: What do they want to watch him for?

RAGNAR: They like to see him obliged to stay below; they know he'd never dare climb, even to the top of his own house.

HILDE: So that's why they're here, is it?

RAGNAR: Yes—all these years he's kept us down. We like to see him forced to stay down below himself.

HILDE: Well—you won't see that this time.

RAGNAR: Really? Where will we see him then?

HILDE: High up! High up at the top of the tower! That's where you'll see him!

RAGNAR: Do you expect me to believe that?

HILDE: It is his will to climb to the top—so at the top you shall see him.

RAGNAR: His *will!* Yes, I dare say—but he simply can't do it. He'd get dizzy before he was halfway up. He'd have to crawl down again on his hands and knees!

HERDAL (*Pointing toward the new house*): Look! There goes the foreman up the ladder!

MRS. SOLNESS: He has the wreath to carry too. Oh, I do hope he'll be careful!

RAGNAR (*With a shout of incredulity*): But—it's—

HILDE (*Jubilant*): It's the Master Builder himself!

MRS. SOLNESS (*With a cry of terror*): Yes, it's Halvard! Oh, God! Halvard! Halvard!

HERDAL: Sh! Don't shout to him!

MRS. SOLNESS (*Beside herself*): I must go to him—I must get him to come down!

HERDAL (*Holding on to her*): Stand still—all of you! Not a sound!

HILDE (*Motionless, follows* SOLNESS *with her eyes*): He climbs and he climbs. Higher and higher. Higher and higher! Look! Just look!

RAGNAR (*Scarcely breathing*): He *must* turn back now. He can't do anything else.

HILDE: He climbs and he climbs. He'll soon be at the top now.

MRS. SOLNESS: I shall die of terror. I can't bear to look at him!

HERDAL: Don't watch him then.

HILDE: There he stands on the topmost planks—right at the very top!

HERDAL: No one must move— Do you hear!

HILDE (*Exultant; with quiet intensity*): At last! At last! I see him great and free again!

RAGNAR (*Almost speechless*): But this is—

HILDE: All these ten years I've seen him so! How proud he looks! Wonderfully thrilling all the same. Look at him! Now he's hanging the wreath on the vane!

RAGNAR: But—this is utterly impossible!

HILDE: It *is* the impossible that he's doing now. (*With that indefinable expression in her eyes*) Do you see anyone else up there with him?

RAGNAR: There is no one else.

HILDE: Yes—there's someone he's striving with.

RAGNAR: No—you're mistaken—

HILDE: Don't you hear a song in the air either?

RAGNAR: It must be the wind in the tree tops.

HILDE: I hear a song. A mighty song! (*Shouts with wild joyful ecstasy*) Look! Look! Now he's waving his hat! He's waving to us down here! Oh, wave—wave back to him—for now it is finished! (*Snatches the white shawl from* DR. HERDAL, *waves it and shouts up to* SOLNESS) Hurrah for Master Builder Solness!

HERDAL: Stop it! Stop it—for God's sake!

(*The ladies on the veranda wave their handkerchiefs, and shouts of "Hurrah!" come from the street below. There is a sudden silence—then the crowd bursts into a shriek of horror. A human body, with a few planks and fragments of wood, is seen dimly, crashing down behind the trees.*)

MRS. SOLNESS and the LADIES (*Simultaneously*): He's falling! He's falling!

(MRS. SOLNESS *sways and falls back in a faint. The ladies support her amidst cries and confusion. The crowd in the street breaks through the fence and storms into the garden.* DR. HERDAL *rushes down there too. A short pause.*)

HILDE (*Stares fixedly upward and says as though petrified*): My Master Builder.

RAGNAR (*Trembling, leans against the railing*): He must have been killed outright—smashed to pieces.

ONE OF THE LADIES (*As* MRS. SOLNESS *is being helped into the house*): Run for the Doctor—

RAGNAR: I can't move—

LADY: Then call down to him!

RAGNAR (*Makes an effort to call out*): Is there any hope? Is he still alive?

A VOICE FROM BELOW: The Master Builder is dead.

ANOTHER VOICE (*Nearer*): His whole head is crushed in—he fell right into the stone quarry.

HILDE (*Turns to* RAGNAR *and says quietly*): I can't see him up there any more.

RAGNAR: What a ghastly thing. So—after all—he couldn't do it.

HILDE (*As though under a spell, with a quiet triumph*): But he climbed to the very top. And I heard harps in the air. (*Waves the shawl and cries out with wild intensity*) *My—my* Master Builder!

CURTAIN